AF835364

Public Expenditure Economics

an introductory application of welfare economics

European Economic Series

Other titles:
Sturmey & Pearce: Economic Analysis
Nicholson: Economic Statistics and Problems
Jackson: Wages and Labour Economics

Public expenditure economics

an introductory application of welfare economics

Robert Millward
Lecturer in Economics
University of Manchester

McGRAW-HILL · LONDON

New York · St Louis · San Francisco · Düsseldorf
Johannesburg · Kuala Lumpur · Mexico · Montreal
New Delhi · Panama · Rio de Janeiro · Singapore · Sydney
Toronto

Published by
McGRAW-HILL Publishing Company Limited
MAIDENHEAD · BERKSHIRE · ENGLAND.

07 094148 3

Copyright © 1971 McGraw-Hill Publishing Company Limited. All rights reserved. No part of this publication may be reproduced, stored in a retrieval system, or transmitted, in any form or by any means, electronic, mechanical, photocopying, recording, or otherwise, without the prior permission of McGraw-Hill Publishing Company Limited.

PRINTED AND BOUND IN GREAT BRITAIN

Preface

The activities and operations of individual government departments and enterprises are becoming an important area of interest for economists. It is not simply a matter of an increased willingness to seek economists' advice —though this is true. More important is the recent abundance of literature on this subject area in the academic journals. Much of this is concerned with the theory of public goods and externalities, and, on the applied side, with cost-benefit analysis. But marginal cost pricing has also been a major issue, certainly in the UK, partly because of the very interesting empirical work on costs now proceeding in the electricity and transport sectors. This area has, at least as its starting point, the theory of welfare economics. Economics students usually have considerable difficulty—quite understandably—in getting much out of welfare theory. On the other side of the coin, the empirical studies are not only more easy to digest, but their fundamental premises are sometimes accepted fairly uncritically. This book explores the middleground between pure welfare theory and empirical studies. While some of the more abstruse areas of welfare theory are not explored, it is hoped that the early chapters will provide a fairly clear exposition of some of the main theories in welfare economics. Empirical studies are referred to but they are not an important part of the book. The reader who wishes to have an idea of the content may turn to the general introduction (Chapter 1) but, in brief, Part I, in addition to the general discussion of welfare economics looks at indivisibilities, the use of consumer and producer surplus analysis, public good theory, externalities, and theoretical aspects of public investment criteria. The general applications in Part II explore 'general' issues such as short- and long-run marginal costs, financing deficits, historic costs, indivisibilities again, peak loads, some general valuation problems commonly encountered in cost-benefit analysis, budget constraints, and income distribution objectives.

The prime aim is to provide a systematic exposition of these problems intelligible to someone with an introductory knowledge of micro-economics. In most British universities this will probably mean third-year undergraduates and also postgraduate students. For American courses, the book will be more useful at the graduate level. However, I hope that those administrators, economists, and engineers working in the public sector will also be able to derive much from it. Standard propositions in demand and production theory are assumed to be known, but I have, in fact, treated investment criteria and capital budgeting almost from first principles since coverage of this area in micro-economics texts is not uniform and it is, of course, a prerequisite to understanding some of the problems of social time preference and the social opportunity cost of the funds used by the public sector. I have not, however, entered into the protracted debate on present value versus internal rate of return. The latter is but a proxy to the present value approach which —since we are, here, primarily concerned with theory and general principles —dominates the book. There is *some* discussion of the debate and the reader is introduced to the concept of the internal rate of return, but this is mainly to provide an appreciation of the work of those writers on public investment who persist in using the internal rate of return approach. It is difficult to devise a term that adequately describes the area of analysis, but I hope fellow economists will view the title of the book with some sympathy. This is patently not an analysis of the role of public expenditure in macro-economic policy but, even setting that aside, I have had to deal only cavalierly with the problems of uncertainty and capital accumulation. The whole subject of human capital and the economics of health and education is alluded to only in the most superficial way. There is no discussion of foreign trade issues nor of the special problems faced by underdeveloped countries. I can only offer the excuse that the book would otherwise have become unmanageable.

Some of the analysis will, I hope, shed new light on the problems in this area. A book whose main aim is exposition and synthesis must however benefit considerably from the work of others. Of the American writers, O. Eckstein, J. Hirschleifer, R. N. McKean, S. A. Marglin, and P. O. Steiner have contributed considerably to many of the areas explored in this book, and, on more purely theoretical subjects, particularly public goods, I have benefited from the writings of J. M. Buchanan and P. A. Samuelson. My admitted parochialism has restricted my knowledge of French contributions to those articles that have been translated, and M. Boiteux and P. Massé have featured strongly in this respect. The articles of R. Turvey and E. J. Mishan have clarified many issues and other important UK contributions have come from M. E. Beesley, C. D. Foster, R. L. Meek, and M. H. Peston.

The initial manuscript was completed while I was teaching at Manchester University and before I took up a government appointment as an economic adviser to the East African Community. I must first of all thank the many students who attended my lectures and seminars at Manchester for their part in my understanding of many of the issues in this book. Dr J. J. Warford was unfortunately on leave of absence in the United States while the main draft was being made, but our earlier discussions of this subject area gave me a good base from which to work. I am grateful also to Professor A. R. Prest for comments on the initial conception of the nature of the book, and I can only guess at how my understanding of some fine points of analysis have been considerably improved by frequent discussions with Mr W. Peters. Mr P. Devine looked at first drafts of selected chapters and his comments proved extremely helpful. To a large extent this is a contentious area of economics and the usual disclaimer has particular force. My colleagues have absolutely no responsibility for the approach that I eventually chose, let alone any technical errors or omissions.

The main work was undertaken from 1967 to 1969 and I am grateful to my wife—to whom this book is dedicated—for kindly tolerating all that this implied in our home life and also for providing encouragement at each stage of the work, as well as helping out on typing. I should like also to thank Mrs J. Wild for undertaking the bulk of the typing. Miss K. Deighnan helped at one stage by typing a chapter when everyone was busy. Last, but certainly not least, I should like to acknowledge the skilful work of Mrs A. Furlong and Mrs M. Watts in designing and drafting the diagrams.

R. MILLWARD

To Pauly

Contents

Preface v

1. GENERAL INTRODUCTION 1

PART 1: THEORY

2. THE BASIC THEORY OF RESOURCE ALLOCATION
   - 2.1. National welfare 9
   - 2.2. The Pareto optimum 13
   - 2.3. A formal analysis 26
   - 2.4. The search for a unique solution 30

3. ECONOMIC EFFICIENCY AND EXPENDITURE CRITERIA
   - 3.1. Price patterns 35
   - 3.2. Private enterprise systems 42
   - 3.3. Social ownership and public enterprises 48
   - 3.4. Comparing gains and losses 57
   - 3.5. Social surplus analysis and indivisibilities 60
   - 3.6. Distribution and compensation tests 73
   - Appendix 82

4. A REVIEW OF OBJECTIVES AND POSSIBLE DECISION RULES
   - 4.1. Welfare economics, policy recommendations, and economic efficiency 85
   - 4.2 A formal analysis of the theory of second-best 100

5. PUBLIC GOODS, EXTERNALITIES, AND RETURNS TO SCALE
   - 5.1. Introduction 109
   - 5.2. Unpriced natural resources 112
   - 5.3. The decreasing cost problem 118
   - 5.4. Public goods and external economies 131
   - 5.5. Summary and review 141
   - 5.6. Externalities and 'efficient' solutions 145
   - 5.7. Distributional factors 161

6. THE PLANNING HORIZON AND TIME-STREAM ASPECTS OF PUBLIC INVESTMENT

6.1. Introduction 163
6.2. The time dimension of Pareto efficiency 166
6.3. Market derived investment rules and the preferences of the present generation 182
6.4. Social time preference 195
Appendix 199

PART 2: GENERAL APPLICATIONS

7. MARGINAL COST PRICING

7.1. Introduction 203
7.2. Cost minimization and choice of production technique 211
7.3. Pricing and optimal investment 218
7.4. Expanding capacity and long-run marginal cost 226
7.5. Excess capacity 236
7.6. Balancing the books, and other difficulties 242

8. JOINT COSTS, INDIVISIBILITIES, AND PEAK LOADS

8.1. General issues 252
8.2. Capacity indivisibilities 255
8.3. The peak load problem 265

9. PROBLEMS IN COST/BENEFIT ESTIMATION

9.1. The basis of 'cost-benefit analysis' 278
9.2. Specification of a project 283
9.3. Examples of techniques used to value project outputs 290
9.4. Economy-wide effects 298
9.5. Public investment: effects on the private sector 310
9.6. Criteria and financing for public investment 316
9.7. Summary of time-stream issues 328

10. ALTERNATIVE OBJECTIVES AND ADDITIONAL CONSTRAINTS

10.1. General issues 331
10.2. Budget allocation 334
10.3. Income distribution objectives and expenditure criteria 346
Appendix 358

11. CONCLUSION 364

Reading guide 365
List of abbreviations 369
Index 370

1. General introduction

This is a book about the content rather than the total of public expenditure. As a vehicle for altering the degree of utilization of all resources in the economy, public expenditure has been of key interest to economists ever since Keynes' *General Theory*. We are here more interested in the criteria used to decide which particular items are to make up the total, rather than in an analysis of the use of the total as a macro-stabilizer. In particular, the concern is with the contribution that economic theory can make to, for example, the choice between nuclear or coal-fired electricity generating plants or between the various sites for the third London Airport; to the policy of those parts of the public sector for whose goods and services prices are levied as in the UK nationalized industries; the contribution of economics to investment decisions involving new or improved roads, hospitals, water reservoirs, or the exploitation of discoveries of new sources of coal or natural gas. One could put the matter in a stronger form by saying that the issues involve whether, for example, the proposed motorway 'box' round London is a *better* scheme than a system of licences for cars using central areas, or whether the lump-sum water rate levied on domestic households *should* be replaced by direct metering and pricing of water consumption. In this latter form the issues take on a distinct normative air, and since they are often expressed in such terms, we shall find ourselves very much concerned with pinning down the fundamental values behind such statements.

In some respects, and particularly in terms of the more applied problems, this is a fairly new subject area for economists. True, the pricing policy of public utilities has for a long time been the subject of discussion by economists. Pigou, for example, was not the first to look at railway rates or the public operation of industries, yet even his work is now fifty years old.[1] In addition, of course, it was Pigou who first fully explored the divergencies between social and private valuation. And finally we shall see that much of the pure theory behind these studies has, at least as its starting point, the analysis of theoretical welfare economics and this has a long tradition, at least in this century. Nevertheless, the period since the early 1950s has seen a tremendous spurt in the attention devoted to, first of all, the theoretical aspects of externalities, indivisibilities, and 'public' goods, and of public investment

[1] A. C. Pigou, *The Economics of Welfare*, chapters XV and XIX, Macmillan, 1920.

criteria. On the applied side, French engineers and economists pioneered, in the electricity and transport sectors, some important studies relating to pricing and investment. The development of techniques for evaluating transport projects in the UK, and the increased attention of American economists to the studies made by engineers of many of the large-scale water-resource development plans, has stimulated a tremendous amount of interest in other parts of the public sector. The influx of economists to government work in the UK in the 1960s had the effect—amongst others—of reviving interest in the relationship between prices and costs in the public corporations, a subject which had received a battery of attention in the economic journals during the immediate post-war period when large parts of the fuel and transport sectors were nationalized. In addition, the economics of education has, since the late 1950s, become a major growth subject itself and large sections of educational activity are, in many countries, found within the public sector.

Part of the explanation for these developments may be attributable to the marked rise in the portion of national expenditure taken by the public sector in recent years. Following the approach of Peacock and Wiseman,[2] in the inter-war period of 1920–37 government expenditure in the UK at 1900 prices showed small oscillations around 25 per cent of gross national product. By the early 1950s this had grown to roughly 40 per cent—and this excludes the investment of nationalized industries—and has since shown no sign of being reduced significantly. On the other side of the coin, the level of the inter-war period itself represents a considerable increase over the nineteenth-century level. In 1792 the ratio—in so far as one can tell from the data—was roughly 10 per cent and 100 years later it was still at this level. Interest in public expenditure economics is probably, then, as much a reflection of the general growth of economics as a subject, as an effect of the growth in government expenditure. In fact, we have to be careful about the use of the term 'public expenditure economics'. First of all, large parts of the discussion relate to what is traditionally known as public enterprise (or public utility) economics, but much is applicable to areas such as water-resource development and roads and also to what are traditionally known as the 'social services'. Moreover, much of the theoretical basis to applied studies in these other areas is the same—as we shall see—as that underlying public enterprise economics. In sum, the term public expenditure economics is not as pretentious as it first appears. Secondly, the book is concerned only with certain aspects of public expenditure; in particular, it has as its main theme the analysis of techniques that are increasingly being used to evaluate items of public expenditure. In this respect it is very much concerned with the traditional approach of looking at prescriptions for government policy, and, partly because of this, the subject of welfare economics plays an important role.

[2] A. T. Peacock and J. Wiseman, *The Growth of Public Expenditure in the United Kingdom*, 2 Ed., Tables 1 and A–6, Allen & Unwin, 1967.

Another approach—which in my view is complementary rather than alternative—stems from the question: what actually *determines* the content and total of public expenditure? This question has also been largely ignored by economists for a long time. However, since 1960 or thereabouts, there has been a number of attempts to develop theories relevant to this issue. Much of this work has been done by American economists and is concerned both with the motivation of governments and with the economic characteristics of goods commonly produced in the public sector. In addition, the Peacock and Wiseman work constitutes a pioneering study in the UK of the statistical basis for this subject area. Although we make some brief allusions to the theoretical developments as part of our whole discussion of 'public goods' in chapter 5, the book is not concerned with these issues. In many respects they constitute an entirely different set of problems and, in addition, they are as yet fairly undeveloped.

Granted this basic approach, consider the form of the analysis in this book. Our main concern is with what might be termed 'general principles'. On the one hand there will be, for reasons shortly to be described, an exposition of the basic principles of theoretical welfare economics, including a considerable discussion of those theoretical developments—such as the analysis of public goods and public investment criteria—which are related directly to public sector activities. The application of this theory in Part II is in fairly general terms; we shall be discussing, for example, the valuation principles implicit in criteria used to choose between various types of public irrigation schemes or various locations for the development of a country's ports and harbours; or, as another example, the suggestions that have been made in electricity and transport for changing the price structure given the presence of daily and seasonal peaks in the demand patterns. That is, we shall not be describing any particular investment project in detail, nor be concerned with the current economic problems facing individual parts of the public sector, though throughout the second part of the book the discussion will be fully illustrated by particular cases and actual problems. A second feature of the nature of the analysis provides a point of departure for chapter 2. It has been suggested so far that the individual items of public expenditure form the subject matter—investment projects, output supplies, particular input choices, and so on. Most people would probably agree that for any one of these activities the relevant approach is to compare the advantages of having it or doing it with the disadvantages. This book is concerned both with exploring the definitions that can be attached to advantages and disadvantages, and with a systematic analysis of the relationship between the two. In fact, in relation to outputs, inputs, and projects in a particular part of the public sector, we might say that our concern is with the maximization of advantages minus disadvantages, subject to various constraints relating to, for example, the availability of resources or administrative feasibility. In programming terms it is a matter of maximizing the objective, or the objective function, subject to various constraints. Now even if objectives could be defined easily, there would still be a lot of interest in exploring the relevance and implications of constraints in the public sector and in deriving the 'decision rules' that emerged from the maximization problem. But it is the definition of objectives that widens the scope of the subject area, for the more interesting definitions will relate to advantages and disadvantages for the country as a whole rather than for any particular public enterprise or government department. Now theoretical welfare economics has been very much concerned with exploring exactly these issues. To undertake a public investment project because it raises national (or social, or community) *welfare* is to use a form of words which conveys nothing more than the equally vague concepts of advantages and disadvantages. Moreover, the setting for discussing these items in welfare economics has been the problem of allocating resources between uses, and so it is a subject with obvious relevance to the analysis of the content of public expenditure. This is then the starting point of chapter 2.

Plan of the book

Chapters 2 and 3 provide an exposition of some of the basic theorems in welfare economics, with chapter 3 geared more closely to problems likely to arise in the public sector; in particular, this latter chapter makes some introductory comments on marginal cost pricing, looks in depth at the use of consumer and producer surplus for the evaluation of indivisible changes, and considers the relevance of compensation tests in a partial equilibrium setting. The two chapters are the springboard for the rest of the book and chapter 4 provides, as well as a discussion of the second-best problem, a review of the conclusions that can be drawn from traditional welfare economics. It is a key chapter and the first part of it warrants a re-reading after the later chapters have been digested. Chapter 5 then provides a theoretical analysis of problems particularly common in those activities often found in the public sector of many countries; it looks at the theory of 'public' goods and externalities and evaluates the significance of decreasing costs and other returns to scale problems. Part I of the book ends by analysing, in chapter 6, the time-dimension of most of these issues.

Part II on general applications opens with chapter 7, entitled 'Marginal Cost Pricing'; this is mainly concerned with those parts of the public sector where prices are levied, and links the problem of pricing closely to that of investment. Chapter 8, as its title indicates, examines the technical difficulties raised by the existence of joint costs, indivisibilities, and peak loads, and this follows the pricing chapter because these difficulties have often been discussed in the context of pricing, though, as we make clear, the analysis has relevance for goods and services for which prices are not normally levied. The production of, and investment in, such goods and services forms the kernel of chapter 9 which explores the techniques used in cost-benefit analysis and, in addition, provides a discussion of public investment criteria of a more applied kind than that in chapter 6. The 'efficiency' approach to project evaluation, pricing and investment decisions has very much dominated the applied work done by economists, but chapter 10 looks at some alternatives and examines certain suggestions that have been made for incorporating distributional objectives directly into public expenditure criteria. In addition, this chapter examines budget constraints in some detail.

The book closes with some concluding remarks in chapter 11. A brief guide to the contents of each chapter is given at some point in the first few pages of each chapter. Throughout the book the titles of journals and a few economic institutions are given in an abbreviated form and a key to these abbreviations is given after chapter 11. Many references to the literature are made in the footnotes of the text, and these often include comments on the work in question, but an introductory guide to the literature is given at the end of the book.

Mathematics

All mathematical material has been presented in separate sections, footnotes, or appendices, and the general reader can miss these out without significantly detracting from his understanding of the book. Considerable use is made of symbols and notation in much of the text, but the non-mathematically orientated student need not be frightened of this; the notation does not involve any mathematics and a serious student of economics should have no difficulty. In fact, the mathematics in the separate sections is itself elementary, involving mostly the use of Lagrangean multipliers, and those who wish to read further in the journals would do well to equip themselves with these techniques; some references are given in section 3 of chapter 2.

Part 1 : Theory

2. The basic theory of resource allocation

2.1 National welfare

The problem of choosing the best way of allocating resources between uses is formally quite straightforward. Define 'best' in terms of something to be maximized, set out the constraints in terms of available resources, and the problem can be solved. In fact the main part of this chapter will involve the search for a maximand. It is precisely what is meant by 'best' that forms the major part of the analysis. But, the retort may be, surely the aim is to maximize national welfare? One could go along with this if only we knew what the phrase 'national welfare' meant. Perhaps one could start by saying that national welfare is some amalgam of the welfares of the constituent members of the population. Traditionally, the foundations of theoretical welfare economics has been concerned with trying to attach some precision to this 'amalgam' of welfares and, of course, in pinpointing what we mean by the welfare of an individual.[1] Let us, therefore, look at the problem in two

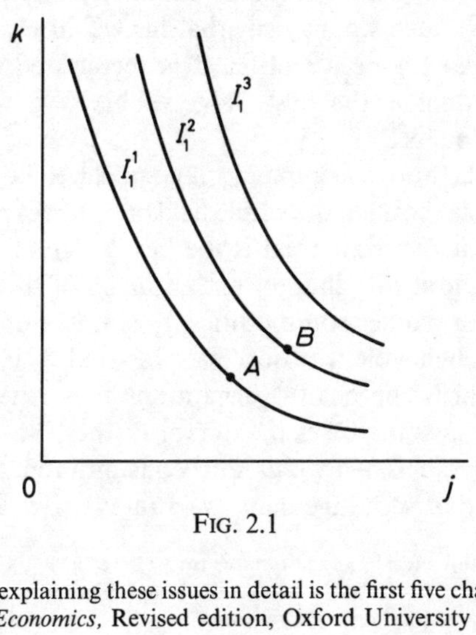

FIG. 2.1

[1] The best source for explaining these issues in detail is the first five chapters of I. M. D. Little, *A Critique of Welfare Economics*, Revised edition, Oxford University Press, 1957.

stages, one which considers the meaning of individual welfare and the second which looks at national welfare.

When economics students are introduced to the theory of consumer choice they learn that an individual's actual purchases of the various goods available can be viewed as reflecting two sets of forces. One is the money data on prices and consumers' income. The other is the individual's preferences, often illustrated diagrammatically by an indifference map. Such a map is produced in Fig. 2.1 where the indifference curves, I_1^1, I_1^2 and so on, have the usual meaning of showing the various combinations of two goods, *j* and *k* in this instance, between which the individual is deemed to be indifferent. Now it is very easy to slip into a way of thinking that implies that higher indifference curves represent higher levels of welfare for the individual, i.e., the individual gets 'better off' the higher is his actual consumption point. If we accept this interpretation then it means we have solved our first problem—we have, in other words, a device which indicates when an individual's welfare increases. But does an indifference map—or a utility function in more general terms[2]—indicate an individual's welfare? It depends what you mean by 'welfare'. Strictly speaking all that a utility function represents is a collection of probable choices that an individual will make. It tells us for example that if the individual is given the choice of a bundle *A* or bundle *B* as shown in Fig. 2.1 he will choose bundle *B*. That is all the information provided. However, if the assumption is made that the individual is interested solely in his own welfare and *that he is the best judge of his own welfare*, then the indifference map can be viewed as indicating when the individual's welfare increases. Notice we are not saying that the individual or anyone else can attach a cardinal number to utility or welfare. The proposition is simply that if an individual chooses one thing (bundle *A*) when he could have had the other (bundle *B*), then we may say that his welfare is higher with *A* than with *B* provided that, to be scientific, it is recognized that this implicitly assumes the individual is the best judge of his own welfare, well-being, utility, call it what you like.

Now, although the above argument may appear to be rather laboured, it is in fact quite a crucial point in the whole field of public expenditure appraisal. The assumption that the individual is the best judge of his own well-being will be used throughout this chapter and in much of this book. Is it always valid? Certainly for some commodities it seems dubious. What about health? Are we, as benevolent observers, prepared to let individuals make free choices as regards the health precautions they make? Or are we prepared to argue that in some cases the doctor or the National Health Service knows better. Is free choice in cigarette consumption a good thing, or is some governmental discouragement warranted? Do individuals always

[2] The term 'utility' will be used as synonymous for welfare throughout the book. Moreover, the phrase 'marginal utility' will also be used even though there is no pretence that utility can be measured; it aids understanding in many cases.

know what vaccinations or innoculations they 'need'? Are students aged 8 years or 14 years or 19 years, the best judge of what type and quality of education is 'best' for them? Notice the argument is not concerned with the fact that some people have less income than others; that is a separate point. It is concerned with what one might loosely refer to as the relevance and virtues of free choice. We shall provisionally equate welfare increases with the choices made by individuals, but the argument that an individual is the best judge of his own well-being *is* a value judgement, and one that needs to be continuously borne in mind. We shall have occasion to consider its relevance at a number of points in the book, particularly in chapters 4 and 10.

Accepting this approach to individual welfare, what can be said about national welfare? There are probably as many definitions of national welfare —or 'the national interest' in one of its disguises—as there are adults in the population. Perhaps one might follow on from the discussion of the previous section by saying that the national welfare is simply the arithmetic sum of the welfare of the individuals in the community? However, to start with, it has already been implied that an individual's welfare cannot be measured in quantitative terms. Secondly, even if we perpetrated the fiction of Mr Jones' 'utiles' or other bastardizations, there is no obvious way of adding Jones' utiles to Brown's utiles. It would mean that one would have to have some predetermined way of weighting one individual's welfare against another's. Writers in theoretical welfare economics have now rejected the possibility of making such inter-personal comparisons of utility. Where does one go from there? A famous—or infamous, for some people—Italian writer, Vilfredo Pareto advanced a definition of an increase in national welfare which has been used in welfare economics. This, in some respects, is a very mild definition with which few, it would appear, would wish to quibble. His definition was that it is a good thing socially—i.e., national welfare rises—*when one person in the community is made better off and no one else suffers.* Notice this does not require any inter-personal comparisons of utilities but simply the observation of whether, in relation to some particular change in circumstances, any person or persons become better off and whether any person(s) gets worse off. The full significance of this Pareto criterion will emerge in the course of this chapter and the next two, as we explore the various ways of allocating resources. With this background we may now proceed.

Plan of chapter

The approach will be as follows. Certain characteristics of the resources of a 'model' economy will be described. An attempt will then be made to solve for the 'best' way of allocating these resources. What will *not* be discussed in this chapter are the possible devices that could be used to achieve these solutions: a discussion of the manner in which various types of social organizations would have to act to achieve these solutions is taken up in the next chapter. To crystallize the reader's understanding of this approach, he might think of someone—a benevolent dictator or an omniscient economist—who has all the information at his finger-tips and who, having solved the problem, could order the various resources into various uses. In particular, this will emphasize that the analysis need have no connection with market systems; these and other 'devices' are considered later.

Consider then a model where the basic resources of the economy consist of land and population. We may consider a time period short enough to permit a realistic assumption that these stocks of resources are fixed. Capital, and the production of it, pose problems which are better dealt with separately, and this is postponed to a later chapter. The population comprises a large number of individuals; though the population stock is fixed, the quantity of factor services that they can supply is viewed as variable—the quantity of man-hours of a particular grade of labour, for example, is to be determined. Variations in human input supply arise because we shall assume such services enter the individual utility functions; generally a person's welfare will be inversely related to the quantity of services he supplies. It will simplify matters if we further provisionally assume that non-human inputs also enter the preference functions. Now this assumption one would normally associate with an economy of well-defined property rights, where every physical resource is owned by individuals as opposed to the state. An individual, then, may not be willing to supply all of the factor services of a resource on the grounds that he wishes to use or consume some himself. While this provides an example of what we have in mind here, it is important to avoid the presumption that supplying factor services automatically guarantees some return by way of commodities or other types of payment; the individuals do not own their factor services in this sense, and what rewards a person gets or how many services he has to supply is something to be determined in the analysis. In any case many of the resources of an economy will be in fixed supply—they will not enter preference functions—and this possibility is explicitly catered for in later chapters. The assumption merely simplifies some of the expositional material. The positive elements in the individual utility functions will be commodities or outputs. The negative items are input supplies. We assume that there are large numbers of firms[3] in the economy, in each of which there is a certain given technological relationship between inputs and outputs; formally, each firm has a production function.

Finally, there are three issues which raise problems which we delay discussing until later chapters. First we assume that each commodity can be produced at constant returns to scale; doubling all inputs, including entre-

[3] We are cheating here since there is nothing special about firms; they are a form of social organization which we might have considered later on. This refinement is however ignored. See J. de V. Graaf, *Theoretical Welfare Economics,* p. 16, Cambridge University Press, 1957.

preneurship will just double output; different assumptions pose considerable problems. Secondly, we shall assume that the production function of a firm depends solely on its use of inputs and outputs; similar remarks apply to the utility functions. External effects such as my enjoyment of the park being affected by the volume of your transistor are ruled out. Thirdly, we shall assume that all inputs and outputs are perfectly divisible so that we can talk of marginal adjustments without worry.[4]

2.2 The Pareto optimum

Production

Although in the final analysis no one problem can be considered on its own, it is useful to approach the general issue of resource allocation in stages. The first problem is a technological one. If it is assumed that more of any output (and/or less of any input), other things being equal, is a good thing, then there are likely to be certain points about the organization of production that can be made without resort to welfare considerations. Although the production problems are fairly straightforward we shall spend some time on them, since it is a useful area in which to introduce certain analytical techniques which will be used throughout the book. Changes in the organization of production are viewed here as involving moving inputs and outputs between firms. Suppose that we take a fixed quantity of inputs and a particular distribution of these inputs between various firms. If it is possible to move inputs from one firm to another and increase the quantity of at least one output, then we may say that production is not optimally organized. The production problem can thus be viewed as discovering how outputs and inputs should be allocated between firms so that:

(a) No further shuffling would increase the quantity of one commodity without decreasing the quantity of another, given a fixed quantity of inputs, and,

(b) it is impossible, for any given stock of commodities, to decrease the use of one input without increasing the use of others.

Where such conditions are met production is deemed to be optimally organized. This does not mean there will be a unique distribution of inputs and outputs between firms; there may be several distributions with such characteristics.

The solution to this problem is as follows. In the previous section the economy was taken to comprise a large number of firms, individuals, inputs, and outputs. To handle all these items simultaneously requires the use of some elementary mathematics. Considerable insight to the problem can

[4] Note that implicitly we shall be assuming that each person or firm consumes and supplies some quantity of every good. This also is not necessary but instead of the simple equality conditions we derive later, some would have to be inequalities. A further point is that we shall assume all our functions are differentiable and no solutions involve kinks or corners.

however be provided if we consider only small numbers. This we shall do to start with since it is also a situation which can be illustrated diagrammatically; in addition, the case of large numbers can be explained intuitively with this analysis as background. Later on, for those readers willing and able to tackle a more formal approach, the more realistic situation of large numbers will be considered rigorously. An acquaintance with the more rigorous approach certainly aids understanding of the issues, but the more general reader can skip it. For the problem of production consider, therefore, the situation where there are simply two outputs, two inputs, and two firms. The two inputs are denoted as j and k and the production function of one of the firms, say firm number 2, is indicated by the *isoproduct map* of Fig. 2.2 where I_2^1, I_2^2, etc., are the lines of equal quantities of some output, say, commodity number 2. We may re-interpret our previous diagram, Fig. 2.1, as the isoproduct map of firm 1 producing commodity 1 from the two inputs, j and k.

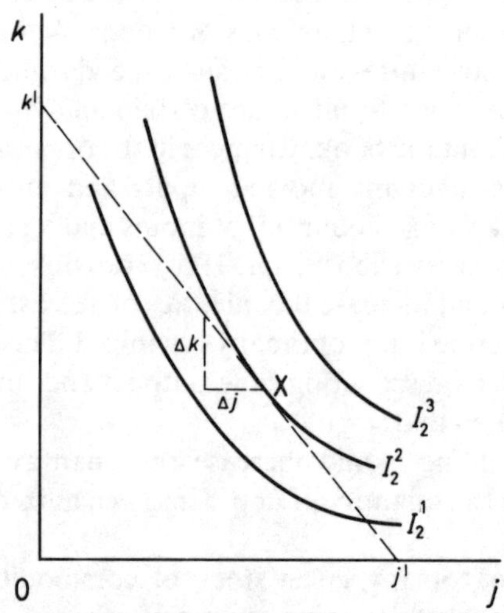

FIG. 2.2

An approach to the production problem would be to set the quantities of j and k at some particular level, and then examine how this fixed stock is to be distributed between the two firms so that the maximum quantity of output 1 is produced given particular levels for output 2. This can be accomplished by joining the two diagrams into a box as shown in Fig. 2.3. Firm 1's origin is at 0_1 with its isoproduct map I_1^1, I_1^2, etc., in the same position as before. Firm 2's origin is now however at 0_2 with its isoproduct lines increasing outwards in a south-westerly direction from I_2^1 to I_2^2, etc. The main function of the box is to fix the total quantities of the two inputs available to the firms; the fixed levels are 0_2j^* $(= 0_1k^*)$ and 0_2k^* $(= 0_1j^*)$. All points in the box constitute particular distributions of the input stocks between the

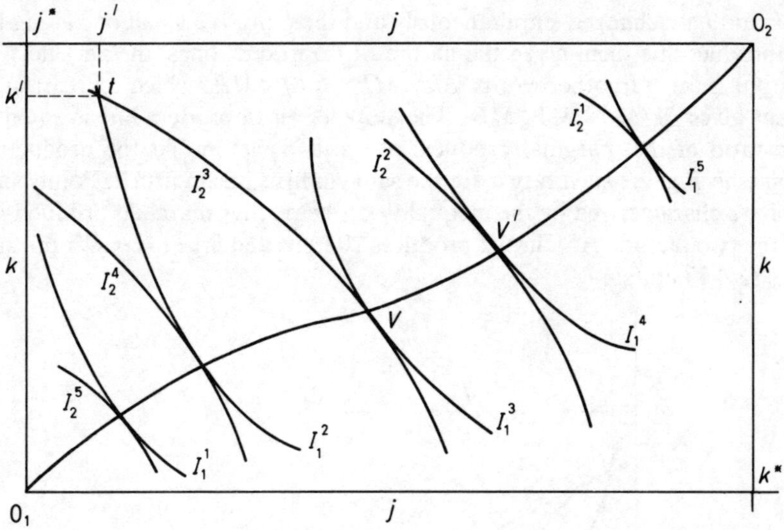

FIG. 2.3

two firms. At point t for example firm 1 gets $0_1k'$ of input k, the rest, $k'j^*$, going to the other firm; $0_2j'$ of j goes to firm 2, the rest going to firm 1. Suppose we fix firm 2's output at I_2^3, which might constitute say 20 units of commodity 2, and inquire about the distribution of the inputs between the two firms which will maximize output 1. Clearly the distribution will have to be somewhere along I_2^3 and, given the normal curvature of isoproduct lines, the solution distribution is at V where I_2^3 touches the highest possible isoproduct line of firm 1. Point V is characterized by the tangency of I_2^3 and I_1^3. If the output of 2 had been fixed at I_2^2, say 15 units, then the optimal point is given by V'. Points such as V and V' have the characteristic that it is not possible, by reshuffling inputs between firms, to increase the output of one commodity without decreasing that of the other. All the tangency positions will, therefore, have this characteristic and the line connecting these positions, $0_1VV'0_2$, is called a contract curve. All points on the curve are Pareto production points.

The economic meaning of the tangency positions can be seen if it is remembered that the slope of an isoproduct line represents the marginal rate at which the inputs can be exchanged without affecting total output, and it is equal to the relative marginal productivity of the two factors. At point X on Fig. 2.2, for example, the marginal rate of transformation between k and j in firm 2 is represented by the slope of the tangent $j'k'$. More precisely, if we consider the small dotted triangle, then the slope of $j'k'$ is given by $\Delta k/\Delta j$. Now consider a small increase in the use of k from point X, holding the quantity of j constant; the associated change in output will be $\Delta k \times MP_k$ where MP_k is the marginal product of input k; alternatively a reduction in the use of j, holding k constant, would cause a decrease in output of $\Delta j \times MP_j$.

If k and j are changed simultaneously and the move is a small one along the isoproduct line then, given the nature of isoproduct lines, the net effect on output is zero. In other words, $\Delta k \times MP_k = \Delta j \times MP_j$, which on rearrangement gives $\Delta k/\Delta j = MP_j/MP_k$. The slope of an isoproduct line is equal to the ratio of the marginal products of the two factors. At the production points in Fig. 2.3 such ratios are the same in firm 1 as in firm 2. Points such as t are characterized by the inequality of the relative marginal productivity of the two factors. At t, firm 2 produces 20 units and firm 1 is on X_1^2 producing, say, 10 units.

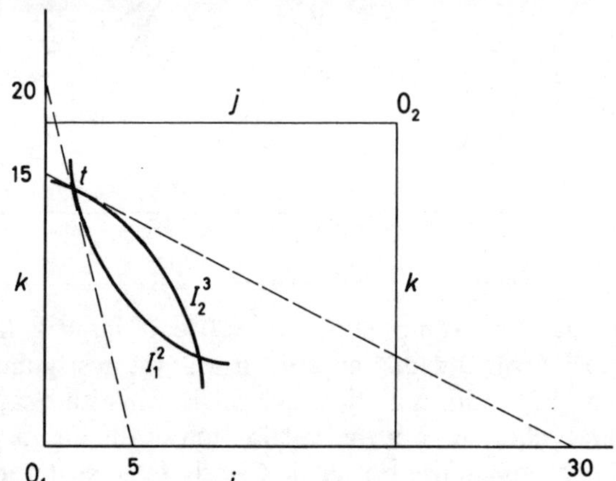

FIG. 2.4

Figure 2.4 presents an arithmetic example. In firm 1 the relative productivity of the two factors is such that on the margin at t, $5j$ is equal to $20k$; i.e., $1j = 4k$; if it gives up one unit of j, four units of k will just permit the firm to keep output at 10 units. For firm 2, $1j = 0{\cdot}5k$, so that k is relatively more productive in firm 2 and j is relatively more productive in firm 1. To this extent mutual swopping of j and k could increase the output of both firms, as long as the trading rate is anywhere between the two existing rates. Suppose, for example, that for every unit of j transferred to firm 1, firm 2 gets a unit of k in exchange. Firm 1 can produce more since it only has to surrender $1k$ to obtain one extra unit of j; firm 2 can produce more since it has received more than 0·5 units of k in exchange for one j. Clearly the boundary of possibilities at which at least one firm's output is increased is shown by the ellipse in Fig. 2.4. All we have done here is to demonstrate fully what the previous results implied; if the transformation rates between two inputs are not the same, the output of one commodity can be increased without decreasing that of the other commodity. The problem is clearly the same as that encountered in international trade theory, where the issue involves the allocation of production between two countries.

General implications

Although in this example much play has been made of the shuffling of inputs between firms and of the exchange rates at which the factors are moved, this does not have any implications about how resources *are* to be shifted. To re-emphasize, it is not until the next chapter that devices for achieving the optimum conditions will be considered. It may aid understanding, however, to think of the above transfers as being effected by the commands of the benevolent despot.

A further point relates to the boundary of feasible production in this 2-firm economy. If, in fact, the services of the two factors are fixed in quantity, then the production limits would be indicated by the maximal quantities of the two commodities that can be produced. The contract curve of Fig. 2.3 can be redrawn into the output dimension of Fig. 2.5, in the form of the familiar production possibility line, $l'l$, whose slope indicates the technically most efficient way of transforming one commodity into another. At any point on it the rate of transformation, therefore, indicates the marginal cost of one commodity in terms of another when production has been optimally organized.

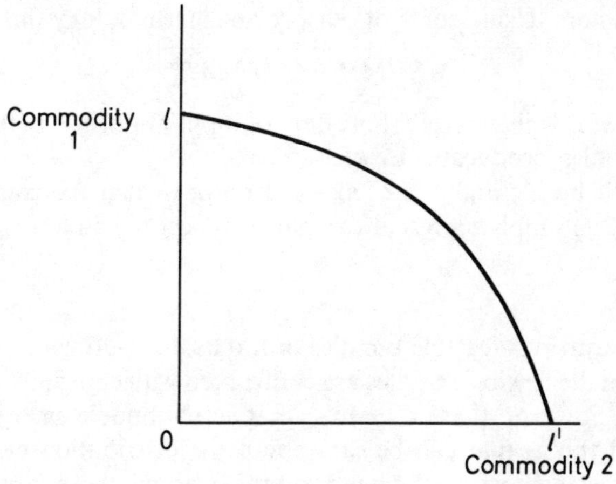

FIG. 2.5

The conditions under which it has been drawn are quite special, since inputs are assumed to be in fixed supply and do not actually appear in the formulations of production possibilities. However, the logic of the analysis can be used to indicate—intuitively rather than formally—the situation where inputs are in variable supply and, moreover, the case where there are large numbers of firms, inputs, and outputs. If the term 'goods' is used to encompass both inputs and outputs, then Pareto optimality in production requires that the rate at which it is possible to transform one good into another should be the same in all firms where such transfers are effected.

Otherwise, some outputs could be increased without requiring a larger total of inputs, or input usage could be decreased without affecting outputs. If we now think of k and j as goods, i.e., inputs *or* outputs, if further we think of v as the number of firms in the economy and if, finally, we take any two of these, say, firm a and firm b, then the general form of the Pareto production condition could be written as:

$$MRT^a_{k,j} = MRT^b_{k,j} \qquad \begin{aligned} a,b &= 1 \ldots v \\ j,k &= 1 \ldots n \end{aligned} \tag{2.1}$$

where $MRT^a_{k,j}$, etc., is the marginal rate of transformation between k and j in firm a. The condition implies that such transformation rates should be the same in all firms and for any pair of the n 'goods' in the economy. In more detail we see that:

(a) If k is an input and j is an output, then the transformation rate could be interpreted as the marginal product of k in terms of j, and the production condition requires that this be the same in all firms where k is used to produce j; clearly if this did not hold, the output of j could be increased by reallocating k between firms.

(b) If both are inputs, the ratios represent the relative marginal productivity of the two factors. Using some of our previous terminology this means

$$MP^a_j/MP^a_k = MP^b_j/MP^b_k \tag{2.2}$$

where MP^a_j, etc., is the marginal product of input j in firm a in terms of, say, some output also producable by k.

(c) Finally, if both j and k are taken as outputs then the transformation rates in eq. (2.1) simply represent the marginal cost of j, in terms of k.

Exchange

Which of the various feasible bundles of inputs and outputs is 'best' will be decided when the feasible bundles are confronted with consumer preferences. It turns out, however, that no matter what actual bundle emerges there are a number of things that can be said about the distribution of any bundle between *individuals*, without saying anything about the relative merits of different bundles. In other words, if we select a particular bundle comprising fixed totals of inputs and outputs, we may consider evaluating the various possible ways of distributing this bundle between individuals. Thus, before considering the general allocation problem, another sub-problem, this time the so-called exchange problem, is considered.

Clearly, a given stock of goods can be distributed in a number of ways depending on whether one favours one consumer rather than another. Since we are not prepared at this stage to compare the benefit (utility) received by one person with that received by another, it would appear that there is little that can be said about distribution. However the Pareto criterion for a social improvement, a criterion that has been adopted in this chapter, does enable one to specify good and bad characteristics for the distribution of a given bundle of goods. Since the Pareto criterion sanctions any change which renders one person better off without making another worse off, then, if from any particular distribution of the given bundle such a move is possible, this distribution is deemed to be sub-optimal. Changes are effected by shuffling goods between individuals, and an optimal distribution is defined to exist when no Pareto improvements can be made by further changes. The techniques for discovering the characteristics of such optimal distributions are the same as those used in the production problem. Taking any given bundle of goods, we would hold the welfares of every individual but one, at prescribed levels. The welfare level of the one individual could then be increased up to its maximum. At such a maximum a Pareto optimal distribution of the fixed stock of goods has been achieved. Taking the case of two individuals, the previous diagrams can be used to illustrate this point. Figures 2.1 and 2.2 can now be interpreted as relating to two consumers. The curves[5] in these diagrams are now taken to represent *indifference curves* between, say, two outputs j and k. The tangency positions in the box of Fig. 2.3 represent positions from which it is not possible to make one person better off without at the same time making someone else worse off; all points on the contract curve represent Pareto optimal distributions of the fixed quantities of commodities, 0_2j^* and 0_2k^*. The slope of each consumer's indifference curve is the same at these points. Since such slopes represent the ratio of the marginal utilities from the outputs, or marginal subjective rates of substitution in modern terminology, then if, between any pair of commodities, such rates are not the same for all consumers, Pareto improvements can be effected. Again one can demonstrate arithmetically that at points such as t in Fig. 2.4, one or both persons could be made better off by redistributing the bundle of goods.

More generally, if one thinks of an economy with m individuals, typified by person i and person d, and n 'goods' typified by k and j, then the distribution of any stock of 'goods' is only Pareto optimal when

$$MRS^i_{k,j} = MRS^d_{k,j} \qquad \begin{matrix} i,d = 1 \ldots m \\ j,k = 1 \ldots n \end{matrix} \tag{2.3}$$

where $MRS^i_{k,j}$, etc., represents person i's marginal subjective rate of substitution between k and j. The reader is left to work out the meaning of 2.3 when j and/or k are inputs.

The general optimum and community indifference maps

It is now possible to consider the basic problem of the 'best' way of allocating

[5] An important difference now is that cardinal numbers cannot be attached to these utility levels.

resources between uses. Two points have been established so far. Firstly, the conditions have been established under which the maximal attainable outputs can be extracted from any given supply of inputs, and under which the quantity of inputs needed to produce any given set of outputs is minimized. The conditions which characterize this production frontier are that inputs and outputs should be so allocated between firms that the *MRT* between any pair of goods is the same in each production location. Secondly, it has been demonstrated that any given stock of goods cannot be optimally distributed between the various consumers (or factor suppliers) if the *MRS* between any two goods is not equal for all persons, since otherwise Pareto improvements could occur.

Allocating resources to promote the national welfare is a phrase that means many things to many people. We agreed, in the introduction to this chapter, to provisionally assume that national welfare was some amalgam of the welfares of the various individuals in the community; it was not, in other words, to be regarded as anything imposed or dreamed up by a government, for example, although we shall consider this possibility in the later applied chapters. Having said this, one can guess intuitively from the start that unless we are prepared to say something about the welfare of one person *vis-à-vis* another, there will not be a unique solution to the allocation problem; that, for example, there will not be one bundle of goods B^1 distributed in a particular way which cannot be 'bettered'. If a different bundle B^2, with a particular distribution, was taken then clearly some people might be worse off and some better off than with B^1. Unless a criterion is available for comparing different people's welfare, the relative merits of B^1 and B^2 cannot be evaluated. Although we shall find this is largely true, it is also true that the Pareto criterion for an improvement in national welfare permits one to say quite a bit about resource allocation without resort to such inter-personal comparisons of utility. In other words, if 'one person being better off without someone else being worse off' is regarded as a good thing then certain points can be made. The so-called general optimum condition holds when it is not possible, by changing the assortment and distribution of the technologically feasible sets of inputs and outputs, to effect Pareto improvements.

The requirements for attaining this condition can be established if we first of all recall the discussion of the exchange conditions. These were derived by maximizing one person's welfare subject to the rest of the community being held at particular welfare levels, and subject to a specified stock of goods. Increasing one person's utility whilst holding others constant constitutes a Pareto improvement. If this maximization process were repeated subject this time not to a specified stock of goods but to the constraint of the community production function, then the result which would emerge would be the required one. To demonstrate this point diagrammatically it is necessary to digress briefly and explain the concept of the so-called community indifference map,[6] a device which has also other uses which are exploited in later chapters. As before, the number of variables is kept down, this time to two consumers and two commodities, *j* and *k*, produceable from a fixed supply of inputs. Now the first thing to note is that an increase in one person's welfare while holding others constant can be achieved in a variety of ways. Person 1 could be given a large quantity of commodity *k* and not much extra *j*, or a lot of *j* and only a small increase in *k*; in fact, there is an infinity of possible ways of increasing person 1's welfare. In the two-person world of our simple model, person 2 constitutes the rest of the community. His welfare is fixed at a particular level denoted by I_2^1, and first of all we might consider the various ways of achieving I_2^1 and a certain welfare level for person 1, I_1^1.

One possibility would be the bundle of *k* and *j* indicated in Fig. 2.6 by point *t*, which constitutes person 2's origin of the box 0_1wtz. The distribution of this bundle between the two consumers is indicated by point *D* where the two indifference curves I_2^1 and I_1^1 are tangential; it is an efficient distribution in the sense that, from *D* no Pareto moves can be made within the box. Another possibility would be *t′* distributed according to *D′*. Visually, the

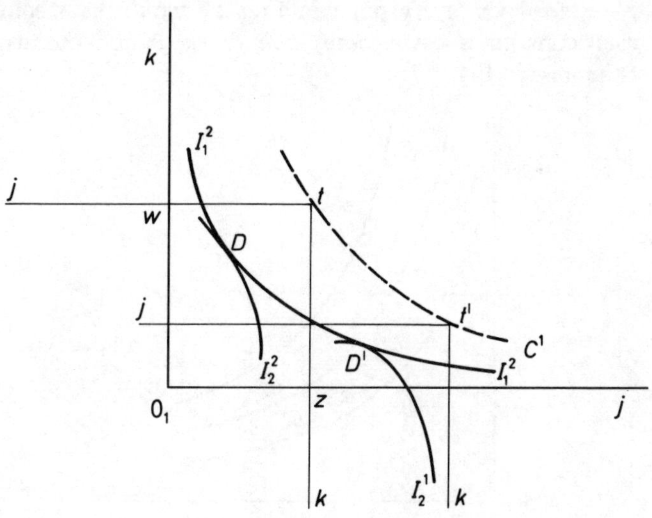

FIG. 2.6

[6] Devised initially by T. B. Scitovsky in his paper 'A Note on Welfare Propositions in Economics', *Review of Economic Studies*, November 1941, and reproduced in *Readings in Welfare Economics*, Editors K. J. Arrow and T. B. Scitovsky, AEA, Allen and Unwin, 1969. E. J. Mishan has made considerable use of this device in many of his writings. See, for example, 'The Principle of Compensation Reconsidered', *JPE*, 1952, No. 4, as well as his excellent paper, 'A Survey of Welfare Economics', *EJ*, June 1960, reproduced in *Welfare Economics: Five Introductory Essays*, E. J. Mishan, Random House, 1967, and in *Surveys of Economic Theory*, **I**, AEA and Royal Economic Society, Macmillan, 1965.

move from t to t' can be thought of as person 2's origin being shifted in a south-easterly direction, ensuring all the time that I_2^1 is tangential to I_1^1, and stopping at a particular point t', effectively forming a new box. Clearly, it is possible to trace out a large number of points like t and t', which have the characteristic that the two individuals get no more or less than the utility levels I_1^1 and I_2^1. The dotted line C^1 is deemed to connect such points, and C^1 effectively traces out the minimum bundles of k and j, and their associated distribution, sufficient to keep the two individuals on their respective indifference curves.

Curves like C^1 are called *community indifference lines* because they show the various bundles of j and k between which the community (the two individuals in this case) is indifferent. Movements along C^1 have no effect on the welfares of the members of the community. If different values were taken for their prescribed welfare levels a different curve would emerge. If for example we took I_1^2 (where $I_1^2 > I_1^1$) and kept person 2 at I_2^1, a new curve (C^2) could be derived. Given the normal shape of individual indifference maps, C^2 will be everywhere to the north east of C^1, as in Fig. 2.7, since at every point on C^2, person 1 is better off and person 2's welfare is unchanged. If the exercise were pursued, each time holding person 2 at his prescribed welfare level, every point in Fig. 2.7 would be accounted for, and the result constitutes a *community indifference map*. Note two characteristics of the map in Fig. 2.7:

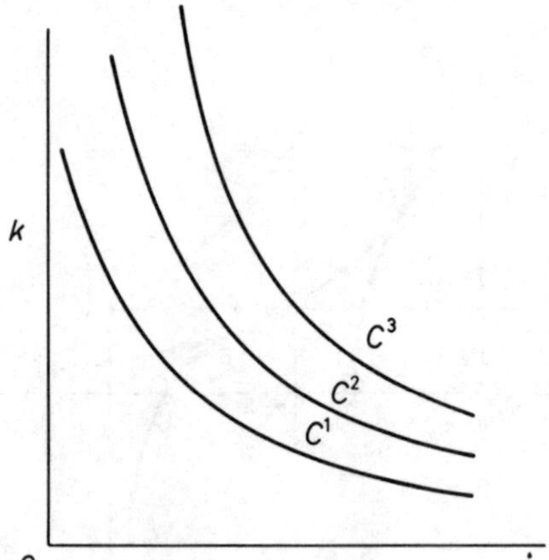

FIG. 2.7

(a) At any point on any curve the $MRS_{k,j}$ is the same for both consumers.
(b) Movements up the map from C^1 to C^2 to C^3, etc., constitute Pareto improvements.

Whereas for an individual an indifference map is unique, there is not one unique community indifference map[7] even if there are only two people in

[7] Except if every member of the community had exactly similar utility functions.

the economy. This is easily seen if we consider constructing a map on the basis of I_1^1, I_2^1, then I_1^1, I_2^2, then I_1^1, I_2^3, etc. Both characteristics (a) and (b) are met, but the map would clearly have a different shape from that in Fig. 2.7, since the new construction advances person 2's welfare while person 1 is held at a prescribed level I_1^1. Similarly, one could rank on the basis of $I_1^1+I_2^1$; $I_1^1+I_2^2$; $I_1^2+I_2^2$; etc., and another different map would emerge. This is a very important point, the significance of which will become apparent later on.

Note finally that if characteristic (b) is not specified, the map could involve C lines which crossed; an example would be $I_1^1+I_2^1$; $I_1^1+I_1^2$; $I_1^2+I_2^1$; etc.; on the third curve person 1 is better off and person 2 *worse off* than on the second line. Since, however, we are only interested in the Pareto criterion at this stage this latter point need not detain us.

The significance of the general optimum

It is now possible to return to the main stream of the analysis. To illustrate the implications of the general optimum condition, the community indifference map of Fig. 2.8(a) has been drawn up, it is assumed, on the basis of holding person 2 at some welfare level, I_2^1. The map indicates the range of possibilities open to us if we want to do the best for person 1 given the constraint that person 2 is at I_2^1. The production constraint is to be represented by the production frontier of Fig. 2.5, and this is reproduced as ll' on Fig. 2.8(a). Only at M are there no feasible opportunities for Pareto

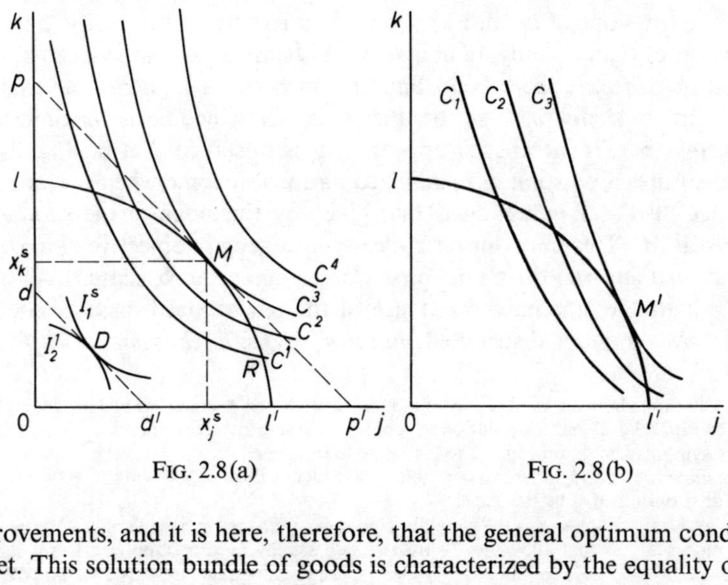

FIG. 2.8 (a) FIG. 2.8 (b)

improvements, and it is here, therefore, that the general optimum condition is met. This solution bundle of goods is characterized by the equality of the slopes of the community indifference curve and the production frontier.

Since these represent $MRS_{k,j}$ and $MRT_{k,j}$, respectively, then the general optimum condition requires that they be equal. Point R is not a maximum, since by producing less j and more k, we can move up the community indifference map, and such movements constitute Pareto improvements. Put another way the (common) marginal benefit of j (in terms of k) is less than the (common) marginal cost of j (in terms of k), and thus less j and more k are called for. The solution then comprises a bundle of outputs $x_j^s + x_k^s$, distributed among consumers[8] according to point D, with person 1 on I_1^s and the solving value for person 2's utility level is the initially prescribed amount, I_2^1.

But, as we have been continuously emphasizing, there is nothing unique about this solution if the Pareto criterion is the sole criterion used for evaluating social improvements. Using a community indifference map—C_1, C_2, C_3, etc., on Fig. 2.8(b)—which ranks the two persons' welfares in a different way from Fig. 2.8(a), one would finish up on the same production frontier but at a different[9] point, M'. At both M and M', the general optimum condition is satisfied. What is interesting is that, as long as we regard 'everyone being better off' as a good thing, then irrespective of the weights we attach to different people's welfare, the three Pareto conditions are *necessary* conditions for a welfare optimum. A further point of interest is that on Fig. 2.8(a), 'national income' is maximized at M. Since money prices and income do not enter this model, national income can only be measured in real terms in relation to some numeraire commodity. All outputs might, for example, be valued in terms of j, that is, by using the community's relative evaluation of goods in terms of j. In this simple model the appropriate valuing device would be the slope of pp' in Fig. 2.8(a). Readers can easily verify that, if all commodities (j and k only, of course, in this simple case) are valued at these 'accounting prices', there is no bundle which has a higher value than M. Why then is M not *the best* bundle if national income is maximized by producing there? The answer appears if it is observed that on Fig. 2.8(b), M' constitutes a position of maximized national income when the 'accounting price' used for valuation is that given by the slope of the production frontier at M'. This point makes it clear why a general objective of maximizing national income does not, on its own, make much sense.[10] To get a unique figure for the maximized size of the pie we need to say something about how the pie is distributed. *In other words, in choosing which feasible*

[8] To determine how the fixed supply of inputs is distributed between the two producing firms, return to Fig. 2.3 and find the point on the contract curve which corresponds to point M. Note that the symbols k and j on Fig. 2.1 to 2.4 relate to inputs.

[9] Recalling footnote 7, if the two consumers have identical tastes the solution bundle (though not its distribution) will be the same.

[10] In addition, this case has the simplification that inputs are in fixed supply. Dropping this assumption requires that allowance be made for losses involved in supplying factor services. Maximizing the value of commodities is, clearly, then inadequate and only a welfare objective has an unambiguous meaning.

bundle of goods to produce, the problem of the distribution of welfare between individuals cannot be separated from that of allocating resources.

We may finally now consider the significance of the general optimum conditions in the more realistic situation of large numbers of inputs, outputs, firms, individuals, and where the supply of inputs is not fixed. The logic of our previous analysis indicates the nature of the solutions. All one needs to do is to replace the phrase 'outputs' (or commodities) by 'goods', where this encompasses both inputs and outputs. The subjective substitution rate between any two 'goods' has to be equal to the technical transformation rate. In other words, the general optimum condition requires that

$$MRS_{k,j} = MRT_{k,j} \qquad k,j = 1 \ldots n \tag{2.4}$$

Notice four things about this:

(a) No labels for firms or individuals are given in eq. (2.4). It implicitly recognizes a subjective substitution rate, $MRS_{k,j}$, 'common' to all individuals. That is, we have demonstrated that $MRS^1_{k,j}$ has got to be the same as $MRS^2_{k,j}$, $MRS^3_{k,j}$, and so on. The 'common' rate is indicated by $MRS_{k,j}$ and the same point applies on the production side.

(b) If j and k are viewed as outputs, then the analysis suggests that resources be so allocated between commodities that the rate at which it is technically possible to transform k into j should be equal to individuals' (common) relative evaluation of the two commodities. If we think of k as serving the role of a numeraire good then the subjective substitution rate between k and j could be thought of as consumers' evaluation of, or benefit from, j, in terms of k. On p. 18 it was established that the transformation rate represented the opportunity cost of one good in terms of another. The Pareto optimum conditions thus require that the production of a commodity j should be pursued until the marginal benefit of j (in terms of k) should equal its marginal opportunity cost.

(c) If k is an input then the marginal cost of j is measured directly in terms of inputs, and the equality with marginal benefit implies that the rate at which individuals weigh the loss (disutility) in providing factor services against the benefit of the product of these services, should be equal to the rate at which it is possible to transform factor services into commodities.

(d) The rate at which factor suppliers are prepared to switch their supplies should be equal to the rate at which it is technically possible to do so.

The solution that emerges from the maximization process involves a situation where it is not possible, by any of the feasible methods available—shifting inputs and outputs between production locations, redistributing commodities, and factor supplies between persons—to make any people better off without at the same time rendering some others worse off. But, and this is the crucial point, there is no unique solution. Many possible combinations of inputs and outputs and distributions between firms and individuals can be consistent with the general optimum condition. The condition, in other words, is a necessary one for maximizing national welfare, as defined, but it is not a sufficient condition.

The general reader may now miss the next section, but those wishing to obtain further insight into the Pareto conditions need to read the more rigorous analysis of these conditions given in this next section.

2.3 A formal analysis

Explanation of techniques: production as an example

The derivation of the Pareto conditions is basically a problem of maximizing a function subject to constraints. In the case of *production*, the issue is one of discovering under what conditions it is impossible to produce more of any output (or use less of any input) without increasing the total of inputs (or without detracting from the total supply of outputs). It follows that if the output of any one commodity is maximized with all the other inputs and outputs held at fixed totals, then the solution to this problem will, in fact, give us exactly the result required. Clearly, which particular commodity we choose as the maximand (or which input we take as the minimand if an input is selected) is immaterial. We assume then a context of n goods in the economy —where 'goods' encompasses inputs and outputs—and a large number (v) of firms. Each firm has a production function relating inputs to outputs and this, for say firm a, is in the implicit form:

$$f_a(x_1^a, \ldots, x_n^a) = 0 \tag{2.5}$$

where x_n^a, etc., is the volume of the nth good produced or used by firm a. The total of any good, say n, summed over all firms is indicated by X_n.

The approach is as follows. Set the levels of all inputs and outputs except one, say output X_1, at fixed levels denoted by X_2^*, X_3^*, etc. Though the distribution of good 2 is something to be determined, the restriction means that in the solution the total of good 2, summed over all firms, must equal X_2^*; i.e., that $x_2^1 + x_2^2 + \ldots + x_2^v = X_2^*$. Now maximize X_1 subject to these restrictions and, of course, to the restriction of the production functions. The solution values would then indicate a situation where it is not possible to produce more of any commodity without producing less of others or using more inputs. This is the sort of result we want. The appropriate Lagrangean expression[11] is, therefore,

$$L = X_1 - \sum_{j=2}^{j=n} \phi_j (x_j^1 + x_j^2 + \ldots + x_j^v - X_j^*) - \sum_{a=1}^{a=v} \lambda_a f_a(x_1^a, \ldots, x_n^a) \tag{2.6}$$

[11] This maximizing technique is one of the few pieces of mathematics used in this book and familiarity with it is extremely useful in public expenditure economics. For exposition and economic uses see, for example, W. J. Baumol, *Economic Theory and Operations Analysis*, 2 Ed., chapter 4, Prentice-Hall, 1965, or J. M. Henderson and R. E. Quandt, *Microeconomic Theory: A Mathematical Approach*, section A-3 of the appendix, McGraw-Hill, 1958.

where the ϕ's and λ's are the, as yet, undetermined multipliers. The first-order conditions[12] are, therefore,

$$\delta L/\delta x_j^a = (-)\phi_j - \lambda_a\, \delta f_a/\delta x_j^a = 0 \qquad \begin{array}{l} a \;= 1 \ldots v \\ j \;= 1 \ldots n \\ \phi_1 = \;(-)1 \end{array} \tag{2.7}$$

The right-hand side of eq. (2.7) indicates that there will be n such equations for each of the v firms. Clearly, the same general types of expression would have emerged if other goods had been used as maximand (or minimand if an input were used). The meaning of the multipliers will be discussed later, but to get to the important conclusions we observe that from eq. (2.7) for commodity number 1:

$$\lambda_a = 1/F_1^a \qquad a = 1 \ldots v \tag{2.8}$$

Here and henceforth $\delta f_a/\delta x_j^a$ is denoted by F_j^a. It follows that

$$(-)\phi_j = F_j^a/F_1^a \qquad a = 1 \ldots v; j = 1 \ldots n \tag{2.9}$$

Finally, re-arrangement of eq. (2.9) leads to the main result:

$$F_j^a/F_k^a = F_j^b/F_k^b \qquad a, b = 1 \ldots v \qquad j, k = 1 \ldots n \tag{2.10}$$

Expressions such as F_j^a indicate, for an increase in j, what has to be given up, in firm a, if more of output j is produced; with j as an input it indicates what can be produced from extra j. Ratios such as F_j^a/F_k^a thus represent the rate at which k can be transformed into j in firm a. We could, for example, write such ratios as $\delta x_j^a/\delta x_k^a$. Instead they will be denoted by $MRT_{k,j}^a$, to emphasize that they represent the marginal rate of transformation between the two goods. Thus, the main result of eq. (2.10) will be represented by:

$$MRT_{k,j}^a = MRT_{k,j}^b \qquad a, b = 1 \ldots v; j, k = 1 \ldots n \tag{2.11}$$

which implies that if such switching rates are not the same in all firms then production is not optimally organized. Clearly eq. (2.11) is the same as eq. (2.1) which we derived intuitively.

The vn equations in eq. (2.7), together with the two sets of constraints, can, given knowledge of the production functions, enable us to solve for X_1 as a function of the assumed levels for the X_j^*'s. Given values for the X_j^*'s the maximum value for X_1 can be determined. The solution will involve a particular distribution of the various inputs between uses. As already noted, taking different levels for the X_j^*'s or choosing a different good for maximand, would not alter the character of the first-order conditions in eq. (2.11), and it is these conditions which are of most interest. Now if we repeated the process of eq. (2.6), using different levels for the X_j^*'s, each process would yield

[12] The full first-order conditions would also include $\delta L/\delta\phi_j$ and $\delta L/\delta\lambda_a$ which are necessary to introduce for actual solving. Note also that we shall be assuming throughout that the appropriate second-order conditions are always met.

a maximum value for X_1 given levels for the other goods. Clearly, this can be carried on indefinitely and the sum total of the results constitutes information on the maximum (minimum) value any given output (input) can take, associated with given values for the other goods. This information describes the production frontier for the economy—the boundary of feasible production opportunities associated with the given technology; a simple version is given by the production possibility line of Fig. 2.5. Such a boundary is called the community production function or social transformation function[13] and is of the form

$$F(X_1, \ldots, X_n) = 0 \tag{2.12}$$

indicating, in general, that it is a function of both outputs and inputs.

Finally, a word on the meaning of the multipliers in the maximization problem. Both the ϕ's and the λ's were used to constrain the maximand and can, in fact, be regarded as the cost of these constraints. The expression for ϕ_j in eq. (2.9) reveals that it can be thought of as the cost of extra output j in terms of what would have to be given up of the maximand, good 1; if j is an input, then ϕ_j represents the marginal social productiveness of j in terms of the extra amounts of good 1 that can be produced (or released in the case of good 1 being an input). On the other hand, the λ's indicate the cost of the constraints imposed by the production functions and eq. (2.8) indicates that λ_a represents the marginal productiveness in firm a of extra inputs (in terms of output 1) or, alternatively, the marginal cost of extra output in terms of input 1.

The exchange and general optimum conditions

Looking now at the Pareto *exchange* problem, similar issues are involved. We now allow that the economy contains a large number, m, of individuals. Each has a utility function of the form, for person i, of

$$U_i = U_i(x_1^i, \ldots, x_n^i) \tag{2.13}$$

where x_n^i is person i's consumption of commodity n, or supply when n is an input. The solution to the exchange problem is as follows.

Fix the totals of goods at levels X_1^*, X_2^*, etc. Set the (arbitrary indexes of) utility of all consumers except one at particular levels U_2^*, U_3^*, etc., and maximize the utility of person 1 subject to these restrictions and, of course, to the constraints of the utility functions. The solution values would then indicate a situation where it is not possible to make one person better off without making someone else worse off; such a result constitutes an optimal distribution as defined before. The appropriate Lagrangean expression is:

[13] See de Graaf, *op. cit.*, appendix to chapter II, for a formal derivation of the social transformation function.

$$L = U_1 - \sum_{j=1}^{n} \lambda_j(x_j^1 + x_j^2 \ldots + x_j^m - X_j^*) - \sum_{i=2}^{m} \phi_i(U_i - U_i^*) \qquad (2.14)$$

where, though similar symbols are used, the multipliers have no connection with those used for production.

Letting U_j^i denote $\delta U_i/\delta x_j^i$, etc., the first-order conditions for a maximum can be rearranged to read:

$$U_j^i/U_k^i = U_j^d/U_k^d \qquad i, d = 1 \ldots m; \quad j, k = 1 \ldots n \qquad (2.15)$$

which is similar to eq. (2.10) for production. Since U_j^i, etc., represents the marginal utility to person i from an extra unit of j (or disutility if j is a factor service supplied), then the ratios in eq. (2.15) represent the individuals' marginal rates of substitution between the two goods; the rate at which, in other words, a person could switch k for j and keep his welfare at the same level. A given bundle of goods is optimally distributed only when such substitution rates are the same for all persons. In other words, eq. (2.15) can be written as:

$$MRS_{k,j}^i = MRS_{k,j}^d \qquad j, d = 1 \ldots m; \quad j, k = 1 \ldots n \qquad (2.16)$$

Clearly, this expression is nothing more than a repeat of eq. (2.3), derived intuitively before.

As we suggested in the general discussion, the *general optimum condition* can be derived by repeating the exchange maximization process subject this time, not to a specified stock of goods, but to the constraint of the community production function, eq. (2.12). Again, the result which would emerge would be the required one. The appropriate Lagrangean expression is, therefore:

$$L = U_1 - \lambda F(X_1, \ldots, X_n) - \sum_{i=2}^{m} \phi_i(U_i - U_i^*) \qquad (2.17)$$

The first-order conditions are obtained by maximizing this expression with respect to each of the goods for each person. Denoting $\delta F/\delta X_j$ by F_j etc., these first-order conditions when rearranged read:

$$U_j^i/U_k^i = F_j/F_k \qquad i = 1 \ldots m; \quad j, k = 1 \ldots n \qquad (2.18)$$

The left-hand side of this expression represents the subjective substitution rate for person i between the two goods j and k. The discussion of exchange problems has already established that this rate has to be the same for all persons and, in fact, eq. (2.18) itself implies that it is a common rate. The right-hand side needs more explanation. F_j represents the partial derivative of the community production function with respect to a change in j; if the change was extra output j, then F_j could, for example, be thought of as the extra inputs needed. The whole ratio thus represents the economy's technologically most efficient way of transforming k into j and, given the previous analysis of production problems, this transformation rate is the same in all production locations where k is transformed into j. Equation (2.18) thus requires that the rate at which people are prepared to switch k for j should be equal to the rate at which it is technically feasible to do so. This result can, therefore, be written as:

$$MRS_{k,j} = MRT_{k,j} \qquad k, j = 1 \ldots n \tag{2.19}$$

where $MRS_{k,j}$ is the common marginal subjective substitution rate and $MRT_{k,j}$ is the transformation rate which will also be common to all firms which transform k into j. Equation (2.19) is, of course, exactly the same as eq. (2.4), which we derived intuitively before.

The solution that emerges from the maximization process involves a situation where it is not possible, by any redistributions of outputs and inputs between firms and individuals, to make any people better off without at the same time rendering some others worse off. The solution to eq. (2.17) involves the prescribed levels of welfare $U_2^* \ldots U_m^*$, a solution for the level of U_1 and solutions for the levels of the x_j^i's. This latter, of course, would imply determinate totals for the goods $X_1 \ldots X_n$. It is fairly obvious that if different prescribed levels for $U_2 \ldots U_m$ were taken, the same Pareto conditions would emerge. But the solution bundle of goods would be different and so, as we predicted, there is no unique solution to the problem of allocating resources if our only guide for determining improvements in national welfare is the Pareto criterion. To the extent that in the second case we attach more weight to certain persons' welfare, then their preferences for goods will influence the character of the solution bundle. It is possible then that *all* of the feasible sets of inputs and outputs described by the community production function could appear as solution bundles as we go through different maximization processes. To repeat what we said in the general discussion, in choosing which feasible bundle of goods to produce, the problem of the distribution of welfare between individuals cannot be separated from that of allocating resources.

2.4 The search for a unique solution

Unless a *particular* community indifference map is taken—that is, unless we attach explicit particular weights to different people's welfare—it is likely that most, if not all, of the feasible bundles of outputs shown on the production frontier could be Pareto efficient. The analysis that has been developed constitutes the core of what might be called the 'grand design', the search for a method of choosing a best bundle of goods. The indeterminancy which remains can, in principle, be solved, and in the next section we shall briefly demonstrate how this is done. But the solution involves theoretical techniques which, though tidying-up the analysis, have as yet hardly any operational significance and, therefore, before doing so, we may summarize the main elements and implications of the analysis developed up to this point.

(a) The Pareto conditions can be regarded as necessary (though not sufficient) conditions for the achievement of the 'grand design'. As we have seen, they leave an indeterminancy in the selection of bundles. What can be said about the relative merits of the feasible bundles? A number of points can be made, and Fig. 2.9 will be used to illustrate them.

For bundles within the frontier, no matter what their distribution, there will usually be a range of other bundles to which they are potentially inferior in the sense that Pareto improvements could be made. In Fig. 2.9, for example, the distribution of bundle *Z* is given by point *E*. Pareto improvements are possible if a move is made to points like *Z'*, provided that the distribution is in accordance with the community indifference map C_a^1, C_a^2, etc., the slope of C_a^1 at *Z* being equal to the slope of the indifference curves at *E*. This is tantamount to saying that the production condition is met.

Similarly, bundle *Y* distributed according to point *L* does not meet the exchange condition.

Finally, a bundle such as *Y'* will be superior to bundle *Y* distributed according to *D*, provided that the distribution of *Y'* corresponds to the community indifference map C_b^1, C_b^2, etc., where the slope of C_b^1 at *Y* equals the slope of the indifference curves at *D*. This is tantamount to requiring that the general optimum condition is met.

But note that in no circumstances could we say, *without qualification*, that *Z'* is better than *Z*, *Y'* better than *Y*, since there may be *some* distributions of the new bundles which do not constitute Pareto improvements on the old bundle. This is the point that Samuelson[14] has insisted on, and we shall return to these matters in a later chapter.

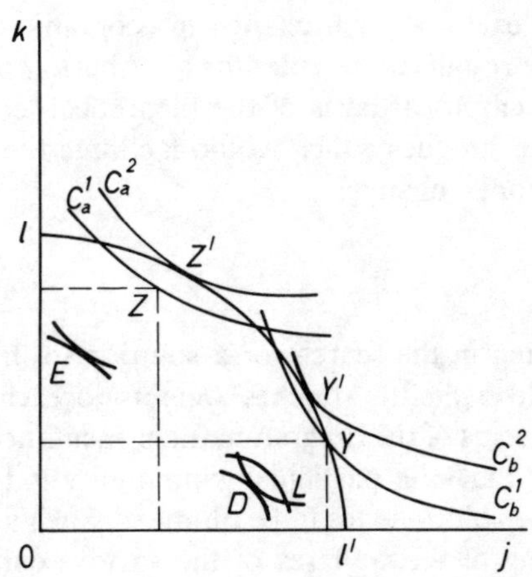

FIG. 2.9

[14] P. A. Samuelson, 'Evaluation of Real National Income', *OEP*, No. 1, 1950. Reproduced in *Readings in Welfare Economics, op. cit.*

(b) One point implicit in the analysis is that the conditions are of an all-or-nothing nature. If, for some reason, one of the conditions cannot be implemented, then the other conditions are no longer necessarily desirable. If, for example, the transformation rate between two inputs is not everywhere the same, then this will affect the production of outputs and thus the actual quantity of goods available. This point is very important and will be reconsidered later on, particularly in connection with the problem of 'second best'.
(c) For future reference the reader is invited to think of the Pareto conditions as comprising the three main conditions of production, exchange, and general optimum each containing three sub-conditions:
(i) as between outputs,
(ii) as between inputs, and,
(iii) as between inputs and outputs.
(d) They are derived from a criterion—'it is a good thing if someone is better off and no one is worse off'—which is really quite weak, in the sense that many changes in economic circumstances in real life usually involve some people suffering.
(e) The way that the distribution issue is tackled will become apparent as the analysis develops in the book, and in particular when we examine how (models of) various types of social systems implicitly deal with the allocation and distribution problems. But we can usefully look ahead and indicate that there will be broadly two lines of approach:
(i) On the one hand, we will envisage certain methods being used to promote the attainment of the Pareto conditions and certain different methods being used to promote distributional aims.
(ii) An approach which, in practice, may be either a substitute for, or complementary to, (i) is to examine each change in economic circumstances and evaluate it with some rough *ad hoc* rules for distribution, as opposed, that is, to searching for the empirical basis of the theoretical techniques discussed in the next section, techniques which would facilitate the ranking, distribution-wise, of all economic changes.

Bliss

What has been lacking in the search for a solution to the 'grand design' is some function which explicitly attaches weights to each person's welfare. Clearly, thinking in terms of the diagrammatic presentations, if we had good reasons for thinking that one particular community indifference map was correct, then a unique solution would be obtained. Such a map would imply a particular weighting of the welfares of the various constituent members of the community. Such a *social welfare function* would, therefore, express national welfare as a weighted sum of the welfares of the individuals in the economy.

The literature in theoretical welfare economics abounds with discussions involving the use of social welfare functions and its kindred brethren, such as utility possibility lines and welfare frontiers. We have chosen to avoid much of this, for the simple reason that it is doubtful whether a social welfare function could be derived in a way which was consistent with the sovereignty of individual preferences. While you and I might both agree to support more aid to Southern Italy, it is doubtful whether your evaluation of the relative importance of my welfare accords with my evaluation. Of course, our dictator does not have the same qualms, and for him there may well be a particular set of welfare weights he wishes to use; but obviously this is not based on the preferences of individuals in the economy. To the extent that our theoretical apparatus rests on *individual* preferences, the social welfare function does not have much of a role. At the same time, it is important to bear in mind that in the later applied work we shall, among other things, try to take account of some of the government's objectives in the fields of income distribution, etc. and so we are not throwing views on distribution out of the window. They will be an important consideration. What we are suggesting is that it does not appear that there is one 'right' and unique solution to the problem of resource allocation if the sole guide-line is the individual preferences of people in the community.

For those readers who would like to see how social welfare functions tie up formally with the previous analysis, we can proceed by suggesting that national welfare, W, is some function of the welfare or utility levels of the various individuals in the economy. In particular, we may write

$$W = W(U_1, U_2, \ldots, U_m) \tag{2.20}$$

Although W can be arbitrary in its numerical size (cf. individual utility functions) it does provide us with a maximand, so that the Utopian bundle of goods which gives community 'bliss' is attained by maximizing W, subject to the constraint solely of the community production function. We shall assume that W, called a social welfare function, whatever its particular characteristics, does have the general characteristic that it sanctions Pareto improvements, i.e., that $\delta W/\delta U_i > 0$ $(i = 1 \ldots m)$. Note, incidentally, that since each person's utility is a function of the goods he consumes, then the social welfare function could be written in the form analogous to a *particular* community indifference map, and this information is sufficient to determine a unique bundle of goods on Fig. 2.8 and Fig. 2.9. Keeping to the more general form of the social welfare function, the problem can be seen as maximizing:

$$L = W - \lambda F(X_1, \ldots, X_n) \tag{2.21}$$

Denoting $\delta W/\delta U_i$ by W_i the first-order conditions include

$$\delta L/\delta x_j^i = W_i\, U_j^i - \lambda F_j = 0 \qquad \begin{array}{l} i = 1 \ldots m \\ j = 1 \ldots n \end{array} \tag{2.22}$$

giving

$$\lambda = W_i \, U_j^i / F_j \qquad i = 1 \ldots m; \quad j = 1 \ldots n \tag{2.23}$$

Taking j as an output, this result indicates that the social value of the extra utility ultimately accruing from the use of any inputs, should be the same, irrespective of which commodity is produced by these inputs or which consumers received the commodity. Also, we have:

$$W_1 U_j^1 = W_2 U_j^2 = \ldots = W_m U_j^m \qquad j = 1 \ldots n \tag{2.24}$$

which indicates that any good cannot be optimally distributed among consumers if the net marginal *social* utility, which accrues from switching the good from one person to another, is not zero. The reader can easily verify that the first-order conditions imply the satisfaction of the exchange and general optimum conditions as given by eq. (2.18); eq. (2.18) is a result of a particular form of a Paretian social welfare function, namely, that we do the best for person 1 subject to the rest of the community being at certain prescribed levels. In other words, no matter how the welfare weights are distributed between persons, as long as 'someone being better off and no-one worse off' is a move which is sanctioned by the social welfare function, the optimum conditions are required in all cases. This brings out formally the point already made that the Pareto conditions are *necessary* conditions in the achievement of the 'grand design'. As long as W involves the Paretian characteristic that $W_i > 0$, then the Pareto conditions can be derived from the maximization process, without need to specify the particular form of W.

3. Economic efficiency and expenditure criteria

3.1 Price patterns

The omniscient economist and benevolent dictator who featured in the previous chapter have enough knowledge to deal with the problem of resource allocation. Since they are familiar with all the production and utility functions, the general equilibrium problem can be solved. At least the dictator can, since he will have his own views on what relative weights should be attached to various people's welfare; the omniscient economist still has difficulties if he is not prepared to exercise his own opinion on what constitutes a proper distribution of welfare. But when we leave such myths and think perhaps of a government facing these problems, the most striking point is the almost insuperable quantity of knowledge that it would have to acquire to actually solve the problem. In general, we shall assume that governments—and even their planning boards!—do not have this knowledge. It is for this reason, as noted in chapter 2, that the function of subsequent analysis will be to search for general rules of behaviour for the firms and individuals in the economy, which will both guide the economy to a desired result and reduce the volume of knowledge needed by the government in whatever turns out to be its required role.

Plan of chapter

In the first three sections of this chapter the chief subject of interest will be the attainment of Pareto efficiency, and social systems will be described as efficient if the allocation of resources is Pareto efficient. As we have seen, there will not be one unique allocation which meets this criterion and neither is there anything inherently, ethically desirable in having a Pareto efficient solution. We shall examine such allocations because

(a) their achievement constitutes *one* of the objectives which could usefully be pursued by public expenditure decision-takers; why we take this line will not be justified until the next chapter, where the relevance of these models and the general methodology of their application will be reviewed; and,

(b) the analysis will indicate what determines the *actual* distribution of welfare in various (models of) social systems and what scope exists for changing this distribution.

Now, in the analysis of the optimum conditions all items were discussed in real terms—outputs, inputs, production rates, utility—but it is an important feature of the results of chapter 2 that a set of constants (the transformation rate between inputs, for example, which was required to be constant for all firms) is embedded in the solutions, and these constants could correspond in a money economy to the various prices exacted for services rendered. This issue we take up immediately. In section 3.2 an economy where all resources are privately owned is examined. Next follows, in section 3.3, a simple model where all non-human resources are publicly owned. This will introduce the first points about public sector decision rules, and these are further developed in the context of a mixed economy. The final three sections consider both the problem of allowing that all inputs and outputs are not perfectly divisible —as we have implicitly assumed so far—and also wider objectives other than efficiency. Consider then first of all a number of points about price patterns.

Required price features

From the basic theory of resource allocation there emerged a set of requirements involving certain exchange rates between goods, where, as before, the term 'goods' encompasses inputs and outputs. The rate at which it is technically possible to transform one good into another was required to be the same in all firms; similarly, the rate at which persons evaluated one good in terms of another was required to be constant over persons and, in addition, to be equal to the technical exchange rate. Now, in a money economy goods are exchanged at prices, and it is but a small step to see that the attainment of the optimum conditions requires that these prices have certain characteristics. For ease in following the analysis, the reader is reminded of the point made on p. 32, that there are effectively 9 optimum conditions.

Consider, for example, the production sector's choice of commodities (or outputs) to produce. The Pareto production condition requires that the technical transformation rate between any two commodities should be the same in all firms. It could be met by ensuring that the selling price of any commodity is the same, no matter which firm produces it, and ensuring that, in every firm, the production of commodities is organized so that the technical transformation rate between any pair of commodities is equal to their relative selling prices. Previously, the transformation rate between two commodities j and k, has been written, for some typical firm a, as $MRT^a_{k.j}$. Let us now write this in a more explicit form as $(\Delta k/\Delta j)^a$; it represents[1],

[1] Those readers who tackled the formal analysis of section 2.3 will realize that we are using $(\Delta k/\Delta j)^a$ for F^a_j/F^a_k, where F^a_j, etc., is the partial derivative of the firm's production function with respect to j. In fact, of course, in calculus terms, F^a_j/F^a_k can be written as $\delta x^a_k/\delta x^a_j$.

in other words, the rate at which k has to be surrendered to get more j. The proposition is therefore that, taking firm a as one of many firms in the economy, and k and j as two of the many commodities, production should be arranged so that

$$P_j^a/P_k^a = (\Delta k/\Delta j)^a \qquad (3.1)$$

where P_j^a, etc., is the selling price of commodity j in firm a. Given the requirement that the selling price of any commodity is the same in every firm, the price ratio in eq. (3.1) will also be a common one, the transformation rate will, therefore, be the same in every firm and the Pareto production condition as between any two outputs will be met. How these two points are 'ensured' is something that will be considered in the later sections; at this stage it is useful simply to concentrate on the price features. A significant point about the second requirement is that it is price ratios that count; the absolute price level does not matter.[2]

Turning to the person sector, the requirements are similar to those for production. The Pareto condition is met by

(a) ensuring that the buying price of any commodity is the same for each of the large number of consumers,[3] and,

(b) ensuring that the individual so arranges his consumption that,[4] taking one particular person i,

$$P_j^i/P_k^i = U_j^i/U_k^i \qquad (3.2)$$

Here P_j^i, etc., represents the price paid by individual i for commodity j. Expressions such as U_j^i indicate the marginal utility to person i from commodity j, so that the ratio U_j^i/U_k^i represents[5] person i's marginal subjective substitution rate between j and k. Given the common price ratio, the substitution rate would then be the same for all consumers. Further, if we also ensure that the two sectors' prices are the same, then it would follow that the general optimum condition would be met, since the common price ratio would be equal to both the technical and the subjective substitution rates; the last two, in other words, would be equal.

[2] However, this is really tied up with the whole treatment of money balances and this brings in some formidable issues. For an introductory link-up with the analysis here see J. M. Henderson and R. E. Quandt, *Micro-Economic Theory: A Mathematical Approach,* chapter 5, McGraw-Hill, 1958.

[3] Strictly speaking it is not necessary that consumers pay the same price for each unit of a commodity they consume; all that is necessary is that prices paid for the *marginal* unit each consumer takes, should be the same for all consumers. Intra-marginal units could command different prices. This point has some significance later on. Generally, however, we shall assume every unit commands the same price.

[4] Equation (3.2) will be recognized as the equilibrium condition for utility maximization in consumer demand theory. This gives a clear hint to one of the behavioural requirements that will be considered in later sections of this chapter.

[5] In fact, one might write this substitution rate as $(\Delta k/\Delta j)^i$, but we keep it in the form of the utility ratios to avoid confusion with the notation for production.

So far commodities only have been considered. The reader can probably see that, formally, the rest of the price features follow the same pattern. The general point is that as between any two 'goods', Pareto optimality is ensured if their prices are uniform over persons and firms, if the person sector adjusts its consumption so that the subjective substitution rate is equal to the price ratio, and if production is pursued until the transformation rate is equal to the relative prices. Rather than spell out these requirements for the remaining 6 Pareto conditions, we concentrate on the implications of these requirements.

Marginal costs and prices

In considering the allocation of inputs it is useful to introduce some new terminology distinguishing between inputs and outputs. Henceforth, there will be outputs (or commodities) typified by j and k and inputs typified by l. Assuming that the Pareto production condition between inputs is met, it is now possible to say something about the relationship between prices and costs. This can be seen in the context of eq. (3.1). Suppose both these commodities j and k use input l, whose price is W_l^p, the superscript p indicating that it is a price common to the production sector. Now the marginal money cost of j in firm a is given by $W_l^p\,(\Delta l/\Delta j)^a$, i.e., by the extra inputs needed for an extra unit of j, multiplied by the input price. Notice that, since $\Delta j/\Delta l$ is the marginal product of input l in terms of j, then marginal cost is equal to the input price divided by marginal product. Now if both sides of eq. (3.1) are divided by $(\Delta l)^a W_l^p$, then rearrangement gives:

$$P_j \div [W_l^p(\Delta l/\Delta j)^a] = P_k \div [W_l^p(\Delta l/\Delta k)^a] = R^a \tag{3.3}$$

where P_j and P_k have lost their labels for firm a to indicate our previous requirement that output selling prices are common to all firms. The expression indicates that the ratio of price to marginal cost in firm a is required to be the same for all commodities; the constant ratio is given an arbitrary value R^a. Now this is simply an implication of the points already developed. But the Pareto production condition between inputs and outputs requires that transformation rates such as $(\Delta l/\Delta j)^a$ be the same in all firms. This can be achieved if it is ensured that the ratio of price to marginal cost is the same in all firms, as well as for all commodities, since then we would have:

$$P_j = RW_l^p(\Delta l/\Delta j)^a \tag{3.4}$$

Since P_j, W_l^p, and R are common to all firms, the proposal that every firm adjusts its operations so that eq. (3.4) is met will guarantee that the transformation rate between input and output is the same in all firms. This requirement, that prices be everywhere equi-proportional to marginal costs, incidentally, also guarantees the fulfilment of the other Pareto *production* conditions, provided that input and output prices are common to all firms.

Now it is an interesting point, and one to which we shall return later, that if all inputs are in fixed supply, ensuring that prices are everywhere equi-proportional to marginal costs is a sufficient device for attaining the Pareto conditions.[6] This is because, under conditions of fixity, the inputs would not enter the individual utility functions, they are there and available irrespective of economic factors. Many of the non-human resources associated with land may well fall into this category. This does not mean they are fixed in their usage and, in fact, the characteristics of their allocation between uses has already been mentioned. The fact that these inputs do not enter the preference functions means that the remaining Pareto conditions not yet considered are redundant, since each of these involves the welfare effects of adjusting the supply of inputs. In these circumstances, the price features so far considered are sufficient for the attainment of Pareto optimality.

A complete picture of possible price features emerges if it is allowed that the remaining Pareto conditions *are* relevant, i.e., that inputs do enter utility functions. Ensuring that input price ratios are uniform over persons and firms, and that the two sectors adjust their supplies and usage so that these ratios are equal to the subjective substitution rate and transformation rate respectively, will be sufficient for the attainment of the exchange and general optimum conditions between inputs. There now only remain the conditions between inputs and outputs. The exchange condition necessitates that personal consumption and supplies be so arranged that for every individual typified by person i

$$P_j/W_l = U^i_j/U^i_l \tag{3.5}$$

for, given that the price ratio is common to all individuals, everyone's substitution rate will be the same. Finally, the general optimum condition between inputs and outputs can be considered in relation to the two price features indicated by eq. (3.4) and eq. (3.5). Each of these guarantees that the two 'real' transformation and substitution rates are uniform over their respective sectors. But taken together the price patterns imply (bearing in mind that $W^p_l = W_l$) that the subjective rate is R times the technical rate, whereas the general optimum condition requires that they be equal. If R exceeds unity then prices are in excess of marginal costs. The implication of this is that consumers' evaluation of extra product j in terms of the inputs they are prepared to supply in exchange, exceeds the rate at which it is technologically necessary to give up inputs to obtain more output. More j is therefore warranted; output should be increased until the two rates are equal—until, in other words, price equals marginal cost. Formally this means eq. (3.4) has to be replaced by:

$$P_j = W_l(\Delta l/\Delta j) \tag{3.6}$$

[6] There is a qualification necessary when intermediate or producer goods are involved—more on this later.

implying that R is set equal to unity. *Thus proportionality of prices to marginal costs is not enough; they have to be equal.*

The requirement that prices be equal to marginal costs is the money economy equivalent to the 'real' rules discussed in the previous chapter. In particular on p. 25 we demonstrated that the output of any commodity had to be pushed to the point where marginal benefit was equal to marginal cost. Put otherwise, the condition in eq. (3.6) corresponds to a familiar intuitive idea that each class of factor be so allocated between activities that the 'value' of its services is everywhere the same. This can easily be seen by rearranging eq. (3.6) to give:

$$W_l = P_j(\Delta j/\Delta l) \tag{3.7}$$

Since the transformation rate here represents the marginal product of the factor l in terms of output j, then the right-hand side of eq. (3.7) can be interpreted as the value of the marginal product of the factor, which, granted uniform factor prices, is required to be the same in all its uses.[7] However, the transition from 'real' rules to rules involving prices is not yet complete, since we have not really explained in what sense the word 'value' is being used or why prices can be interpreted as marginal 'benefit'. Similarly, whilst $W_l(\Delta l/\Delta j)$ may easily be understood as representing marginal money costs, one might inquire in what sense the expression represents 'real' costs?

A feature of the price patterns that have emerged is that, for each consumer, the marginal utility per dollar or pound of outlay is the same for every commodity. This can be seen from eq. (3.2) where U^i_j/P^i_j represents this ratio for commodity j, and eq. (3.2) implies that this ratio, for consumer i, is the same for all commodities. Suppose that, for the ith consumer, we denote this constant ratio by M^i. Since a characteristic of the price patterns is that prices are the same for all consumers, then it follows that if there are m consumers in the economy:

$$P_j = U^1_j/M^1 = U^2_j/M^2 = \ldots = U^i_j/M^i = \ldots = U^m_j/M^m \tag{3.8}$$

Similar points apply if a different commodity is taken. Thus, P_j represents a dollar measure of the marginal benefit to the consumer of an extra unit of j. 'Benefit' is used in the sense that it constitutes the quantity of money he would just be prepared to give up to get an extra unit; 'just' is used, here, in the sense that exchanging P_j dollars for one unit of j renders him no better or worse off. What he gets is U^i_j; what he would otherwise have received for P_j dollars is P_jM^i: on the margin, these two are equal. It is in this sense that the term 'value' is used in denoting $P_j(\Delta j/\Delta l)$ as the value of the marginal product of a factor. By similar reasoning, W_l constitutes the minimum

[7] The price/marginal cost equality was stated as a rule by A. P. Lerner in his *Economics of Control*, Macmillan, 1944. In its other version as requiring the equality of returns to a factor it has appeared in numerous places. E. J. Mishan calls it the 'allocative rule' and uses it in his exposition of the optimum conditions. See *A Survey of Welfare Economics: 1939–59* cited in chapter 2.

compensation a person would require for providing one more unit of factor l; in this sense, $W_l(\Delta l/\Delta j)$ reflects the 'real' marginal cost of an extra unit of j. To the extent that non-human resources are in fixed supply, their prices cannot be interpreted in this way, since such inputs have no welfare effect, they do not enter utility functions. The prices to the production sector are simply at a level which rations out the limited and fixed supply among the various firms in the economy. In fact, no matter who owns such factors, whether it be the state or individuals, it is irrelevant what payment they *receive*—they are available, by assumption, irrespective of economic forces.[8]

Intermediate goods

Finally, two points concerning *intermediate goods*. Firstly, such goods will not enter the individual utility functions and all the exchange conditions are redundant, as also are two of the general optimum conditions. The remaining conditions can be analysed if we think of an input l being used to produce an intermediate good, g,—say raw cotton—which is itself an input for firms manufacturing a final good j. Now, while the producer good does not enter preference functions, both l and j do, and the general optimum condition requires that $U_j/U_l = (\Delta l/\Delta j)$. The second part of this equation is really a compound of two transformation rates and, thus, the general optimum conditions will be fulfilled if

$$P_j/W_l = (\Delta l/\Delta g) \times (\Delta g/\Delta j) \qquad (3.9)$$

Provided that the usual point about transformation rates and prices applies both in the sector producing g and in the sector producing j, then eq. (3.9) will emerge as long as the buying and selling prices of the producer good are the same.

A second feature of producer goods can be seen if the case of fixed input supply is considered. We have already seen that in such circumstances the proportionality of prices and marginal costs was advanced as a sufficient rule. As long as some goods cannot be used as both intermediate and final goods, no problems arise. Consider, however, items like water and coal which do have this characteristic. Following the rule, the price of g when sold as a final good would be, say, R times its marginal cost. The costs of another final good j relate to the use of g in its role as producer good. The price of j would be, therefore, R times marginal cost. But if this marginal cost was calculated with g at the same price as when sold as a final good, the transformation rate between the two final goods would not be equal to their relative prices.

Following the proportionality rule:

$$P_j = RP_g^p\,(\Delta g/\Delta j) \text{ and } P_g^c = RW_l\,(\Delta l/\Delta g)$$

[8] Cf. One can tax the income of a factor in fixed supply, such as land, without any effect on the volume of its services.

where the superscripts, p and c, indicate the prices of the good in question in its role as both producer and consumer good. The relative prices of the two final goods are:

$$P_j/P_g^c = (\Delta g/\Delta j)\,[(P_g^p/W_l)/(\Delta l/\Delta g)]$$

In order that the general optimum conditions between the two final goods hold, it is necessary, granted that the prices of the final goods are uniform over consumers, that the expression in square brackets be equal to unity. In other words, that

$$P_g^p = W_l(\Delta l/\Delta g)$$

The price of g as an intermediate good should be *equal* to marginal costs.

In these circumstances, if domestic water is sold at a price above marginal cost, the industrial users of water must be charged a price equal to marginal cost. Of course, this may not be feasible, but, in any case, viewing the proportionality thesis as a normative rule, it would be much simpler in this context to make the proportionality equal to unity.

3.2 Private enterprise systems

In the spirit of some of the myths discussed previously, one could perhaps think of a government with sufficient knowledge and sufficient dictatorial power to solve the allocation problem in the money-economy environment. Given some predilection for a particular distribution of welfare, it could 'instruct' the production sector to manufacture the solution quantities of output, pay the solution factor prices and the solution output prices, and so on. Fortunately there is no need, in theory, for such central information and direction. Whether resources are primarily privately owned or publicly owned—and the degree of ownership constitutes the sole distinguishing feature between various social systems that will be considered here—a decentralized structure can do the job, certainly if Pareto efficiency is the only objective. The previous section has cleared much of the ground, and it is useful to summarize the four main features of the required price patterns:

(a) Prices of each class of variable input and output to be uniform over the person and production sectors.

(b) Prices of inputs in fixed supply and of intermediate goods to be uniform over the production sector.

(c) Personal consumption patterns to be so arranged that subjective substitution rates between 'goods' equal their respective prices.

(d) Outputs and inputs to be increased in each industry until the price of the product equals marginal cost.

The private enterprise system to be considered is one where every input, whether human or non-human, and including entrepreneurship, is privately owned; implicit in this is that the production of all intermediate goods is in private control.[9] The methodology of the analysis is to detail the required characteristics of the economy, and the required behavioural rules of the persons and social organizations in the economy, which would ensure that the price features did emerge.[10] To the extent that private enterprise systems involve goods being exchanged on markets, it should be fairly obvious that 'perfect' markets will ensure that points (a) and (b) are met. If there are large numbers of participators on both sides of the market and if factors and commodities are freely mobile, then common prices will be established for both the buying and selling sides of the market. Further, if the market is allowed to clear, prices will be the same for both buyers and sellers.[11]

It now remains[12] to demonstrate that if firms are profit-maximizers and individuals are utility-maximizers, features (c) and (d) will be satisfied. Taking the person sector first, it is a well-known conclusion of demand theory that the condition in (c) is met when consumers maximize utility. The conventional illustration of this is a two-dimensional diagram pinpointing a consumer's equilibrium purchases of commodities. If the reader will take the trouble to return to Fig. 2.2. in the previous chapter, the line $k'j'$ can be viewed as indicating the possibilities open to the consumer as between two commodities j and k, given his income and their prices. With the consumer's preferences indicated by the indifference map, I_2^1, I_2^2, etc., utility is maximized at X. This point is characterized by the tangency of the consumer's budget line with his highest attainable indifference curve. Since the slopes of these two represent the relative price ratio and the marginal subjective rate of substitution, respectively, then characteristic (c)—or more explicitly eq. (3.2)—is met. Broadly, the same points apply to the individual's supply of factor services.[13] In general, his utility function will contain factor services and, moreover, his money income will depend on how many of these he is willing to supply and what rewards they command in the market.

Looking now at the production sector, it is a well-known proposition of micro-economics that profit-maximization entails an equilibrium position

[9] This, of course, is a very extreme case. If everything were in private control it would mean that, as well as railways and atomic research being in private hands, so also would be the administration of justice, the road system, flood relief, etc. However, we do here assume a role for government, certainly in the context of income distribution. Note also that it is possible to demonstrate, using certain models, that if some of the above services were left to private enterprise, little or no services would emerge! This is one point developed in the later chapter on external effects.

[10] Although the specification of required behavioural rules has (implicitly, if not always explicitly) characterized the literature in welfare economics, some recent work by O. A. Davis and A. Whinston has, among other things, demonstrated this point most forcibly. See 'Welfare Economics and the Theory of the Second Best', *Review of Economic Studies,* January 1965, and 'Piecemeal Policy in the Theory of Second Best', in the July 1967 issue of the same journal.

[11] For inputs in fixed supply some qualification can be made to this; cf. above p. 39.

[12] There are, of course, many implications of this model and these will emerge in the course of the book. In particular, section 3.3 includes some of the implications at the industry level.

[13] The appropriate indifference curve diagram, when inputs and outputs are involved, would have a commodity on one axis and leisure (i.e. not supplying labour services) on the other. The familiar leisure/good analysis can then be performed.

for the individual firm where marginal revenue equals marginal cost. Provided that within each commodity market there are a large number of firms, then any one firm will be a price-taker, so that for it, marginal revenue will be equal to price. Marginal costs will, therefore, be equal to price as point (d) required, and this will also ensure that the other production requirements explicitly or implicitly described in the previous section will be met. For example, it was implied there that the choice of inputs be such that the technical rate of substitution between any two inputs should be the same in all firms. Considering Fig. 2.2 again, we may now think of the axes as relating to two *inputs*, j and k, and the curves as indicating a firm's isoproduct map. If firms are profit-maximizers, then by definition they are also cost minimizers. If the price ratio of the two inputs is indicated by the slope of the line $k'j'$, then attempting to minimize the cost of any output level, such as I_2^2, requires that the input bundle be chosen where the price line is tangential to an isoproduct line—bundle X in this case. And this position is characterized by the equality of relative input prices and the relative marginal productivity of the two factors, i.e., $\Delta k/\Delta j$ (cf. discussion on pp. 15–16). Granted uniform factor prices, the equality of the relative productivity of the two factors in all locations is guaranteed.

Of course, one of the factors of production, entrepreneurship or 'organization', may not receive a reward just equal to the value of its marginal product. Even if we allow that all firms within an industry are of equal efficiency—entrepreneurs are homogeneous—if the number of these firms is in limited fixed supply each earns abnormal profits. If our slice of time is viewed as being long enough to permit the number of firms to vary, then a requirement of free entry will ensure that the abnormal profits are competed away, so that effectively entrepreneurship gets paid (by way of 'normal' profits) an

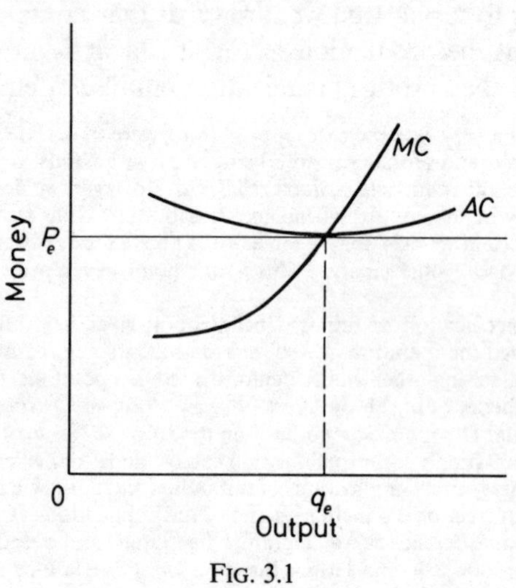

FIG. 3.1

amount equal to the value of its services. Thus the classic solution—shown in Fig. 3.1—emerges with the typical firm's average cost[14] (AC) equal to the final price P_e. The number of firms in an industry will be one of the factors which affect the actual solution quantities of inputs and outputs and, generally, this solution will involve all markets being in equilibrium.

The allocation of resources and the distribution of income

A social system, then, where all resources are privately owned and which has the outlined characteristics, will involve an allocation of resources which is Pareto efficient. While such an economy would constitute a sufficient condition for Pareto efficiency, it is, of course, not a necessary condition since, as we shall see, economies where many of the resources are socially owned can also achieve efficient solutions. The student familiar with micro-economic theory will recognize that models of perfect competition usually have most of the characteristics examined above,[15] and this provides the basis for the contention that perfect competition leads to an efficient allocation of resources.

It is pertinent to reiterate that there is nothing fundamentally desirable about the result achieved so far, since there is nothing to suggest that the actual distribution of welfare is intrinsically commendable. Let us consider the general features of the solution bundle of goods and its distribution. An individual's welfare is determined by how many commodities he consumes and how many human inputs—man-hours of work, for example—he supplies. His ability to obtain access to commodities is governed by the size of his money income, which in turn depends on the quantity of man-hours he works, on the quantity of non-human resources he owns, and on the prices that these services command in the market. Since, in our model, the rewards of a factor are equal to the value of their marginal products, then such rewards will be affected by the factors' physical productivity and by the relative scarcity, both of the factors themselves and the commodities

[14] The marginal and average cost curves in Fig. 3.1 can be interpreted as long-run curves. Note that, whether short-run or long-run, these represent costs to the *firm* and the shape of the curves reflect influences *internal* to the firm. Rising long-run firm costs, for example, are often associated in the orthodox theory of the firm with difficulties in managing large enterprises. Whatever the reason, it is important to distinguish between firms' costs and product costs. The latter is the relevant concept in the later discussion of constant returns to scale and constant/rising cost situations.

[15] However, they need not have. In competitive models it is possible to postulate firms insisting on fixed hours of work from their employees, and so some 'mobility' is lost. This point has often been made by E. J. Mishan. See for example 'Second Thoughts on Second Best', *OEP*, p. 210, October 1962. Factor suppliers cannot adjust their supplies in the way they would like, i.e., eq. (3.5) cannot be realized. Prices are equal to marginal money cost as in eq. (3.6), but W can no longer be regarded as reflecting the 'real' cost of factor services. Perfect competition is, therefore, strictly neither a necessary nor sufficient condition for the attainment of Pareto efficiency, though it gets very close to being sufficient.

produceable from them. Given, then, certain technological and market relationships, a person's welfare is broadly determined by his willingness to work, the type of skills he has and the quantity of other factors he owns. In a world of fixed input supplies, the pattern of resource ownership will be crucial in determining the solution bundle of goods and its distribution.

This can be illustrated if the reader will turn back to Fig. 2.8(a) in the previous chapter. This diagram depicts an economy where there are but two of each of the items—firms, consumers, products, fixed inputs. Bundle M can be taken as the solution totals of the commodities j and k with the solution price ratio pp'. To see how this bundle is produced read off[16] the appropriate point, say V, on the contract curve in Fig. 2.3, and this will indicate how much each firm produced. The tangent at this point indicates the relative solution prices for the 2 inputs which will be equal to their relative marginal productivity. If, then, person 1 owns, say 60 per cent of both inputs, with person 2 owning the rest, then their relative money incomes are known. Returning to Fig. 2.8(a), the distribution of the commodities between the two members of the community is determined by their relative money incomes. The line dd' indicates the relative prices of the two commodities and the budget constraint of each consumer. The distribution point D indicates that person 1, with origin at O, finishes up on I_1^s, his highest attainable indifference curve; person 2 with origin at M is on I_2^1. Clearly, the choice of the bundle reflects both the tastes of the consumers (for j and k) and their relative purchasing power.

Of course, a government with power to tax and transfer purchasing power could alter the actual distribution of welfare that emerges. If some people receive money transfers from the state this gives them greater access to goods at the expense of those members of the community who have been taxed. But the chief difficulty, and one which forms one of the main elements of the study of 'Public Finance', is how these taxes and transfers are to be levied. An income tax distorts the relationship between the subjective substitution rate involving work and product and the market prices of such goods. If producers operate on the basis of these prices, the general optimum condition is not realized. Similar remarks apply to the whole gamut of typical present-day taxes. In order that the optimum conditions be unaffected it is necessary to devise taxes and transfers unrelated to the economic variables which affect allocation patterns. Such 'lump-sum' devices—certainly if they are to be any use in affecting the distribution of welfare—are however difficult, if not impossible, to invent. Poll taxes seem the only possibility. Suppose, for example, it is decided to 'improve' the distribution of income by granting transfers to the employees of the railway industry—a recognized low-paid source of employment. Such transfers could well provide inducements for new entrants to the industry with the market wage driven further down. Factor suppliers are adjusting to rewards which do not reflect the trans-

[16] Note the axes of Fig. 2.3 should be interpreted as representing quantities of 2 inputs.

formation rate on the production side; they are adjusting to the market-wage plus the state bonus for working in such industries. Strictly speaking, these issues constitute an almost insuperable problem and we return to them in later chapters.

Private ownership of resources, then, in a context of perfect markets in which each member is a maximizer of either profit or utility, leads to a bundle of goods from which it is not possible to make anyone better off without others suffering. It is interesting to recall that many of the early discussions of welfare economics were couched in a framework of private ownership. Studies of allocation problems in economics in the UK began by attempting to answer the question 'what determines prices' rather than 'what determines welfare'. Interest in price formation led to the development of theories concerning the nature of markets. When, later, the nature of the issue was reversed and the question was posed 'how ought resources to be allocated', it is easy to understand how the question became more one of 'what do our studies of markets indicate about the best method of allocating privately owned resources'. It is not surprising, therefore, that some of the early welfare economists slipped almost unconsciously into championing fully-fledged market systems (subject, of course, to certain qualifications) and the free play of self-interest in allocating *privately* owned resources, and their conclusions could easily be viewed as necessary requirements for the promotion of welfare. Pigou, for example, felt that

> . . . obstacles in the way of that distribution of resources which self-interest tends to bring about will render the value of the marginal social net products of resources more unequal and so will damage the national dividend.[17]

As we shall see, however, appropriate rules can be designed for an economy where social ownership is the main feature. At the same time (a model of) a perfectly competitive system is a very ingenious 'device' for the attainment of Pareto efficiency. Given that from the specification of the optimum conditions there emerges a set of exchange rates whose role can be taken by prices, then no central controls are necessary to ensure that factor returns are everywhere equal; the invisible hand establishes a set of common prices throughout the economy to which each of the myriad of buying and selling units respond.[18]

To the extent that prices would be in excess of marginal costs, production

[17] *The Economics of Welfare*, p. 126, Macmillan, 1920.

[18] These characteristics of a competitive system and, also, the circumstances under which (kinks, corners, increasing returns to scale, for example) the exchange rates emanating from the optimum conditions may not be appropriable by a private market system, are admirably set out in two articles by F. M. Bator. See 'The Simple Analytics of Welfare Maximization', *AER*, March 1957, and 'The Anatomy of Market Failure', *QJE*, August, 1958. Both of these articles have been reproduced in, W. Briet and H. M. Hochman (Ed.), *Readings in Micro-Economics*, Holt, Rinehart, and Winston, 1968.

by monopolies fails as a device for securing Pareto efficiency. This proposition, of course, begs most of the questions about the evaluation of monopolistic practices since our analysis is essentially in static terms; it is this rather than any of our later discussions of capital expenditure and externalities which qualifies the usefulness of the conclusions. Whether or not *changing* from a monopoly position to a large number of firms would, in a world of changing and complex technology, lead to a more Pareto efficient solution is something beyond the bounds of our simplest analysis. One point of historical interest in the literature[19] relates to the circumstances under which monopolies could be Pareto efficient. We have seen[20] that when factor supplies are completely inelastic some of the Pareto conditions are redundant, and prices which are everywhere equi-proportional to marginal costs will suffice. If each industry then had an equal degree of monopoly the associated use and distribution of outputs and inputs would be Pareto efficient. Those readers desirous of testing their rigorous knowledge of these behavioural rules might attempt to formulate them mathematically, to see how they match up to the Pareto efficiency conditions spelled out in section 2.3.

3.3 Social ownership and public enterprises

Market socialism

Socialist economies take a variety of forms and the study of them has become a major field of interest within economics itself.[21] Our aim here will solely be to examine a simple model of an economy where resources are primarily publicly owned, and to examine what behavioural rules need to be followed if Pareto efficiency is to be achieved. In this section the discussion will be on a fairly broad canvas leaving, until the next section, a fuller introduction to production rules for the public enterprise, it will only be an introduction since we are now approaching the major subject of interest in the book.

Suppose then that while the population of the economy still provides many factor services—its own human skills—all non-human resources (including inputs in fixed supply) and all intermediate goods are 'owned' by the state. All the commodities in the economy are publicly produced and, provisionally, we shall assume there is, for each commodity, just one firm or 'Ministry' responsible for production decisions. At the same time we allow that any input has a number of different uses, so that generally there will be a number of public firms wishing to use each factor. The problems involved will not take much time to deal with for the earlier parts of this chapter have provided the basic analysis. The four price features detailed on p. 42 have to be

[19] See, for example, R. F. Khan, 'Some Notes on Ideal Output', *EJ*, March, 1935.
[20] p. 39. above.
[21] For a recent exposition of allocation problems in a socialist state see A. Bergson, 'Market Socialism Revisited', *JPE*, October, 1967.

attained. Again, for simplicity of exposition, intermediate goods will be ignored. In the output market as long as there is a large number of buyers and the market is allowed to clear—given the supply function of the public firm—the first price feature will be met for commodities. For inputs large numbers of buyers and sellers on both sides of the market will ensure that all participators are price-takers. With the market clearing, the price on both sides is equated. If, for any input, there are not sufficient public firms buying it to guarantee that producers are price-takers, then clearly some central government intervention would be necessary to ensure uniform prices.[22]

As far as the production sector is concerned, the fourth price feature provides the behavioural rule required of each public firm. The production of each commodity is pursued up to the point where price equals marginal cost. In this model one firm controls the whole production process for each commodity. In practice, production technologies will usually involve large numbers of plants, and under certain circumstances it is possible to devolve much of the decision taking to the plant level. This possibility is considered in the next section. As far as the person sector is concerned, as before, utility maximization will guarantee that the third required price feature is met. However, not all of the income generated in this economy goes directly to the person sector. To the extent that each firm earns a surplus as payment for entrepreneurship this goes to the state. Further, the rewards paid to non-human inputs also accrue to the state. It might be thought that no money transactions need take place in a public firm's use of public inputs. If these inputs are in fixed supply no compensation for disutilities rendered is necessary. However, the 'efficient' allocation of these inputs between firms is required and so at least a shadow price will have to be used. In practice then a money transaction will greatly simplify the allocation problem. The general point is that the state has income which has, it is assumed in this model, to be disbursed to the members of the community. Thus the income/expenditure constraint for each consumer will, in those circumstances, be determined not only by the range of human inputs he possesses but also by the amount of transfer income he gets from the state.

The implications are clearly that the distribution of welfare in this type of economy is still partly determined by 'marginal productivity principles' but greater scope, in theory, is provided in this model for government control of income distribution, to the extent that a large part of income generated initially goes to the state. However, the problem of devising taxes and transfers which do not disrupt the attainment of Pareto efficiency still remains.

Mixed economies and public enterprise operation

Most Western economies are characterized by both a public and a private

[22] As an alternative, and particularly if a public firm were the sole purchaser of an input, behavioural rules will have to be drawn up for such purposes. These are noted in the next section.

production sector. The optimum conditions require both mobility of all outputs and inputs and their adjustment in each sector, so that the value of the marginal product of each type of input is everywhere the same. If it was a reasonable assumption that perfect competition reigned in the private sector, then clearly the rules drawn up for the public firms in the market socialism model are applicable now to the public enterprises in a mixed economy. If for any reason the price patterns in the private sector do not correspond to the required patterns, then clearly we might have to rethink our rules for the public sector. It has been established on p. 32 above that that the Pareto conditions are of an all-or-nothing nature. If one condition cannot be fulfilled then the other conditions are not necessarily any longer desirable. If, then, in parts of the private sector the price pattern is inappropriate, we shall have to consider what this implies about the achievement of Pareto efficiency. This is discussed under the heading of 'second-best' in a later chapter. For the time being it is assumed that private sector price patterns are 'right'.

In the market socialism model, public expenditure decisions were considered on a broad equilibrium canvas. It is now time to make a closer examination of the implications of the piecemeal policy conclusions for individual sectors. Consider, then, one such sector involved in, say, the production of coal (j). Assume

(a) that all prices other than that of coal are fixed, and,

(b) all inputs to coal are in perfectly elastic supply.

The first assumption allows us to consider a partial equilibrium demand curve for coal as indicated by the D line in Fig. 3.2. The second point, taken in conjunction with an assumed constancy of returns to scale, means that

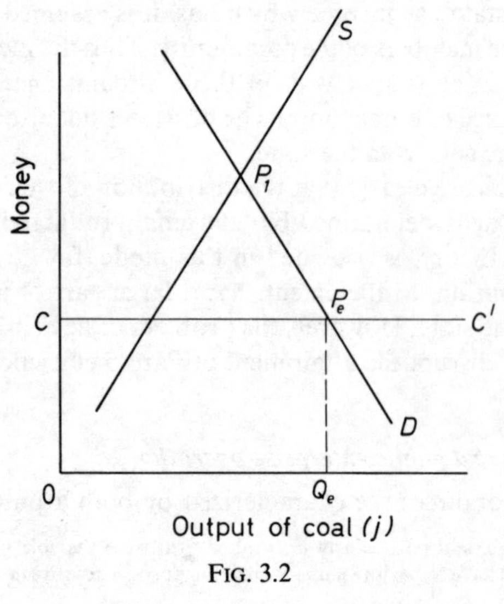

FIG. 3.2

the average money costs of producing coal are constant; this 'constant cost' situation is illustrated by the CC' line in the diagram. For any particular factor of production, say, labour (l), the technological transformation rate, $(\Delta l/\Delta j)$, would be constant at each output level and so $W_l\,(\Delta l/\Delta j)$—marginal costs for the product—would be constant and equal to OC. For a public enterprise controlling the whole output, the price/marginal cost rule would indicate producing Q_e at price P_e, which in this situation contains the incidental accounting advantage that total expenditure is just covered by receipts.[23]

Compare this with the competitive solution of private enterprise. It makes sense to postulate a myriad of firms producing this commodity when constant returns to scale are involved. Doubling all inputs (including entrepreneurship) does not more than double output, and so we can think of output being finely divided between the large number of firms. But we often think of industry supply curves as being upward sloping like the S curve in Fig. 3.2. If all the firms are identical, then, with all other factors in perfectly elastic supply, the upward slope of the S curve must correspond to a situation where the remaining factor, entrepreneurship, is not in perfectly elastic supply; the number of firms is fixed. The S curve would correspond to a short-run supply curve; the market price would be P_1 and each firm earns abnormal profits. If the number of firms is variable, and if we persisted with our assumption of identical firms, then free entry would shift the supply curve

[23] Difficulties would arise if losses were involved and this will be an issue considered in later parts of the book. Here, the assumption of constant returns to scale obviates the accounting problems—it is important to note the whole analysis is in terms of the *product* and not the plant or firm—and the existence of more than one factor does not invalidate the point. If three factors, z, l, and b, are used in the manufacture of product j, then the production relation can be written as $X_j = f_j\,(h_z, h_l, h_b)$, where h_l, etc. is the quantity of input l. If this function involves constant returns to scale, then it must be homogeneous of degree one, in which case, by Euler's Theorem, it has the property that:

$$X_j = F_z h_z + F_l h_l + F_b h_b \tag{1}$$

where F_z, etc., are partial derivatives representing the marginal products of the factors in terms of the output X_j. Multiplying both sides of eq. (1) by P_j gives:

$$P_j X_j = (P_j F_z) h_z + (P_j F_l) h_l + (P_j F_b) h_b \tag{2}$$

Now $(P_j F_z)$, etc., constitutes the value of the marginal product of the factor and, so, *if* factors *are* given a reward equal to this, then the product is exhausted—total revenue, $P_j X_j$, equals total expenditure—since eq. (2) can be written as:

$$P_j X_j = W_z h_z + W_l h_l + W_b h_b \tag{3}$$

Another way of looking at this would be to suppose that b constitutes a socially owned factor with l and z as private human resources. The returns to the socially owned factor could then be considered as the residual (B) of revenue after payments have been made to other factors. This means:

$$B = P_j X_j - W_z h_z - W_l h_l \tag{4}$$

and if z and l are employed up to the point where their reward equals the value of their marginal product, then the product will be just exhausted if the employment of the socially owned factor is increased in the same way.

to the right, lowering the market price with P_e and Q_e as the long-run equilibrium solution; the position of each firm would then be typified by Fig. 3.1. In effect then, the line CC' in Fig. 3.2 would correspond to the long-run supply schedule of the perfectly competitive industry. It is in this sense that we can see a symmetry between the public industry and private industry solution. In examining Pareto efficient outputs we need not restrict ourselves, even with constant returns to scale for the product, to constant cost situations; later we may consider rising cost situations.

The above remarks do give a lead to possible further devolvement of decision taking from the 'Ministry' responsible for coal to the plant (or colliery) managers. If there were a large number of plants in the industry, then each plant manager could be instructed to maximize profits. To the extent that the number of plants is large, then each plant is a price-taker and so, in maximizing profits, the situation would be similar to that of a profit maximizing firm, in a perfectly competitive industry. Of course, the non-human factors are publicly owned and the real issue may well be whether there is any inducement for plant operators to seek profit. If the number of plants is insufficiently large for each manager to be a price-taker a different solution would be in order; prices would have to be fixed by the Ministry. In fact, in both sets of circumstances the Ministry or industry planning board has an important role, that of ensuring that the price/marginal cost equality holds for the product or industry. In the case where the plants really are price-takers, this means the planning board has to increase the number of plants when the price exceeds marginal cost and decrease it when there is a short fall. When it is 'fixing' the ruling price it has to ensure that the supply of output emanating from the profit-maximizing plants equals demand at this price. In both cases the board's role is equivalent to that achieved by the free entry of firms in a perfectly competitive model. This kind of analysis was popular in the discussion by economists such as Lange and Lerner in the 1930s on the efficiency or otherwise of socialist economies.[24] In fact, in current analysis of public sector pricing decisions in mixed economies, the approach in some cases is more one of viewing the decision-takers as having an eye for the effect of their policies on the whole industry; attempts to measure costs, for example, in environments where there is considerable interdependence between the various parts of the production system, such as in transport and electricity supply, must of necessity be

[24] The challenge was made by Mises that, in a collectivized economy, efficient allocation was impossible simply because of the sheer administrative burden. The 'Ministries' would have to decide output/input targets for each plant and effectively solve the whole general equilibrium system. As far as the argument is related to economic models, this point has been invalidated in this chapter and this is precisely how Lange and Lerner replied to Mises. The relevant references are F. Hayek (Ed.), *Collectivist Economic Planning*, 1945, which contains Mises's paper as chapter II; O. Lange's article 'On the Economic Theory of Socialism' is in the October issue of *Review of Economic Studies*, 1936, while *The Economics of Control, op. cit.*, contains the main points made by Lerner in previous articles.

couched in a general framework.[25] More formally, we shall see in a later chapter that if increasing returns to scale operate, the above decentralized structure runs into difficulties in the achievement of Pareto efficient outcomes. In practice, the scope for decentralizing decision-taking will depend on the characteristics of the product and its technology and can, therefore, be expected to vary from industry to industry. At this stage, it is useful to pursue the assumption of there being one public firm responsible for the product, e.g., the Central Electricity Generating Board or British Railways, and to analyse its appropriate output/input adjustments.

Rising costs

In the factor market the implications of the constant cost case are straightforward. Effectively, the public industry would be required to adjust its use of any factor to the point where the factor price was equal to the value of its marginal product, as specified in eq. (3.7). Again, a symmetry can be found with the purchases of a perfectly competitive industry. Suppose, now, that some (or all) of the inputs are not in completely elastic supply to this sector. The coal industry might be envisaged as the sole purchaser of a particular kind of labour skill. In the analysis of individual utility functions, it was assumed that providing human factor services involved an increasing disutility. The supply curve of such services will, therefore, be upward sloping and the supply price of factor services an increasing function of the quantity

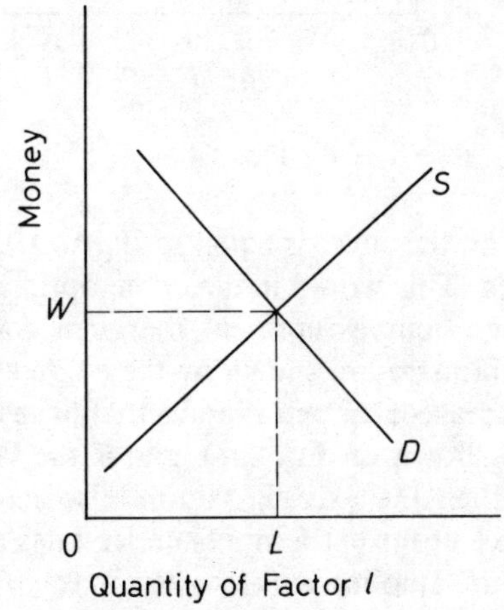

FIG. 3.3

[25] In the later parts of the book where applied studies are referred to, this point will be amply demonstrated. For recent examples see the *Economic Journal* for March 1968 which contains two reports on the cost studies being made in the UK electricity supply industry. Also relevant is 'Road Track Costs', Ministry of Transport, HMSO, 1968.

supplied. Since the public industry's purchases are to be determined by the condition that $W_l = P_j(\Delta j/\Delta l)$ then the D curve in Fig. 3.3 may be viewed as indicating, for various levels of the factor price, the associated volume of factor usage which would realize this condition. Clearly then, W, L, constitutes its equilibrium position. Again, a private industry's purchases will be symmetrical if each buying firm is a price-taker.

Now, this assumption of some inelasticity in factor supply has some important implications which can best be seen if the output market is re-examined. If a factor is in inelastic supply, then the curve analogous to CC' in Fig. 3.2 showing the average money cost of the product would rise like the S line in Fig. 3.4, even though constant returns to scale is still the order of

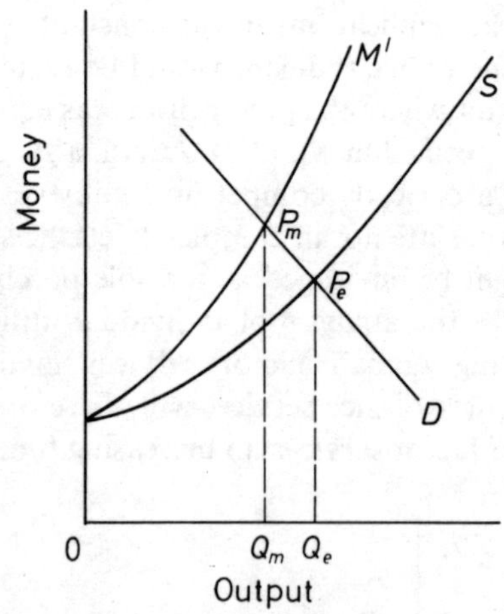

FIG. 3.4

the day. Each point on the curve is equal to $W_l(\Delta l/\Delta j)$, but though $(\Delta l/\Delta j)$ is constant, W_l is rising. This would indicate the optimal output is Q_e. But in what sense does the S curve represent marginal costs? Marginal money costs to the public industry are shown by the curve (M') marginal to the S line. As output is increased, the extra inputs that have to be attracted require a higher reward (as shown on Fig. 3.3), and if the same reward has to be paid to all inputs, then the existing factors also receive higher payment. Thus, the supply price of the extra inputs understates marginal outlay to the public industry by an amount equal to the extra payments made to the existing factors. But it is clear that these marginal money costs do not represent what were referred to before as 'real' marginal costs. The new wage represents the minimum compensation the extra inputs must get to supply their services, but the minimum compensation for the previous units is less than this—it must be since they have already expressed willingness to supply their services at a lower wage. The extra payments they now get, therefore, constitute a 'surplus' above their transfer earnings—it constitutes economic rent—and does not represent a money measure of the real cost (loss) of their services. Clearly, this rent arises only because of the restriction we have imposed throughout on our price patterns, that if any person supplies a number of units of any factor the factor payment is the same for all units.[26] Otherwise one could differentiate between each unit supplied and no surplus would accrue. Note, also that this surplus is the counterpart, on the factor supply side, to the consumer surplus that accrues through each unit of each output that a person buys being subject to the same price. In fact, when we get into the realm of surplus analysis it is necessary to tread very carefully, since there are a number of pitfalls, which we shall consider in the next sections of this chapter.

Consider now the implications of the above cost situation for the perfectly competitive industry. The point can be illustrated if the firms in the industry use land whose supply is subject to some (or even complete) inelasticity. Expansion of output is effected by more and more (identical) firms entering the industry but with each expansion the price of the scarce factor is bid up. In (long-run) equilibrium, each firm's marginal and average cost is equal to P_e as in Fig. 3.1 and Fig. 3.4, and land-owners earn rents. The costs of every existing firm in the industry are raised on the advent of a new entrant, but each (new) firm effectively ignores the influence of his own actions on the economic position of other firms. In such cases 'external effects' are said to exist, and we shall have a lot to say about these in a later chapter. In this particular context, however, it is precisely because each firm ignores these external effects that the perfectly competitive industry's output is 'right' in the sense of being Pareto efficient. Discussion of this topic by, among others, Pigou, had led initially to the erroneous conclusion that P_m in Fig. 3.4 was the 'right' industry output on the grounds that M' represented marginal costs. This was later rectified and led Viner[27] to term the phenomenon pecuniary external diseconomies. 'External diseconomies' in the sense that expansion by one firm has cost-raising effects external to itself; 'pecuniary' in the sense that the extra money costs do not represent the real cost (loss) of extra inputs; they are simply a surplus payment. In fact, this phenomenon always arises when firms are competing for some factor in inelastic supply; the normal market forces bid up the price to each buying firm.[28]

Note finally that the rising S curve in Fig. 3.4 could also represent inelasticity in the supply of 'entrepreneurship'. If the number of firms is

[26] Cf. p. 37 above and footnote [3].

[27] The debate is well surveyed in the paper by H. S. Ellis and W. Fellner, 'External Economies and Diseconomies', *AER*, 1943. It is reproduced as chapter 12 in the AEA's *Readings in Price Theory,* Allen & Unwin, 1953, where J. Viner's article—'Cost Curves and Supply Curves' initially written in 1931—can also be found.

[28] For this reason, E. J. Mishan thinks the term pecuniary external diseconomies is unnecessary. See 'Reflections on Recent Developments in the Concept of External Effects', *Canadian Journal of Economics and Political Science,* February 1965; reproduced in his *Welfare Economics: Five Introductory Essays* cited in the previous chapter.

actually fixed, then each (identical) firm could earn a surplus above normal profits and the S curve would correspond to a short-run supply curve. Alternatively, rising costs would arise if each firm were not identical—entrepreneurs are of differing efficiency, for example—such that even if the number of firms is not fixed, costs rise. The 'marginal' firm's average and marginal cost would be equal to P_e (cf. Fig. 3.1) while the other firms earn surpluses.[29]

Interpreting prices as benefits and losses

To tie up the discussion in this section it is useful to note the following point. When consumers are in equilibrium the price of output represents the value to them of the marginal unit; this we demonstrated on p. 40, and said that this value or benefit could be interpreted as the maximum the consumer would pay to obtain this unit; symmetrical remarks applied to the marginal units of factor supplies. In addition to this, Pareto efficient solutions involved the benefit of the marginal unit being equal to the real loss involved in supplying it. Thus, the Pareto conditions imply a *criterion* for evaluating a change in economic circumstances, such as a change in output, namely that marginal benefit exceeds marginal loss; that the maximum the gainers are prepared to pay for the change exceeds the minimum compensation required by the losers. If such a change *does* take place (i.e. compensation *is* paid) 'everyone' is better off and, when all such changes have been exhausted, it is impossible by further changes to make 'everyone' better off—we will have a Pareto efficient solution. Now consider Fig. 3.4 and ignore the M' line. It is tempting to argue in the following way. Where the market is in equilibrium at P_e, the benefit of a marginal unit of output is P_e, and the ordinates of the demand curve could represent the benefit of each unit of output, so that the total area under the curve indicates the maximum amount of money consumers are prepared to pay for various outputs—total benefit. The area under the supply curve may be viewed in a similar way. Thus, the rule of setting price equal to marginal cost is in fact an equilibrium condition for the maximization of a surplus—total benefit minus total loss.

Omitted from this analysis, however, is the point that as output and price change, consumer purchases are being adjusted in other markets as well as this one. Thus prices could be changing elsewhere, and the D curve (and the S curve) is a partial curve drawn up on the *ceteris paribus* assumption that other prices are constant. Further, even if other prices were constant, consumer expenditure could be changing in these other markets. Interpreting supply and demand curves in this way merits, therefore, closer examination.

[29] An analogy with a public industry would be the cost situation in electricity supply industries, where there are plants of differing efficiency arranged in an order of merit. Setting price equal to the average running cost of the marginal (highest cost) generating plant leads to surpluses for the other plants.

Further, many changes in economic life, including those involving public expenditure—new airports, railway lines, lower (higher) prices, less scientific research—involve some people gaining and others *actually* losing. This forces the problem of the distribution of welfare, largely ignored so far in this chapter, right to the surface. Finally, some, if not many, changes in economic life—water barrages, Channel Tunnels, etc.—can be quite large and the question arises whether the tools of marginal analysis can still be applied and, if not, what the alternatives are. In other words, even ignoring the time-dimension of the services provided by such projects, there are problems posed by the large change in the structure of the bundle of goods and services consumed. All these issues are considered in the remainder of this chapter.

3.4 Comparing gains and losses

Drawing up criteria to facilitate the assessment of the economic worth of public expenditures is, broadly, the very subject matter of this whole book. The rest of this chapter draws on implications of the previous analysis and considers some further technical problems; but it remains very much in the simple type of environment considered so far. Public expenditures often involve the provision of capital assets whose services are spread out over time; in practice, cost functions do not have the simple shapes assumed so far; some public sector activities generate external effects on other sectors in the economy. The environment, in which public expenditure criteria are now to be considered, is assumed to be lacking any of these sorts of complications. It will help if the discussion continues to revolve round a particular representative sector and if an especially crucial assumption, that elsewhere prices are equal to marginal costs, is also allowed to continue. The analysis is however quite general, in two senses. Firstly, the approach will largely be one of considering a particular change in public expenditure, and evaluating whether such a change is worthwhile; in this sense it requires an analysis of the general points associated with changes in economic circumstances, whether they involve public or private expenditure. Secondly 'changes' in public expenditure can take a variety of forms and the analysis relates to all such types. As well as the usual interpretation as change in output (of say electricity supply) or in input (extra resources for the health services), the analysis encompasses variations in the size of an input, such as various possible sizes of a water barrage, or a motorway; it also applies to mutually exclusive projects, e.g., an irrigation scheme or subsidy to farmers, and to all sorts of various policy options.

Now, the discussion so far in this chapter has already implicitly provided us with a criterion for doing this job. For any small activity—such as a small increase in output—we are instructed to compare the gain or value with the loss (or cost). It has been demonstrated that the former is indicated by the ruling market price, and the latter by marginal cost. Evaluating each marginal activity in this way takes us to the frontier. All changes which effect Pareto improvements are then exhausted. It was also demonstrated that this criterion could be interpreted as a compensation test, namely, that it involved comparing the maximum the gainers would be prepared to pay to have the new situation, with the minimum compensation required by the losers—the providers of factor services, for example. If a criterion is available why bother any further about this matter? Three important reasons are:

(a) In practice, some public expenditure activities are not small. North Sea Gas, road programmes, new power stations, all may constitute large jumps on both the output side and in the demand for factor services. Since the price/marginal cost criterion was derived from an analysis in which all changes could be viewed as marginal, it is not necessarily appropriate for use in a world where perfect divisibility is not always present.

(b) Many changes involve some people actually losing. One way in which this can occur is when changes in tastes or production possibilities in a market economy cause price changes favourable for some and unfavourable for those whose factor reward has fallen or whose main purchases have experienced a rise in price. Similarly many kinds of government measures—abolition of meat imports through a foot and mouth scare, new taxes, standards, or subsidies—can lead to both gains and losses to the members of the community. The point is, of course, that such situations cannot be handled by the criterion used so far. The Pareto criterion sanctions any activity where some people gain and none lose. To handle a situation where some people *actually* lose necessitates the development of a wider criterion for evaluating social changes.

(c) In practice, some activities may not be matched by money transactions. Factor services, for example, are provided without reward. Consumers may gain benefits for which little or no direct payment is made. The latter is a phenomenon quite common in the public sector where goods and services are financed from taxation with little direct pricing; health, education, and research and development provide obvious cases, but items such as roads and water supply in some countries also fall into this category. While getting something for nothing seems quite plausible, providing factor services without compensation seems at first sight unlikely. However, one has only to think of the noise, fumes, and general inconveniences involved in our congested world to see examples, even though we do not usually think of these as constituting the supply of services. Why such effects occur and why money transactions are not involved is something which will be discussed in the later chapter on external effects. The general point is that both these phenomena are important for public expenditure decisions. To the extent that on both the gain and the loss side prices are inappropriate, one issue is discovering what the appropriate prices would have been. This is something which we deal with in the second part of the book. What is particularly relevant at this stage is that, even if we knew what the appropriate prices were, the fact that some people do actually lose from such activities—compensation is not paid—means that again we are dealing with a situation that cannot be handled by the criterion available so far.

The general issue that emerges from points (b) and (c) is that we may wish to consider other objectives besides simply Pareto efficiency. Particular types of distribution of welfare may be an important aim. One way to achieve this is to incorporate distributional objectives into criteria for social improvement. This approach involves quite a sharp methodological break from the previous analysis. The efficiency objective is geared towards particular criteria for increases in national welfare. It is possible—as we showed in section 3.3—to devolve all the decision-taking pertaining to this objective to individual sector level, i.e., the firm (or industry) and the individual. It was briefly pointed out at the end of chapter 2 that this cannot be done for distributional objectives. If the sovereignty of individual preferences is held paramount no schemes for distributional changes could emerge from such a setting. If we now wish to talk of incorporating distributional objectives into our criteria for social improvement, we have to drop the idea that individual preferences are the sole governing factor. Instead such objectives must be thought of as being imposed by a government or some executive branch of government. This possibility is an inherent characteristic of both decision-taking in practice, and of economic studies in this field, though of course there are some who think economists have nothing to contribute in these matters.[30]

Compensating income variations

A feature common to all three points is that for any activity the gain must be compared with the loss. Our concern will now be to examine both *definitions and measures* of the gains and losses ensuing from an activity. There is a considerable literature on these problems since it involves the very foundations of welfare economics, but we shall be fairly ruthless in our selection of the important issues. In particular our approach will be determined very much by the theme running throughout the book—that the primary concern is with the search for and derivation of criteria and rules

[30] Cf. J. M. Buchanan's view that

'. . . a consistent methodological position does not allow the introduction of non-individualistic norms in *either* allocation *or* distribution . . . When non-individualistic norms are introduced, the domain of economics, *as I define the discipline,* is abandoned. . . . it will be objected that my approach amounts to an 'opting out' of the discussion of many interesting and highly important issues of applied economic policy. So it does, but I can see no personal excuse for joining other economists in an attempt to hoodwink the public into thinking that we make more sense out of these issues than analysis allows, or that economists have a hot line to God.'

Economica, May 1968, 'What Kind of Redistribution Do We Want', pp. 188–9 and footnote 2. (Buchanan's italics.)

appropriate for individual sector decision-taking. It is policy conclusions usable in a partial piece-meal setting that are of most interest.

The next section is concerned with non-marginal changes and to simplify the issues it will be helpful if the following criterion for social improvement is provisionally—but only provisionally—accepted: Criterion (1): Someone *could* be made better off by the activity without others suffering.

This means that while the activity may involve some groups of people losing, the size of the gain more than offsets this: more precisely the gainers could compensate the losers and still be better off than the initial position.[31] In this context, the gainers will have some maximum amount of money they would be prepared to pay for the change; maximum in the sense that if this amount were extracted from them they would be no better or worse off. Similarly the potential losers will have some minimum compensation they would require to accept the change. If the former exceeds the latter the activity is warranted on the basis of criterion (1). These amounts of money are termed *compensating variations in income*[32] since they constitute those variations which would have to be made to a person's money income in order that his welfare remains at its initial level when the activity occurs. In the gainers' case it is a matter of taking money income from him; the losers would receive compensation. However—and this is an important point—under criterion (1) these income variations are hypothetical since we are not requiring that 'everyone' *is* better off; it is not necessary that compensation be paid although of course those activities which do involve the losers being compensated are encompassed by this criterion. As such the criterion is of limited use, since one thing that would be important would be the identity of the gainers and losers; if the losers were a poor section of the community and no compensation were paid, such a change may well not be accepted by a government. However, it is used only provisionally, and the distributional aspects will be considered later on. Note, finally, that if all possible positive net gain moves are undertaken this will lead us to a distribution of resources which is 'efficient'; if for further activities the gainers cannot 'overcompensate' the losers, Pareto optimality has been achieved.[33]

3.5 Social surplus analysis and indivisibilities

When all inputs and outputs are perfectly divisible the price/marginal cost

[31] Often termed the Kaldor-Hicks test after the two economists associated with its initial conception. See N. Kaldor, 'Welfare Propositions of Economics and Interpersonal Comparisons of Utility', *EJ*, September 1939, and J. R. Hicks, 'The Foundations of Welfare Economics', in the December 1939 issue of this journal. These tests were developed in a much wider setting than that contemplated here. Kaldor's article has been reproduced in K. J. Arrow and T. Scitovsky (Ed.), *Readings in Welfare Economics*, AEA, Allen & Unwin, 1969.

[32] Due to J. R. Hicks. See 'The Rehabilitation of Consumers' Surplus', *R. Economic Studies,* 1940/1, No. 2, reproduced in *Readings in Welfare Economics, op. cit.*

[33] Unfortunately this is not quite true, strictly speaking. The point is taken up later on, but at this stage it can be taken as roughly correct.

rule will sanction all activities which meet criterion (1). This is because, as we have seen, market prices can be interpreted as the compensating income variations. The meaning and significance of indivisibilities is more fully discussed in the later chapter on returns to scale, but the implications at this stage could be seen if it were supposed that an activity involved a large increase of output.[34] A Channel Tunnel for example is to be constructed and, in a static world, this may be viewed as leading to a considerable increase in the volume of cross-channel services and, therefore, to a significant fall in their price. Treating the new lower price as an indicator of the gain to the consumer would surely be misleading, since some of the potential customers may well be prepared to pay more than this for some of the units involved in the jump—measurement problems aside. Similarly the old price would be an over-estimate since—ignoring quality changes—none of the new units of output were purchased when price was at that level. If output increases take this form then ruling market prices can no longer be regarded as reflecting the benefit of this extra output to the consumer. It then becomes necessary to search for *an alternative method of measuring* the benefit. Clearly, the same point applies on the supply side—'marginal' cost loses its meaning for an indivisible change. Note that, in practice, all changes of more than one unit of output need not be non-marginal. As Little says,

> a good test of whether an increase in production is marginal or not is to ask whether it would be possible to sell the increased number of units . . . for significantly more than they in fact sell, if discrimination between customers were possible.[35]

Empirically large changes might be possible for some goods without any marked effect on prices, so in practice judgement needs to be exercized.

The role that market prices play in marginal analysis is that of indicating, in a simple observable manner, certain things about individual utility functions. In the search for an alternative measure in the presence of indivisibilities, clearly the utility functions will contain all the required information. However, this is not an operationally significant source. It is assumed here that the public expenditure decision-taker may have a knowledge of the relevant partial supply and demand curves; he knows in other words how the quantity of the good in question would vary with price if marginal changes were possible and if all other prices are constant. Even if such direct knowledge is not available, it is reasonable to allow that there may be methods of

[34] The general basis of surplus analysis is also applicable to two other problems. One is the introduction of new goods which cannot really be handled by 'marginal' analysis. Secondly, in the specification of the Pareto conditions in chapter 2 the second-order conditions were always assumed to be met. Their significance is that while we might be at the summit of some welfare 'hill', there may be an even bigger hill in the distance. The marginal analysis could lead us to the top of the 'hillock', but could not help us in deciding whether a jump to another hill would be even better.

[35] I. M. D. Little, *A Critique of Welfare Economics,* 2 Ed., pp. 167–8, OUP, 1957.

acquiring basically the same type of information. It is fairly common practice in cost/benefit analysis to assess demand prices by some variation on the alternative cost approach.[36] Without going into detail at this stage, this procedure involves assessing the demand price for any particular service by estimating the costs of achieving the function of this service by an alternative method (e.g. transport by rail instead of canal). Whatever the method of obtaining such information, it is now our purpose to indicate how and under what circumstances such data can indicate the gains and losses associated with indivisible changes.

Consumer surplus

The main issues can be seen if the demand side of the problem is considered; the results apply symmetrically to the supply side. The activity in question could be thought of as an increased quantity of product *x*, and looking at one consumer brings out the main points. It is assumed that for all other outputs, price equals marginal cost; this is in fact quite crucial and dropping it poses problems discussed in the next chapter. The issues can be seen by examining the consumer's choices of *x* and money income (*y*) in which case, if all income is spent and if we further assume factor services do not enter the utility function, *y* represents expenditure on all other commodities. In these circumstances the slopes of the indifference curves in Fig. 3.5, representing

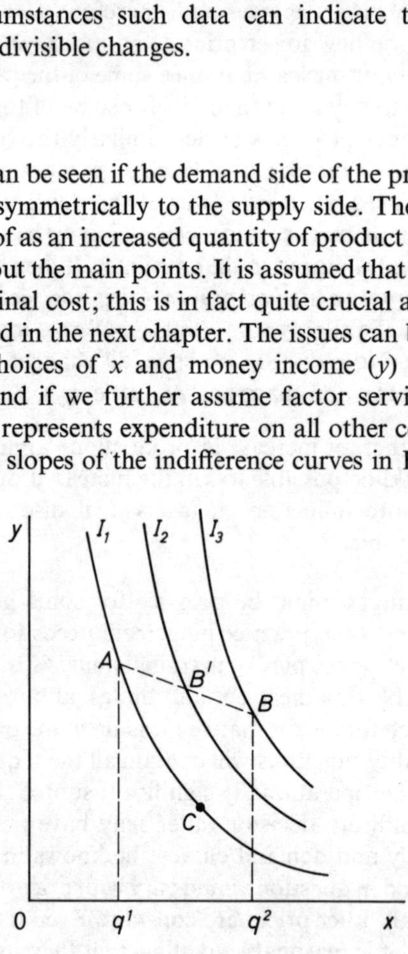

FIG. 3.5

substitution rates between *y* and *x* ($MRS_{y,x}$), constitute U_x/M, where U_x is the marginal utility of *x* and *M* is the marginal utility of income (or money) to the consumer.

[36] Cf. P. O. Steiner, 'The Role of Alternative Cost in Project Design and Selection', *QJE*, August 1965.

First of all, it is useful to introduce a measure of the extent to which the consumer benefits from an activity, which will serve as a benchmark. Suppose initially the consumer is in equilibrium at A, and then money income and/or all prices change in a series of small steps which leads the consumer to move to B along the dotted line AB^1B. Since the slopes of the indifference curves that are traversed in this move represent the evaluation of extra x in terms of money, then if we summed these measures over the whole move we would have a money measure of the evaluation that the consumer attaches to the extra q^1q^2 of x occasioned by the income/price changes. It is a money measure of the benefit the consumer gets from the change, but it is not at all clear what significance attaches to the measure. It certainly is not related to a demand curve measure, since we allowed that the move could represent changes not only in the price of x but also in other prices and money income. Neither is it immediately obvious, at first sight, what correspondence there is to the Hicksian compensating variation.

Suppose however it is postulated that the extra purchases of x are occasioned by a fall in the price of x, with all other prices and the consumer's money income constant. Assume secondly and more restrictively that total expenditure on x remains constant—the consumer has a unitary price elasticity of demand for x. Such a situation is shown on Fig. 3.6 where the

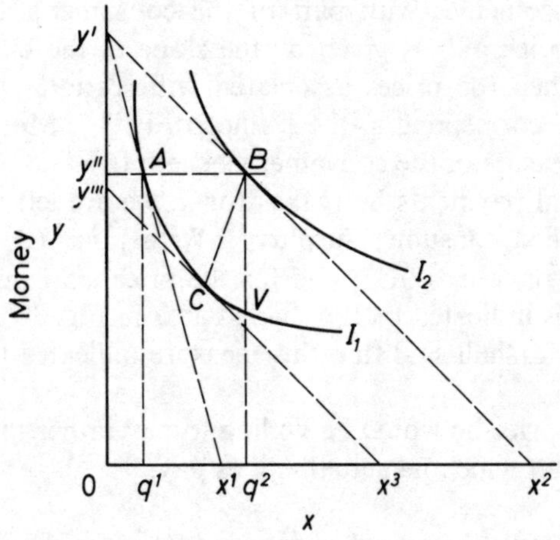

FIG. 3.6

consumer's money income throughout remains at y'. Starting from A, the change in relative prices from x^1y' to x^2y' shifts him from A to B with expenditure on x at the constant level $y'y''$. Let the money evaluation of extra x, as defined before, be plotted on Fig. 3.7 where the vertical is a money axis and the horizontal a quantity of x axis. Given a normal shape for the indifference map, the evaluation of x would gradually decrease as more x

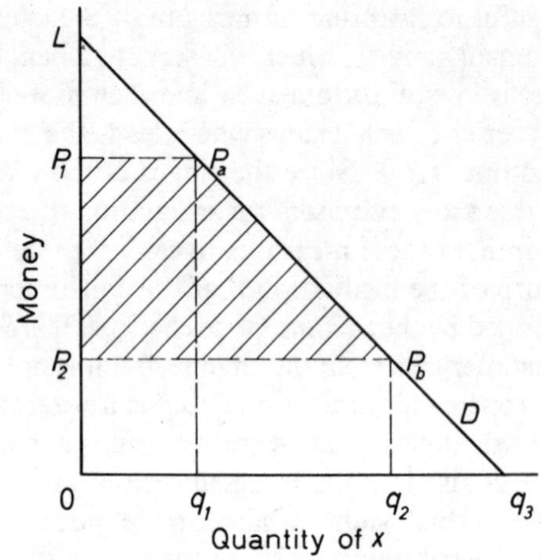

FIG. 3.7

is consumed. Starting with an assumed level of P_a, the evaluation of each extra unit of x is indicated by the line connecting P_a and P_b and, summed over all the extra units the money measure, is $P_aP_bq_2q_1$. Now, it should be clear that the line P_aP_b coincides with part of the consumer's demand curve. Since the *absolute* price of x is given by the slope of the budget lines like $y'x^1$ on Fig. 3.6, then the prices associated with various quantities—the demand curve—will correspond to the D line in Fig. 3.7. More generally, if, from this money measure of the consumer's benefit from or evaluation of x, we deduct the actual payments he makes for x, we are left with a surplus which Marshall called consumer surplus.[37] With price P_a, the surplus is LP_aP_1, with a zero price it is $0Lq_3$ and for the price fall from P_a to P_b the increase in surplus is indicated by the shaded area in Fig. 3.7.

Unfortunately, Marshall said that this measure indicated the

> . . . excess of the price he would be willing to pay rather than go without the thing, over that which he actually does pay.[38]

This *definition* is clearly close to the income variations developed later by Hicks, but even in the restricted circumstances of this example the demand curve measure and the compensating income variation do not coincide. The latter is indicated in Fig. 3.6 by $y'y'''$, since if this amount of money were extracted from the consumer at B, he would be shifted back to C at

[37] A. Marshall, *Principles of Economics*, 8 Ed., Macmillan, 1936, Book III, chapter VI. This measure also corresponds to the concept of consumer 'gain' developed by D. M. Winch in 'Consumer Surplus and the Compensation Principle', *AER*, June 1965.

[38] *Op. cit.*, p. 124.

his initial welfare level. It constitutes the maximum amount of money that could be taken from the consumer if, allowing him the price fall from $y'x^1$ to $y'x^2 (= y'''x^3)$, he is to be kept on his initial indifference curve I_1; the move from B to C will be recognized as a version of the income effect of consumer demand theory.[39]

To see the full implications of this case, it is useful to recall some points about consumer equilibrium touched on in the first section of this chapter (pp. 37, 40). For every good, typified by j, consumer equilibrium is characterized by $P_j = U_j/M$. As the consumer moves from A to B in Fig. 3.6 the prices of all goods other than x, are constant. Further total expenditure and, therefore, total consumption on each of the other goods is constant. It follows that, taking j as typical of the other goods, P_j and U_j are constant and, therefore, M is constant for the equilibrium conditions to hold. Thus, as the consumption of x increases, though U_x/M is falling, the marginal utility of income is constant. What this means is that, in the demand curve measures, the extra utility ensuing from the increased quantity of x is converted to money terms at a constant rate. Suppose, for example, the measure were £50; this indicates that in, say, moving back from B to A the consumer would lose a total amount of utility, say U^*, equal to fifty times the utility of his last £ spent at B. This case of a constant marginal utility of money corresponds to the assumption that Marshall made in publicizing his measure. However, this does not guarantee—and this point was made explicit by Winch[40]—that M is constant over *different* consumption paths. In particular if, from B, the consumer moves along the BC path, there is no guarantee that the marginal utility of money is constant. In fact, given that in Fig. 3.6, the income effect is positive, M will be rising in the move from B to C.[41] If then the consumer is at B and £50 *were* extracted from him, his total loss of utility would be greater than U^*, since each £1 decrease in income constitutes a larger loss of utility than that lost from the first £ extracted *at B*. To ensure that the loss of utility is the same from B to C as from B to A, *less* than £50 must be extracted from him. It follows that the two money measures of surplus are different, and that the compensating income variation for a price fall is less than the demand curve measure, as long as along the BC path the income effect is positive.

Further insight into these issues is provided if we translate the idea of the compensating income variation to the usual price/quantity dimensions. Suppose we wished to plot the consumer's evaluation of extra units of x on the assumption that the extractable surplus *was in fact taken away at each stage*. This would mean that the consumer gets no better or worse off, and the relevant measure would be the slope of the indifference curve I_1

[39] There is, of course, another version of the income effect and this corresponds to yet a further definition of surplus. We introduce this later on in the chapter.

[40] *Op. cit.*, section C.

[41] P_x is constant but U_x will be rising as consumption of x diminishes; to maintain the equilibrium condition, M must be rising.

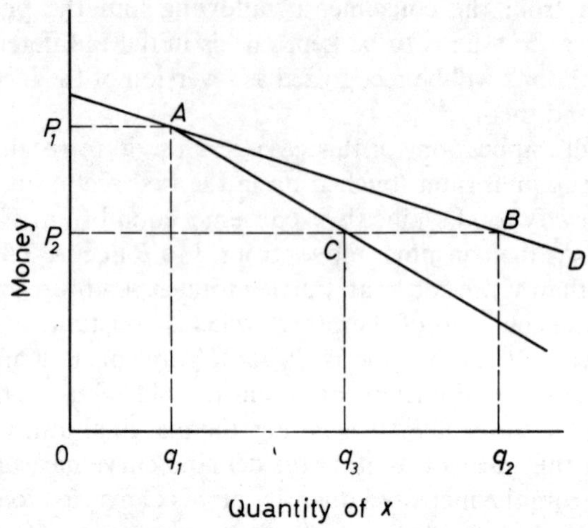

FIG. 3.8

in Fig. 3.6 as the consumer proceeds down it from A to C and beyond. This is plotted as the line AC in Fig. 3.8.

As might be expected from the previous analysis, the evaluation of extra x is less than on the demand curve. Along AC the consumer's utility is at a lower level than along the demand curve, and his evaluation of x in terms of money will be so much lower.[42] This is Hicks' *compensated demand curve*,[43] and it indicates that if price did jump—a non-marginal change, in other words—from P_1 to P_2, you could extract P_1ACP_2 from him and render him no better or worse off than before the change; clearly, P_1ACP_2 is equal to $y'y'''$ on Fig. 3.6. The shortfall of this with the demand curve measure, arises from the fact that for each of the intermediate steps between P_1 and P_2 each price fall benefits the non-exacted surplus on the uncompensated curve, as well as the basic purchasing possibilities.

Notice that the quantity q_2 which the consumer purchases on the demand curve with price P_2 is greater than the quantity he takes if compensation is exacted for the price fall, q_3. If, when compensation is exacted, the consumer was somehow to be restricted to taking the new quantity q_2, at the new price, then the maximum income extractable would be less than the previous measure. On Fig. 3.6 the relevant measure would be BV, and this measure is called the quantity compensating variation in income, to distinguish it from the previous measure whose full title is the price compensating variation in

[42] With normal, that is not inferior, goods the shape of the indifference map is such that as one moves up any vertical from the horizontal axis the slopes of the curves increase. Thus on Fig. 3.6, the $MRS_{y,x}$ ($= U_x/M$) increases up any vertical. It follows that along AB the $MRS_{y,x}$ will be everywhere greater than the $MRS_{y,x}$ directly below it on the I_1 line.

[43] *A Revision of Demand Theory,* chapter 8, Oxford University Press, 1956.

income.[44] In equilibrium analysis the quantity measure seems of doubtful usefulness since the consumer would not normally remain at V in Fig. 3.6, given the new price ratio. However, it is not always possible in practice to reasonably assume that equilibrium positions are attainable, and so the quantity variations may have a part to play.

Application of the analysis

It is time to take a breather from these rigours and inquire about the significance of the analysis. The general point made is that, in the situation postulated, the maximum amount of money that can be taken from a consumer for a favourable change in economic circumstance will usually be different—in fact smaller for a price fall with normal goods—than the demand curve measure. Secondly, the reasons for the difference have been closely examined, and these can shed light on a question that immediately occurs—under what circumstances would the two be equal? The short answer is: when the marginal utility of money is constant over all the relevant paths in the range of output/price changes under consideration. This sort of constancy would mean that the income effect of the price change is zero. On Fig. 3.6 the consumer's tastes would be such that taking money income from the consumer at B would shift him vertically down to a position like V. Starting from A, the effect of the fall in the price of x would lead him to consume the same quantity of x whether he moves along the AB path or down the I_1 indifference curve.[45] On Fig. 3.8 the two demand curves would coincide, as say the D line. If price fell from P_1 to P_2 he would move from A to B, and no matter what money income you took from him he would remain at B. Of course if you did take money income from him he would be worse off—expenditure on other goods would decrease. The demand curve measure, P_1ABP_2, indicates what is the maximum that can be taken without reducing his welfare level below what it was at the starting point A.

Thus, to advance the use of the demand curve to indicate an alternative measure of consumer benefit—interpreted as the maximum he is prepared to pay—when non-marginal changes are involved requires that the marginal utility of money be (at least) roughly constant. It is, now, useful to look at the significance of the other conditions. A second constraint used in the exposition was that the price elasticity of demand for the good in question, be

[44] The quantity variation seems the closest approximation to Marshall's *definition* of consumer surplus. These points were first made by A. M. Henderson and prompted Hicks to set out the possible measures of surplus—including those alluded to in our footnote of p. 65—in some detail. The relevant sources are 'Consumers Surplus and the Compensating Variation', *R. Economic Studies,* 1940/1, No. 2, and Hicks's 'The Four Consumers' Surpluses' is in the No. 1 issue of the same journal for 1943. The quantity measures are used, for example, by E. J. Mishan, in analysing 'Welfare Criteria for External Effects', AER, September 1961.

[45] Implying that over the relevant ranges, the indifference curves are parallel in the sense that up any vertical from the x axis, their slopes are the same. U_x/M is constant and so are both the numerator and the denominator.

equal to unity; this is in fact not binding and can be quickly swept out of the way. It was merely used to simplify the exposition. We may take the move from *A* to *B* in Fig. 3.5 to exhibit the more general case, though of course it is still assumed that the prices of all goods other than *x* are constant. Plotting U_x/M as one moves along *AB* will again correspond to the information given on the partial equilibrium demand curve. *M* could be rising or falling as real income changes when the price of *x* falls. Where expenditure on other goods is rising as in the case of Fig. 3.5 *M* will be falling, in the move from *B* to *A*. This, of course, is quite consistent with *M* rising as *money* income decreases in moves such as those from *B* to *C*. With *M* varying along both the *BA* and *BC* paths then, as Winch says,

> . . . neither the Hicksian measurements nor the Marshallian triangle are in money of constant marginal utility, but the reason for the variations . . . differs.[46]

The analogy with the previous analysis is that, even if *M* were rising from *B* to *A*, its rise will be quicker, for each unit decrease in *x*, if the consumer is moved from *B* to *C* than if moved from *B* to *A*, and so again the demand curve measure will exceed the compensating income variations.[47] If the income effect were zero then it is easy to demonstrate that *M* will be constant over all the relevant paths, and so again the two measures would coincide.

A third condition that can be examined is quite crucial and forms the basis of the usefulness or otherwise of surplus analysis. This is the requirement that all prices other than *x* be constant. In the application of surplus analysis to particular problems it is probably not disastrous, in some instances, to assume that for the activity in question, our first requirement—that the marginal utility of money be constant—will be met. This is often dealt with by assuming that the change is not so big as to markedly affect the consumer's total budgetary decisions.[48] In fact Fig. 3.8 makes it clear that the smaller

[46] *Op. cit.*, p. 402.

[47] Suppose *B* was above *A* so that in moving from *B* to *A*, expenditure on other goods is falling and *M* is rising. At any particular point on the *BA* path, the marginal evaluation of *x* (U_x/M) is greater than that at the same quantity of *x*—that is directly below the particular point— on the *BC* path. If U_x/M is greater, then with U_x the same, *M* must have risen more slowly on the *BA* path since of course at *B*, *M* was the same for both.

[48] Cf. The assumption of

> '. . . constant marginal utility of income for consumers' goods . . . [is] . . . essential not only to the expression of efficiency in terms of willingness to pay but also to the equating of a beneficiary's willingness to pay for the output he receives with the area under his demand curve . . . [The expenditure on] . . . system outputs that are consumers' goods (for example, electric energy and water consumed in the home), however . . . is likely to be sufficiently small in relation to an individual's total income to justify the simplifying assumption of constant marginal utility of income over the range of increase . . . [in expenditure on] . . . system outputs that are consumers' goods.'

S. A. Marglin, 'Objectives of Water-Resource Development: A General Statement', p. 37. Produced as chapter 2 of *Design of Water Resource Systems,* by A. Maass and others, Harvard University Press, 1962.

is the change in the quantity of x, the smaller is the discrepancy between the demand curve measure and the income variation. If an infinitesimally small change is involved the difference can be ignored, and we are effectively back into the realm of evaluating changes by using the ruling prices of inputs and outputs—the price/marginal cost comparison. In a similar vein one could assume that although the expenditure (by consumers of x) on other goods is changing, other prices remain constant because:

(a) The other sectors are (fortunately) constant cost industries so that variations in output do not affect prices, or

(b) changes in 'other' expenditure, even summed over all consumers of x, are small in relation to the total size of these other industries so that effectively their prices are undisturbed even if they are, say, rising cost industries. Certainly, if neither of these assumptions is warrantable for the problem at hand, the use of the demand curve measure is very dubious. Returning again to Fig. 3.5, but now allowing that the change in relative prices constitutes absolute price changes for other goods as well as x, the summing of the $MRS_{y,x}$ over the AB path will again give a money measure of the gain to the consumer—in fact, this was the benchmark we started with on p. 63. But this will have no correspondence with areas under *partial* demand curves. The Hicksian variation is still obtainable from the utility function, but as long as it remains there and is not observable in another form little use can be made of it in practice.

Notice, however, that various policy measures may lead to changes in only a small number of prices in the economy. If it were a reasonable assumption that no factor supplier or consumer were involved in more than one market then the partial surplus analysis could be used to calculate gains and losses in the various markets.

Social surplus maximization

The idea of a person earning a surplus from his market activities has traditionally been more popularly understood in relation to factor supplies. The fact that the receipts from the supply of factor services may include an element of surplus, namely economic rent, is more widely appreciated than consumer surplus, and this may arise from the tangible existence of certain payments for the use of land which fall into this category. Students of micro-economics will recognize the shaded area above the supply curve (S) in Fig. 3.9 as the usual representation of rent as the amount paid to a factor '. . . in excess of the minimum amount necessary to keep that factor in its present occupation'.[49]

But it should be clear that this economic surplus is conceptually no different from the consumer surplus. The rigorous derivation of both types of surplus necessitates an examination of the individuals' utility functions, since both

[49] K. E. Boulding, *Economic Analysis*, p. 227, Harper and Bros., 1948.

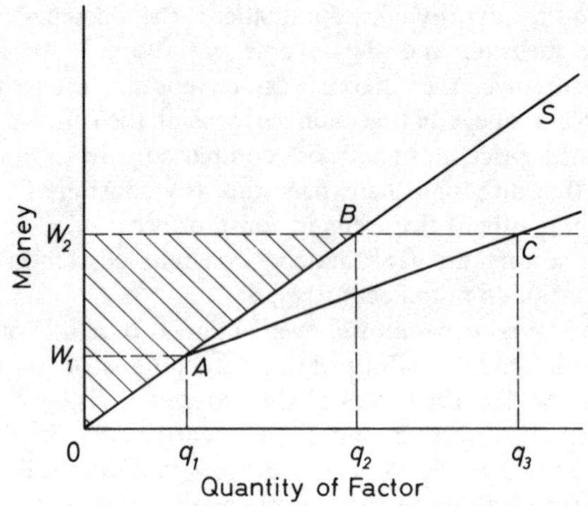

FIG. 3.9

constitute attempts to measure the welfare aspects of economic changes. To this extent the definition of rent as a surplus above transfer earnings, though providing a simple loose guide to the basic concept, is insufficiently general.[50] The conventional measures of rent arise from inelasticity in factor supplies and such inelasticity implies, ultimately, certain points about the way factor services affect individual utility. It follows then that 'consumers' surplus . . . is one species of economic rent, as Marshall was at pains to point out. There are also factor-owners' surpluses, workers' surpluses, and lenders' surpluses, among others'.[51] The derivation of factor surplus is symmetrical[52] with that of consumer surplus, and the *AC* line of Fig. 3.9 can be thought of as a compensated supply curve in much the same way as the compensated demand curve of Fig. 3.8. Given a starting point of *A*, the ordinates of *AC* indicate the minimum compensation required by the factor-owner for extra factor services. If, then, the factor return jumped from W_1 to W_2 it would be possible to extract from him an amount of money equal to the area W_1W_2CA, and he would be no better or worse off than when he started; this is the price compensating income variation again. The supply curve measure of the *increase* in surplus is the area W_1W_2BA, and thus falls short of the other measure by the area *ABC* in the diagram. The relative positions of the compensated and uncompensated supply curves reflect the fact that movements up the latter involve the consumer's welfare rising. Since in the

[50] Cf. 'Rent as a Measure of Welfare Change', *AER*, June 1959, where E. J. Mishan examines definitions of factor surpluses symmetrical with the Hicksian consumer surpluses. This article is reproduced in *Welfare Economics: Five Introductory Essays*, Random House, 1967.

[51] C. D. Foster, 'Surplus Criteria for Investment', *BOUIS*, November 1960, p. 343.

[52] At the same time the transition is not straightforward; a fuller explanation is given in the appendix to this chapter.

normal case a person's evaluation of 'goods' is greater the higher is his welfare level then *AS* will lie above *AC*.[53]

All 'goods' in the economy can thus be viewed as giving rise to rents or surpluses. The surplus depicted by a supply curve on a diagram involving quantities of *output*, as in Fig. 3.10, represents the amalgam of surpluses

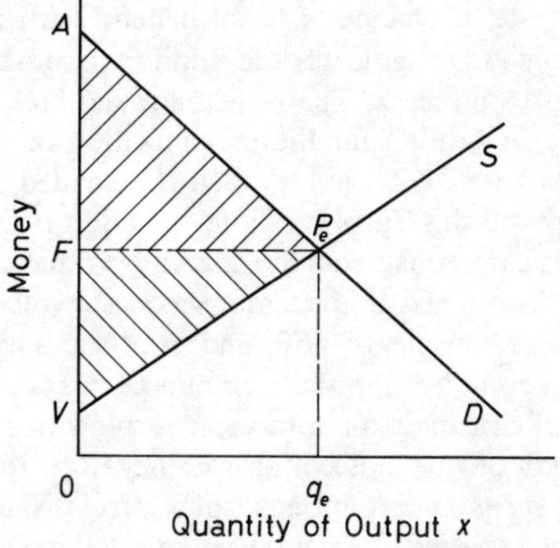

FIG. 3.10

accruing to the owners of the various inputs (including entrepreneurship) used in the production process. Before considering the implications of this, it is relevant to note one point about the supply side of these issues. The conditions under which the supply curve can be treated as indicating surpluses from factor services are the same as those operating on the demand side. But changes of the price in question may well, for factors, involve a significant change in the budgetary possibilities of the individual and, thus, have a significant effect on the marginal utility of income. To this extent

> . . . the area above the individual's supply curve especially in the case of only one productive service, is a much less reliable index of the surplus welfare than the area under his demand curve for any one good.[54]

However, since there appears to be no alternative to using this device, we will simply have to bear its short-comings in mind.

It is now time to bring together some of the implications of the supply and demand issues. If the supply curve in Fig. 3.10 *is* derived, ultimately, from the utility functions of the various individuals supplying the inputs,

[53] Cf. above p. 66.
[54] Mishan, *op. cit.*, p. 393.

then it will be a 'real' marginal cost line in the sense alluded to in the earlier parts of this chapter. What is interesting to see when the demand and supply issues are brought together is the relationship between the price/marginal cost rule and surplus analysis. Given the conditions under which surplus analysis is applicable, the ordinates of the demand curve indicate consumer benefit from commodity x; they indicate the maximum the consumer is prepared to pay for extra x. The demand curve in these circumstances indicates then the rate of change of 'total benefit' with respect to output. Similarly, the supply curve indicates the minimum compensation required by factor-owners to produce x. The price/marginal cost rule may then be seen as a first-order condition for the maximization of a surplus—namely total benefit minus total cost. In Fig. 3.10 the shaded area indicates the maximized amount of this surplus. Note, in addition, that this surplus constitutes two elements, consumers' surplus and producer surplus, the latter term being used to encompass all the factor services involved. At the solution quantity q_e, consumer surplus is AFP_e and producer surplus is VFP_e. The price/marginal cost conditions in these circumstances is a marginal rule for the maximization of consumer and producer surplus. In some instances one or other surplus may be non-existent or even negative. In the constant cost case of Fig. 3.2 there is no producer surplus precisely because all factors were assumed to be in perfectly elastic supply *to that industry*.

At first sight it would seem that a very useful maximand has been discovered. The term 'social surplus' was coined by Hicks[55] to indicate total benefit minus total cost, and maximizing this surplus constitutes a behavioural rule applicable to both marginal and non-marginal changes.[56] It appears to give us a quite general 'efficiency' objective. It should by now be clear, however, that even if distributional aims are ignored, the rule is applicable only in quite limited circumstances. The most crucial restriction is that surplus analysis is applicable only when changes in price patterns are quite limited. Prices, other than that of the commodity in question, can vary but the individuals involved must not, strictly speaking consume more than one of the goods.[57] This restriction does not apply to the price/marginal cost rule which is usable when all changes are marginal; here all one requires is

[55] *The Rehabilitation of Consumers' Surplus, op. cit.* Hicks was in fact more ambitious than we have been in that he attempted to allow for the possibility of price changes and price/marginal cost discrepancies, elsewhere in the economy. We have already hinted at the difficulties inherent in such possibilities, but a fuller discussion of what can be done in these circumstances is delayed until the next chapter.

[56] This behavioural rule is implied in many of the discussions of optimal pricing and investment policies for public enterprises. Few have treated the point explicitly, but, O. E. Williamson has set out the points in a formal but simple manner. See 'Peak-Load Pricing and Optimal Capacity under Indivisibility Constraints', *AER*, 1966, reproduced as chapter 3 of *Public Enterprise,* ed. R. Turvey, Penguin Modern Economics Series, 1968.

[57] It follows that the marginal social surplus from extra output can be indicated by the difference between the ordinates of the demand and supply curves only—again sticking to purism—when no individual is both a consumer of the product and an owner of factor services used in production.

that public enterprises simply compare ruling input and output prices. When non-marginal changes are involved the partial supply and demand curves constitute an operational source for information about the utility functions, but they require that the changes in question are *in fact* partial. Social surplus maximization is, then, a relevant practical rule in certain circumstances. In addition, as we shall see in later parts of the book, it is a useful analytical device which sheds light on some problems where the price/marginal cost rule is not very helpful.

3.6 Distribution and compensation tests

Those readers who have anticipated some interesting insights into the distributional aspects of economic changes will, I am afraid, be disappointed. It is probably not unfair to say that while welfare economists have successfully pinpointed the intractable relationship between efficiency and distribution, this constitutes the limit of their achievements. No distributional 'rules' have been devised analogous to the efficiency 'rules'. The same point applies on the empirical side of our subject area. I am not aware myself—though I shall willingly stand corrected on this—of any competent cost-benefit study, for example, which had anything intrinsically significant to say about distributional objectives or even about the distributional effects of the scheme. This is not to say, of course, that decision takers have not implicitly allowed for some distributional effects.

In one sense this is not surprising since in the theoretical analysis of the relationship between efficiency and distribution, there has emerged the general point—alluded to at a number of points in the book so far—that the basic value judgement necessary for the use of economic analysis, more or less precludes anything significant being said about distribution. Distributional problems involve essentially the assignment of weights to the welfares of the constituent members of the community. The basic value judgement used in our analysis is that individual preferences are to count. As we have seen in section 2.4, schemes for assigning welfare weights consistent with the sovereignty of individual preferences seem impossible. Thus, we have to push the boat out to the decision-takers. We have to say to them 'here is the limit of the analysis of the welfare aspects of this project in so far as we cannot go further without any specified predilection for particular welfare distributions'.

There is, of course, some guide that can be given to decision-takers, if only to point out the broad implications of different distributional objectives, and we shall try to do this in certain sections of the second half of this book; at this stage some general points are observed. In this chapter we have been looking at particular changes in economic circumstances, an analysis which characterizes particular changes in public expenditure. The criterion used so far involves a hypothetical comparison of gain and loss. Merely to indicate that the gainers from a scheme such as the construction of a new airport may be primarily the more affluent sections of the community, while the losers—inhabitants of the surrounding area for example who are uncompensated for the extra noise—could be quite poor, should suggest that a simple gain/loss criterion is inadequate for any decision-takers interested in real income distribution.

There seem to be two broad ways of indicating the distributional aspects of economic changes:

(a) Calculate the gains and losses in the manner indicated already and then explain how this is linked to distribution. Assuming that, for the project in question, any losers are not compensated then criterion (1) discussed on p. 60, has the following implication. The effects of the projects are such that it would be possible to rearrange the distribution of the bundle of goods that emerges from the new project in such a way that, as compared to the pre-project situation, some people are better off and no one has suffered. Now, the change from the pre-project situation to the hypothetical version of the new bundle in effect constitutes a Pareto improvement. The first question is, then, is the decision-taker happy about such a change? We have so far made the judgement that such changes *are* acceptable and, thus, we will assume the decision-taker would also take this view-point although one could argue the toss even about this type of change.[58] A second question to ask the decision-taker arises from the point that the above Pareto change is, for this project, hypothetical. In actual fact the losers are not compensated and, thus, the relevant question is 'do you approve of the distributional changes involved in moving from the hypothetical version of the new bundle to its actual version'. Both these questions—less formally presented of course!—may help the decision-taker to make up his mind. Both questions arise from welfare economists' analysis of the effects of economic changes. The discussion of 'welfare criteria' in the literature has had a much broader canvas than the partial piece-meal environment applicable to our problems, but the same general points apply. Moreover, it is important to point out that economists are not in full agreement by any means on the usefulness of asking the two questions above!

(b) The second line of approach is basically no different from the first in that it forces the decision-taker to be explicit about his distributional preferences. We could attach different weights to the various benefits and costs ensuing from the project and, thus, indicate to the decision-taker the different answers that could emerge from a gain/loss comparison, depending on how we distribute the weights. Even in the case where compensation is

[58] In the wider setting of general equilibrium analysis of welfare criteria this question appears to be one of the issues in dispute. In particular J. E. Meade's 'A Review of I. M. D. Little, A Critique of Welfare Economics', *EJ*, March 1959, implies some doubt about whether it is useful to regard 'everyone being better off' as a universally acceptable criterion for social improvement. A brief summary of the subsequent debate can be found in Winch's paper (*op. cit.*) and also in E. J. Mishan's article, 'The Recent Debate on Welfare Criteria', *OEP*, July 1965.

paid the gain/loss criterion, particularly when one is comparing one project with another, involves, as Foster has clearly put it, the value judgement

> that any man's pound of benefit is to have equal weight with any other man's pound of benefit; and similarly that any man's pound of cost is to weigh the same as any other man's. . . . The point is that there is no refutable reason why we should accept that a pound's benefit (or cost) is to count the same to whomsoever it accrues. Society—if society is the decision maker—can employ any system of weights it pleases. For instance, to take a trivial example, it could state that any fall in book-makers' profits is not to be counted as a social cost of a given investment but an equivalent benefit; this is an intelligible value judgement.[59]

In canvassing this second approach as a possibility it might appear that we are welching on our dismissal of the social welfare function. This device was rejected only on the grounds that searching for some fundamentally scientific basis for it, seemed a cul-de-sac. In a sense, to talk of assigning weights to benefits and costs *is* using a social welfare function; but (a) we allow that the weights are ultimately to be chosen by the government, and (b) we are not requiring the government's decision-taker to rank all conceivable distributions of the feasible sets of outputs and inputs in the economy. He is confronted only with the possibilities afforded by the public sector projects available.

This is not to say that in practice the use of simple, so-called 'neutral', gain/loss tests is to be rejected out of hand. In so far as they provide basic information necessary for illuminating the distributional aspects of economic changes, they have clearly a part to play. Further, empirical techniques and knowledge is still rudimentary in many instances and it is certainly praiseworthy that attempts are being made to provide the basic data for a gain/loss test;[60] it may well be that even this is enough for decision-takers to chew on at present. More on all these matters in the next chapter.

Some complications[61]

Given the likely relevance of a gain/loss test, it is necessary to point out certain ambiguities that can arise from the problem—ignored so far—that the measures of gain and loss are not unique. This is a problem that has

[59] *Op. cit.*, pp. 349, 350.

[60] Cf. A. A. Walter's praise of the pioneering work of Foster and Beesley on the economic assessment of the Victoria Underground Tube, that 'the authors . . . have fearlessly tried to quantify, while theorists have still been carping about nice points of principle'. See *JRSS*, Series A, Part I, 1963, 'Estimating the Social Benefit of Constructing an Underground Railway in London (With Discussion).' C. D. Foster and M. E. Beesley, p. 81, reproduced in *Readings in Welfare Economics, op. cit.*, and also in *Transport*, Ed. D. Munby, Penguin Modern Economics Series, 1968.

[61] The rest of this chapter can be omitted on a first reading.

bedevilled the discussion of 'welfare criteria' in its more general setting, in that the test of gainers being able to 'overcompensate' losers is unable in some instances to give a straight answer. In the partial equilibrium setting the problem essentially arises from the fact that, as the change in question takes place, the marginal utility of income is also changing. We have already established that differences can arise between the compensating income variations and the measures using the curves of partial equilibrium analysis because of this factor, and our conclusion was that, to the extent that the partial curves constitute the main likely operational data source, they are useful only in situations when real income changes are small. The arguments that are now pursued are useful, then, only in so far as they give further understanding to the more fundamental problems involved in devising criteria for public expenditure appraisal. The issues only arise when real income changes are not so small as to be ignored.

The main feature of the compensating variations is that they are concerned with keeping the individual in question at his starting welfare level when the economic change—price fall, a fall in a factor's reward, an increase in consumption—takes place. His income is adjusted in such a way (upward or downward) that he is compensated for experiencing the change. An alternative approach, but one in the same spirit, would be to deny him the change in question but so adjust his income that he attains the welfare level he would have had with the change. In this approach, then, he is denied the experience of the change but his welfare level is equilibrated to what it would have been with the change. These money adjustments are, therefore, called *equilibrating* income variations and, thus, for a potential wage-rate fall for a factor supplier the variation would involve taking income from him. This, then, gives us two general types of measure of surplus—in addition to the measure of the partial equilibrium curves—and they will normally differ in size. In both measures the income variations ensure that the individual keeps a particular welfare level—for the compensating variation it is the initial level and for the equilibrating it is the 'new' level. If, then, the change is a favourable one, the initial welfare level will be lower than the new level. We shall shortly illustrate that this implies that the equilibrating variation is the higher of the two in many circumstances. The careful reader will however probably have already spotted the basic point that, since an individual's evaluation of 'normal commodities' is higher the higher is his welfare level, then the compensating variation will be the lower of the two for a favourable change in economic circumstance (price fall, increases in commodities) and the higher of the two for an unfavourable change.

The implications of these points can be seen if we take a particular instance of a consumer experiencing a price fall for commodity x—a favourable change in other words. Starting at A on indifference curve I^1 in Fig. 3.11, the consumer moves to B when price falls from y_1x_1 to y_1x_2. The compensating variation for this change is y_1y_2, and this can be interpreted as the maximum

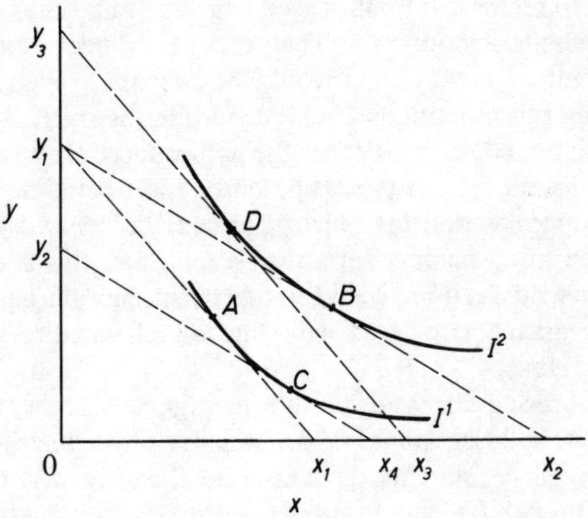

FIG. 3.11

the consumer would be prepared to pay to get the change. The price equilibrating variation in income is y_1y_3 since, keeping the old price level ($y_1x_1 = y_3x_3$), this is the amount we would have to give him if the I^2 welfare level is to be attained (at D). Further, it can be interpreted as the minimum compensation he would require if requested to forego the favourable price change. By analogy with the early discussion of a compensated demand curve, the equilibrating variation in this case is associated with the evaluation of extra x (or not having x!) along the I^2 indifference curve and, thus, the equilibrating surplus is greater than the demand curve measure and, therefore, greater than the compensating variation.[62]

The above points constitute the essence of the difficulties associated with measuring gains and losses in a partial setting, and it is now possible to indicate the general significance of these problems. Imagine a particular potential policy change involving some members of the community gaining because the price of a commodity falls, while others lose through a rise in the price of another commodity. The UK Post Office raises its charges for letter deliveries and this, by reducing the demands on the Exchequer permits

[62] This can be indicated on Fig. 3.8, by plotting the minimum compensation the individual would require for giving up x as he moves along the I^2 indifference curve in Fig. 3.11 from B to D and beyond. Clearly, this line will lie above the demand curve in Fig. 3.8, and the reader is left to work out the precise area which indicates the equilibrating income variation for the price fall from P_1 to P_2. Two further points can be mentioned at this juncture. Firstly, a quantity equilibrating income variation can be conceived of as the surplus relating to changes in quantity of output (or input). Following the Marshall definitions this would, more precisely, be the variation in income necessary to attain the new welfare level and, at the same time, keeping the old prices and the old quantities (cf. Henderson, *op. cit.*). Secondly, if the marginal utility of income is constant over all the relevant ranges, then the equilibrating variations will coincide with the partial demand curves and, therefore, with the compensating variations.

the government to increase the subsidy on eggs and milk, thus benefiting the consumers of these commodities.[63] The potential gainers would have some maximum amount of money they would be prepared to pay to have the change. Denoting this amount as C^G, we could, in the spirit of the gain/loss test considered so far, compare this with the minimum compensation required by the potential losers—C^L. A typical potential loser could be thought of as being initially at point B on Fig. 3.11; the price rises from y_1x_2 to y_1x_1 and, thus, the compensating income variation is y_1y_3, and this is the minimum compensation he would require if expected to experience the change. Clearly, these are the measures associated with the test of whether gainers could 'overcompensate' losers.

The analysis of the equilibrating variations suggests another test involving gains and losses. The losers might be prepared to pay something to prevent the change taking place; starting again at point B on Fig. 3.11 the maximum the individual is prepared to pay to avoid the price rise is y_1y_2; this is the price equilibrating variation for a price rise and so we will denote it by E^L. If the change were avoided the consumers of eggs and milk would need compensating if they are to be rendered at least as well off as if they had had the change; clearly the relevant measure of this is the equilibrating variation for a price fall—E^G. The alternate test then involves comparing the maximum the potential losers would be prepared to pay to avoid the change, with the minimum compensation required by the potential gainers; could the losers bribe the gainers to forego the change? In one sense this test involves allowing the change to take place, and then inquiring whether the users of postal services could bribe the consumers of eggs and milk to have the policy change reversed. We are inquiring whether 'everyone' could be made better off—criterion (1) in other words—by moving from the new situation back to the old situation. It may be useful then to call this alternative comparison the 'backward test', implying that if it is met the backward move is warranted; this will distinguish it from the question 'can the gainers compensate the losers' which we call the 'forward test'.[64]

[63] These price changes could conceptually be consistent with the use of partial equilibrium curves, but it does not matter here since we are allowing that the marginal utility of income could change markedly.

[64] We have seen that the forward test can be thought of as comprising two moves. Firstly, a move from the initial bundle of goods to a hypothetical bundle in which 'everyone' is better (or worse) off than with the initial bundle. The second move involves converting the hypothetical bundle to the actual new bundle. If the forward test is met, it implies that there is some redistributed version of the new bundle in which everyone is better off than the actual old bundle. Similarly, the backward test can be thought of as moving first of all from the actual old bundle to a hypothetical version of the old bundle; secondly, one moves from this bundle to the actual new bundle. If the backward test is *not* met this implies that the actual new bundle involves 'everyone' being better off than some redistributed version of the old bundle. In both tests one of the moves constitutes a Pareto improvement. Notice, however, that in the forward test this is a move to a *hypothetical* version of the new bundle while in the backward test it is a move to the *actual* version of the new bundle. It is for this reason—cf. footnote on p. 60—that the 'gainers being able to overcompensate losers' test may not be satisfied in moving to a

The compensation tests re-examined

At first sight all these refinements are somewhat dubious, since it seems crazy that there could be any contradiction between the tests. However, granted that there is no unique measure of gain (or loss) in principle different answers *can* be given by the two tests. Clearly, many changes may involve both the forward test being met and the backward test not being met and, prior to a further discussion of distribution, we might provisionally assume such changes are to be recommended. Granted this, three broad problems remain to be analysed:

(a) the case where both tests are met

(b) the case where neither test is met

(c) the effects of introducing distributional consideration.

(a) It is important to be clear about the circumstances under which both tests could be met. One element is the fact that there are different measures of gain and loss; if the real income effects of the change are negligible then the 'paradox' would not arise. In the more general setting of the discussion of welfare criteria, where the whole structure and distribution of the bundle of goods in the economy is changing, the paradox was first pointed out by Scitovsky[65] and the basic cause here is the changing relative evaluation of goods—or, putting it another way, the problem arises both from real income changes and changes in relative prices. A second element is the hypothetical nature of the compensation tests. If, in the forward move, compensation were actually paid then again no paradox can arise.

Now in the partial setting it turns out that, in many cases, if the forward test is met the backward test will not be met. Irrespective of whether the changes involve commodity price movements or changes in quantity of input and output without price changes, we may write:[66]

Forward test met: $C^G > C^L$

Backward test not met: $E^G > E^L$

Take the case of price changes for postal services and agricultural goods. If all these commodities are normal (i.e. non-inferior) then an implication of the analysis throughout this chapter is that $E^G > C^G$ and $C^L > E^L$. It, therefore, follows that if the forward test is met then the backward test will not be met. The same points apply if we think of the change as involving changes in the quantity of commodities available to a consumer (or input services required from a factor owner) with no price changes involved.

Pareto efficient point since, with this test, Pareto moves are made only to hypothetical versions of the new bundle. In the backward test the comparison, in the Pareto move, is with the actual new bundle and so this is the test that will take us to a Pareto efficient point. See Little's, *Critique, op cit.*, pp. 108–11 for a fuller discussion of these matters.

---

[65] 'A Note on Welfare Propositions in Economics', T. Scitovsky, RES, November 1941, reproduced in *Readings in Welfare Economics, op. cit.*

[66] Terms like C^G, E^L, etc., in other words are now used to indicate income variations whether of the quantity or price variety.

Mishan[67] gives a nice example where a piece of land is in the control of a local government authority and is used by the local residents for recreational purposes. The possibility arises of allowing the land to be used by business interests for construction purposes. In effect, such a policy would be to the detriment of the local residents whom one could regard as at present receiving a free good. For them the change involves giving up commodities (land), and there would be equilibrating and compensating measures of the effect of the proposed withdrawal of the free good on their welfare levels. Similarly, there would be two measures for the potential gainers from the policy change —the local business interests who would have acquired the land without charge. Again, no contradiction arises from the two tests as long as land is a normal good; the reader can verify this with the use of Fig. 3.11, leaving out the price lines and viewing x as quantities of land and y, as before, as money income.

In so far as we are interested in general cases, there are two instances where the two tests disagree. One is where the commodity in question is 'inferior', implying that consumers' evaluation of it (in terms of money income) would decrease as their welfare levels rose. If milk is an inferior good then, in the previous example, $E^L < C^L$ and, thus, when the forward test is met there is no guarantee that $E^G < E^L$. This sort of situation could quite reasonably be viewed as a special case. The second instance concerns changes in factor rewards and cannot be lightly dismissed. If a factor of production constitutes a 'normal good' for its owner, then it is possible to demonstrate that for unfavourable price changes—wage decreases that is—$C^L < E^L$ and, therefore, again a paradox can arise. Essentially this problem arises from the fact that factor services enter negatively into the utility functions. Wage falls are associated with decreases in factor services, but while the former is an unfavourable change, the latter taken on its own is favourable. There would, in any case, be certain amounts of money which the factor owner would be prepared to pay in exchange for a reduction in his services all other things being equal. When the wage *does* fall then the compensation he requires for this is less than the money that you could take from him if, without the wage fall, his welfare is to be equilibrated to the lower level to which the wage fall would have pushed him. For those interested a fuller demonstration of this point is given in the appendix.

(b) Even if the above paradoxes did not arise, there is an additional problem. If the forward test is not met but the backward test is, then we could provisionally allow that the move is not to be recommended—that is, pending distributional considerations. But inherent in the discussion of 'normal' commodities is the possibility of a situation where the gainers cannot overcompensate the losers, but neither is one able to justify the backward move—the losers could not bribe the gainers to forego the change. On the forward test losses exceed gains, but on the backward test losses also exceed

[67] 'Welfare Criteria for External Effects', *op. cit.*

gains. We are, in other words, assuming a ranking of $E^G > E^L > C^L > C^G$ which is consistent with the commodities being 'normal'. Even if we are distributionally neutral[68] the compensation tests cannot help us in deciding whether to undertake the change. For some particular project for example, the move looks bad from the pre-project viewpoint but if the project were undertaken then, retrospectively, the move appears to have been worthwhile.

(c) It is worth repeating that much of the data necessary to make the above distinctions in empirical studies is, clearly, lacking at present. Crude information on prices, alternative costs, and rough implications about the nature of partial equilibrium curves is the basic raw material as yet available. If the necessary knowledge were available then, following on from the section on distribution, there would be further analytical points that would have to be put to the decision-maker in terms of the effects of the project or policy change. We need not spell these out. What can be done here, by way of summary, is to set out various general types of changes which could well have universal acceptance. Suppose that the potential gainers and losers from the project can be classified (fortunately!) as homogenous groups being either poor or rich. The distributional effects of the change can then be described as 'good' if the gainers are the poor and the losers are the rich, and 'bad' if the reverse holds. Consider 3 cases:

(i) 'Everyone' *is* better off if the project is undertaken. If the distributional effect is favourable it seems likely that such a change would command acceptance by decision-takers. This means compensation is actually paid so that the potential losers do not actually suffer. The distributional clause is added to cover the point that 'everyone' being better off is consistent with small groups of people gaining quite a lot and others, though not losing, not gaining much. Even if the distributional effect is bad, some decision-takers, would not be averse to recommending this change on the grounds that at least no one suffers. However, the requirement that compensation is paid means that this criterion will not embrace many projects or policy changes.

(ii) The forward test is met. Again, project recommended if the distributional effect is favourable. This conforms to the earlier discussion of distributional issues, but note that we are not requiring that the backward test be non-fulfilled. We are allowing that the backward test could be met or not met, since even if it were met we could not favour the backward move on the grounds that this would be distributionally unfavourable. Even though the losers could bribe the gainers to move back, the fact that the bribe would not be paid—the test is hypothetical—means the poor would not be compensated for the backward move, and so we

[68] The word 'neutral' is used as short-hand, but it should be clear from the earlier discussion that this is an emotive word. Counting every £ of benefit and cost at face value, no matter to whom they apply, is in effect countenancing a predilection for the existing distribution of income and wealth.

rule it out. If the identity of the gainers and losers were reversed we would definitely recommend against having the change (if the backward test is met), since the poor would experience an uncompensated loss if the project were undertaken, and this loss is more sizeable than the compensation required by the rich to forego the change.

(iii) The backward test is not met. Project recommended if distributional effect of forward move is favourable even if the forward test is not met. If the gainers were the rich and the losers were the poor from the forward move, then we would definitely recommend against the change when the forward test was not met.

Of course these cases will not cover all possible policy changes or projects. We have refrained, for example, from commenting on a change where the forward test is met and the backward is not met but the distributional effect is unfavourable. Similarly a project involving a favourable distributional effect but where the forward move cannot be warranted and, moreover, the backward move can be warranted by the compensation test, poses tricky questions. All these cases are concerned with broad magnitudes and in the final analysis it is the decision-taker who makes the distributional judgements. Enough has been said to indicate where problems can arise!

Appendix

Factor rewards and surplus analysis

The analysis of economic surpluses in the context of payments to factors of production is a straight transition from the consumer surplus discussions, but some further interpretation is needed. In addition, there are few sources

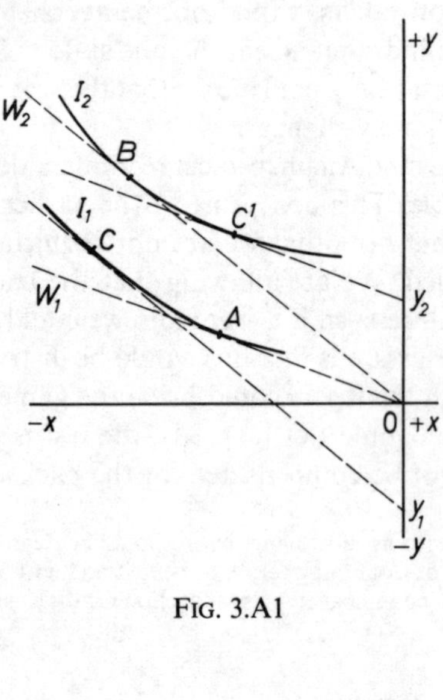

FIG. 3.A1

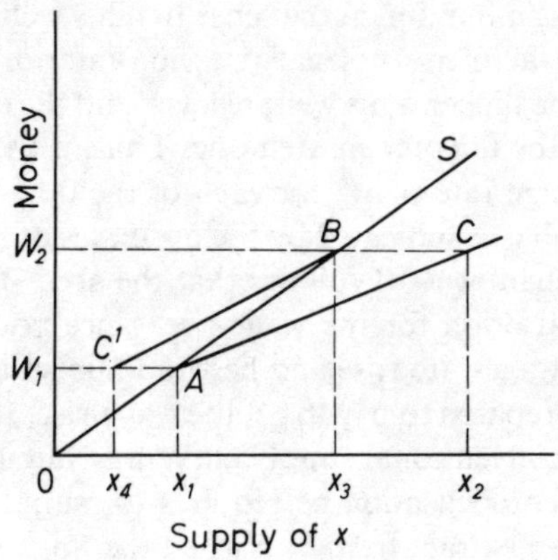

FIG. 3.A2

which treat it satisfactorily; one exception is Mishan's article[69] on which part of the subsequent analysis rests.

Fig. 3.A1 illustrates most of the relevant points. The supply of labour services by an individual is treated as involving the giving up of x. The y axis has the same meaning as before—money income—so that price lines like $0W_1$ and $0W_2$ are associated with particular wage-rates. With a wage-rate W_1, the individual is in equilibrium at point A on indifference curve I_1. If the wage-rate rises to W_2, he moves to point B supplying more labour services. If the prices of all other 'goods' are constant, then the slopes of the indifference curves traversed in this move correspond to the ordinates of the partial equilibrium supply curve (S) shown in Fig. 3.A2. For this sort of change one cannot talk of an 'income effect', since money income is not constant—it is something determined in the analysis. We can however—following Mishan—think of the wage-rise as involving a 'welfare effect'. Holding the wage-rate at its new level, the individual could be moved back from B to C by taking away lump sums of money income—'lump sum' in the sense that the receipt or withdrawal of these sums is unrelated to the quantity of factor services supplied. It follows that $0y_1$ is the price compensating variation in income, since if this is extracted when the wage rate rises the individual finishes up at C, no better or worse off than at A. (The line Cy_1 is drawn parallel to $0W_2$.)

The connection with the conventional measure of economic rent can be seen if the individual's evaluation of extra supplies of x is observed as one moves along the I_1 indifference curve from A to C and beyond. By analogy with the consumer analysis in this chapter, we may plot these observations on Fig. 3.A2 as the line from A to C and beyond. This line represents a compensated supply curve indicating the minimum compensation he requires

[69] 'Rent as a Measure of Welfare Change', *op. cit.*

for supplying extra x; minimum in the sense that his welfare level is constant along this path. If the factor x is 'normal' (i.e., non-inferior) then his evaluation of it will be greater the higher is his welfare level, and the compensated supply curve will lie below the uncompensated one. Thus, if the individual is at C, having received a wage-rate of W_1 for each of the $0x_1$ units and payments for the extra x_1x_2 units, as indicated by the ordinates of the AC line, he is no better or worse off than at A. It follows that the area W_2CAW_1 is the compensating income variation for the wage-rise, since you could extract this from him when the wage-rate rose and he would finish up at C. It indicates the maximum he is prepared to pay to get the wage-rise. It is a larger measure of surplus than the conventional supply curve measure (W_1W_2BA) because, since along AC the compensation he requires for supplying extra x is less, the maximum one can extract from him when the wage *does* rise is so much higher.

The equilibrating variation on the other hand is indicated by $0y_2$ on Fig. 3.A1 and the area $W_1W_2BC^1$ on Fig. 3.A2. The former needs little explanation since $0y_2$ is clearly the lump-sum compensation that would be required to put him on indifference curve I_2 (at C^1) if the wage were kept at its lower level ($0W_1 = y_2C^1$). Consider the individual's evaluation of x as he moves down the I_2 indifference curve from B to C^1 and beyond. He is actually prepared to pay money to reduce his supply of x, and these money measures are plotted as the ordinates of the line BC^1 in Fig. 3.A2. Point C^1 can be interpreted in the following way. Starting from B with an income of $0W_2Bx_3$—associated with the higher welfare level—he moves down the line BC^1 in Fig. 3.A2, paying out money to facilitate a reduction in his labour services. At C^1, supplying $0x_4$ labour services and holding a net income of $(0W_2Bx_3)$—$(Bx_3x_4C^1)$, he is no better or worse off than at B. It follows that, if he starts at A and there is a potential wage-rise to W_2, one need only give him an amount of money equal to $W_1C^1BW_2$ if the wage-rise is denied but his welfare is to be equilibrated to the higher level. Thus, this area constitutes the equilibrating variation for the wage-rise.

The crucial point for the discussion of welfare criteria is that, for a favourable change in economic circumstances, i.e., a wage-rise, the compensating variation exceeds the equilibrating. Similarly for a wage fall the equilibrating variation will exceed the compensating. The maximum he is prepared to pay to avoid the wage-fall (i.e., from W_2, starting at B, to W_1) exceeds the minimum compensation he requires for experiencing it. As pointed out in the text of the chapter, the difference with consumer analysis arises from the fact that favourable price changes (wage-rises) are associated with unfavourable quantity changes (increases in factor-services), whereas the two are in step in the case of commodity purchases.

4. A review of objectives and possible decision rules

4.1 Welfare economics, policy recommendations, and economic efficiency

The previous two chapters provide the backcloth to many of the applications of welfare economics in areas such as international trade problems, tax analysis, and monopolistic practices. They are, also, the base from which stems many of the applied studies in public expenditure economics. This chapter considers the general relevance of this background, and what we have to say here is extremely important in appreciating the significance of the applied work. In fact, the first part of this chapter should be re-read after the later parts of the book have been studied. First of all let us, very briefly, recap on the main points emerging from the previous chapters. Granted a particular definition of an 'increase in the welfare of an individual', certain 'efficiency' conditions were derived which characterized an economy in which national welfare was maximized, in the particular sense that no change would make any individual(s) better off without at the same time rendering others worse off. Unfortunately, there is not one but a number of possible arrangements for distributing goods between individuals and firms which meet these conditions. Associated with these efficiency conditions are certain required price patterns. These are achievable by a private enterprise economy provided it is characterized by some fairly stringent conditions, such as perfect competition, free mobility of factors of production, and so on. In addition, the price patterns are achievable when some or all factors of production are publicly owned, provided that each public enterprise, agency, or government department adjusts operations so that price equals marginal cost, and provided that the private sector—when the economy is a 'mixed' one—meets the characteristics specified before. Some technical problems about marginal-cost pricing were briefly explored. In addition, we demonstrated that although the Pareto efficiency conditions are drawn up in a context where all goods are perfectly divisible, the efficiency costs and benefits associated with indivisible changes can, in certain circumstances, be handled by the use of consumer and producer surplus analysis. Associated with all these devices for achieving the required price features are certain implications for the distribution of money income and welfare. If these are not 'ideal' in any sense, then taxes and transfers could be used to effect the ideal solution and at the same time retain the required efficient price patterns. Unfortunately, in theory, these taxes and transfers have to be of a lump sum kind and, since there are no useful fiscal weapons which meet this condition, we are led into an impasse. Partly because of this, an alternative approach to such 'blue-prints' has been attempted. This involves the idea of considering a change in economic circumstances and in trying to specify in what way one could weight the gains and losses associated with such a change. Despite the considerable effort that has gone into this search, the only general conclusion is that the size of the gains and losses should not be the only consideration; the identity of the parties involved is a relevant consideration for any decision-taker interested in distributional issues.

'Applied' studies of public expenditure

Although this brief survey indicates that there are a number of qualifications to be made to some of the suggested public sector decision rules, insufficient stress has been placed so far on the magnitude and significance of these qualifications and on the dubious nature of some of the assumptions implicit in the analysis. We propose, shortly, to bring these out more clearly. Prior to this, it will prove useful to indicate briefly how welfare economics has been 'applied' in the field of public expenditure—to give, in other words, a very brief bird's-eye view of some of the subjects explored in later chapters. First of all, we may note that the discussion of the previous chapters has not been particularly 'special' to the public sector. What has been indicated is that if part of the economy is under public ownership certain decision rules can, in principle, be pursued, which are Pareto efficient in the same way that a perfectly competitive private economy achieves such efficiency. Implicit in this is the recognition that many public agencies may have near monopolies of the goods they produce, and profit-maximization in these circumstances would be inappropriate. But many products and services traditionally found in the public sector of many economies have special characteristics. In particular, items like health, education, transport, broadcasting, defence, water resource development, and many others, exhibit strong 'externalities' or 'public good' properties in economists' jargon. In addition, indivisibilities and scale economies seem also to be common in such services. The next chapter, therefore, explores the theoretical aspects of these problems in more depth. In some respects, it might have seemed more appropriate to start our whole analysis with these issues. There are two good reasons for not doing this. One is that the analysis of externalities, indivisibilities, and the like, uses the basic techniques considered in the previous chapters, and it is important to fully understand these principles in a fairly simple environment. Secondly, it is simply not true that one can divide the economy up into public and private on the basis that the former contains all the goods and services giving rise to externalities, etc. Governments, in practice, undertake activities to meet a wide range of objectives and bring goods and services under public ownership for all sorts of reasons. In addition, of course, activities commonly found in the private sector are not bereft of externalities, to put it mildly. However, we must not play this down too much; the theory of 'public' goods, externalities, and scale economies is a key aspect of public expenditure economics, and we shall spend considerable time on these issues in the next chapter.

Looking at the more applied parts of the subject area, it is probably not unfair to suggest that the criterion of economic efficiency has dominated the very useful work that has been done so far. The equation of the 'benefits' of an activity with the willingness to pay of consumers, and its costs with the compensation required by input suppliers, has characterized the economic evaluation of public expenditure. Four aspects of this will briefly illustrate the point:

(a) Most of the so-called *cost-benefit* studies of public sector projects have been concerned with goods and services for which prices are not normally levied. Irrigation schemes in places as far apart as California and India have been subject to investigations where benefits are estimated by calculating the effects on farmers' profitability. Analyses of transport projects have considered effects on journey cost savings. Early attempts to evaluate health programmes and accident prevention rested on some estimates of the market value of goods and services, otherwise lost if people were withdrawn from the labour force. In all such cases 'benefits' are equated with the willingness to pay of parties affected by the project in question.

(b) The more sophisticated work on *pricing in public corporations* has been directed towards relating prices to marginal costs. Some pioneering work has been done in the French electricity industry, and the UK industry seems to be following this approach. In fact, in 1967 a government White Paper suggested that for all the UK nationalized industries

> . . . prices need to be reasonably related to costs at the margin and to be designed to promote the efficient use of resources within industry.[1]

The issue was taken up by a number of bodies. The National Board for Prices and Incomes, for example, commented in 1968

> . . . on the costing methods employed by the Post Office. Although we were impressed at the thoroughness with which this was done we did not consider that the results took sufficient account of long-run marginal costs . . . to provide an appropriate basis for decisions on tariffs.

[1] *Nationalised Industries: A Review of Economic and Financial Objectives*, p. 8, Cmnd 3437, HMSO, November 1967.

The Board's study was published in March, and in July they were able to report that the

> . . . Post Office intend to examine the application of long-run marginal costing to future pricing policy. . . .[2]

As a second example one may take the Board's report on the nationalized Gas Council and Area Boards where they

> . . . suggested that the industry should introduce experimental tariffs approximating to the structure of marginal costs, and that it should attempt a systematic calculation of these costs.[3]

(c) The apparently innocuous injunction to choose between production techniques—or more generally to choose between various methods of achieving some objective—on the basis of *minimizing costs* is, when the logic is pursued, fundamentally based on the premise that economic efficiency is of paramount importance. Some fairly complicated procedures are at present involved in choosing, for example, between coal-fired, nuclear, and hydro-electricity plants; in the end these all boil down to the cost-minimization approach and the argument that social costs are included does not invalidate the point, since, as we shall see, such allowances are usually based on market-type valuations.

(d) One does not need to have private ownership or public corporations to use a price system, and many of the suggestions for introducing pricing schemes for roads, water-supply, university education, blood-transfusions and the like, relate, certainly in the UK, to activities within the control of the public sector. Most of these suggestions are closely based on the logic of economic efficiency, and the more sophisticated the suggestions, the more do they approximate the price/marginal (social) cost rule.

The conclusions of welfare economics

With this as a background let us now consider what welfare economics has to offer by way of policy implications. The main point is, of course, that far from generating any decision rules, welfare economics only warns against ascribing any welfare significance to such rules. If we are to be truly scientific —following the lead of theorists like[4] Little, de Graaf, and Nath—we have

[2] The Board's report was published as *Post Office Charges,* Cmnd 3574, HMSO, March 1968. The two quotations are, however, taken from pp. 43–4 of the Board's *Third General Report: August 1967 to July 1968*, Cmnd 3715, HMSO, July 1968.

[3] The Board's report was published as *Gas Prices (Second Report),* Cmnd 3924, HMSO, February 1969, but the quotation is taken from p. 54 of its *Fourth General Report: July 1968 to July 1969*, Cmnd 4130, HMSO, July 1969.

[4] See I. M. D. Little, *A Critique of Welfare Economics,* 2 Ed., Oxford University Press, 1957; J. de V. Graaf, *Theoretical Welfare Economics,* Cambridge University Press, 1957; S. K. Nath, *A Re-appraisal of Welfare Economics,* Routledge and Kegan Paul, 1969.

to recognize that the main implication of welfare economics is that some of the standard 'conclusions' are pitted with qualifications. In particular, the implications of theoretical welfare economics may be stated baldly as:

(a) There is nothing ethically desirable about the price patterns associated with Pareto-type efficiency (nor with the surplus solutions of the indivisibility problem) because, among other things:

- (i) They are based on the value-judgement that the individual is the best judge of his own well-being, which is, in some cases, open to argument.
- (ii) They are, to put it kindly, 'neutral' with respect to income distribution.
- (iii) They assume individuals have perfect foresight.
- (iv) There is no allowance for persuasive advertising.
- (v) They assume that each individual's welfare is unaffected by any of the devices used to achieve efficiency.

(b) It follows that there is nothing inherently desirable about social organizations which achieve such solutions; that is:

- (i) Even if a private enterprise system was perfectly competitive, and one ignored externalities, indivisibilities, and advertising, there is still the problem that the use of a price system has little welfare significance if the distribution of income emanating from the pattern of resource ownership is not 'ideal' nor if consumers do not really know what, for example, health precautions they really 'need'. The use of the tax/transfer mechanism for dealing with income distribution is open to the theoretical objections that the taxes have to be lump sums. Moreover, if one ignores the above, there is still the problem that if indivisibilities and externalities *are* important phenomena perfect competition does not even achieve 'efficient' solutions; that is, it is *not* true, to be rigorous, that there

  > . . . is at the foundation of normative (welfare) economics a presumption that free competition will promote the efficient performance of economic activities.[5]

- (ii) Similarly, the public sector decision rule of setting price equal to marginal cost; the techniques of evaluating indivisible changes by surplus analysis, and of evaluating unpriced goods and services by cost/benefit analysis; the suggestions for introducing price systems; and, finally, the whole theoretical apparatus—to be described in the next chapter—of dealing with 'public goods' and the like, are all subject to basic qualifications regarding the use of price systems or using the logic of a price system.

(c) Even if we ignored the above points, there is still a formidable problem for public expenditure appraisal—that of the 'second-best' problem. The efficiency rule of setting price equal to marginal cost in the public sector requires that the private sector meets all of the requirements for Pareto

[5] H. G. Johnson, 'Problems of Efficiency in Monetary Management', *JPE*, p. 972, September/October 1968.

efficiency. But it is clear that this does not hold as long as the private sector includes some imperfections in market structure, is subject to taxes, and investment incentives, and contains uncorrected externalities.

In addition, it has been argued that the efficiency rules themselves are open to a number of criticisms. What does marginal cost mean; is it short-term or long-term; what happens if marginal is less than average cost; surplus analysis, as we have seen, is itself subject to numerous qualifications; many of the benefits of public projects cannot be measured; what is the appropriate interest rate to use for evaluating public investment projects: is it possible to allow for external effects? These relevant issues are considered in other parts of the book. They are, in a sense, technical problems of a different kind from points (a), (b) and (c) above. The latter are common to all the more technical areas of public expenditure economics, and it is useful to treat them separately here.

Now the bald statements of the 'impossibility' theorems of welfare economics would appear to suggest that economics has nothing to offer with respect to any of the 'normative' aspects of public expenditure. And, strictly speaking, this *is* true. On the other hand, *decisions still have to be made*. The chief virtue of welfare economics is, in my opinion, to make it clear that none of the suggestions for evaluating public expenditure—nor policies in other areas like international trade, tax analysis, monopolistic practices—can really be given any ethical significance. To appreciate why welfare economists, like Little and de Graaf, spent so much time pinning down the value judgements involved in certain prescriptions in the field of resource allocation, it is extremely instructive to look through A. C. Pigou's, *The Economics of Welfare*, MacMillan, 1920, or A. P. Lerner's *The Economics of Control*, MacMillan, 1944 *sub-titled* 'Principles of Welfare Economics'. Here one finds the price system given a welfare significance which is clearly not warranted. There are, unfortunately, no universal truths that have been discovered about national welfare. This does not mean that good reasons cannot be advanced for this policy or that. It means simply that one cannot, strictly speaking, appeal to welfare economics for support for many of the proposed decision rules. As long as we recognize that the 'good reasons' are simply arguments based on particular value judgements—often of a political nature—then we have learnt our lesson.

Consumers' needs and choices, and the problem of second-best

Of the numerous qualifications to the 'efficiency' rules, there seem to be three that are fairly crucial and worth exploring further, namely, the problem of consumer 'rationality'—for want of a better phrase—income distribution, and 'second-best'. We consider them in that order.

(a) *Consumer rationality:* An important aspect of this problem and one which is crucial to the whole analysis of public expenditure, is involved with the value judgement, mentioned in chapter 2, that the individual is the best judge of his own well-being. It is the first peg in the argument that the free choices made by an individual in, for example, a market environment, indicate something about his real 'needs'. It is the first peg in the proposition that the benefits of any public project can be taken as the willingness to pay of project consumers. It is, therefore, one of the first questions that must be considered in deciding for any good or service whether any price system or willingness to pay criterion is appropriate. We have already hinted that in areas like health and education, governments do appear to have taken a paternalistic role, though part of this is probably accountable to income-distribution problems. The more complex our world becomes the less likely does it appear that we, as laymen, will be fully knowledgeable of the effects of some of our consumption patterns. Of course, paternalism itself carries dangers, again of an intangible nature, and so the argument is not one-sided. Informative advertising clearly has a role here but, in practice, particularly in the private sector, an even bigger influence is that of persuasive advertising. Even if one decided that price systems are inappropriate for certain services because of these reasons, this does not mean economic analysis has no contribution to make. It means if anything that systematic analysis is needed for the evaluation of different objectives. The economist, for example, could take general objectives like 'the provision to all of equal access to health services' or 'free education for everyone up to the age of eighteen' or 'complete withdrawal from East of Suez by 1980', and analyse both the meaning of such objectives and various alternative courses of action. We return to this theme in chapter 10. The problem of uncertainty has also been mentioned in relation to consumers, but we propose to look at this issue in the context of investment decisions in chapter 6: it is as well to say here, however, that the main conclusion is nothing more than that, in relation to any project or output supplies, 'allowances will have to be made', since this is still a fairly underdeveloped part of economics.

(b) *Income distribution:* It was demonstrated in chapter 2 that Pareto efficiency is not associated with one unique pattern of resource allocation but can be consistent with several such allocations, depending on how one weights the welfares of the various individuals in the economy. In purely formal terms, this indeterminancy can be removed if a particular system of weights is introduced—if a social welfare function is used. No such function can rest, however, on the preferences of individuals in an economy. A government imposed system of weights will do the job and, in a sense, this is one way of saying that a government has certain objectives in the context of income-distribution. The basic approach would be to let the economy reach *a* Pareto efficient point—by following the various 'efficiency' rules—and then shift it to the *desired* Pareto point by levying taxes and transfers to redistribute income. An example will probably help. Government subsidies to housing imply that certain people may receive houses when the costs are greater than what these people are willing to pay—the efficiency rule is not followed. Take the extreme case where the houses in question cost £2,000 each but are in fact provided free, that is, they are financed from central government revenue rather than from the income of the residents. The benefit to the residents in this case is equal to the total amount they would have been willing to pay—say, £1,500. The implication of the efficiency/tax/transfer approach is that less resources are used if no subsidy is given to residents, but they receive general transfer income of £1,500. The saving is £500 and the residents—who now move to different types of houses—are no worse off than they were before; they previously had a 'consumer surplus' of £1,500 and they still enjoy this, but now it is in the form of a direct money grant. In practice, free provision is unusual and subsidized housing usually involves part of the cost being borne by residents, but the argument still applies.

This approach to income distribution is the second peg in the argument that market prices indicate something about consumers' need; it is 'better', on this argument, to effect distributional aims not by 'distorting' resource allocation but by use of the tax/transfer mechanism. Against this approach, two important counter-arguments can be developed. One to which we have already referred is that theoretically the taxes and transfers that are levied to effect distributional aims should not themselves be related to any magnitudes affecting production, work, or consumption, otherwise some further distortions will be created. They have to be of the mythical lump-sum variety. Even if one ignored this point, there is the whole problem that such measures may not always be feasible or desirable. It may be so much easier—in terms, say, of identification—to grant real income increases to particular 'needy' groups by subsidizing goods and services. It may be less humiliating to receive subsidized housing, milk, and welfare services than to receive unemployment pay or public assistance grants. Moreover, when one looks at public sector pricing and investment schemes, the distributive impact is not always immediately discernible nor is it, probably, always appreciated by decision-takers in the government sector. There is, therefore, no clear-cut solution either way and in chapter 10 we take a look at some of the recent suggestions for allowing for income distribution in the assessment of public expenditure projects.

(c) *Second-best:* To fully appreciate the problem of second-best, it is useful to go back to first principles, since it is a problem which is, intrinsically, bound up with the initial specification of the Pareto conditions. A rigorous exposition of the problem is presented in section 2 of this chapter, but the more general reader can miss this out. It will be recalled that chapters 2 and 3 proceeded as follows. Granted certain constraints provided by the available production technology, the analysis specified positions of 'maximum welfare' in the sense that from these positions no individual(s) could be made better off without others suffering. Associated with these Pareto conditions were certain price patterns, and the analysis proceeded to describe the various *behavioural rules* required of institutions, firms, and individuals in a number of different environments—private ownership, market socialism, mixed economies—and the various required characteristics of these environments. There was no presumption that governments would be able to control the behavioural rules of all these bodies. In fact, in a mixed economy many of the behavioural rules of the private sector can be taken as largely fixed. As long, however, as the actual rules and characteristics of the private sector correspond to those required—profit and utility maximization, perfect competition, and so on—certain behavioural rules can be prescribed for the 'controlled sector', that is, the public sector.

The problem arises when the actual behavioural rules and characteristics of the 'uncontrolled' sector do not conform to those required. In effect this means there is *an additional constraint* on the over-all maximization problem, namely, that the behaviour of certain firms and individuals deviates from the required behaviour as specified in the initial analysis. The solution to this is to repeat the maximization process subject to the additional constraint(s). The new set of behaviour rules for the controlled sector will contain an allowance for the behaviour of the deviant(s). One can see intuitively that the result will not be as 'good' as the first. Social welfare will be less in the second situation, for it is subject to an additional constraint. For this reason, the new efficiency conditions are known as the 'second-best' Pareto conditions, and the new set of behavioural rules for the controlled sector are a second-best set. It is our purpose, here, to see how the second-best differs from the first best. Notice that this is what Davis and Whinston[6] have called a partial piece-meal approach. It may well be that, say, the private sector is not as much out of the reach of government policy as we have implied. To the extent, however, that one is interested in decision rules for public enterprises and individual government departments, it is realistic to treat the private sector as 'uncontrolled'. We are interested in those weapons of policy that relate to the operations of particular public agencies rather than weapons like investment incentives, corporate taxes, or monopoly legislation, notwithstanding that the latter, in practice, do have a part to play.

Now, clearly, for certain institutions, firms, etc., the second-best rules will not differ from the first. That is, to state the obvious, the behaviour of the non-controlled sector is the same; except for the deviants these will be the first-best behaviour rules; in principle, part of the controlled government sector need experience no change and the issue is, therefore, one of specifying the size of that part of the controlled sector that has to change from first-best to second-best rules and the nature of these changes. There are two general factors at work here. Firstly, if externalities are present between producers or consumers in the public sector and producers or consumers in the private

[6] O. A. Davis and A. Whinston, 'Piecemeal Policy in the Theory of Second Best', *Review of Economic Studies,* July, 1967.

sector, then a deviation in the behaviour of a producer or consumer in the private sector will cause the required behavioural rules for part of the controlled public production sector to change from the first-best conditions. Clearly, we are here anticipating some of the next chapter's discussion, but it is sufficient to understand at this stage that externalities are defined to be present when a firm's production or an individual's utility is directly affected by a real variable within the control of another firm or individual. If a private cotton mill with noisy machinery is located near to a state hospital, then the latter's operations are directly affected by the amount of production that goes on in the cotton mill. If the cotton mill is not required to pay compensation, then it will adjust its activities in a way that takes no account of the costs imposed on the state hospital. The cotton mill is a 'deviant' whose actual behaviour—producing to the point where price equals marginal private cost—deviates from the required rule, to produce where price is equal to marginal social cost, where the latter includes all costs. The second-best rules for the state hospital would, therefore, involve an allowance for this constraint; it would mean choosing its location under the constraint that the cotton mill's activities are unchangeable: it might mean the state financing the insulation of the hospital from noise and so on. Clearly, if the cotton mill is, *in addition,* in an imperfect market, and exerts some monopoly control and this, also, is 'uncontrollable' then the normative behaviour rule for the hospital becomes even more complicated.

The second general factor and probably of much more importance is the general interrelationship that occurs through firms and individuals via market forces. To the extent that, for example, the UK nationalized gas industry's sales depend partly on the price of competing fuels, then if, for example, the privately owned oil refining industry's operations diverge from the required behavioural rules, it is no longer certain that the first-best rules for the gas industry—price at marginal cost—are any longer desirable. The argument is not exclusively concerned with goods and services where prices are levied. Some of the techniques, which we have briefly suggested can be used for estimating 'benefits' in water-resource development, road investment, and so on, are essentially dependent on related industries operating the required behavioural rules. Similarly, the technique of estimating the 'surpluses' that accrue from indivisible changes depend, as we saw in the previous chapter, on the existence of efficient behavioural rules in the rest of the economy. Having said this, we shall proceed to illustrate the problem of market inter-relationships in the context of an enterprise's pricing policy. To the extent that, in the fuel example, the oil refining industry is monopolistic or subject to government taxes, then oil prices are in excess of marginal costs. Private bus operators in the UK pay certain taxes—purchase tax on vehicles, petrol duty—and, on the other side of the coin, escape paying directly for the use of the road system, so that their prices are also unlikely to be equal to marginal costs; in which case demand for British Railways' services will be different from what it would have been if bus prices were equal to marginal costs. Perhaps one could get round this by suggesting that the ratio between price and marginal cost, in British Railways, should attempt to approximate to that in the private bus companies, and that the gas industry should approximate the ratio in the oil industry. The trouble with this is that, in principle, the effects are widespread. Both bus and rail services are, in the end, substitute sources of expenditure for consumers for other goods and services. Working through, the demand for state financed postal services may be affected. This does not mean that all of the public sector will necessarily be affected; the more rigorous analysis in section 2 of this chapter describes the factors determining the limit of these effects. Another suggestion[7] is that to the extent that, in general, prices in the private sector are above marginal costs because taxes are more common than subsidies and that market structure imperfections will tend to work in this direction, then perhaps one might raise all public sector prices above marginal costs by amount roughly related to the excess in the private sector. Leaving measurement problems on one side, this, however, is also subject to qualifications. The presumption is that the 'related' goods and services are substitutes. But what if they are complements? Manufacturers of gas appliances are subject to a purchase tax. Since the demand for such appliances is complementary to that of gas, the second-best rule for the publicly owned gas supply industry would, in this context, imply a price less than marginal cost. Finally, hidden subsidies are not all that unimportant, particularly in transport—think of the 'social costs' of noise, fumes, and congestion caused by road transport. The chief conclusions that must be drawn, therefore, from the *theoretical* analysis are that the second-best rules for public sector decision-taking will be very different from the standard Pareto conditions, that they will be fairly complicated and that, therefore, they will be difficult to implement.

An impasse?

How then does one deal with these formidable issues? In particular, how does one reconcile the use of the efficiency criterion in many applied studies with the emptiness of this criterion as revealed in theoretical welfare economics? There is a vast and growing gap between the two lines of analysis though, on the more applied side, there have been some recent attempts to reconstruct public expenditure criteria making allowances for things like income distribution, and we discuss this in chapter 10. There seem to be two general lines of approach to this issue. One is to argue that decision-takers in the public sector *are* interested in a number of objectives, one of which is

[7] Cf. M. J. Farrell, 'In Defence of Public Utility Price Theory', *OEP,* February 1958; an amended version appears as chapter 2 of *Public Enterprise,* Ed. R. Turvey, Penguin Modern Economics, 1968, and the discussion of second-best can be found on pp. 47–50.

'economic efficiency'. In this sense economists are 'merely' analysing the logic of catering for such an objective, without necessarily committing themselves to saying whether they, personally, think it is a useful objective. This is somewhat similar to J. de Graaf's suggestion that

> . . . the economist cannot say at what level the National Coal Board should set the price of coal. He can merely make clear . . . the probable consequences of setting it at various different levels.[8]

What de Graaf does not make explicit is that, among the probable consequences, decision-takers are likely to be interested in the effect on the welfare of the various individuals in society. They will not simply be interested in the effect of the price of coal on other prices, or the portion of the money income of certain groups that is devoted to coal. They will be interested in what economists have to say about the 'welfare' of an individual, and they might well want to ascribe some welfare significance to, for example, setting price equal to marginal costs. Nevertheless, this whole approach is broadly one which brings the issues of public expenditure economics within the context of what is known as 'positive economics', in that the economist is concerned with analysing the logic of a particular definition of welfare without necessarily advocating that the definition contains any universal truth; it is simply a definition. There is, of course, one important difference with the conventional 'positive' studies of macro-economics, growth theory, and so on. This is that the predictions are more or less impossible to test. The predictions concerning a particular change in the pricing policy of the NCB, are, say, that some people's welfare rises. If one opts for the particular definition of welfare used in chapter 2, then the only way to discover whether an individual's welfare has risen is to ask him—a procedure which we are told is extremely unscientific in the social sciences. As many writers on theoretical welfare economics have said, one can, therefore, only test the theory by considering whether the assumptions are realistic—a methodological approach which is often scorned in other areas of economics but which appears to be the only possible approach in this area.

For these reasons, the rest of this book could, to a large extent, be treated as being positive economics. Most of the 'efficient' solutions to externalities, appropriate investment criteria, price policy, and so on, could be treated as involving simply the logical implications of a particular policy objective. Moreover, some of the things we have to say, on income distribution, for example, and other 'non-efficiency' objectives, could also be viewed simply as analysing the logic of different objectives. This leaves the economist as not much more than a human computer. Moreover, with the inheritance of the literature on welfare economics, and with familiarity with techniques used in the applied studies, it would be foolish to suppose that an economist would

[8] *Op. cit.*, p. 171.

always keep to this role[9] or that his interest would be maintained in such a role. A second main approach would, therefore, be for the economist to advocate certain policies making the value judgements and unsubstantiated assertions *clearly explicit.*[10] For this reason, the following section, for what it is worth, attempts to set forth the author's own attitude to these issues, to indicate a general approach to the use of the efficiency and other criteria. This will incidentally include some discussion of the second-best problem, since in the end this also seems to require, if not an act of faith, at least an act of judgement.

A suggested approach

While there are many problems associated with using those decision rules often canvassed for public expenditure, what we have to say here concentrates mainly on the three items which were described before as being fairly crucial, namely, consumer rationality, income distribution, and second-best. This is not a programme for action but a set of suggestions for approaching the problems. One of the first things that has to be decided is the extent to which one feels confident in the value judgement that the individual is the best judge of his own well-being. By 'decided' we mean that this ability is probably different for different products, and there seems to be a case for thinking that broad distinctions can be made between different types of goods and services. I, personally, would think it is a dubious assumption in areas of the public sector such as health and education, and probably a number of others. For these sorts of services a paternalistic approach seems justifiable, and the 'traditional' analysis of the previous three chapters has only limited relevance. This case is not concerned with the fact that such services involve externalities—as they may well do—nor with the problem of income distribution. In addition, it is also true, as we have already hinted, that there is considerable scope in these areas for looking at the costs of alternative methods of achieving some objective; for example, the costs of a slaughter policy as opposed to a vaccination programme in relation to the control of animal foot-and-mouth diseases. What we are saying is that the equation of the 'benefits' or 'advantages' of public projects in these areas with *willingness to pay,* rests fundamentally on the proposition that the individual is the best judge of his own well-being and this we would wish to dispute.

The second main part of our approach relates to income distribution and it

[9] It is tempting to go further and agree with Lord Poole: 'People never want advice; they want to be told what to do; that's one of the great secrets of life.' The remark is attributed to him by A. Howard and R. West in *The Making of the Prime Minister,* p. 135, Jonathan Cape, 1965.

[10] I cannot fully share R. Turvey's '. . . personal feeling . . . that the value judgements made by economists are, by and large, better than those made by non-economists!' *EJ*, March 1963, p. 96 of the paper 'Present value versus Internal Rate of Return—An Essay in the Theory of the Third Best'.

recognizes two points. Whereas it would ease matters considerably if one could assume that the distribution of income can be dealt with by the tax/transfer mechanism, it is more realistic to accept that there are limits to this and, moreover, that the full distributive effect of using price systems or analogues to them (cf. cost-benefit analysis) will not be realized. We have, briefly, described the arguments behind this already in this chapter and we explore them in more depth in chapter 10. Now, since any change in the price/output decisions of a public enterprise, or any public investment project, always has distributive effects, it would appear that the implications of our approach are that price and investment policies in the public sector should pay no concern to 'efficiency' objectives. However, the second point in our approach to income distribution matters—more formally it is a constraint—is that it is probably not feasible in all instances to require public sector decision-takers to take distributive effects into account;[11] that the head of the Post Office should not be required to be continuously allowing for distributional matters in pricing and investment policies. What we do suggest is that in routine operating matters for parts of the public sector not excluded by the considerations of the previous paragraph, the 'efficiency' approach of using a price system or using the logic of a price system is relevant. This is to be supplemented partly by the use of the tax/transfer mechanism to effect distributional aims. Finally, and most importantly in matters relating to pricing and investment which are not of a routine nature, we think distributional considerations can usefully be introduced. Where the dividing line lies is not something we wish to pin down exactly, but the sort of decisions in which distributional considerations could be introduced are:

(a) Situations where existing capacity is likely to be more or less fixed over long periods, thereby leading to long-term 'shortages' as we experienced in the fuel sector in the UK in the decade after 1945.

(b) Specific once-and-for-all projects, such as the third London airport scheme, which often, in addition, involve 'externalities'.

(c) The *introduction* of pricing to goods and services previously subject to some kind of non-price rationing; examples in the UK would include the suggestions for pricing roads, water-supply, and parking facilities.

(d) Major changes in pricing procedures, such as switching from average-cost pricing in electricity supply to time-of-day differentials, to reflect marginal costs.

Granted these two major points, both of which are essentially concerned with the extent to which market prices reflect consumer 'needs', this still leaves large areas of the public sector where we think there is scope for using the 'efficiency' approach to the extent that it does indicate some of consumers' preferences, and, in addition, it has the traditionally expounded advantages

[11] R. Turvey has made this point on a number of occasions. See, for example, *Optimal Pricing and Investment in Electricity Supply,* pp. 86–7, Allen & Unwin, 1968.

of being a decentralized but easily administered system. By the efficiency approach we mean either:

(a) Levying prices for goods and services and relating these prices to costs, or,

(b) Where price systems cannot be used because of externalities or indivisibilities, the use of decision rules, based on consumers' willingness to pay and input suppliers' required rewards, i.e., techniques which are based, as we shall see, on the same valuation principles as a system of prices.

The more sophisticated are the solutions in (a) and (b), the more they will tend towards the price/marginal cost rule and related concepts to be discussed in later chapters. Having said this, we must now recognize that these sorts of solutions are subject to the more technical but formidable problem of second-best; that, for example, the suggestion of pricing public sector outputs at marginal cost, rests, to be theoretically correct, on the presumption that prices are equal to marginal costs in the rest of the economy. In fact, as well as the high level problem of pricing, there are more mundane issues involved, such as whether the Post Office bases its choice between different letter-sorting machines on the size of the money costs involved. In addition, as well as the overall constraints on Pareto efficiency provided by distortions in the private sector, there are some policy decisions that are made in the public sector which can be treated in no other way than being an additional constraint. Thus ever since 1961 the UK nationalized industries have been required to earn certain target financial surpluses. In effect this constitutes a constraint on 'efficient' pricing in such industries.[12]

Now, it may well be that in the dim and distant future techniques of analysis will be so refined and decision-takers so used to economic analysis that some of the complicated solutions to the second-best problem can be overcome. Incidentally, a further reason has emerged in this section for thinking that these solutions are complex, namely, that we have excluded certain areas from efficiency considerations; optimal resource allocation is now related to different types of objectives in different parts of the economy. While we may, in the long run, overcome these problems, decisions have to be made now. Perhaps we give up? But this means nothing more than that the nationalized industries will, in practice, be asked to maximize profits or break even. It seems possible to argue that something better than this can be achieved. The argument is that though the effects of distortions are in principle widespread, some of the more 'immediate' and nearby effects are the most important. One tries, in other words, to optimize within broad sectors; to ensure, for example, that within the transport sector relative transformation rates are roughly related to relative substitution rates. This means allowing in the UK environment for private and public buses, state railways and road track, private and public road vehicles and, if we are

[12] For an exploration of the implication of this constraint see R. Rees, 'Second-Best Rules for Public Enterprise Pricing', *Economica,* August 1968.

ambitious, domestic airlines and perhaps even coastal shipping. Thinking in terms of prices, the price/marginal cost configurations in public enterprises—allowing for some flexibility in control over the private enterprises—would be manipulated to achieve optimization within such broad sectors. By doing this, one could not, of course, be sure that too much or too little transport as a whole was being provided, but this is the price paid for sub-optimization. In more detail, some recent suggestions by R. Turvey[13] are in this spirit. He would firstly base choice of technique on the cost-minimization approach, allowing for the largest and more tractable externalities and market imperfections. A public enterprise's product would be sold at a price whose relationship to marginal cost approximated to that in competing private enterprises, and adjustments in taxes on the latter would be used as far as possible to ensure, for this group as a whole, that the price/marginal cost ratio does not get too much out of line with that in the rest of the economy. This rule has to be modified for sales by one public enterprise to another for reasons that we discussed in the previous chapter (pp. 41–42), so that here Turvey would have the price set equal to marginal cost. There may well be points at which one could quibble with this and situations where it is not helpful, but the broad approach seems useful. Finally, it should not be forgotten that the more use is made of general equilibrium policy weapons—such as taxes and investment incentives—the less the onus is put on the partial equilibrium operations of public enterprises as vehicles for allowing for discrepancies in the private sector. If over time the general policy measures become more refined, the nearer will the second-best rules for the public sector approximate the simpler first-best rules.

4.2 A formal analysis of the theory of second-best[14]

The proposition that the Pareto efficiency conditions are of an all-or-nothing nature has long been recognized. Moreover, in the decade after 1945, a number of problems arose in areas such as international trade, tax analysis, as well as public enterprise pricing, which were essentially related to the all-or-nothing characteristic. In particular, it was noticed that if distortions existed in part of the system, following the 'efficiency rule' in other parts of the system could make matters worse. If some countries have trade barriers, then free trade in the rest of the world is not necessarily the best solution. It was not however until Lipsey and Lancaster[15] formalized the problem in 1956 that the full formidable nature of second-best problems was appreciated.

[13] 'The Second-Best Case for Marginal-Cost Pricing', chapter 15 of *Public Economics*, Ed. J. Margolis and H. Guitton, Macmillan, 1969. This volume is a collection of papers presented at the International Economic Association's conference at Biaritz in November 1966. There is a discussion of Turvey's paper on pp. 547–50.

[14] This section can be omitted by the more general reader.

[15] R. G. Lipsey and R. K. Lancaster, 'The General Theory of Second Best', *Review of Economic Studies*, No. 1, 1956.

It was these two writers who made it clear that, on the one hand, the 'correct' second-best solution involved repeating the basic welfare maximization process subject to new constraints relating to the behaviour of the 'deviants' and, on the other hand, that the optimal second-best rules for the 'controlled sector' such as a public enterprise, were likely to be fairly complicated. Part of the problem in using the Lipsey and Lancaster model is that it does not focus on the behaviour of individuals and firms, but remains very much in an industry setting. A paper in 1965 by Davis and Whinston[16] clarified this point and, moreover, considerably improved our understanding of the second-best problem, though the basic difficulties for policy that emerged from the Lipsey and Lancaster paper have hardly been reduced. It is still true, as we pointed out in the previous section, that most of the rough allowances for second best are theoretically incorrect, and it was for this reason that the suggestions in the previous section were self-evidently of an arbitrary nature.

A reformulation of the Pareto conditions

To start with, one needs a model from which the standard Pareto efficiency conditions can be derived. One could use the summary model expounded in the last few pages of chapter 2; that is, where a social welfare function is maximized subject to the constraint of a social (i.e., community) production function. This sort of approach is insufficiently detailed for present purposes. The models used in section 2.3 (together with the analysis of behaviour rules in sections 3.2 and 3.3) are more appropriate, but the exposition there has the drawback that the maximization process was sub-divided into the three compartments of production, exchange, and general optimum. To fully appreciate the second-best problem it is useful to have a model where all these three issues are integrated. That is, we require a maximization process, the solution to which will determine, simultaneously, the distribution of inputs and outputs between production locations and between individuals. The starting point is an economy of m individuals, and a function which attaches weights to the welfare of each of these individuals. A social welfare function is required such as that in eq. (2.20), and we reproduce it, here, as:

$$W = W(U_1, \ldots, U_m) \tag{4.1}$$

where U_m, etc., is the utility function of person m. There is no pretence that such a function can be based on the individual preferences of the members of the population. The main point of the analysis is to derive the efficiency conditions, and these can be derived without specifying the form of the social welfare function as long as it is of the general Paretian variety, i.e., it sanctions

[16] O. A. Davis and A. Whinston, 'Welfare Economics and the Theory of Second Best', *Review of Economic Studies,* January 1965. Our exposition draws considerably from this article; the approach has been simplified by expressing everything in calculus terms, though we have had to cheat occasionally to keep to this. Davis and Whinston's exposition is in the format of a programming problem.

any change which renders someone better off and no one worse off ($\delta W/\delta U_i > 0$ *for* $i = 1 \ldots m$). There are $1 \ldots n$ outputs (or commodities) and $1 \ldots s$ inputs, and each individual utility function will include these so that for some typical person i, the utility function, U_i, is given by an expression like eq. (3.10). As before, we postulate $1 \ldots v$ firms, and the production function of firm a, typical of all firms, is of the form,

$$f_a = (x_1^a, \ldots, x_n^a; h_1^a, \ldots h_s^a) = 0$$

Here x_n^a is the quantity of commodity n produced by firm a and h_s^a is the quantity of input s that it uses. Now, in chapter 2, the efficiency conditions, in production for example, were derived by maximizing the output of one commodity under the constraint that all other inputs and outputs were at fixed levels. In the present context, all outputs and inputs are treated as variable, but there is a constraint analogous to the one in chapter 2; this is, that the total production of any commodity should be equal to the total amount of commodities consumed by the person sector. It is, in a sense, a market clearing condition. If terms like x_j^i represent, as in the previous chapters, the quantity of output j consumed by person i, then the constraint for commodities is:

$$\sum_{i=1}^{i=m} x_j^i = \sum_{a=1}^{a=v} x_j^a \qquad j = 1 \ldots n \tag{4.2}$$

Similarly for inputs there is the constraint:

$$\sum_{i=1}^{m} h_l^i = \sum_{a=1}^{v} h_l^a \qquad l = 1 \ldots s \tag{4.3}$$

It is now possible to specify the overall problem, which is one of maximizing eq. (4.1) subject to the market clearing conditions in eq. (4.2) and eq. (4.3), and subject to the technological constraints provided by the production functions in each firm. This can be formulated into the following Lagrangean expression, where Λ_j, Π_l and Φ_a are the undetermined Lagrangean multipliers:

$$L = W(U_1, \ldots, U_m) - \sum_{j=1}^{n} \Lambda_j \left(\sum_{i=1}^{m} x_j^i - \sum_{a=1}^{v} x_j^a \right)$$
$$- \sum_{l=1}^{s} \Pi_l \left(\sum_{i=1}^{m} h_l^i - \sum_{a=1}^{v} h_l^a \right)$$
$$- \sum_{a=1}^{v} \Phi_a f_a(x_1^a, \ldots, x_n^a; h_1^a, \ldots, h_s^a) \tag{4.4}$$

The first-order conditions for a maximum are found by differentiating L with respect to each input and output, for each individual and firm, and setting the results equal to zero. Using W_i as the shorthand for $\delta W/\delta U_i$ and terms like F_l^a and U_j^i, as in previous chapters, for $\delta f_a/\delta x_j^a$ and $\delta U_i/\delta x_j^i$ respectively, we have:[17]

[17] It is assumed that all second-order conditions are met.

$$\delta L/\delta x_j^i = W_i U_j^i - \Lambda_j = 0 \qquad i = 1 \ldots m; j = 1 \ldots n \tag{4.5}$$
$$\delta L/\delta h_l^i = W_i U_l^i - \Pi_l = 0 \qquad i = 1 \ldots m; l = 1 \ldots s \tag{4.6}$$
$$\delta L/\delta x_j^a = \Lambda_j - \Phi_a F_j^a = 0 \qquad a = 1 \ldots v; \ j = 1 \ldots n \tag{4.7}$$
$$\delta L/\delta h_l^a = \Pi_l - \Phi_a F_l^a = 0 \qquad a = 1 \ldots v; \ l = 1 \ldots s \tag{4.8}$$

If, in addition, L was differentiated with respect to the multipliers, then the resulting total of equations would enable one to solve for the values of x_j^i, x_j^a, h_l^i, h_l^a. Of more interest in the present context are the Pareto efficiency conditions, which can be derived by rearrangement and substitution of the above four equations to give:

$$U_j^i/U_l^i = \Lambda_j/\Pi_l = F_j^a/F_l^a \qquad \begin{array}{l} a = 1 \ldots v; i = 1 \ldots m; \\ l = 1 \ldots s; j = 1 \ldots n \end{array} \tag{4.9}$$

Here the conditions are expressed in terms of an input and an output but, clearly, similar expressions could be derived as between any two outputs or as between any two inputs. With this qualification, eq. (4.9) contains the conditions of Pareto efficiency, since it requires that marginal substitution rates be the same for all individuals, that transformation rates be the same in all firms, and that the two sets of rates are themselves equal. In a money economy, the Λ_j's and Π_l's are equivalent to prices and, in fact, formally in this model they represent the 'cost' of the market-clearing constraints. If they are replaced by P_j and P_l—the price of commodity j and the wage-rate of labour services, l—then the resulting expression indicates the required price patterns and the requirements for production and consumption arrangements, namely,

$$U_j^i/U_l^i = P_j/P_l = F_j^a/F_l^a \qquad \begin{array}{l} a = 1 \ldots v; i = 1 \ldots m; \\ l = 1 \ldots s; j = 1 \ldots n \end{array} \tag{4.10}$$

Implicit in eq. (4.10) is that P_j should equal the marginal costs of producing j in terms of labour services, l. This provides the required operating principle for publicly owned enterprises. For an economy of privately-owned resources, profit and utility maximization in a context of perfect markets will also generate eq. (4.10). This we spelled out in chapter 3, but it is useful, for exposition of the second-best problem, to briefly set out the private sector's required behavioural rules. As far as individuals are concerned we postulate, as in chapter 3, their maximizing utility, subject to a budget constraint, so that for the ith consumer the process is represented by

$$L_i = U_i - M^i\left(\sum_{j=1}^{n} x_j^i P_j + \sum_{l=1}^{s} h_l^i P_l\right) \tag{4.11}$$

where M^i is the Lagrangean multiplier, and where factor services, h_l^i, will implicitly be negative. The first-order maximum conditions when the individual is a price taker are:

$$\delta L_i/\delta x_j^i = U_j^i - M^i P_j = 0 \qquad j = 1 \ldots n \tag{4.12}$$
$$\delta L_i/\delta h_l^i = U_l^i - M^i P_l = 0 \qquad l = 1 \ldots s \tag{4.13}$$

which on rearrangement give:

$$M^i = U_j^i/P_j = U_l^i/P_l \qquad j = 1 \ldots n; l = 1 \ldots s \tag{4.14}$$

Since P_j and P_l are common to all individuals, part of the requirements in eq. (4.10) have been met. Turning now to production, each firm is viewed as maximizing profit subject to the constraint of its production function. For the *a*th firm the maximization process is written as

$$L_a = \sum_{j=1}^{n} x_j^a P_j + \sum_{l=1}^{s} h_l^a P_l - \phi_a f_a(x_1^a, \ldots, x_n^a; h_1^a, \ldots, h_s^a) \tag{4.15}$$

where ϕ_a is the undetermined multiplier. The first-order conditions are

$$\delta L_a/\delta x_j^a = P_j - \phi_a F_j^a = 0 \qquad j = 1 \ldots n \tag{4.16}$$
$$\delta L_a/\delta h_l^a = P_l - \phi_a F_l^a = 0 \qquad l = 1 \ldots s \tag{4.17}$$

On rearrangement these give

$$\phi_a = P_j F_j^a = P_l/F_l^a \qquad j = 1 \ldots n; l = 1 \ldots s \tag{4.18}$$

and this indicates the price/marginal cost condition required in eq. (4.10). It may be noticed from equations (4.5), (4.6), (4.12), and (4.13) that, given that the role of Λ_j and Π_l are taken over by prices P_j and P_l, then $M^i = 1/W_i$. Since we observed in chapter 3 that the multiplier in the individual's maximization process, M^i, is equal to the marginal utility of income, then this, in the final solution, is equal to (the reciprocal of) the social weight given to the individual's marginal purchases or input supplies. For similar reasons, ϕ_a is clearly equal to Φ_a.

The second-best solution

As we noted in the first part of this chapter, a second-best problem is defined to exist when one or more of the actual behavioural rules in an economy are different from the required behavioural rules and, moreover, that the behaviour of the deviant(s) cannot be changed. It follows that, in this new situation, changes may be necessary in the required rules for the rest of the economy. To discover what determines the scope of the required changes, it is necessary to repeat the whole maximization process with an additional constraint that the behaviour of some firm(s) or individual(s) is fixed in a particular way. Clearly, social welfare will be less in this new situation and for this reason it is called a second best solution. As an example[18] suppose firm *b* has a private monopoly over product *k*. The firm is not, therefore, a

[18] This is partly based on one of Davis and Whinston's examples in their 1965 paper in the *Review of Economic Studies, op. cit.*

price-taker like firm a in the above equations. Firm b's price is now a function of quantity demanded. That is:

$$P_k = f_k(x_k^b) \tag{4.19}$$

and eq. (4.19) is the market demand function for k. If firm b is a profit-maximizer, then equilibrium output will be where marginal cost equals marginal revenue, rather than price. This characteristic of firm b's behaviour would, therefore, have to be added as a constraint on the basic welfare maximization process. This we may do in two stages, firstly by specifying the actual behaviour of the monopolist more rigorously, and then converting it into the terminology of the basic welfare maximand. It will simplify matters if firm b is assumed to produce only the one output, k, in which case his maximization process can be written as:

$$L_b = x_k^b P_k + \sum_{l=1}^{s} h_l^b P_l - \phi_b f_b(x_k^b; h_1^b, \ldots, h_s^b) \tag{4.20}$$

If firm b exerts no monopolistic influence in the factor market, then the first-order conditions for its use of factors is given by:

$$\delta L_b/\delta h_l^b = P_l - \phi_b F_l^b = 0 \qquad l = 1 \ldots s \tag{4.21}$$

The price it has to pay for factors is unaffected by the volume of purchases. In the product market however, the equilibrium condition, remembering eq. (4.19), is

$$\delta L_b/\delta x_k^b = [(x_k^b\, \delta P_k/\delta x_k^b) + P_k] - \phi_b F_k^b = 0 \tag{4.22}$$

The expression in square brackets is the partial differential of total revenue with respect to output—that is, marginal revenue.[19] From eq. (4.21) and eq. (4.22) we have

$$(x_k^b\, \delta P_k/\delta x_k^b) + P_k - P_l F_k^b/F_l^b = 0 \qquad l = 1 \ldots s \tag{4.23}$$

which presents the equality of marginal revenue and marginal cost more rigorously. This is the constraint that has to be added to the overall maximization process, but it has first to be changed into the latter's terminology by replacing P_l by Π_l and P_k by Λ_k

Equation (4.23) then becomes:

$$(x_k^b\, \delta\Lambda_k/\delta x_k^b) + \Lambda_k - \Pi_l F_k^b/F_l^b = 0 \qquad l = 1 \ldots s \tag{4.24}$$

This, then, is to be an additional constraint on the overall welfare maximand. We do not need to write this out in full but simply note that, using Ψ as the additional Lagrangean multiplier, the following expression has to be added to eq. (4.4).

[19] Since the elasticity of demand is $e = (x_k^b/P_k)\,(\delta P_k/\delta x_k^b)$, then the expression in square brackets implies that marginal revenue is equal to $P_k(1+e)$, a familiar representation of the relationship between average and marginal revenue.

$$-\sum_{l=1}^{s}\Psi_l[(x_k^b\,\delta\Lambda_k/\delta x_k^b)+\Lambda_k-\Pi_l\,F_k^b/F_l^b] \quad (4.25)$$

Clearly, the first-order conditions, eq. (4.5) to (4.8), would all be affected. In effect, to each of these conditions as initially specified would have to be added the partial derivative of eq. (4.25) with respect to the variable in question. That is, the second-best efficiency conditions are:

$$\delta L/\delta x_j^i = W_i U_j^i - \Lambda_j - \left\{\sum_{l=1}^{s}\Psi_l\,\delta[\quad]/\delta x_j^i\right\} = 0$$

$$i = 1\ldots m; j = 1\ldots n \quad (4.5a)$$

where [ ] refers to the items in the square brackets of the previous equation. Similarly, we have

$$\delta L/\delta h_l^i = W_i U_l^i - \Pi_l - \left\{\sum_{l=1}^{s}\Psi_l\,\delta[\quad]/\delta h_l^i\right\} = 0$$

$$i = 1\ldots m; l = 1\ldots s \quad (4.6a)$$

$$\delta L/\delta x_j^a = \Lambda_j - \Phi_a F_j^a - \left\{\sum_{l=1}^{s}\Psi_l\,\delta[\quad]/\delta x_j^a\right\} = 0$$

$$a = 1\ldots v; j = 1\ldots n \quad (4.7a)$$

$$\delta L/\delta h_l^a = \Pi_l - \Phi_a F_l^a - \left\{\sum_{l=1}^{s}\Psi_l\,\delta[\quad]/\delta h_l^a\right\} = 0$$

$$a = 1\ldots v; l = 1\ldots s \quad (4.8a)$$

The general point is that, for any firm or individual for which { } is zero, the *second-best conditions are the same as the first-best.* In general, we suggested in the first part of this chapter that this depended on the extent of externalities and the market interdependency between decision units. In the example of an economy with one monopolist, this means that { } would be non-zero for other firms if the monopolist's production function was affected by production in these other firms; or if k was a substitute or complementary good for consumers in relation to other goods, then the market demand function would show an interdependency. In the conditions specified in our model so far, no such interdependencies exist. Let us now postulate such a problem and see how one actually solves it—that is, see how one has to change the required behaviour rules for those sectors amenable to control.

An example

The product of the monopolist might be taken as a substitute commodity for one produced in the public sector. Take k as the output of a monopolistic oil firm, and j as the output of the publicly-owned gas industry. The market demand for k is a function of the price of k and the price of j. Or, in the inverse terminology of eq. (4.19), consumers' willingness to pay for extra k depends on the quantity of k and the quantity of j. That is

$$P_k = f_k(x_k^b, x_j^a) \quad \text{and} \quad P_j = f_j(x_j^a, x_k^b) \tag{4.26}$$

The equilibrium condition for the monopolist is, however, still given by eq. (4.23) as long as he does not make any strategic move to alter the quantity of gas. As long as the oil producer is the only deviant, then the second-best solution is given by adding, as before, eq. (4.25) to the basic welfare maximand of eq. (4.4). Looking now at the new efficiency conditions in eq. (4.5a) to (4.8a), clearly $\{\quad\}$ will be zero for all expressions save eq. (4.7a). If we further assume that firm a, the publicly owned gas industry, produces nothing but gas (i.e., the specification that $j = 1 \ldots n$ in eq. (4.7a) is redundant for firm a, the gas industry), then *the second-best rules are the same as the first-best rules for all firms and individuals in the economy except the gas industry and, of course, the deviant firm b.* This ability, to locate the range of decision units affected, was explained by Davis and Whinston. Before looking at the nature of the expression, $\delta[\quad]/\delta x_j^a$, in eq. (4.7a), we have to specify precisely how, if only formally, the second-best solution can be achieved. One approach would be to levy taxes on the oil industry. Though relevant in general, this type of policy action is not the type implied in second-best theory. The latter is implicitly concerned with what Davis and Whinston[20] call a partial piece-meal approach, in that the concern is with deriving new behavioural rules for, say, public enterprises operating in a partial equilibrium setting. It presumes that general policies, like the use of taxes, are circumscribed, even if for only short periods. The second-best solution is, therefore, attained by altering the behavioural rule of part of the controlled sector. In particular, we add to the gas industry's 'first-best' behavioural rule, the constraint that its competitor's price is above marginal costs. Now, in the first-best environment, it was required that the public industry adjusts its supplies of gas until price equals marginal cost. We could put this in a different way, namely, that it is required to maximize profits but take prices as given—to ignore, in other words, any monopolistic influence it has in either product and factor markets. In this case, its behaviour is described by eq. (4.15) to (4.18) save that the firm produces only the one product, j. To solve the second-best problem we repeat this profit-maximization but subject, now, to the additional constraint described by eq. (4.23). That is, the new maximand becomes:

[20] M. McManus in a paper, 'Private and Social Costs in the Theory of Second Best', *Review of Economic Studies,* July 1967, advanced a critique of Davis and Whinston's work (in *Review of Economic Studies,* 1965, *op. cit.*) which rested basically on *general* policy measures—such as the standard Pigovian tax solution—which are precluded in the second-best approach. Davis and Whinston's reply (in the same journal issue as McManus's paper and entitled 'Piecemeal Policy in the Theory of Second Best' *op. cit.*) presents, in our view, the correct interpretation of the methodology of second-best theories.

$$L_a' = x_j^a P_j + \sum_{l=1}^{s} h_l^a P_l - \phi_a f_a(x_j^a; h_1^a, \ldots, h_s^a)$$

$$- \sum_{l=1}^{s} \psi_l [(x_k^b \delta P_k / \delta x_k^b) + P_k - P_l F_k^b / F_l^b] \qquad (4.15a)$$

where ψ is the additional Lagrangean multiplier. The first-order conditions for a maximum are:

$$\delta L_a / \delta x_j^a = P_j - \phi_a F_j^a - \sum_{l=1}^{s} \psi_l \delta[\quad] / \delta x_j^a = 0 \qquad (4.16a)$$

where the square-bracketed term is the same as in the previous equation; the expression $\delta[\quad]/\delta h_l^a$ will be zero and so the other main equilibrium condition is, simply:

$$\delta L_a' / \delta h_l^a = P_l - \phi_a F_l^a = 0 \qquad l = 1 \ldots s \qquad (4.17a)$$

which is the same as eq. (4.17). Equation (4.16a) is the one that has changed. Converting this into the terminology of the basic welfare maximand would require that we recognize that P_j is equivalent to Λ_j, that $P_k = \Lambda_k$, $P_l = \Pi_l$, $\phi_a = \Phi_a$, and $\psi_l = \Psi_l$. We then see that eq. (4.16a) is equal to eq. (4.7a). Since the latter is the required second-best efficiency condition, then we have demonstrated that it *will* be achieved if the behaviour of the deviant is added as a constraint to the controlled sector's maximand. Notice that eq. (4.16a) and eq. (4.17a) together imply:

$$P_j = (P_l F_j^a / F_l^a) + \sum_{l=1}^{s} \psi_l \delta[\quad] / \delta x_j^a \qquad (4.27)$$

The price of j has to diverge from its marginal cost. Granted that the value of ψ_l is solvable, this divergence depends essentially on the sign and magnitude of the cross-elasticities of demand between j and k. Given the expression for [ ] in eq. (4.15a) we have

$$\delta[\quad] / \delta x_j^a = [x_k^b \delta(\delta P_k / \delta x_k^b) / \delta x_j^a] + \delta P_k / \delta x_j^a \qquad (4.28)$$

If the quantity demanded of oil is inversely related to the price of gas, then the price of j will have to be less than marginal cost—the complementarity case; if a substitute relation is involved, the price of gas will have to be raised above marginal cost. The general point is, however, that as long as one admits that the number of deviants is not likely to be small, then expressions like eq. (4.28) will become fairly complicated, and certainly no easy rule of thumb can be theoretically satisfactory.

The Davis and Whinston contribution has clarified issues, but has not really reduced any of the policy difficulties. In practice, it still looks as though rough guesses will have to be made of the major potential distortions, as we suggested in the first part of this chapter.

5. Public goods, externalities, and returns to scale

5.1 Introduction

One of the major claims to fame of the so-called father of welfare economics, A. C. Pigou, is his highlighting the potentiality of divergences between private and social valuation. This divergence has been used by subsequent writers as a weapon in criticizing the private enterprise system and in supporting government interference in such a system. The 'social valuation' of an activity conveys something rather grandiose. In fact, economists use this terminology to refer to a relatively mundane concept. The social valuation of an activity is nothing more than the benefits and costs defined in chapter 3. Thus, the social cost of producing some commodity is the compensation required by the various suppliers of inputs. The social benefit of the goods and services produced is the willingness to pay of all benefited parties. The distinction between 'private' and 'social' arises when one assumes decisions are not all taken by the central government of a country. When decisions to undertake activities are made by firms, individuals, municipal authorities, nationalized industries, etc., then they are known as 'private' decisions and will, therefore, in practice be normally evaluated in relation to the costs and benefits facing them—the 'private' value of the costs and benefits, in other words. Now, clearly, there are a large number of reasons why such private and social values diverge. One factor, thinking in terms of a private enterprise system, would be the type of market structure. If firm X is buying supplies from a monopolist, then the private cost to X will exceed the social cost to the extent that the monopolist's price exceeds real marginal costs. Another factor is that some activity may generate 'side effects' experienced by people other than the decision taker. If my neighbours are innoculated against some contagious disease I benefit as well as them, to the extent that my chances of being infected are reduced; private benefit is less than social benefit. Whatever the cause of the divergence between private and social, the key point to remember is that the fundamental principles of valuation are no different from those discussed before. The emphasis remains on individual preferences and neither does 'social' connote any allowances for income distribution matters.

The main focus of this chapter is on two factors which can cause divergences between private and social valuation. One is the problem of side-effects, a problem whose modern name is 'externality'. In fact, this was the factor primarily in Pigou's mind in thinking of divergences between private and social valuation. Now, to pin down a definition of externality is not so easy as it might first appear. Why it is difficult to define will emerge in the course of the chapter. For the time being, however, we will not be led far astray by Pigou's remarks that

> . . . marginal trade net product falls short of marginal social net product, because incidental services are performed to third parties from whom it is technically difficult to exact payment . . . [and exceeds it when there is the] . . . technical difficulty of enforcing compensation for incidental dis-services . . . .[1]

The basic idea, then, is that one person's (or firm's) actions affect another's, and such services or disservices do not pass through the normal market process. A private enterprise system might then have difficulties in expropriating all the social benefits and costs of activities, which give rise to these external effects. Another difficulty may arise for a private enterprise system if one drops the assumption—made in chapter 2—that all products can be produced at constant returns to scale; in particular, if sizeable increasing returns to scale are present, private markets may have difficulties in achieving Pareto efficient outcomes. Both these factors are not trivial problems. In fact, activities commonly found in the public sector of many mixed economies — railways, roads, health services, education, etc.—often do appear, as will be demonstrated throughout the chapter, to contain one or both of these factors.[2]

Two caveats are in order in relation to the subsequent discussion of externality. First of all, perhaps one of the most important examples of external effects also raises most problems from the policy angle. External effects can arise, not simply because the producing and consuming *activities* of one individual affects other people, but also because one person's real

[1] *The Economics of Welfare*, pp. 160, 161. Macmillan, 1920.

[2] In fact, one writer, P. A. Samuelson, thinks that—let alone those activities commonly found in the public sector—goods exhibiting externality and/or increasing returns to scale are quite pervasive throughout the economy. Goods exhibiting either of these characteristics are termed 'public goods' by Samuelson.

> '"A public good is one that enters two or more person's utility." What are we left with? Two poles and a continuum in between? No. With a knife-edge pole of the private good case, and with *all* the rest of the world in the public good domain . . .'

See 'Pure Theory of Public Expenditure and Taxation' International Economic Association Conference, Biaritz, 1966, proceedings published as *Public Economics*, Ed. J. Margolis and H. Guitton, Macmillan, 1969. The Samuelson quote is on p. 108.

income, standard of living, welfare, call it what you want, affects others. This is the standard 'keeping up with the Jones'' problem, but it may well be empirically very important. On a wider canvas, underdeveloped countries, seeing the affluence of others, may feel worse off than 'objectively' they are—though, of course, objectively their living standards *are* low. The problem, even restricting oneself to such demonstration effects within a country, is what does one do about it. Do we reduce some group's income level simply because they make other people 'feel' worse off? This is an issue we propose to ignore, and the subsequent discussion of externality relates more closely to more tractable side effects. A second issue is that divergences between private and social valuations do, in a sense, arise when we allow that, in contrast to the implied assumptions of chapters 2 and 3, decisions are usually taken in a context of uncertainty. Here again, normal market trading can run into difficulties in terms of 'efficiency'. When products are connected by complementary and substitute relations, then the decision to produce a good may depend on how much of other goods are going to be produced. In the presence of uncertainty there could then be over or under commitment of resources to the good in question. Some centralized producing arrangement spanning the whole range of relevant products may overcome this; in the UK, for example, the fuel sector is predominantly under public ownership, and these issues may be mitigated by some co-ordination in investment plans. The general point, however, is that decentralized production arrangements run into these problems and they are intrinsic to a market system. They may be particularly important in under-developed countries where sets of industries are being developed.[3] They are not, however, the sort of 'externality' featuring in this chapter. Our concern, then, is to be with those external effects broadly consistent with a static equilibrium analysis where uncertainty is largely absent.

For expositional purposes three simplifications are made:

(a) The primary focus of attention will be on the 'efficiency' aspects. As we made clear in the previous chapter, distributional issues affect all discussions of market problems; similarly, the problems of individual choice and individual welfare are still relevant. No *new* issues are raised in the discussion of externalities and returns to scale, and so they will be largely ignored. However, in the later parts of the chapter, policy proposals are discussed and distributional factors are re-introduced in the final section.

(b) Similarly, the whole problem of second-best is pertinent to any policy conclusions in this area but again no new issues are raised. For expositional purpose it is, therefore, ignored.

(c) Many examples of externalities and non-constant returns to scale involve activities whose effects are spread out through time. The use of capital and

[3] See 'Two Concepts of External Economies', T. Scitovsky, *JPE*, April 1954, for further discussion of these issues. This article has been reproduced in *Readings in Welfare Economics*, Ed. K. S. Arrow and T. Scitovsky, AEA, Allen & Unwin, 1969.

investment decisions are inevitably involved. However, the issues are quite separate and a full discussion of capital and investment decisions is delayed until the next chapter.

Plan of chapter

The chapter has been arranged in the following way. Some fundamental factors which lead to the existence of external effects are discussed in sections 2 and 4. The emphasis is on factors *causing* external effects to arise, rather than on policy implications. The main problem of non-constant returns to scale arises when there are scale *economies* and this is most suitably analysed in section 3, prior to the section 4 discussion of public goods.[4] The rest of the chapter concentrates on externalities, and section 5 both re-caps on the analysis up to that point and paves the way for a discussion of policy proposals by re-considering the problem of the definition of externality. Section 6 then looks at policy proposals geared towards 'efficient' solutions, and section 7 finally introduces distributional considerations.

5.2 Unpriced natural resources

Some activities which give rise to unfavourable side-effects—or external diseconomies as they are sometimes called—can usefully be analysed from the point of view of their exploiting some natural resource. Drilling for products like natural gas or oil, deep-sea fishing, and congestion of one form or another exhibit the problem. Take roads as one type of asset that could become congested; when traffic flows are heavy, additional vehicles on the road slow up the existing traffic and this would, normally, lengthen the time taken to perform a journey and increase the existing vehicles' operating costs; for both these reasons the cost of introducing an extra car on to a busy road comprises not only the vehicle's 'own' costs but the additional costs placed on the existing traffic. Similarly, in the case of oil wells, new extracting firms lower the 'oil table' and thus make it more difficult for the existing firms; the more fishing fleets there are, the less accessible is the stock of fish.[5] The existence of these external effects is explained by the absence of any price for a factor of production used by the firms. This 'unpaid factor' is road space in the case of congested streets, and the stocks of oil, gas, and fish in the other examples. To see why this is so, it is useful to examine how economists first analysed this problem.

[4] The three 'causes' of market failure correspond to the three highlighted by F. M. Bator, but our analysis of decreasing costs and public goods differs in a number of important respects. See 'The Anatomy of Market Failure', *QJE,* August 1958, reproduced as ch. 31 of *Readings in Micro-Economics,* Ed. W. Breit and H. M. Hochman, Holt, Rinehart and Winston, 1968.

[5] See for example 'Optimisation and Sub-Optimisation in Fishery Regulations'. R. Turvey, *AER*, March 1964.

Pigou on increasing costs

In a way, the problem originated in Pigou's assertion that competitive industries subject to increasing cost would not produce at the Pareto efficient output, that their output would be excessive and should be reduced by levying a tax. We have already seen on p. 55, that if rising industry costs are due to the rise in price of some input then the proposition that 'ideal' and actual output diverge is incorrect. Recanting on this case, Pigou, however, claimed that the proposition was true when the rise in costs was due to decreases in the physical productivity of the factors employed in the industry. In effect, Pigou was talking about products whose production functions were subject to decreasing returns to scale,[6] implying that the average money costs of manufacturing the product, even with constant input prices, rose as the industry expanded. Figure 5.1 is similar to Figs. 3.2 and 3.3 but now the line showing average

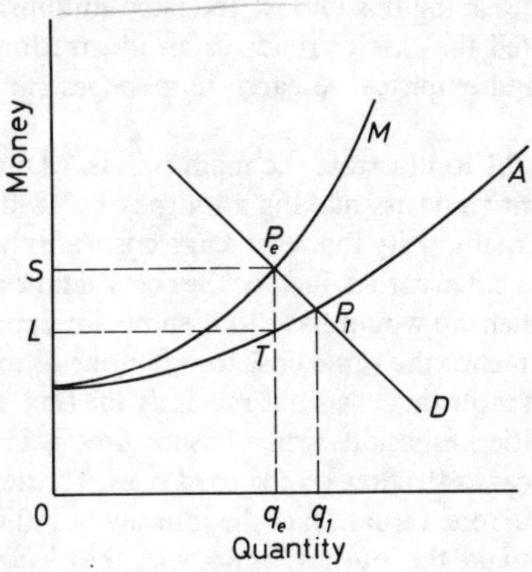

FIG. 5.1

money costs of the product, *A*, rises not because of rising input prices but because the 'productivity' of these inputs is decreasing. When a new firm enters the industry not only are its costs higher than those of the existing firms at the old output, but it raises the costs of the existing firm, and these extra costs are *real costs not intra-marginal rents as they were in the case of rising input prices.* In a competitive situation, each firm will ignore these external effects; the industry's supply schedule will be *A* and the equilibrium

[6] On p. 936 Pigou says that

> . . . the reason why diminishing returns in terms of money appear . . . is, in general, not that the money price of factors employed is increased, but that the proportionate combination of different factors which it is most economical to employ when $(x+\Delta x)$ units of commodities are being provided is a less efficient proportionate combination than that which it is most economical to employ when x units are being produced; and the extra cost involved in this fact is real, not merely nominal. (*op. cit.*).

output will be at P_1. The external effects are incorporated into the M line, which indicates the way in which total real costs change as the industry expands; it indicates the real marginal costs of output. The M line has the same geometric relationship to the A line as the marginal and average cost curves in the theory of the firm, but here they represent *industry costs.*

The excess of marginal over average costs represents extra costs that a new firm occasions for the existing firms. Since these extra costs are real, then optimal output is determined by the intersection of the industry demand curve with the marginal cost line. Thus, whereas the competitive output is at q_1 where price equals what one might call marginal private cost, optimal output is at q_e where price equals marginal social cost. The Pigovian solution would involve levying a tax on each firm's output so that the scale of the industry is reduced to q_e. Clearly, in terms of Fig. 5.1 the optimal tax is P_eT; with each firm paying this impost, industry equilibrium would be at q_e. Pigou himself quoted the case of roads as an illustration, and much of the recent discussion and empirical research into *congestion taxes* rests on this analysis.

We can use Fig. 5.1 to illustrate the main points.[7] Think, for example, of a large number of private cars making a journey by road from one town to another; assume for simplicity that each car's costs are the same. A vehicle's 'costs' will, as we indicated earlier, include the costs of time as well as operating expenses. Strictly then we would have to assume, for expositional purposes, that each driver attaches the same cost to one hour of journey time. In the empirical studies of motoring costs it is precisely the time element that causes most of the difficulties, especially when leisure time is involved. The A line shows the cost per car as the flow on the road rises. The demand curve can be interpreted as the drivers' valuation of the journey; it indicates what they are prepared to pay to make the journey. Since what they *have to pay* is indicated by the A line, then the actual flow of traffic on the road will be q_1. But an extra car on the road occasions costs which it does not itself bear; at flow q_e the marginal car's costs are q_eT but, in addition, by slowing down the existing traffic, it raises the costs of other cars by a total amount equal to TP_e. Thus, beyond flow q_e, each additional vehicle's valuation of the journey (as indicated by the ordinates of the demand curve) is less than the total additional costs it occasions (as shown by the M line). The Pareto efficient flow is therefore at q_e where price equals marginal cost; or, in the surplus terminology of chapter 3, consumer plus producer surplus is maximized at q_e. The

[7] More refined versions of Fig. 5.1 can be found in 'The Theory and Measurement of Private and Social Cost of Highway Congestion', A. A. Walters, *Econometrica,* October 1961, reproduced in *Transport,* Ed. D. Munby, Penguin Modern Economics, 1968. For further discussion of optimum congestion taxes for the UK see his 'Empirical Evidence on Optimum Motor Taxes for the UK', *Applied Statistics,* November 1961, and also the report of the Smeed Committee on *Road Pricing: The Economic and Technical Possibilities,* Ministry of Transport, HMSO, 1964. For some discussion of distributional issues see 'Congestion and Welfare—An Examination of the Case for a Congestion Tax', C. Sharp, *EJ,* December 1966.

proposal would then be to introduce metering devices to facilitate the levying of a tax, TP_e, on each vehicle. The usual proposals involve either driver-operated meters, or meters actuated by electronic impulses from roadside installations. Other suggestions for pricing include special licences for the centre of cities. Keeping to the case of a tax, total congestion tax receipts would then be given by the area SP_eLT in the diagram. Giving £1 of benefit or loss the same weight to whomsoever it accrues, then the overall net gain is the total of congestion tax receipts less the fall in consumer surplus for those motorists still on the road and the loss of consumer surplus for those who have left the road. The reader is left to demonstrate that, with the general shape of curves given in Fig. 5.1, this net gain will be positive. This net gain would then have to be compared with the costs of introducing meters.

The unpaid factor

In one sense it is possible to refute Pigou's suggestion that the competitive industry's output will be wrong, and in analysing this possibility we shall unearth the basic cause of the externality. A few years after the publication of *The Economics of Welfare*, the American economist F. H. Knight suggested that Pigou's analysis left out of consideration an important factor of production, namely, land. Road space is in fact a scarce resource unaccounted for in the standard conclusion. Pigou's illustration related to the advantages that his taxing suggestions would have in shifting vehicles from a narrow congested road to a broader less congested road. But, as Knight says, if

> . . . the roads are assumed to be subject to private appropriation and exploitation precisely the ideal solution which would be established by the imaginary tax will be brought about through the operations of ordinary economic motives. . . . The owner of the narrow road can charge for its use a toll representing its 'superiority' over the free road, in accordance with the theory of rent, which is as old as Ricardian economics.[8]

In other words, the congestion tax receipts are effectively a payment for the use of road space, a rental payment necessary to secure efficient use of a scarce factor of production. The real marginal cost of output in a fully competitive situation consists, then, of the payments that the marginal firm has to make for capital, labour, and land. It does *not* include any increases in the payments that existing firms have to make for factors whose prices are rising; it excludes, in other words, *intra-marginal* rents paid to capital, labour, *and land.* In practice, of course, in many countries not only are roads not under private control but are not priced by the public authorities responsible for

[8] 'Some Fallacies in the Interpretation of Social Cost', *QJE*, pp. 586–7, August 1924, reproduced as chapter 8 of *Readings in Price Theory*, AEA, Allen & Unwin, 1953, and also in *Readings in Welfare Economics, op. cit.*

them. And, basically, the same point applies to the other examples.[9] The pool of oil is a common property resource unpriced, as is also the stock of fish in the fishing example. In fact, stretching one's imagination slightly this 'unpaid factor' explanation could be used for some other examples of external diseconomies. The hoariest one of them all is probably the

> . . . smoke in large towns [which] inflicts a heavy uncharged loss on the community, in injury to buildings and vegetables, expenses for washing clothes and cleaning rooms, expenses for the provision of extra artificial light, and in many other ways. (Pigou again !)[10]

If *air* were priced, the problem would be solved in the same way as road space. Perhaps if we could price 'quietness', the noise problem would also be reduced to Pareto efficient levels!

For the main examples, the fact that some factor is not 'booked' leads to these 'ownership externalities' as Bator would call them. And this seems a fairly adequate explanation of the immediate cause of these externalities. There are two important ways, however, in which further explanation is required. Firstly, the traditional analysis does not have much to say about how the parties would react given the existence of external effects. We need to abandon the broad spectrum of the industry and pick up the microscope, to examine the behaviour of firms and individuals. Much of the modern writing has been related to this issue and we take it up in a later part of this chapter. Secondly, many of the examples quoted seem to involve problems in addition to the external diseconomy issue. Why are not roads normally priced? Would a private competitive industry provide an 'efficient' supply of roads, bridges, oil wells, etc. There seems to be a strong element of *indivisibility* in some of these examples. It is now appropriate, therefore, to look at the problems of decreasing cost, increasing returns to scale, and indivisibility.

However, before doing this, let us conclude this section by tightening up our understanding of the 'unpaid factor' and its relationship to the initial idea of decreasing returns to scale. Whether or not any product does exhibit constant or decreasing returns to scale is an empirical question. What Knight was implicitly saying was that the production function exhibits decreasing returns to scale only because some factor has not been included in that function. If output is denoted by X, capital by K, labour by L, and land

[9] Another writer who talks of 'decreasing returns' in the same way as Pigou is M. Boiteux who, together with other French engineers and economists, has done some important applied work in public enterprise economics. (See later chapters.) In relation to the generation of electricity supply by the French nationalized undertaking—Electricité de France—Boiteux claims that 'Decreasing returns appear in hydroelectricity as sites are exhausted. A tendency to decreasing returns appear in thermal electricity, with the exhaustion of available rivers. . . .' Is Boiteux not implying there is an ('unbooked'?) factor, land, and it is in inelastic supply? See 'Electrical Energy: Facts, Problems and Prospects', p. 25, originally published in 1960 and reproduced as chapter 1 of *Marginal Cost Pricing in Practice,* Ed. J. R. Nelson, Prentice-Hall, 1964.

[10] *Op. cit.*, pp. 160–1.

or road space by S, then we can write the production function as $X = f(K, L, S)$. *If* this function exhibits constant returns to scale, then when the factor S is 'unbooked' the effective function for the industry is $X = f(K, L)$, and this would then exhibit decreasing returns if our law of diminishing returns has anything in it. In analysing external diseconomies Meade[11] used a similar approach and it is useful, if only in highlighting the relationship between Pigou's tax and the returns that road space would get if privately owned. Suppose, to start with, that road space is privately owned. Suppose, further, that capital hires the other factors, i.e., undertakes the job of entrepreneurship and effectively determines the size of the industry. Capital will increase in this industry as long as the return it gets (r per unit) exceeds its opportunity cost—the return it can earn elsewhere. Capital's total returns in this industry (Kr) equal the total value of sales (XP), less expenditure on labour and road space. On normal profit-maximizing assumptions it would employ the accompanying factors until the value of their marginal products (V_l and V_s respectively) equals their prices. We can, therefore, write:

$$Kr = XP - (V_l L) - (V_s S) \tag{5.1}$$

But we know that if the production function $X = f(K, L, S)$ exhibits constant returns to scale then:[12]

$$XP = V_k K + V_l L + V_s S \tag{5.2}$$

where V_k is the value of the marginal product of capital. In this case substitution gives

$$Kr = V_k K \tag{5.3}$$

and since capital extends its own usage to the point where r equals capital's opportunity cost, then this opportunity cost is, in industry equilibrium, equal to the value of the marginal product of capital—the Pareto efficient solution.

On the other hand, if road space is not 'booked', capital's receipts are:

$$Kr = XP - (V_l L) \tag{5.1a}$$

With the 'effective' production function, $X = f(K, L)$, exhibiting decreasing returns to scale we have[13]

[11] See 'External Economies and Diseconomies in a Competitive Situation', J. E. Meade, *EJ*, March, 1952, and the criticism in E. J. Mishan's 'Reflections on Recent Developments in the Concept of External Effects', *Canadian Journal of Economics and Political Science*, p. 22, February 1965. This latter has been reproduced in *Welfare Economics: Five Introductory Essays*, Random House, 1967. Meade's article has been reproduced in *Readings in Welfare Economics, op. cit.*

[12] See footnote on p. 51 of chapter 3.

[13] Following on from the previous footnote, Euler's theorem states that if a production function $X = f(K, L)$ is homogeneous of degree $(1-t)$ then $X(1-t) = F_k K + F_l L$, where F_k and F_l are partial derivatives, or in this case the factors' marginal products. Multiplying both sides by the price of the product, P, and rearranging gives eq. (5.2a) in the text. With constant returns to scale t is equal to O; with decreasing returns it is a positive fraction, and with increasing returns to scale t is negative.

$$XP = (V_k K + V_l L)/(1-t) \qquad (5.2a)$$

where t is a positive fraction.

In contrast to before, where capital's receipts were equal to $V_k K$, we now find, by substituting, that:

$$Kr = V_k K + t(XP) \qquad (5.3a)$$

In other words, capital's receipts (which in equilibrium are also equal to its opportunity cost) exceed the value of its marginal product and there is, therefore, excessive capital in the industry. The Pigou solution involves levying a tax so that capital is restricted to the efficient point. Looking at the last equation we see that the appropriate tax would be at a rate t on the value of sales, since then capital's net receipts (again equal to its opportunity cost elsewhere) would equal the value of its marginal product. It is clear that the tax receipts, tXP, are equivalent to the returns to land ($V_s S$) in the case where land is privately owned. The tax *rate* is equal to the share of roads in the total value of output.

5.3 The decreasing cost problem

Economists have long recognized that if industries (i.e., products) experience decreasing costs, considerable problems arise in achieving optimality. Unfortunately, while the problem has long been recognized it has also been, and probably still is, an area open to dispute. Definitionally, decreasing costs arise because the price of some inputs fall as the industry expands its purchases, and/or the product exhibits increasing returns to scale. Provisionally, we shall ignore the possibility of input prices falling and concentrate on the idea that the average money costs of producing the product actually fall as

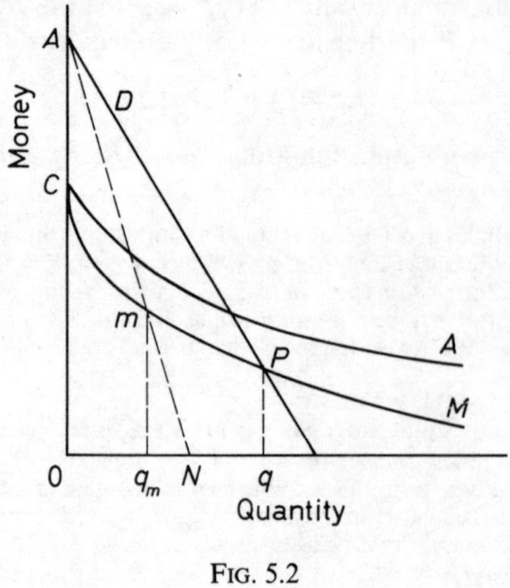

FIG. 5.2

the scale of the industry increases. Notice that we are talking about the industry and not the firm. In this sense the problem is symmetrical to the rising cost discussion of the previous section. The *A* line of Fig. 5.2 plots average costs of output—capital, labour, land—as a function of scale. Notice also that, with all factors variable, we are not talking about the fall in average costs that arises through spreading fixed overheads over a larger and larger output—it is not the first part of the *U* in the firm's short-run average cost curve. Notice, further, that the scale economies are large in relation to the total size of the market. In Fig. 5.2 the demand curve represents consumer demand for the *product*, and here it cuts the industry average cost line as it is still falling. We cannot, therefore, be thinking about those 'internal' scale economies associated with the declining part of the competitive firm's long-run average cost line; these are usually assumed to lead 'quickly' to 'internal' diseconomies and to a rise in the firm's long-run average cost curve; the firm remains small in relation to the total market and its operations consistent with a constant-cost perfectly competitive industry.[14]

The concept, then, relates to scale economies of considerable magnitude in relation to market demand. Are there any products which exhibit such economies? Traditionally economic writers have assumed that railways, gas and electricity supply, and the like exhibit such tendencies. Again Pigou had something to say.

> In view of the great engineering cost of preparing a suitable [railway track] . . . it will, obviously be much less expensive to have one or, at most, a few railways providing the whole of the transport service between any two assigned points, than to have this service undertaken by a great number of railways, each performing an insignificant proportion of the whole service. Similar remarks hold good of the industries of furnishing water, gas, electricity or tramway service to a town. The existence of many separate establishments involves a large number of main pipes, wires and rails. . . . Therefore the existence of many separate establishments implies the investment of a great quantity of capital in mains that are only employed up to a very small proportion of their capacity. There is an obvious economy in avoiding such investment.[15]

There are two points to note about this type of explanation. The first is that, as well as being a theory about the shape of the product's production function, this characteristic has been used to suggest that such industries have a tendency to monopolization. This is a dynamic issue well outside the bounds of our analysis. However, it does raise a related matter. Could the scale economies arise in such a way as to be consistent with the *existence* of a competitive industry? Are there circumstances under which one could

[14] Cf. the analysis in chapter 3 pp. 51, 52.
[15] *Op. cit.* p. 219.

envisage the industry being subject to scale economies and yet, at the same time, comprising a large number of competitive firms? Such a possibility has been advanced, but we shall delay analysing it to a later part of this section of the chapter.

The second point is that the way product costs do vary with output is an empirical question. In the UK we have only just started to attempt to estimate cost functions for public enterprises like electricity, roads, and railways. Sufficient evidence has been collected to suggest that cost functions for these sorts of products are much more complicated than we could possibly imply by two-dimensional diagrams.[16] Furthermore, even introspective reflection suggests that some scale economies may fall neither into the category of 'very large in relation to market demand' nor into the category of those economies 'quickly' submerged by problems of managerial diseconomies. What about bridges—across the Severn or across (or under) the Channel? How big does a theatre have to be before its services weigh heavily in the market? These latter points we shall try and bear in mind. As for the point of empiricism, there are still some points of general interest that can usefully be made and we shall now proceed with them.

Pareto efficiency and increasing returns to scale

Consider the industry of Fig. 5.2 in a 'partial' setting, and assume that any changes in the consumption of its product have negligible real income effects on consumers. We can then analyse the 'efficient' scale of industry output in terms of surplus analysis. The optimal output is where total benefit less cost (consumer + producer surplus) is maximized. Consumer benefit from output is indicated by the area under the demand curve. Total cost is indicated by the area under the marginal cost line, *M*. The efficient scale is, therefore, at q since the surplus is there at a maximum—indicated by area *APC*; the marginal unit is characterized by the equality of marginal benefit and marginal cost (qP).

Now, suppose we accept Pigou's inference that, left to private enterprise, a monopoly would develop. How would it fare? On standard profit-maximizing assumptions it would produce at q_m where marginal cost equals marginal revenue (on the dotted line *AN*) rather than marginal benefit; output is sub-optimal. Moreover, the demand and cost curves could be such that although at some output the social surplus is positive, at no output are profits positive; the reader can verify this by re-drawing the demand curve so that the monopolist's price is less than average cost. The monopoly then fails by both 'structure' and 'incentive'.[17] An oft-quoted loophole arises if—

[16] Many indications of this will be given in the later parts of the book but one illuminating example is *The Determination of Costs of Expansion of an Interconnected System of Production and Distribution of Electricity* by M. Boiteux and P. Stasi, originally published in 1952, and reproduced as chapter 5 of Nelson (*op. cit.*).

[17] As Bator would put the matter (*op. cit.*).

and if is the crucial word—the monopolist can discriminate in its charges as between consumers. If it can discriminate perfectly, then its marginal revenue curve *is* now the demand curve and its profit-maximizing output is at q. All the social surplus is expropriated as producer surplus with consumer surplus zero.

Coming nearer to earth, how would the public enterprise have to behave? In chapter 3 we envisaged the public firm's economic decisions being determined centrally; this sort of approach becomes particularly relevant when sizeable scale economies are involved. The 'plant' becomes the industry and the devolvement of decision-taking to a large number of plant managers—reasonable enough in the constant returns to scale case of chapter 3—does not make any sense in this new context. If the public enterprise followed the rules suggested in earlier chapters—to adjust output until price equals marginal cost—then, clearly, in the context of Fig. 5.2 the optimal output would emerge. In fact, socialist economists writing in the 1930s gleefully reflected that they would not have discovered this 'superiority' of socialized industry over private industry, had they not been stirred to investigate such problems by the assertions of von Mises and the like that socialism was not consistent with a rational economic system.[18] Aside from politics, there are, however, two problems with this solution. One is that marginal-cost pricing with increasing returns to scale may mean total revenue less than total expenditure. The budget is over-exhausted.[19] To the extent that scale economies are at some stage exhausted and decreasing returns set in, then, with price equalling marginal cost in the latter range of output, deficits need not necessarily always arise when there are sizeable scale economies. But when they do, one immediately meets the problem of how to finance them. The main suggestions in this context have been to use general taxation, but we propose to leave a discussion of this to the later part of the book when marginal-cost pricing is discussed in some detail. However, it is as well to say here that welfare economics has little of a constructive nature to contribute in this matter.

The second problem is that the rule price at marginal-cost may in some cases be wrong! Basically, this arises because increasing returns to scale are a form of indivisibility.[20] Since real costs actually fall as output rises, one

[18] Cf. the discussion and references in chapter 3 p. 52 and footnote.

[19] This is the symmetrical proposition to the case of decreasing returns to scale where, with one resource 'unbooked', the budget is not exhausted. When all factors are used to the point where their opportunity cost equals the value of their marginal products, then total revenue exceeds the total of such opportunity costs when there are decreasing returns to scale (cf. previous section) and falls short in the case of increasing returns to scale.

[20] One can, in a sense, get round the 'existence' of increasing returns to scale by saying that there is, somewhere, an indivisible factor which is being used in production. If all factors, including this one, are doubled then output will also double—constant returns to scale. Is this helpful? It is similar to the idea that decreasing returns arise only because some factor is 'unbooked'. Now we saw that *in some cases*—congestion, etc.—focusing on the unbooked factor was useful and meaningful. But it would be silly to deny the existence of non-constant returns to scale in *all* cases by using this argument, since one could not always do something about it.

cannot consider each unit increase on its own; all the units are linked together in one package. Formally, this means that the demand and cost curves could be such that the output at which price equals marginal cost involves a negative social surplus. Total benefit falls short of total cost in Fig. 5.3 despite the

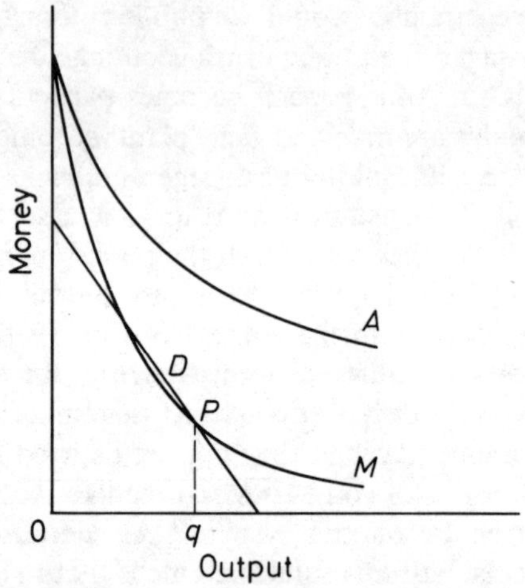

FIG. 5.3

fact that marginal benefit equals marginal cost at output *q*. As a general rule then 'marginal' cost pricing falls down, when, as we might expect, it is used in circumstances where it is not appropriate—when, in other words, a non-marginal (indivisible) evaluation is required. The public enterprise would have to estimate the sum of consumer evaluations of output and compare this with costs. Each consumer can purchase different quantities of the good, but the public enterprise must discover the shape of the whole demand curve. Samuelson, particularly, has emphasized this point.

> It is not enough in the decreasing cost case to come closer to marginal cost pricing in the Lange-Lerner manner, making up the deficits by general taxation. . . . I like my cider sour; you like it sweet. With constant returns to scale we could both get what we want, or at least what we deserve. But with initial indivisibilities or other forms of increasing returns what I get will depend on what you get. (This is true even if we pay in the form of fees the marginal costs of our separate consumption.). . . . Now, how can a society decide on the product mix which will maximize a specified social

If the physics of our world does have non-constant returns to scale characteristics—inside volume of sphere equals input (output), surface area equals output (input)—that is that. For further discussion, see 'Euler's Theorem and the Problem of Distribution', J. Robinson, *EJ*, September 1934, reproduced as chapter 24 of *Readings in Micro-economics* (*op. cit.*).

welfare function? It must weigh in all the different individuals' utilities from each decision.[21]

Joint supply

Scale economies are pervasive throughout the economy but the main problem, particularly when one starts to think of examples, is evaluating how they fit into a market context. This issue becomes particularly acute if we think of the cases where the cost functions do not exhibit the smooth slopes of those in our diagrams. The provision of some services involves a fairly large outlay on construction resources, in such a way that 'output' can be expanded up to certain capacity limits with only little further expenditure. To return to a previous example, a recent report put the capital cost of constructing a Channel Tunnel between England and France at £102·7 million; the study was based on the assumption that the Tunnel would be open in 1969, thereafter the expansion of facilities to cover traffic growth necessitated annual capital expenditure averaging less than £1 million for the next fifty years.[22] Clearly, there would be some operating expenses involved in running the Tunnel as there would also be in other less extreme examples. Theatres, bridges, circuses, swimming pools all have one characteristic similar to the Tunnel, namely, that if a service is provided for one consumer, other people *could* use these assets at hardly any extra construction cost to the supplier—at least up to the capacity limit—and without detracting from the first consumer's purchases. In such a situation we would say that services are jointly supplied.[23] It will prove useful to pin down our meaning of this concept, since it will crop up again in the context of 'public goods' in the next section. Joint supply

[21] 'Aspects of Public Expenditure Theories', *R of Economics and Statistics*, p. 336, November 1958, reproduced in *The Collected Scientific Papers of Paul A. Samuelson*, **II**, Ed. J. E. Stiglitz, MIT Press, 1966. The comment that 'what I get will depend on what you get' will also, one would have thought, apply to industries subject to rising cost because of factor inelasticities though the implications are different. An additional but different point mentioned by Samuelson about decreasing cost situations is a further theoretical drawback to the price/marginal cost rule. 'As soon as decreasing cost and diversity of product appear, we have the difficult non-local "total conditions" to determine what finite mix of product is optimal. This involves a terrible social computation problem: we must scan the almost infinite number of possible products and select the best configuration; we cannot feel our way to the optimum but must make judgement at a distance to determine the "optimum optimorum"' (*Ibid.* p. 336.).

[22] See *Proposals for a Fixed Channel Link*, Cmnd 2137, HMSO, 1963, Appendices 5 and 6, reproduced in *Transport*, *op. cit.* The capital costs are for the Tunnel proper excluding terminal installations, railway equipment, etc., and are in undiscounted terms—the hypothetical construction period was six years. The comparable figure for a Channel Bridge was £275 million. See also 'The Channel Tunnel: Investment Appraisals', A. H. Watson, *Public Administration*, Spring 1967.

[23] The term 'joint supply' has been used to cover cases other than that discussed here. We use it very much in the spirit of R. A. Musgrave when he says that a

> '. . . circus performance involves joint consumption on the part of those who attend.'

The Theory of Public Finance, p. 10, footnote. McGraw-Hill, 1959.

to some defined group of people is said to exist if the supply of services to one person permits the rest of the group to be supplied at zero extra cost. This does not mean services will automatically be supplied to all of the group. It means that the minimum size of theatre is usually such that, up to some capacity limit, the construction cost is unaffected by the number of people who are going to use it.

In a sense, then, joint supply to a group of people is no more expensive than supplying only *one* of them—what one might call 'single supply'. Further, assuming that people are not bothered about having to share, joint supply is much cheaper than what one might call 'separate supply', where each person has his own theatre, swimming pool, etc.

For these sorts of examples there is an indivisibility in the nature of supply and, in principle, it is simply an extreme version of the smooth increasing returns to scale discussed before. Suppose, for example, we simplified the case of the Tunnel by assuming that only capital costs are involved.[24] Assume further that demand is expected to be more or less constant over time. In this case we could compare the annual demand for the Tunnel with its 'equivalent' *annual* capital cost.[25] This means we can keep to the standard price/quantity diagrams. On Fig. 5.4, the capacity of the Tunnel is assumed to be very large in relation to market demand and so these capacity limits

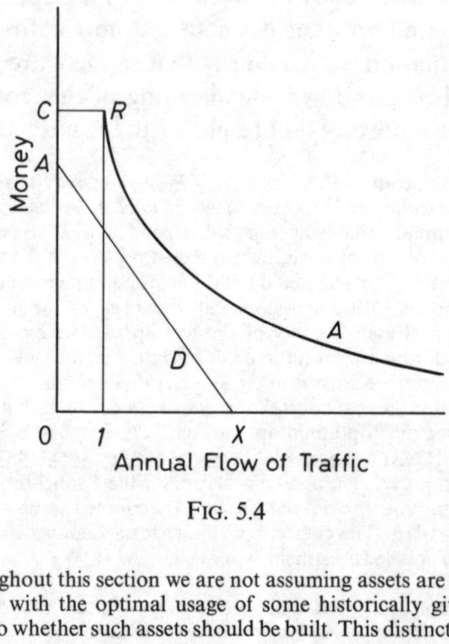

FIG. 5.4

[24] Notice that throughout this section we are not assuming assets are inherited from the past. We are not concerned with the optimal usage of some historically given asset, but with the 'long-run' decision as to whether such assets should be built. This distinction between 'historical' and 'planned' costs is pursued in the applied chapters on pricing.

[25] Formally, the base year capital cost figure is converted (by a discounting formula) into an annual sum, the flow of which over the life of the asset has a present value equal to the base year figure. More on this in the applied chapters.

are not considered at this stage. The capital cost is *OC*; in fact, it has been drawn in an exaggerated slice, *OCR*1, to indicate that whether only one vehicle used the tunnel or large numbers used it, the capital cost is the same. Marginal costs are difficult to think of, but in a sense the marginal cost line takes the path of *CR*1, and then follows the horizontal axis through *X*. The *A* line indicates total (capital) costs divided by output. The basic problem is, then, the same as the smooth curve diagrams. If the price/marginal cost rule is pursued then this means setting price at zero and allowing a traffic volume of *X*. But is the Tunnel worth building? We have to use surplus analysis; it is worth building if total benefit exceeds total cost—if, in other words, the area under the demand curve (*OAX*) exceeds the capital cost (*OCR*1). If the Tunnel is to be publicly owned, it would mean estimating the shape of the demand curve and then the public operators would compare this with the capital cost; if the criterion is met, the Tunnel is built but no tolls are charged.

In this situation, then, a comparison of revenue with expenditure is the wrong criterion and this is where a private market would fail. Given the position of the average cost line in Fig. 5.4, no uniform toll would raise enough revenue to cover expenditure; in some cases of course a financial surplus may well be possible. Present proposals involve the levying of tolls for the Channel Tunnel, but the Ministry of Transport's report does not assess the viability of the Tunnel in terms of revenue and expenditure; implicitly, they are trying to estimate demand curves (see the report, *op. cit.*, for details). The crucial issue then becomes the size of the distortion effect due to the existence of tolls; i.e., how much traffic, which would be willing to pay the marginal costs of their using the Tunnel, will be excluded to the extent that the toll exceeds such marginal costs. A similar issue relates to the tolls charged on the recently constructed Severn Bridge. At the time of writing the charge is of the order of 2*s.* 6*d.* per vehicle, so that for long-distance traffic the distortion effect is probably minimal. This problem has long been recognized by economists. In fact, as long ago as 1844 the French engineer Jules Dupuit[26] spotted the basic issue and discussed solutions in terms of canals and bridges. Of course, as he pointed out, if perfect discrimination is possible, then, as we noted before, a 'profitability' criterion would be right; the perfectly discriminating monopolist's toll income is equal to total benefit: but is such discrimination feasible on such a scale?

Competition with joint supply

Let us now consider the applicability of this analysis to some of the other examples of joint supply that have been suggested. If the cost of the Tunnel is denoted by *JMC* (i.e., the joint cost of an extra (marginal) tunnel) and the

[26] A translated version of his article appears in *International Economic Papers*, 1952. This paper 'On the Measurement of the Utility of Public Works', has been reproduced as chapter 1 of *Transport*, *op. cit.*, and also in *Readings in Welfare Economics*, *op. cit.*

benefit accruing to the ith consumer (or consumption unit) as E_i, then the criterion as to whether the tunnel be built is:

$$JMC < E_1 + E_2 + \ldots + E_n \quad (5.4)$$

The joint cost is to be compared with the sum of the consumers' evaluation of the Tunnel. Now, the capital costs of assets like theatres, bridges, circuses, and even shared swimming pools, are clearly joint to the users and a similar sort of criterion would apply. But we would not in all these instances necessarily suggest that provision by a private enterprise system would be inefficient —in the Pareto sense. Why is this? The crucial element is the various *dimensions* to scale in all these examples. Large towns often have a number of theatres, swimming pools, and so on. As well as the number of people using such assets, another output dimension is then the number of such assets. And this dimension clearly becomes crucial in deciding whether a competitive system could achieve optimality. Certainly for run-of-the-mill theatres, shared swimming pools, and cinemas one could envisage such replication. Now replication would normally only arise when the existing facilities are being fully used. This point is illustrated on Fig. 5.5. Here we have retained the

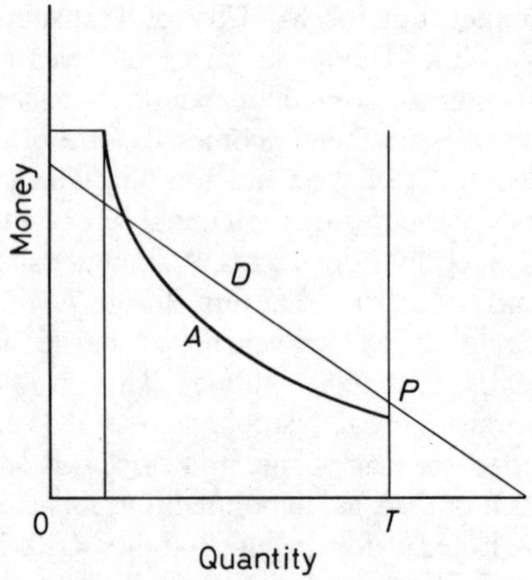

FIG. 5.5

same demand situation, but assumed that there is a rigid capacity limit at T. In this case, total net benefit is maximized by fully using capacity and levying a price of P. Marginal costs become indeterminate at T and the price is necessary to restrict consumption to those most willing to pay. Notice that, in practice, it may well be possible to extend capacity beyond T, and then the issue becomes what is the optimal size for the asset. We shall return to these issues in the later applied chapters, but at this stage we can ignore these possibilities. The crucial thing to recognize when replication and capacity limits appear, is that the demand curve for this asset may well flatten out. If this asset is no longer the sole source of supply, then in the extreme the demand curve becomes horizontal as in Fig. 5.6. This diagram can be thought of as

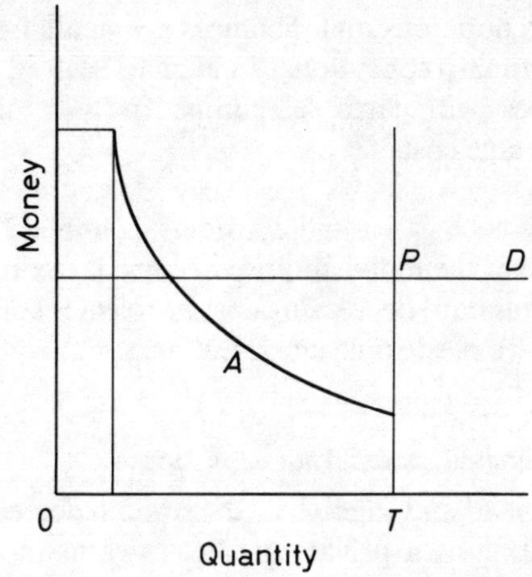

FIG. 5.6

relating to a firm in competitive industry. With price, P, profits are earned but competition would usually reduce these to normal levels. In practice, markets for such services may well be characterized by situations intermediate between the two extremes. In both cases optimality would be characterized by extending the number of such assets (along a JMC schedule) until

$$JMC = P_1 + P_2 + \dots + P_n \tag{5.5}$$

where P_2 is the price paid by person 2 etc. This then would be the characteristic of the marginal 'theatre', pool, etc. In cases similar to Fig. 5.5, some sort of discrimination may well be required for optimality; in others the prices P_1, P_2, etc., could tend to equality with sufficient competition between suppliers. A further complication with these sorts of assets is that the characteristic of services being shared means the old congestion problem re-appears. The more crowded is the swimming pool the smaller is my enjoyment of it. In fact, for some people it may work the other way—their pleasure increases the more people there are. The swimming pool owner has then to decide on both its optimal physical size and the optimal number of members.[27]

In summary, then, jointness in supply need not necessarily imply inefficiency on the part of a private enterprise system. Samuelson appears to have something like the above analysis in mind in the following passage.

[27] These issues can be pursued in J. M. Buchanan's 'An Economic Theory of Clubs', *Economica,* February 1965.

> Consider cinemas in a large town. Because of deviations from constant returns to scale (indivisibilities, if you like), my well-being depends on your being willing to watch movies and in fact I might get a greater thrill out of a film if I watch it in the same room with hundreds of other people. . . . But, if the town is populous and distances are small, free enterprise might well result in optimal replication of cinema theatres, each operating at capacity audiences, with fares set competitively at short and long-run marginal and average costs.[28]

It is when one leaves such cases, and considers examples like the Tunnel and bridges and roads, that the indivisibilities become large in relation to market demand. Here, the standard decreasing cost problem is still relevant although in the final analysis we need some empirical help.

Competition and Marshallian external economies

Although both Marshall and Pigou saw the smooth decreasing cost situation of Fig. 5.2 as encouraging a private market towards monopolization, they also thought there were certain types of scale economies consistent with the existence of perfect competition. What 'rescued' competition was the concept of external economies. The argument, due primarily to Marshall, was that as the scale of the industry expanded the productivity of each firm increased. Each new firm occasioned economies external to itself but internal to the industry. Subsequent writers had difficulty not only in understanding precisely what Marshall meant but also in finding examples consistent with static market analysis.[29]

> There are those external economies which result from the general progress of the industrial environment . . . [particularly] . . . the growth of correlated branches of industry which mutually assist one another, perhaps being concentrated in the same localities, but anyhow availing themselves of the modern facilities for communication offered by steam transport, by the telegraph and by the printing press.[30]

Clearly these are 'irreversible' economies which cannot be fitted into static analysis. Oft-quoted examples, which seem to be nearer the mark, are the cases of coal-mines and afforestation. A new colliery has to pump water out of its shafts and, in so doing, lowers the general water-table and thus benefits

[28] IEA conference paper, *op. cit.*, p. 110.

[29] This, and Pigou's discussion of returns to scale, led to J. H. Clapham's famous complaint that such analysis was not much use if we could not put actual industries into any of these categories. See 'On Empty Economic Boxes', *EJ*, 1922. This, and further contributions by Pigou, D. H. Robertson, P. Sraffa, Ellis, and Fellner can be found in *Readings in Price Theory* (*op. cit.*).

[30] A. Marshall, *Principles of Economics*, 8 Ed., pp. 317 and 441, Macmillan, 1936.

neighbouring collieries (cf. the symmetry with oil wells and external diseconomies). Similarly, if a farmer plants trees to provide wind-breaks or prevent soil erosion or induce rainfall, his action may often benefit neighbouring farmers.

In terms of Fig. 5.7 this implies that the competitive industry will produce

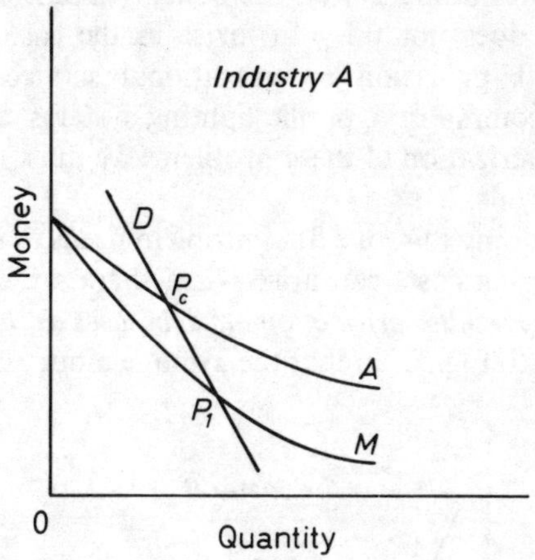

FIG. 5.7

at P_c, with each of the myriad of firms operating in long-run equilibrium with the price P_c equal to the firms' short and long-run marginal and average costs. The *A* line corresponds to the competitive industry's supply line. But the marginal 'social' cost is less than the marginal private cost, because each new firm lowers the costs of existing firms and these are *real* cost reductions; we are still assuming input prices are unaffected by industry scale. The *M* line indicates, then, real marginal social costs so that optimal output is at P_e, a larger output than the competitive one. The optimal output is thus defined by the same condition as before but, because competitive firms ignore the external effects, the industry's actual output is wrong.

One can see the symmetry between this situation and Pigou's decreasing returns problem, and as might be expected the Marshall/Pigou recommendation is to provide a government subsidy or

> . . . bounty on such a commodity . . . [causing] . . . so great a fall in its price to the consumer, that the consequent increase of consumers' surplus may exceed the total payments made by the State to the producers. . . .[31]

There are two problems associated with this sort of analysis. One is that the concept of external economies seems to step across industry boundaries.

[31] Marshall, *ibid.*, p. 469.

In the afforestation case, for example, one could think of a separate industry concerned with afforestation; are we then saying that this industry's output is 'wrong', or that the farming industry's output and/or 'purchases' are wrong?[32] Secondly, there are clearly many other examples of external economies which do not seem to be adequately characterized by the above analysis. If the chief characteristic of afforestation is that the benefit cannot be restricted to one farmer alone, then does not this also arise in the case of health services (immunization, etc.), provision of educational services (your education benefits the whole community), public lighting systems, and so on? To find an adequate characterization of these problems we must turn to the modern theory of 'public' goods.

However, before doing this, one final problem needs to be briefly explored. In principle, decreasing costs can arise when there are constant returns to scale but where the *purchase price of inputs decreases as the industry expands.* Figure 5.8 is similar to Fig. 5.7 in that the average money costs of the product

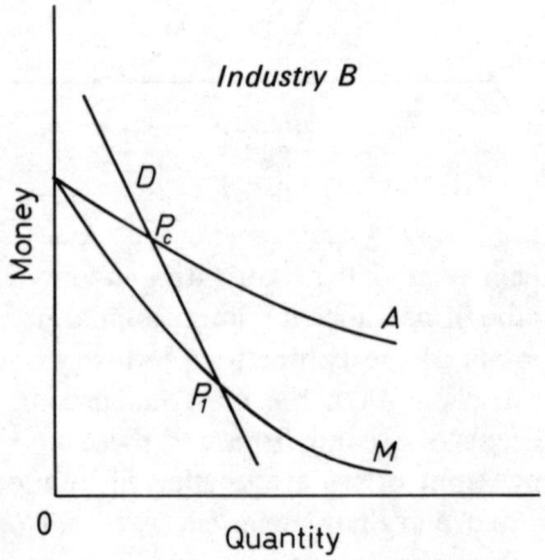

FIG. 5.8

fall as industry output rises, but now this fall is assumed to be due not to a change in the productivity of the factors but to decreases in their price. Again this could lead a private market to monopoly, but we can also think of a competitive industry existing in much the same way as before. The perfectly competitive industry's equilibrium is at P_c in Fig. 5.8; as new firms enter the industry they lower the costs of the existing firms, but such external effects are ignored by any one firm. The issue now is whether the *optimal* output is

[32] This is the main problem in interpreting Meade's proposition (*op. cit.*, pp. 61–6), that externalities could arise when there were 'atmosphere' effects. He assumed that rain induced by a timber industry led to increasing returns to scale in the farming industry. But afforestation has public good properties—to anticipate the next section's analysis—and whether the farming industry exhibits increasing, constant, or decreasing returns to scale, is an entirely separate problem. See Bator (*op. cit.*, pp. 372–3) for a good critique of Meade's example.

at P_c or at P_1. In effect, then, it is necessary to decide whether marginal social cost is indicated by the *A* line or the *M* line. The key to the problem is found by examining the cause of the falling input price. If the industry supplying the inputs (say industry *A*) is a decreasing cost industry itself, then the purchasing industry (say *B*) will experience decreasing costs. But if *A*'s decreasing costs are due to *its* input prices falling as it expands, then we are back where we started. In other words, if any industry experiences falling input prices then, in static analysis, there must, somewhere in the economy, be another industry experiencing real scale economies.

Suppose then industry *B* (to be represented by Fig. 5.8) has constant returns to scale but experiences falling input prices because one of its suppliers (industry *A* in Fig. 5.7) experiences increasing returns to scale. To discover *B*'s marginal social costs we cannot assume industry *A* is run by private enterprise, for *A*'s price and output—unless subsidized—would be wrong. Suppose then that *A* is a public enterprise setting price equal to marginal cost so that its supply curve is the *M* line in Fig. 5.7. If a new firm enters *B* and requires supplies from *A*, the real cost of the extra resources required is indicated by *A*'s marginal cost; thus *A*'s marginal unit of output would command a lower price than previous units; the new firm in *B* gets the benefit of this lower price. This lower price is also paid to all of *A*'s intra-marginal units; but this does not represent a real saving; the intra-marginal units in *A* have transfer payments greater than the marginal price. The money saving to existing firms in *B* is not then a real saving, and the fact that the new firm in *B* *ignores* these savings guarantees that *B*'s actual output at P_c is also the optimal one. The fact that the intra-marginal units in *A* experience a loss is *precisely* the over-exhaustion problem of increasing returns to scale; that is, that total revenue is insufficient to cover the factors' opportunity costs when they are employed up to the point where the value of their marginal products just equals such opportunity costs, i.e., when price equals marginal cost.[33]

5.4 Public goods and external economies

Using the Pigovian definition of externality, *external economies* are increasingly being recognized as pervasive characteristics of modern states. Some of the 'indirect' benefits of education fall clearly into this category. Consider two instances given by M. H. Peston.

> Education is conducive to law and order and lowers the demand for a police force and other crime prevention devices ... [also] ... The value of an individual's ability to read or write depends on other people's ability to do the same. This is one example of a whole class of communication

[33] Cf. p. 121 above and footnotes. The loss experienced by *A*'s intra-marginal units is the symmetrical causative factor to the intra-marginal rents in the case where rising industry costs are due to inelastic input supplies. If *A* could perfectly discriminate in its selling policy the loss would not arise.

externalities. Consider the value of a telephone system from this standpoint.[34]

The first example has recently been looking somewhat sick, but both indicate the sort of interdependencies viewed as characterizing external economies. Another major sector throwing up similar sorts of problems is that concerned with

> . . . 'environmental' or 'public' health services, that is, services like clean water supply, the disposal of sewage and refuse, the clearing of central sources of infection and so on, which confer their benefits generally and indiscriminately on the inhabitants of some relevant area.[35]

There are, in addition, clearly other activities whose services are conferred generally and indiscriminately. For a very long time it has been recognized that lighting systems—lighthouses, street lighting—have this characteristic. Various forms of defensive activities like flood-relief and national defence expenditures benefit parts or the whole of a community. Finally, there are many aesthetic side effects that arise in our congested world, some of which are fairly localized—I like the flowers in your garden and enjoy listening to your transistor—and others more widespread—we all like the architecture of the new Town Hall.

Now, what is the chief characteristic of these examples? It is that, if one person is supplied with certain services, other people automatically receive services. Flood-relief usually involves the construction of levées and similar devices which, if 'supplied' to my neighbours, would usually involve my also benefiting. There are a number of things to notice about this characterization of external economies. First of all, in many instances, the indirect benefits conferred will not be technologically exactly the same as the direct benefits. Although I will benefit from your innoculation against malaria, this is not a perfect substitute for my getting innoculated. In a more extreme case, your benefits from your newly-constructed house are clearly physically different from my benefits—my aesthetic pleasure from its architectural design. Secondly, the characterization is general to externality in that the indirect services rendered could be a diseconomy; your fence could cut-off the sun from my garden. Thirdly, the relevant group affected differs in size in each example ranging from the small group cases of transistors, to 'regional'

[34] 'The Theory of Spillovers and its Connection with Education', *Public Finance*, No. 21, p. 186, 1966. (A reproduction of a Paper presented at the 21st meeting of the International Institute of Public Finance, 1965.) There are, of course, many other instances of divergences between private and social valuations in education—as Peston points out—but many of these are dynamic in nature and do not come within the scope of the present discussion.

[35] 'Efficiency in Government Spending: Social Services: Health', D. S. Lees, p. 178. This is a paper presented at the 22nd meeting of the International Institute of Public Finance, 1966. The proceedings have been published, by the Institute, as *Efficiency in Government Spending*, 1967.

groups in flood-relief and some of the health cases, to nationwide effects in the case of the national defence.

Samuelson's polar case

To highlight the important analytic features of some of these examples, let us provisionally ignore the first two qualifications. Think, that is, of the services in question being physically identical for all the affected parties and conferring a positive benefit on them. Defence, lighthouses, and certain types of flood-relief are probably near to this polar model. In effect, then, everyone consumes the same quantity of this good; it is 'collectively' consumed. This does not mean each person attaches the same evaluation to the good. What it does mean is that the good simultaneously enters the utility function of each member of the group. For this reason, such goods have been called 'public' or 'collective' goods. The 'publicness' of a good is not a political term but a technical term, used to suggest the characteristic that the goods are consumed collectively. Although there is a long history of this concept among economics writers, the key features of 'public' goods, their distinction from 'private' goods, and relationship to the concept of externality, were first rigorously presented by Samuelson. His

> . . . basic assumption is an oversharp distinction between the following two kinds of goods; (i) A *private* consumption good, like bread, whose total can be parcelled out among two or more persons, with one man having a loaf less if another gets a loaf more. Thus if X_1 is total bread, and X_1^1 and X_1^2, are the respective private consumptions of Man 1 and Man 2, we can say that the total equals the sum of the separate consumptions—or $X_1 = X_1^1 + X_1^2$. (ii) A *public* consumption good, like an outdoor circus or national defence, which is provided for each person to enjoy or not according to his tastes. I assume the public good can be varied in total quantity and write X_2 for its magnitude. It differs from a private consumption good in that each man's consumption of it, $X_2^1 = X_2^2$ respectively, is related to the total X_2 by a condition of *equality* rather than of summation. Thus, by definition, $X_2^1 = X_2^2$ and $X_2^2 = X_2$. Obviously, I am introducing a strong polar case.[36]

[36] 'Diagrammatic Exposition of a Theory of Public Expenditure', *Review of Economics and Statistics*, p. 350, November 1955, reproduced in *Collected Scientific Papers . . ., op. cit.* This latter also contains his initial mathematical exposition of the problem in 'The Pure Theory of Public Expenditure', *Review of Economics and Statistics*, November 1954, an article which has also been reproduced in *Readings in Welfare Economics, op. cit.* A rigorous derivation of the propositions in the next paragraph of the text can be given if it is recalled, from chapter 2, that the Pareto conditions are first-order conditions for the maximization of some weighted sum of individuals' welfare. This weighted sum—the social welfare function—we may write as $W = W(U_1, U_2, \ldots, U_i, \ldots, U_m)$ where U_i, etc., is person i's total utility. Let there be a private good whose total is Y, and a public good whose total is denoted by X. Individual i's utility function is $U_i = U_i(X^i, Y^i)$ where X^i is person i's consumption of the public good. Finally, let there

Thus your national defence *is also* my national defence. Sitting next to you on the beach, your radio programme is my radio programme. What is the Pareto efficient quantity of such goods? If extra expenditure on such items is undertaken, its benefit is indicated by the sum of the benefits accruing to each member of the group affected. The criterion would then be that extra units of defence, etc., are worth producing if the sum of consumers' evaluation exceeds the extra cost. Denoting this extra or marginal cost by MC, and the marginal evaluation of the ith consumer by E_i, we have that supply is Pareto efficient when:

$$MC = E_1 + E_2 + \ldots E_i \ldots + E_m \tag{5.6}$$

m being the size of the group involved. Notice, immediately, the similarity with the joint cost problem discussed in the previous section (eq. (5.4)). We shall discuss this similarity shortly.

The characteristics of eq. (5.6) can be represented diagrammatically if the usual assumptions necessary for partial analysis are made.[37] If the public

---

be a production function, $F(X, Y) = 0$, indicating the maximal produceable quantities of X and Y given certain (fixed) factor supplies and given a certain technology. If the production function is constrained by λ, then the Lagrangean expression to be maximized is:

$$L = W - \lambda F(X,Y) \tag{1}$$

Following standard procedure, for the private good we would have:

$$\delta L/\delta Y^i = W^i U_v^i - \lambda F_y = 0 \qquad i = 1 \ldots m \tag{2}$$

In this expression W^i is used to denote $\delta W/\delta U^i$; U_y^i represents $\delta U_i/\delta Y^i$; F_y is the partial derivative of the production function with respect to Y. When we come to the public good we need to remember Samuelson's definitions which in our notation would mean $X^1 = X^2 \ldots - X^i \ldots = X^m = X_2$. We cannot, therefore, increase X^1 without at the same time increasing X^2, X^3, and so on. It follows that the condition analogous to (2) is:

$$\delta L/\delta X = W^1 U_x^1 + W^2 U^2 + \ldots + W^m U_x^m - \lambda F_x = 0 \tag{3}$$

Given this, it is now simply a matter of rearranging terms to get the Pareto conditions. We have:

$$F_x/F_y = (W^1 U_x^1 + \ldots + W^m U_x^m)/W^i U_y^i \qquad i = 1 \ldots m \tag{4}$$

Now an implication of (2) is:

$$W^1 U_y^1 = W^2 U_y^2 \ldots = W^m U_y^m \tag{5}$$

It follows that the W's in eq. (4) cancel out leaving:

$$F_x/F_y = U_x^1/U_y^1 + U_x^2/U_y^2 + \ldots + U_x^m/U_y^m \tag{6}$$

Now the left-hand side of eq. (6) is the production transformation rate—the marginal cost of X in terms of Y. Similarly, the items on the right-hand side are the consumers' evaluation of X (in terms of Y). Thus eq. (5) is equivalent to eq (5.6) in the text.

[37] Namely, that all other prices are constant and each consumer's marginal utility of income remains unchanged. Those who want to see public good diagrams similar to those used to depict Pareto optimality in the private goods world of chapter 2 might proceed as follows. Construct a community indifference map for two persons with a public good on one axis and a private good on the other. Introduction of a production possibility line will then give *a* Pareto efficient point. Then check Samuelson's *Diagrammatic Exposition. . . .* (*op. cit.*) to see if you are right.

good can be produced at constant costs then we have a marginal cost line like MC in Fig. 5.9. For simplicity only two consumers are taken. The ordinates of D_1 indicate person 1's marginal evaluation of national defence and similarly D_2. Given the constraint that both consume the same quantities aggregate demand (D) has to be obtained, not by summing horizontally as would be the case with normal private goods, but by summing vertically. One sums consumers' evaluation of each unit. Clearly the Pareto efficient supply is q. How would a private market fare? Though it is difficult to think of defence in such a context the analysis has general applicability and the question is relevant. The full policy implications of externalities are not discussed until a later part of this chapter, but two possibilities can be mentioned here. Firstly, one can guess intuitively that private sale is going to be difficult because no

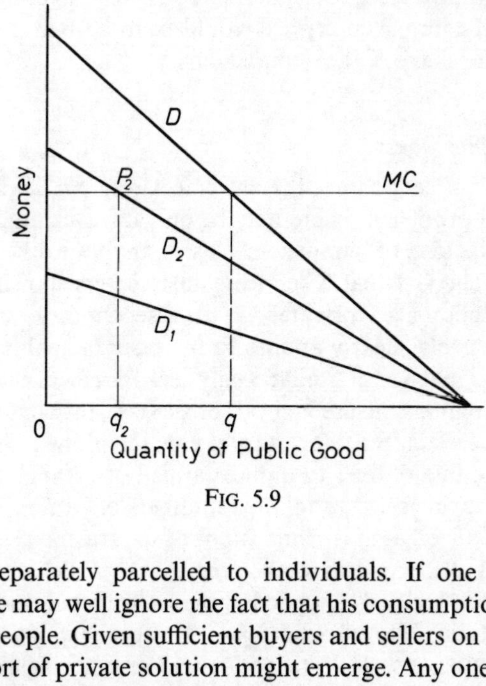

FIG. 5.9

units can be separately parcelled to individuals. If one individual *were* supplied then he may well ignore the fact that his consumption automatically benefits other people. Given sufficient buyers and sellers on both sides of the market some sort of private solution might emerge. Any one individual such as person 2 might well be prepared to buy some units. In this case the marginal unit of sale would be characterized by point P_2 on Fig. 5.9, namely that:

$$MC = E_2 \tag{5.7}$$

which is clearly a non-Pareto solution. In many cases the required outlay may be prohibitive for any one person so that no sales emerge from a private market. In fact, there is a better reason for thinking this may well result. This arises when large numbers of people are involved and is the important point made by Samuelson. Given the collective nature of the services rendered, it might be thought that some collective voluntary contributions might be forthcoming. But if the good is supplied at all, I will automatically benefit no matter to whom the supply is allegedly directed and no matter who pays for it. For this reason, I would tend to understate my preferences for the good; I would 'under-reveal' my willingness to pay in a way that I would never do for 'private' goods; if I did this for the latter I just would not get the goods. But by ducking my share in this case, I rest my hope on the possibility that others will contribute in which case I would still benefit. Since each and every individual might argue in this way, then normal market forces would not fully reveal the community's preferences for this good. This 'free-rider' problem, if correct, implies then that such goods can only be provided through the political process, by governments in other words. Although the characteristics of an optimal solution are known, it is not possible to get there by ordinary market forces. The public enterprise would be in no better position; it also needs to know the shape of the demand curve.

Some general implications

As in other areas of economics, the extreme case gives helpful insights into the more general problems. There may be only a few examples which fit the polar case, but the idea of 'publicness' clearly applies to the other examples of externalities. The fact that a service cannot be consumed 'privately'—or a factor of production used 'privately' in the diseconomy case—but has to be consumed 'collectively' clearly applies to the cases of health, education, and so on, and one could use a similar analytical framework. Although many examples relate to final consumer goods or services, the concept can embrace producer goods. In fact, the afforestation case mentioned above is one such instance. The planting of trees to induce rainfall or prevent soil erosion will, in many cases, provide services to large numbers of farmers simultaneously; here a public producer good is being supplied to farmers.

Although we have emphasized that the term 'public' is only a technical term in our usage, it is clearly a loaded phrase. The theory does not imply that *only* goods exhibiting the extreme form of externality 'should' be publicly provided. Economics has little to contribute in deciding the relative sizes of the private and public sectors and, in this book, we have purposely avoided what 'should' constitute the items of public expenditure. However, the theory of public goods perhaps does indicate a minimum list of services which 'ought' to be provided publicly—defence, justice, etc.—if only because the private sector would have great difficulty in providing them. One could, in addition, look on public goods theory as a *positive* theory about the size of the public sector. But its predictions would not be supported by the facts of present-day economic systems. Much government activity and spending—housing, transfer payments, income taxes, incentive payments, to mention but a few—are undertaken for objectives, like improving the distribution of income, stabilization policy or encouraging economic growth, wider than that envisaged in public goods theory.[38] Its predictions would not have been far out for the nineteenth century and before. At this time the list of publicly provided services was quite small and perhaps did relate closely to 'what the private sector cannot possibly do'. This, no doubt, partly explains why all the great treatises on 'Public Finance' had very little to say on public expenditure. In many cases it was a matter of taking expenditure as given—to be minimized as far as possible—and then examining how best to raise taxes to finance it. Those who did look at expenditure came immediately up against the problem that the items in question—administration of law and order, defence, etc.—were subject to the difficulties of our polar public good case; the levying of tax-prices on the basis of benefit received would be impossible to implement.[39]

One final general point about public goods can be noted here. Some writers have felt that public goods raise problems for the distribution of income different from those raised by private goods. In Musgrave's exposition we are invited to think of an economy starting with a given potentiality for producing private goods. If public goods are to be produced and consumed, then their optimal volume can only be determined by specifying how we are to distribute the costs of such public goods (in terms of private goods surrendered). Thus, the location of a Pareto efficient point requires some weighting of the welfares of various individuals in a society. There will not be just one Pareto efficient volume of public goods but a large number, each associated with a particular distribution of welfare.

> To choose among these solutions, a social welfare-function is required.... This need not arise in the allocation of resources between various private wants where various individuals may consume different amounts of any one product. The simple welfare condition leads to a single solution and

[38] However, there is a growing literature, particularly in the USA, using the standard public good theory as a starting point, which examines the development of the public sector in terms of its satisfying wants which private provision is incapable of doing. Much of this borders on the study of political institutions and political theory. See J. M. Buchanan's *The Demand and Supply of Public Goods*, Rand, McNally & Co., 1968, for discussion and references.

[39] See Musgrave, *op. cit.*, chapter 4 for a history of the benefit theory of taxation. This trend in 'Public Finance' texts has continued through to this century. Samuelson has remarked in *Aspects of Public Expenditure Theories, op. cit.* that in Pigou's great work on *A Study of Public Finance*, Macmillan, 1920, there are only four pages on the pure theory of public expenditure and, even if one includes transfer and exhaustive expenditure and the pricing of public utilities, the total comes to only about twenty pages. In fact, an indication that the study of the 'micro' aspects of public expenditure is a fairly recent development can be found if the contents of more up-to-date texts are examined. In the works of Musgrave, Prest, and Williams one finds—aside from 'macro' problems—something on pure public goods theory (though there is nothing in Williams), on transfer payments and, in addition, Musgrave has a section on decreasing cost industries, but this is all. These texts were written in the late 1950s early 60s. See A. R. Prest, *Public Finance* 1 Ed. Wiedenfeld & Nicolson, 1960, and A. Williams, *Public Finance and Budgetary Policy*. The Minerva Series No. 8, Allen & Unwin, 1963.

the optimal allocation of resources is determined uniquely on the basis of a given state of distribution.[40]

But this is surely misleading. If one started off with possibilities of producing and consuming certain private goods, and then another private good emerged as a possibility, exactly the same issues arise; one would have to specify how the gains are to be distributed to get *a* Pareto efficient point. In fact, Samuelson has made this clear in a recent paper where he emphasizes that the key difference with private goods is the non-revealment of preferences. If we were to suppose consumers did, for some 'irrational' reason, reveal their preferences then one gets a solution similar to the private goods case where the Pareto efficient point is determined crucially by the initial ownership of factors of production.[41] What does perhaps remain of the Musgrave thesis is that, to the extent that a decentralized price system cannot be used for public goods, then the distribution of welfare problem is made explicit in the decision to produce public goods. One cannot 'let the market do it' and then effect movements along the welfare frontier by lump-sum transfers and taxes.[42]

Joint supply, externality, and public goods[43]

Reflecting on the examples given of joint supply in section 5.3, and on the examples of external economies and public goods, the reader will have noticed that some sort of 'jointness' appears in the supply arrangements in both cases. This section explores their similarities and differences. In both cases, services are provided by the production of certain assets or goods and we may distinguish between two kinds of jointness:

[40] *Op. cit.* p. 84. A. R. Prest and R. Turvey are among those who think that

> . . . even if the non-revealment of preferences problem is ignored, there is still another major snag, in that there is no single best solution but rather a multiplicity of alternative optimum solutions.

See 'Cost-Benefit Analysis: A Survey', *EJ*, December 1965, p. 696, reproduced in *Surveys of Economic Theory,* **III,** AEA and RES, Macmillan, 1966.

[41] See Samuelson's 1966 IEA paper (*op. cit.*) where he suggests that Musgrave

> . . . seems to be saying that Pareto-optimality is unique for private goods but not for public: in fact, neither is unique and the same distributional problem arises.

(pp. 104–5, footnote).

[42] Some recent work by M. A. McGuire and H. Aaron analyses the relationship between financing methods for public goods and the separability of the allocation/distribution issues. See 'Efficiency and Equity in the Optimal Supply of a Public Good' *R Econ. and Statistics.* February 1969.

[43] This section draws on parts of my paper 'Exclusion Costs, External Economies and Market Failure', *OEP,* March 1970. For a different view see 'Joint Supply, Externality, and Optimality', J. M. Buchanan, *Economica,* November 1966, and 'Public Goods and Public Policy', J. G. Head, *Public Finance,* No. 4, 1962.

(a) One situation is where the services of these assets are such that if one person, in a relevant group, is supplied with such services other people in the group *can* be supplied at zero extra cost. This conforms to our previous definitions of joint supply, and is exemplified by indoor theatres, swimming pools, etc.

(b) The examples of external economies like health immunization, flood-relief, etc., have the characteristic that if one person is supplied the other members of the relevant group *will* also be supplied at zero extra cost to the supplier.

The phrase 'joint supply' has been used in a variety of ways by economists[44] but here we shall use it only in relation to (a), and shall provisionally term (b) 'automatic joint supply'. In searching for an explanation of public goods Musgrave observed that a consumer

> ... is excluded from the enjoyment of any particular commodity or service unless he is willing to pay the stipulated price to the owner. This may be referred to as the *exclusion principle*.... The benefits resulting from [public goods] will accrue to all who live in the particular place or society where the services are rendered. [But each person] ... knows that his benefit will be independent of his particular contribution. [Therefore in public goods] ... we must combine the condition of joint consumption with that of inapplicability of the exclusion principle.[45]

In other words, the services of such goods not only exhibit joint supply but, in addition, it is very costly to exclude people from the services. Now, for most services supplied in our economic systems in a sense exclusion facilities are undertaken by the supplier. In practice, it may well be impossible to differentiate in a firm's total costs between what one might call production and exclusion costs. In many cases, also, exclusion costs are probably negligible: this would certainly apply for tangible goods and even for some services—warm cinemas already have the basis for exclusion possibilities. But, granted that in principle at least exclusion facilities are undertaken, it is important to remember why they are. They are necessary if it is decided to charge prices or more generally to reveal the demand curve.[46]

[44] Musgrave, as we have already suggested, uses the phrase in the manner adopted in this text. Buchanan's usage (*Economica*, 1966, *op. cit.*) appears to embrace both (a) and (b) though he starts off with an analogy to Marshallian joint supply. Marshall was thinking of the cows/meat/hide problem; at first sight this appears to be directly relevant to the public good/decreasing cost issue but, as Samuelson has recently shown, Marshallian joint supply does not create any problems for private markets. See 'Contrast between Welfare Conditions for Joint Supply and Public Goods', P. A. Samuelson, *R Econ. Stats.*, February 1969.

[45] *Op. cit.*, pp. 9–10 and footnotes. His emphasis.

[46] One qualification to this is that much of the work in cost/benefit analysis, as we shall see, is concerned with estimating the demand curve. Often this proceeds by estimating what it would cost the potential customers if they used another source; if they do not use the proposed canal, what would it cost them by rail. To this extent the public enterprise can dispense with exclusion facilities.

The key point is that if for certain services, exclusion facilities are costly then it is cheaper to provide on an 'automatic joint supply' basis than to supply even *one* person on his own; 'automatic joint supply' is cheaper than 'single' supply! Thus for cinemas, swimming pools, etc., with negligible exclusion costs, joint supply is cheaper than separate supply and not much more expensive (in terms of construction costs) than 'single' supply. For flood-relief, health immunization, public lighting, etc., *automatic joint supply is much less expensive than even single supply, let alone separate supply.* In fact, it is difficult to think of devices that could exclude people from the services of some of these assets. Since private enterprise requires exclusion facilities to levy prices then, when they are prohibitive, private enterprise will not operate. If 'automatic joint supply' is used, then we run into the under-revealment problem, for of course the reader will by now realize that automatic joint supply is equivalent to saying that the activity gives rise to external economies.

Notice that these problems are not avoided if a public enterprise is supplying the service. Following the rules discussed before, it also needs knowledge of the demand curve. Thus, whereas the public enterprise could, in principle, achieve an 'efficient' solution in the joint supply and decreasing cost problems which render difficulties for private enterprise, it is faced with the same problems as private enterprise when exclusion costs become large. Notice also that exclusion facilities are, in principle, necessary for all commodities and so it seems that externalities are perhaps best characterized as arising when exclusion costs become high; the Pareto-relevant opportunities missed for standard commodities and services are probably negligible. This gives a clue to the observed similarity of equations (5.4) and (5.6). In eq. (5.6) the cost item implicitly leaves out the cost of exclusion facilities. In eq. (5.4) these exclusion costs are included but implicitly taken to be negligible.

The point that exclusion facilities are, in principle, necessary for all market supplied commodities, raises some further points. First of all it means that externalities could, in theory, arise if production inputs exhibited no indivisibilities, if in other words there were constant returns to scale in production. On these grounds one could quibble with Musgrave's definition of public goods but, in practice, it is difficult to think of examples. Moreover, most of the examples of public goods and external economies *do* in practice seem to exhibit joint supply; that is, even if exclusion were possible one might still have problems for private markets because of the extreme indivisibilities in production costs. Thus Samuelson instanced broadcasting:

> The Federal Communications Commission is now trying to make up its mind about permitting subscription television. You might think that the case where a programme comes over the air and is available for any set owner to tune in on is a perfect example of my public good. And in a way it is. But you would be wrong to think that the essence of the phenomenon

is inherent in the fact that the broadcaster is not able to refuse the service to whatever individuals he pleases. For in this case, by the use of unscramblers, it is technically possible to limit the consumption of a particular broadcast, to any specified group of individuals. . . . [However] . . . what, after all, are the true marginal costs of having one extra family tune in on the programme? They are literally zero . . . [Thus] . . . our well-known optimum principle that goods should be priced at their marginal costs would not be realized in the case of subscription broadcasting.[47]

A somewhat similar problem arises in reverse for roads and bridges, which seem to include a multitude of efficiency problems. There may, on one hand, be extreme indivisibilities in producing a road system for a country; in addition, the exclusion facilities necessary to levy prices may be very costly, particularly in heavily populated areas such as the UK; finally, there is the congestion problem.

Samuelson, in fact, uses the term 'public good' to cover our external economy/public good cases *and* the case of decreasing costs. Similarly, other writers have equated decreasing costs with externality.[48] While one can see that similar sorts of conceptual problems are involved (summing benefits over persons) and that both provide difficulties for a decentralized private enterprise system, we think it better to distinguish between the two concepts. They raise separate issues and, as we have emphasized, whereas the public enterprise has the same difficulties as private markets in the public good/ external economy cases, it can, in principle at least, 'solve' the decreasing cost problem.

5.5 Summary and review

The key points made in this chapter so far are:

(a) If products exhibit decreasing costs—aside from those caused by factor price changes—private enterprise systems run into difficulties in achieving Pareto efficient solutions. In principle, public enterprises can achieve efficiency.

(b) With extreme forms of decreasing costs—joint supply in our terminology — the same points apply. However, mere jointness does not necessarily imply private enterprise failure. Provided the indivisibilities are not very large in relation to market demand, it is possible to conceive of private markets

[47] *Aspects of Public Expenditure Theories*, *op. cit.*, p. 335. Further discussion of the broadcasting case can be found in the *Journal of Law and Economics*, October 1964; there, a piece by J. Minasian, 'Television Pricing and the Theory of Public Goods', drew forth a counter blast from Samuelson, 'Public Goods and Subscription TV: Correction of the Record'.

[48] Samuelson's usage is indicated in the passages omitted—to avoid confusion—in the above quotation. Buchanan in his *Demand and Supply of Public Goods*, *op. cit.*, also uses 'public' in this way. In his *Anatomy of Market Failure*, *op. cit.*, Bator, in fact, calls increasing returns to scale, 'technical externality' and his conclusions are similar to those of Head, *op. cit.*

providing efficient supplies—the swimming pools, cinemas cases. When indivisibilities become large, as they may do in the case of roads and bridges, the private market failure problem returns.

(c) Externalities arise when goods or services are supplied 'collectively' (i.e., automatic joint supply) rather than 'privately'. An extreme model of this, where large numbers of people each simultaneously consume the same good, indicates that any market device, whether private or public, will fail in achieving efficient supply because the demand curve will not be revealed.

(d) In practice, the collectively supplied goods are not always homogeneous. Goods of different characteristics can be provided and some could be 'bads'. The various examples of externalities also involve different sizes of groups affected.

(e) For goods giving rise to externalities, 'collective' supply is cheaper not only than 'separate' supply but cheaper even than supplying just *one* person on his own, i.e., 'single' supply. This arises because the technology of these activities is such that the facilities needed to exclude people are very costly. This constitutes the chief difference with the simple joint supply cases where exclusion can easily be carried out.

(f) In this terminology, external *diseconomies* arise when the cheapest way of performing some activity involves automatically supplying 'bads' to other people. However, in some instances, particularly the reciprocal-type diseconomies examples of congestions, etc., a more fundamental and meaningful cause, particularly bearing in mind policy implications, is that the affected parties are all using some factor of production for which no payment is made and this is the basic reason for divergences between competitive market behaviour and ideal output.

In the rest of this chapter we shall leave the problem of decreasing costs and concentrate on externalities. The above summary points indicate that our prime concern so far has been with exploring the forces that give rise to externalities. It is now appropriate to turn to policy implications. Now the traditional solution, following the lead of Pigou, is the tax/subsidy approach. Those people or firms responsible for creating external diseconomies are to be taxed on the grounds that their activities are excessive in as much as they ignore these external effects. The existence of external economies in particular sectors suggest insufficient resources are allocated to these sectors and, thus, a subsidy is warranted. Pigou did not, however, look very closely at how the parties in question would react to the existence of external effects. This is precisely what modern writers have done. If I find your radio particularly wearisome at 9.00 a.m. on Sunday mornings, I might try to dissuade you from playing it; if an up-stream dyeing factory spoils the water which a downstream firm wants to use for cooling purposes, the latter might even provide economic incentives for the dye firm to reduce its water spoilage. It is, in fact, the potentialities of *economic* action in these situations that needs exploring. To do this it is necessary to pin down the definition of externality more precisely. Granted a market environment, the issue is one of expressing precisely what we mean when we say that an externality exists. One problem with the Pigovian definition (see p. 110) is that, though it hypothesizes that interdependence exists, the affected parties might not want to do anything about it if it is economically insignificant. Further, it is not clear what variables of the individuals or firms are affected; is it profits or the production function for example?

Defining externality

As it turns out, a full understanding of why it is difficult to pin down a definition of externality requires some knowledge of topics we are about to discuss in the next section. However, the following suggestions, in an article[49] by J. M. Buchanan and W. C. Stubblebine, come pretty close to a satisfactory treatment. Since the issue is to concentrate on the idea of interdependence, the actual locale—whether it is more concerned with production effects like smoke or individuals using radios—does not matter. They take the case where person *B*'s consumption actions affect another person *A* since:

> . . . we shall find no cause for discussing production and consumption externalities separately. Essentially the same analysis applies in either case. In what follows, 'firms' may be substituted for 'individuals' and 'production functions' for 'utility functions' without modifying the central conclusions. . . . We define an external effect, *an externality*, to be present when
>
> $$U^A = U^A(X_1, X_2, \ldots, X_m, Y_1) \qquad (1)$$
>
> This states that the utility of an individual, *A*, is dependent upon the 'activities', $(X_1, X_2, \ldots, X_m)$, that are exclusively under his own control or authority, but also upon another . . . activity, Y_1, which is, by definition, under the control of a second individual, *B* . . . .

The concept is, then, firmly put into the realm of the real forces of production and welfare. The crucial aspect of the quote is the way the variables are defined. Clearly, my welfare is affected by whether the local toffee-firm is going to produce this year; that is not under my control, but neither does it matter since what enters my utility function is *my* consumption of toffee, something clearly within my control. Now, clearly, for some types of external effect *A* may be affected by large changes in *B*'s activities but not by small changes; to be rigorous one would want to allow for this in the definition; however, we shall ignore such refinements. More important is that *B*'s activity should actually affect *A*'s welfare; that the marginal utility (or disutility) to

[49] 'Externality', *Economica*, November 1962. The quotations in the next few paragraphs can be found on pp. 371–4. This article has been reproduced as chapter 32 of *Readings in Micro-Economics*, *op. cit.*, and also in *Readings in Welfare Economics*, *op. cit.*

A from extra Y_1 should not be zero. Further if *A* is not affected when *B* is in his own best position—his equilibrium position—this would not be an important external effect. If *B*'s equilibrium quantity of Y_1 is denoted by $\overline{Y}_1$, and if *A*'s marginal utility is denoted by U^A_{Y1}, then Buchanan and Stubblebine's further points can now be understood.

An externality is defined as *potentially relevant* when the activity, to the extent that it is actually performed, generates *any* desire on the part of the externally benefited (damaged) party (*A*) to modify the behaviour of the party empowered to take action (*B*) through trade, persuasion, compromise, agreement, convention, collective action, etc. An externality which, to the extent that it is performed, exerts no such influence is defined as *irrelevant*. Note that, so long as (1) holds, an externality remains; utility functions remain interdependent. A potentially relevant marginal externality exists when,

$$U^A_{Y1}\Big|_{Y_1 = \overline{Y_1}} \neq 0 \tag{7}$$

This is a potentially relevant marginal external economy when (7) is greater than zero, a diseconomy when (7) is less than zero.

Though somewhat pedantic, this certainly clears some ground. Now it becomes clear that, in analysing the direct interaction of situations where potentially relevant external effects exist, policy proposals will involve one or both parties changing the scale and even the nature of their activities. And the issue is going to revolve round whether such moves are worth while. If you have to remove your fence because it prevents the sun reaching my house, then all other things being equal, such a move would make me better off and you worse off. We are back, in other words, in the world of evaluating changes in economic circumstances discussed in chapter 3, and that chapter's discussion of appropriate criteria becomes relevant. Now, distributional factors enter *all* the problems of this chapter though we have chosen to ignore them so far. The new situation simply makes them explicit. If someone's gain has to be compared with someone else's loss then a weighting system is needed. To start with we shall assume that £1 of benefit or loss is the same no matter who experiences it. In this case we could use a standard criterion discussed in chapter 3, namely that a change is worth while if the gain exceeds the loss—the 'gainers could compensate losers' criterion. However, it is also necessary to remember that if the changes in question have sizeable real income effects on the parties affected then there is no unique measure of gain and loss[50]—another point explored in chapter 3. Again we shall provisionally ignore this, by assuming changes in the parties' marginal utility of income

[50] E. J. Mishan has analysed both the real income issue and the distributional problem in 'Welfare Criteria for External Effects', *AER*, 1961 September, and in his book, *The Costs of Economic Growth*, Staples Press, 1967, Part 2.

are negligible. The important point at this stage is that, given that the removal of an external effect will promote losses as well as gains, then all potentially relevant external effects are not necessarily to be modified; it may not be 'efficient' to change the existing situation. The mere existence of such effects does not then necessarily imply inefficiency. This leads on to Buchanan and Stubblebine's further point.

> An externality is defined to be Pareto-relevant when the extent of the activity may be modified in such a way that the externally affected party, *A*, can be made better off without the acting party, *B*, being made worse off. That is to say, 'gains from trade' characterize the Pareto-relevant externality, trade that takes the form of some change in the activity of *B* as his part of the bargain.

We are now in a position to explore such possibilities.

5.6 Externalities and 'efficient' solutions

It is helpful, in analysing solutions to external effects, to work in terms of some practical examples. To make a choice, only diseconomies will be considered though the analysis applies '*mutatis mutandis*' to external economies. The following four cases indicate some of the wide characteristics that external effects can take and, to facilitate understanding of some of the proposals made by certain economists, two of the examples are taken from previous writings.

(a) An airport is to be located not far from a built-up area whose residents object to the potential noise nuisance.

(b) A municipal authority owns a piece of land which at present is allowed to be used by families for recreational purposes. Local business interests are keen to use the land for building; to this extent the local residents would suffer if they lost these recreational facilities.[51]

(c) Jones is a 'do-it-yourself' maniac. His particular DIY bent is for home-brewed beer which, however, produces noxious fumes, offensive to Brown, his neighbour.

(d) A cattle-raiser's land borders on a farmer's potato field; often the cattle stray into the farmer's field and destroy part of the crop.[52]

In all cases one can think of two groups of people involved. The persons or group undertaking the activity which generates the external effect—airport authorities, Jones, etc.—are to be thought of as gaining from this activity and are thus denoted as group *G*, the gainers. Those suffering from the side-effects of *G*'s activity (the local residents, farmer, etc.) can be thought of as experi-

[51] Cf. Mishan, *AER*, 1961, *op. cit.*

[52] This is R. H. Coase's chief illustrative example in his paper, 'The Problem of Social Cost', *J of Law and Economics*, October 1960, reproduced as chapter 30 of *Readings in Micro-Economics*, *op. cit.*, to which future page references refer.

encing an economic loss—albeit perhaps difficult to quantify—and they are, therefore, to be denoted as group *L*, the losers. Now, one thing common to most of the examples is that the nature and size of the external effect will be affected by a number of technological factors. For one thing, its importance will depend on the scale of *G*'s activity—how much of the recreational land the local builders are allowed to use, how many cattle are being reared, and so on. In addition, in coming to a solution one would also want to examine the possibilities of changes in the location of the airport, or the recreational facilities, or of constructing fences between the cattle-raisers' land and the farmer's. To start with, however, we shall assume the nature of the activity is fixed: then later on we can examine alternative technological arrangements.

The simplest case

Although the location of the airport, building site, etc., is to be taken as given, the scale of activity can be taken as variable. In other words the economic loss experienced by group *L* may vary with the size of *G*'s activity. In practice, in some cases, there may just be a once and for all effect. Brown's troubles may only be mitigated if Jones completely stops brewing beer. However, it would be overlooking some possible solutions if scale effects were ignored and so, to take it to its logical extreme, we shall assume *G*'s activity can be varied in small amounts and each marginal increase adds to *L*'s losses. The problem is one then of evaluating the gains and losses from each change in scale of *G*'s activity. Now what are these gains and losses? Formally, *G*'s activity enters as a variable in *L*'s utility functions (or production function in the case of the farmer). To the extent that this effect is potentially relevant, there will be an economic value for *L*'s loss. In some cases, financial effects will be experienced, e.g., the farmer's potato receipts fall. But the existence of an economic value for the loss does not depend on their being financial effects. In general, *the loss can be defined as the money compensation group L requires in order that they be no worse off when (a change in) G's activity takes place, than they would be if it did not take place.* The recreational land case is somewhat similar to the old problem of congestion, in that the local residents are using a piece of land for which they actually might be prepared to pay but which they use effectively as a free good. The consumer surplus that they thereby derive indicates, in theory, the money compensation they would require for giving up (a part of) the land. Analogously, though somewhat more tortuously, the potential sufferers from the airport and Jones' beer also attach some money value to their present bliss.[53] The farmer's case raises an additional point. The value of his potato crop might at first glance appear to be the relevant measure. But, after only a little experience of the cattle's meanderings, he would presumably reduce his planned cultivation. In so doing he will lose on potato receipts but also he will save on the cost of accompanying

[53] What they are giving up is quiet or fume-less air!

factors, such as seeds, labour, even machines in the long-run. The farmer's loss is, therefore, equal to his fall in producer surplus—the value of the crop less the opportunity cost of all other factors. The point is a quite general one, the difference in the other cases being simply that such opportunity costs are zero.

It will help if this is formalized. Let the potential economic loss to group L from an increase in the scale of G's activity be denoted as N_L. This 'net' loss[54] consists of this group's evaluation of those pursuits it might lose, E_L, less the cost of these pursuits, O_L. We thus have that $N_L = E_L - O_L$. Exactly similar reasoning applies for the gainers. *The gain is equal to the maximum they are prepared to pay to undertake (a change in) their activity.* This we may denote by $N_G = E_G - O_G$. For the airport authorities, builders, and cattle-raisers this can be thought of as their producer surplus; for Jones it is consumer surplus. Clearly these measures, particularly for the losers, would be difficult to quantify. However, inability to quantify has often been used as an excuse for doing nothing and, since we are interested in principles here, we shall assume that, if necessary, some rough estimates of these economic magnitudes are obtainable. Since the economic values in question relate to changes in the scale of G's activity, then the criterion for deciding whether such a change is worthwhile is:

$$N_G > N_L \tag{5.8}$$

Assume that G's marginal net gain decreases as the size of his activity increases—a standard sort of assumption in economics—and that L's marginal loss increases. It follows that *optimality* is achieved when the scale of G's activity is such that for a marginal change N_G equals N_L, or putting it another way:

$$E_G - O_G = E_L - O_L. \tag{5.9}$$

A diagram will probably help. In Fig. 5.10, the scale of G's activity is indicated on the horizontal axis.[55] The gains to group G and the losses to L are both

[54] To the extent that the measures of loss relate to L's pursuits, we are departing from the approach which focuses on G's activity. The principle is no different however. Instead of talking of L's evaluation of G's activity, we talk of L's evaluation of those pursuits which G's activity prevents. This emphasis is better for discussion of subsequent problems. Notice, also, the formal link between 'evaluations' and the utility function. For the most general case, allowing for changes in the marginal utility of income, we should drop the money terminology involved in E_L—and E_G for that matter—and think of L's marginal rate of substitution between the pursuit in question and some numeraire commodity. In the approach which focuses on G's activity entering L's utility function, it would be L's marginal rate of substitution between G's activity and the numeraire. If the latter is called commodity h, and G's activity is denoted by s, then the substitution rate is U_s^L/U_h^L where U_h^L is the marginal utility to one person (of the L group) of commodity h and U_s^L is his marginal (dis)utility from G's activity. The whole analysis could be conducted in this terminology. Cf. Buchanan and Stubblebine, *op. cit.*

[55] Versions of this diagram can be found in Mishan's *Welfare Criteria for External Effects op. cit.*, and in R. Turvey's article 'On Divergences between Private and Social Cost', *Economica*, August, 1963.

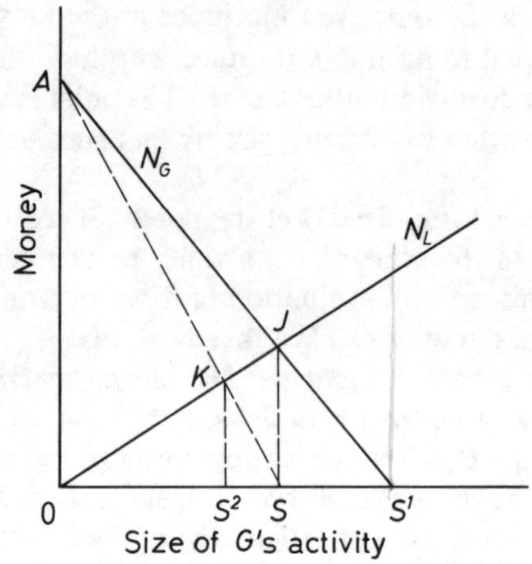

FIG. 5.10

expressed as a function of scale, and are indicated by the N_G and N_L lines respectively. Clearly the optimal scale is S, the dotted line AS indicating G's marginal gains net of L's marginal losses.

So much for efficiency. The question is how do we get there. This is where the legal system comes in, since the interdependencies and side-effects characteristic of externality—particularly of the diseconomy variety—often involve problems of property rights and who has the right to do what. If the laws of a country actually require compensation for such side-effects, then this will obviously have an effect on the actual solution and may well bring the actual solution close to the optimum. Suppose that G is obliged to compensate L for their losses, in the general sense of rendering L as well off as they would have been in the absence of G's activities. In this case, the compensation payment is exactly equal to the loss discussed above $(E_L - O_L)$. Now in the absence of such a requirement we might suppose G would adjust the scale of their activities to maximize their own private net gain; they would, in other words, undertake all those changes for which N_G was positive and in equilibrium.

$$E_G - O_G = 0, \tag{5.10}$$

that is, the profit on the marginal unit is zero. Given our assumptions, this would involve a larger scale of output than the optimum. They would operate at S^1 on Fig. 5.10. But, if they have to pay compensation, then they would compare the gross value of their activity not simply with their own costs, O_G, but with the compensation payments as well. In other words the actual equilibrium would be when

$$E_G = O_G + (E_L - O_L). \tag{5.11}$$

They compare marginal benefit not with marginal private cost but with marginal 'social cost'. Clearly eq. (5.11), the actual solution, is the same as eq. (5.9), the optimal solution, as one might expect.

On the other hand, if compensation is not required, then we might expect eq. (5.10) to characterize the actual solution and this is, clearly, not optimal. But are we not overlooking the possibility that group L might try to dissuade G from pursuing their activities? In principle L could take economic action; they might provide incentives for G to reduce the scale of their activities or eliminate them completely. What incentive would group G need to reduce their activities? For each reduction in scale G loses N_G and this, therefore, is the minimum compensation they would require. What incentive payment can group L afford? On each unit L loses an amount equal to N_L—which of course varies with each unit—and if, by paying any amount less than N_L they could induce G to reduce their activities, then group L would be better off. Thus, mutual beneficial trading could take place as long as $N_L > N_G$. Assuming this does take place, L could thereby bribe G to reduce their activities to the point where N_L was equal to N_G; further reductions would not take place because the minimum needed by G exceeds the maximum bribe payments group L would offer. Put another way, G would pick its scale of activity by comparing the gross value of its activity with the private cost and the likely bribe payments from L. The actual equilibrium is again described by eq. (5.11) which is also the optimal one.

Thus, we come to the somewhat startling conclusion that:

(a) The presence or absence of legal rights does not affect the actual output,
(b) this actual output is also the optimal one, and
(c) this optimal position does not necessitate the complete stoppage of the activity giving rise to the external effect.

These possibilities emerge from the work of Coase, Buçhanan, and Stubblebine. By recognizing that the elimination of the external effect would mean economic losses for those 'responsible' for its existence as well as benefits to the currently injured parties, the analysis suggests a trade-off is required. Further, by mooting the possibility of the parties' engaging in bartering, it allows that these potential gains from trade or 'inefficiences' are exploited. In effect, the compensation payments or bribe offers, both set a shadow cost to G's activities over and above that group's own private costs. In terms of policy, the key problem raised is that the mere existence of external effects does not mean anything need be done about them. As Buchanan and Stubblebine would say, potentially relevant external effects exist in the final optimal position of our cases above, but these are not Pareto-relevant.

Alternative technological arrangements

Imagine the relief afforded by the above analysis to the supporters of the price system. The market mechanism is 'saved'. All those nasty Pigovian externality blemishes do not matter! There are, of course, a number of questionable assumptions in the analysis which need considering. Nevertheless, the tax/subsidy solution does also need re-considering. To these and other qualifications we shall shortly turn. However, before doing this, let us keep within the spirit of the simple model and now briefly consider the sort of possibilities that arise when we admit of alternative locations for the airport, or the existence of alternative land for the farmer to grow his potatoes or for the children to play on. This will also have the incidental advantage of indicating some of the more complex issues that arise in any 'real-life' cases.

The new setting admits of technical possibilities not existing in the previous analysis. It follows that not only may actual outcomes be different but the *optimal* solution has also to be *redefined*. We now have to choose between different scales and *kinds* of activity for G and L. Two examples will make the key points. In the first one, we consider some technological alternatives for group L. Coase's farmer may for example have some alternative land on which he could grow his potatoes; by definition this has to be inferior to the original piece of land otherwise the farmer would have preferred it in any case. His profits when using the inferior land are N_L^1 where $N_L^1 < N_L$. Similarly, there may be alternative land available in the recreational case. Although the local families' benefit from this alternative is the same (and equal to E_L), there are certain costs involved in using it ($O_L^1 > 0 = O_L$); one could think of this in terms of travel costs or payments having to be made for access. Again then, we have $N_L^1 < N_L$. The issue now, therefore, is whether it is better that (a change in) G's activity takes place and L is located elsewhere, than that G's activity does not take place and L stays put. In other words, the case where G's activity takes place and L stays put is now irrelevant since Coase's farmer or local families should in any case move on the assumption that N_L^1 is positive.

It is, therefore, a matter of deciding whether over-all social net benefits are larger in one situation rather than the other. If G's activity does not take place, group L are allowed to pursue their better option and the social net benefit is N_L. If G's activity does take place and group L shifts, then over-all net benefits are $N_G + N_L^1$. Thus, the criterion as to whether it is better for L to relocate is that:

$$N_G + N_L^1 > N_L. \quad (5.12)$$

Again we may consider whether the actual solution will accord with the optimum. Where there are no legal restrictions on G's activity, L would normally shift to their inferior position. Could L dissuade G from undertaking their activity? Thinking in terms of the farming example, the farmer would experience a fall in profits equivalent to $N_L - N_L^1$; thus, if he could discourage G's activities by offering any amount up to $N_L - N_L^1$, then he, the farmer, staying on his better land, would be better off. As before, the cattle-raiser would require N_G as compensation for not rearing his cattle. Thus L would be unable to curtail G's activities as long as:

$$N_G > N_L - N_L^1 \tag{5.13}$$

Thus the actual decision process, eq. (5.13), accords with the optimal one, eq. (5.12). Similarly if G is obliged by law to compensate L, then it would pay G to try and induce L to relocate. That is, whereas normal compensation would be N_L, if L were to relocate, G need only pay an amount of compensation equal to L's fall in surplus, $N_L - N_L^1$; this is clearly cheaper for G as long as N_L^1 is positive. Since then $N_L - N_L^1$ is the compensation L would require, and since N_G is the maximum G would be prepared to pay, then whether G is able to produce and to induce group L to shift is given by eq. (5.13). Again actual and optimal solutions coincide.

More generally, there will be technical possibilities for changing the nature of the activity that generates the external effect. This could mean completely eliminating the external effect, e.g., the local builders relocate elsewhere, or at least reducing its force, e.g., Jones switches to a less smelly form of beer-brewing. A general example which would illustrate these sort of problems is the case where an alternative site is available for the airport—less profitable for the airport authorities—but this is not so far away from the residential area that all noise effects are eliminated. With this sort of change the new profits of the airport authorities are less than on the original site ($N_G^1 < N_G$), but the economic losses imposed on local residents, though still existing, are lower than previously. These losses could be expressed in the following way. With no airport at all the local residents have the benefit of a quiet environment, the economic value of which is N_L. If the airport is built on the original site this value falls to zero; on the proposed new site it would only fall to N_L^1. In a sense there are three options available:

(a) The airport keeps to the original site and the local residents get the full blast. In this illustration we can drop the idea of scale and simply think of a once-and-for-all change, though analytically one could pursue the idea of differences in the size of the airport.

(b) The airport is not built at all and group L suffer no economic losses.

(c) An alternative site is used thus reducing losses to group L.

Now our previous discussion implicitly dealt with the choice between (a) and (b), and we saw that the optimal choice would emerge if there were compensation or bartering possibilities. Suppose then we assume the outcome of this is that (a) is to be preferred to (b) because $N_G > N_L$. It is now, therefore, a matter of deciding whether (c) is preferable to (a). If the airport is built on the original site in the (a)-type solution, then social net benefits are N_G. If the alternative site were taken, social net benefits are $N_G^1 + N_L^1$. It follows that the new site is better if:

$$N_G^1 + N_L^1 > N_G. \tag{5.14}$$

This, then, is the efficiency criterion and we may again inquire what actual criterion will be used. If the airport authorities are required by law to compensate people suffering from the noise, then they would choose the second site only if it were of advantage to them to do so. Although on the new site operating profits are only N_G^1 and less than on the original site, compensation payments are also lower; by building on the new site local residents suffer to the tune of only $N_L - N_L^1$, as opposed to N_L on the old site. Thus, the airport authorities will compare over-all profits on the old site, $(N_G - N_L)$, with over-all profits on the new site. The new site is chosen if:

$$N_G^1 - (N_L - N_L^1) > N_G - N_L \tag{5.15}$$

and this is equivalent to the optimal criterion, eq. (5.14), since the N_L's cancel out. On the other hand, if the airport authorities are not legally obliged to compensate they would choose the original site. The local residents cannot dissuade the authorities from building on the old site—for by assumption $N_L < N_G$—but could they be induced to shift to the new site? On the old site group L's net benefits are zero, but they would rise to N_L^1 if the airport were re-located. Thus N_L^1 is L's maximum bribe offer. G would need $N_G - N_G^1$ as compensation for shifting locale and, thus, the local inhabitants can induce a move to the new site as long as:

$$N_L^1 > N_G - N_G^1. \tag{5.16}$$

And again this is equivalent to the optimal criterion, eq. (5.14).

Before leaving this general problem, it would be amiss if mention was not made of one special kind of technological alternative which is relevant to the case of external diseconomies. This is the possibility of constructing 'exclusion facilities' which eliminate or mitigate the external effect. Thus, it may be technically feasible to provide sound-insulation facilities in each house located near to the airport. More mundanely in the farming example, a fence could be erected to prevent the cattle from straying. Clearly these sorts of possibilities would, in practice, have to be considered as one of the many options available including relocation of potential gainers and losers. Suppose, however, we keep the example simple by assuming that re-location is not feasible. The issue—thinking in terms of Coase's cattle—is whether it is optimal to build a fence and what criteria would, given compensation or bartering possibilities, actually be used in deciding whether the fence is built. Suppose that again a once-and-for-all effect is considered, and that the construction costs of the fence are denoted by F. Suppose further that, *without* the technical possibility of the fence, the optimal solution is for the cattle-raiser to pursue his activities on the grounds that $N_G > N_L$. In this case, social net benefit is equal to N_G. If a fence can be built and if, for simplicity, it is assumed that the measures of potential profits are unaffected—that, for example, the cattle are no worse off by not having access to the farmer's field—then overall social net benefit with the fence constructed is $N_G + N_L - F$. It follows then that it is optimal to erect the fence if:

$$N_G + N_L - F > N_G \tag{5.17}$$

that is, if $N_L > F$. Where the legal system imposes no restrictions on the cattle-raiser's activity, the question becomes whether the farmer's criterion in deciding to build a fence accords with the optimal decision rule. If the farmer constructs the fence he has to pay for it, but he gains in potato profits an amount equal to N_L. Thus, he builds the fence if $N_L > F$, which accords with the optimal criterion, eq. (5.17). Similarly, if the cattle-raiser is obliged by law to pay compensation then he will build the fence if what he would otherwise have to lay out in compensation payments—L's losses, N_L—exceeds the fencing costs. Thus, the actual criterion determining the cattle-raiser's decision, $N_L > F$, is also the optimal one.

Some qualifications and implications

There are two aspects to the sort of analysis used so far in the discussion of policy. One is that to the extent that there is an external effect for which compensation is not paid, all Pareto-relevant opportunities might be exhausted by private trading. Secondly, there is the normative aspect which one writer expressed as follows:

> . . . when negotiation is possible, the case for government intervention is one of justice not of economic efficiency.[56]

This statement sheds more light on the limited nature of the economists' concept of efficiency than anything else, but the argument *is* consistent with an analysis which focuses its attention on efficiency. Let us first consider the validity of the first point.

Firstly, keeping fairly close to the spirit of the previous analysis there is the possibility that some sort of dissimulation on the part of either group could prevent the actual solution from according with the optimum. For example, if the party 'creating' an external diseconomy is obliged by law to pay compensation, then the injured party might try to exaggerate the size of its losses. In the agricultural example, the farmer might threaten to use unprofitable farming land. If the farmer gets *any* positive payment at all he will have gained. One point to bear in mind here[57] is that in long-run equilibrium the cattle-raiser's revenue will fall to a level just equal to the opportunity costs of all his factors of production—including capital and/or entrepreneurship. If then group L's demands are biting deeply into G's profits, G may eventually shift location. The farmer will have to play his cards carefully. Looking at the other sort of situation where no legal rights exist, G's activities are scaled down by group L's incentive payment. Again, presumably, G could dissimulate as to their own self-maximizing position. The

[56] *On Divergences between Private and Social Cost*, R. Turvey, *op. cit.*, p. 313.
[57] This is mentioned by Coase, *op. cit.*

cattle-raiser could threaten to use land which he normally would not consider.

A second, and much more important point, is that when large numbers of people are involved the possibility of bartering solutions obviously is considerably reduced. In the airport example it would be necessary for all the nearby inhabitants to collectively try to dissuade the airport authorities to change their mind. People are not without initiative in this respect—the pressure groups that emerge in the issue of London's third airport is a case in point—and local resident associations are a familiar institution. But whether one can think of this in terms of economic action is a different matter. In fact, for cases like airports and noise and the classic instances of smoke, one is very near to the difficulties of the Samuelsonian pure public good with its free-rider problem. Eliminating the scale of the activity or mitigating its effects simultaneously confers benefits on large numbers of people. To this extent each and every person likely to benefit will under-reveal their willingness to pay for these benefits. If the airport is not built or its size reduced, the benefit to local inhabitants in our previous terminology is indicated by, $N_L = E_L - O_L$. Now O_L in this example is zero. Further one could think of E_L as being the benefits summed over each member of the group, say $E_1 + E_2 + \dots E_m$. The 'cost' of achieving these benefits is indicated by the fall in profits of the airport authorities $(E_G - O_G)$. Thus, this 'cost' is worth undertaking if:

$$E_G - O_G < E_1 + E_2 + \dots E_m \tag{5.18}$$

which is exactly equivalent to the criterion implied in the public good equation (5.6); there the 'cost' is denoted by MC.

Thirdly, consider the feasibility of bartering in relation to the classic Pigovian tax/subsidy solutions. Even if one thinks of small numbers of people involved, bartering mechanisms seem a dubious analytic concept. It is true that where small businesses are involved, if there is not any bartering there may well still be resort, on the part of the injured person, to the legal system to exact compensation; Coase has provided many examples of this.[58] Even in the neighbour/neighbour externality examples—your wall cuts off the light from my house—people do resort to law occasionally. Do they also, where compensation is not likely to be forthcoming, try economic incentives in the mould of the bartering theory? Empirically this is, of course, difficult to answer since mere inaction may simply indicate that the external effects are not Pareto-relevant. But even in the case of small business, I am personally very doubtful that injured parties would think of such a line of action—only those demned economists would think of that! Some brief points about legal compensation will be made shortly, but let us now suppose bartering and compensation are ruled out. It is here that the tax/subsidy scheme becomes relevant. A brief return to Fig. 5.10 will demonstrate the main point. Think,

[58] See his article (*op. cit.*), sections V and VII in particular.

in other words, of the scale of G's activity as being the only option available. With no restrictions, G operates at S^1 and, in the absence of bartering, stays there. Clearly to restrict G to the optimal point, S, a tax would have to be levied on G's activity at a rate equal to the losses imposed on L. If one could differentiate between units, then the tax per unit would rise as G increased output.[59] G's marginal profit after tax is indicated by the dotted line AS. At output S, G's marginal tax is JS and his marginal net gain is zero. The taxes thus simulate the job that compensation payments had in the previous analysis. Of course, if the two groups are willing to barter then the tax solution could be wrong. At S there are opportunities for mutually beneficial trade. The value that L attaches to further reductions in the scale of G's activity is indicated by the ordinates of the N_L line. For reductions over the range SS^2 this exceeds the net profits *after tax*, that G would forgo. Thus L could bribe G to move back to K. In these circumstances the tax authorities would have to ensure that the *tax proceeds were passed on to the injured parties*, and to make it clear that these payments are only paid if G remains at point S. In other words, the taxes would really have to be compensation payments. This, incidentally, does raise a problem about what we mean by externality and at the end of this section we will re-consider our definitions.

The diagram does make it clear that *the tax must be calculated in relation to the injured parties' economic losses*, even if payment to the latter is unnecessary on allocative grounds, because of the absence of bartering possibilities. This is simply because, if the tax is not precisely related to group L's losses, G cannot be guaranteed to move to point S. This is clearly an important point and raises problems in calculating the tax.[60] Exactly the same issue arises in the case where compensation is required by law. If this compensation is not drawn up in relation to the sufferer's economic losses, there is no guarantee that an efficient solution will emerge. Suppose that, in the farming example, the cattle-raiser is required to meet the fall in the value of the potato crop. The latter has been denoted by E_L. It would then follow that the cattle-raiser's own equilibrium position will be where:

$$E_G - O_G = E_L \tag{5.19}$$

as opposed to the optimal solution of eq. (5.9). The two are only the same if O_L is zero, if, in other words, the factors of production used by the farmer have no opportunity costs. What could well happen here then is that, on experiencing the cattle's meanderings, the farmer, far from reducing his planned cultivation, will actually keep it at the same level to increase his compensation receipts. The cattle-raiser's herd becomes sub-optimal in size as he adjusts

[59] In the absence of 'income effects' the same result can be achieved by levying a uniform tax rate equivalent to the distance JS on Fig. 5.10.

[60] A similar point has been made by C. R. Plott in relation to a firm producing a good or service, X, and the firm incidentally also 'produces' smoke. The tax must be levied on smoke (or the input responsible for smoke) and not on X; if, however, there is only one input this does not matter. See 'Externalities and Corrective Taxes', *Economica*, February 1966.

to eq. (5.19) as opposed to eq. (5.9).[61] In practice, compensation payments may be completely unrelated, as one might expect, to concepts of economic efficiency. Coase provides some good examples of this, one of the nicest involved

> ... the case of Bass v Gregory ... [where] ... fresh air was drawn in ... [by a public house, the Jolly Anglers, through a well in a near-by yard and this well] ... facilitated the production of beer but foul air was expelled through the well which made life in the adjoining properties less pleasant. ... The judge ... held that the public house had ... legal right ... to the current of air ... by the 'doctrine of lost grant'. ... The economic problem was to decide which to choose: a lower cost of beer and worsened amenities in adjoining houses or a higher cost of beer and improved amenities. In deciding this question, the 'doctrine of lost grant' is about as relevant as the colour of the judges' eyes.[62]

What unfortunately emerges from all this is that appropriate government action is going to require an awful lot of information. In the simplest case of Fig. 5.10, the shape of the curves would have to be known to calculate the appropriate tax rate, assuming that it has been established that bartering will not take place. When alternative technological arrangements are introduced the problem becomes immense. However, such a setting is not uncommon in economic policy and rough guesses may have to be tried. While the optimum size of your fence may be 5 feet, no fence may be better than one of 20 feet. We are also trying to make some guesses at optimum airport location, which may well be better than leaving it to airport authorities themselves. Note also that, where external effects involve firms, it clearly becomes possible that mergers might be profitable because of the very existence of the external effect. In this way the externalities are 'internalized'.[63]

Finally, consider the problem of defining externality. It's a play on words since I think we know what the problem is about. If it is said—as Buchanan and Stubblebine have done and as we have suggested—that the Pigovian tax solution may be wrong, then one is perhaps being unfair on Pigou. His definition relates the concept of externality to situations where, for 'technical' considerations, trade does *not* take place. Our analysis suggests that the Pigovian tax could take one away from the efficient solution. But this only arises because trade does take place. Thus a recent contributor, S. K. Nath,[64] argues that the Pigovian solution is correct when an externality is defined

[61] In addition, in general the tax or compensation payments would have to be calculated with a view to how G would best maximize his position. For discussion of this see 'On the Theory of Optimum Externality', F. T. Dolbear, *AER*, March 1967.

[62] I have pieced this paragraph together from pp. 433–4 of Coase's article, *op. cit.*

[63] For more discussion of this see 'Externalities, Welfare and the Theory of Games', O. A. Davis and A. Whinston, *JPE*, June 1962.

[64] *A Re-Appraisal of Welfare Economics*, chapter IV, Routledge and Kegan Paul, 1969.

as *existing* only when trade has not taken place. (This does not exclude the possibility of its being Pareto irrelevant.) Remember Buchanan and Stubblebine were thinking of person *B*'s consumption of Y_1 entering person *A*'s utility function. If one uses Buchanan and Stubblebine's notation of *A*, *B*, and Y_1, then Nath's definition of externality, a sharper version of Pigou's, would read as follows. An

> ... externality ... exists *when* the utility of *A* is favourably affected by any change ... of *B*'s consumptions of Y_1 *and when A* does *not* make an appropriate payment of *B* for this, so that *B* reaches his equilibrium ... by equating the market price of Y_1 with *only* the marginal utility in money terms to *himself* of his consumption of it. However if *A* and *B* are able to trade, and do trade with each other ... then there is *no* externality ...[65]

Thus Nath is, in a way, fairer to Pigou. The key difference between the two sets of writers is that, on the one hand, Buchanan and Stubblebine implicitly presuppose that when there is interdependence (i.e., their definition of an externality *existing*) there is *a priori* likely to be difficulties in trade. Nath's formulation does not make this presumption; for him an externality exists only when, with interdependence, no trade has taken place. On balance, the Buchanan and Stubblebine approach seems better since by pre-supposing trade difficulties it sheds light on the way various possible mechanisms, including bartering, taxes, and compensation, can take one to a Pareto efficient solution.[66]

The measures of gain and loss

In analysing optimal outcomes, the criterion used has simply been that, for any change, the gain should exceed the loss or, more precisely, that the maximum that the potential gainers are prepared to pay for the change exceeds the minimum compensation required by the losers. It has, further, so far been assumed implicitly that this measure of gain is equivalent to the compensation the gainers would require if they had to forgo the change, and that the measure of loss was equivalent to the maximum the potential losers would be prepared to pay to prevent the change taking place. In other words, the assumption of a unique measure for the gains and losses ensures

[65] This is a straight quote from Nath (p. 68) replacing *g*, *r*, and X_k by *A*,*B*, and Y_1 respectively; the emphasis is his.

[66] E. J. Mishan, has another definition.

> 'External effects may be said to arise where relevant effects of production or welfare go wholly or partially unpriced.'

Reflections on Recent Developments in the Concept of External Effects, *op. cit.* p. 6. This seems to be somewhere in between the other two sets of authors, in that the reference to pricing implies that there certainly is not a normal market for this service.

that the question 'could the gainers overcompensate the losers?' is the same as asking 'could the losers bribe the gainers to forgo the change?' This assumption was crucial in demonstrating that, when bartering is possible, the absence or presence of legal rights did not affect the actual outcome. The analysis of chapter 3 made it clear that there need not be this uniqueness in the measures, if the change in question leads to sizeable real income changes. The issue is *not* unimportant. If, for example, the minimum compensation needed by local families to put up with the withdrawal of their recreational facilities is much greater—as we shall demonstrate—than the maximum amount of money they are prepared to pay to try and keep them then, clearly, the way that rights are granted by the legal system is going to be extremely important in determining the actual outcome. Further, if any policy moves are made in relation to external effects then, in many cases, this will not simply be a routine operating problem but a major decision; airports, smoke abatement schemes, and so on make the point. It then becomes important to ascertain relevant measures and to recognize that, if the change is sizeable, there could be this non-uniqueness in the measures. And finally, should we decide to take an interest in the identity of the parties involved—whether the potential losers are a low-income group for example—the issue becomes doubly important.

An important characteristic of external effects, which aids understanding of this issue, is that the parties in question are consuming or producing some commodity or service for which, for one reason or another, technical considerations are likely to inhibit normal market trading. The cattle-raiser is effectively using the farmer's land; the children of the local families are allowed by the municipal authority to use land without payment. Although more difficult to visualize, the same point applies to the airport's use of (initially noise-less) air and Jones' use of (fume-less) air. The 'efficiency' considerations of the previous section have been concerned to discover what value the affected parties attach to this commodity, and the 'efficiency criterion' (gains > loss) allocates it to that party whose valuation is greater. When this allocation takes place it could have an important effect on the parties' real incomes. If residents lose their quietness because of the airport they could be significantly worse off. When we, therefore, inquire what valuation the parties' attach to this commodity the answer may well depend on whether we pose the question 'before' or 'after'. In other words it is the *quantity equilibrating and compensating income variations* that are the measures in question (see chapter 3, pp. 66, 67, 76–82).

When, for example, we ask people located near to the likely airport site what they are prepared to pay to prevent the airport being located there, we are effectively asking them to attach a value to the quietness, on the assumption that the airport *is already there.* When they are asked what compensation they would need should the airport be built, the question is effectively posed in a situation where they are enjoying the solitude of no airport. Thus, their welfare level is higher in the second circumstance than the first. On the usual assumption that a consumer's valuation of normal goods, i.e., non-inferior goods, is higher, the higher is his real income level (see chapter 3, p. 66), then his valuation of quietness is higher in the second situation than the first. The minimum compensation he requires for having the airport is greater than the amount of money he is prepared to pay to avoid it.[67] We might denote these two measures for the potential losers as N_{CL} and N_{EL}, respectively, where N_{CL}, compensation required, exceeds the maximum they are prepared to pay to try to prevent the change. The latter, N_{EL}, is the *equilibrating income variation* in that it indicates what adjustment one would have to make to the person's money income, should the change—unfavourable in this instance—not take place, in order that his welfare is at the same level that it would have been if the change *had* taken place. The N_{EL} thus involves, in this instance, taking money from him. By similar reasoning for the potential gainers, the compensating income variation, N_{CG},—the maximum Jones is prepared to pay to be allowed to brew his beer—is less than the minimum they require if they do not undertake the activity, N_{EG}. We thus have:

$$N_{EG} > N_{CG} \quad \text{and} \quad N_{CL} > N_{EL} \tag{5.20}$$

The main issues arising from this can be best considered diagrammatically. Figure 5.11 has been constructed in a similar manner to Fig. 5.10 save that there are now two measures of *G*'s marginal gain and two measures of marginal loss.[68] Consider first of all the relationship between the four measures in the range of output 0 to T^1. The points that can be made about scale increases in this range apply equally to any changes—including those of the once-and-for-all variety. The key characteristic is that the maximum the potential gainers are prepared to pay to have the change (N_{CG}), exceeds the minimum compensation required by the losers (N_{CL}) and in addition $N_{EG} > N_{EL}$—the losers could not bribe the gainers to forgo such changes. For this type of change, the two tests do not give contradictory results. Similarly, for those sorts of changes the economic effects of which are typified by the scale of *G*'s activity from T^3 to T^4, the gainers cannot compensate the

[67] Few writers have *explicitly* considered the problems of real income changes nor, moreover the distributional matters referred to in the next section. Mishan in his *AER* 1961 article, *op. cit.*, and his book *Costs of Economic Growth*, *op. cit.*, is an important exception. Those readers having difficulties in visualizing the two situations under which the money measures are ascertained might find the following helpful. Suppose I have a ticket for a UK/US athletics match at White City. You want to go but have not got a ticket and all alternative sources, including the touts, have yielded nothing. Now, we may inquire about the economic value of the ticket to you. Its face quoted price is irrelevant; that is an historic cost—or bygones are bygones as the economist would put it. Suppose you offer me 10s. for it, this amount being the maximum you are prepared to pay for it. Now, suppose I actually give you the ticket free. A few minutes later someone tries to buy it from you. How much would you want? The proposition in the text implies that—granted that athletics matches constitute a 'normal' good—the minimum compensation you require for giving up the ticket is greater than 10s. For an indifference curve treatment of this point see Mishan's *AER*, 1961 article, *op. cit.*

[68] Cf. the diagram in Mishan, *AER*, 1961, *op. cit.*

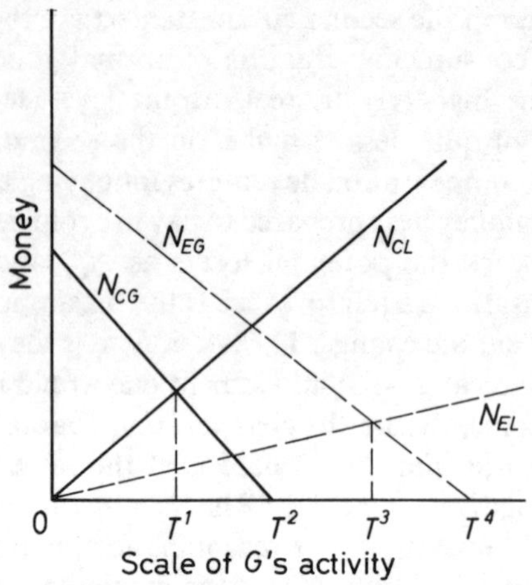

FIG. 5.11

losers and, moreover, the losers could bribe the gainers to forgo the change ($N_{EL} > N_{EG}$); or, putting it another way, by reducing scale in this range the gainers from such a change (group *L*) could compensate the losers (group *G*). This means then that, if the legal system does not give group *L* any rights, then *G* would normally try to produce at T^4; to the extent that group *L* can, and are willing to, barter, the scale of *G*'s activity would be pushed back to T^3. If, on the other hand, the law requires *G* to compensate, or if a tax is levied equivalent to *L*'s losses, then *G* would undertake all those output increases in the range 0 to T^1, but would actually stop at T^1. It follows that, when the changes in question give rise to sizeable real-income effects, *the actual outcome* is *affected by the legal system.* When compensation is required *G* will not expand beyond T^1 because thereafter $N_{CG} < N_{CL}$; if there are no such legal restrictions, *L* will not be able to reduce *G*'s activities below T^3 for in the range T^1 to T^3, $N_{EL} < N_{EG}$. *Moreover, it is not clear, given these possibilities, what is the optimum scale.* If 'optimum' is defined in relation to the 'gainers can compensate losers' test, then it depends on whether one regards *O* or T^4 as the normal starting point. If the latter then T^3 is the optimum; if the former, T^1 is the optimum. Moreover, what does 'normal starting point' mean? One could think of it in terms of the existing set of regards 0 or T^4 as the normal starting point. If the latter then T^3 is the 'normal starting point'; if compensation is already written into the existing legal system then 0 becomes the 'normal starting point'. But the existing set of property rights does not have any necessary significance for allocative economics—as Coase's case law studies make clear. Of course, one could perhaps come to a determinate decision about changes similar to those in the T^1T^3 range, if one had some preferences concerning the affected parties. The distributional issue is made explicit, but it has a much wider significance.

5.7 Distributional factors

Do it if the gains exceed the loss irrespective of whether the losers are compensated. That is the criterion implied in the 'efficient solutions' which have dominated the discussion in this chapter. The acceptability of this sort of criterion depends on the sort of issues discussed in chapters 3 and 4. It depends, among other things, on the 'proper' state of income distribution and on the feasibility of achieving this state by means other than 'tampering' with the allocation of resources. Granted feasibility problems, how could one allow for distributional issues in the policy proposals for external effects? Implied in the discussion of the previous chapter is the view that there are certain decisions which allow one to introduce distributional considerations fairly easily. Some of the examples of external effects would appear to fit into this category. Many public sector schemes, like the granting of site rights to airport authorities or the construction of airports when this activity is publicly owned; the drawing-up of zoning plans; smoke abatement schemes; flood-relief programmes; etc., involve fairly major once-and-for-all decisions where distributional considerations could be incorporated. In addition, where solutions involve the permanent introduction of pricing schemes, e.g., a Ministry of Roads selling road space, or meter schemes for water supply, there also should income distribution effects be calculated and considered, in our opinion.

We can, here, briefly indicate some of the issues involved. Assuming bartering solutions are not likely to emerge, and provisionally assuming unique measures for the gains and losses involved, suppose that gains exceed losses in the conventional way. The policy proposals might then be confronted with the following two questions:

(a) Are the losers compensated? If the policy proposals involve an affirmative answer, this itself, in the case of external diseconomies, would constitute a major change in our existing ways of life.

(b) If the losers are not compensated, do they constitute a low-income group in the economy? If they do, one would want to strongly query the policy proposals. Of course one has a problem in defining who the losers are. Do building firms have an unalienable right to belch dust all round the place? Do we call them 'the losers' to the extent that this external effect is reduced? Or is a zero fog to be the 'norm', in which case it is the bleary-eyed natives who are the losers. Presumably most of us would want to take the second view for the reason that it is beyond the natives' control and this, certainly, is the assumption behind questions (a) and (b).

Distributional factors become particularly relevant in instances where, because of the magnitude of the external effect, there are no unique measures of gains and losses. The three policy criteria considered in chapter 4 become relevant. That is, some relevant tests to which the policy proposals could be submitted are:

(a) Can the gainers 'overcompensate' the losers and do they compensate them?
(b) Can the gainers compensate the losers and is the distributional effect, in the absence of compensation, favourable?
(c) Is it impossible for the losers to bribe the gainers to forgo the change, and, in the absence of compensation, is the distributional effect favourable.

Activities, like those in the range of scale 0 to T^1, in Fig. 5.11, which give rise to external effects, would be warranted if the law required compensation, on the grounds that they meet criterion (a). If the law does not guarantee compensation but the gainers could be roughly classified as poor and the losers as rich, then these activities would be warranted on the basis of criterion (b). If the distributional effect were unfavourable—the roles are reversed—the acceptability of the change becomes questionable even though 'gain' exceeds 'loss'. Where the gainers are the rich then we may have to reject some of the 'efficient' solutions. However if, for activities like those in the range of output T^3T^4, the gainers are the rich, then such activities meet neither criterion (b) nor criterion (c). Here a problem would arise if the gainers were the poor. For those external effects, typified by output increases in the range T^1 to T^3, where the 'efficiency' tests contradict, distributional considerations can bring a determinateness to optimality. If the distributional effect is favourable, then such activities would be warranted on the basis of criterion (c), since $N_{EG} > N_{EL}$ for such changes. This, incidentally, means that if the law requires compensation, the *actual outcome would not be optimal* since for such activities the gainers cannot compensate the losers and, thus, group G would not undertake them. Similarly, if the distributional effect is unfavourable—the gainers are the rich and the losers are the poor— and there are no legal safeguards for compensation, the actual outcome will not be optimal, since G would undertake these activities despite the fact that no compensation to the poor is paid and that in any case the poor's required compensation exceeds the maximum the rich are prepared to pay to undertake the change. There are clearly a number of other situations which the reader could fruitfully analyse with the techniques suggested here.

6. The planning horizon and time-stream aspects of public investment

6.1 Introduction

The analysis of resource allocation has, up to this stage in the book, been related to a rather curious sort of world. In considering the basic fundamentals in chapter 2, it was assumed that there was a large number of individuals whose welfare was to be maximized in some sense. The problems were considered through the eyes of some benevolent dictator or omniscient economist, and we saw that a unique solution distribution of resources necessitated some explicit weighting system to 'add' the welfares of different people; formally, a social welfare function had to be introduced. What was particularly restrictive was the fact that, implicitly, only one slice of time, such as 'this year', was considered; the analysis was quite adequate if the Day of Judgement was expected to occur for everyone at the end of 'this year'. It is the purpose of this chapter to explore some of the implications of dropping this assumption.

Allowing for something called 'the future', suggests that the welfare of each individual will now be affected by his expectation of producing and consuming, not only this year, but next year, the year after, and so on. The goods that enter his utility function should now be given a time-dimension; a simple illustration would be where a consumer has but two consumption possibilities, bread this year (y_0) and bread next year (y_1); his welfare function could then be written as $U = U(y_0, y_1)$. Further, recognition must be paid to the possibility that new members of the community will be born sometime in the future. This suggests another problem which we have slurred over so far. Are the individuals to which the previous analysis related to be viewed as including children making decisions on their own consumption and production? Generally, we shall assume that the decision-takers are heads of households, and the consumption patterns of the constituent members of the household are included in the decision-takers' utility functions. But the children will grow up and their future welfare when they become decision-takers—age 16, 17, 18—must be considered. A second general possibility that emerges when 'the future' is considered, is the economic potentiality of methods of production involving using factor services this year to produce goods which can produce further goods next year and thereafter. It is this possibility of the production of capital that enlarges the content of this chapter since, of course, much of public expenditure involves the use of capital.

Within our spectrum now are not simply the *m* individuals of today and their dependants, but tomorrow's adults and tomorrow's children. A quite fundamental problem has now to be faced, namely, precisely *whose* welfare is to be maximized?; who is to be included in the maximand? We call this fundamental since it is something on which our mythical benevolent dictator or omniscient economist has to make a decision. Is the welfare of the generation living from 2040–2109 to be embraced in the maximand as well as the present generation. There is no fundamental truth to be uncovered here; to say that the expected population into infinity is to be included is simply one possible answer; but it is basically of no different nature to declaring for the present generation. Whatever group is demarcated the choice is essentially a value judgement.[1] It is similar to the sort of value judgement involved in the simple model where a weighting system had to be drawn up to pinpoint a solution to the resource allocation problem. In fact, this new problem is also one involving the distribution of welfare—this time as between generations. The demarcation decision does have an effect on the required distribution of resources and, to see this, let us consider a very simple case.

Suppose, in contrast to the above points, that the existing population comprises *m* adults. 'This year' is 1970 and the omniscient economist assumes that by the year 2040 all of the *m* persons will have died. Neither the omniscient economist nor the individuals themselves know precisely when, in the intervening period, any one person will die, but all assume that, for them, the Day of Judgement will not be beyond the last day of 2039. However, the omniscient economist is also, fortunately, relatively immortal and he knows that in 2040 a new group of persons will suddenly spring to life.[2] Moreover, they are all adults and their maximum expectation of life is a further seventy years; we let the omniscient economist pass away also in 2109! Now we can, without specifying the logic of this very precisely, suggest that the methods of production and the distribution of resources and welfare in 1970, in the next year, and thereafter, will depend, concerned as the omniscient economist is to maximize welfare, on whether one or both generations are included in the maximand. If, for example, it is simply the first group that is of interest then it is likely that the implications of the welfare maximization process would be that at the end of 2039 all physical capital in the economy would be

[1] Cf. J. De Graaf *Theoretical Welfare Economics,* chapter VI, Cambridge University Press, 1957.

[2] Cf. The models in S. A. Marglin's 'The Social Rate of Discount and the Optimal Rate of Investment', *QJE*, February 1963.

practically exhausted. If assets are constructed during the period 1970–2039, then that part of their services which would accrue after the terminal date is completely irrelevant in determining the economic worth of such assets, since those people whose welfare is being maximized could not unfortunately enjoy such services. With this creed, the new generation would start from scratch. The general point then is that, assuming scarcity of resources prevails throughout, whatever is decided about the present generation's welfare depends on whether the welfare of future generations is to be included in the maximand.

Some may object to this conclusion—even ignoring the simplified nature of the model—on the following grounds. The welfare maximand used in the analysis implicitly is assumed to be an individualistic one; that is the welfare of any one person is to be considered in relation to his own individual preferences. In this case, an individual's utility function may contain—as an argument—provision for future generations. This could take the form either of a provision for their children—dropping one of the simplifications of the model—or an altruistic desire to see the next generation as a whole starting with at least *some* roads, steel plant, mineral resources, etc. To the extent that this is empirically valid, some of the worries about future generations are reduced. In fact, there are a number of other factors that need discussing in this context and this will be done later. But the basic value judgement is still inescapable. Various social systems deal with the time-dimension problem in various ways; implicit in these solutions is the catering for the welfare of particular individuals. To assess whether this is 'good' or 'bad' necessitates our having, or the government having, a benchmark for comparison. This is the purpose of the maximand and whether the solution of any given type of social system is 'good' will, therefore, depend on which individuals' welfare have been included in the government's maximand.

Plan of chapter

As before, we shall be examining market devices for dealing with these problems. The arguments can become complex and the following procedure is used here. First of all the simple model outlined above will be retained. Further, we shall take the first generation (1970–2039) as the people whose welfare is to be maximized, and assume that only their own consumption of goods enters their utility functions. The necessary conditions for welfare maximization that emerge in this setting are of a similar kind to those discussed before in chapter 2, but now with a time dimension. Moreover they are, given certain further simplifying assumptions to be made shortly, appropriable by a market system whether of the private ownership or public ownership variety. In this context, certain conventional decision rules can be derived for a public enterprise's use of capital. Section 6.3, though retaining the idea of maximizing the welfare of the present generation, relaxes the simplifying assumptions of the model and some important points about market failure in the context of investment decisions is discussed. Section 6.4 then reverts to the problem discussed in this introduction—precisely what weighting should governments or planners give to the welfare of different generations.

6.2 The time dimension of Pareto efficiency

The basic model in mind differs from that used in chapters 2 and 3 in the following way. In their utility functions, individuals—now to be regarded as adults with no children—have commodities and factor services relating to each of the seventy years from 1970 onwards. Similarly, there are firms each of whose production functions include these items; in addition, the production functions will include capital goods as both inputs, to the extent that they will be used to produce future commodities, and outputs, to the extent that other factor services are used to produce such capital goods. Granted, then, some system of weighting one individual's welfare against another, a solution distribution of resources for each of the seventy years can be determined. This, then, is how the benevolent dictator would proceed, and we shall assume that he has perfect knowledge of the future so that he can make investment decisions without much difficulty. Further, in line with previous analysis, the weighting system used i.e., the social welfare function, is assumed to sanction all Pareto improvements. It then follows that a set of necessary Pareto conditions can be derived somewhat similar to those discussed before. Since the achievement of Pareto efficiency is one of the policy objectives to which we think public expenditure decisions can be directed, then this concept will be examined. As before, however, it is important to remember there is nothing inherently desirable about this and the decision rules that emerge can only play the same role as those discussed in the earlier chapters—the price/marginal cost rule, for example.

We, therefore, proceed by first of all setting out the Pareto conditions. Emanating from these are the set of required price features which are examined. Thirdly, the required behavioural rules and institutions are specified in the context of both privately- and publicly-owned resources. Thus, the basic plan is similar to that used for the simple model of the earlier chapters. However, it would be rather tedious to set out the analysis in the same formal detail and so the key features only will be examined.

Before discussing these features two background points need to be made. Firstly, the production of capital goods is effected by the use now of factor services which, if the economy is fully employed, could otherwise have produced consumption goods now. Whether or not it is worthwhile to use such roundabout methods of production clearly, therefore, depends on a balancing of the gain in future consumption goods against the loss of present-day consumption goods. What *will* be assumed is that there are certain products for which such production methods do give a net positive yield in the sense that, giving one loaf tomorrow the same weight as one loaf today, the gain in future goods more than makes up for the loss of present goods. We shall, however, be skating over any discussion of the factors that determine the degree of capital usage in the economy; these and other problems in capital theory are too complex for satisfactory treatment in this text.

The assumption of a net positive yield attainable by some capital using production methods does not imply that such methods are desirable in the welfare sense. This can only be answered by looking at how the population weights the gain and loss involved, and the background to this constitutes the second introductory point. In consumer demand theory it is often assumed that goods similar in every respect other than the date of consumption are not identical goods for the individual. More precisely, the assumption is that individuals will, other things being equal, prefer present goods (y_0) to future goods (y_1). This, therefore, implies that U_{y0}/U_{y_1} exceeds unity, where U_{y_0}, etc., is the person's marginal utility from extra bread this year. A traditional way of expressing this is to say that the consumer has a positive-time preference for the present.[3] A *rate* of time preference is defined in the following way. If present goods are surrendered, Δy_0, then the future goods necessary to compensate for this, Δy_1, will be numerically greater. The size of this difference when expressed as a proportion of the present-day goods given up constitutes the time preference rate. Denoting the latter as r_t we have:

$$r_t = [(\Delta y_1 - \Delta y_0)/\Delta y_0]_c \tag{6.1}$$

Here and henceforth the subscript c is used simply to indicate that we are talking about the person sector's consumption decisions. Now, since $U_{y0}/U_{y_1} = (\Delta y_1/\Delta y_0)_c$ then[4]

$$U_{y0}/U_{y_1} = 1 + r_t \tag{6.2}$$

A positive value for r_t is often justified on the grounds that people dislike waiting or are impatient to spend, so that to give up one loaf this year requires more than one loaf in compensation next year. But why are people impatient? One reason might be that individuals are uncertain about what consumption goods they are going to get next year. This is a fair point, but is ruled out at this stage because, firstly, the problem in hand is one for the benevolent dictator and he, by assumption, has perfect knowledge of the future. Secondly, in examining whether market systems can achieve the efficient solutions to the overall problem it will be assumed, provisionally,

[3] It needs noting that if the view is taken that one cannot talk about a person's utility in any meaningful sense, then the concept of time preference is also meaningless. This is but one aspect of a general problem which was discussed in chapter 2; again, however, we feel that such phrases aid understanding of the underlying ideas and they are therefore retained for this reason.

[4] Strictly speaking, since $(\Delta y_1/\Delta y_0)_c$ will normally be negative, then the substitution rate will be equal to $(-)(1+r_t)$.

that individuals have perfect knowledge of the future. In the absence of the factor of uncertainty, two arguments have been advanced to suggest individuals would still have a positive time preference. One point is that the time of death is not known with certainty. Although the benevolent dictator knows what consumption goods an individual would receive in any year within the assumed time-span, he is not certain that this person will be there to enjoy them. The chances that the individual will die before the terminal date can lead to a positive time preference rate. Eckstein has in fact suggested that we could derive a measure for r_t based on the probability of not surviving the next year. For the USA, the latter range from 0·04 for those who have not advanced beyond their early teens to 7·45 for those people aged 80 to 84.

> Or to cite a long-run figure, a twenty-year-old person looking ahead to a date fifty years away should discount at an average annual rate of 0·09 per cent.[5]

It is assumed in the basic model used here that a positive time preference is held by consumers and the mortality issue is one factor assumed to work in this direction. Another factor that has been advanced, working in the same way, arises when the individual has an expectation of a rising welfare level over time. Taken in conjunction with an assumption of diminishing marginal utility of real income, this would imply again that U_{y_0}/U_{y_1} exceeds unity and the substitution rate would then imply a positive time preference rate. One final point on time preference can be noted. The analysis here rests essentially on individual preferences; it is not a government imposed rate or a 'planner's time preference' in the sense of reflecting any social weighting of present and future; this possibility is however explored in section 6.4. In summary, the two background points concerning capitalistic production methods and time preference imply that another 'trade-off' relationship is involved in our basic welfare theory, namely, labour produced jam today or machine produced jam tomorrow; we are now in a position to spell this out.

The pure efficiency conditions

If any two years within the model's time-span of seventy years are taken, most of the insights into the inter-temporal Pareto conditions can be adequately presented. We shall do this and, further, take the two years 'this year' (1970) and 'next year'. Looking at the seventy years simultaneously is a messy procedure quite unnecessary at this stage, but the multi-period aspects will be discussed in a later section. Moreover, the following simple schedule of

[5] 'A Survey of the Theory of Public Expenditure Criteria', O. Eckstein. Last chapter in *Public Finances: Needs, Sources and Utilisation*, p. 457, NBER, Princeton, 1961, The data relates to 1950 and the source is the UN.

'goods' will be sufficient to highlight the key features. There will be but two consumption goods, y_0 and y_1 as described before. There is 'this year' only one class of factor service, labour (l); 'next year' it is assumed for simplicity that no labour services are available; anticipating some of the market models this implies no income from labour services next year. Factor services next year come from a capital good (j) which is constructed this year.

There are, then, the three Pareto conditions for exchange, production, and the general optimum. In examining the exchange condition earlier on in this book, it was seen that any given stock of goods could not be optimally organized if the marginal substitution rate between any two goods was not the same for all consumers. In the present context it is therefore required that the ratio U_{y_0}/U_{y_1} be the same for all the m individuals, otherwise Pareto relevant redistributions of goods are possible; that is, some people could be made better off without others suffering. Figure 6.1 introduces some diagram-

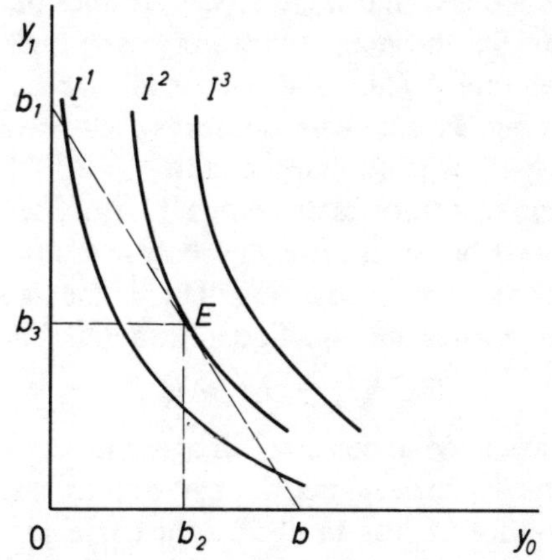

FIG. 6.1

matic techniques which, throughout, will prove helpful in illustrating some of the problems. A consumer's utility function is represented by the indifference lines I^1, I^2, etc. With y_1 and y_0 on the axes, the slope of an indifference curve at a point such as E, constitutes $(\Delta y_1/\Delta y_0)_c$. Moreover, recalling eq. (6.2), the requirement that the slope of the indifference curve at the consumption point be the same for all consumers, implies that there should be a common time preference rate.[6] If all possibilities were to be allowed for, one would have to cater for labour services entering the utility function and the three sub-conditions of exchange[7] could be derived. But there should be no need to spell this out.

[6] If at any point such as E on Fig. 6.1, the time-preference rate is assumed to be positive, then diagrammatically the slope of the indifference curve should exceed 45° since it is equal to $-(1+r_t)$.

[7] Cf. the point mentioned on p. 32, that in the general case there are effectively nine Pareto conditions.

Capital goods are not affected by the exchange conditions because they do not enter preference functions. They are affected by the Pareto production conditions which, recalling chapters 2 and 3, seek to ensure that resources are so distributed between firms that the output of no commodity can be increased without decreasing that of another, and that the use of no input can be decreased without increasing the use of another. This requires, first of all, that the rate at which it is technically possible to transform labour into the capital good should be the same in all firms effecting such a transformation. Let us denote such a rate as $\Delta j/\Delta l$, remembering throughout that we are referring now to production (and not exchange rates in the person sector). Similarly, it is also required that the production transformation rates, $\Delta l/\Delta y_0$ and $\Delta y_1/\Delta j$, are required to be common over the production sector. Within any one firm these three transformation rates imply an important fourth one, namely $\Delta y_1/\Delta y_0$, and this will also be common over firms if the other ones are.[8] In fact, even if our firm does not itself produce the capital good but simply uses it as input for the manufacture of next year's bread, provided that the transformation rate, $\Delta j/\Delta l$, is the same in all places where such capital goods are produced, then the rate between this year's bread and next year's will still be common over the production sector.

The general optimum condition is met when it is not possible, by changing the distribution of goods between firms and between individuals, to render anyone better off without others suffering. This is met when the technical and subjective switching rates are equalized; formally, that:

$$U_{y_0}/U_{y_1} = \Delta y_1/\Delta y_0 \tag{6.3}$$

where both ratios are assumed to be common over the person and production sectors respectively. In two dimensions, this can be illustrated if a production possibility line is introduced. Thus, in Fig. 6.2 the curve qq^1 is taken to represent the maximal produceable quantities of y_0 and y_1, given an assumed fixed stock of labour. It, therefore, incorporates information about the transformation possibilities between the four 'goods' y_0, l, j, and y_1, and its slope represents the rate of transformation between y_0 and y_1.

The map C^1, C^2, etc., constitutes a particular community indifference map, movements up which represent Pareto improvements; at M, the possibilities of such improvements are exhausted and here the general optimum condition is met. Equation (6.3) is characterized on the diagram by the tangency of the production and indifference lines.[9] The solution point M thus implies a

[8] That is: $\Delta y_l/\Delta y_0 = (\Delta y_1/\Delta j)\times(\Delta j/\Delta l)\times(\Delta l/\Delta y_0)$.
Those who have read the more rigorous parts of chapter 2 and 3 will realize that we are now implying a production function for a firm of the form $F(l,y_0,j,y_1) = O$. Denoting the partial derivature of this function with respect to j as F_j, etc., then the transformation rate $\Delta y_1/\Delta j$ would be written as F_j/F_{y_1}. The above equation would then read:

$$F_{y_0}/F_{y_1} = (F_j/F_{y_1})\times(F_l/F_j)\times(F_{y_0}/F_l).$$

[9] Those readers feeling somewhat lost with the terminology should re-read chapter 2, particularly pp. 13–26.

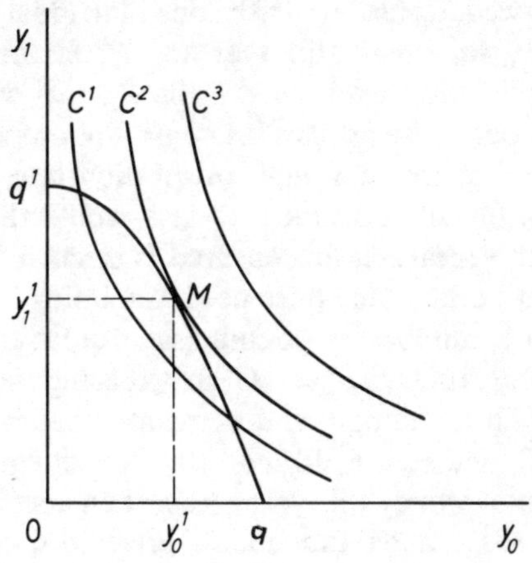

FIG. 6.2

particular distribution of consumption over time namely y_0^1 of bread this year and y_1^1 next year. But, of course, there is nothing unique about the point M since it depends on the use of a *particular* community indifference map; it depends, as we were at pains to point out in chapter 2, on the specific distribution of welfare as between individuals, implied by this map. One final point on the pure efficiency conditions. In the spirit of the time preference rate in the person sector, one might conceive of a rate of return to the use of capital on the production side. Let us define such a rate as $(\Delta y_1 - \Delta y_0)/\Delta y_0$, where the y's now refer to production, and denote it by R_{y_1, y_0}. The transformation rate, $\Delta y_1/\Delta y_0$, is therefore equal to $(1+R_{y_1, y_0})$. It follows, bearing in mind eq. (6.2), that the general optimum condition, eq. (6.3), is equivalent to:[10]

$$r_t = R_{y_1, y_0} \tag{6.4}$$

Pareto efficiency requires that the distribution of resources be so arranged that the rate of return from using capitalistic production methods is, on the margin, just equal to individuals' rate of time preference. The criterion for balancing future gains against present sacrifices has been derived.

Required price features

Following the basic plan, the features of the price system in a money economy which correspond to the 'real' exchange rates of the previous section, can

[10] The notation used here and in most of this chapter omits labels for persons and firms. But the text itself should make it clear under what circumstances r_t, for example, is referring to an individual, or to some common time-preference rate. To spell out the labels would make the exposition unnecessarily complicated.

now be briefly reviewed. Consider, firstly, one individual in the person sector faced with prices P_0 for bread this year and P_1 for bread next year. The exchange condition would then be met if these prices were the same for all persons and if each person so adjusts his consumption pattern that the price ratio, P_0/P_1, is equal to the marginal substitution rate, U_{y0}/U_{y1}. For if the prices are the same for all consumers so also would the substitution rates be the same. How these features are 'ensured' is discussed in the next section. One very important point which does need examining is the meaning of the prices. P_0 refers to a number of pounds (say 10) incurrable this year; P_1 refers to pounds incurrable next year. Clearly this number could be different because of changes in the supply and demand situation for bread. Even if they are the same, P_1 and P_0 (i.e., 10_0 and 10_1) are not equivalent. The reason is that the provision of money this year rather than next is a service in scarce supply; in other words, granted individuals' preference for present consumption and granted the superiority of some capitalistic production methods requiring finance this year, the supply of funds this year is a service in scarce supply and would therefore normally command a price; this price is the ruling interest rate in the market for the scarce service, the money market. It follows that £10 now is equivalent to £10$(1+r_m)$ next year, r_m being the market rate of interest. Further, £10 next year is equivalent to £10/$(1+r_m)$ this year; the latter amount is usually called the *present value* of £10 incurrable or receivable next year; the ratio $1/(1+r_m)$ is a *discount rate* which converts future items into equivalent present values. Returning to our main theme, it follows, assuming the absolute price of bread is the same in both years, that[11] $P_0 = P_1(1+r_m)$. The price ratio is thus equal to $(1+r_m)$ and, therefore, remembering that $U_{y0}/U_{y1} = 1+r_t$, the required price features in the person sector are:

$$r_m = r_t \tag{6.5}$$

In other words, if commodity prices are the same for all persons, then it is required that the rate of interest be the same for all persons and that each individual adjusts his consumption and saving decisions so that eq. (6.5) is satisfied.

In the production sector the prices of all 'goods' would have to be the same in all firms so that if, for any pair of goods, each firm makes output/input adjustments so that the price ratio is equal to the transformation rate, then such rates would, as required, be common over the production sector. If the reader recalls the analysis in chapter 3, this would imply that in the production of this year's bread from labour services, the familiar price/marginal cost rule should be pursued. A similar rule applies for those firms producing capital goods from labour and for that sector using capital goods as an input in the production of next year's bread. If these rules are followed then an import-

[11] To make the issue quite clear suppose the interest rate is 20 per cent. The equality then indicates that £10 incurred this year is equivalent to £12 incurred next year.

ant implication concerns the relationship between bread this year and next year; the rules would imply the following price feature:

$$P_0/P_1 = \Delta y_1/\Delta y_0 \tag{6.6}$$

This can be re-arranged to give a familiar 'investment' rule:

$$r_m = R_{y_1,\, y_0} \tag{6.7}$$

Namely, that for the marginal 'project', the rate of return in the production sector should just equal the rate of interest. Finally, if the interest rate and the price of goods are the same in both the production and the person sector, then the rate of return will be equal to consumers' time preference rate. The general optimum condition, eq. (6.4), will have been met.

Privately owned resources

We are now in a position to examine the behavioural rules required in a money economy for the achievement of Pareto efficiency. It is the derivation of public investment rules—rules to guide a public agency's use of capital—that is the main aim, but it is useful to first of all consider how the above price features are appropriable by a private market system. In fact the person sector's behaviour is something common to both types of situation. It is required, firstly, that not only the prices of goods but also the rate of interest should be the same for all the *m* individuals in the economy. This will be met if there is perfect competition between them in all markets including the capital market. Clearly, the required features of the capital market appear very restrictive. But the uniform interest rate only arises because of the simplifications of the model. Nevertheless, the perfectness of the market is something we shall have cause to call into question later on. Given this, it should now be fairly obvious that it is necessary for consumers to maximize utility in order that eq. (6.5) is realized. This can be illustrated in Fig. 6.1 where the consumer can be thought of as having an income in the first year equivalent to Ob of the consumption good y_0. If he refrains from buying such goods, then he can earn interest on the saving; this, together with the savings, is returnable next year. The budget line bb_1 thus indicates the maximum purchaseable quantities of y_0 and y_1, given the consumer's income, prices, and the rate of interest. The slope is equal to $(1+r_m)$ and the line itself is one of constant present value;[12] all combinations on bb_1 have a present value equivalent to Ob of current consumption goods. Utility is maximized at E with bb_2 savings financing Ob_3 consumption next year. E is characterized by the equality of the slopes of the budget and indifference lines, and so eq. (6.5) is guaranteed.

[12] Keeping to the assumption of the same prices for bread this year and next year let us denote the constant present value by C, in which case the equation of the budget line is $y_0P_0+y_1P_1-C = 0$. If the consumer maximizes $U(y_1y_0)$ subject to this constraint, then the first-order conditions can be shown to imply eq. (6.5).

In the simplified version of the production sector used so far, there are three outputs, namely capital goods plus two 'kinds' of bread. The requirement that these outputs be expanded until price equals marginal cost, necessitates, in a system of private ownership, free mobility of factors, perfect markets, and profit maximization by the producing firms. As we demonstrated in the previous section this will guarantee that the overall rate of return in the production sector between next year's consumption goods and this year's, will, on the margin, be just equal to the rate of interest. This is simply a translation of the analysis of chapter 3; what does need spelling out is the precise meaning of this for those firms using capital goods. Suppose that in this private economy there are two producing sectors, one manufacturing bread, the other machines. These machines can be used to make bread but they will not be available until next year, since the whole of this year is needed for their construction. Labour is used not only for producing this year's bread but also in the construction of machines. The problem is that the labour used to produce machines must be paid this year. It will help if we provisionally assume that the consumption good sector contracts for and pays for capital goods this year; it finances this by borrowing this year on the capital market; next year it receives the machines, and the receipts from the sales of next year's bread are used in part to pay off the loan and cover interest charges on the loan. The complete 'external' financing of the investment is a questionable assumption, but it will be closely examined later on.

What then, are the profits which the sector producing consumption goods is deemed to maximize? Consider a firm engaged in the production of y_0 and y_1. In its manufacture of y_1 the *cash flow* this year is zero, since its payments to the capital goods industry are balanced by the inflow of funds from the capital market. Next year the receipts from y_1 constitute a cash inflow; in *undiscounted* terms this amount is denoted by Py_1. The repayment of the loan and interest charges comprise next year's outflow and this is $P_j(1+r_m)j$ where machines are denoted by j and their price by P_j. Next year's profits are the difference between these two items. It is usual in the context of investment decisions like this to express cash flows in present value terms. The *discounted present value of total profits* (A) is, therefore, in this instance given by multiplying the cash flow in each year by the discount rate.[13] Thus:

$$A = (y_1 P/1+r_m) - jP_j \tag{6.8}$$

This is simply total revenue from y_1 (in present value terms) minus total costs (simply capital outlays). If the firm is a profit maximizer then its equilibrium position will be characterized by the equality of marginal revenue and marginal cost. Thinking of a marginal change involving extra bread

[13] Since in this simple case the net cash flow in the base year is zero then effectively, all we are doing is multiplying next year's net cash flow by next year's discount rate, $1/1+r_m$.

next year (Δy_1) and extra capital this year (Δj), then if the firm is a price-taker its equilibrium[14] is characterized by:

$$P/1+r_m = P_j(\Delta j/\Delta y_1) \tag{6.9}$$

Since the left-hand side is equal to P_1 then the familiar price/marginal cost condition can be seen. It is because the items occur in different years that we have had to be careful about the meaning of the condition. In the context of private ownership it is met because profit-maximizing firms will expand their use of capital until the discounted present value of profits for the marginal project is just zero; this is precisely what eq. (6.9) means. To see the implications for a particular change in output or an individual investment project we may rearrange eq. (6.9) to get:

$$(P\Delta y_1/1+r_m)-P_j\Delta j = 0 \tag{6.10}$$

The left-hand side of this expression *formulates the effects of the project in a particular way and this formulation is usually called the net discounted present value* (NDPV). An investment rule associated with this is to accept a project if its NDPV is positive; for the marginal project the NDPV will be virtually zero as eq. (6.10) implies. The point that profit-maximization implies assessing the discounted present value of profits is now a fairly familiar investment rule. At least it is familiar to economists. It is not until recently that discounted cash flow analysis has invaded private industry, though there are good reasons for explaining this. However, we are stepping ahead of the story. One final point may be made. The above analysis makes it clear that the use of a present value assessment automatically allows for the disbursement of interest charges and the methods of paying off the loan. If future receipts are discounted, it is not necessary to incluue interest charges as a cost of a particular project.

The public sector

Even if all non-human resources were publicly owned in an economy, decisions concerning the trade-off between present and future consumption goods are inescapable. Further, criteria for the allocation of scarce capital funds between uses is obviously required. If market devices are used to solve these problems then the previous analysis gives us most of the leads. Provided that the equality of prices and marginal costs operates in the private sector of a mixed economy, then rules for the public part of such an economy take the same form as those for a 'market socialism' solution. Henceforth we shall then be thinking of the operations of public agencies in an essentially

[14] If the production function in the footnote of p. 170, is constrained by a Lagrangean multiplier ϕ then, written out in full, the first order conditions for maximizing (6.8) are: $\delta A/\delta y_1 = P/(1+r_m)$ $\phi F_{y1} = 0$ and $\delta A/\delta j = (-)P_j - \phi F_j = 0$. An expression for ϕ emerges as $\phi = P/(1+r_m)F_{y1} = (-)P_j/F_j$. Since the transformation rate, (F_{y1}/F_j) will normally be negative, then the above when rearranged, implies eq. (6.9).

mixed type of economy like the USA or the UK; particularly in mind will be the use of capital goods to produce consumption goods next year. In fact, public enterprises in these countries often use capital goods to produce intermediate goods such as electricity and irrigation water, but this complication is ignored until the second half of the book where general applications are considered.

There are three points that can be made:

(a) In line with the conventions of earlier chapters we may think of the public enterprise as making decisions on the output of the whole industry. The aim again is the adjustment of output until price equals marginal cost but now the time-dimension has to be incorporated. Clearly the enterprise should not, given its monopolistic position, maximize profits, but its appropriate guideline is the investment criterion involved in eq. (6.9) and (6.10). That is, each extra quantity of output should be evaluated by comparing price with marginal cost or, more explicitly, it should undertake all those projects or output increases for which the NDPV is positive, taking prices as given. Whereas in the discussion of private firms, competition was assumed to guarantee that the firm is a price-taker, in this case the public enterprise has to ignore its ability to tilt the demand curve. In fact, there could clearly be a large number of reasons why NDPV of *profits* is an inappropriate rule; as well as the monopolistic positions there may be external effects of one sort or another. These issues can be encompassed by the rule that it is the NDPV of social benefits and social costs which the enterprise is required to evaluate, and to undertake projects when this amount is positive. It will be useful if, at this stage, we briefly set this out formally. Let the net social benefits in years 0 and 1 for a particular project be represented by C_0 and C_1 respectively. It follows that the public firm's equilibrium is given by:

$$(C_1/1+r_m)-C_0 = 0 \tag{6.11}$$

where the left-hand side indicates the NDPV of social net benefits from a particular project which, in this case, is the one on the margin. Clearly, in some circumstances C_1 may represent nothing more than extra receipts, $P\Delta y_1$ when the change is small; in other circumstances it would represent a wide variety of factors. By encompassing all of these in C_1, concentration on the time-stream aspects is facilitated.

(b) The analysis throughout the whole of this chapter has implicitly assumed all factors and outputs are perfectly divisible. Clearly, capital is a factor most likely to be subject to some form of indivisibility. Public sector projects such as roads, dams, etc., often involve large jumps on both the input and output side so that prices could change considerably. In these circumstances the 'marginal' rules become inappropriate, but our discussion of surplus analysis has provided the techniques which, in some situations, can deal with these problems. The full operational implications of this are discussed in the later chapters on cost/benefit analysis. Here we may simply note that if for example

Δy_1 was quite large then, instead of C_1 being represented by extra receipts, one would have to use some estimate of the area under the demand curve.

(c) Investment rules in both private and public industry often, in practice, involve the idea of rates of return. Moreover, in our discussion of Pareto efficiency we discussed the rate of return between present and future consumption goods. The use of rates of return in investment analysis can, as will be indicated later, be quite misleading. In the two-period world of our present model they are however unambiguous.[15] In trying to derive a rate of return in the production of y_1 from machines, the early definitions cannot be used since y_1 and j are physically non-comparable. One could, however, think of a rate of return (R_{C_1,C_0}) in terms of the undiscounted net social benefits of a project expressed as a proportion of the capital cost. Thus:

$$R_{C_1,C_0} = (C_1 - C_0)/C_0 \tag{6.12}$$

This can be rearranged to get the following interesting expression:

$$(C_1/1 + R_{C_1,C_0}) - C_0 = 0 \tag{6.13}$$

R_{C_1,C_0} therefore emerges as that rate of interest which, when used for discounting renders the NDPV of a project equal to zero.[16] This concept appears in economics under a number of names. It is Keynes's marginal efficiency of capital and, in micro-economics, often goes under the heading of the 'internal rate of return'.[17] An investment criterion, associated with this, is to undertake a project if the rate of return exceeds the market rate of interest, so that on the margin the two are equal. Intuitively, one can perhaps guess that in the simple circumstances of our model this criterion is equivalent to the NDPV criterion. Formally, if r_m is substituted for R_{C_1,C_0} in eq. (6.12), then the terms, when rearranged, read that the NDPV of the marginal project, using r_m for discounting, should be zero.

We have now come to an important point of the analysis in this chapter. All the features of the very simplest type of model have been explored. We shall now step by step introduce more and more realistic assumptions. Firstly, some special problems concerning the finance of investment are considered. Then in section 6.3 we start off with a discussion of multi-period

[15] Except when indivisibilities are involved. Projects which are mutually exclusive are a form of indivisibility, and problems can arise in using the rate of return rule. For a discussion of this see J. Hirschleifer 'On the Theory of Optimal Investment Decisions', *JPE*, August 1958, reproduced in *The Management of Corporate Capital*, Ed. E. Solomon, The Free Press of Glencoe, 1959.

[16] Similarly for private investment projects, one could, in the context of the previous discussion of private firms, define $R_{y_1,j}$ as the undiscounted net profits of a project expressed as a proportion of the capital cost. One would then have

$$(P_0\Delta y_1/1 + R_{y_1,j}) - P_j\Delta j = 0$$

[17] For a discussion of these terms and concepts see, 'The Rate of Interest, Fisher's Rate of Return Over Cost and Keynes' Internal Rate of Return', A. A. Alchian, *AER*, December 1955, reproduced in Solomon, *op. cit.*

analysis, which paves the way for a number of qualifications that have to be made to the investment rules discussed so far.

The finance of investment[18]

Whereas we have been assuming that production decisions are made entirely separately from consumption decisions, in practice the two are often made simultaneously. By buying houses, cars, refrigerators, etc., individuals make production decisions, and the benefits are in non-cash form accruing directly to the persons concerned. Decision-takers within private firms act (or are assumed to act) on behalf of shareholders. Distributed profits constitute, for shareholders, a command over consumption goods. If, then, they have any preferences regarding the time-path of consumption, investment decisions within the firm need to take this into account. For the owner/manager the issue is unavoidable. A particularly crucial decision in this context would be how much of present profits to plough-back into the firm; it is here that the problem of financing investments is raised and it is appropriate, now, to drop the assumption of complete external borrowing and consider the degree of self-financing as a variable. The analysis of this problem raises important points about investment criteria, and it is here that the relevance for public investment decisions emerges.

The following simplified case for a private firm illustrates the main points. Suppose that the firm's *production* of consumption goods this year is fixed. The *profits* from this, expressed in terms of this year's consumption good, y_0, are equal to $0b$ in Fig. 6.3. We now admit of three immediate possibilities

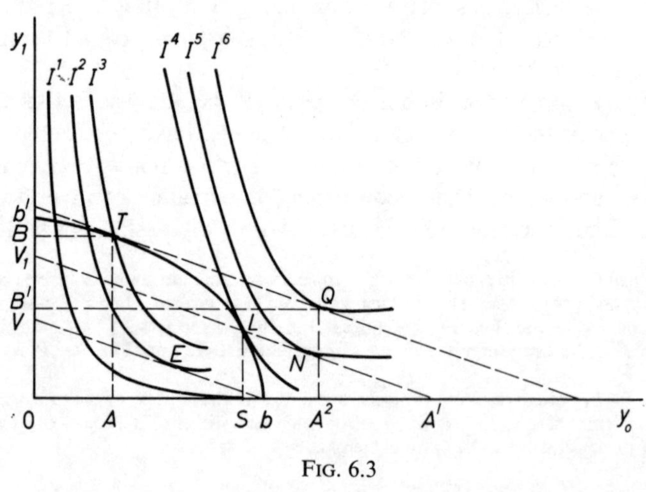

FIG. 6.3

[18] This section can be omitted on a first reading. It draws partly on an important article by J. Hirschleifer, *op. cit.* Figure 6.3 is adapted from Hirschleifer's diagrams. His main concern is with the theoretical background of the prolonged discussion of investment criteria in the 1950s. Some of this debate, as well as Hirschleifer's article, can be found in Solomon, *op. cit.*

open to the owners. Firstly, they could actually use all the profits to consume at b. Secondly, they could lend part of their income, as the consumer did in our previous analysis, by moving along the 'market opportunity line', bV; again the slope of this is deemed to be $(1+r_m)$. The indifference map I^1, I^2, etc., purports to represent the shareholders preferences between present and future consumption and, clearly, the best position in this context is at E, implying that part of current profits is loaned in the money market. However the firm, thirdly, has certain productive opportunities indicated by the bb^1 line. This line[19] indicates how the firm can transform current consumption goods into future consumption goods by the use of capital. The transformation is not done directly in the firm but indirectly, through the sacrifice of current income to finance the acquisition of capital goods. For the shareholders, consuming at L is superior to E. At L part of present income is used to purchase OS of consumption goods; the remaining income (= Sb in terms of y_0) is used to purchase capital goods; these produce income next year equivalent to SL of next year's consumption goods (y_1). An even better position at N could be achieved if money was borrowed facilitating a left-right movement down the market line V^1A^1. Given this sort of possibility it should be now clear that the best move for the shareholders taking into account both productive and market opportunities is to produce at T and consume at Q. In other words, while the firm's base year income is $0b$ (in terms of y_1) its total consumption is actually $0A^2$. The difference is financed from borrowings in the money market. Next year's income of $0B$, in terms of y_1, derives from the use of capital goods whose acquisition is financed by borrowing, this year, money equivalent to Ab of y_0. Thus its total borrowings are AA^2. Next year's income of $0B$ is used in part, B^1B, to pay off the loan and interest charges; the rest, $0B^1$ is consumed next year. Clearly 'consumers' can be thought of as going through a similar process. Given, for example, an income from his factor services this year, the individual decides how much to consume this year, how much deposit to put down on a house, what size of house to build (the productive investment) and how much mortgage to take out.

Two general points emerge from this:

(a) Given prices for the consumption goods, the market lines in Fig. 6.3 can be thought of as lines of constant present value of profits to the firm, the constant amount being higher the farther from the origin is the line. Thus, all the combinations of y_0 and y_1 along the line V^1A^1 are equivalent, given prices and the market rate of interest, to $0A^1$ of y_0. In moving up the production possibility line from b, the firm is therefore increasing the present value of profits and at T these are maximized, so that the NDPV of the marginal project at T is equal to zero. The slope of the production line reflects indirectly the transformation rate between y_0 and y_1 and is thus equal to $(1+R_{y_1, y_0})$ as

[19] Such lines can be used in a variety of ways. Notice that in the interpretation here it does *not* show the quantity of y_0 *produced by the firm*.

defined before. Since the slope of the market line is $(1+r_m)$ then, at T, r_m is equal to R_{y_1, y_0}. Clearly in this simple situation R_{y_1, y_0} is equal to $R_{y_1, j}$, and so the standard investment rules apply to get to T. But shareholders do not like the consumption pattern implied by point T; in fact T is inferior to L where the rate of return is just equal to the time preference rate. Borrowing[20] provides the bridge between production and consumption, and at Q the time-preference rate is equal to the market rate of interest. Since the latter is also equal to the overall rate of return between y_0 and y_1, then Pareto efficiency is achieved, assuming as before that these prices are the same for all other consumers and producers.[21]

(b) Perhaps *the* important point of all this is to highlight the fact that the conventional investment criteria breakdown in the sense that they do not lead the decision-taker to the final solution. They clearly represent necessary conditions since the decision-taker has, in a sense, to move to T before going to Q. But the rules do not indicate anything about optimal financing procedure.[22]

What are the implications of all this for the public enterprise? The first thing to discover is the analogue, in the public firm, to the distributable profits of the private firm. Clearly such profits constitute a payment either for capital funds supplied in the past or as a payment for entrepreneurship. The latter we can, to be realistic, rule out and treat such payment as going directly to internal executives of the public enterprise. Since it would further be realistic to assume that there is no equity capital in the public sector,[23] it becomes questionable whether there is any income comparable to private profits, certainly if optimal pricing is pursued. All receipts would be used in paying off the factors of production including, for capital assets, the fixed interest charges of bond-holders; even when assets are compulsorily acquired, compensation by way of government bonds is usually paid; this was certainly the case in the nationalization of the fuel and transport industries in the UK in the late 1940s. There remains however three possibilities. The income attributable to a particular factor of production, compulsorily purchased in the past, could exceed outgoings on it because the outgoings are a compensation payment and the statutes have decreed a fairly sub-economic level for them; or more simply, past policy has decreed the genera-

[20] Note that a lending solution is quite possible.

[21] A general algebraic representation of the problem, allowing for the firms to produce a variable amount of y_0 from labour services, would envisage the firm maximizing the utility function subject to two sets of constraints. One would be a production function. The second constraint would be that total expenditure on the consumption goods should not exceed the surplus of receipts from the production of consumption goods over outlays on labour and capital.

[22] And this was one of the key points of Hirschleifer's article, *op. cit.*

[23] Although this possibility has been canvassed for the nationalized industries in the UK. For a discussion of the various possible sources of finances for these bodies see 'Finance of the Nationalised Industries', D. Munby, *BOUIS*, May 1959.

tion of a surplus to self-finance a part of future investment.[24] A second possibility, following Cuban practice, would be where no compensation was paid when assets were brought into the public sector. Thirdly, of course, there is taxation raised in as non-distortive way as possible.

Granted that we are concerned here simply with Pareto efficiency, what exactly can a public enterprise do with the funds raised? Figure 6.4, which

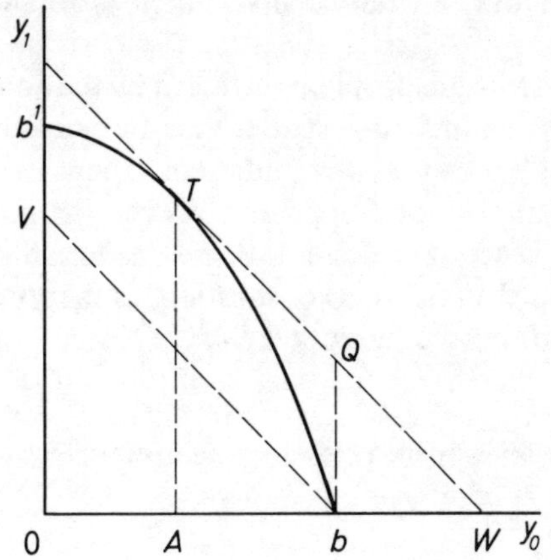

FIG. 6.4

reproduces the productive opportunity line, indicates some possibilities. Firstly, there does not appear to be much point in lending money along the market line *bV*. Acting on behalf of the community it would only be lending money back to itself. Of course if it is distributed to the general public, to be consistent this will have to be performed in a non-distortive manner. Clearly, as far as productive investment goes, it should operate at *T*. But how much borrowing should be undertaken? On efficiency grounds there seems no point in 'consuming' beyond O*b* since the state would then be borrowing from the general public only to return it to them. On income distribution grounds such a possibility, however, may be a useful device. A further possibility would be to distribute all current income and finance all the investment by borrowing as implied by point *Q*. At the other extreme *Ab* of current income could be withheld so that the investment is completely self-financed. In both cases the general public is effectively supplying the funds and, on these grounds, perhaps it does not matter. Once practical matters are introduced the choice may be important. It may, for example, be administratively or politically easier to finance public investment from current surpluses than

[24] Cf. the suggestions in *The Financial and Economic Obligations of the Nationalised Industries*, Cmnd. 1337, HMSO, London, April 1961.

to raise additional taxes or to use the money market.[25] The size of the funds raised may be such as to constitute a non-marginal change so it may not be a matter of indifference whether they are saved or spent. All of these issues are very relevant to the assessment of public investment projects, and we shall try in various parts of the rest of the book to incorporate allowances for them. If the simple model is kept, however, the degree of self-financing, on efficiency grounds, appears to be unimportant. For the time being it will, to make a choice, be assumed that all public investment is financed on the money market.

One final pointer to future problems is raised by the analysis in this section. Throughout it is individual preferences that have counted. It is the time preference rate of individuals acting under conditions of free choice that has been deemed to be important. Suppose, however, the government itself has views on time preference. Are there any reasons for thinking that the time preference rate implied in the market solutions is inappropriate? These and related matters are discussed in section 6.4.

6.3 Market derived investment rules and the preferences of the present generation

Introduction

The main theme of the analysis in this chapter so far has been the derivation of Pareto efficient investment rules for the public sector, within the context of a maximization model relating to the welfare of the present generation. The broad conclusion is that assuming the benefits and costs of particular changes or projects have been correctly estimated for each year, then the rule is to invest if the NDPV is positive, where items are discounted by a market rate of interest. It is the purpose of this section to consider the viability of this rule taking into account a more 'realistic world' than that alluded to so far.

But first, one simplification of the previous analysis can be removed. An horizon of seventy years was initially considered but only two of those years, 'this year' (1970) and 'next year', were examined in highlighting the features

[25] S. A. Marglin suggests that

> '. . . the level of new federal investment is little affected by the extent to which the benefits of earlier investment are recaptured . . . [by sales revenue]. On the other hand, such recapturing may well be a crucial factor in determining the level of state and local public investment in the U.S., and of all public investment in underdeveloped countries, since government investment in those countries depends much more on the extent to which the government is able to pre-empt resources from the consumption sector of the economy.'

See 'Economic Factors Affecting System Design', p. 205 and footnote, chapter 4 of *Design of Water Resource Systems*, A. Maass and Others, Harvard University Press, 1962. For the view that the increased degree of self-financing required by the 1961 White Paper, *op cit.*, of the Nationalized Industries in the UK, was due to the embarrassment that their current methods of financing was making for the government's monetary policy, see 'Old Problems and New Policies in the Nationalised Industries', M. V. Posner, *District Bank Review*, December 1962.

of a Pareto efficient inter-temporal allocation of resources. If the whole seventy years are considered, then it is necessary to allow that individuals will have expectations of supplying factor services and consuming commodities for each of these seventy years; similarly, firms will be engaged in production throughout the period and capital projects initiated in any one year may provide benefits for a series of years into the future. Moreover, projects may involve capital outlays for more than one period. We can allow for some of these points by denoting the net social benefits in year t, of a capital project, as C_t. Thus, a particular project may involve $C_0, C_1, C_2, \ldots C_n$, the notation covering the possibility that capital costs for this project may be incurred in years 1 and 2 for example, as well as the base year. Secondly, the multi-period case necessitates our recognizing that consumers will have time preference rates covering all these years. In principle, the rate of time-preference between periods 0 and 1 need not be the same as that between 4 and 5 or 1 and 5. Clearly, however, Pareto efficiency would still require that the market rate of interest as between any two periods be the same for all consumers and producers.

This means, therefore, that we would require public enterprises to discount future items at the rate of interest appropriate to each year. Thus $C_1/(1+r_1)$ is the present value of C_1, where r_1 is the market-interest rate between periods 0 and 1. Similarly, the present value of C_2 is $C_2/(1+r_1)(1+r_2)$, where r_2 is the rate between periods 1 and 2.[26] In practice, it is usually assumed that there are no reasons for expecting interest rates to vary in this way, in which case one gets the following expression for the net discounted present value of a public project:

$$\text{NDPV} = C_0+[C_1/1+r_m]+[C_2/(1+r_m)^2]+\ldots+[C_n/(1+r_m)^n] \quad (6.14)$$

The investment rule associated with this is to undertake projects if the NDPV is positive.[27] Previously we presented an alternative criterion in terms of comparing a project's rate of return with the market interest rate. Once one moves into multi-period analysis, rates of return become particularly dubious concepts. We could follow the logic of our previous analysis by defining the rate of return as that interest rate which, when used for discounting, renders the NDPV of eq. (6.14) equal to zero. This is the conventional definition of the internal rate of return, but what it means in economic terms is not clear. There has been considerable discussion in the literature on the compatibility of the internal rate of return investment criterion with the NDPV rule. Much of this applies equally to both public and private

[26] The cumulative value of £10, invested in the base period, is, at the end of the first year, $10(1+r_1)$. At the end of the second year it is $10(1+r_1)+r_2 10(1+r_1) = 10(1+r_1)(1+r_2)$. Thus, the present value of £10 received in period 2 is $10/(1+r_1)(1+r_2)$.

[27] If the assumption of a varying interest rate is maintained, then the NDPV is given by:

$$C_0+[C_1/1+r_1]+[C_2/(1+r_1)(1+r_2)]+\ldots+ [C_n/(1+r_1)(1+r_2)\ldots(1+r_n)].$$

investment criteria. We shall not for that reason, review this literature,[28] and throughout the book we will stick fairly closely to the use of the NDPV approach. However, three points may be briefly made:

(a) For any enterprise, whether public or private, the appropriate investment decision rule depends both on what is being maximized and what constraints exist.[29] If, for example, a public enterprise is required to achieve a certain target surplus over a five-year period and if, further, certain products or services *have* to be provided—both of these applied, to a certain extent, in the UK nationalized industries in the period 1961–67—then the appropriate decision rule for any one investment project could be unrelated to either of the standard investment rules. Also, as we shall see in the later part of the book, if capital funds are in restricted supply, ranking devices, such as NDPV per pound of base year capital cost, may be in order.

(b) Since we *have* specified maximands, in terms of either profits or social net benefits and since, further, no constraints have been assumed, the NDPV approach emerges as the logical rule in the setting considered so far. Briefly, the internal rate of return is a proxy to the NDPV approach; the former may have certain practical advantages, but since it does not always give the same results as the NDPV approach, for theoretical purposes it is rejected here.

(c) Because the internal rate of return is only a proxy to the NDPV approach, it can in some circumstances rank projects in a different way. However, when investment projects involve base year outlays and have returns in the form of either a perpetual income stream or a return in just one year, then the situation corresponds closely to the two-period world discussed in the previous section and, in ranking projects, the two rules give exactly the same results.[30] Since this sort of situation crops up a number of times in the public investment literature, a proof of this assertion is given in the appendix to this chapter.

Given this more comprehensive version of the investment rule we may now consider some of the basic assumptions underlying its applicability. Two general objectives to which it is related will not at this stage be questioned. One is that it is the preferences of the present generation that matter; secondly, the assumption that Pareto efficiency is all that matters is also retained.

[28] Solomon's book, *op. cit.*, contains some of the earlier material. For a further development of Hirschleifer's critique, *op. cit.*, of the internal rate of return see 'Formal Criteria for Investment Decisions', M. J. Bailey, *JPE*, October 1959. Other work on this topic includes 'Present Value Versus Internal Rate of Return: An Essay in the Theory of the Third Best'. R. Turvey, *EJ*, March 1963; 'The Problem of Time Stream Evaluation: Present Value Versus Internal Rate of Return Rules', J. S. Flemming and M. S. Feldstein, *BOUIS*, February 1964: Section B of 'Investment Criteria for Public Enterprises' by P. D. Henderson, in *Public Enterprise*, Ed. R. Turvey, 1968, an amended version of an article in *BOUIS* February 1965 with a similar title; 'A Proposed Normalisation Procedure for Public Investment Criteria', E. J. Mishan, *EJ*, December 1967.

[29] Cf. Turvey's discussion of the 'Beeching Minimand' and the 'Stalinist Maximand' (*op. cit.*, *EJ*, March 1963).

[30] Subject again to the problem of indivisibilities.

Market imperfections

The existence of imperfections in product and factor markets closely related to public sector markets implies, as we saw in chapter 4, that considerable qualifications have to be made to the general applicability of certain of the allocative rules. The same general point applies to the market for capital funds. The use of a market interest rate for discounting the effects of a public project rests on an assumed perfection in this market. But, of course, individuals (and firms) cannot borrow in unlimited amounts at the ruling market rate. This is partly because of the problems of risk which we discuss later on; partly also it reflects the fact that the government traditionally makes much use of the capital market in its monetary policy to effect much wider objectives than that considered here. In total, as Eckstein has said, the capital market is

> . . . rife with rationing, ignorance, differential tax treatments, reluctance to finance investment from external funds, slow adjustment processes, etc., which destroy the normative significance of actual rates found in the market. The enormous gaps between investing and savings rates in the system, with savers typically receiving 3 per cent and investment decisions being made at 20 per cent and more (and yielding similar 'ex post' returns), is strong evidence against the pure classical view.[31]

Two other sorts of imperfections may be considered to illustrate the sort of issues involved. If there are sizeable differences (between borrowing and lending rates) over and above any transactions costs, then, as Hirschleifer has demonstrated,[32] the equilibrium position for a private firm may involve the worthwhileness of projects being defined in relation to the firm's own time preference rate which could differ from either of the market interest rates. Market rates may not, therefore, reflect the time preference rate of private individuals. Secondly, a fairly common source of imperfection is the tax levied on corporate profits. Setting aside any divergences between private and social benefit arising from monopolistic power, external effects, etc., the social yield of capital funds in the private sector may be taken as being indicated by the gross profit stream; the net yield to private investors is less than this by the amount of the tax. This is, therefore, important both because it will have an effect on the level of interest rates and also because any funds transferred to the public sector from the private sector will have a private valuation which underestimates the social yield.

The effect that market imperfections and the other problems of risk, etc. discussed below, have on the way one evaluates public investment projects is a major topic itself and it is more appropriately explored in the context of the more practical issues of the second part of the book. Here we concentrate

[31] *Op. cit.*, p. 503.
[32] *Op. cit.*

on exposing the main likely causes for the inappropriateness of the simple NDPV rule. It is, however, worth pointing out at this stage that the relevant allowance may not simply be one of tampering with the interest rate used for discounting. To hint at some of these issues consider the case of the corporate profits tax. The volume of private investment is, in this context, sub-optimal. One approach would be to recognize that policy constraints are such that private investment cannot be subsidized and the level of the tax is unalterable. Suppose the public projects in question are those for which no direct sales revenue accrues; new hospitals, government research and development, and to a certain extent road construction, would be examples in the UK. Suppose, further, that all the costs of these projects are financed by floating government bonds at a rate of interest which, in a risk-free and perfectly competitive situation, is also equal to the rates on other types of funds.[33] Suppose, in addition, that the purchasers of these bonds would otherwise have channelled their funds into private investment. The constraints on policy would then imply a second-best solution which aimed at ensuring that funds are transferred from one use (the private sector) to another (the public projects) only if their social value in the latter exceeds the former. As a part solution to this one might make the assumption that the alternative private uses of the funds are near the margin; that is, the NDPV of the forgone alternatives, for the *private investor,* is near to zero. Thinking then of options involving base year capital costs of £K, the assumption of 'marginality' implies that the net present value of profits, before depreciation but after tax, is roughly equal to £K. Thus, the nominal amount of the transferred funds, £K, indicates their alternative private use value; but given our assumptions, the social value will be greater than this, say £K^*. In evaluating public projects one could, therefore, allow for the corporate profits tax by calculating the NDPV of the public project using as a measure of capital costs, not the nominal cost, £K, but a 'shadow value', £K^*. Remember, however, this is purely illustrative; the precise circumstances would have to be spelt out more carefully to get a definitive answer.[34]

[33] This situation has features similar to that used in W. J. Baumol's discourse 'On the Social Rate of Discount', *AER*, September 1968.

[34] For example one would want to know to what extent private investment would be stimulated by the benefits of the public project. Note that, in the very simplest sort of cases, the suggested procedure can be shown to be equivalent to using a different interest rate for discounting; more precisely to calculating the present value of the benefits of the public project, using for discounting a measure of the gross rate of return in private industry, and comparing this with the nominal cost of funds. This approach, typified in Baumol's article (*op. cit.*), where effectively all investment options yield perpetuities, though possibly useful in certain circumstances, is—as we shall see when we explore such suggestions in the later part of the book—misleading to the extent that it concentrates on what is known as a social discount *rate*. The issues remain clearer if attention is concentrated on the *absolute* alternative present use value of transferred funds. Similarly, in certain circumstances, the suggested procedure in the text is equivalent to imputing the tax rate to the public project's benefits and then comparing their present value—discounted at the market interest rate—with the nominal cost of funds.

Uncertainty

Broadly there are two main issues involved:

(a) What are the implications for welfare economics and particularly the allocative rules, of the fact that in practice economic decisions have to be made within a context of uncertainty whereas the standard welfare model is drawn up without this complication?

(b) How can public expenditure criteria be adapted to allow for the problem that the time stream of benefits and costs is not known with certainty?

In relation to the first point, the general issue is that the uncertainty associated with the general political and economic situation, while clearly also applicable to the 'one year model' of previous chapters, becomes very important in the context of saving and investment decisions. People making these decisions do not know, with certainty, what will be the structure of relative prices or the general price level next year and further into the future. But such information is precisely what is assumed in the analysis which ascribed normative significance to the current interest rate. A related issue is that the failure of markets to provide information in instances of interdependent production decisions—a point alluded to in an earlier discussion (see p. 111)—becomes particularly relevant when investment decisions are involved. The development of a new railway may depend on being able to expropriate some receipts from potential new farmers in the area; the existence of uncertainty means firms and industries have inadequate information on the investment decisions of other firms.

What can be done? One approach, at the academic level, is to draw up new Pareto conditions making specific allowances for uncertainty. In fact, there are other factors loosely related to time which affect individual welfare which we have largely ignored, e.g., desire for stability, time path of reactions to economic events. In a sense, then, we are calling for a dynamic theory of welfare economics. The short answer is that, not surprisingly, little has been done in this context. A second approach, related specifically to uncertainty, would be to improve the methods of disseminating information in markets by, for example, the stimulation of research and information services. A third approach, complementary to the second, is to take the line that the suggested investment rules should be roughly adhered to but specific allowance, in public investment decisions, should be made for the existence of uncertainty. It is here that we return to the second main issue mentioned at the beginning of this section. Now, in practice, allowance for uncertainty often takes on fairly crude forms. One way is to attach a fairly short economic life to a project. In some instances a premium is added to the discount rate. Some of these methods will be referred to in the latter part of the book. At the theoretical level a whole range of new techniques are being introduced.[35]

[35] For introductory discussions to both crude and sophisticated solutions see Eckstein, *op. cit.* section 5 , and section E of Henderson, *op. cit.* For a lengthier treatment see pp. 129–58 of 'Basic Economic and Technological Concepts: A General Statement', by R. Dorfman, which forms chapter 3 of Maass, *op. cit.*

This book is not the place to evaluate all these procedures, for two reasons. One is that most of the issues have no special significance for public investment decisions—they relate to all such decisions whether undertaken in the private or public sector. Moreover, it is a major subject area to which we could not possibly do justice in the context of this book.

There is, however, one aspect of this which does need mentioning. To the extent that private firms do make allowances for uncertainty by incorporating a risk premium in their discount rate, then market interest rates will in general include risk premia. The previous analysis suggested that market rates are to be used for discounting the time-stream of public sector projects because they reflect something about the preferences of the present generation with respect to present and future consumption. Now, public expenditure may be subject to different sorts of risks than private expenditure and, thus, it becomes questionable whether market rates should be taken gross of the risk allowance. One solution would be to take the market rate net of the risk premium and then make specific allowances for the public project which could, if deemed appropriate, mean adding back a risk premium. In fact some economists[36] have gone further, and argued that since the government undertakes a very large range of projects, then under the law of large numbers, certain types of risk can be ignored. Thinking in terms of the illustrative decision rules of the previous section this would mean discounting the benefits of the public programme at a market interest rate net of risk premia; then this would be compared with the alternative use value of funds used to finance the project. This alternative use value would, following the same principles, be calculated by discounting the time stream with a rate which allowed for the risks of private projects. Of course, in the absence of external effects, taxes, etc., this alternative use value would be indicated by the nominal cost of funds if the private projects could be treated as marginal. These last few remarks do have particular relevance when we consider an argument by Baumol[37] that the large number argument can be applied to private projects. On this basis, from *society's* viewpoint, private projects are equally riskless and the alternative social use value of the transferred funds exceeds their nominal cost to the extent that the allowance for risk can be ignored.[38]

[36] For example, P. A. Samuelson:

'One can look at much of government as primarily a device for mutual reinsurance. General Motors can borrow at a lower rate than American Motors because it is a pooler of more independent risks. It would be absurd for G.M. to apply the same high risk-interest discount factor to a particular venture that A.M. must apply. The same holds for We, Inc., which is a better pooler of risks than G.M.'

'Principles of Efficiency: Discussion', p. 96, *AEA Papers and Proceedings of 76th Meeting*, published May, 1964.

[37] *Op. cit.*

[38] Because he examines a very special case—a point alluded to above in footnote on p. 186—Baumol's investment rule becomes fairly simple, namely to compare the face value of the transferred funds with the benefits of the public projects, discounting the latter at the market interest rate inclusive of risk premium.

The appropriate decision rules for public investment appear to be growing into a formidable problem, whichever viewpoint one takes. However, to avoid dramatization, it should be remembered that these are only part of the issues involved in assessing public projects and, in practice, as we shall demonstrate in the second part of the book, certain simplifying procedures can be used.

The social productivity of investment

Another reason for questioning the validity of the standard investment rule, arises from a further argument suggesting that private investment could have a social value exceeding its value to the private individuals making the decision. Again the implication would be that the nominal cost of funds used by the public sector is less than their social value in the private sector. The argument—most frequently referred to by M. S. Feldstein[39]—is as follows. Those people responsible for making investment decisions in the private sector concern themselves with the streams of output value or benefit, net of operating costs; i.e., it is the return to capital that matters. But investment projects increase the future incomes of owners of factors of production other than capital; as such, then, it is the total value of output that should be compared with capital costs and not simply the return to capital. In instances where benefit/cost ratios have been deemed relevant for investment decisions, this takes on the suggestion that it is the capital/output ratio that matters. Essentially, this implies that one should ignore future operating costs. Put this way the issue, as stressed by Henderson,[40] is clearly whether these accompanying factors of production have any alternative use value. One could not dispute that many of the large investment projects, particularly those associated with technical innovation, may have large effects on all factor incomes; in the extreme case of a pool of unemployed (or disguisedly unemployed) labour force in underdeveloped countries, the criterion might prove relevant. But the main point is that it all depends on the extent of alternative use value and, as a *general* rule—concerned as we are in this section of the chapter with 'efficiency'—it has no place.

Voluntary provision for future generations

Although the basic premise in this chapter so far has been one of catering for the welfare of the present generation, this is not inconsistent with resources being invested to yield benefits for the future generation. If the present generation itself *desires* to make such provision then this is something

[39] See 'Net Social Benefit Calculation and the Public Investment Decision', *OEP*, March 1964; 'The Social Time Preference Discount Rate in Cost Benefit Analysis', *EJ*, June 1964; 'Opportunity Cost Calculations in Cost Benefit Analysis', *Public Finance*, No. 2, 1964.
[40] *Op. cit.*, p. 120.

which comes within the scope of our maximand. This desire may arise for a variety of reasons. Firstly, in the simple model used up to this point it was hypothesized that the present generation comprises *m* adults, all of whom were assumed to die seventy years from now. In practice, the economic decisions made by adults will be affected by their desire to make provision for their children when they grow up; their saving for example will be affected by a need for income for their children in the future, as well as for their own consumption purposes. Further, when people die the benefits of their past saving and investment may be passed on to their children. To this extent, inheritance taxes and death duties make such saving and investing less attractive than otherwise so that the private yield is less than social benefit.[41]

Secondly, individuals may have some altruistic desire to make provision for the future generation. Clearly, people do in practice privately make such provision if only by way of charitable expenditure on things like buildings glorifying our national heritage and cathedrals—though on second thoughts the latter may be more related to insurance than altruism. An argument has been advanced—most explicitly by S. A. Marglin[42]—that the private contributions that people make may be a very poor indication of the desire they have for providing benefits for the future generation. The reasoning is that the market does not adequately allow such preferences to be expressed; that provision for the future takes on 'public good' characteristics necessitating collective provision by the government.

A grossly simplified example will make the key points.[43] Suppose we return to our very simple model of two distinct generations, but make it even simpler by assuming that there are only two items affecting me as a typical member of the present generation. One is the total consumption by the next generation (X), the other is my total consumption during my life-span (Y). In this simple two-period model[44] these are the only items which enter my utility function. I can, in addition, make certain productive investments yielding X which involve giving up some of my present potential consumption. My overall problem is one of maximizing utility, $U = U(Y,X)$, subject to the constraint of the production relationships between X and Y. Bearing in mind our previous discussions of this sort of maximization problem, the equilibrium condition, with respect to X and Y, would be characterized by the equality of the marginal subjective rate of substitution and the marginal rate of transformation. If expressions like U_x are used to

[41] Cf. Baumol, *op. cit.* This indicates, if anything, the 'depths' to which the 'efficiency' criterion can take us.

[42] 'The Social Rate of Discount and the Optimal Rate of Investment', *QJE*, February 1963. For the way this is to be integrated into investment decision rules see his *Economic Factors Affecting System Design*, *op. cit.*, and his book *Public Investment Criteria*, 'Studies in the Development of India', No. 4, 1967.

[43] Parts of the foregoing draw on Marglin's *QJE*, article, *op. cit.*

[44] The two-period characteristic allows one to talk of rates of return which have some economic meaning. Cf. the appendix to this chapter.

denote the marginal utility of X, and if the production transformation rate is written as $\Delta X/\Delta Y$ then we can write this condition as follows:

$$(\Delta X/\Delta Y) - U_y/U_x = 0 \tag{6.15}$$

The substitution rate indicates how much consumption by the next generation would compensate me for giving up a unit of my own present consumption. The transformation rate indicates how much extra consumption *will* accrue to the next generation per unit of my forgone present consumption. Thus, it is of benefit to me to give up Y as long as the transformation rate exceeds the substitution rate. Recalling the discussion in the earlier part of this chapter concerning rates of return and time preference, eq. (6.15) is equivalent to:

$$(1+R_{y,x}) - (1+r_a) = 0, \quad \text{that is}$$

$$R_{y,x} - r_a = 0 \tag{6.16}$$

$R_{y,x}$ is the productive rate of return; r_a is my rate of time preference between my present consumption and the consumption of the next generation; it is what might be called an individual's altruistic time preference rate.[45] The left-hand side of eq. (6.16), to be denoted, say, by N, indicates my overall net benefit per pound/dollar of forgone present consumption. Thus, the rule is to 'invest' if N is positive. Let us consider some 'likely' figures for the variables. To be generous towards the criterion one might hypothesize—following Marglin—that production would double, i.e., $R_{y,x}$ equals 1 (or 100 in percentage terms). An assumption that an individual would surrender £1 now for every £10 received by the future generation is also probably generous; the altruistic time preference rate is therefore 900 per cent. Despite this generosity, N is negative—I would not invest. Granted similar sorts of opportunities and preferences for my contemporaries, they also would not invest for the same reason.

However, my pleasure from the thought of provision being made for the future generation is independent of who makes that provision. If some person other than myself makes this provision so much the better.[46] I may attach some disutility to some of my contemporaries' giving up consumption possibilities and, thus, whether *I think* it is a good thing for *other* people to invest will involve a balancing of my 'psychic' welfare gain from the increased consumption of the next generation against my 'psychic' welfare loss from the reduced consumption of my contemporaries. My subjective substitution rate between these two items is U_x/U_v, where U_v is my marginal utility from

[45] Cf. Marglin, *op. cit.*, *QJE*, p. 107, 1963.

[46] In fact—as Marglin cutely observed—an individual may well rank some positive expenditure by all of the present generation, including himself, above the possibility of all not making a contribution. But even better would be the case where he alone is exempted! See *QJE* article, *op. cit.*, p. 100.

the consumption (V) of a typical contemporary. If the possibilities of transforming units of V into units of X are indicated by $\Delta X/\Delta V$, then *I* think it would be a good thing for *another* person to give up some present consumption if:

$$(\Delta X/\Delta V) - U_v/U_x > 0 \tag{6.17}$$

The transformation rate is, we assume, no different from the previous one and can, therefore, be written as $1+R_{y,x}$. More insight into the substitution rate is given if it is expressed in terms of my own consumption; that is, it could be written in the form $(U_v/U_y)/(U_x/U_y)$. Now, we know that the denominator is equivalent to $1/(1+r_a)$. The numerator indicates the rate—which may of course be quite low—at which I am prepared to surrender some of my consumption goods for the benefit of my contemporaries; it could, therefore, be written in the form $1/(1+r_c)$, where r_c is a rate of preference defined in a similar way to r_a, but relating to my own and my contemporaries' consumption. In total then, if the left-hand side of eq. (6.17) is denoted by N^1 then:

$$N^1 = (1+R_{y,x}) - (1+r_a/1+r_c) \tag{6.18}$$

N^1, therefore, indicates the net benefit to me per pound/dollar of consumption foregone by one of my contemporaries.

Now, if figures similar to those used previously are inserted in eq. (6.18), we find that N^1 could well be positive. As before $R_{y,x}$ is taken as 1 and r_a as 9. Suppose—following Marglin—that present individuals attach more significance to the consumption of contemporaries than to that of the next generation; that is, for every £10 received by a contemporary I am prepared to contribute, say, 30s., implying a value for r_c of 560 per cent (or 5·6). With these figures N^1 comes out as $+0{\cdot}5$. Thus, the main conclusion is that, whereas I am not prepared to invest for the benefit of the next generation (N is negative), I do think it would be a good thing if someone else did ($N^1 > 0$). But, of course, the someone else would not invest for precisely the same reasons that inhibited me. What does now appear to be quite possible is that, if all of us were enforced to simultaneously invest, we all might well regard this as a good thing. Suppose, for example, there are m individuals in the population and each person invests £1. My benefit from the increased consumption of the next generation is not related exclusively to my own investment. If the net benefit to me from the collective venture is denoted by N_i, we have:

$$N_i = N + N^1(m-1) \tag{6.19}$$

and on the basis of the previous figures N_i turns out to be positive as long as m exceeds 17. Whether or not the whole £m investment is warranted is determined by the criterion that:

$$N_1 + N_2 + \ldots + N_i + \ldots + N_m > 0 \tag{6.20}$$

This formulation allows for the possibility that people have different preferences. If, however, it were assumed that preferences are roughly similar, then the left-hand side of eq. (6.20) is equivalent to $N_i \times m$; in this case, the decision to collectively invest simply depends on whether N_i is positive. Further, if the population is large, then in the expression for N_i, eq. (6.19), the contribution of N becomes insignificant and N_i is roughly equivalent to N^1. In other words, the issue as to whether it is worthwhile for all of us to invest collectively depends on the same things as whether I think it is worthwhile for you alone to invest.

Granted then the basic assumptions, a collective expenditure on—i.e., government provision for—the next generation is warranted on the basis of individual preferences. These preferences cannot be expressed through a market because the expenditure has public good characteristics. If other people invest, I cannot be excluded from deriving pleasure from the thought of provision being made for the next generation. This exclusion difficulty is exactly the same sort of thing which arises for standard large-number public good examples such as health immunization, flood-relief, and defence. In such cases, we noted in the previous chapter that expenditure is warranted if it is less than *the sum of the benefits* accruing to the population in question, (see p. 134). This is precisely what eq. (6.20) says. There, the N_i's relate to benefit net of the assumed expenditure of £1 per person.

Collective aspects of public investment: summary and conclusions

The main point of this analysis is that it is a further nail in the coffin of market interest rates in terms of their normative significance. The arguments about provision for the next generation are still in terms of the individual preferences of the present generation, but we have seen that some desires for this provision cannot be expressed through the market and will not, therefore, be reflected in market rates of interest. However, before we are carried away with this let us remember two points. Firstly, the conclusions clearly rest on both the assumed level for the variables and on some of the analytical assumptions. The Marglin formulations are very sensitive to quite small changes in the data. As G. Tullock[47] has pointed out, if the present generation is taken to be only slightly less generous in its consideration for the next generation, collective investment may not be warrantable. Suppose that for £10 of extra benefits to the next generation, the typical present-day individual is prepared to sacrifice 15s. rather than £1. The value of N^1, the crucial item, then becomes $-0{\cdot}4$. Further, an important issue more or less avoided by the simplifying assumptions, is the distribution of the benefits among the next generation and the distribution of the costs among the present generation.

[47] 'The Social Rate of Discount and the Optimal Rate of Investment: Comment', *QJE*, May 1964. For more criticism of Marglin's approach see 'Further Comment' by R. C. Lind in the same issue.

Even if the future beneficiaries were expected to be primarily the poorer sections of the community, they may be much less deserving than today's poor if only because income levels are generally expected to rise over time.

Secondly, setting aside these qualifications, we might consider the implication of the basic ideas for the evaluation of public investment. The chief point is that individuals may want government to weight benefits to future generations more highly than they themselves are able to do in their own market transactions. An individual's decisions, with respect to his own present consumption and *his own* future consumption, is to be guided by the private time preference rates discussed in the earlier part of this chapter. However, he will wish the government to assess investment projects in a way which reflects his preferences with respect to the future generation, i.e., to use a time preference rate which reflects the altruistic desires which he cannot make effective in the market. Such a rate is sometimes called a 'social' or 'planners' time preference rate, and would generally be expected to be less than the private rate. The terminology—as we shall see in the next section—encompasses a wide range of factors, but here we use the phrase simply in the context of the altruistic desires of the present generation. What would such a rate be in terms of previous concepts? *My* social time preference rate would relate to the balancing of consumption units sacrificed by the present generation, against consumption units received by the next generation. If one thought of m units being involved in both cases, then this would give a measure of my 'social time preference rate'; more precisely, a measure of $1+r_s$ where r_s is such a rate. We have

$$1+r_s = [U_y+U_v(m-1)]/mU_x \tag{6.21}$$

If m is large, then my own sacrifice, U_y, could be taken as insignificant in relation to the rest of the numerator. Further, since the difference between m and $m-1$ also becomes insignificant, then the right-hand side of eq. (6.21) is equivalent to U_v/U_x. Bearing in mind equations (6.17) and (6.18) this means:

$$r_s = (1+r_a/1+r_c)-1 \tag{6.22}$$

The rate of interest, r_s, to be used in discounting the time-stream of public investment projects, reflects the way an individual weights his own present consumption against both the consumption of the next generation and the consumption of his contemporaries. How do we discover what such a rate would be for an economy? Marglin has suggested that one could perhaps derive an implied rate from the planned investment level of current government policy. The currently chosen growth rate, on this argument, would imply a particular level of national investment implying in turn, given full employment, a sacrifice of present consumption. If governments chose their growth rates solely in relation to the problems outlined in this section then there may be something in this, but of course in practice the rate is influenced by much wider objectives.

6.4 Social time preference

In the simplest type of competitive model, market interest rates play the role of a weighting system. They implicitly attach weights to items occurring at different points of time, and make all such items commensurable by the weighting system. The nub of this chapter has been to examine whether a market-derived weighting system is the one we want. This section both reviews the analysis and extends its scope. In the course of evaluating the normative significance of interest rates we have had to look at the whole process of investment decisions—at least from the viewpoint of economic theory. Some of the qualifications to using conventional investment criteria have related to other factors beside the interest rate. Thus, the existence of taxes on the profits of private investment is not directly connected with the system one uses to weight the time-stream of benefits and costs of a public project. Clearly, it is something we may wish to allow for since public investment usually means a reduction of investment opportunities in the private sector, and the foregone value of such transferred funds should be an important item in deciding on the worthwhileness of public projects. A possible approach to this sort of problem was suggested on p. 186. The point is that, in this section, we wish to concentrate on the interest rate aspect of investment decisions, notwithstanding that in drawing up investment decision rules in the later part of the book, these 'other' factors will be relevant.

We might, then, assume that all non-interest rate matters have been dealt with in specifying the measures of the benefits and costs over time of public projects, and the issue is now one of deciding on an appropriate interest rate or weighting system to make the items commensurable.[48] The appropriate device is a *planners' or social time preference rate*.[49] This is but a name. It means, simply, that the government should use an interest rate which reflects its own weighting of present and future. Why should this not correspond to a market interest rate? The arguments that have been advanced against using market rates can be arranged into five sections, all of which approach the issue from a distinctly different standpoint:

(a) *Technical Limitations.* If one regards market behaviour as indicating

[48] This point, I think, brings out clearly why the present value approach is much more illuminating than the internal rate of return. Rates of return pretend to ascribe some unique figure to the value of an investment. But if by 'value' we mean—as in common practice—some absolute standard which can be compared with, say, present day consumption, then this depends on what weights are attached to benefits and costs occurring at different points of time. Cf.

> 'Use of present value does, and use of an internal rate of return does not involve a discount rate representing our relative evaluation of current and postponed returns and costs. If, therefore, we care about the relative futurity of gains and losses, if, that is to say, the maximand is a present value, the internal rate of return is the wrong criterion, and that is that.'

R. Turvey, *op. cit.*, p. 96. (*EJ*, 1963).

[49] This terminology is used frequently by O. Eckstein. See 'A Survey of the Theory of Public Expenditure Criteria', *op. cit.*, pp. 453–60, and *Water Resource Development*, pp. 94–104, Harvard University Press, 1958.

something about a person's welfare; if one is concerned only with the welfare of the present generation; if the achievement of Pareto efficiency in relation to this generation is to be the guiding rule; even given all these assumptions one could still reject the normative significance of interest rates. The problems of imperfections in the capital market, the role of uncertainty, and the 'collective' nature of some of the desires of the present generation—all the matters discussed in section 6.3 in other words—all constitute what might be called 'technical' limitations to the usefulness of market interest rates.

(b) *The Distribution of Income and Wealth.* As with other prices in the economy, market interest rates will reflect the current distribution of income and wealth.[50] In assessing the benefit and cost time stream of public sector projects, the government may wish to use a different set of weights than that which reflects those groups whose influence on market interest rates is strongest. This approach then recognizes that Pareto efficiency may not be the sole policy objective. It would mean discounting rates higher or lower than current rates. A higher rate could be in order, for example, particularly for those projects involving unpriced outputs—social services, etc.—if the government felt that the present poor are more deserving than the future poor.

(c) *Preferences and Welfare.* As we stressed in chapter 4, market behaviour may not indicate much about a person's welfare, over and above the income distribution argument, if he is not the best judge of his own well-being. Some economists have suggested that this may be particularly true in the way individuals assess the future. Pigou felt that, generally speaking,

> . . . everybody prefers present pleasures or satisfactions of given magnitude to future pleasures or satisfactions of equal magnitude, even when the latter are perfectly certain to occur. But this preference for present pleasures does not . . . imply that a present pleasure of given magnitude is any *greater* than a future pleasure of the same magnitude. It implies only that our telescopic faculty is defective, and that we, therefore, see future pleasures, as it were, on a diminished scale. That this is the right explanation is proved by the fact that exactly the same diminution is experienced when, apart from our tendency to forget ungratifying incidents, we contemplate the past. . . . This reveals a far-reaching economic disharmony. For it implies that people distribute their resources between the present, the near future and the remote future on the basis of wholly irrational preferences.[51]

Pigou, then, would favour a lower discounting rate than that implied in market behaviour. In fact in a much broader spectrum, whether any 'rationality' can be imputed to some economic decisions involving the future seems

[50] Cf. M. S. Feldstein, *op. cit.*, *EJ*, p. 364, 1964.

[51] A. C. Pigou, *The Economics of Welfare*, pp. 24–5, Macmillan, 1920.

questionable. Time itself sees a change in an individual's values; experience of 'life' can revolutionize one's retrospective judgement of past decisions. This seems to be particularly important in relation to that type of expenditure which changes our values, i.e., education. Many recent suggestions in the UK for bringing outlays on higher education within the nexus of the price system, impute a rationality to decisions taken at age 18 which seems highly questionable. Can students assess the benefit stream that arises from incurring educational expenditure when the latter is in part designed to promote a re-assessment of what life is all about? Further, as Collard has said, this is a

> highly complex investment decision . . . [and] . . . is to be made either by young people or by parents on their behalf. To assume anything like the degree of rationality required is absurd apart from any effect the proposal would have on the class distribution of education . . . [In] . . . the field of medicine general practitioners, mostly intelligent men, find it impossible to sort out the rival claims of drug manufacturers. The bombardment of parents with educational literature would surely be just as useless and perhaps positively harmful. A 'wrong' choice is so important here that we cannot agree that bad choosers 'can learn to choose wisely by being allowed to choose and at first by choosing wrongly'.[52]

(d) *Political and Market Preferences.* Still thinking along the lines that it is the preferences of the present generation that matter, it has been suggested by Marglin[53] that individuals may have desires for provision to be made for the next generation over and above those that are actually expressed (charitable expenditure) and those that are technically difficult to express in a market (the 'collective good' argument). This arises because individuals wish governments to do things which they, as individuals, would never do. It is different from the 'collective good' argument which rests on what could perhaps be called hedonistic altruism. Marglin has labelled this approach, the 'schizophrenic view', since it sees an individual as both citizen and economic man. Clearly, the argument is not restricted to this context alone. Compare A. J. Ayer's thinking on the pros and cons of sending his children to state schools.

> If the independent schools enjoy an educational advantage, it is mainly because the more privileged parents continue to send their children to them. So, if one believes in social equality, should not one set an example by having one's children educated in the public sector, even at some small cost to them? This would be a very strong argument, if there were any great likelihood that one's example would be widely followed; but in fact there is not. . . . Political action will be needed to strip them of their privileged

[52] D. Collard, *The New Right*, p. 7, Fabian Tract 387.
[53] Most explicitly in the *QJE* article (*op. cit.* pp. 98–9).

positions. . . . In the meantime, like most other parents, we shall do what appears to be the most advantageous for our son.[54]

(e) *Whose Needs are Relevant?* But most of these arguments do not address themselves to, perhaps, the most important issue in the context of public investment decisions. Are the preferences of the present generation to be the only ones that matter? We come back then to the issue raised at the beginning of this chapter. Much of the writings of American economists—if I might be allowed this generalization—rest on the view that not only do individual preferences count but also only present individuals count. This concentration on 'individualism' thus requires a further value judgement when time is introduced. Moreover, there is a deeper point raised by Graaf.

> Very occasionally there may be unanimity on the location of the horizon. Then we can claim that our welfare theory has a true individualist basis. But if there is not unanimity, or only unanimity within a certain group, we have in effect a paternalist element at the foundation of our theory. For to say anything at all about welfare on an individualist basis we must demarcate the group of individuals in which we are interested; to demarcate the group we must fix the horizon; and the horizon fixed must, so to speak, be paternalistically imposed on all who do not happen to share our view of its 'proper' location. It is important to bear this in mind when evaluating the claim that welfare economics can be satisfactorily based on individual preferences.[55]

As a means of weighting the time stream of effects of public investment, market interest rates have, then, no necessary normative significance. The relevant weighting system would depend on the extent to which the government attached importance to the welfare of unborn generations. A government may well want to take account of some of the preferences of the present generation, and market interest rates may well be a useful starting point. But the general conclusion must be that of Feldstein, namely

> . . . to allow administrative determination of the . . . [social time preference rate] . . . with whatever weight to the welfare of future generations . . . democratic administrators would allow.[56]

This does not mean economic analysis has no part to play in this. The appropriate rate will depend on trends in consumption and population over time.

[54] The *Sunday Times*, London, 16 July 1967.

[55] J. De V. Graaf, *op. cit.*, p. 96.

[56] *Op. cit.*, *EJ*, p. 367, 1964. Feldstein's article is also concerned with exploring the factors which would affect the rate. The view advanced in the last sentence of our chapter has also been expressed by both Baumol (*op. cit.*, p. 801) and E. J. Mishan, 'Criteria for Public Expenditure Appraisal: Some Simplifying Suggestions' *JPE*, p. 140 fn., April 1967.

Given certain technical possibilities, one would want to know how items like consumption per head could vary over time. These and other matters should rightly be reviewed in choosing a rate. My own personal view, for example, would be that given present expectations of a rising income level we ought, perhaps, to pay more attention to some of the needs of the present population and let the future take care of itself.

Appendix

Net present value and internal rate of return

We wish, in this appendix, to describe two situations where the net discounted present value (NDPV) rule and internal rate of return (IRR) rule lead to the same result in ranking projects. In both situations all projects are viewed as involving a base year capital outlay of £K. In the first situation returns for one project, A, take the form of a constant amount, £a, each year into infinity. Now, the present value of such a stream, using an assumed appropriate interest rate, r, is given by a very simple expression, namely, a/r. The proof is as follows:

The present value of a stream of constant annuities (equal to a) up to year n when written out in full, is given by S where:

$$S = aD + aD^2 + \ldots + aD^n$$

Here, for simplicity, $1/(1+r)$ is represented by D. The stream, S, is a geometric progression which can be simplified in the following way:

$$SD = aD^2 + aD^3 + \ldots + aD^{n+1}$$

$$\therefore \quad S - SD = aD(1 - D^n)$$

$$\therefore \quad S = aD(1 - D^n)/(1 - D)$$

Replacing D by $1/(1+r)$ and cancelling out gives:

$$S = [1 - (1/1+r)^n]a/r$$

If n is very large and r is positive, then $1/(1+r)^n$ approaches zero, in which case we have: $S = a/r$.

It follows that for an investment involving a constant annuity of £a and a base year capital outlay of £K the NDPV is given by:

$$(a/r) - K \tag{6.A1}$$

The associated rule is to choose that project with the higher NDPV. If another project, B, involves the same base year capital cost then, clearly, the ranking rule is equivalent to simply observing whether the constant annual return in the other project, say b, is bigger than a. In these circumstances, the interest rate plays no role in the ranking; this is similar to the two-period model of the early part of the chapter where, with two projects involving the same base year capital cost, the ranking process would involve simply observing the size of undiscounted net profits (or net social benefits if a public firm is involved) in the 'next' year. Now the IRR criterion is to choose between A and B on the basis of the size of the rate of return. Since however the IRR is defined as that rate of interest which, when used for discounting, renders the NDPV equal to zero, then we can see from expression (6.A1) that, for project A it is equal to a/K, and for B it would be b/K. Thus, the two ranking devices are equivalent. On both criteria A is better than B if $a > b$.

In the second situation, returns accrue in only one year. Denoting this year by n, and letting the return for project A be K_A, we have that the NDPV is:

$$[K_A/(1+r)^n]-K \tag{6.A2}$$

A similar sort of expression would describe the NDPV of project B, save that K_B would be substituted for K_A. Clearly, again, choosing the project with the higher NDPV is equivalent to observing whether K_A is greater or less than K_B; the interest rate is again irrelevant. Now an expression for the IRR for project A, say R_A, can be obtained if (6.A2) is set equal to zero and r replaced by R_A. Rearrangement of terms would then give:

$$R_A = \sqrt[n]{K_A/K}-1 \tag{6.A3}$$

The IRR for project B, say R_B, would be expressed in a similar way, save that K_A would be replaced by K_B. Again it would follow that if $K_A > K_B$ then $R_A > R_B$. Thus, as with the NDPV method it is K_A and K_B alone that are crucial. The two methods rank in the same way.

Part 2: General Applications

7. Marginal cost pricing

7.1 Introduction

Much of the analysis in the second part of this book takes place in the context described in the first part of chapter 4, and a re-reading of this will prove useful in appreciating the significance of the analysis of general applications. For example, a discussion of pricing policies appropriate for governmentally supplied goods and services can be conducted at a number of different levels. One could consider whether it is feasible (in the technical sense) to levy prices —the public good problem. Secondly, even if it is feasible to levy prices one has to decide whether a price system achieves the desired objectives; some of the considerations that are relevant are the extent to which a price system reflects consumers' needs and the implications for income distribution. Thirdly, appropriate policies, even within the context of allocative efficiency, will depend on the significance of second-best and externalities. All of these wide issues were considered in chapter 4. We shall, here, be concerned with a third level of discussion, one which explores the technical problems of marginal-cost pricing, given a background that for certain parts of the public sector prices should be related to such costs. Although we have argued that in some instances some discrepancies between prices and marginal costs will be necessary because of second-best and externality problems, this chapter proceeds very much as if such problems did not exist. Where it seems particularly relevant to mention these wider factors, this is done, but continuous qualification is unnecessary.

The main concern is, then, with analysing the logic of an optimizing process. This process involves the maximization of benefit less cost—assumed here to be indicated by market data—subject to the constraint of the production technology and subject also to some wider feasibility constraints discussed towards the end of the chapter. Granted this context it follows that part of what follows has direct optimizing implications for private firms. It is not often recognized that, subject to the necessary qualifications regarding the monopolistic/monopsonistic power of some public enterprises, many of the technical problems of marginal cost pricing apply to profit-maximizing firms. In this sense there is nothing special about public sector activities. Another general point is worth bearing in mind. An important subject of interest in this chapter is the meaning of costs. To the economist costs partly depend on output requirements which themselves depend on prices. Thus prices and costs are interdependent. In deciding on alternative methods of production, one cannot take existing forecasts of demand as given since demand depends on price which depends on costs. In practice this interdependence, which is an important part of the economist's set of tools, cannot always be catered for in planning output. One has to take demand and price as more or less given, notwithstanding that eventually some repercussions will be felt. To this extent a public enterprise is behaving almost like the textbook competitive price-taker. Something like this appears to operate in electricity supply.

> In principle, there is of course a feedback between the forecast load growth which it is planned to meet and the plant programme. Costs depend on the programme and help to determine tariffs, which in turn affect the growth of the load. To bring this interdependence into a formal analysis of optimising the plant programme would not be helpful, however, since it is impossible to take account of it in practice, simultaneously determining future tariff levels and the plant programme. It is just not possible either to predict the demand relationship between load, tariffs and other fuel prices several years ahead or to predict what price relativities will then be. Thus the feed back can only be taken into account implicitly and iteratively: each year's plant programme aims to meet a load which is forecast in the light, among many other things, of anticipated trends in electricity tariffs relative to the prices of other fuels; these anticipated trends in turn reflect the expected development of costs, depending, among other things, upon investment decisions already taken. Each time a new forecast is made for, say, six years ahead it may be different from the forecast made the previous year for seven years ahead.[1]

We mention this general point at this stage because no allowance is made for it in the subsequent analysis, though it does implicitly crop up in the later discussion of feasibility constraints.

Plan of chapter

Three final points relate to exposition. The price paid by an enterprise for a factor of production is assumed to be independent of the quantities purchased. This sort of market problem was discussed in chapter 3, and in this chapter similar issues arise in the context of final good prices. It is unnecessary to analyse again the static aspects of factor price changes; changes over time, because of inflation or technical change, will however be a feature of the later discussion. A second point is that the analysis will be conducted in a partial equilibrium setting. For expositional simplicity, output/input changes

[1] R. Turvey, *Optimal Pricing and Investment in Electricity Supply*, p. 13, Allen & Unwin, 1968.

in the sector in question will be treated as if they had no significant effect on the real incomes of consumers and factor suppliers, nor on prices in the rest of the economy. This allows one to use the areas under demand and cost curves as measures of the compensating income variations arising from changes in output or input; that is (in line with the discussion in chapter 3), such areas indicate *total* consumer benefit and total economic costs at each production level. Some of the problems posed when changes in the public sector cause price changes elsewhere are analysed in chapter 9. Those changes which do, in fact, involve indivisible jumps are considered in the next chapter, which also looks at the problem of peak loads. For the time being, it is assumed that all inputs and outputs are perfectly divisible. A third point relates to investment decisions. We saw in chapter 6 that the investment criterion associated with Pareto-type efficiency is the one which accepts projects whose net discounted present value (NDPV) of social benefits and costs is positive. Although the broad relationship between this criterion and pricing decisions was analysed in chapter 6, this present chapter is primarily concerned with a more detailed consideration. At the same time, three problems associated with public investment decisions are ignored here. One is the implication of using an interest rate different from current market rates; we assume that some rate, r, has been chosen as the appropriate one. The implication of this in general for the public sector's use of capital funds is considered in a later chapter. Secondly, the problems that risk allowances, profits taxes, and the like—also discussed in chapter 6—cause for investment decision rules are also not considered until a later chapter. Thirdly, limitations on the availability of funds can also alter the appropriate decision rule; here, it is assumed that no such constraints exist. The point is that, should allowances be made for these issues, the decision would be a major policy issue which would not be taken by an individual enterprise. They can properly be discussed in a separate chapter.

The contents of this chapter are as follows. A key point concerning the level of prices is discussed in the very next sub-section. Then in section 7.2 some introductory points concerning choice of production technique are explored in the context of a new public enterprise with a new product—starting from scratch, in other words. Section 7.3 looks at pricing and optimal capacity in the same context. In section 7.4 this relationship is examined in the more realistic context of an enterprise with an inherited volume of capacity. Section 7.5 considers the important relationships between short and long-run pricing when there is excess capacity, and finally, section 7.6 explores some general difficulties associated with marginal cost pricing.

A general theoretical principle concerning prices

At any point in time an enterprise's stock of capital assets is fixed. In practice, this fixity of an enterprise's *capacity* may apply for considerable periods of time. There may be over a year's gap between the decision to introduce new railway engines and their introduction. Telephone capacity in the UK has usually taken much longer. Within such periods it is often the case that the only way output or services can be expanded is *by using the existing capacity more intensively*—by laying out more on the 'running costs' of labour, fuel, raw materials, and so on. Slightly different procedures sometimes operate; the UK Electricity industry at one time used to hire gas-turbine units when demand was particularly heavy; even here, however, the rental payments were effectively a running cost for the industry. This characteristic was largely ignored in the discussion of pricing in chapter 3. What it does mean is that in these circumstances the use of the enterprise's existing capacity entails no economic costs. The purchase price of the capital assets is not a cost which is incurred within this period. It is what economists call a historic cost. Since the 'efficient' use of resources and 'efficient' output scales are defined in relation to benefits and costs incurrable within the time-period in question, then the historic cost of existing assets is irrelevant in such decisions. The only economic costs involved relate to labour, fuel, and raw materials. There are two qualifications to this. The enterprise's existing assets may have a scrap value or, putting it more generally, the capacity may have a use value in locations alternative to the existing one. For items like plant, machinery, and rail track this may well be very low if only because there are large costs involved in shifting locale or in scrapping; in this case, the historic costs are irretrievably 'sunken'. For assets like land, particularly in urban areas, there will be a considerable 'opportunity cost' which in some circumstances might be realizable within the period in question. A second qualification is that the use of assets may involve some user cost, to the extent that maintenance work is needed to keep up the quality of its services. Though it cannot be parcelled out to individual vehicles, road surface maintenance involves economic costs that can probably be ascribed to groups of traffic. However, this sort of cost clearly can be incorporated under the umbrella heading of running costs. In addition we shall assume, henceforth, unless otherwise stated, that existing capacity has no alternative use value.

This keeps intact the proposition that within such periods the only economic costs are running costs. In Fig. 7.1 these costs are plotted as a function of output, and take the path of the *S* line which is the enterprise's short-run marginal cost line. One could think of this cost function in a number of ways. Where the enterprise has a large number of plants one might think of increasing output being met by using more and more of the existing plants. In electricity supply, for example, it is usual to arrange existing plants in an 'order of merit' on the basis of fuel and other running costs. For fairly low output levels nuclear plants provide most of the electricity, because their *running* costs are low *vis à vis* the conventional coal plants. Output can be increased by bringing in the coal plants; some of these have higher fuel costs

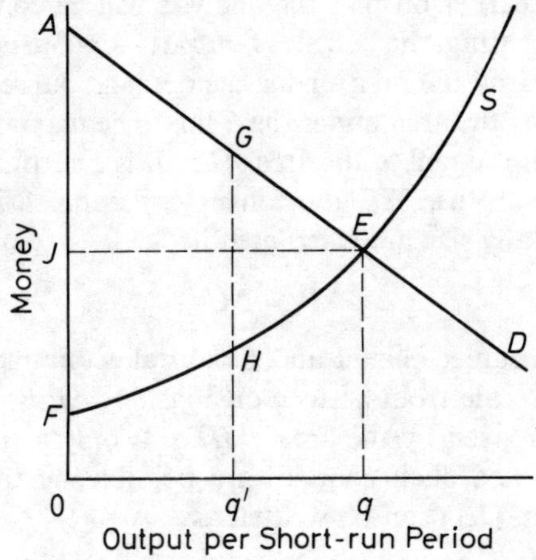

FIG. 7.1

than others and so the high-cost coal plants are only introduced when the required output is high. In this sense then the ordinates of the *S* line indicate the running cost (per unit of output) of the 'marginal' plant.[2] Of course, we have cheated slightly in the definition of short-run marginal costs since each plant will normally produce more than one unit of output. The unit running costs of the 'marginal' plant is then an average of the plant's running costs. Provided there are a large number of plants, however, this point is trivial. Similar points apply in a general sense to other activities often carried out in the public sector. Alternatively, the rise in the *S* line could be thought of in terms of rising running costs as each plant in a system is used more intensively. Within this context, then, optimal output is at q where price equals short-run marginal cost. To pave the way for future discussion it is useful to briefly re-cap on the interpretation of this, discussed in chapter 3. The optimal output is that output at which benefit minus cost is maximized.[3]

[2] The cost structure in electricity is, of course, much more complicated than this.

[3] The analysis can more rigorously be presented as follows. Total consumer benefit, as defined earlier on in this section, is given by the area under the demand curve. Here, it is relevant to look at the demand curve vertically expressing price as a function of quantity, rather than the usual 'horizontal' approach of expressing quantity as a function of price. The demand curve equation is, therefore, $P = f(q)$, where P is price and q is quantity demanded. Total consumer benefit may, therefore, be written as

$$(TB) = \int_{O}^{Q} f(q)\delta q \qquad (1)$$

Total short-run costs may be expressed directly as a function of output; that is,

$$(TC) = C(q) \qquad (2)$$

Since we suggested earlier on that the analysis will be conducted in a truly partial equilibrium setting, the benefit of output—or consumer evaluation of output—is indicated by the area under the demand curve. Total economic costs are indicated by the area under the *S* line. The maximand is, therefore, greatest at q where it is equal to the area *AEF*. It is a surplus comprising two elements, producer surplus, *JEF*, and consumer surplus *AJE*. In other words, output increases of any size are warranted if:

$$\Delta B > \Delta C \tag{7.1}$$

where B is total consumer benefit and C is total economic costs. Thus, for the large change in scale from q^1 to q on Fig. 7.1, ΔB is given by the area $GEqq^1$ whilst ΔC is given by the area q^1HEq. If only a small change from output q is made—and such changes are possible by the assumption of divisibility—then eq. (7.1) can be written as:

$$P > SMC \tag{7.2}$$

where P is the ruling price and SMC is short-run marginal cost. All changes which meet eq. (7.2) are undertaken so that optimality is characterized by the equality of price (or marginal benefit) and marginal cost.

Now, there is an important element in this analysis which pervades the whole discussion of pricing. No matter what time-period is taken, one can assume realistically that variations in output can take place by varying the volume of running costs;[4] short-run marginal costs will always be a relevant way of changing output. Within some time-spans output can also be altered by changing the volume of capacity, but the shorter the time-span the less likely is this possibility. Granted this—and granted the context, namely that 'efficiency' is the relevant criterion, that problems of second-best,

---

The surplus to be maximized, *S*, is therefore:

$$S = (TB) - (TC) \tag{3}$$

The equilibrium condition is found by differentiating (3) with respect to output and setting the result equal to zero. That is we have:

$$f(q) - \delta C(q)/\delta q = 0 \tag{4}$$

The first term is simply price and the second term is (short-run) marginal cost. Equation (4) is, therefore, similar to eq. (7.2) in the text.

[4] In practice, some running costs may be variable within very short-periods such as a week—some raw materials could fall into this category—and others may be 'fixed' for any periods less than say two months; labour supplies probably have this characteristic in many sectors. The key issue is whether it is economic to consider very short-periods. If, because of potential inconvenience to customers and the enterprise itself, price changes within periods of less than six months are ruled out then it becomes relevant to talk of the short-period as six months rather than nine months and rather than one month. The text makes a distinction between running costs and capacity costs which may well be a relevant distinction in practice. However, none of these considerations affect the subsequent analysis of pricing. Even if a daily period were taken, the general relationship between prices (equal to short-run marginal costs) and the costs of all factors not variable in such time-periods, still holds. This point is re-examined in the later parts of this chapter.

externality, and so on can be ignored—it follows that, in theory, price should always be equal to short-run marginal costs. *Irrespective of the existing size of capacity or the possibilities of altering it, output should always be adjusted to the point where price equals short-run marginal cost.* If *SMC* is less than price, then net benefits can accrue from expanding the use of existing capacity; if price is less than short-run marginal cost then, by making a short-run contraction, the saving in running costs exceeds the loss in consumer benefits. This, at first sight, raises considerable problems; if price is unrelated to the costs of capital assets how do we know when to build them? If built, how are these costs to be financed? What is the relevance of long-run marginal cost? These problems have been the subject of much discussion by economists. In the UK, for example, particularly in the decade following the nationalization of the fuel and transport industries, the journal literature was full of discussions of marginal-cost pricing, and the issue of short-run or long-run costs was a key feature of the discussion. In fact, it was French economists (and engineers) working in the public sector who solved most of these problems. This they did by considering the relationship of investment policy to price policy. In particular, they addressed themselves to a key question: what is the optimal volume of capacity? In other words, while price policy is closely bound up with the use of existing capacity—by definition, since prices allocate existing resources—there is a related set of decisions which will ultimately affect the level of prices, namely, the decisions about whether existing capacity is larger or smaller than optimal. Although one might not be able to change capacity 'now', one can certainly *decide* whether an increase or decrease in its volume is warranted. And eventually *at some point of time* capacity can be changed. Otherwise how did the present volume of capacity come into existence! A key proposition about the relationship between pricing and capacity decisions can be taken from the writings of the French economist M. Boiteux;

> Provided there is an optimal investment policy, short-term pricing is also long-term pricing, and there is no longer any contradiction between the two.[5]

It is this proposition and its implications that will be examined in the next section.

Physical capacity limits

However, before doing this there is one qualification that needs to be made

[5] 'Peak-Load Pricing', p. 70. This is an article which appeared originally as 'La tarification des demandes en pointe: application de la théorie de la vente au coût marginal'. An edited translation appeared under the above English title in the *Journal of Business*, April 1960. This was reproduced as chapter 4 of *Marginal Cost Pricing in Practice*, Ed. J. R. Nelson, Prentice-Hall, 1964. The page references are to Nelson's book.

to the previous suggestion that price should always equal short-run marginal costs. Whereas traditional cost theory assumes smoothly rising SMC curves, in practice cost functions do not always fall neatly into this box. In some cases the cost function may, after a point, start rising fairly steeply so that marginal costs become very high. On an existing road, for example, where economic costs comprise maintenance items and vehicle costs, as traffic flows increase marginal costs may become very high; the SMC curve in fact may cut backward if output is defined as traffic flow per unit of time.[6] Much plant and machinery may be inflexible in this sense. At the extreme there may be rigid capacity limits to the use of existing capacity. If one assumed that running costs were constant per unit of output up to a capacity limit, *q*, then short-run marginal costs take the path of *ALG* in Fig. 7.2. In other words, they are

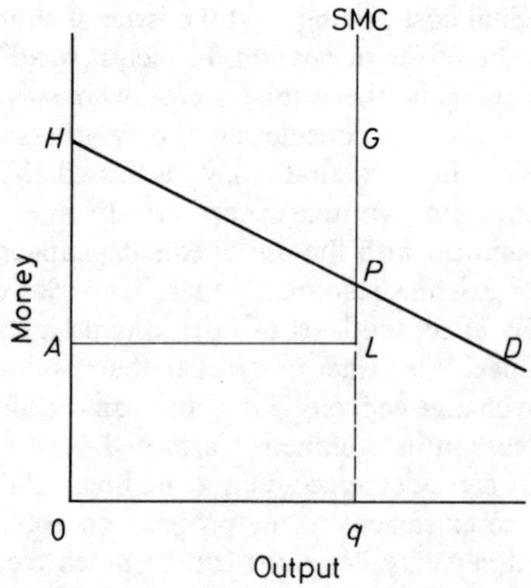

FIG. 7.2

constant and equal to *OA*, up to the capacity limit, and thereafter they are infinite. This case of rigid capacity raises issues which crop up time and time again in the pricing field. We are not suggesting that any cost function in practice looks like that in Fig. 7.2, but it does illustrate the sort of issues that arise when there are rigid limits.[7] What is optimal price and output? If the

[6] See, for example, 'The Theory and Measurement of Private and Social Cost of Highway Congestion', by A. A. Walters, *Econometrica*, October 1961; reproduced as Chapter 7 of *Transport*, edited by D. Munby, Penguin Modern Economic Series, 1968.

[7] Boiteux thinks the case of rigidity is fairly common. The curve in Fig. 7.2

'. . . is seen to be the extreme case of a progressively less flexible curve, the arms of which approach their asymptotes. . . . Many industrial plants are near to . . . [the type of Fig. 7.2] . . . than to . . . [the type in Fig. 7.1] . . . and should be treated as being of rigid capacity.'

(*op. cit*., p. 65).

demand curve had cut the SMC line along its horizontal segment then, clearly, the optimal price would have to be equal to unit running costs. But in Fig. 7.2 the *D* curve cuts the vertical segment. Marginal cash operating costs are *OA*, but if price is set at this level there is excess demand. On wider grounds of equity, distributional considerations, and so on, it may in practice be decided to set price at this level and engage in some form of rationing. On grounds of Pareto-type efficiency the solution however is clearcut. Total benefit minus total cost is maximized by selling output *q* at price *P*; the maximized amount of producer and consumer surplus is indicated by the area *HPLA*. This is not marginal cost pricing if costs are thought of in terms of cash operating costs. But marginal cost pricing is not the objective; it is a method. The objective is the maximization of total consumer benefit subject to the constraints of resource availability. Some have condemned the solution as 'charging what the traffic will bear';[8] the condemnation is correct—this *is* the appropriate solution in this context! One way of understanding the solution is to see that price, in effect, is equal to the next best alternative use value of the resources. Whereas this normally would relate to using the factors of production in some other locale, here the next best use is to sell to the consumer just excluded. His evaluation of the marginal unit is just short of *P* and this exceeds the factors' use value elsewhere as indicated by *OA*. One could then think of price being always equal to marginal opportunity cost,[9] the latter being whichever is the higher of the two items just mentioned. If it be understood that 'short-run marginal costs' refers to opportunity cost in this sense, then the proposition that price should always be equal to short-run marginal cost can be retained.

7.2 Cost minimization and choice of production technique

In the traditional theory of the firm, discussion of the optimality of capacity usually takes place in the context of the firm's long-run production decisions —a context where all factors are taken as variable. What is often not recognized is that these long-run decisions are usually viewed as taking place in very special circumstances, namely, that no capacity is inherited from the past. It is very rare in practice that one 'starts from scratch'. New roads, hospitals, railway lines, and electricity generating plants are, in practice, invariably additions to an existing stock of assets. And the existence of such an inherited stock considerably complicates the economics of new capacity.

[8] R. L. Meek made this one of his criticisms of the French economists' rationale for the 'Tarif Vert' of the French Nationalized Electricity body, Electricité de France. See 'An Application of Marginal Cost Pricing: The "Green Tariff" in Theory and Practice', *JIE*, July and November 1963 (p. 218, July). However, he appears to have changed his mind on this and accepted that marginal cost pricing is not an objective but simply a means; see 'The New Bulk Supply Tariff for Electricity', *EJ*, p. 56, March 1968.

[9] Two people have made this point explicitly. See 'Peak Loads and Efficient Pricing: Comment', by J. Hirschleifer, *QJE*, p. 458, August 1958, and R. Turvey's 'Marginal Cost Pricing in Practice', *Economica*, pp. 429–30, November 1964.

To provide three-lane motorway services raises different engineering and economic issues when a two-lane motorway already exists than if one was starting from scratch. In integrated systems new capacity may actually affect the amount of use made of the old capacity; in electricity supply, new nuclear plants invariably lead to reduced usage of existing coal-fired plants. Since the existing capacity was first introduced both technology and factor prices could have changed. These very relevant issues we provisionally side-step by *assuming that the enterprise is starting from scratch;* later on in this chapter the issues are re-introduced. A second expositional assumption to be made is that the required assets can all be introduced simultaneously. There is a gestation period between decision-taking and actual operation of capacity, but this period is taken to be the same for all assets. Decisions concerning the optimality of capacity are, clearly, going to be concerned with the benefits and costs of different output scales. The problem can be analysed in two stages. First of all it is necessary to estimate the costs of different levels of capacity. Here, one is concerned with the optimal plant mix, technique, and factor combination appropriate to each scale. It should be fairly obvious from the earlier chapters of this book that, provided the prices paid by the public agency for factors of production truly reflect the social cost of using these factors—that second-best and externality problems have been accounted for in other words—then the efficiency criterion pervading this chapter requires that the enterprise minimizes the cost of producing any given output. Given information on the minimum costs of various capacity scales, one can go on to consider the optimal scale in terms of both benefits and costs.

'Least cost optimal' capacity

Choosing the least cost methods of providing various output levels raises problems which will be familiar to any one who has read a micro-economics text. Here the aim will be to concentrate on certain features important for the determination of optimal prices. In practice, choosing between different methods of producing a given output is not as simple as a cost comparison might imply. To return to some previous examples, in integrated systems one often has to look at the system in its entirety in assessing any one individual project. In electricity, choices are usually made between coal, nuclear, and hydro generating plants. Each will operate in the system in a different way, and one has to allow for the full effect on system costs when a plant is introduced as well as consider the plant's 'own' costs. The use of hydro plants is complicated by the uncertainties associated with water supply and some estimates have usually to be made about 'expected' climatic conditions. A problem more connected with time is the motorway example alluded to earlier on. Traffic flows may not be large enough to make a three-lane motorway physically necessary now. However, if a two-lane road is built now and extension to three lanes made in say ten years time the undiscounted total of construction costs would usually be larger than for the once-and-for-all three-lane construction. Here, then, the issue becomes one of choosing between the present value of two time-streams of costs; the rate of interest then becomes a crucial variable—the higher it is, the more favourable is the method which delays the construction of the third lane. Different techniques of production also often involve assets with different lengths of life; in the UK electricity industry an allowance of twenty years is usually made for a nuclear plant and thirty years for coal plants; to guarantee that different techniques are being compared on an equivalent basis, one would have to standardize the time-span by taking a period of say sixty years (the lowest common multiple), or by assuming indefinite replacement.[10]

It is practically impossible to simultaneously consider all these complications, and for expositional purposes simplifications have to be made. However, the problem of time-stream does need explicit treatment. Suppose that a planning period is decided on which is long enough to cover the differences in lengths of life of different kinds of capacity. Secondly, let us make the very strong assumptions that demand is going to be constant over each year of the planning period, that plant running costs do not rise with age, and that no technical advances or general price rises are expected over the planning period. For any output level, i.e. say 20,000 units per annum for each year of the planning period, that technique of production is chosen which involves the least present value of costs. The larger the output the greater will be the scale of capacity, and for each output level one has a present value figure for the chosen production method. Capital costs will often be spread over time. It would help if we could think of capital costs as a once-and-for-all outlay. This can be done if the capital cost outlays are summed and the interest charges paid during the construction period are included. Thus, if construction starts in January 1970, operation starts in January 1973, and construction costs are incurred in the January's of 1970, 71, and 72—K_0, K_1 and K_2 respectively—then the cumulative value of capital costs by January 1973 is

[10] There is a growing literature on choice of technique in the public sector, even if one restricts the terms of reference to micro-aspects and to electricity and transport. A nice illustration of the motorway problem can be found in 'Some Aspects of the Economics of the MI', M. Beesley, *JIE*, July 1962. The choice of plants in electricity is often viewed as involving the so-called global problem of planning the broad outlines of the plant structure. For this, programming techniques are used. Then substitution at the 'margin' takes place on the basis of conventional cost comparisons. A general discussion of these issues can be found in an article by R. L. Meek, 'The Allocation of Expenditure in the Electricity Supply Industry: Some Methodological Problems', *SJPE*, February 1963, reproduced in *Public Expenditure: Appraisal and Control*, Ed. by A. T. Peacock and D. J. Robertson, Oliver & Boyd, 1963. More detail can be found in the early chapters of Turvey's *Optimal Pricing and Investment in Electricity Supply*, *op. cit.* A very useful survey of some of the problems—system interdependence, differing lives, differing capacities, and so on—which arise in the 'marginal' problem, has been made by M. G. Webb in his 'Some Principles Involved in the Economic Comparison of Power Stations', *Manchester School*, January 1967.

$$K_0(1+r)^3+K_1(1+r)^2+K_2(1+r) = K,$$

where r is the assumed appropriate interest rate. If future operating costs are discounted back to January 1973, then effectively all costs are being expressed in terms of January 1973 values. The 'least cost optimal' capacity figures constitute, then, a capital cost item plus the present value of a stream of annual running costs. Where replacement of capital items is subsumed in the planning period, then the present value of such items is included as part of the base-year capital cost figure. Now, to the extent that output is going to be constant each year, the annual running cost items can usefully be represented on the standard two-dimensional diagram. The S^1, S^2, and S^3 lines of Fig. 7.3 indicate the annual marginal running cost functions for three different

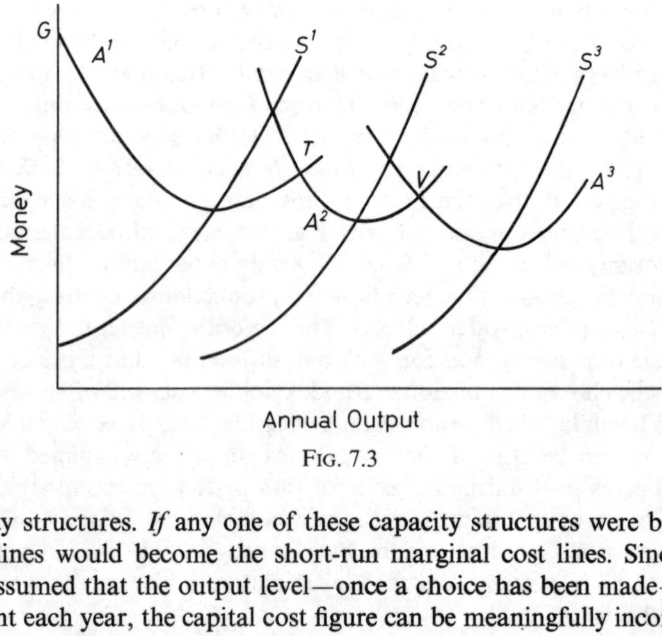

FIG. 7.3

capacity structures. *If* any one of these capacity structures were built then the S lines would become the short-run marginal cost lines. Since it has been assumed that the output level—once a choice has been made—will be constant each year, the capital cost figure can be meaningfully incorporated into the diagram.

The appropriate concept is the *annual equivalent capital cost*. There will, in other words, be some annual sum, say £a, which, if incurred annually over the planning period, constitutes a time stream of money outlays whose present value is equivalent to the base-year capital cost. This annual sum does not represent a real variable; resources are actually committed in the base-year (or replacement year). It is an analytic device useful for bringing capital costs into a diagrammatic treatment. The point is that in evaluating, say, two different methods for producing a given output one could use the criterion: prefer that method the present value of whose stream of costs is lower. When running costs are constant per annum this is equivalent to the criterion: prefer that method with the lower *annual equivalent cost*, where this is the sum of annual running costs and the annual equivalent capital cost. Similarly, if one was evaluating the benefits and costs of a project, one could either calculate the net discounted present value in the normal way, or, if annual benefits and running costs are constant, one could see whether annual benefits exceed annual costs where the latter is defined as before.[11] How is the annual equivalent capital cost calculated? It was demonstrated in the appendix to chapter 6 that the present value of a constant annual sum, a, incurred (or received) over n years, is equal to $(1-D^n)a/r$, where D was a symbol used to represent the discount factor, $1/(1+r)$. Calculation of the equivalent annual capital cost involves the reverse procedure. If K is the base-year capital cost figure, then the equivalent annual figure is:

$$a = Kr/(1-D^n) \tag{7.3}$$

When n is very large, D^n approaches zero, so that a takes the form of the returns to a perpetuity, i.e., the annual interest charges on the base year figure. Incidentally, in the UK public sector, an identical concept is often used for both project evaluation and accounting. This so-called *annual capital charge* consists of two items. Provision for accounting depreciation is, in both the local government authorities and the nationalized industries, often made on a sinking fund basis. When a loan is obtained to finance a project the authorities will put away into a fund (usually for reinvestment elsewhere) a certain amount each year. This provision is usually the same each year, and it is necessary to estimate the minimum amount that need be put away such that, allowing for interest (through the reinvestment), the cumulative value at the end of the project's life is just sufficient to pay off the loan. It can be demonstrated[12] that, if K is the initial loan, r is the annual

[11] Many apparently different investment criteria are equivalent in certain circumstances. See, for example, R. L. Meek's 'Ideal and Reality in the Choice between Alternative Techniques', *OEP*, November 1964.

[12] Suppose £x is put aside for reinvestment at the end of each year. The provision made in the first year will, at the end of the period, have a cumulative or terminal value of $x(1+r)^{n-1}$. The terminal value of the second year provision will be $x(1+r)^{n-2}$. Let the sum of such terminal values for all years be K. We have:

$$K = x(1+r)^{n-1}+x(1+r)^{n-2}+\ldots+x(1+r)^{n-(n-1)}+x(1+r)^{n-n}$$

$$\therefore \quad K = x(1+r)^{n-1}+x(1+r)^{n-2}+\ldots+x(1+r)+1$$

$$\therefore \quad K = x[1+(1+r)+(1+r)^2+\ldots+(1+r)^{n-1}]$$

As in the appendix to chapter 6, we have here a geometric progression which simplifies to:

$$K = x[1-(1+r)^n]/[1-(1+r)] = x[(1+r)^n-1]/r$$

This then is the sum which would cumulate if £x were invested annually for each year of the period. Alternatively, we have:

$$x = Kr/[(1+r)^n-1]$$

and this is the annual sum that would have to be invested if £K were to be cumulated in n years time. For further discussion of the annual capital charge see A. J. Merrett and A. Sykes, *The Finance and Analysis of Capital Projects*, pp. 3–15, 39–42, and 165–71, Longmans, 1963.

interest that can be obtained from reinvestment, and n is the project life, the annual sum is equal to $Kr/[(1+r)^n-1]$. This is the first part of the capital charge. The second part is the annual interest payment—Kr, if we assume the interest rate is the same—that has to be paid to the bodies granting the loan. Thus the annual capital charge, a', is:

$$a' = Kr+\{Kr/[(1+r)^n-1]\} \tag{7.4}$$

By rearranging terms, it is seen that a' is the same as a. The annual capital charge is then an annual constant amount, the present value of whose time-stream is equal to the base-year capital cost (or loan), and whose value is sufficient to pay off interest charges on the loan and provide for eventual redemption of the loan.

Short and long-run marginal costs

To return to the main stream of the analysis, the A^1 line in Fig. 7.3, thus, represents the 'annual costs' of the first of the three capacity structures; it comprises the annual equivalent capital cost per unit of output, plus annual running costs per unit of output. The A^2 and A^3 lines refer to different and larger capacity structures. With only these three possibilities, capacity structure 1 is the least cost method for output scales less than T. Beyond T however capacity structure 2 becomes the cheaper method, at least up to output V; for scales of output larger than V the largest capacity structure, type 3, is best. Thinking in terms of roads one might envisage three possibilities for a particular route, a formed earth road, a gravel surfaced road, and a two-lane sealed road. Running costs relate to vehicle operation and road maintenance; the type of road one wants will, therefore, depend on the expected traffic flows.[13] Whatever the context, Fig. 7.3 implies some indivisibility in the use of capacity. The scalloped line passing through GTV and then taking the path of A^3 is, effectively, the enterprise's long-run average cost curve. It indicates the minimum cost of various output levels where one is starting from scratch. If we could assume that capacity is perfectly divisible, then such cost curves become smooth. Although only two capacity structures are shown on Fig. 7.4, perfect divisibility is assumed, and this generates the familiar smooth long-run average cost curve (LAC).

Now, such curves have a characteristic crucial for the level of prices. If a particular volume of capacity is decided on, say that associated with S^1, then A^1 effectively *becomes* the enterprise's short-run average cost curve. Of course *then* only running costs would be economic costs. We may denote lines like A^1 and A^2 as short-run average cost curves, but must remember that our whole discussion is in the planning stage: all costs *are* economic before capacity is built. Students of micro-economics will remember that

[13] Some of the implications of such indivisibilities can be found in 'Investment Criteria and Road Pricing', G. M. Neutze, *Manchester School*, January 1966.

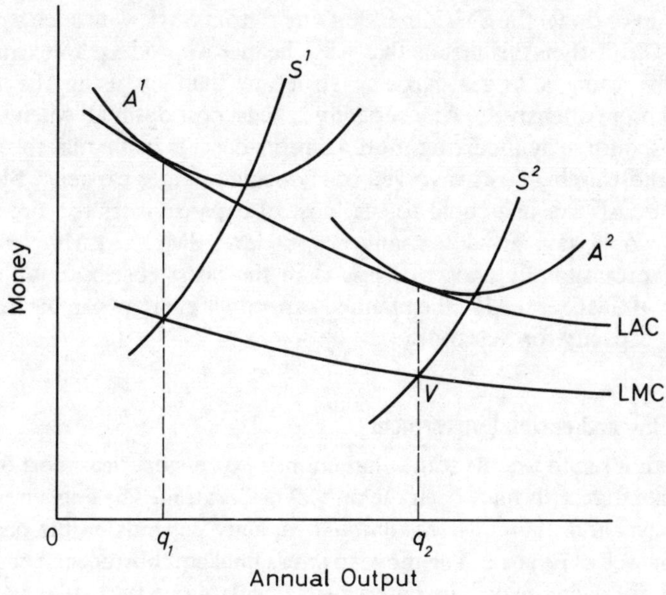

FIG. 7.4

in those output ranges where long-run average cost is falling, the LAC line is tangential to the falling part of the short-run average cost curves. Falling long-run costs indicate, to the extent that one is talking of products and industries, increasing returns to scale. It is not suggested that this is a general phenomenon; the situation is used here because, diagrammatically, it indicates fairly clearly a crucial point. This point relates to outputs like q_1 and q_2. For output q_1 capacity structure 1 (i.e., that associated with A^1 and S^1) is the 'least cost optimal' structure; similarly capacity structure 2 is the least cost method of producing q_2. At such outputs, not only is the LAC line tangential to the A^1 line associated with the 'right' structure, but *short-run marginal costs with such a capacity structure are equal to long-run marginal costs.* When capacity is optimally adjusted, in terms of least cost, LAC is always equal to SAC. Therefore, long-run *total* costs equal short-run *total* costs. For a very small change in output, the change in short-run total costs equals the change in long-run total costs. But the former is the definition of SMC and the latter is the definition of long-run marginal cost, LMC. It follows that, at such outputs, SMC and LMC are equal.[14] The intuitive explanation of this is that, with any given capacity, output can be varied by

[14] This point can be more rigorously demonstrated with algebra or further diagrams. A useful introductory algebraic treatment can be found in K. J. Cohen and R. M. Cyert, *Theory of the Firm*, pp. 138–49, Prentice-Hall, 1965. Long-run total cost diagrams can be found in Boiteux (*op. cit.*) and Meek (*JIE*, July 1963, *op. cit.*).

moving up or down the SMC line. If at any output SMC with such a capacity exceeds LMC, then this means that it is cheaper to produce an extra unit of output by using a larger capacity structure than by using the planned capacity more intensively. Any capacity is 'least cost optimal' when the costs of raising output by incurring more running costs is just equal to the extra capital and running costs involved in choosing a larger capacity. Short-run marginal costs are just equal to the 'cost of expansion' as the French economists would say. Thus if at any output level SMC $>$ LMC, the actual capacity provisionally chosen is less than the 'least cost optimal' scale of capacity. If SMC $<$ LMC, the planned capacity is greater than the 'least cost optimal' capacity for that output.

7.3 Pricing and optimal investment

We have chosen to use the somewhat clumsy expression, 'least cost optimal', to indicate that costs have been the only consideration. The final choice of *an* output level and, therefore, *the optimal* capacity depends on the benefits of output as well as its costs. The move towards final equilibrium can be thought of in the following way. The enterprise considers one particular volume of capacity, the capital and running costs of which are known. Once installed, the optimal usage of this capacity would require that output be adjusted to the point where price equals short-run marginal costs. If at this output SMC $>$ LMC, then the planners know that this output can be produced more cheaply—from the point of view of capital and running costs—by using a larger capacity structure. In this case, the provisionally planned investment is sub-optimal. A larger capacity structure would entail a different set of short-run marginal costs and, therefore, a different price and output. If at this higher output SMC $>$ LMC, then further capacity increases are warranted, and so on. As long as $P =$ SMC, extensions of capacity are warranted as long as SMC $>$ LMC. The optimal volume of capacity is achieved when SMC $=$ LMC. In other words, the final optimal volume of output and capacity is characterized by the condition:

$$P = \text{SMC} = \text{LMC} \tag{7.5}$$

The extra capital and running costs involved in increasing output by extending capacity is just equal to the cost of using the planned capacity more intensively. Moreover, these costs are just equal to the value of such extra output as indicated by consumer benefit. Therefore, as long as capacity is least cost optimal, pricing at short-run marginal costs is equivalent to pricing at long-run marginal cost—the French proposition has been demonstrated. Figure 7.5 illustrates this proposition and involves, in contrast to the previous diagram, the case of constant returns to scale. If capacity structure 1 is built, price would have to be at P^1. But this capacity is not the least cost optimal capacity for output q^1. LMC is less than P^1 ($=$ SMC),

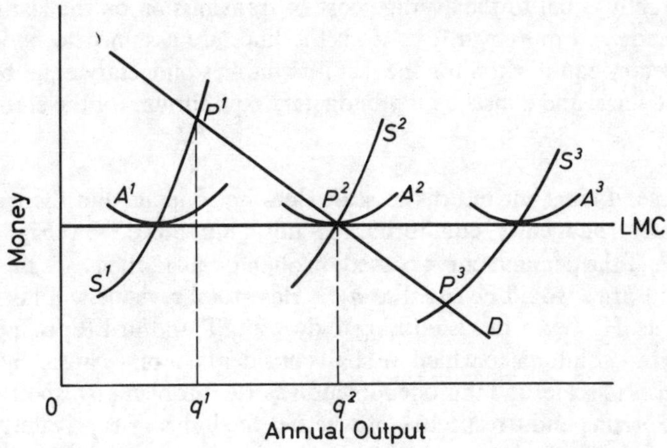

FIG. 7.5

and a larger capacity size is warranted. Similarly, if capacity structure 3 were built, price would be at P^3, but at such an output SMC $<$ LMC; planned capacity is too big. Optimal output and capacity is at q^2 with price, P^2, equal to both short and long-run marginal costs.

The assumption of constant returns to scale means that no scale economies appear as the overall capacity is increased or as the number of plants in a system are increased. It means that when capacity is least cost optimal for any particular output then this output involves producing where short-run average costs, for a small change, are constant. SMC = LMC at the minimum point of the short-run average cost lines. And this, of course, means that price is not only equal to SMC (and LMC) but also SAC (and LAC). Total revenue covers all costs. The capital and running costs of expanding capacity are constant. Boiteux in one of his articles appears to have something like this in mind. He is thinking of transmission lines carrying electricity, the chief 'running costs' of which are the energy 'losses' that occur during transmission. He assumes

> . . . that the enterprise has a large number of identical lines providing the same transmission service and carrying the same loads. If these lines are 'too' loaded, another will be built. The fixed charges [i.e., capital costs] of the whole system will increase by the amount of fixed charges for the additional line but the total cost of the losses will decrease because the load carried by each line will be less. If the annual gain realised from cutting the losses is greater than the annual cost arising from the increase in fixed charges, the lines had indeed 'too' heavy a load and it was correct to build another; . . . [when the] . . . level of optimum plant is reached, the marginal cost of transmission on any line whatsoever of the network will

> be exactly equal to the average cost of transmission on the last line constructed; . . . moreover, . . . if all the lines are assumed to be identical, budgetary equilibrium for the last line implies budgetary equilibrium for all the lines, and consequently budgetary equilibrium for the entire operation.[15]

Of course, if constant returns to scale does not operate and there *are* scale economies, budgetary equilibrium is not guaranteed. On Fig. 7.4, for example, if the demand curve passed through point V, then q_2 is the optimal scale and price would be equal to q_2V. Here total revenue will fall short of total costs. However, this is nothing to do with SR and/or LR pricing. This is a problem—solutions to which we shall consider later on—caused by increasing returns to scale, and this phenomenon causes problems irrespective of the form of pricing and irrespective of whether the industry is privately or publicly owned. This point emerged most clearly in section 5.3. The difficulties about the equivalence of SR and LR pricing are a separate issue. They can appear once one drops the assumption used so far that no capacity is inherited from the past. More generally, they arise when adjustment to optimal capacity cannot be easily or quickly made. As R. Turvey has said,

> . . . the argument about whether public enterprises should set prices equal to long-run or short-run marginal cost is only meaningful when capacity is not optimal.[16]

Such situations are the subject of sections 4 and 5 of this chapter.

Project benefits and costs

Prior to this, some further explanation is required about the relationship between pricing and investment. In the above analysis, investment decisions can be viewed as being made entirely independently of pricing decisions. In other words, as long as those responsible for operations and pricing can be relied on to make short-run output adjustments to ensure the equality of price and short-run marginal cost, then the investment planners need not compare long-run marginal costs with price but merely with short-run marginal costs. All they have to do is ensure that the output level, whatever it is, is being produced by the least cost optimal capacity structure. Similarly, those responsible for setting price can simply adjust to short-run marginal costs; they need not worry about the correspondence with long-run marginal

[15] The chief problem in interpreting this is that one is never sure whether Boiteux is thinking of additions to capacity inherited from the past. See 'Marginal Cost Pricing', pp. 55–6. This article originally appeared as 'La Vente au coût marginal', *Revue Française de l'Énergie*, December 1956. Its translated form is produced as chapter 3 of Nelson, *op. cit.*, to which the page references refer.

[16] 'Marginal Cost', *EJ*, p. 283, June 1969.

costs as long as the investment planners are undertaking all worthwhile investments. This proposition becomes particularly relevant in the case of inherited capacity, when new capacity is an addition to an existing stock—more on this later. Something like this division of function appears to operate in Electricité de France. However, the general points concerning the equivalence of SR and LR pricing do not rely on this context. One could think of projects being evaluated, simultaneously, in relation to both costs and benefits. We need to consider, then, the investment criterion suggested in the introduction to this chapter—to undertake a project if the net discounted present value (NDPV) of social benefits and costs is positive—in relation to pricing problems. One can think of decisions in the planning stage where the issue is whether a particular volume of capacity is to be preferred to a smaller volume. By definition, this will imply a criterion for arriving at the optimal volume of capacity. The extra capacity means that there will be a time-stream of extra output over the planning period, consumer evaluation of which represents the benefit side of the problem. In any one year these benefits constitute a part of the area under the demand curve. Thus, the extra benefit for a particular year could be thought of as the area $q^1P^1P^2q^2$ in Fig. 7.5. Denoting such benefits in year t as ΔB_t, and similarly denoting the extra capital and running costs, in year t, occasioned by the choice of a larger capacity, as ΔC_t, we have that the investment is worthwhile if:

$$\sum_{t=0}^{t=n} \Delta B_t D^t > \sum_{t=0}^{t=n} \Delta C_t D^t \tag{7.6}$$

where D is the discount rate, and n is the planning period in years. This means, simply, that the present value of the flow of extra benefits should exceed the present value of the flow of extra capital and running costs. Let[17] the extra capital costs involve simply an additional £K in the base year. Let the extra output produced in year t be ΔQ_t, and the extra running cost per unit of extra output be b_t. The extra benefits in year t constitute the extra area under the demand curve that would arise should the larger scale of capacity be chosen. Thus, the price in the second situation would be lower. Denoting P_1 and P_2 as the prices—and these, of course, would be equal to short-run marginal costs in each case respectively—the increased benefits in year t can be approximated by $\frac{1}{2}(P_1+P_2)_t\Delta Q_t$. This formulation will be precisely correct if the demand curve in year t is a straight line. We have now that the investment is warranted if:

$$\sum_{t=0}^{t=n} \tfrac{1}{2}(P_1+P_2)_t\, \Delta Q_t D^t > K + \sum_{t=0}^{t=n} b_t\, \Delta Q_t D^t \tag{7.7}$$

If the extra output, annual benefits, and running costs are going to be constant for each year of the period, then the present value formulation is equivalent

[17] Some of the formulations used here and in other parts of this chapter draw on parts of R. Turvey's exposition in 'Marginal Cost Pricing in Practice', *op. cit.*

to comparing annually equivalent items. If a_1 is taken as the annual capital cost 'equivalent' to K, then the following is equivalent to (7.7):

$$\tfrac{1}{2}(P_1+P_2)\Delta Q > a_1+b\Delta Q \tag{7.8}$$

where the absence of time-labels implies that items are constant each year. This certainly simplifies the decision. Granted that there are no expectations of demand and/or running costs changing over time, then one simply compares the surplus of first-year benefits over first-year running costs, with the equivalent annual capital cost. Finally, if perfect divisibility of capacity is possible, then a small change in output can be considered. This can be effected by dividing the above expression by ΔQ. If only small changes are considered, then the difference between P_1 and P_2 disappears and the extra annual benefits can be denoted as P. If $a_1/\Delta Q$ is denoted by a, then eq. (7.8) simplifies to:

$$P > a+b \tag{7.9}$$

Since a is the equivalent annual capital cost per unit of output, then the criterion is to choose the larger capacity—producing one extra unit of output per annum—if price exceeds the extra annual costs. The latter is clearly equal to long-run marginal cost, and so eq. (7.9) implies that capacity is optimal when P = LMC. Granted, then, that prices will always be set at short-run marginal costs, the criterion of accepting investments if the NDPV of benefits and costs is positive, guarantees that optimal capacity will be characterized by the equality of short and long-run marginal costs and prices.

Physical capacity limits

This approach becomes particularly relevant when capacity is subject to rigid capacity limits. In these cases, price may have to exceed short-run marginal running costs; it may have to be equal to the wider concept of short-run marginal (opportunity) cost discussed in the introduction to this chapter. Since at any given output the latter is not known independently of prices, then the investment planners need to analyse the consumer benefits of investment decisions; looking only at running costs will be inadequate. The formulations of the four equations above become the appropriate decision rules, the prime difference with the previous context being that, now, when capacity is optimal price will exceed marginal running cost. When the capacity structure comprises a large number of independent plants, price exceeds marginal running cost on the 'marginal' plant.

A simple illustration of this issue is shown in Fig. 7.6. Because of its drastic simplifications, the situation depicted will be used on a number of occasions later on to demonstrate some general points about marginal cost pricing.[18]

[18] O. E. Williamson used this case in his analysis of 'Peak-Load Pricing and Optimal Capacity under Indivisibility Constraints', *AER*, September 1966, reproduced as chapter 3 of *Public Enterprise*, Ed. R. Turvey, Penguin Modern Economic Series, 1968.

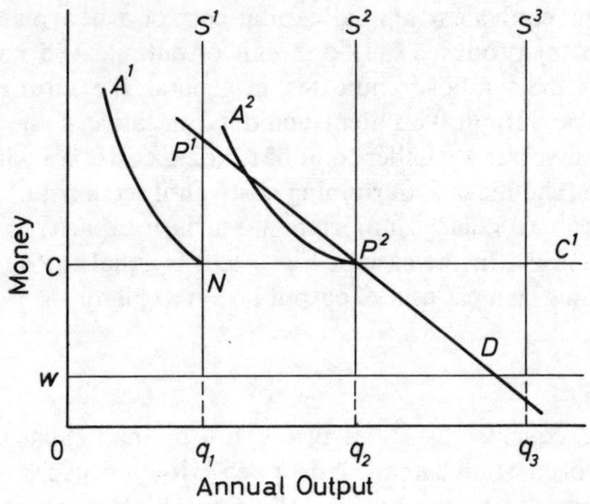

FIG. 7.6

One can think of this as a situation where the product can be produced by a capacity structure exhibiting constant returns to scale, and where this structure exhibits rigid capacity limits. The least cost capacity structure for output q_1 is that whose short-run marginal cost line is S^1. With such a structure, output increases up to q_1 involve a constant marginal running cost of Ow; no output greater than q_1 can be produced without introducing new capacity. Similarly, S^2 is the short-run marginal cost line of that capacity structure which is least-cost optimal for output q_2, and running costs are also unit constant, this time up to q_2. The A^1 and A^2 lines indicate short-run average costs which, at the outputs for which these structures are least-cost optimal, are the same and equal to marginal (and average) running cost per unit of output plus the annual equivalent capital cost per unit of output, i.e., $Ow+wC$, on the diagram. If one further allows that capacity is perfectly divisible, then CC^1 is the long-run marginal (and average) cost line. A situation which would meet this case would be where there were a large number of small identical capital assets or plants, each with rigid capacity limits, and on each of which running costs per unit of output were constant and the same. Thus, should the capacity structure associated with S^1 be chosen, price would be set at P^1 on the basis of the points made in the introduction to this chapter. Should S^2 be chosen, the price would have to be P^2. Choosing the large structure in preference to the smaller would be warranted on the basis of the investment criterion implied in eq. (7.8)—change in benefit exceeds change in annual equivalent cost. More generally, granted perfect divisibility, a larger capacity than q_1 is warranted since price exceeds LMC. The optimal capacity is at q_2 with price P^2. Notice that short-run marginal cost (equal to price) exceeds short-run marginal running cost by an amount just equal to the equivalent annual capital cost of a new plant, assuming that this new plant produces only one unit of output. And notice, finally, that in eq. (7.9), the symbol b indicates, in general, the *extra* running cost per unit of extra output. This item could be negative if the choice of a larger capacity involves a smaller total of running costs. We will defer a full discussion of the significance of running costs until section 4 of this chapter, since it becomes particularly important when new capacity is an addition to an inherited stock. In the case of Fig. 7.6, it is equal to Ow, that is, it is simply the running cost per unit of output on a new plant.

Demand variations

Are the general conclusions about prices and optimal capacity affected if the assumption of constant demand is dropped? How is capacity to be planned if demand is expected to rise and/or fall over the planning period? A key word here is 'expected'; it is anticipated demand trends that are under discussion. Granted uncertainty about future trends, some risk factors will usually have to be attached to demand estimates.[19] In addition, unexpected demand changes raise problems when extensions to or contractions of an existing stock of capacity cannot be affected immediately; this latter point is discussed in the next section. Aside from these very important matters and granted the continued assumption of constant technology, planning for demand variations does not present any major new issues. Some points of interpretation are needed however. Over the planning period, the annual demand function will not be constant. Any particular planned volume of capacity will have an associated annual short-run marginal cost function. In practice, this function itself could shift over time to the extent that as the capacity gets older it becomes more difficult to operate. For any set of outputs over the planning period, further choices are presented if the rate and costs of ageing differ on different types of plant. Which plants are appropriate may well depend, therefore, on the pattern of demand over the planning period. For simplicity we will ignore this and assume the annual SMC function remains constant. If, then, demand varies over time then the optimal price with the capacity under consideration will also vary over time; this applies whether the plant is flexible, i.e., output can be varied over large ranges by changing running costs, so that output and short-run marginal running costs are different each year; or whether capacity has rigid limits, in which case although price varies actual output could be the same each year. Notice that this means capacity may be 'under-utilized' in some years. Take

[19] Some interesting discussion on the security margins used in planning the generating plant programme in the UK electricity supply industry can be found in a number of articles in *The Manchester School*. See 'Capital Costs and the Peak Problem in Electricity Supply', R. W. Bates, May 1963. A comment by M. A. Crew appeared in September 1967 together with a reply by Bates. See also 'Security Margin Decisions in the Electricity Supply Industry, 1955–67', C. M. Cannon, *The Manchester School*, 1970.

the two/three-lane motorway example discussed earlier in this section of the chapter. Granted knowledge of rising traffic flows over time, a lower present value of costs may be involved if the three-lane carriage-way is built now with less than capacity utilization in the first few years, than if a two-lane carriage-way is constructed and fully used now and expensive extension facilities built on later.

Now, if a larger volume of capacity is considered, this will involve a different set of annual outputs, prices, and running costs, and in each year one would normally expect output to be larger and price lower. But eq. (7.7) still constitutes the appropriate criterion for deciding whether the larger capacity is to be preferred; that is, the present value of the stream of extra annual benefits minus extra annual running costs—both of which can vary each year—has to exceed the additional base-year capital outlay involved in choosing the larger structure. Capacity increases are then warranted if this criterion is met, and capacity is optimal when the two items are just equal. Thus, the approach is basically no different from the one used before. The chief difference is that one cannot choose between the two structures by simply comparing the first-year annual benefits with the sum of first-year annual running costs plus the annually equivalent capital cost. Both benefits and running costs are going to change over time, and so it is appropriate to leave it in the present value formulation. How do we know if there is going to be budgetary equilibrium when the optimal volume of capacity is chosen? Intuitively, the reader can probably see that this depends on the same factor as before, namely, the constancy of returns to scale. It is usual, of course, to think of this in terms of a two-dimensional diagram. Although we have indicated that looking at the first-year annual items is misleading, it is possible to get a correct formulation in annual terms. The procedure is somewhat tortuous, and is basically unnecessary in making capacity decisions, but it will probably be useful to spell it out so that the relationship with the diagrams is clarified.

First of all let us convert the formulations of eq. (7.7) to the 'marginal change' case. Let K^1 be the additional base-year capital costs occasioned if a slightly higher volume of capacity is chosen; capable that is of producing one extra unit of output per annum over the planning period. This means that ΔQ_t is equal to 1 for all values of t, and so in each year the running cost item is b_t which, therefore, represents the change in running costs that would occur if a larger capacity is chosen and one extra unit of output is produced. Similarly, in the left-hand side of eq. (7.7), ΔQ_t will disappear and the difference between P_1 and P_2 will disappear; extra benefit in year t could then be denoted as P_t. The criterion for a small change is, therefore:

$$\sum_{t=0}^{n} P_t D^t > K^1 + \sum_{t=0}^{n} b_t D^t \qquad (7.10)$$

Everything is in present value terms and refers to a marginal change in the flow of output. Now, a few pages back we saw that the base-year capital cost figure could be converted to an annually equivalent item. Equation (7.3) gave a formula for doing this. All the items in eq. (7.10) could be converted into equivalent annual terms using the same method. Thus, the left-hand side could be multiplied by $(r/1-D^n)$ to give an expression, say P^*, which indicated the annual equivalent (extra) benefit; in other words, the present value of the constant annual term, P^*, over the planning period is equivalent to the left-hand side of eq. (7.10) – the present value of the flow of actual benefits. The analogous concept for the running costs could be denoted as b^*. For the capital cost we would have our old friend, a, the equivalent annual capital cost for a unit increase in capacity. Thus, in deciding whether a higher volume of capacity is warranted, the use of the present value criterion in eq. (7.10) is equivalent to the following criterion:

$$P^* > a + b^* \tag{7.11}$$

This could be represented on diagrams like those in Figs. 7.5 and 7.6, but one would have to remember that such items would not be real variables. They do not represent the extra annual benefits or changes in running costs that actually occur in any year; this is in contrast to P and b in eq. (7.9), where extra benefits and changes in running costs *are* constant (by assumption) each year. The symbols in eq. (7.11) represent annual equivalent items; the annual capital cost concept is also not real in this sense; resources are actually committed in the base-year with nothing thereafter—a is an accounting device. However, they do indicate that despite demand variations the relationship between pricing and investment is the same. Capacity is optimal when the (annually equivalent) price is equal to (annually equivalent) long-run marginal cost, and, if scale returns are constant, such a price and capacity guarantee budgetary equilibrium.

7.4 Expanding capacity and long-run marginal cost

In the year 1972 most investment decisions in any industry will involve additions to or subtractions from an existing stock of assets. There will be few decisions made in the context of the last section where the enterprise is starting from scratch. If the existing capacity is being changed then, for some reason, actual capacity diverges from the optimal volume. This can arise because new technological opportunities have emerged, e.g., North Sea Gas is discovered; it can arise because of changes in relative factor prices, i.e., capital-intensive techniques become more favourable. For the time being however these complications are ignored. Divergences between actual and optimal capacity can still arise because of factors broadly consistent with the previous analysis. Thus, for example, when a public enterprise does start from scratch it may not be possible to introduce all the required capacity at the same time because of outside constraints[20] such as availability of funds and construction limitations; the stock of assets can only be built up slowly. Secondly, it may not be possible to adjust immediately to unexpected changes in demand. Should demand rise in 1972 over its previous level, it may well be a number of years before the required new capacity can be introduced. These gestation periods would then be an important reason why inherited capacity is sub-optimal. In the UK there is a time-span of about six years between deciding to introduce a new electricity generating plant and its first year of operation; the numerous administrative difficulties that have to be overcome in order to get planning permission for use of the chosen site is one of the big problems. The reverse side of the coin is when demand contracts. If the existing assets have a number of years' 'physical' life left in them, one has to decide how this 'spare' capacity is to be used and how prices are to be set.

Basic principles

Although the same broad theoretical principles are involved in the expanding and contracting cases, once practical matters such as administrative constraints and other wider factors are introduced, different issues tend to emerge, and so it is useful to treat the two problems separately. Some of the features of the problems posed by an expanding enterprise can be shown with the help of Fig. 7.7. 'Now' is, say, 1972 and the enterprise has inherited from the past a capacity with a rigid limit of Oq_1. At the earliest new capacity can be

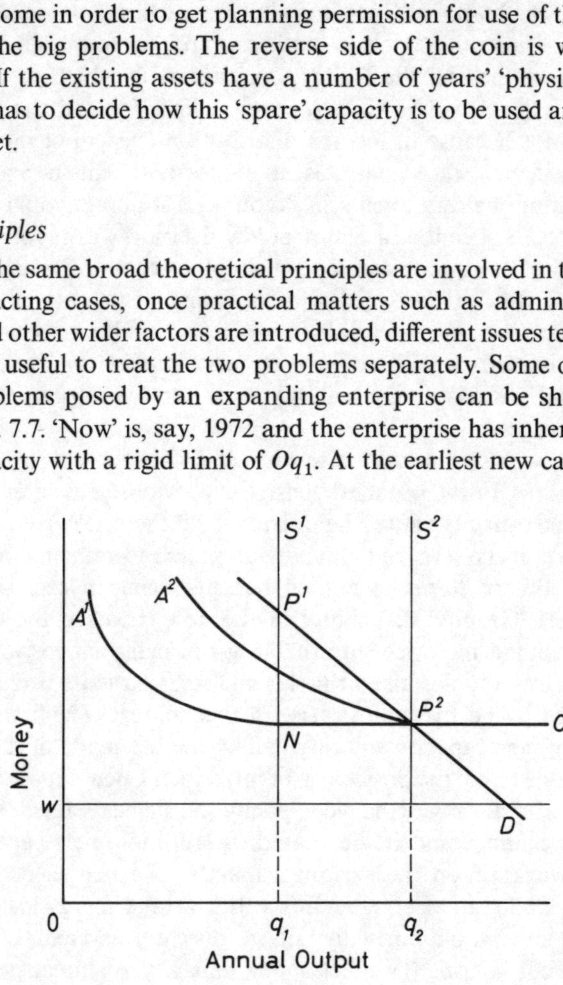

FIG. 7.7

[20] One has to be careful in interpreting these. Constraints on capital could be interpreted as meaning that the face cost of capital assets understates the alternative use of the resources and/or the funds. These points are explored in a later chapter.

introduced only in 1975. For the next few years the annual demand would have to be restricted to q_1 by levying a price P^1. This is the logic of the efficiency criterion though, as we inferred earlier, wider factors may be good arguments for doing something different. Should the commodity in question be an important item in the budgets of low income groups, rationing may be 'better' if it is feasible and if other redistributive measures are partly circumscribed. Something akin to the elements of this situation occurred in the UK in the early fifties. Then there was a coal 'shortage' in the sense that at ruling prices certain demands were not met because of rationing. Some economists were critical of the National Coal Board's prices which were much less than marginal costs—definition unclear, but loosely related to marginal collieries' running costs. In the end the Ridley Committee, in which many of these issues were discussed, published a report[21] which rejected the solution of raising prices not because of income distribution effects but more because of inflationary fears. Since coal was an important item in poor people's budgets, distributional arguments in favour of rationing would have been good arguments. Notice that a major policy decision was involved here. In the normal run of things we suggested in chapter 4 that individual industries cannot, realistically, be burdened with pursuing distributional objectives. Notice also that rationing is feasible in other parts of the public sector. The UK electricity industry was, up to the 1960s, continually trying to catch up on a rising demand. Invariably the inability to do this led to power-cuts rather than price increases.

Consider, now, the issues that arise when it *does* become possible to introduce new capacity. In the broadest sense the previous principles still apply, namely, that the capacity should be introduced if the NDPV of benefits and costs is positive; if the level of demand is expected to remain constant, one could express this in terms of annual benefits being in excess of annual equivalent costs. Granted divisibility in the new capacity, the criterion is equivalent to comparing price with the long-run marginal cost of *extending* output, and prices should fall to this level. The main issue is clarifying the meaning of LMC, and two points arise in this context. The first is that the introduction of new capacity will often affect the use made of the inherited stock. On the one hand, the possibility of introducing new capacity raises the question as to whether any of the old capacity should be retained; in this case, the use of old plants could be decreased. In addition, new capacity could reduce 'over-working' on the existing capacity. If a new electricity transmission line is added to existing facilities the average energy losses on each of the existing lines would normally fall. In this case, a systems cost analysis is necessary in considering the effect of new capacity. A similar point applies to new roads which reduce congestion and maintenance costs on competitive routes.

[21] *Report of Committee on a National Policy for the Use of Fuel and Power Resources*, Cmnd 8647, HMSO, July 1952.

A second feature of expansion is that—even with no changes in technology—decisions involving new capacity relate to different technological circumstances compared with the case where the enterprise is starting from scratch. This point is often overlooked. In examining criteria for increases in capacity we were, previously, comparing two hypothetical volumes of output and inquiring whether it would be better to have the larger capacity than the smaller. In the new situation we are comparing a particular hypothetical volume of capacity with an *existing* lower volume. Take the case of a water barrage controlling a river's flow for irrigation, flood-relief, and land reclamation. Whereas before we were considering a high water barrage as opposed to a lower one on the same site, or two very low ones on different sites, the issue now is whether it is warrantable, say, to *add* 50 feet to the height of an existing barrage. Clearly design and, therefore, cost considerations are different in the two cases. The two- or three-lane motorway example is a similar instance. In principle, in the 'planning from scratch' case, one could be comparing two very different capacity structures. When capacity is inherited from the past, a wholly new capacity structure would normally not be economically justifiable.

For these reasons one must be careful in specifying the meaning of capital and running costs and particularly in using two-dimensional diagrams. The very simplest sort of case is where the inherited capacity consists of a number of rigid plants, all of which are identical. The new capacity is exactly the same and all have the same unit running costs. The effect of the new capacity is simply to extend the existing capacity limit. In other words, one has the sort of situation depicted in Fig. 7.7, where the rigid capacity limit to annual output is extended from q_1 to q_2. Old capacity is replaced when it physically expires. Net additions to capacity can be looked at simply in terms of their own costs and the benefits of the extra outputs. New capacity reduces the 'ration price' used to restrict usage of the scarce rigid capacity. The line *from* N to C^1 can be interpreted as the long-run marginal cost of *extending* output; it comprises the unit running cost plus the equivalent annual capital cost per unit of output of new capacity.

If, in 1972, inherited capacity is equal to Oq_1 in Fig. 7.7, and if new capacity cannot be introduced until 1975, then price is fixed at P^1 for 1972, 73, and 74, granted that demand is constant throughout. In 1975 new capacity is introduced, price is lowered to P^2, and capacity is optimal. In the absence of further demand changes annual output remains at q_2. What is the relationship between price and the total costs of old and new capacity? Because of the constancy of returns to scale over the range of output q_1 to q_2, the total revenue from this output—area $NP^2q_2q_1$—just covers the annual capital and running costs for the whole of the new capacity. Now, running costs per unit of output on the old capacity are the same as on the new. It follows that the total revenue from all output will cover the running and capital costs of *all* the capacity, if the new capacity is technically identical to the old, and if its purchase price is exactly the same as the old plant. These extremely simple assumptions are necessary if we are to be able to use the A^1 and A^2 lines of Fig. 7.7 to refer to the case of inherited capacity. The A^1 line can then be interpreted as indicating the annual fixed charges and running costs of the old plants, expressed per unit of output of the old capacity. The fixed charges are not of course an economic cost. They play no part in determining the scale of output in 1972, 1973, or 1974. Neither do they affect whether the capacity extension is made in 1975. They constitute the book entry—of depreciation and interest charges—that the accountant will be making each year for the old assets. The A^2 line, thus, contains a rag-bag of items, namely, annual running costs, the annual equivalent capital cost of the planned new capacity, and the annual fixed charges of the old capacity, all expressed per unit of total output. This 'average cost' is just equal to price P^2 at output q_2 because of the special assumptions made. In effect, one has a large number of small plants each identical, some purchased at different dates from others, but all at the same price.

Capacity expansion and effects on old plants

It would be more realistic to allow that variations in output on inherited capacity can be effected only by changing the total of running costs. The assumption that unit running cost is a universal constant is too simple. It is more likely that increasing the use of the old capacity leads to rising marginal costs. At the same time such characteristics need explaining. Why should running costs vary in this way? One reason might be that the existing stock of plants reflects the changes in technology that have occurred in the history of the enterprise. The younger the plant is, the more technically advanced it is likely to be. If improvements in technique partly take the form of lowering unit running costs, then the existing capacity may comprise a large number of plants each with different unit running costs. Increased use of the existing capacity is effected by bringing in more and more of the old plants. Thus, the existing stock of electricity generating stations in the UK will comprise nuclear plants with very low running costs, new coal and gas-fired plants, and finally some old-fashioned coal-fired plants. Short-run marginal costs then reflect a profile of the history of the industry. Another factor which could cause rising short-run costs is the ability to operate plants at different degrees of intensity. Increased use of capacity is effected, here, by more intensive use of each plant, but each plant's average running costs rise the greater is the intensity of this use. The examples of system interdependence like transmission lines and roads, fall into this category. Finally short-run marginal costs could rise, in the absence of the above two factors, if the unit running costs of operation and maintenance on a plant rise as the plant gets older; ageing increases the difficulty of operating the plants. Again, then, the existing stock of plants reflects the industry's history; each plant was purchased at a different date, and so 'now' average system running cost is higher the more is use made of the older plants.

To indicate the main implications of rising marginal cost schedules, it will be assumed that inherited capacity consists of a large number of plants each purchased at different dates, and that unit running costs are higher on the older plants simply because they are more difficult to operate. The implications of the first two factors—technology changes and system interdependence—can be briefly indicated later on. Once capacity changes become possible the first question that arises is whether some of the old plant should be retired. The enterprise inherits a capacity structure, in say 1974, on which short-run marginal costs are given by the S^1 line in Fig. 7.8. Its rise indicates

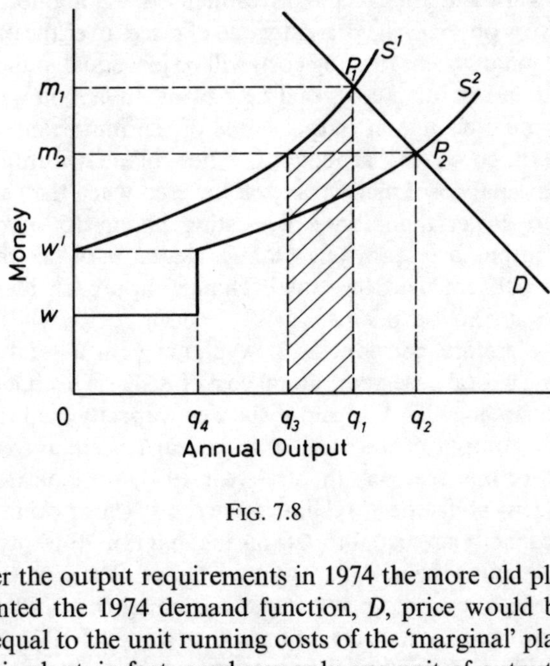

FIG. 7.8

that the higher the output requirements in 1974 the more old plants have to be used. Granted the 1974 demand function, *D*, price would be set at P_1. This price is equal to the unit running costs of the 'marginal' plant—m_1. Let us suppose this plant, in fact, produces only one unit of output. Is it worth while to retire this plant and introduce a new plant in 1974, costing K^1 with a capacity of one unit? The planning period is taken to be the life-span of the new plant (*n* years). During this period, the old plant would in any case have terminated its physical life. The unit of output in question would, therefore, in any case be produced by a different plant in later years; and this plant's costs could be different from those on the present plant. This certainly complicates the issue. To see the basic principles of the replacement decision let us make the very unrealistic assumption that over the planning period the old plant *could be* retained, albeit at a rising unit running cost. This assumption can be relaxed later on. Now then, the issue is simply whether the flow of running costs using the old plant is greater or less than the flow of capital and running costs using the new plant. The new plant's unit running costs—u_t in year t—would normally be lower than those on the old plant (m_{1t}). It is appropriate then to replace the old plant if:

$$\sum_{t=0}^{n} m_{1t}D^t > K^1 + \sum_{t=0}^{n} u_t D^t \tag{7.12}$$

This is simply one version of the old maxim: replace if running cost of old exceeds total costs of new. Here, it is made explicit that estimates will have to be made of the running costs of the two types of plant over the planning period. Now, the reader will no doubt notice that, provided that price in each year is equated to marginal running costs (m_{1t}), then the standard relationship between pricing and investment is maintained, namely, that when capacity is optimal, the present value of prices over the planning period (equal to marginal system running cost) will be just equal to the present value of the capital and running costs of a new plant. In fact, however, by taking only a very small change in output some of the important aspects of this problem are obscured. In particular, if a new plant *is* introduced then the short-run marginal cost function is itself lowered when the new plant's running costs are lower than those of existing plants. It follows that a net increase in output over previous planned levels may be warranted. This possibility is subsumed in the 'small change' approach above. It is now appropriate to make it explicit.

Consider, therefore, introducing new plants with a total capacity of T units involving a total base-year capital cost of K. If the net increase in output in year t is denoted[22] by ΔQ_t, and if the new capacity is always fully used, then the fall in output of the old plants in year t is equal to $(T-\Delta Q_t)$. The implications for one year, say the first year 1974, are indicated on Fig. 7.8. The new capacity shifts the SMC line to the right. The low unit running costs on the new capacity are equal to Ow on the diagram. For any output levels up to $0q_4(= T$ units) the new plants only are used. Thereafter, the old plants are used. The least cost old plant has unit running costs of $0w^1$. Thus, with the new set-up, this would be the first plant used should 1974 output requirements exceed $0q_4$. Thereafter, short-run marginal costs rise as before, and so the new short-run marginal cost line takes the path of S^2. The new price would be P_2; this means marginal running cost has fallen, that is, some old plants which would otherwise have been used are now left idle. In fact, the new 'marginal' plant is that with running costs of m_2. We have, then, that the net increase in annual output (ΔQ_t in general terms) is, for this first year, equal to q_1q_2 in Fig. 7.8; the fall in production by old plants (in general, $T-\Delta Q_t$) is q_3q_1; the physical capacity of the new plants (T units) is equal to $q_3q_2 = 0q_4$. Notice that the saving in running costs, through the discontinued

[22] Some of the forgoing algebraic formulations draw on Turvey's *Marginal Cost Pricing in Practice, op. cit.*

use of some of the old plants, is indicated by the shaded area in Fig. 7.8. A rough approximation to this area would be the average of the old and new marginal costs multiplied by the fall in quantity; that is, for year t, $\frac{1}{2}(m_1+m_2)_t\,(T-\Delta Q_t)$.

Is it worth while to introduce the new capacity? On the one hand, there is the benefit of the extra output to consumers which we can approximate in the normal way, for year t, as $\frac{1}{2}(P_1+P_2)_t\Delta Q_t$. Against this, there is the capital cost and the overall effect on running costs. It should now be clear that this latter consists of the running costs of the new plants $(u_t T)$ less the fall in costs of old plants. Thus the new capacity is warranted if:[23]

$$\sum_{t=0}^{n} \tfrac{1}{2}(P_1+P_2)_t\Delta Q_t D^t > K + \sum_{t=0}^{n} [u_t T - \tfrac{1}{2}(m_1+m_2)_t(T-\Delta Q_t)]D^t \quad (7.13)$$

If prices (P_1, P_2) are always set equal to marginal running costs (m_1, m_2), then the above expression cancels out to:

$$\sum_{0}^{n} \tfrac{1}{2}(m_1+m_2)_t T D^t > K + \sum_{0}^{n} u_t T D^t \quad (7.14)$$

The flow of output from the new plants, valued at marginal system running cost, should, when discounted to the present, exceed the present value of the flow of these plants' own capital and operating costs. To tie up with the previous discussion, a small change can be evaluated by considering a capacity costing $K/T = K^1$. Dividing the other items in eq. (7.14) by T, and noting that the difference between m_1 and m_2 disappears, the condition that emerges is none other than eq. (7.12). Capacity is optimal when all such warrantable extensions to the existing stock of plants is exhausted. Granted then that price (P_t) is always set equal to marginal (system) running cost (m_{1t}) then the optimal solution is characterized by:

$$\sum_{0}^{n} P_t D^t = K^1 + \sum_{0}^{n} u_t D^t \quad (7.15)$$

Here, one has perhaps the best indication of the significance of the French propositions about short- and long-term pricing. It is couched in the more complicated environment of a capacity inherited from the past. The set of prices over the planning period are equal to marginal (system) running costs; the running costs of very new capacity are less than this, and the surpluses thus earned over the period in question, are, when capacity is optimal, just sufficient to cover the per unit capital charges on such new capacity.[24] This

[23] To be even more general one would want to allow that the annual output of the new capacity might decrease over time so that in eq. (7.13), T could be replaced by Td_t, where d_t is the degree of utilization of the new capacity in year t.

[24] Diagrams lose most of their usefulness when the context becomes so complicated. One could convert all the time flows of costs into annually equivalent terms as suggested before. Then an annually equivalent long-run marginal cost line could be drawn starting from the existing volume of output. But such diagrams hardly shed new light on the problem.

does not, of course, mean that capital charges on all the inherited capacity are necessarily covered. However, the new capacity in this example differs from the old only to the extent that increased age renders the plants more difficult to operate; unit running costs rise with age. In other respects all capacity is identical; the new capacity incorporates no new technology and its purchase price is the same as the old. In these circumstances, provided there are no economies consequent on the increased scale of operations, i.e., constant returns to scale prevail, a price covering long-run marginal cost, or more explicitly a set of prices covering the time flow of costs resulting from an expansion of capacity, guarantees the recovery of all accounting costs.

Relaxing the assumptions

It is now appropriate to inject some realism into the analysis, by dropping some of the drastic simplifications that were made for expository purposes. First of all, it is probably useful to bring out the implications of the analysis for one cost situation not so far considered. Short-run cost functions could well, in practice, be some amalgam of the smooth and rigid cases. That is, while output can be varied in the short-run by bringing in more and more of the old plants, there will usually be some finite limit to this. If each plant is inflexible then, effectively, one has an SMC line which rises up to some capacity point; thereafter SMC is infinite. Such a situation is indicated in Fig. 7.9 where the rigid capacity limit is at q. Should annual demand functions be in positions like the D' line, then the previous analysis applies. With demand curves like D'', prices would have to exceed marginal running cost (m on Fig. 7.9), to soak up the excess demand. If the optimal volume of capacity, during part or all of its life-span, exhibits such characteristics, then this means

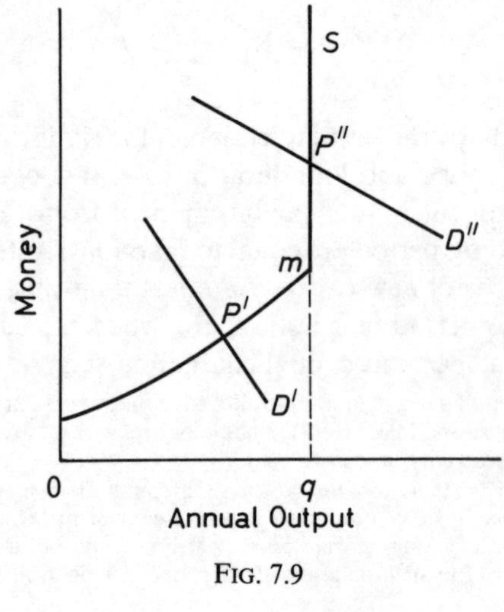

FIG. 7.9

prices not only exceed the unit running costs of new plants but also the unit running costs on old plants 'marginal' to the system. Thinking in terms of eq. (7.15), let us denote the excess of price over marginal running costs in year t as E_t. It follows that if m_{1t}—marginal running cost in year t—is deducted from both sides of this expression one has:

$$\sum_0^n E_t D^t = K^1 - \sum_0^n (m_{1t} - u_t) D^t \qquad (7.16)$$

The last part of this expression constitutes the flow of running cost savings that a new plant would achieve. When price has to be raised above marginal running cost to soak up demand then, when capacity is optimal, such surpluses are equal to the capital cost of a new plant less the savings that such a plant would make over the old plant it replaces. If plant operating costs do not rise with age, then we are back into the world of Fig. 7.7. In terms of eq. (7.16), m_{1t} and u_t would be the same, so that the surpluses are just equal, when capacity is optimal, to the capital cost of a new plant.

Most of these points apply if rising SMC costs are attributable to the flexibility with which plant can be operated. New electrical transmission capacity may both expand the load carried and, in addition, save on the running cost of existing facilities; system interdependence exists. The basic approach of Fig. 7.8 and related expressions is applicable. The existing facilities are not now necessarily retired on the advent of new capacity; they are used less intensively but running costs are still saved.

Another assumption made in the exposition was that all of the capacity inherited at the starting date (1974) could have been retained over the planning horizon. But if the new capacity is physically identical to the old then all of the old plants would come to the end of their physical life during the planning horizon, since the latter is defined in relation to the life of the new plant. The decision to introduce new capacity in 1974 was partly a replacement decision so, to this extent, the decision is concerned with the optimal timing of the replacement decision; the old plants would in any case be replaced at some time in the future if only because they physically expire. Given assumptions about the pattern of demand, a complicated simulation exercise would be required to find the optimal pattern of plant replacement and capacity expansion. This exercise becomes particularly complicated when there is system interdependence, as in electricity transmission facilities. Of course, electricity is also characterized by another factor which considerably complicates the analysis of system costs. If demand is uneven throughout the year, the problem of peak loads arises since electricity cannot be stored. An interdependence between the costs of generating plants then appears. We shall have much more to say on this when the phenomenon of peak loads is analysed in the next chapter. An additional general point is that there may well be a secular upward trend in demand; capacity increases will then be adjusting to an optimal size partly with respect to given demand functions and partly to shifts in these functions over time. Basically, the same fundamental principles are in operation, but the exercise is more complicated. An indication of some of the general points that arise in such a context can be found in R. Turvey's article on 'Marginal Cost'.[25]

A fourth assumption that was made in our elementary exposition was to take technology as given and constant. Relaxing this point can bring in a whole host of considerations.[26] There are two aspects, however, which are particularly pertinent to the problem of marginal cost pricing. Firstly, technological advances often lower the unit running costs of production. The schedule of marginal costs associated with an inherited volume of capacity will, therefore, reflect the technological history of the industry. Secondly, the cost of new plants—that is the discounted sum of running and capital costs—will in real terms be lower than old plants. To the extent that prices, with optimal capacity, are equal to long-run marginal costs, then the costs they cover are those of new plants. Budgetary equilibrium—even with constant returns to scale—is no longer guaranteed. Total revenue would cover all accounting costs if all the existing capacity were new. If we 'start from scratch' with new capacity then, initially, all accounting costs are covered. In practice, decisions now relate to additions to an inherited stock of plants. Therefore, the larger the proportion of older plants in the existing capacity the larger, *ceteris paribus*, will be the accounting deficit. The *ceteris paribus* qualification is very important, since our world is characterized not only by technological advances but by inflation. The propositions hold good in real terms but accounting balances are in money terms, and the historic cost of plants acquired in the 1950s are much less of a burden when prices have been rising. Prices are related to short-run marginal costs, and this means revenue is related to running costs at 1974 prices—to 1974 labour, raw material, and fuel prices. The budget balance then will depend on not only the rate of technological advance but also the rate of inflation. Further points on budgetary equilibrium are considered at a later point in this chapter.

7.5 Excess capacity

Many of the classic problems of short-run and long-run pricing arise when the existing inherited capacity exceeds its optimal size. Basically, such excess capacity arises if demand has been over-estimated;[27] the actual level of demand falls short of that anticipated when capacity plans were made. Some of the key issues can be highlighted without resort to many of the complications of the previous section. We can take a world of constant technology and constant factor prices. In Fig. 7.10, the inherited capacity in some year,

[25] *Op. cit.* This paper also explores some of the waste land between the world of the economist and the depreciation and amortization concepts of the accountant.

[26] See W. G. Salter's *Productivity and Technical Change*, Cambridge University Press, 1960, for an excellent treatment of these issues.

[27] One could plan for over-capacity however (cf. above pp. 224, 225).

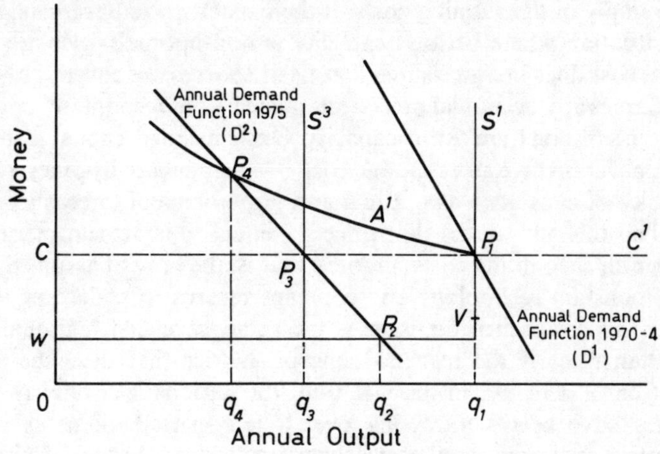

FIG. 7.10

say 1974, is such that, when used to its maximum, q_1 output can be produced at a unit running cost of Ow; capacity comprises a large number of small identical plants, each with rigid limits, and on each of which unit running costs are Ow. S^1 is then the short-run marginal cost line and with the demand curve, D^1, the optimal price is P_1. One might think of this capacity as having been introduced in say, 1970. In 1974 the capital charges on this capacity are not an economic cost. However, the annual fixed charges (plus running costs) per unit of output, as indicated by the A^1 line, are in fact just covered by the price. In other words, an optimal decision with respect to capacity size was made in 1970 and, granted constant returns to scale with this capacity, the optimal price covers all costs. If demand remains constant over the life of this capacity annual output would remain at q_1. Suppose, however, that after a number of years, say in 1975, demand unexpectedly contracts. The 1975 level of demand is indicated in the diagram by D^2. Following the basic pricing principle, price should therefore fall to P_2 and granted no further demand changes in subsequent years, remain there.

The key issue is, of course, that revenue, though covering all economic costs does not cover the fixed charges of the inherited capacity—at output q_2 price is less than 'average cost'. This is *not* fundamentally because 'capacity is not being fully utilized'. If demand had only contracted slightly, such that the new demand curve intersected the S^1 vertical at V, capacity would be fully used, but price, though exceeding unit running costs, still does not cover average cost. Given the demand curve, D^2, why not raise price to P_4 so that all 'costs' are covered? On the efficiency criterion this would not be correct for the excluded consumers—the output range q_4q_2—are prepared to pay amounts (as indicated by the ordinates of the demand curve) in excess of the only costs that are occasioned in supplying them. These economic costs consist simply of the running costs of the capacity. We have here, then, the classic situation where because capacity is non-optimal, price at short-run marginal cost does not guarantee that fixed charges are covered by revenue. These charges are the annual provisions made by the accountant for depreciation and interest on the existing capacity. Once installed, capital assets during their life never involve an economic cost[28]—bygones are bygones—but if the past choice of capacity was optimal and good demand forecasts have been made, then this guarantees that price set equal to short-run marginal cost will cover all accounting costs; granted that is, the present assumed environment of constant technology and constant returns to scale. For the profit maximizing private firm the issue is the same, save that marginal revenue rather than price is the relevant concept. Notice that the issue is one of contraction of demand. In the UK both the nationalized railway and coal industries have been contracting over a long-period. Some of the early contributors to the marginal cost debate emphasized that in such industries, particularly the railways, fixed charges are a very high portion of total accounting costs. They gave the impression that this was the main issue.[29] Fundamentally it is irrelevant. True, the higher is the portion of fixed costs the greater, *ceteris paribus*, is the size of the accounting deficit. But this reflects the magnitude of the problem rather than its nature. It is the non-optimality of capacity which is crucial.

It is easy to exaggerate these problems if it is not remembered that, at some point of time, assets come to the end of their physical life. If, for example, some of the assets expire in 1978, one has then to decide which, if any of them, are to be renewed. The replacement decision, in other words, brings one back to long-run considerations and clearly it is then that adjustments to optimal capacity can be made. To take the simplest sort of case, suppose that *all* the capacity comes up for renewal in 1978, that unit running costs on the replacements are the same as on the old equipment, and that the equivalent annual capital cost[30] per unit of output of the new capacity is equal to wC on Fig. 7.10. Granted divisibility in this new capacity, we have effectively a 1978 long-run marginal cost curve which is shown on the diagram by the dotted line CC^1. In these circumstances if the level of demand is expected to remain at D^2 over the life of this new capacity, the optimal volume of capacity is q_3, associated with the short-run marginal cost line S^3. In 1978, then, price would rise to P_3. The previously unused capacity—q_2q_1—is not renewed, and neither is the capacity which previously supplied the output q_3q_2. It is only economic,

[28] Subject to the scrap value qualification.

[29] See for example, E. H. Phelps-Brown, *A Course in Applied Economics*, Pitman, 1951, chapter VIII, pp. 229–30; also 'The Pricing Policy of the Nationalised Industries', F. Cassell, *Lloyds Bank Review*, p. 5, October 1956.

[30] Notice that assets with the same base-year capital cost will have different annual equivalent costs if their expected lives are different. The larger is the expected life the smaller is the equivalent annual cost. This can be seen in the formula of eq. (7.3). The assumed life is given by n and the larger it is the smaller is D^n, since D is a fraction. The smaller D^n is the smaller is a.

in other words, to renew the capacity responsible for the Oq_3 output. Thus, at some time, the excess capacity problem is overcome. Its magnitude will depend not only on the portion of total 'costs' occupied by fixed costs but also on the *durability* of the assets in question; the longer is their physical life, the longer does the deficit have to be borne. It is possible to imagine some assets whose use *never* involves an economic cost. This would apply to assets with a continually everlasting life—'permanent assets' in Arthur Lewis' terminology[31]—and whose scrap or alternative use value is zero. To a certain extent, the costs involved in developing land for railway tracks fall into this category. They involve a once-and-for-all expenditure which will never need repeating. The price paid for the land itself could also come into this category, if its attractiveness decreases over time so that the present alternative use value is low. Some of British Rail's rural tracks may well fit this label; in urban areas quite the reverse has happened—the value of some central sites is now very high.

An example from British Rail

A practical implication of this analysis is that, when decisions to reduce capacity are being taken, it is very important to be clear on the meaning of costs. The 'unprofitability' of some of British Rail's passenger and goods services is a case in point. This is an enterprise the demand for whose services has been declining over a long period with the development of alternative transport facilities. At the same time many of its assets like stations, bridges, rail track, marshalling yards, have very long physical lives. An issue which became of some public concern was the criteria used by BR to decide on the closure of passenger services. There is some evidence[32] to indicate that BR have been using rather dubious criteria. Now railway closures may well have a number of side-effects, such as increased congestion on the roads and curtailment of the development of a growth region. These are very important issues but not the ones in question. We are simply referring to the internal effects on BR itself. For any particular track, BR in the 1950s used to compare the likely loss of (system) annual revenue should closure take place with not only movement, maintenance, and signalling costs—which we can loosely refer to as running or direct costs—but also the annual fixed depreciation and interest charges of assets on the line. But many of these assets would not need renewing for a number of years into the future—with fairly routine maintenance, bridges, for example, can have physical lives in excess of fifty years—and their use now occasions no economic cost. Only movement, maintenance, and signalling can reasonably be categorized as involving economic costs 'this year'. (Of course, it is important to bear in mind that the

[31] See 'Fixed Costs', W. A. Lewis, *Economica*, November 1946. This has been reproduced as a chapter in his book *Overhead Costs*, Allen & Unwin, 1949, and also as chapter 2 of *Transport op. cit*.

[32] See 'The Withdrawal of Railway Services', M. Howe and G. Mills, *EJ*, June 1960.

Beeching Report[33] revealed that on many tracks not even these direct costs were covered by revenue.) The consumers' council for the industry, the Transport Users' Consultative Committee, felt that only 'direct factual savings' were relevant. In general, however, the issue has a time-dimension. Take a simple case where closure investigation is made in, say, 1972 and for the foreseeable future only two of the existing assets, a station and a bridge, need renewing—both in, say, 1980. One would first see whether revenue in 1972 covers 1972 direct costs. If it does, then the line is kept open and remains open over the next seven years provided this surplus is maintained. At the beginning of 1980 one has to decide whether to renew the station and the bridge; if they are not renewed the line closes down. Making the best estimates possible over the life of the new assets one compares the present value of the stream of revenue, which would otherwise be lost, with the capital cost of the station and bridge and the present value of the stream of direct costs. If the annual surplus of revenue over direct costs is expected to remain constant, then this is equivalent to comparing this annual surplus with the equivalent annual capital cost of the station and the bridge.[34] Notice that, even if this comparison turns out to be unfavourable, *one would still keep the line open to 1979*. What did emerge from the complaints of the TUCC was that an agreed compromise scheme was concluded. This involved comparing the annual surplus with the annual capital charge on those assets likely to need renewing over the next five years. Moreover, the estimated capital replacement costs were written off over five years;[35] the annual capital charge, in other words, implicitly assumed a life of only five years. Thus the method was still fairly unfavourable to the retention of these lines since, for any given capital cost, the annual charge is smaller the greater is the assumed life. On the other hand, renewals after five years are ignored though no doubt the line could be reconsidered at a later date.

The problem of fluctuating prices

So far, in this chapter, we have followed fairly closely the logic of the theory. More practical matters—such as avoiding deficits—are considered in the final section of this chapter. One issue is, however, worth raising at this stage and it is illustrated by Fig. 7.10. To re-cap, this example implied an initial

[33] *The Re-shaping of British Railways*, British Railways Board, Ministry of Transport, HMSO, 1963.

[34] Howe and Mills, *op. cit.*, present this in a different way. They suggest that the issue is to discover those time periods over which the cumulative sum of the discounted values of revenue less costs, is positive. This is equivalent to the formulation in our text, granted the assumptions made there.

[35] Howe and Mills illustrated their arguments by data from the passenger services on the St Ives–Kettering line. In the official figures for estimated annual savings from withdrawal of services was an entry of £57,000, covering 'provisions for renewals saved'. £32,000 of this constituted one-fifth of the £160,000 that would have to be spent within five years on a bridge in need of renewal. According to Howe and Mills, interest charges were not included in the agreed scheme, because of some confusion in the evidence put by the British Transport Commission!

price of P_1 in 1970 when capacity installations were made; in the next five years price remains at this level. Then in 1975 when demand contracts, price falls to P_2. It stays there until 1978 when capacity is contracted causing a rise in price to P_3. In other words, if capacity adjustments cannot be made immediately but *are* eventually made, there could be considerable fluctuation in the product price. The same point applies in the expansion case of Fig. 7.7. This can cause not only administrative inconvenience to the supplier but also disruption to the consumer. Because of this a number of economists have suggested that prices should relate *to the optimal volume of capacity that is expected to emerge*; or, put another way one actually sets price equal to long-run marginal cost. Turvey has argued that the

> . . . nature of the marginal-cost concept required can thus be ascertained only with reference to the objective function, to the constraints and to the amount of information available . . . [Two constraints] . . . which seem to be of fair generality at least in the field of public enterprise pricing . . . suggest the usefulness of a marginal-cost concept which relates to permanent rather than to temporary increments of output. The first is that prices or tariff structures cannot be changed frequently but have to be fixed for two or three years. One reason for this is the institutional hurdles that have to be gone through in order to introduce a change; the other is the cost to the enterprise and the inconvenience to consumers which it involves. The second constraint—more accurately it is a demand characteristic—is that consumers' decisions are frequently long-term ones, since they involve the acquisition of durable complementary goods. A decision by a new consumer to heat a room by gas, for example, requires the acquisition of a gas fire which he will expect to use for several years. Thus prices both have to endure for some years and have an impact on consumers which will frequently endure for some years. The marginal-cost concept which is relevant to pricing decisions consequently relates to permanent output changes.[36]

Boiteux,[37] for somewhat similar reasons, also suggests setting price at long-run marginal cost.

As far as expanding capacity is concerned, setting price at long-run marginal cost would, in many cases, mean excess demand as Fig. 7.7 illustrates. This is all right as long as rationing is feasible—as it is in electricity supply which

[36] 'Marginal Cost', *op. cit.*, pp. 287–8.

[37] See 'Peak-Load Pricing', *op. cit.*, section 2.3. Another French contributor to this issue is Gabriel Dessus. He appears, however, to be relying, rather hopefully, on demand contracting at a relatively slow rate and the existence of only a few under-employed assets. See 'The General Principles of Rate Fixing in Public Utilities'. The original title of this paper was 'Les Principes Généraux de la Tarification dans les Services Publics', and it was presented at the Brussels meeting of the Union Internationale des Producteurs et Distributeurs d'Energie Electrique, September 1949. The translated version appeared in *International Economic Papers*, No. 1, 1951 and is reproduced as chapter 2 of Nelson, *op. cit.*

Boiteux primarily has in mind. In the case of excess capacity the avoidance of short-run pricing may also have an additional advantage of reducing the accounting deficit. By raising price from P_2 to P_3 in Fig. 7.10 the total deficit is reduced, though it is not removed—P_3 lies below the A^1 line. We are now able to see—from hindsight—that some of the earlier UK discussion[38] on marginal-cost pricing was not very clear. However, one of the contributors, Lewis, made suggestions equivalent to requiring that price be set at long-run marginal cost. What is interesting about Lewis's work is the fairly close proximity to the modern analysis of pricing, even though the basic characteristics of prices when capacity is optimally adjusted are not explicitly and clearly analysed as they are in the French writings. To the extent that Fig. 7.10 refers to assets which have a finite life, Lewis would say they are non-permanent assets[39] and involve a long-run escapable cost. Of these assets, those which could earn revenue sufficient to cover long-run costs should be retained; these are 'renewable' assets, and on Fig. 7.10 refer to the Oq_3 range of capacity. That capacity 'responsible' for the q_2q_1 range is not used now; the remaining capacity—for q_3q_2—is non-renewable in Lewis's terminology and should also be closed down now. Since effective capacity would then become Oq_3, prices would rise to P_3—the long-run level. The result would be that the revenue earned by the capacity in use would cover all its costs. The capacity closed down would, of course, involve no running costs, but its fixed charges would still have to be met. This Lewis views as past mistaken investment which should be borne by the supplier, that is, these losses would have to be financed from general government revenue. On the other hand, if all these assets are 'permanent', only the q_2q_1 capacity should be closed down. Lewis is, in other words, recognizing here that when an asset's life is very large the policy of setting price at long-run marginal cost may involve sizeable economic losses. Where the excess capacity is short-lived, not much is foregone by closing it down.

7.6 Balancing the books, and other difficulties

Marginal cost pricing has been a fairly contentious subject area in economics. This is partly due to the fact that its advocates can be attacked at a number of different levels. One concerns the pros and cons of using any price system, whatsoever, in governmental supply of goods and services. Whether one can ascribe any *welfare* significance to marginal-cost pricing is dubious as we pointed out in chapter 4, where many of these more 'philosophical' points were discussed. A second level of attack rests on whether marginal-cost pricing can be defended, even on 'efficiency' grounds, when there are second-

[38] For a survey of some of these contributions see Nancy Ruggles' 'Recent Developments in the Theory of Marginal Cost Pricing', *Review of Economic Studies*, 1949, reproduced as chapter 1 of *Public Enterprise, op. cit.*

[39] *Op. cit.* Notice that throughout we have been assuming that capacity is divisible. The reference is, then, to Lewis's 'non-permanent divisible' assets.

best, externality problems, and the like, in the economy. A practical but arbitrary approach to these issues was also considered in chapter 4. A third, lower-level, of attack directs its attention to the technical problems of relating prices to marginal costs. It is to some of these last issues that we now turn.

It is hoped that some of the criticisms, that have been directed against marginal-cost pricing, will already have been dispelled in this chapter. One stricture is that the definition of marginal cost is arbitrary. Wiseman for example has suggested that the marginal cost rule implies that once

> ... the sacrifices necessary to create a durable and specific asset have been made ... no further opportunity costs are created by its later use. The opportunity costs having been borne in the past, no account should be taken of them in deciding current prices, even though *this results in losses*.... [Welfare criteria] ... would seem to imply consideration of a time-period at least as long as the lowest common multiple of the life-span of the factors concerned. If the marginal-cost rule is conceived in terms of a time-period shorter than this, then not all opportunity costs *requisite* to the manufacture of the product concerned can be *imputed* to that product, and the time-period chosen must itself be arbitrary, so that the marginal cost rule becomes simply a statement that outlays on factors of some specified durability should be ignored in deciding prices.... The figure treated as marginal cost will thus depend upon the time-period selected.[40]

To the extent that this is a theoretical comment on marginal cost pricing, it is incorrect. The theory indicates that output should always be adjusted if net benefits can accrue from such adjustments. At the extreme this might mean adjusting output at the end of each week. If we take periods up to a month, the range of factors of production that are variable is increased; labour supplies may well take this long. In deciding on price levels an important consideration is whether it is *economic* to have prices varying over such short periods. In our analysis we proposed a distinction between on the one hand labour, raw materials, and fuel, and, on the other hand, the costs of new capacity, primarily because such running costs are a relevant way of increasing output over fairly short periods and that for shorter periods price fluctuations would not be worthwhile. What is 'economic' is not arbitrary in Wiseman's sense; our proposition about the benefits of avoiding price fluctuations may be wrong, but that is a different matter. Wiseman was more concerned with the fact that capital costs would only be covered if one took a longish period. Marginal-cost pricing is certainly not arbitrary in this sense; prices are related to those costs that vary in the shortest run deemed economic to consider; whether capital costs are covered depends on the optimality of capacity, scale economies, technology, inflation, etc. *It does not depend on*

[40] 'The Theory of Public Utility Price—an Empty Box', J. Wiseman, *OEP*, pp. 59–60 February 1957 (my italics).

how long a period is taken to define marginal costs. In fact, if one takes very short periods one is more likely to come up against rigid capacity limits so that 'short-run' marginal costs and, therefore, price are very high! Moreover, those like Turvey and Boiteux who advocate pricing at long-run marginal cost justify it precisely on the grounds that shorter planning periods would entail uneconomic price fluctuations. A similar criticism can be found in Phelps Browns' book,[41] where the basic approach involves analysing what items should be included in marginal costs. In many cases the calculation of marginal cash costs is irrelevant; if capacity is fixed the appropriate price is that which clears demand at full capacity utilization. It is the non-recognition of capacity limits which is often a key explanation to some of the problems raised. This point becomes particularly important when there are indivisibilities, a topic explored in the next chapter. More generally, the main implication of the French theory of optimal capacity is as follows. Granted some period of time to which it is deemed economic to relate prices, the costs of all those factors of production—whether capital, *or* labour, *or* raw materials—*not* variable in this time-period, will be covered by the 'short-run' price provided the inherited volume of such factors is optimal (and, of course, provided there are no problems of returns to scale and/or technological advances).

One final point in this context is the difficulty involved in measuring marginal costs.[42] This is not disputed, but what is its significance? It is, surely, that we have only just started trying to estimate these sorts of concepts; the subject area is young but initial experience in electricity supply is not discouraging. In any case, all of these points apply to profit-maximization. A sophisticated 'model' profit-maximizer will need a rough knowledge of marginal costs; he will, in principle, price and invest with very much the criteria discussed in this chapter; the same problems arise. Are we doing any more in this chapter than look at the optimizing aspects of efficient price systems?

Accounting and economic costs: a re-cap

An important difficulty raised by marginal cost pricing is the possible emergence of accounting deficits. This point has been stressed and analysed by most of the British contributors to this literature. This, one might say, at the expense of analysing the relationship between pricing and investment and of empirical studies of marginal costs. Now, it is important to be clear on the basic causes making for deficits. A distinguishing characteristic of the UK nationalized industries, throughout most of the post-war period, has been

[41] *Op. cit.*, pp. 233–8 and 242–53.

[42] Durbin was an early writer to stress this. Lerner accepted the observation, but felt that one could improve with experience. See 'Economic Calculus in a Planned Economy', E. F. M. Durbin, *EJ*, p. 679, December 1936, and 'Statics and Dynamics in Socialist Economics', A. P. Lerner, *EJ*, pp. 258–9, June 1937.

the prevalence of low or negative surpluses. The reasons for this are numerous, but none relate to marginal-cost pricing, and it is the extent to which marginal-cost pricing gives rise to deficits that is of chief concern here. Basically we have uncovered three factors:[43]

(a) Technical Change: even if capacity is optimal so that prices equal to short-run marginal costs also equal long-run marginal costs, and even if the current production function exhibits constant returns to scale, total revenue will fall short of accounting costs if technological advance has lowered the cost of new capacity relative to old capacity. However, as we have pointed out, inflation could in principle offset this.

(b) Returns to Scale: in the absence of technical change, prices equal to long-run marginal costs will not produce a budget balance if there are scale economies in the production function.[44] Notice that assets which exhibit indivisibilities, such as bridges and roads, are simply extreme versions of this problem. Some general points about such assets were discussed in sections 5.3 and 5.4. A more detailed analysis is presented in the next chapter, but the general problem of covering financial losses is dealt with here.

(c) Excess Capacity: even with constant returns to scale and no technical advances, financial losses can arise if the existing volume of capacity is too big; prices equal to short-run marginal costs will not even cover long-run marginal costs.

These are three entirely independent factors. Most of the British writers have, until quite recently, concentrated on the last two factors. This partly reflects the natural concentration on public sector activities like transport, where indivisibilities can be important, and the coal and railway industries, both of which have been contracting throughout this century. At the same time, the distinction between excess capacity and scale economies has not always been made clear.[45] The latter involves the very considerable problem

[43] Treatment of the budget balance problem in those French articles which appear in Nelson's collection, *op. cit.*, is rather patchy. In the analysis of methods of financing deficits, British writers score better marks. This is also true of the wider 'welfare' aspects of marginal cost pricing.

[44] If an enterprise produces output ranges exhibiting decreasing returns to scale, surpluses emerge. No one seems to mind that!

[45] For example, M. J. Farrell:

> 'Early discussions were based on . . . the assumption that public utilities operate under conditions of decreasing average cost . . . [in which case] . . . marginal cost is less than average cost. . . . [However it] . . . will usually be only in the short run that average cost exceeds marginal, and in this case the magnitude of marginal cost depends on the (arbitrary) definition of the length of the short-run.'

Farrell seems to be talking about excess capacity, but the proposition that public utilities are characterized by decreasing average cost is, as Farrell implies later in the article, a proposition about the existence of scale economies. Although Farrell is discussing what others have said about marginal-cost pricing—the last part of the quotation is an allusion to Wiseman's criticisms, *op. cit.*—there is nowhere, in the rest of the article, any qualification of the above remarks. See 'In Defence of Public Utility Price Theory', *OEP*, February 1958. An amended version appears as chapter 2 of *Public Enterprise*, 1968, *op. cit.*, and the quotation is taken from this version (p. 45).

of 'over-exhaustion' (see sections 5.2 and 5.3), which applies when all factors of production are variable; excess capacity causes problems because past investment now involves an historic rather than an economic cost. Before looking at some of the suggestions for meeting these accounting deficits, there are three points to bear in mind to get the problem in perspective. The first point is that present knowledge of cost functions in the public sector is fairly thin. Scale economies may not be pervasive; perhaps the only safe *a priori* bet is that indivisibilities may be important in certain parts of transport. In addition, we shall argue in the next chapter that the theoretical significance of indivisibilities, in terms of causing problems for pricing, has probably been exaggerated. The second point is that the 'solution' of raising price to cover average cost does not end the matter. It removes the deficit but, on Pareto efficiency grounds, economic losses are thereby created. In the case of excess capacity, we saw in the previous section of this chapter that these losses are bigger the larger the size of the annual deficit that would otherwise have arisen, and the longer would that deficit have persisted! Thirdly, as already stressed, technological advance may be offset by price rises. Boiteux, writing in 1960, felt that the French Nationalized Electricity Industry had certainly benefited from rising prices. A

> . . . part of the capital investment in Électricité de France was made before the war, and the interest charges relating to this part of the investment have become relatively light on account of the subsequent inflation. . . . Today, average and marginal cost are of about the same order of magnitude. . . . We are not yet cynical enough to calculate the optimum rate of inflation which would continue this fortunate equilibrium indefinitely. But it does exist now.[46]

The early British writers on marginal-cost pricing overlooked this effect of inflation—to be fair the persistent rise in prices was probably not foreseen in the 1945–7 period. It could, in fact, submerge the effects not only of technological advance but also excess capacity and scale economies. If prices are related to 1974 running costs, 1935 capital costs are going to look fairly small beer.

Proposed solutions

Nevertheless, the deficit problem has to be faced. The suggestions that have been made can be arranged into three groups:

(a) A key point to bear in mind is that Pareto efficiency has hardly anything

[46] 'Electrical Energy: Facts, Problems and Prospects', p. 26. This article, originally appeared in *Annales des Mines*, October 1960 under the title, 'L'Energie électrique: données, problèms et perspectives'. It was reprinted in the *Revue Française de l'Energie*, November 1960, and its translated version appears as chapter 1 of Nelson's book, *op. cit.*, to which the page references refer.

to say about accounting problems like deficits. The one conclusion that can be drawn from the efficiency conditions is that the methods of financing should not disturb any of the conditions. The very existence of a deficit implies that consumers of the product are not covering all that product's accounting costs. If payments are actually made to the suppliers of the factors of production in question—holders of fixed interest government bonds, for example—then they must be being paid by the owners of the enterprise, that is the state, that is by 'us' via taxation. Two of the early advocates of marginal cost pricing, Lerner and Hotelling,[47] thinking primarily of the problem of scale economies, suggested financing deficits by central government revenue. But the conventional sources of such revenue—income tax, purchase tax, etc.—are themselves distorters of the efficiency conditions.[48] The only source, in principle, not subject to this difficulty would be a so-called lump sum tax—such as a poll tax—that is, a tax which is not related to variables affecting production, work, and so on. As we pointed out in chapter 3, it is difficult to think of any tax which is completely unrelated to economic magnitudes. An additional argument, that has been used against running state-financed deficits, is that this involves a redistribution of income from tax-payers in general to the consumers of the enterprise's product;[49] that is, moving from average-cost pricing to marginal-cost pricing involves gains greater than losses, but if the losers (tax-payers) are not compensated income distribution has been changed. But is the initial income distribution 'proper' in any sense? Every method of running any enterprise has distributive implications. To use any price system for governmentally supplied services has distributive implications. Using average-cost pricing on London's buses, as opposed to providing them 'free', involves distributive implications. One cannot look at the issue of marginal versus average without requiring some knowledge of the government's general policy on income distribution.

(b) An important difficulty associated with using state finance—one broadly consistent with considerations of allocative efficiency—is the effect that such methods will have on managerial efficiency and managerial incentives.[50] Covering all accounting costs provides a tractable check on managerial methods. Even if the enterprise is allowed to run at a loss there is something to be said—as Henderson[51] has argued—for those who bear the loss, having

[47] See Lerner, *op. cit.*, and also his book *The Economics of Control*, Macmillan, 1946. H. Hotelling's pioneering article on 'The General Welfare in Relation to Problems of Taxation and of Railway and Utility Rates' is in *Econometrica*, April 1938, and has been reproduced in *Readings in Welfare Economics*, Ed. K. J. Arrow and T. Scitovsky, AEA, Allen & Unwin, 1969.

[48] Lerner (in his book, chapter 19), Meade and Coase all stressed this point. See J. E. Meade, 'Price and Output Policy of State Enterprise', *EJ*, December 1944; R. H. Coase, 'The Marginal Cost Controversy', *Economica*, August 1946. Meade's article has been reproduced in *Readings in Welfare Economics, op. cit.*

[49] Cf. Coase, *op. cit.*

[50] Both Henderson and Phelps-Brown, *op. cit.*, of the earlier writers, felt this was important. See 'The Pricing of Public Utility Undertakings', A. M. Henderson, *The Manchester School* No. 3, 1947, reproduced in *Readings in Welfare Economics, op. cit.*

[51] *Op. cit.*

some clear relationship with the enterprise; on these grounds a 'free' local water supply is better financed from local authority rates than central government revenue. The recent proposals in the 1967 White Paper[52] that the UK Nationalized Industries should aim at certain target surpluses, reflects concern that the recently espoused policies of marginal-cost pricing and benefit/cost analysis require some money balance targets, to which managers can usefully direct their attentions. However, the main point at this stage is simply that general subsidies to public industries contain the danger of laxness in managerial efficiency. Partly because of this, there have been a number of suggestions for attempting, as far as possible, to require public enterprise to balance their books in one way or another. Two suggestions in this spirit try to avoid distortions of the marginalist principle. Neither, however, seem particularly practical. One method would be to differentiate between each consumer in levying prices. By discriminating in this way all of the consumers' surplus is expropriated as enterprise net revenue—producer surplus—but Pareto efficiency is unimpaired.[53] This method would certainly solve the scale economies problem—discriminatory tolls on a bridge being the classic case[54]—and might reduce much of the deficit in the excess capacity and technical change situations. If the reader will turn back to the excess capacity problem in Fig. 7.10, he will see that perfect discrimination between each of the Oq_2 consumers, associated with the 1975 demand function, would in fact more than cover all accounting costs. Much of the discussion by British writers is flavoured by the ability of the railways, since the First World War, to discriminate between broad groups of transport merchandise. In fact, with the growth of road transport, this price system became distinctly unfavourable to the railways, since fares on different routes and for different consignments were completely unrelated to costs.[55] The point about discrimination is, however, that generally it is just not feasible to operate it finely enough to capture surpluses. A similar point applies to a closely related suggestion concerning the use of two-part tariffs.[56] The running part of such a tariff is to be related to marginal costs and the fixed part is to be used to expropriate consumer surplus. But how are such *individual* surpluses to be discovered?

[52] *Nationalized Industries: A Review of Economic and Financial Objectives*, Cmnd 3437, pp. 12–14, HMSO, November 1967.

[53] The French economist Dupuit was the first to recognize this possibility (cf. discussion and references in section 5.3 below). Both Henderson, *op. cit.*, and E. W. Clemens ('Price Discrimination in Decreasing Cost Industries', *AER*, December 1941) considered discrimination as a possibility; Hotelling, *op. cit.*, recognized the argument but rejected the solution on feasibility grounds.

[54] Cf. section 5.3 and section 8.2.

[55] Many of Gilbert Walker's writings indicate this clearly. See for example, 'Transport Policy Before and After 1953', *OEP*, March 1953.

[56] See Lewis, *op. cit.*; similar ideas underlie another of his articles, though it is primarily directed at the peak problem—'The Two-Part Tariff', *Economica*, August 1941, reproduced in *Overhead Costs, op. cit.*

(c) More manageable suggestions have been made, however. Two-part tariffs have been advocated in which the running charge is related to marginal costs as before, and the fixed part is so levied that all other accounting costs are recouped, but without the requirement that it be related to individual consumer surpluses.[57] Various forms of average-cost pricing have been suggested. The most sophisticated analysis is that of C. D. Foster[58], who makes it clear that some average-cost pricing policies are vastly different from others. The UK nationalized industries were, in the period up to the early 1960s, required to cover all costs taking one year with another. In practice, this led individual enterprises simply to ensure that over all the system, total revenue covered total accounting costs. One could, however, clearly cover such costs and at the same time have different prices for different services rendered. One could insist on different parts of the National Coal Board paying their way as well as the industry as a whole. Similarly, prices could be based very much on the marginalist principle and yet cover total costs. One could, for example, calculate prices for electricity based on time of day and season of year; to the extent that marginal costs differ in these different periods—as we shall argue in the next chapter—some differentials would remain even if in each period prices were raised above marginal costs. Seasonal and daily differentials are a characteristic of the 'Tarif Vert' levied since 1956 by Électricité de France on its high-voltage (industrial) consumers. Boiteux, as we have already seen, has suggested that in Électricité de France inflation has considerably reduced the disparity between current marginal costs and average accounting cost.

> There is, however, a slight divergence between average and marginal cost cost—of the order of 7 per cent. The deficit of 7 per cent has been covered by increasing the schedules of marginal prices obtained, so as to reduce the most extreme differences between new and old tariffs. This is not so arbitrary as it seems to be at first sight, once one allows for the readaptation of demand to the new level of price.[59]

What can be said about all these suggestions? The first point is that no unique general solution is available; all practical 'solutions' distort the efficiency conditions in one way or another. Secondly, the problem of knowing how to deal with deficits is very much a problem of the constraints on policy measures. Formally, we might say[60] that, setting aside distributive considerations, the maximand of benefits and costs is constrained not only by the production function but also by administrative and other constraints, not

[57] Wilson, Coase, and Phelps-Brown all treat this as a possibility. (See previous footnotes and T. Wilson, 'Price and Output Policy of State Enterprises', *EJ*, December 1945.)

[58] *The Transport Problem*, Blackie, 1963, particularly Part I.

[59] *Electrical Energy: Facts, Problems and Prospects*, p. 26, *op. cit.*

[60] Cf. The Turvey quotation on p. 241 above. See also his piece on 'How Rational Economic Decisions are Made', *Lloyds Bank Review*, January 1968.

directly measurable in the economist's language of benefits and costs. These constraints will vary for each product of the public sector. Moreover, they may not in some cases be significant. It is worth repeating that we are still in an *a priori* world; the accounting deficits that might arise from marginal-cost pricing may for some products be trivial. True, we have claimed that indivisibilities may be important in the provision of certain transport services, like roads. But we do not yet know even whether it is 'economic' to introduce *any* price system for roads. In general, a safe suggestion is that time and effort is best spent in discussing these issues at the product level. We—perhaps unwisely—venture a few general points.

Setting aside the problem of indivisibilities, provided the deficits that may arise are not going to run into astronomic proportions, there seems some case for using certain of the methods described in (c) above; this, on the grounds that covering all accounting costs is likely to be a target understood by enterprise executives and that it avoids the administrative (and political?) difficulties of operating a subsidy scheme. This means that prices are based on marginal costs plus adjustments to cover all accounting costs. The context of this suggestion needs stressing. Firstly, this is not a suggestion for using a price system in all parts of the public sector. Such general issues are discussed in chapter 4. In addition second-best, externality, and income distribution problems are not being ignored. These issues, as we also stressed in the previous chapter and also in chapter 4, cannot be dealt with on a routine basis by enterprise executives. At the least, second-best problems require a general approach by government or bodies responsible for say the Nationalized Industries as a whole. Similarly, externality problems are probably better dealt with on an *ad hoc*, once-and-for-all basis. Income distribution is a major policy issue. Social objectives which cannot be put into simple economic terms—'subsidizing' the Scottish Highlands—need special treatment. Some of these issues may well involve specific subsidies being given to the industries. Our suggestions, then, about prices relate to more routine matters in sectors where it has been decided that a price system ought to be used. Granted this, there is a second general point which arises when one allows that the potential deficits in some circumstances could be quite large. In the normal run of things, we adopt the suggestion that prices should be levied at a level which would emerge when capacity is optimal. If there is considerable excess capacity this could still mean a deficit, smaller perhaps than if prices were kept at short-run marginal costs, but still there. Moreover, if the excess capacity is likely to persist there are considerable economic losses involved in raising prices to long-run marginal costs. Something akin to this was certainly the case in the UK railway system. In these circumstances, it would seem to be useful that a specific subsidy be granted to the industry otherwise there will be gross under-utilization for lengthy periods of a capacity involving little economic costs. Similarly, when capacity is sub-optimal, rationing, when feasible, could be used to restrict demand with price at its long-run level. Should the shortages be expected to persist over a period as long as say a decade, a major policy decision would be in order to decide between a market clearing price —with its distributive implications—and physical rationing schemes.[61]

[61] Some of these suggestions are not all that different from some of the suggestions in the 1967 White Paper, *op. cit.*, although that paper is considerably blemished by the section on costs. It is really a pity that in such a pioneering government paper, the key concept of costs is very loosely used.

8. Joint costs, indivisibilities, and peak loads

8.1 General issues

Activities commonly found in the public sector often raise some of the more intriguing problems of micro-economics. The prevalence of joint costs is one such issue. In its many guises it can considerably complicate pricing policy, and it is this aspect which dominates this chapter. By jointness in costs we mean that certain functions can be best produced in such a way that if one function is provided the others can be provided at zero extra cost. A train often carries both passengers and small parcels. The train's fuel costs and the engine's capital cost are joint to both the passenger and parcel functions. It is cheaper to provide these services jointly rather than have a separate train for each function. Costs which are truly joint to various functions are such that, if any one function is provided for, all the other functions can be met at zero extra cost. Now, jointness manifests itself in a number of ways and four which are of particular interest in the public expenditure field are:

(a) Multi-purpose Projects and Facilities: many large public projects particularly those connected with water-resource development are multi-purpose. In the USA, the Tennessee Valley Authority, the Bureau of Reclamation, and the Corps of Engineers have constructed many such schemes.

> A typical multi-purpose project will include a dam which is used to provide flood-control, stream-flow regulation for navigation, seasonal or annual carry-over of water for irrigation, as well as long- and short-term storage for hydro-electric power. Some of the costs, such as expenditures for electric generating equipment or for irrigation pumping facilities, can be assigned to one of the purposes, but much of the investment, especially the dam and reservoir, is necessary for each purpose.[2]

[1] To get maximum benefit from this chapter, the reader should have read chapter 5 (sections 2–4) as well as chapter 7.

[2] O. Eckstein, *Water-Resource Development*, p. 259, Harvard University Press, 1958.

The suggested barrages across the Dee Estuary and Morecambe Bay in the UK, provide a road as well as water-storage facilities. In all these cases, part of the construction cost is joint to different products or services. Examples are rife in transport. In a recent study of a railway line in the UK, the annual running and maintenance costs of the track and signalling were estimated at £90,000. British Rail officials suggested that if passenger services alone were withdrawn only £12,000 would be saved, while if only freight services were withdrawn nothing would be saved. Thus, these costs comprise an element of £12,000 which is a separable or avoidable cost attributable to passengers plus an amount, £78,000, representing a cost joint to passengers and freight, avoidable, in other words, only if both freight and passenger services were simultaneously withdrawn.[3]

(b) Indivisibilities: costs may be joint not only over different products but also over different units of the same product; for simplicity we call only this type of jointness 'indivisibility', though the term is often used by writers to cover other examples of jointness. Since the capital and running costs of a passenger bus are largely independent of the number of passengers, then they are joint to the various users. This corresponds to the indivisibility problem discussed in chapter 5 where services are jointly supplied. Buses, railway carriages, cinemas, theatres, parks, museums, road and rail track, all appear to exhibit some degree of joint supply.

(c) Investment Decisions: many capital assets physically depreciate, not as a function of usage but more because of age. It follows that the cost of such assets are joint to the various slices of time in their lifespan. No part of such capital costs can be attributed to any one of these slices of time. This was implicitly allowed for in the net discounted present value formulation of the investment decisions in the previous chapter. The plants in question were viewed as providing services over a certain horizon and the base-year capital outlay on these plants was compared, not with benefit (net of running costs) in any one year, but with the (discounted) *sum* of benefits over the plants' lives.

(d) Peak Loads: a special case of jointness over time is provided by the phenomenon of peak loads. Now, the capital cost of any asset or machine is clearly joint to the various hours, days, and weeks of the year as it is to different years in its life-span. We distinguish between years because interest payments are often made annually. Within the year, variations in demand can often be ignored since stock-piling can even out production over the year. When, however, the product is non-storable—as for many public sector activities like rail services, electricity supply, etc.—then the time at which a particular demand is made becomes important, especially if total demand does show

[3] This is taken from a project with which I was involved. See *A Study of Transport in the Furness Area of Lancashire*, Report to the M. of Transport, N.W. Economic Planning Council, February 1967. A general discussion of joint costs in railway operations can be found in chapter III of this report.

considerable variation; again this is also characteristic of public services in transport, fuel, and education. The problem is how 'efficient' prices are to be determined in such circumstances, and how these prices relate to capacity costs which are joint to the various periods of demand within the year.

Multi-purpose projects

Some of the general points associated with joint costs can be indicated in relation to multi-purpose projects. This will pave the way for more detailed analysis of the two major topics of interest, indivisibilities and peak loads. The first thing to recognize is that, for any multi-purpose facility, there are usually some 'separable' costs as well as joint costs. The total construction costs of a water-barrage topped by a road may include some separable costs. Clearly, the road surface and its signalling equipment fall into this category; similarly, facilities for water pumping are directly attributable to the water facilities. When signalling equipment is planned for a railway line part of the capital cost—as well as the running cost as indicated in our earlier example—will be attributable to passenger services which require a higher standard of service than freight. But, in both these examples, a large part of the capital cost will be joint to the various purposes. If prices can be levied for the various purposes involved a question that arises—granted the suggestions in the previous chapter for relating prices to costs—is how to allocate the joint costs to these various purposes. Attempts are often made. Sometimes they are allocated on the basis of engineering data on the proportionate use of capacity; sometimes on decisions as to priority of use.[4] The point is, however, that the question itself is misconceived. If the cost is truly joint then, on grounds of economic efficiency, no allocation is possible. Neither is it necessary. How do we know whether the asset should be constructed? The principle is straightforward. Multi-purpose projects are worth building if the *sum* of consumer benefits from each purpose (net of separable costs) exceeds the joint cost item. Where the enterprise levies prices—and where the variation in output is too small to disturb these prices—then the principle is that the revenue from the extra output, net of separable costs and summed over all purposes, should exceed the joint cost. It is like the conventional investment decision where the jointness arises through time. For a plant producing only one product, the (discounted) *sum* of net receipts over the various slices of time in the plant's life is compared with the capital cost. Since multi-purpose ventures often involve capital, then they contain two elements of jointness, that arising through time and that arising from the variety of services produced.

One final point needs to be made about multi-purpose facilities, and this is that the extent of jointness can easily be exaggerated. Take the water-barrage as an example. Suppose that after deducting the separable costs of the road

[4] Cf. Eckstein, *op. cit.*, chapter IX.

surface and water-pumping facilities, the construction cost is £40 million. It is most likely that related investment options are available. If a barrage for water-storage alone were considered then the same services (and benefits) could perhaps be produced by designing a slimmer barrage costing only say £30 million. Similarly, should a road only be considered, a small viaduct across the river or estuary may be adequate to provide the same benefits to road traffic and this costs say £20 million. In assessing the multi-purpose venture it would, in these circumstances, be insufficient to go ahead simply because the sum of road and water benefits exceed £40 million. The saving in cost through not catering for road traffic is £10 million. This is a separable cost for road traffic; if their benefits fall short of £10 million, then it is better simply to build the slimmer barrage costing £30 million which will be less than the benefits of the water supply. Put another way, the additional costs involved in the multi-purpose project as opposed to the more modest water-barrage, exceed the additional benefits. By similar reasoning, water-supply involves a separable cost of £20 million. The true joint cost of the multi-purpose project is then only £10 million, and it is this which the sum of road and water benefits, net in each case of all separable costs defined above, must exceed for the joint venture to be worth while. The more general problem is that the width of the road and the height of the barrage may both be variable. Separable marginal costs for each additional 5 yards of road or 10 feet of barrage height could be calculated. Of course, in all these cases all the asset's opportunity cost becomes joint to the various purposes *once it has been constructed.* But, in any case, what are these opportunity costs? They are the scrap or alternative use value of the sunken resources, an amount which may well be trivial. The initial capital outlay is now an historic cost. But, as we know from our discussion of optimal capacity in the previous chapter, as long as no unforeseen demand changes occur, these historic costs will be covered by prices.

8.2 Capacity indivisibilities

This section draws together various points made previously throughout the book, and extends their scope. This can most usefully be done with the aid of Fig. 8.1. Imagine a situation where a product or service is to be supplied, and one is planning the optimal scale of capacity and deciding on the appropriate price. No capacity is inherited from the past; all the plants in the potential new capacity have the same life; further, all have the same unit running costs —equal to *Ou* in Fig. 8.1. The plants' running costs remain the same throughout their life, a life which abruptly ends for all of them after say twenty years. In other words, to concentrate on the issue of indivisibility all the complicating factors discussed in the previous chapter are ignored. Further, if we assume demand remains constant, then optimal capacity size and optimal prices can be evaluated with reference to annual benefit, annual running cost,

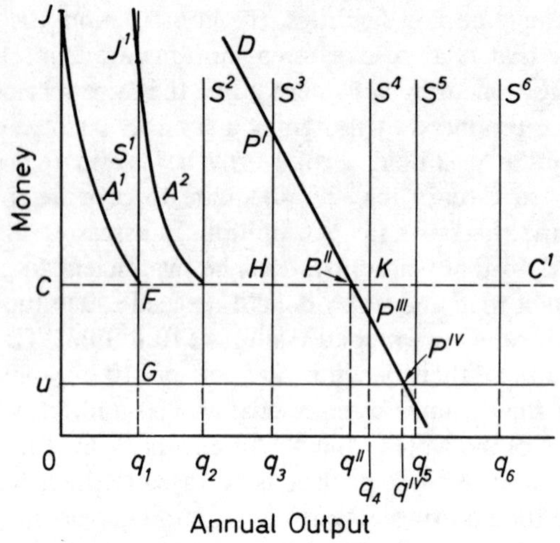

FIG. 8.1

and annual 'equivalent' capital cost. This will give the same results as comparing the present value of the flow of annual benefits with capital costs and the present value of the flow of annual running costs.

One possible level for capacity is q_1, so that if capacity is subject to rigid limits the (annual) short-run marginal cost function is S^1. Other capacity levels are indicated by S^2, S^3, S^4, S^5, S^6. *Indivisibilities would exist if we assumed that these were the only possible capacity sizes.* To increase capacity beyond q_1 the minimum 'jump' is to build the larger capacity associated with S^2. One can produce an annual output intermediate between q_1 and q_2 only by introducing a plant structure whose maximum capacity is q_2; to produce such an intermediate output level one would have to build the S^2 size, and run it at less than maximum potential. Similarly, the minimum possible positive scale of capacity is q_1, and we can examine this particular capacity level to see how capital costs enter the picture. The annual equivalent capital cost of this capacity is given by uJ on Fig. 8.1. This is a cost joint to the $0q_1$ units of output, in the sense that if one unit is supplied the other units can be supplied at zero extra (capital) cost. Expressed per unit of the q_1 output that this capacity can produce, it is equal to $FG(= uC)$. (The A^1 line indicates average total costs.) It is assumed that, for all the other capacity sizes, the average capital cost is also equal to uC; average total costs with capacity structure 2—indicated by A^2—is, at full capacity, just equal to OC. Therefore, subject to the indivisibility conditions, the production function exhibits constant returns to scale.[5] Despite this assumed constancy, problems for pricing remain. The dotted line CC^1 indicates unit running cost plus the

[5] Cf. The production function used by O. E. Williamson in his exposition of **'Peak Load Pricing and Optimal Capacity Under Indivisibility Constraints'**, cited in previous chapter.

average capital cost as defined. Now, *if* capacity *were* perfectly divisible, CC^1 would represent long-run marginal cost. Price would be set at P'', equal to short-run marginal (and average) cost; since q'' capacity is the optimal level, this price also equals long-run marginal (and average) cost. But capacity is not perfectly divisible, and a smooth LMC line does not exist. Long-run marginal costs if anything follow the path of $JuGJ^1$, etc. What is the optimal capacity size? If S^3 capacity were built, price would be P'; at least this capacity size is warranted since annual benefit, as indicated by the area under the demand curve, exceeds annual running costs and equivalent annual capital costs ($0C \times 0q_3$). Would an even bigger plant structure be better? If the S^4 capacity were chosen, price would be at P'''; such an increase is warranted on the efficiency criterion on the grounds that the extra annual benefit (area $q_3P'P'''q_4$) exceeds the extra annual costs (area q_3HKq_4). An even larger capacity is not warranted since the extra costs outweigh the extra benefits. Thus, following the basic logic of the theory, q_4 is the optimal capacity size with price set at P'''.

The problem is, of course, that such a solution involves a budget deficit. The point is more strikingly demonstrated if increasing scale beyond S^3 involved jumping to S^5, i.e., S^4 did not exist. In these circumstances unqualified pursuit of the theory would indicate building capacity structure S^5, running it at less than full capacity and selling output q^{iv} at price P^{iv}, the resultant revenue covering only running costs. This situation—devoid of any of the *different* problems of inherited capacity, unforeseen demand changes, technical change, factor price movements—exhibits the key problem of indivisibility that, because capacity cannot be finely adjusted, its optimal volume may involve so setting price that a budget deficit arises. The deficit arises not because of any divergence between actual capacity and optimal capacity; it is caused by the lumpiness of the capital input.

Some examples from transport

Let us, now, consider the implications of this analysis for assets which have traditionally been thought to give rise to indivisibility. Many can be found in the field of transport. The capital cost—and fuel costs to a certain extent—of a bus, are joint to the various users. French economists like to quote the

> ... example of 'the traveller to Calais' ... who gets to the station Paris-Nord just in time to board the Calais-bound train. If unoccupied seats are available, the cost of transporting our traveller will, in practice, be nil. But if it is necessary to put on an additional coach ... run an extra train ... lay a new track ... or widen the Chantilly Bridge, the cost of moving this last traveller mounts with astonishing rapidity.[6]

[6] G. Dessus, article cited in previous chapter, pp. 42–3.

There are a number of points that can be made about these sorts of examples:

(a) The mere existence of indivisibility does not imply a price equal to unit running costs, as some writers have implied. What is often forgotten is that the basic end of the theory is the maximization of total benefit minus total cost; with rigid capacity limits this may well involve a price in excess of unit running costs even if there are indivisibilities. We are not suggesting that this price will always cover all long-run costs; if the demand curve in Fig. 8.1 had cut S^4 at point K, this would indeed have been fortuitous.[7] All we are saying is that, if the indivisibilities are not big, then optimal prices are on *a priori* grounds, just as likely to resemble P' or P''' as P^{iv}. One must then judge C. D. Foster to be *incorrect* in this

> . . . example of a train. While the train is not full, the SRMC of carrying another passenger is virtually zero. When full it is the cost of running another train, but *as soon as* the extra train is provided it falls to zero again. In this example the SRMC and therefore the price, will always be zero since *either* there is no more room on the train and no one else can be carried *or* there is room on the train and it costs nothing to carry another.[8]

Price is set equal to short-run marginal *opportunity* cost not cash cost.[9] In deciding prices the planning of an optimal volume of capacity is a crucial issue, and lack of reference to this problem is a further factor in explaining why indivisibilities are often assumed to cause larger problems than they actually do. Thus, I. M. D. Little suggests that it is a

> common sense value judgement . . . [that] . . . people should be allowed to use something as much as they like if it costs nothing. We may ask why

[7] Moreover, even if this happy result emerged, one could not strictly say that price is equal to long-run *marginal* cost. At no point on Fig. 8.1 is long-run marginal cost equal to $0C$. All one can say is that, if price is equal to $0C$ (and capacity is fully used—i.e., the demand curve intersects S^4 at K) all long run costs are covered. This is the one qualification that one has to make to Dessus's otherwise excellent discussion of indivisibilities.

> 'We will suppose that a coach has seating accommodation for eighty passengers, and that this will be the maximum number of passengers allowed to travel per coach . . . the problem of determining the number of coaches to be run has to be considered not in terms of one additional passenger per day, but in terms of *a group of eighty additional passengers per day*. The cost of transporting such an additional group is equal to the daily cost of running the required supplementary coach. The number of groups of eighty passengers to be conveyed each day, and thus the number of coaches to be brought into service, is determined by charging a fare which, when paid by eighty passengers, will cover the daily cost of commissioning the marginal coach. *It is in this manner that the indeterminancy of marginal transport cost (relatively to coaches) is circumvented: its magnitude is equal to the eightieth part of the marginal coach's running cost.*'

(G. Dessus, *op. cit*., pp. 43–4, the emphasis in the last sentence is mine). It is not, for one cannot parcel out a joint cost.

[8] *The Transport Problem*, p. 313, Blackie and Son, 1963 (his emphasis).

[9] Cf. The discussion in the introduction to the previous chapter.

an exception is always made in the case of transport. There is nothing more obvious than that, if a bus or train or ship is running half empty, it would cost next to nothing to carry an extra passenger. Part of the answer lies in the equation of supply and demand. . . . The theoretical pricing rule, when marginal cost is zero, is 'lower price until the service is fully used—if necessary to zero'. This could hardly be done in the case of buses or trains. Everyone would wait until the last moment for the price to come down, when there would be a horrid scramble.[10]

It is true that demand is never known for certainty. But this is quite a general problem. In a world of uncertainty, estimates and forecasts of demand have to be made; one certainly would not mess around with prices the way Little is suggesting.

(b) Notice that many transport facilities may be 'half empty' only in certain parts of the day or year. This is part of the problem of peak loads to be considered in the next section.

(c) If we wished to be theoretical purists, it would be possible to argue that short-run marginal costs start rising, in some of the examples, before full capacity. Congestion costs may arise early on. Long-run marginal cost may not then exhibit as many discontinuities, but the issue is probably trivial for 'small' assets like buses and trains.

(d) The key issue about indivisibilities is their size. It is apparent that Fig. 8.1 illustrates a situation where there is fair amount of choice with respect to the size of capacity; the number and size of buses and trains can be varied. The deficit problem can be overcome by choosing a smaller stock of coaches than that associated with S^4. With S^3, the associated price more than covers all costs. True, we cannot be fully certain that even this stock will always be fully used nor that excessive congestion would not at times occur. But as we said before, this is intrinsic to the problem of uncertainty and applies whatever price is chosen. The question that arises is the size of the 'efficiency' loss involved in having one less coach. In Fig. 8.1 this loss is equal to area $q_3P'P'''q_4$ minus area q_3HKq_4. Against this, one has to balance the intangible benefits, not allowed for in the simple pricing theory, of avoiding a deficit; the administrative advantages of avoiding all the financing problems discussed in the previous chapter; the fine analysis that would be needed to discover whether the extra cost of an additional coach are more than covered by what additional passengers would be *prepared* to pay (as opposed to what they would actually pay). It would not then be unrealistic to suggest that, where indivisibilities are not large—and the buses and trains examples are presumably in this category—the indivisibility problem can be circumvented by choosing capacity in such a way that it will be fully used and prices cover long-run costs. This position is very much in symmetry with the discussion in chapter 5 of other assets giving rise to 'small' indivisibilities—cinemas,

[10] 'A Critique of Welfare Economics', OUP, p. 195, 1957.

theatres, swimming pools. There we suggested that, in such cases, there were no strong reasons for thinking that 'efficient' supplies could not emerge from a competitive environment; because the indivisibilities are small, replication could allow a competitive industry to roughly approximate a Pareto efficient solution.

Of course, if demand decreases in some unforeseen way or if demand forecasts have been widely optimistic then, at any point in time, inherited capacity may be too big. Again, strict adherence to the theory would indicate prices would not fully cover capital charges. *But this is an entirely separate problem*; it has nothing to do with indivisibilities, as the last chapter should have made clear. Where the indivisibility problem becomes important is when such indivisibility occurs on a large scale. As Dessus's example implies, the costs of railway track can be joint to many train services and, therefore, to very large numbers of passengers. In the end one needs some empirical help on these issues; the losses through building a track system slightly smaller than the 'optimal' size may not be great. But when one moves into the field of tracks, roads, bridges, the previous devices for circumventing the indivisibility issue cannot always be justified and it is to this problem that we now turn.

Large indivisibilities

It should be remembered that in the transport examples of large indivisibilities—roads, bridges, and the like—and in other services like broadcasting and large parks, indivisibilities are but part of the problem. For one thing, congestion can become important. Secondly, in most of these examples there are technical difficulties in levying prices related to usage. 'Exclusion costs' become important and externality/public good problems arise. However, this latter issue was discussed in an earlier chapter (see section 5.4). To concentrate on the indivisibility issue, it is more appropriate to think of roads and bridges and assume prices can be levied if necessary. Our arguments are purely illustrative. It would be inappropriate to attempt more since economists, accountants, and engineers have only begun to attempt costing studies of the complex problems that a road system raises.

Figure 8.2 is practically a reproduction of Fig. 5.4, and it illustrates the standard extreme case of indivisibility. The equivalent annual capital cost of a road or bridge is given by $0J$; expressed per unit of traffic, this cost is smaller the greater is the flow—as the average cost line, A, indicates. Given the demand curve, D, the optimal price or toll on this asset, in the absence of any running costs, would be zero; that is, Oq units of traffic would be allowed to use the bridge. Is it worth building? The efficiency criterion implies a comparison of annual benefit with annual cost. In this case it is, therefore, a matter of discovering whether the area under the demand curve exceeds the annual capital cost. A comparison of revenue with expenditure is the wrong criterion. The right criterion is difficult to use, though we shall see in the next chapter

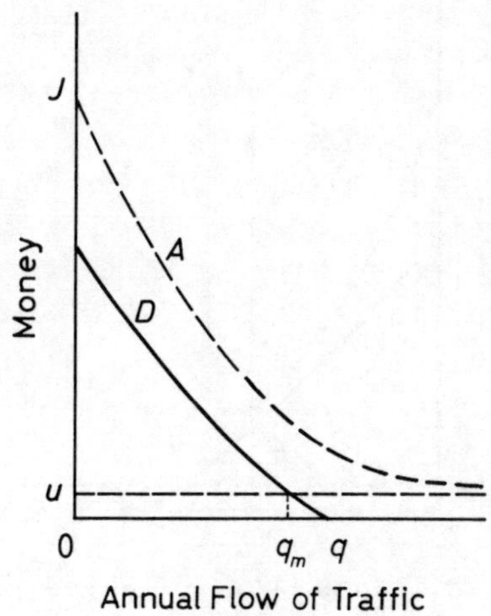

FIG. 8.2

that techniques are now being developed to estimate areas under demand curves. The associated problem which is our chief concern here is that 'optimality' implies a budget deficit—in fact revenue is zero.

Three points may be noted about this simple case. Firstly roads and bridges need maintenance, and so there are usually some running costs. Suppose in Fig. 8.2 unit maintenance costs are constant and equal to $0u$, so that the A line now represents capital plus maintenance costs per unit of traffic. The only difference now is that traffic is restricted to q_m rather than q. That is, on the assumption that prices can be levied, such prices just cover maintenance costs. Secondly, it is worth reiterating that the requirement of low tolls is not due to any divergence between optimal and actual capacity. If the bridge had been inherited from the past, then its capital cost would be irrelevant in deciding present usage.[11] But in this analysis we are in the planning stage—the bridge's construction costs are an economic cost—and the budget deficit problem arises from the extreme indivisibility involved.

Thirdly, the traditional analysis using Fig. 8.2 is too extreme. Roads and bridges do not have an infinite capacity. They are often fully used, and so very low tolls are not a necessary characteristic of 'efficient' usage of such assets. There are two aspects to this issue, and it is useful to treat them separately though in practice they are inter-linked. Figure 8.3 introduces the idea of a rigid capacity limit to the road or bridge. We may suppose that the minimum-sized bridge that can be constructed is one with a capacity limit of q_1. If this bridge were built, maximization of total benefit minus total

[11] Should the bridge's inherited capacity diverge from the optimal, an additional complication is the longevity of the physical life of assets like this. Once sunken, the resources may never again have any alternative use. For this reason, Lewis would say that the use of such 'permanent indivisible' assets never involves an economic cost. (*Fixed Costs*, cited in previous chapter).

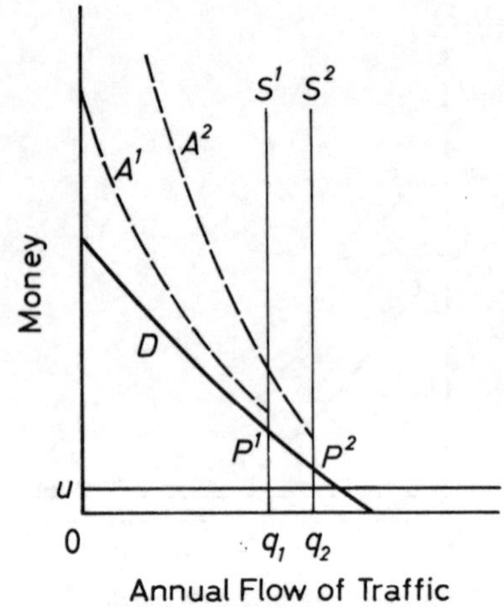

FIG. 8.3

cost would require a price of P^1. There still is no guarantee that the costs of the bridge will be recovered—P^1 is less than average cost, as indicated by the A^1 line—but the size of the deficit is certainly reduced. In addition, it will not usually be a simple matter of a bridge or nothing; the size of the bridge itself could often be extended. A slightly larger capacity of q_2 may be possible. This extension is warrantable if the extra annual benefit (area $q_1P^1P^2q_2$), net of extra maintenance costs, exceeds the extra capital costs involved in choosing the large size.[12] Such considerations are often ignored in evaluating indivisibilities. The scope that exists for tailoring the size of assets may considerably reduce the deficit problems that arise with assets like roads, bridges, railway track, etc. As F. M. Bator has said,

> As economists we can cajole or bully engineers into designing processes and installations that save on concealed inputs and give smaller maximal service yields, especially when designing for low-income communities.[13]

Once capacity limits are introduced, the problem of congestion appears. The market clearing prices of P^1 and P^2 in Fig. 8.3 partly relate to this. But the issue is more complicated than this diagram indicates. The users of assets like roads and bridges have themselves to incur costs—the operating and

[12] A further problem is that even if, with a small-scale bridge, the market-clearing price does cover all the asset's construction costs, increases in scale may realize scale economies so that the optimal size of bridge and the optimal price may not guarantee full recovery of costs. (Figure 8.3 implies scale economies since average costs with full-capacity utilization of the bigger bridge are less than average costs with full-capacity utilization of the smaller bridge).

[13] 'The Anatomy of Market Failure', *QJE*, p. 377, August 1958, reproduced as chapter 31 of *Readings in Micro-economics*, ed. by W. Breit and H. M. Hochman, Holt, Rinehart, and Winston, 1968.

time costs of a motor vehicle, for example. As we saw in chapter 5, increasing the use of a fixed factor like a road, raises its scarcity value. In the absence of a price for such an asset, the social cost of an extra user rises above that user's own private cost. We may, now, briefly indicate the relationship of this issue to the indivisibility problem of covering the road's capital costs. Again, it is important to stress that this is simply illustrative. In practice, detailed costing studies will be necessary. Suppose that a road is to be constructed, and that there is some minimum limit to its possible size or quality.[14] In the construction and use of the road we may assume three types of cost are involved. Firstly, there are the maintenance costs of the road which we will take to be constant per unit of traffic and further, for simplicity, we will assume that these costs can be recouped from a petrol tax levied on vehicles using the road. The second set of costs are the operating and time costs involved in running the vehicles.[15] These are born by the vehicle users and, while the cost per vehicle may be constant when traffic is fairly light, as traffic volume grows they can be expected to rise. In Fig. 8.4 the dotted line AVC^1 represents the total costs of road maintenance and vehicles expressed per unit of traffic. The rise in these 'average variable costs' is attributable to the rise in vehicle costs as congestion increases. The short-run cost function marginal to this

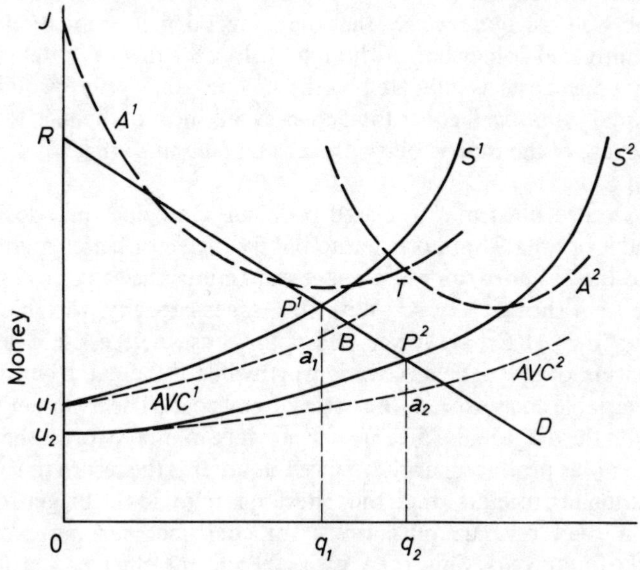

FIG. 8.4

[14] Parts of the foregoing draw on the article by Neutz, cited in the previous chapter.

[15] Strict use of Fig. 8.4 requires the assumption that all vehicles are identical with respect to costs (including the valuation of time). This diagram is adapted from a similar one in the article by Neutz, *op. cit.*

is the S^1 line. It starts off being constant and then, eventually, rises fairly steeply. In its latter parts, therefore, it resembles the S^1 line of Fig. 8.3. Notice that, in the terminology of chapter 5, the AVC^1 line indicates the marginal 'private' cost to road users, whereas the S^1 line indicates marginal social cost. At traffic flow q_1, the marginal vehicle's own costs (including petrol tax) are equal to q_1a_1, but in addition it occasions costs for other vehicles in an amount equal to a_1P^1, so that short-run marginal (social) costs at a traffic volume q_1 are equal to q_1P^1.

The third type of cost is the capital expenditure involved in the planned new road. Its equivalent annual cost is u_1J so that average total cost—capital, vehicle, and maintenance costs expressed per unit of flow—is given by the dotted line A^1. It follows that optimal usage of the road involves a traffic flow of q_1, where marginal benefit equals short-run marginal cost. If it is not possible to price the use of the road then, as we saw in chapter 5, the actual flow would be at B, where marginal benefit equals marginal private cost. All vehicles make a journey if their evaluation of it exceeds the vehicle's own costs. If prices can be levied—by meters, special licences, or tolls, no matter which—then a price of a_1P_1 would have to be exacted for the use of the road. The receipts from this—equal to $a_1P^1 \times 0q_1$—can be thought of as congestion tax revenue, but their economic function is a return to the road as a factor of production. So here again we see that the budget deficit problem of indivisibilities is mitigated somewhat. Although on Fig. 8.4 there is a deficit—P^1 is less than average costs as indicated by the A^1 line—on *a priori* grounds, total revenue could just as well cover total costs as fall short of them. The problem is that, because of the indivisibility, there is no *guarantee* that total costs will be covered.

Figure 8.4 also illustrates a related problem. How does one decide what size of road is optimal? Suppose that to build a bigger or better road involves jumping to the S^2 short-run marginal cost function; the average costs of the bigger road are shown[16] by A^2. With this larger capacity, variable costs at each traffic flow (AVC^2) are lower, and optimal usage necessitates a price or congestion tax of a_2P^2. This move is worthwhile if the extra benefit net of the extra variable costs exceeds the extra capital costs. The extra net benefit is indicated on the diagram by area $u_1P^1P^2u_2$; it is, in other words, the increase in consumer plus producer surplus. Since this latter is the return to road space (or congestion tax receipts), then the criterion is to build the bigger road if the increase in road revenue plus any extra consumer surplus exceeds the additional capital costs. This, then, is the theoretical 'efficiency' criterion for determining the optimum size of the road. The budget problem remains, however. With indivisibilities there is no theoretical guarantee that all costs will be covered from revenue. As we shall see in the next chapter, techniques

[16] If the two sizes of road are the only possibilities, then the scalloped line starting at J following A^1 and then following A^2 from T onwards is, effectively, the long-run average cost curve. It indicates the minimum average cost of catering for various traffic levels.

for evaluating assets like new roads are being developed, though they are only in a rudimentary stage. The pricing problem remains. Whether pricing can or ought to be introduced is still an unresolved issue. Besides technical difficulties, important income distribution factors may be involved. Further, even if the technical problems of metering schemes or licence arrangements can be overcome, there is no guarantee that an 'efficient' pricing scheme will cover all costs precisely, because of the indivisibility problem discussed here. There may be scope for price discrimination in some public sector activities and, as we saw in chapter 5, this can in theory overcome the deficit problem. But its scope seems likely to be fairly limited.[17]

8.3 The peak load problem

The nature of the problem

Throughout this book, the unit of time used most often has been the year. The cost functions of the last chapter were in many cases viewed as relating to output per annum. Such a period allows one to talk realistically of varying the use of labour and raw materials, while at the same time it is short enough to raise the possibility that capital cannot be varied. The choice was arbitrary, but a choice had to be made to indicate the main points concerning pricing. Let us retain this environment, but now recognize that annual output is simply the sum of weekly, or even hourly, outputs. While annual demand and output may be constant over time, this is quite consistent with considerable variations within the year. Products often experience seasonal variations in their demand. In most cases this has no significance. Demand for NCB coal is considerably higher in winter than summer. While sales may show considerable variation, production need not; stock piles can be used to keep weekly production at a fairly constant level. There is no reason for departing from the terminology of annual output, annual prices, and annual costs. The real problem of demand variations arises when they lead to the phenomenon of peak loads which, as Steiner has said,

> ... is characteristically found where the product or service is technologically not storable as in services generally and as with electric power and transportation, both inter- and intra-urban; or where the alternative storage costs are high owing to the bulk or other properties of the products, as in the case of pipe line transportation of petroleum.[18]

Clearly, this is characteristic of services often produced in the public sector. Transport services in both road and rail experience seasonal, daily, and hourly demand variations, and the same applies to transmission lines and generating plants in electricity supply. University lecture rooms are unused

[17] Where larger scale items are involved it may become relevant, as on the railways, to discriminate. J. J. Warford tells me that discrimination might be possible for airports where individual consignments can easily be identified.

[18] 'Peak Loads and Efficient Pricing', P. O. Steiner, *QJE*, p. 585, November 1957.

in the summer. The peak demand for water often coincides, in warm weather periods, with low supply capabilities.

The key point is that, since these services are non-storable, the sub-period within the year at which a demand is made is no longer immaterial. Firstly, unless running costs are a universal constant per unit of output, the short-run cost of an extra unit of output will depend on the level of output (i.e., demand) in the sub-period in question. Secondly, if there are limits to capacity, demand in some sub-periods may fully use this capacity and market-clearing prices may, therefore, differ in different periods. Thirdly, the cost of capacity is joint to the various sub-periods, as it is in the case of coal, but it now becomes relevant to analyse the relationship between the annual capital cost and prices in the various sub-periods. Even if we took a demand cycle of one day, the problem could arise. If, as would be normal, railway staff cannot be engaged for periods less than say ten hours, then a station's daily staffing costs would be joint to the early morning inward commuter rush, the slacker midday period, and the early evening peak period. Basically, the problem is no different from the jointness over time involved in investment decisions. In both cases, the cost of some product or service cannot be attributed to particular slices of time. The significance of variations in demand within a year, as opposed to variations between different years, is that the year is the unit of time often used in calculating interest charges.[19] Demand variations within the year that could be met by stocks would not then have any significance; the cost of any one unit could be treated as the same irrespective of the time during the year it was made. When stocking is not possible, one kilowatt hour of electricity demanded at eleven o'clock on a cold February morning becomes a very different commodity from one demanded on a summer evening.

Now, the first thing to remember is that demand patterns reflect not only consumer preferences but the prices that consumers have to pay. Figure 8.5 averages, over each month, the half-hour of maximum demand on the power stations of the Central Electricity Generating Board in each day of the period April 1959 to March 1960 (excluding Saturdays and Sundays). The seasonal demand for electricity supply is clearly illustrated: in fact, there are in addition important variations within the day not shown in the sketch map. The CEGB supplies Area Boards, who redistribute to final consumers. The relative strengths of demand in the various sub-periods will clearly be affected by the system of prices. Up to fairly recently little differentiation in sub-period prices was made, so that the demand pattern reflects both consumer preferences and a set of largely uniform prices.

Economists have long been familiar with the fundamentals of the theoretical solution to this problem of demand variation. Both Lewis and Houthakker

[19] Of course—and I hope this is clear—it need not be. The half-year may be more appropriate in some instances. Perhaps we should, in any case, use continuous discounting on the grounds that these other periods are simply accounting conventions?

Sketch Map of Daily Maximum Demand Supplied by U.K. Power Stations 1959–60.

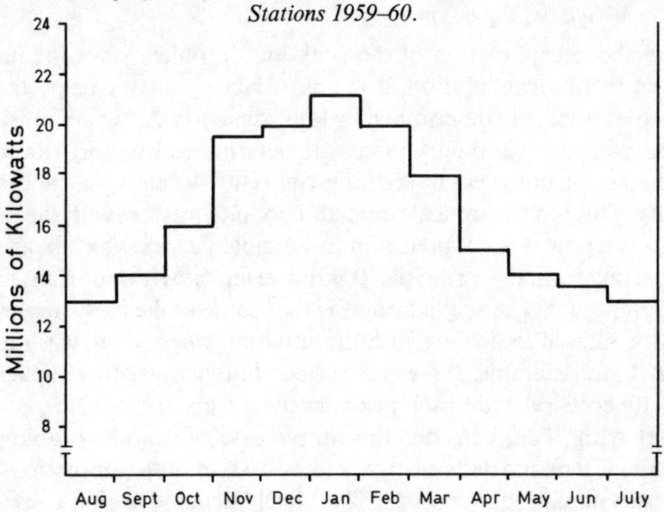

FIG. 8.5

Source: Based on diagram in R. L. Meek's 'The New Bulk Supply Tariff for Electricity', E.J. March 1968.

writing in the immediate post-war period[20] stressed that, when a product is non-storable, the size of capacity needed to meet the demand for the product is determined exclusively by the sub-period in which demand is highest. Thus, in 1959–60, the CEGB's capacity could not have been less than about 21 million kilowatts. Since such a peak period is 'responsible' for capacity then, the argument would go, demands in this period should bear all the capital costs of capacity. In off-peak periods, the capacity is 'already there' and so prices in these periods need cover only running costs. Thus, the suggestion was for season and time-of-day price differentials with the peak price bearing all the capacity charges; commuters would bear the overheads of rail and road track; the morning and evening winter peak demands of electricity would bear the bulk of the fixed charges of generating plants and transmission capacity. In fact, the 'tarif vert' offered by Électricité de France to its high-voltage consumers does distinguish between five periods of the year (including a distinction between different hours of the day), and is as yet one of the few examples of attempts to introduce the principles of marginal-cost pricing to state enterprises.[21]

[20] See 'The Two Part Tariff' (article cited in previous chapter), and 'Electricity Tariffs in Theory and Practice', H. S. Houthakker, *EJ*, March 1951.

[21] For discussion of the green tariff see two articles by M. Boiteux; 'Electrical Energy: Facts, Problems and Prospects', 1960 (cited in previous chapter), and 'Le tarif vert d'Electricité de France', *Revue Française de l'Énergie*, January 1947, a translated version of which appears as chapter 6 of Nelson's edited collection (cited in previous chapter). See also P. Masse's 'Quelques incidences economiques due tarif vert', *Revue Française de l'Énergie*, May 1958, a translated version of which—'Some Economic Effects of the "Tarif Vert"'—also appears as chapter 7 of Nelson. R. L. Meek has also provided an English exposition in his **'The Green Tariff in Theory and Practice'**, cited in previous chapter.

The theory of 'efficient' peak pricing

While the above explanation of the peak-load problem gives the flavour of the correct theoretical solution, it is unsatisfactory in two respects. Firstly, it implies that prices are determined by long-run costs. As we demonstrated in the previous chapter, in theory prices are determined by short-run marginal costs; whether or not these cover long-run costs depends on the optimality of capacity. This is a theoretical point and not inconsistent with the introduction, as in the previous chapter, of non-tangible factors which suggest solutions departing from this principle. It is, however, clearly important to get the principle right first. The second point is that some of the early analyses were somewhat confused in dealing with the situation where there was more than one peak. If, for example, three sub-periods fully use existing capacity, how are capacity costs related to the prices in these three periods?

To start with, then, consider the simple case of a non-storable product whose annual demand falls neatly into two six-month sub-periods, which we may call Summer and Winter. The hourly demand within these periods shows no variation, so we can talk unambiguously of output per six months. We may first consider how any given volume of capacity is to be used; then we can proceed to evaluate its optimal size. It is perhaps worth reiterating here that 'efficient' solutions are the sole concern. Any drastic changes in pricing policy for transport and fuel services will have important distributive implications, which ought not to be ignored in any actual decision. The inherited production possibilities for say 1972 are indicated in Fig. 8.6. The existing capacity comprises a large number of assets or plants, on each of which running costs are unit constant and all equal to $0u$; further, capacity is subject to rigid limits—the maximum six-monthly output is $0q$. In dis-

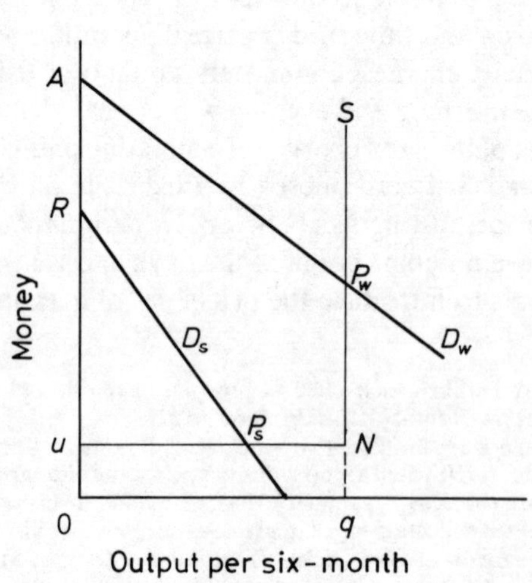

FIG. 8.6

cussing peak loads, it is important to be careful about specifying the time dimension of output. The procedure used mostly in this chapter is to relate output to a period common to the various sub-periods. Granted, then, the six-month winter demand function, D_w, and the six-month summer demand function, D_s, what is optimal output and price in each period? Following the basic efficiency criterion of maximizing total benefit minus total cost, the summer price is set at P_s and the winter price at P_w. The winter demanders fully use capacity, and the summer users are required to simply cover running costs. No other set of outputs and prices can yield a higher net benefit which is here equal to area uRP_s+area uAP_wN. The winter price rations out capacity to those most willing to pay. It is the simplest case. The question now is: Under what circumstances is capacity optimal?

Criteria for evaluating changes in capacity can be fairly complicated if one allows that plant running costs increase as the plants age, if there are expectations of demand and factor price changes, and if new plants incorporate technical advance. These issues were discussed in the previous chapter. To focus on the peak-load problem, suppose that the enterprise in question is starting from scratch with no inherited capacity, that all plants will have the same life, that their running costs are constant over their life, that demand and factor prices are expected to remain constant, and that no technical advance is likely to affect operations in the foreseeable future. Suppose, further, the capacity is perfectly divisible into small plants, each capable of producing one unit of output in each sub-period and for each of which the equivalent *annual* capital cost is equal to an amount, £*a*. Keeping to the simple two period model, Fig. 8.7 shows three of the possible output scales. Should scale q_1 be built with a short-run marginal cost function, S^1, then prices would

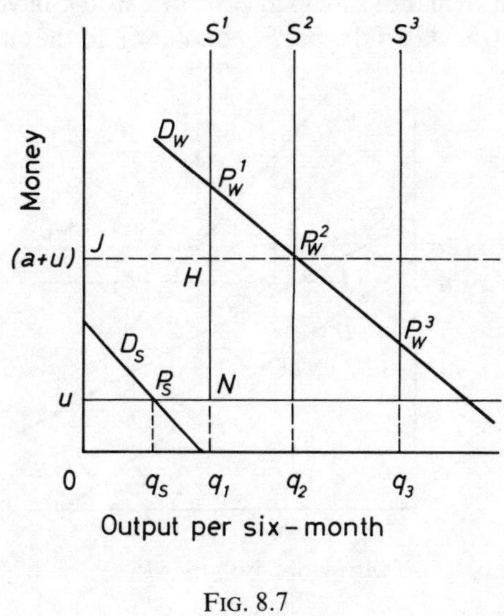

FIG. 8.7

be P_w^1 and P_s. If q_2 were built, the summer price is the same but the winter price falls to P_w^2; similarly, if q_3 capacity is built the winter price is P_w^3. The criterion is that capacity should be built if annual benefit exceeds annual costs. The first sized capacity would certainly be warranted. Annual benefit is the area under the two demand curves at q_s and q_1 respectively. Annual costs comprise running costs in both periods plus the capital cost of capacity. This latter is a cost joint to the two sub-periods, and is equal to aq_1; that is, diagrammatically it is equal to the area $uJHN$. It follows that at least this capacity size is warranted, since the summer demand covers summer running costs while the winter benefit more than covers both winter running costs and the whole of the joint capital costs. Clearly, an extension to capacity q_2 is also warranted by the winter annual benefit. Further increases are not and so optimal capacity is at q_2. Granted, in other words, that the off-peak period covers its running costs and granted further, as we are allowing here, that capacity is finely divisible, increases in capacity are warranted as long as the peak price exceeds peak running cost plus the whole of the capital cost. It is in this very simple case, then, that capacity charges are covered solely by revenue from peak demands.

The shifting peak

Should a system of uniform prices be replaced by one incorporating time differentials, one would normally expect the peak demand to fall and the off-peak demand to rise somewhat. When the difference in the strength of the two demands is not very large, it seems possible that the lower off-peak price could so raise demand that the 'old' off-peak demand becomes greater than the 'old' peak demand. In which case, one would have to change prices again. Thus, if we translated the previous solution to the situation of Fig. 8.8,

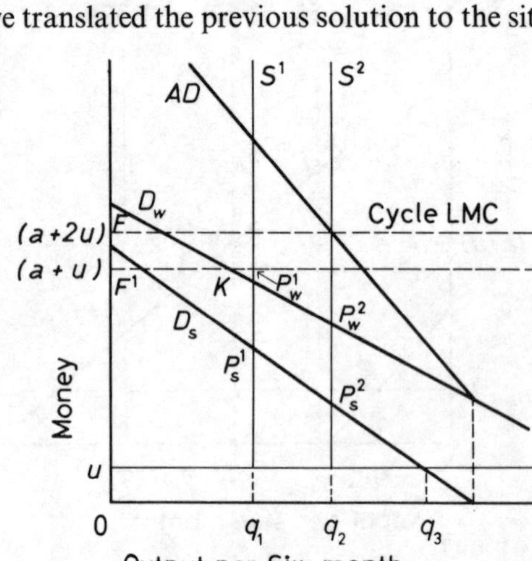

FIG. 8.8

we would find that with a summer price covering running costs only—output q_3—and with a winter price set equal to $(a+u)$ at point K, the 'off-peak' summer demand is now larger than the winter demand! The logic of the previous analysis should have indicated to the reader where this line of thought goes astray. Again, the misconception arises from determining price by long-run costs. If a capacity of size q_1 were built, the 'efficient' prices would be P_w^1 and P_s^1; in other words, *both sub-periods would fully use capacity*. Given this capacity, no other set of prices produces a greater surplus of total benefit over short-run opportunity costs. This kind of situation has been called the *shifting peak* case, to indicate that, in moving from a set of uniform prices where the two demands would differ, 'efficient' prices can eliminate the peak. The example of Fig. 8.7 is called the *firm peak* case, since price differentials do not remove the peak. How, then, is optimal capacity determined in the shifting peak case of Fig. 8.8? We see that the winter demand alone would not warrant the construction of q_1 size capacity, the area under the winter demand curve, at q_1, is less than $(a+u)q_1$. However, the capacity cost is a joint cost to both sub-periods. Such joint expenditures are warrantable if they are less than the sum of the benefits to each purpose, net in each case of 'separable' costs. In the present terminology of peak loads, this means that capacity costs must be less than the sum of the sub-periods' benefits, net in each case of running costs. Probably the best way to see this diagrammatically is to sum the two demand curves vertically to get the aggregate demand curve AD—a line which, therefore, indicates the sum of the two periods' benefits.[22] The ordinate $0F$ is equal to the (equivalent annual) capital cost of one plant plus twice the unit running cost $(a+2u)$. It follows that capacity size q_1 is warrantable, since benefits exceed costs. Granted divisibility in capacity, expansion is warrantable if the sum of the two periods' prices exceed $(a+2u)$. Extensions of capacity are justified if the sum of the two prices exceeds what one might call cycle long-run marginal cost, that is the addition to total cost from increasing capacity and output in *each* sub-period by one unit.[23] Capacity is optimal at q_2 where AD intersects this cycle LMC curve.

Both demands have a part to play in warranting capacity extensions. The formulation is quite general; it holds in the case of Fig. 8.7 where, however, summer benefit net of 'separable' costs is, beyond capacity size q_s, zero. In both these fairly simple cases, the sum of the excess of the two prices over marginal running cost is just equal when capacity is optimal to the (annually equivalent) capital cost of a new plant; granted constant returns to scale, such

[22] The 'solution' to this problem was provided independently by both Boiteux—in 'Peak Load Pricing' (cited in previous chapter)—and Steiner, *op. cit.*, though only the latter used aggregate demand curves. Notice the similarity to Samuelsonian public goods. Here again (as with the standard indivisibility problem) we have jointness, but it *is* technically possible to levy prices—'exclusion costs' are not prohibitive as with flood-relief and health vaccinations. See the latter part of section 5.4 for a fuller discussion of this point.

[23] For simple cost functions, the techniques suggested by J. Hirschleifer seem most useful and Figs. 8.7 and 8.8 follow his approach. See 'Peak Loads and Efficient Pricing: Comment', *QJE*, August 1958.

prices guarantee overall budgetary equilibrium. The split of the year between two equal sub-periods is a simple one, but the analysis is applicable to more complex demand variations. At the extreme, for example, demand for electricity may actually be different in each of the 8,760 hours of the year. In practice, it will not be economic to have prices finely graded into hours, because of the administrative problems involved.[24] But to keep to the theoretical point, prices equal to short-run marginal opportunity costs would then, in principle, be different for each hour of the year. Capacity extensions are warranted if the sum of all these prices, net in each case of running cost, exceeds the annual capital cost, a cost in other words joint to the 8,760 hours of the year. The principle is, therefore, the same though obviously the more complex cases are cumbersome to represent diagrammatically. In fact, even a two-period model is difficult on our type of diagram if the periods are of unequal length. But it is not impossible. Take the case of a winter period of eight months and a summer one of four months. One could redefine the horizontal axis of Fig. 8.8 as output per four months. A demand curve could be introduced equal to half the winter demand. Aggregate demand would then be obtained by adding the four month summer demand to twice the 'winter' demand curve. This aggregate demand curve could then be compared with the cycle LMC—that is $(a+3u)$ where u is defined as running cost per unit of four months output.[25]

One additional point needs mentioning. Steiner has suggested that where one has the shifting peak case—and the more sub-periods there are the more

[24] According to the contributors to Nelson's volume (cited in previous chapter), the 'tarif vert' of Electricité de France distinguishes between five sub-periods of the year. The 'peak' period is two hours of the week-day afternoon from November to February inclusive. (Saturday is defined as a week-day). The 'full-use' hours of winter (defined as the above months plus September) are 6 a.m. to 10 p.m. of each week-day (excluding peak hours). The 'slack' period is the rest of the winter hours. The rest of the year, termed summer, is divided into the full-use hours of 6 a.m. to 10 p.m. of week-days, and the remainder is termed the summer slack hours. Similar divisions are made in the recently revised bulk supply tariff charged by the Central Electricity Generation Board to the UK Area Boards. The months of December and January are grouped on their own. Within these months there is a peak period of about 250 hours covering 8 a.m. to noon and 4.30 p.m. to 6.30 p.m. (excluding Saturdays, Sundays, and holidays). The 'day' period covers 7 a.m. to 11 p.m. (excluding the peak), and the remainder is called the night period. In the 'winter plateau' months of November, February and March, day and night periods only are distinguished; a similar distinction applies for the April to October period (see Meek, *op. cit.*, *EJ*, 1968).

[25] For a better diagrammatic treatment of 'awkward' sub-period lengths see Williamson *op. cit.* We have chosen to avoid his approach for the reason that diagrams are, in any case, only useful in these very simple cost situations. With more realism to the cost function, an algebraic approach is much better. This is probably a suitable point to mention, that if the public agency in question can discriminate between consumers—as for services like electricity supply—then the possibility of offering quantity discounts arises. Should an enterprise wish to do this, the criteria for deciding on capacity extensions are more complicated, though the characteristic of *marginal* prices, when capacity is optimal, is the same. Such discrimination may be very costly in terms of administrative resources and is, moreover, not necessary to guarantee 'efficiency'; when budgetary equilibrium cannot be guaranteed by uniform prices such variability in prices might however be useful. For a discussion of the theoretical aspects of this see 'Peak Loads and Efficient Pricing: Comment', J. M. Buchanan, *QJE*, August 1966.

likely this is—'efficient' prices are discriminatory. If this means nothing more than that price differentials do not reflect cash cost differentials, then he is correct. No one seems to be quite sure what discriminatory means.[26] It certainly has emotive undertones. When capacity is fully utilized, each sub-period's price reflects the intensity of demand—reflects, in other words, the value of the marginal unit to that consumer just excluded. These results are simply first order conditions for the maximization of a surplus. An argument about the maximand would be useful; the argument about 'discrimination' seems irrelevant.

Systems analysis and other complications

One of the simplifications used so far in the analysis of peak loads, has been that unit running costs are a universal constant. Although variable running costs were discussed in the previous chapter, they have a special significance for the peak-load problem and it is important to treat them explicitly. In addition, in this section some of the other simplifications relating to demand and price changes over time, technical progress, plant obsolescence, etc., are briefly integrated into the analysis. To start with, consider a situation where the inherited volume of capacity in some year, say 1972, comprises a large number of small plants each with different unit-running costs. The profile of running costs could be thought of as reflecting the industry's past technological history. New designs for electricity generating plants, buses, roads, reservoirs, have meant lower (real) unit running costs on the newer assets than

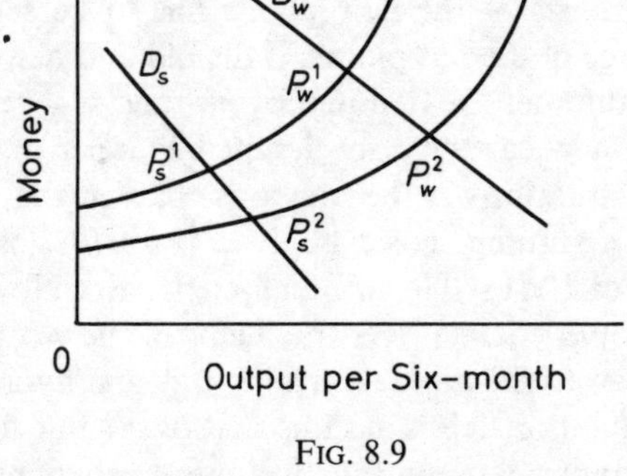

FIG. 8.9

[26] See discussion and references in Hirschleifer, *QJE*, August 1958 (*op. cit.*), and Steiner's reply in the same issue.

on the old. To indicate the main points of the peak load problem, the simple case of two equal periods of demand is adequate. The S^1 line of Fig. 8.9 indicates the six-month short-run marginal cost line, given the capacity inherited in 1972. Its rise indicates that increasing output within each period is effected by bringing into use older and older plants. An alternative environment, consistent with the rising cost line, is where existing capacity can be more intensively used by overtime and shift working, this again causing increased costs. Whatever the reason, the 'efficient' prices, given the demand functions D_s and D_w, are P_s^1 and P_w^1, both equal to the marginal running cost of the respective outputs. Thinking of electricity supply, the price in each sub-period would be equal to the unit running cost of that generating plant which was 'marginal' in the period. So, in these cases, optimal prices *are* equal to a cash cost figure. To be quite general, however, at some point a physical limit to output increases might be met—indicated by the vertical portion of the S^1 line. If any period's demand function had taken a position similar to D^* then price, P_1^*, would exceed marginal running cost at full capacity, m^*, by an amount sufficient to soak up the excess demand.

Keeping, initially, to the D_w and D_s type functions, let us consider the characteristics of the optimal volume of capacity. A move to the S^2 short-run cost function can be effected by introducing new capacity, and the new prices would be P_w^2 and P_s^2. Beyond this point diagrammatic treatments have little advantage. Let us, therefore, use some algebra and denote the extra summer sales as ΔQ_s and the additional consumer benefits in this period as $\frac{1}{2}(P_1+P_2)_s\Delta Q_s$—a formulation similar to those used in the previous chapter (see p. 221). The winter benefits are defined in a similar way. The new capacity is capable of producing, say, T units in each period and so the extra joint capital costs are aT, a being the equivalent annual capital cost per unit of output of the new capacity. If unit-running costs on the new capacity are lower than on any of the old assets, then this new capacity will be *fully used* in both periods. Since price and, therefore, marginal system running cost is lower in each period, it follows that less use is made of the old capacity. So, against the running costs of the new plants has to be set the cost saving through reduced usage of the old plants. If the old and new marginal system running cost in the summer are denoted by m_{1s} and m_{2s}, respectively, and if the running costs of new capacity are denoted as u per unit, then, recalling the analysis of such situations in the previous chapter, the overall change in total summer system running costs is given by: $uT-\frac{1}{2}(m_1+m_2)_s(T-\Delta Q_s)$. A similar expression can be used for winter system costs. Now, annual benefits and running costs could change over the life of the new capacity because of many factors. To keep to the annual terminology and avoid the necessity of a present value formulation, let us assume that over some defined number of years winter and summer demand functions are unchanged, that all the old and new plant's running costs remain constant, that all factor prices remain the same, and that all plants suddenly expire at the end of this defined life-span. It follows that the criterion for introducing the additional capacity is that:[27]

$$\tfrac{1}{2}(P_1+P_2)_s\Delta Q_s+\tfrac{1}{2}(P_1+P_2)_w\Delta Q_w > aT+[2uT-\tfrac{1}{2}(m_1+m_2)_s(T-\Delta Q_s)-\tfrac{1}{2}(m_1+m_2)_w(T-\Delta Q_w)] \qquad (8.1)$$

The sum of additional winter and summer benefits should exceed the joint (annually equivalent) capital cost of the new capacity, plus its running costs in both periods, less the system cost saving in both winter and summer. First of all, note that the formulation is similar to those used in the previous chapter (see eq. (7.13) to (7.16)) save that now various sub-periods of the year are distinguished. Secondly, eq. (8.1) embraces the cases illustrated in Figs. (8.7) and (8.8); for such cases the assumption of a universally constant unit-running cost means that no cost saving is effected on old plants. Thirdly, we have here considered the case where some capacity is inherited from the past, but the expression is applicable to the 'planning from scratch' situation; in the latter the capital outlay would refer to the costs of one capacity structure as opposed to another—not, in other words, simply the capital cost of some new plants as it is in eq. (8.1); similarly, the expression in [ ], would, in the 'planning from scratch' case, relate to the difference between running costs with one completely new system, and running costs with another completely new system. Subject to these qualifications, the expression has broad applicability. Now, in the present assumed environment, price in each period is equal to marginal system running cost: $P_s^1 = m_s^1$, $P_w^2 = m_w^2$, etc. It follows that eq. (8.1) can be simplified to:

$$\tfrac{1}{2}(m_1+m_2)_sT+\tfrac{1}{2}(m_1+m_2)_wT > aT+2uT \qquad (8.2)$$

The output of new capacity, valued at marginal system running cost, should exceed its annual capital and running costs.[28] If capacity is perfectly divisible, then the criterion for introducing a new plant involving only a marginal change in output can be found by dividing eq. (8.2) by T and recognizing that the difference between m_1 and m_2 becomes negligible. We have then:

$$m_s+m_w > a+2u \qquad (8.3)$$

where m_s and m_w are the present marginal system running costs. With $(a+2u)$ defined as the long-run cost of increasing output in both periods by one unit, then we have another illustration of the French proposition, that, provided all worthwhile investments are undertaken—so that on the margin eq. (8.3) becomes *an equality*—short-run pricing is equivalent to long-run pricing and there is no contradiction between the two. Suppose, in one of the periods, demand fully utilizes all existing capacity; the winter demand function, for example, looks like D^* in Fig. 8.9. The new capacity extends the rigid

[27] Some of these formulations are adapted from R. Turvey's 'Marginal Cost Pricing in Practice', *Economica*, November 1964.

[28] Cf. Turvey, *op. cit.*, *Economica*, p. 428, 1964.

capacity limit but the new peak price, P_2^*, still exceeds marginal running cost. In terms of eq. (8.1) this means $T = \Delta Q_w$, and by re-working the algebra we find that when capacity is optimal;

$$m_s + P_w = a + 2u \tag{8.4}$$

Notice that P_w exceeds m_w and, denoting this excess as E_w, we have:

$$E_w = a - (m_w - u) - (m_s - u) \tag{8.5}$$

In the peak period, price is raised above marginal system running cost and the difference, *when capacity is optimal*, is equal to the capital cost of a new plant less the system cost savings that such a plant would achieve in all periods. Notice the difference from the case illustrated in Fig. 8.7; there, running costs are a universal constant, system cost savings are zero, and optimal capacity is characterized by $E_w = a$.

Conclusions

The peak load problem is, then, a special case of jointness through time. Any public enterprise that attempts to incorporate the principles of the solution will be involved in levying different prices in different periods. For some commodities this may not present any technical problems. British Rail have been introducing off-peak discounts for a number of years. For services like electricity supply there are the technical problems of correctly recording the time of consumption. One of the difficulties in extending the 'tarif vert' to Électricité de France's non-industrial consumers, is the high metering costs that could be involved relative to the anticipated benefits. A sophisticated tariff structure will also involve some formidable calculating exercises. For example, in replacing the expository assumptions of constant demand and factor prices and those relating to plant lives, the principles are unaffected but the practical matters become important. Given changes in demand, cost, and plant structure over time, eq. (8.1) will have to be converted into a present value terminology.[29] New plants achieve different cost-savings in

[29] That is it becomes

$$\sum_{t=0}^{t=n} [\tfrac{1}{2}(P_1 + P_2)_{st} \Delta Q_{st} D^t + \tfrac{1}{2}(P_1 + P_2)_{wt} \Delta Q_{wt} D^t] >$$

$$K + \sum_{t=0}^{t=n} [u_t T(d_{wt} + d_{st}) D^t - \tfrac{1}{2}(m_1 + m_2)_{st}(T d_{st} - \Delta Q_{st}) D^t$$

$$- \tfrac{1}{2}(m_1 + m_2)_{wt}(T d_{wt} - \Delta Q_{wt}) D^t]$$

where D is the discount rate, K is the actual base-year capital outlay on the new capacity, t is time in years, n is the life of the new capacity, and d is its percentage degree of utilization. Thus, d_{wt} indicates the percentage degree of utilization of new plants in the winter period of year t. The expression, therefore, says that the present value of the flow of winter and summer benefits, over the life of the new capacity, should exceed the capital outlay plus the present value of the flow of net increases in system running costs, in each period of each year of this time-span.

different periods of the year and in different years of their life—as they get older some of the new nuclear generating plants will themselves be pushed down the order of merit. Whether capacity is optimal can be determined only by knowing whether the flow of system cost changes that a new plant would effect over its life, when discounted to the present and allowing for uncertainty in estimates of demand, more than offsets the capital outlay of such new capacity. Engineers, in sectors like electricity supply, are familiar with systems analysis. Its reconciliation with pricing matters is now the important step.[30]

[30] For some indication of the problems involved see 'Peak Load Pricing' by R. Turvey, *Journal of Political Economy*, February 1968, and his book on electricity supply, cited in the introductory section of the previous chapter.

9. Problems in cost/benefit estimation

9.1 The basis of 'cost-benefit analysis'

The evaluation of the costs and benefits of any activity has been a theme running throughout this book. We have been concerned with analysing the concepts of 'benefit' and 'costs', their relationship to market prices, their 'appropriability' by market systems, their meaning for services commonly supplied by government, and their relevance to public sector pricing policies. The terminology is also applicable to private sector decision-taking; a firm which evaluates the profitability of a new sales campaign is considering the costs and benefits of this venture to itself. Despite the fact that the methodological device of comparing costs with benefits is not new nor restricted to the public sector, over the last decade it has become increasingly fashionable to advocate the use of *cost-benefit analysis*[1] in assessing public sector projects, in particular, investment projects. Partly this reflects an increased ability to measure certain magnitudes; but these techniques are still fairly rudimentary and in some areas non-existent, so some of the support for cost-benefit analysis is overly optimistic if not misinformed. As far as its public locale goes, this is probably traceable to the fact that the first people to use anything like the terminology of benefits and costs in project appraisal were the US Army Corps of Engineers in the early part of this century; these government officials were initially responsible for evaluating river navigational improvements and were obliged by law to look at the 'benefits' of such a scheme. To emphasize that it is costs and benefits incurred by the country as a whole and not individual institutions, and to emphasize that primarily public sector activities are involved, some studies in fact entitle themselves as social benefit and social cost investigations.

The primary task of this chapter is to consider some general problems that arise in public sector activities when benefits and costs are not easily identified or measurable. Characteristic areas of the public sector which raise these problems are water-resources, roads, health, education, research, and defence. It is in these sorts of areas that cost-benefit studies have been directed. Somewhat paradoxically then, 'cost-benefit analysis' is a term used to describe

[1] Or 'benefit-cost' analysis in American parlance.

investigations of public sector activities whose economic costs and benefits are difficult to identify and measure. In fact, these parts of the public sector have up to recently been bereft of any kind of economic analysis; cost-minimizing choice of techniques has only recently (apparently) entered the defence field. For all practical purposes, items occurring at different points of time have often been undifferentiated; this applies to many sectors of government, where the logic of discounting has not been appreciated. It is not necessary to have money values for benefits for a time-weighting system to be relevant.

> In the military field we may ask whether the improved performance of an aeroplane planned to be in service in x years' time more than offsets the strategic advantage of having it available in $x-1$ years' time . . .[2]

So a secondary characteristic of 'cost-benefit analysis' is to employ the language of choice, alternatives foregone, consistency—the everyday tools of the economist. It is the first point, however, the observation and measurement of benefits and costs, on which we wish to focus; only this is at all intrinsically 'special' to the public sector activities mentioned. Now why should there be these difficulties? There seems to be three factors at work. One is that there are good technical reasons for 'normal' market fares being inoperative; indivisibilities, externalities, and 'collective goods' abound. Secondly, prices are not levied for many of these services either because of the technical difficulties of point one or because of wider objectives of policy. Thirdly, the sheer widespread range of the effects of projects in some instances in these sectors suggest a more than routine examination of benefits is required. Given these three general points, the following examples indicate the sort of issues that have been involved:

(a) For some services it is not possible to use a price system, and they are completely financed by taxation. National defence expenditure fully fits this case. Another instance is the flood-relief programme of the US Federal Government, where such services have been subjected to benefit/cost analysis. Over the period 1927 to 1953 the average annual flood damage in the country as a whole was $160 million. The Army Corps of Engineers was required in 1927 to draw up a series of plans for improving America's rivers; these indicated, among other things, that there were many opportunities for flood-control whose costs fell short of the estimated damages avoided. Subsequent to this, the 1936 Flood Control Act officially recognized flood-control as a federal responsibility.[3] The point is that flood-relief has strong 'public' properties; in the terminology of chapter 5, services to an area are jointly

[2] 'Reflections on Public Authority Investment', M. H. Peston; chapter 6, p. 128, of *Public Sector Economics*, Ed. A. R. Prest, Manchester University Press, 1968.

[3] For further discussion of the flood-control programme in the USA see for example O. Eckstein, *Water-Resource Development*, chapter V, Harvard University Press, 1958.

supplied and prices cannot be levied, because of the high costs of exclusion; flood-relief is a 'public' or collective good.

(b) The 'efficient' usage of assets exhibiting large indivisibilities may necessitate very low or zero prices. Since revenue is an inadequate measure of benefit, alternative methods have to be found. Uncongested roads exemplify this sort of problem and the study[4] by a group of engineers and economists of the first motorway—the London to Birmingham M1—has pioneered, in the UK, the technique of evaluating journey savings that such roads produce. Clearly, assets like the Channel Tunnel are of a similar nature, although in all these cases it is important to remember the emphasis on congestion; in its presence different problems emerge. To a certain extent, many recreational facilities like parks, lakes, and reservoirs also include elements of the indivisibility problem.

(c) Some services give rise to side-effects for which compensation is not normally paid. Thus, the search for a third London airport has involved studies of the benefits and costs of various locations taking into account, as far as is possible and measurable, the economic effects of noise. To say that the airport gives rise to an externality indicates that the distinction between this point and (a) is small. A by-product of the services to air travellers—the economic losses created by the noise of aircraft—constitutes a 'public bad'; a reduction of noise to the many nearby residents of an airfield has 'public good' characteristics. Similarly, London Transport's recently opened underground Victoria Line was expected to produce beneficial side-effects—in particular, reduced road congestion—which would not manifest themselves as extra revenue for the London Transport Executive. In fact, the line was expected to show a financial loss for London Transport, and so a study was undertaken to examine whether the line was justifiable if a wider spectrum of benefits and costs was taken.[5]

(d) Some products of the public sector bear low or zero prices, not necessarily because the introduction of a price system is technically impossible, but because of wider objectives of national policy. Part of educational outlays may well fall into this category. It is technically possible to make students pay fees covering the full cash costs of their education or to grant them loans. There may be good reasons for not doing this. Over and above the proposition that

[4] 'London–Birmingham Motorway—Traffic and Economics', T. M. Coburn, M. E. Beesley, and D. J. Reynolds, *Road Research Technical Paper No. 46*, HMSO, 1960.

[5] See 'Estimating the Social Benefit of Constructing an Underground Railway in London', C. D. Foster and M. E. Beesley, *JRSS*, Series A, **126**, Part I, 1963; reproduced in *Readings in Welfare Economics*, Editors K. J. Arrow and T. Scitovsky, AEA, Allen & Unwin, 1969. An abridged version of this article can be found as chapter 9 of *Transport*, Editor D. Munby, Penguin Modern Economics Series, 1968. An additional problem suggesting that financial values were inappropriate indicators of costs and benefits, was that London Transport's fares involve a fair amount of averaging over different routes. This was one of the issues that promoted further discussion of the Victoria Line. See 'Victoria Line: Social Benefit and Finances', Foster and Beesley, *JRSS*, 1965 Series A, Part I, and the Note by F. J. Lloyd in the same journal for 1966, Part II.

the benefits of education are something more than the private benefit to the student,[6] there is the problem of defining private benefit or, rather, reconciling a student's knowledge and expectations of university life with his willingness to pay; can rational economic decisions be ascribed to the student at this point in his life? However, the point here is that in many cases prices are not levied and if one is prepared to overlook the point of 'rationality', then there is some interest in trying to deduce private benefits from earnings performance. Such studies are bedevilled by the statistical problems of isolating the educational force from other 'causes' of differential earnings—family background, residence, IQ level, etc.—but some convincing attempts have been made in the USA. There are other areas of the public sector where the lack of a normal price system cannot solely be ascribed to any of our previous points. Thus, the fact that some types of scientific research and development are undertaken by government, could be rationalized by the argument that no private firm has a sufficiently wide range of products to make use of the benefits of the more 'basic' kind of research. In addition, the charging of low royalties would be justified on the grounds that indivisibilities are involved in the supply of information; after the initial outlay on research staff and equipment which generates the discovery, the marginal costs of 'supplying' the information to others is trivial.[7] But the reason why some research is performed by the public sector cannot always be explained by the above points. Attempts have been made to assess the costs and benefits of certain research projects, and we shall refer to some of these later. In some instances, prices are levied for irrigation water but not related in any close way to willingness to pay; again, therefore, benefits have to be recognized as something more than revenue received.

(e) Finally, there are those projects whose effects either are widespread over products or do not fit easily into existing institutional forms. The Ministry of Housing and Local Government has been concerned at the high cost of providing water supplies to some rural areas in the UK. In cases where new piping facilities are involved, the question arises as to whether it might not be better to relocate the entire resident population. A recent investigation[8] considered this very question in relation to the West Shropshire Water Board's scheme for improving water supplies in the South Atcham area. It involved a consideration of the effects on water supplies, road congestion, public transport, postal services, and so on. The estimation of the benefits of improved water supplies is a fairly impossible exercise in the present UK environment, and so the approach of the investigation was to look at different schemes, consistent with broadly the same objective. These included, on the

[6] Cf. the discussion in section 5.4.

[7] Cf. 'The Simple Economics of Basic Scientific Research', R. R. Nelson, *JPE*, June 1959, and 'Economic Welfare and the Allocation of Resources to Invention', K. J. Arrow, chapter in *The Rate and Direction of Inventive Activity*, NBER, Princeton, 1962.

[8] *The South Atcham Scheme: An Economic Appraisal*, report to the Minister of Housing and Local Government, HMSO, November 1969.

one hand, the 'do-nothing' solution—that is, simply improve the existing facilities—and, on the other hand, various patterns of relocation for the population in question.

The valuation of costs and benefits

Now, a key point about most of these studies is that the valuation of benefits and costs is based on the 'efficiency' concepts discussed at numerous points in this book. The benefit of goods or services produced is interpreted as the willingness to pay of all parties affected by this activity; costs are the minimum compensation required by all input suppliers involved. To give but one example at this stage, it has already been suggested that one of the anticipated effects of flood-control programmes is to reduce the size of the annual value of damages caused by such floods. In principle, people would be willing to pay for flood control services, but because such services have 'public good' characteristics they cannot be sold in the normal way. The US Army Engineers, therefore, attempt to estimate what residents would be prepared to pay for such services. On the assumption that an individual would be prepared to pay at least the value of damages that he would otherwise suffer, then estimates of such damages are taken as the benefit to the individual of the flood-control services. The difficulties do not end there, since the way one estimates damages will be affected by the willingness-to-pay principle. A common procedure, for example, is to estimate property damages by calculating its replacement cost, but should the flood have occurred there is no guarantee that all of this replacement cost would have been incurred.

However, we need not enter into these problems here since the case is used simply to show how the willingness-to-pay principle enters benefit estimation. In specifying benefits and costs, the procedure is therefore one of simulating how the price system would have behaved in the absence of the technical difficulties associated with its usage. Moreover, a second feature of these studies, which is more often implicit rather than explicit, is the presumption that a surplus of benefit over cost indicates that the project is worth undertaking; the gainers *could* compensate the losers even though in many cases—for example, in flood-control where the costs are borne by tax-payers—compensation is not paid. Now, this general basis for estimating benefits and costs—and the efficiency criterion associated with it—has been discussed at length in various parts of this book. Many of the problems associated with its use in the field of public project appraisal are the same as those encountered for pricing. This is sometimes overlooked. It is amazing how the topic of marginal-cost pricing has been bombarded with criticisms, many of which are equally applicable to cost-benefit analysis which often escapes scot-free. The limitations to the use of marginal-cost pricing, caused by the existence of second-best problems, apply with equal force to cost-benefit analysis. The question of whether it would be 'fair' to charge peak-users of electricity a higher price than off-peak users, is no different from a proposal to spend £2 million on a new road scheme in Devon rather than on a new road in East Anglia because the 'benefits' of the former are higher. In both cases, implicit use of willingness-to-pay as a measure of benefit, incorporates income distribution effects and implies something about consumer rationality.

Plan of chapter

Much of the general literature on the theory of cost-benefit analysis is partly concerned with issues like second best, externalities, indivisibilities, and so on. We have dealt with these at length elsewhere. In this chapter we concentrate firstly, in the next section, on identifying the benefits and costs of a project and spelling out precisely what is meant by a project. Section 9.3 then gives examples of some of the methods used to estimate benefits, since these are often the most difficult items to estimate. Section 9.4 explores some further valuation methods with an eye, in particular, to the more widespread effects in the economy as a whole. The relationship between public and private investment is explored in section 9.5. The time-stream aspect of project appraisal is further developed in section 9.6, linking up with the theoretical analysis of public investment criteria in chapter 6; to the extent that the issues are relevant for all types of public investment, then this section's discussion also ties up with the investment criteria used in the previous two chapters. Finally, section 9.7 provides a summary of the time-stream problems. As we have hinted throughout this book, economists in the field of public expenditure economics have had most to say on 'efficiency' problems. Public projects, obviously, do have income distribution effects and these are explored in the next chapter, which also considers some relevant constraints, in particular, the situation where the volume of funds available to a public agency is restricted to arbitrarily prescribed amounts.

9.2 Specification of a project

If one were to try to discover the source of the initial impetus for economic evaluations of public sector activities, it is most likely that the answer would be engineers. In the water-resource sector of the USA, electricity supply in France, and road construction in the UK—where appraisal techniques have probably seen the biggest advance—engineers have traditionally been closely concerned with the economic as well as technical aspects of project appraisal.[9] In historical perspective, economists are really only now starting to make a contribution. Where they can probably make the biggest contribution is in indicating some of the economy-wide effects of individual sector projects, and the economy-wide implications of *selection criteria* used in individual sectors.

[9] The same point applies to pricing problems in electricity supply in the UK and, in particular, France.

To undertake a project, for example, because its costs are less than the saving which the project causes in other resources—cf. the flood-control example—depends on how one values resources saved; if the ruling market price of inputs or outputs is used, the question arises as to whether there is anything sacrosanct about market prices, and so on. In assessing any project, there are two general points that need to be clarified from the beginning. Firstly, it is rarely, if ever, useful to consider one project in isolation. Not only may a particular project have physical side-effects elsewhere—a barrage upstream in a river changes drainage patterns downstream—but using different selection criteria for different projects can have some curious results and, perhaps most important of all, it is important to see how this project affects the total supplies of the services in question, since market prices can be thereby affected. In other words, in assessing one particular river barrage, it is useful to have some idea of its setting in the general context of river-basin development. More generally, it is useful to define as far as possible a sector whose inputs and outputs correspond to or embrace those of the project in question. The second point is that *appropriate* criteria for selection or rejection of a project depends on one's aims in the sector as a whole, and there is, therefore, some advantage in specifying these aims as precisely as possible. As a consequence of these two points, many economists writing about cost-benefit analysis have tended to take a fairly *formal* approach to the whole business of project selection.[10] This certainly has advantages, as we shall see, in understanding some of the valuation procedures. Whether, in decision-taking, such formality is always necessary, particularly bearing in mind the limited nature of some of the statistical information, is not so certain.

The framework

Consider the following approach which, though not necessarily applicable to all types of activities, raises a number of relevant issues. If one followed the dictionary definition of benefits and costs, it would be almost a truism to say that a useful guide for evaluating activities is to undertake a project if benefits exceed costs; for all that this implies is that one compares advantages with disadvantages. For any sector one could set out the overall decision problem as:

Maximize Benefits—Costs
subject to Constraints (a) Production function between inputs and outputs
(b) Budgeted funds available
(c) Others

[10] The prime example is probably S. A. Marglin in two papers surveying these issues. His main audience consists of water engineers who would, therefore, be quite at home with this formality. See 'Objectives of Water-Resource Development: A General Statement' and 'Economic Factors Affecting System Design', chapters 2 and 4 respectively of *Design of Water-Resource Systems*, by A. Maass and others, Harvard University Press, 1962.

This, of course, would cover any definitions of benefits and costs and any form of functional relationship.[11] The particular constraints coming under item (c) may, of course, often be unmeasurable or difficult to specify. Our particular concern at present is with a maximand defined as the sum of benefited parties' willingness-to-pay, and input suppliers' compensation required, and where any £1 of benefit or cost gets the same weight as any other. Secondly, the only constraint considered is that provided by the available production technology. If total benefits and costs as defined are denoted by TB and TC respectively, then we may write the decision problem as:

$$\text{Max.} \quad TB - TC \tag{9.1}$$

s.t. constraint of production function.

Some general problems associated with defining the opportunities afforded by any project can be discussed in the context of this decision process. To be precise, the maximand needs some time-period notation, but such issues can be better dealt with separately in the later sections of this chapter. The maximand thus relates to total benefits and costs incurrable in some defined sector in some time-period. Any one project is but one of the many opportunities subsumed in this formulation. Thus, the benefits symbol could relate to a variety of goods and services producible, i.e.,

$$TB = \sum_{j=1}^{j=s} f_j(x_j) \tag{9.2}$$

where x_j is the volume of the jth good or service.[12] The equation then expresses total benefits as functionally related to the volume of each good or service. If we attempted to obtain even a rough empirical estimate for eq. (9.2) a difficulty encountered in many parts of the public sector is that many services rendered are impossible to measure. Such *intangibles*—fumes caused by road traffic, the aesthetic appeal of certain designs of buildings, recreational facilities—occur also on the input side; in fact, it is not always clear whether they should be categorized as an input or an output, but as long as we know whether they are a 'good' or a 'bad' that is all that matters in this respect. The key issue is whether the measurement and analysis of tangibles is worthwhile if intangibles loom large, and for this each case needs to be considered on its own merits. It should go without saying that sophisticated selection criteria, based on measurable items, are in such circumstances positively dangerous. A second feature of the benefits side is that the formalization of the decision process, in the expressions above, contains the obvious requirement that 'advantages' must be clearly defined and justified. We are

[11] And this means that the decision problem in question may be better solved by techniques like linear programming than the standard differential calculus which pervades this book.

[12] To be even more sophisticated we might allow for joint demand over more than one product. For example, demand for roads between London and Luton will often be joint to the demand for roads between Luton and Leeds.

certainly not suggesting that willingness-to-pay is always the appropriate interpretation, but there are numerous instances in the public sector where the 'advantages' item is very curiously expressed. The so-called 'requirements approach' is one instance. In the UK, for example, public investment in facilities for supplying water is based on the estimates that various boards make of water requirements in the foreseeable future. Acceptable principles for making such estimates

> . . . include consideration of expected population changes, improved housing and domestic appliances, and expected industrial development.[13]

In other words, in estimating demand no price variable is included—and roughly 40 per cent of publicly supplied water is metered. The question of the economic value (however interpreted) of extra supplies has hardly been questioned, and this point applies particularly strongly to the remaining 60 per cent of public supplies which go to the domestic consumer who, after paying a lump-sum charge, is subject to no unit price. There may be good reasons for not levying prices—such as health hazards associated with low water purchases—and for excluding them from demand projections, but these issues are rarely explored in economic terms. Similarly, it may well not be possible in some sectors of the economy to specify policy objectives in any way other than some variation of the requirements approach. Defence expenditure is one example, though here again this does not preclude an examination of the alternatives available and the costs of these alternatives; in fact, this is the sort of work now being undertaken in some defence establishments, particularly in the USA.

A third feature of the benefit side of the decision problem is that eq. (9.2) expresses benefits from any service as functionally related to the quantity of that service provided. To the economist, this would be a standard assumption consistent with a partial equilibrium demand curve. If it does have general validity, then it means some of the estimation procedures have to be carefully used. Consider the example of flood-control again. The replacement cost of items which would otherwise have been destroyed, could be used as a measure of benefit, provided that such repairs would have been undertaken. To raise the possibility that replacement might not otherwise have occurred is, in fact, to imply that benefits are inversely related to scale. Particularly when anticipated annual damages are expected to be high, the value that residents attach to keeping parts of their present property intact may be less than the costs they would have to incur to restore these items should flood-damage take place. Put another way, when present flood-control programmes constitute only small additions to existing protective facilities, the benefit

[13] 'Water "Requirements"—The Investment Decision in the Water Supply Industry', J. J. Warford, *The Manchester School*, p. 87, January 1966; reproduced in a slightly amended form, as chapter 6 of *Public Enterprise*, Ed. R. Turvey, Penguin Modern Economics Series, 1968.

from such marginal additions can be taken as roughly constant; further, if existing facilities are fairly primitive, then these benefits can realistically be measured as alternative replacement cost. If they constitute large additions, marginal benefits may well fall, in which case the use of repair cost makes for over-estimation of the 'value' of damages averted.

Turning now to the other part of the maximand, we may similarly define costs as:

$$\sum_{l=1}^{l=z} f_l(h_l) \tag{9.3}$$

where h_l is the quantity of the lth input. Since costs are to be understood as the minimum compensation required by input suppliers, then they relate to the value of alternatives foregone by using these inputs in this sector. Two aspects of this are worth bringing out. Firstly, the price of inputs may vary with usage, as eq. (9.3) implies; in addition, when the production function is introduced, costs will also vary with output. One fairly obvious implication of this is that any one project is rarely an all or nothing venture. The construction of a new road need not mean a motorway or nothing; its size and quality can, in principle, vary from a single lane sealed road, to a dual-carriageway, to two or three lane motorways. Similarly, the possible barrages in the UK across Morecambe Bay, Solway Firth, and the Wash, for conserving water, can be variable with respect to size. Unfortunately, in practice, by the time benefits are considered, the engineers have often completed feasibility studies and come out with one 'best' solution; the economist's concern with comparing a slightly larger capacity with the ensuing extra benefits is not, at present, catered for in the way these schemes are planned. The second point is that among the many alternatives, foregone by using the inputs in question, is the possibility of private enterprise undertaking the project. This is a point often stressed by American writers,[14] and is a genuine point in the context of resource allocation, though whether the 'efficiency' aspects could ever be separated in practice from political in-fighting is dubious. The possibility being mooted is that some input, say land in a river valley, could be used as a site for a public water barrage, or a public HEP station, or a private HEP station, this example being relevant to the USA rather than the UK. Of course, if this site is privately owned, then granted profit-maximization on the part of the owner, the site would be sold to the highest bidder; that is, to that use which was most profitable. The issue becomes important

[14] To the set of public projects under consideration, Marglin, in his 'Economic Factors Affecting System Design', *op. cit.*, considers a sector (denoted as *S*3) of 'specific external private alternatives'; private projects using the same inputs as the public sector are termed 'technological alternatives', while a private project fulfilling the same function—i.e., producing similar services—as a public project is called an 'economic alternative'. P. O. Steiner had earlier used a similar 'reservoir' of private projects (denoted as *S*2) in the model in his paper, 'Choosing Among Alternative Public Investments in the Water Resource Field', *AER*, December 1959. A similar conceptual framework appears also in Steiner's 'The Role of Alternative Cost in Project Design and Selection', *QJE*, August 1965.

when the government has pre-emptive rights on such an input. In this case, the specification of costs as alternatives foregone requires some governmental evaluation of the social benefits foregone by not using this site for private development. In addition, to be fully consistent, one would want to make such allowances on the output side—private versus government road haulage services. Whether any particular public agency would ever take such an all-embracive view seems doubtful. The third point about costs also relates to alternatives foregone. When costs are financed not by revenue but, as is the case for many of the services discussed here, by taxation or borrowing, then another opportunity cost enters the picture. This is the value of these *funds* in their alternative locale, the private sector. There has been considerable discussion of this issue by economists, but since it is linked closely to investment criteria, we shall postpone discussion until section 5 of this chapter.

Selection criteria

Consider, finally, how selection criteria for individual projects are related to the sector maximand. The expression for benefits and costs are functionally related to the scale of outputs and inputs, respectively. The technological relationship between inputs and outputs would be given by a production function.[15] This is a standard maximization problem which has appeared at numerous points in this book. Provided the functional relationships do not take any unusual form, then equilibrium is characterized by the usual marginal relationships between benefits and costs. Thus, the use of an input should be extended until extra outlays are balanced by the extra benefit ultimately accruing from the use of that input. Similarly, with respect to changes in the output of any good or service, such a change should be undertaken if the extra benefit exceeds the extra cost. Let the change in benefit with respect to an increase in good j be denoted by B_j; the change in cost, say C_j, is a composite of the change in costs with respect to inputs and the techno-

[15] Of the form $f(x_1, \ldots, x_j, \ldots, x_s; h_1, \ldots, h_l, \ldots, h_z) = 0$. Formally the solutions are obtained as follows. Let the maximand of TB−TC, each term defined as in equations (9.2) and (9.3), be constrained by the production function above. Denoting the constraint on this production function as the undetermined Lagrangean multiplier, λ, the first order conditions are:

$$B_{xj} - \lambda F_{xj} = 0 \qquad j = 1 \ldots s$$
$$C_{hl} - \lambda F_{hl} = 0 \qquad l = 1 \ldots z$$

where B_{xj} denotes $\delta \mathrm{TB}/\delta x_j$, and F_{hl} denotes $\delta f/\delta h_l$, etc. Rearranging gives:

$$C_{hl} = b_{xj}(F_{hl}/F_{xj}) \qquad \text{and} \qquad B_{xj} = C_{hl}(F_{xj}/F_{hl})$$

With respect to small changes in either inputs or outputs, marginal benefit equals marginal cost. In the very last equation, the marginal cost of extra output is given as the product of the number of inputs required for an extra unit of output and the price of inputs (assuming the enterprise is a price taker in this respect); this expression is denoted, for a finite change, as C_j in eq. (9.4), while B_{xj} is denoted by B_j.

logical transformation rate between input and output. We have then that the criterion for such a change is:

$$B_j - C_j > 0 \quad \text{or} \quad B_j/C_j > 1 \tag{9.4}$$

This gives a general criterion for evaluating parts of the whole of any project. Notice two points about it. Firstly, though derived from a context where prices are not levied for project outputs, the criterion is related to those discussed before. For very small changes it is similar to the rule of increasing output as long as price exceeds marginal cost. Where large changes are involved, the surplus of benefit over cost in eq. (9.4) is similar to the following two surpluses, each of which are equivalent: (a) The extra output valued at the new ruling price less the cost of inputs valued at the new factor price, plus any consumer surplus and rental elements accruing from the price changes. (b) The increase in the sum of producer and consumer surplus. The second point is that the criterion for project acceptability (and ranking) is that (the change in) benefit minus (the change in) cost should be positive. Some of the early commentators on cost-benefit analysis spent much time discussing the relevance of *benefit-cost ratios*, since they have been a traditional test of water-resource projects in the USA. Of course, our analysis is consistent with *a* use of ratios: namely to accept a project or a change in output if the benefit-cost ratio of this change exceeds unity; as eq. (9.4) implies, this tells us no more than the criterion which accepts all projects whose net benefit is positive.

A guiding light to the assessment of water-resource projects in the USA has been the famous 'Green Book' report to the Federal Inter-Agency River Basin Committee[16] by one of its sub-committees. Through recommending ratios, the 'Green Book' only really suggested excluding projects whose ratio was not equal to one or more. However, there is a danger even in this. One 'interpreter' said that the

> ... rule is not to maximize the ratio, or even to rank projects according to benefit-cost ratios, but is simply to exclude projects with ratios that are less than unity. In practice, however, projects with the higher ratio are inevitably regarded as preferable to those with lower ratios (apart from intangible considerations). For example, the particular reservoir recommended in the Santa Maria Project was the one with the highest benefit-cost ratio.[17]

The key point is that the appropriate criterion depends on the maximand and the constraints. In our specification of the problem, the criterion of positive net benefit is the right criterion. The 'Green Book' dismisses this on the

[16] See *Proposed Practices for Economic Analysis of River Basin Projects*, Sub-Committee on Benefits and Costs, FIARBC, May 1950.

[17] R. N. McKean, *Efficiency in Government Through Systems Analysis*, pp. 107–8 and footnote, Wiley & Sons, 1958. Chapters 2 and 7 contain an excellent critique of the ratio approach.

grounds that large projects are favoured over small. So they are, but this does not matter as long as all interdependencies between projects are clearly formulated and as long as there are no other constraints, for then all the worthwhile small projects will, in any case, be accepted. It is when constraints exist on the size of available funds that such ranking problems emerge, and this was no doubt at the back of the minds of the sub-committee's members. However, it is only confusing to use ratios as a general rule and, to repeat, in the absence of such funds constraints, benefit less cost is the correct selection criterion. We pursue the issue of budget limitations in the next chapter.

9.3 Examples of techniques used to value project outputs

At this stage of the analysis it is useful to indicate, in some detail, the way that the benefits and costs are estimated. Invariably, for parts of the public sector where benefits and costs are not easily measurable, it is the benefits side that poses most problems, and it is this topic that is considered in this section. Broadly, the point is that revenue, if it exists at all, is an inadequate measure of willingness-to-pay. The procedure in many cases is to impute a benefit figure, by examining the effects of the project on parties consuming project services or other people 'downstream' from the project. We do not attempt in this book to explore all the measurement problems that have been raised in cost-benefit analysis nor to survey all the studies undertaken. Our main interest is the basis of valuation, and a few examples only are given to indicate the flavour of the approach often used.[18]

Road investment

Because of indivisibilities in the supply of roads, efficient usage may sometimes require very low prices or tolls. Even though a new road is not expected to generate much toll income nor to be particularly heavily used, it may still be justified on the efficiency criterion that willingness-to-pay exceeds construction cost. With heavy usage, optimal prices may be quite high as congestion increases the scarcity value of such a road. If prices are levied for

[18] A survey of the main cost-benefit studies, at least up to 1965, can be found in 'Cost-Benefit Analysis: A Survey', A. R. Prest and R. Turvey, *EJ*, December 1965, reproduced in *Surveys of Economic Theory*, AEA and Royal Economic Society, Vol. III, Macmillan, and St Martin's Press, 1966. M. S. Feldstein has also written a less technical survey entitled 'Cost-Benefit Analysis and Investment in the Public Sector', *Public Administration*, Winter 1964, and a similar sort of paper is G. H. Peter's 'Cost-Benefit Analysis and Public Expenditure', *Eaton Paper 8*, Institute of Economic Affairs 1966. The Brookings Institution has published the proceedings of two conferences (held in 1963 and 1966) at which detailed studies were described—covering research and development, outdoor recreation, high-school student wastage, aviation, roads, urban renewal, syphilis control, cotton price supports—and, particularly in the second volume, general topics like valuing travel time and accidents, the use of shadow prices, and the relevance of income distribution problems, were discussed. See *Measuring Benefits of Government Investment*, Ed. R. Dorfman, 1965, and *Problems in Public Expenditure Analysis*, Ed. S. B. Chase, 1968.

congested roads, some of the problems of benefit estimation are removed, since toll income or congestion tax receipts will provide a rough approximation to willingness-to-pay. However, roads raise an additional problem, namely, that it may not be technically feasible—or even if feasible it may be too costly—to operate a price system. For both these reasons roads are often not priced and the problem of evaluating new roads is to evaluate the benefits not as revenue accruing to the road provider—say the Ministry of Transport whose *direct* revenue is practically zero—but as benefits actually accruing to road users.[19]

For illustration of the main points we take the case of new uncongested roads, notwithstanding that congested roads raise many further complications. New roads can benefit vehicle-owners in three main ways. Firstly, new roads sometimes reduce the vehicle operating costs of making a journey. A road which involves a significant distance saving may well do this. The possibilities of increasing the average speed of a journey might also reduce operating costs, but empirical work in the UK has played down the significance of this factor; there is some evidence for private cars, for example, that beyond 40m/h, or thereabouts, fuel and other costs may well rise. A second source of benefit is the saving in journey time that a new road effects, either because of distance-saving or because of the higher speeds attainable. It is becoming increasingly recognized that this is probably the biggest benefit from new roads. Unfortunately, it poses some of the largest measurement problems. Data relating to operating costs has been compiled in the UK by the Road Research Laboratory. For each broad class of vehicle—light van, car, medium-sized lorry, and so on—average operating costs per mile can be worked out for various possible speed ranges. Assuming that data on traffic flows likely to shift to a new road has been collected from road censuses and the like, then operating-cost savings can be estimated for each class of vehicle, granted knowledge of distance savings and expected differences in average speeds. For time-savings there are more difficulties. Traditionally, an hour saved in working-time has been valued at the hourly wage-rate of the person involved—commercial traveller, lorry driver, etc.—but leisure time has always been an unknown, and arbitrary estimates have been used ranging from $\frac{1}{4}$ to $\frac{2}{3}$ of the working-time valuation. Much re-thinking on time-savings is now taking place[20] and this work is relevant to other areas of transport like airways. The third main effect of new roads is, in some cases, to reduce accidents. Data is available on expected accident rates on different

[19] For further elaboration of this paragraph see section 5.3 and section 8.2. Notice that road users, of course, do indirectly contribute towards road costs via petrol tax, licence duties, vehicle purchase tax, and so on. The point is that these are largely unrelated to vehicle-mile costs on different stretches of road. For a discussion and estimation of the relationship between tax revenue from road users and road expenditure see A. R. Prest, 'Some Aspects of Road Finance in the UK', *The Manchester School*, September 1963.

[20] For a survey see 'The Value of Time', London Transportation Study Phase III, a background note prepared by the Economic Planning Directorate, Ministry of Transport. See also J. R. Nelson's chapter on 'The Value of Travel Time', in Chase, *op. cit*.

types of road, and the information in any area on the shifts in traffic flow allows one to deduce a figure of the expected decrease in the annual number of accidents as a result of the new road. Differentiation is made between different types of accidents, but while things like property damage are fairly easy to approximate it is the valuation of human life that presents most problems. Present procedure, by road engineers in the UK, is to use some measure of the stream of output lost through the temporary or permanent reduction in the productive capacity of the person involved. For 1965, for example, the figure used for the 'average' accident was £850 per annum. Again, there are obviously problems and limitations to this sort of approach.[21]

Setting the measurement problem aside (!), let us consider the implications of using these figures—and particularly those relating to journey-cost saving—as an indication of the benefit of a road project.[22] Once located on the new road, traffic incurs certain journey costs. The extent to which these fall short of the journey costs that would have been involved on old routes, can be interpreted as the maximum that vehicle-owners are prepared to pay to use the new road. The cost figures differ in principle for each vehicle, so that for some the advantage in shifting routes may be quite small. The only costs borne by the road-provider which vary with usage are maintenance costs which, for expository purposes, we might take to be negligible. Therefore, the only way prices can be levied to both expropriate a sufficient part of road-users' willingness-to-pay to cover construction costs and, at the same time, guarantee 'efficient' use of the new road is by a system of discrimination. If this is not possible, then not only will the 'marginal' user be allowed to use the road free—as would be the case with discrimination—but so would all other users. Notice that the method of estimating benefits is a variant of the 'alternative cost' approach discussed previously in connection with flood-control, and a related problem arises, namely, that some of the traffic on the new road might not otherwise have made a road journey. If some of the users of the new road would otherwise have used bus services, or rail transport, or not made the journey at all, then the use of journey-cost saving becomes a dubious procedure in estimating benefits for such people. This point can be illustrated with a diagram if we make the assumption, purely for expository purposes, that all the vehicles using the new road are identical, both in respect to their operating costs and their owners' valuation of time (see Fig. 9.1). These journey costs per vehicle are indicated by the C^1 line; the assumed constancy implies that the context is one where usage of the road is fairly light. Should these vehicles have made the same journey by the old route, journey costs per vehicle would be as indicated by the C line. Now the demand curve, D, indicates the valuation that the various people

[21] For a pioneering attempt in the UK to estimate some of these magnitudes see 'The Cost of Road Accidents', D. J. Reynolds, *JRSS*, Series A, 1956 Part 4.

[22] The way taxes, such as those on petrol, enter the picture is discussed in the last sub-section of section 4 of this chapter. Present practice is to exclude them from estimates of journey-cost saving.

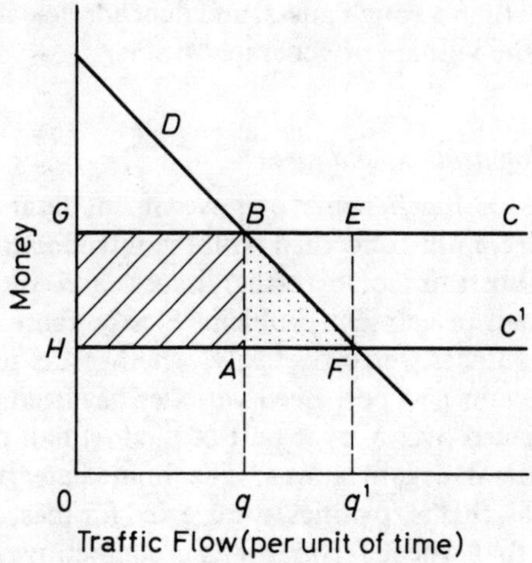

FIG. 9.1

involved attach to making the journey in question. Thus, while the cost of the journey is taken to be the same for each vehicle, each vehicle-owner can in this example attach a different valuation to the journey. On the basis that journeys are made if willingness-to-pay exceeds what has to be paid (journey costs), then the flow on the old road would be Oq per unit of time. When the new road is constructed, this traffic would shift to the new route; such 'diverted' traffic, as it is called, experiences a total journey-cost saving equal to the shaded area in Fig. 9.1. The flow on the new road will actually be Oq^1, the qq^1 group being precisely those people who previously travelled by bus, train, or not at all. The diagram indicates that their benefit from the new road is equal to the dotted area, that is their valuation of the journey net of costs on the new road. It follows that the benefit of the new road to such users is not given by the standard method of journey-cost saving. For this so-called 'generated' traffic, knowledge of the demand curve is required. Since this sort of data is not available the dotted area is sometimes approximated in the following way. The volume of generated traffic on roads like motorways is taken to be roughly of the order of 30 per cent of the diverted traffic. The M1 study used this method, the figure of 30 per cent being derived from experience with Continental motorways. If the size of diverted traffic is known, then so also, with this assumption, is the absolute size of the generated traffic. The area, *ABEF* on Fig. 9.1 is therefore known. In the absence of knowledge of the precise path of the demand curve from *B* to *F*, the assumption is made that it is a straight line. The net benefits to generated traffic are equal, therefore, to one-half of the area *ABEF*. Put another way, each unit of generated traffic is credited with half the cost-saving per vehicle attributed to diverted traffic, and this is the procedure used in road investment in the UK.

It is clearly no more than a rough guess, and depends heavily on the accuracy of the estimate of the volume of generated traffic.[23]

Research and development expenditures

Two investigations of the benefits of government financed research and development activity, both concerned with the introduction of new agricultural techniques, illustrate some further issues, and yet are not all that dissimilar to the road investment problem. Firstly, there is the attempt by Z. Griliches[24] to estimate, retrospectively, whether US public expenditure on research into certain new corn seed varieties has been worthwhile. This research was performed over a large part of the first half of this century by both state and federal organizations. The immediate beneficiaries were farmers but no prices, that is royalties, were levied for these research services. Griliches assumed that wheat farming was a competitive industry, so that any excess profits accruing to farmers from use of the new seed varieties would be passed on as lower prices. The ultimate beneficiaries were, therefore, final consumers and since the first yields from the new seeds came in 1933, the benefits of this 'project' were taken as the flow of annual benefits to final-stage consumers (of bread, dairy products, etc.) from 1933 onwards to infinity. There were two elements in the costs. One was the flow of annual research and development expenditures over the period 1910–55; the data for this was based partly on a mail inquiry to State agricultural experiment stations, partly on direct information from the Department of Agriculture, and partly on some estimates of research expenditure by private seed companies. The other item of cost arose from the production of the new seeds. Given knowledge of the total corn acreage in the USA, the proportion of this using the new seeds and data on seeding rates, Griliches was able to estimate the farming industry's annual purchases of the new variety. The annual cost of the resources used in the production of this seed was estimated by assuming that the seed production industry was competitive, implying that the price of seed was equal to its cost; the expenditure by the farming industry on new seed, therefore, was taken to approximate the cost of the factors of production used to produce the new variety.

The major estimation problem however related to benefits. Suppose one assumed that farming is a constant cost industry so that its long-run supply schedule is horizontal.[25] We can use Fig. 9.1 again to illustrate the main

[23] For more detail of the way engineers in the UK assess road projects, and for some of the implications of the investment criteria involved see my paper 'Road Investment Criteria: A Case Study', *Journal of Transport Economics and Policy*, January 1968. See also 'The Economic Assessment of Returns from Road Works', by G. Charlesworth and J. L. Paisley, *Proceedings of the Institution of Civil Engineers*, November 1959.

[24] 'Research Costs and Social Returns: Hybrid Corn and Related Innovations', *JPE*, October 1958.

[25] Actually Griliches made his estimates under two different assumptions, the other one being that supply was infinitely inelastic. The over-all results were not however greatly affected.

points; the horizontal axis will now measure the annual volume of corn. The introduction of the new varieties effectively reduced the farmers' costs, and we can represent this as the shift in the industry supply line from C to C^1 with the equilibrium position shifted from point B to point F; the benefit to be measured is again the increase in consumer surplus—the sum of the shaded and dotted areas. Now, although the annual value of corn was known—i.e., point F could be located—there was no direct information on the effect of the new varieties on corn prices. Griliches was able to infer the price change from technical data on the productivity of the new seeds. It was estimated that, if the new variety were removed, corn yields would decrease by 13 per cent; that is, $AB/Aq = 0{\cdot}13$. Now the benefit to be measured is rectangle *GEFH* less the area *BEF*, each multiplied by the proportion of the total acreage under the new seed variety. The rectangle is equal to the annual value of corn $\times\, 0{\cdot}13$. The area *BEF* can only be estimated precisely if the shape of the demand curve is known. From work carried out in the US Department of Agriculture the price elasticity of demand, over the range in question, was taken as $(-)0{\cdot}5$. Griliches then had enough information to get the measure he wanted.[26] Expressing every money term at 1955 prices and in terms of 1955 dollars, using a 5 per cent interest rate he was able to conclude that, for every dollar spent on research, the present (1955) value of the flow of benefits net of seeding production costs was roughly 7.5 dollars; that is, an overall social net benefit of 6·5 dollars for each dollar invested in research.

The second example relates to research on new potato harvesters in the UK, undertaken and sponsored jointly by the government's National Research and Development Corporation (NRDC) and the National Institute of Agricultural Engineering (NIAE). Heath and Grossfield attempted to estimate the benefits and costs of this research activity.[27] After numerous trials and tribulations, starting in 1950 with the evaluation of a prize-winning potato harvester, the NRDC eventually in 1956 took over the patent on a trailer-operated experimental model developed by the NIAE. The NRDC then granted a licence to a large engineering firm, who successfully brought the harvester up to marketable standards, and sales have been made in substantial numbers since 1960. Now NRDC did receive royalties from the

[26] If, as Griliches assumes, the demand curve is straight over the range in question, then the area *BEF* is a triangle. It follows that:

$$\begin{aligned}\text{Triangle } BEF &= \tfrac{1}{2}(FE \times BE)\\ FE &= 0{\cdot}13 \times \text{Corn Price } (q^1F).\\ BE &= \text{Elasticity of demand } (e) \times FE \times \text{Corn quantity} \div \text{Corn Price}\\ \text{Triangle } BEF &= \tfrac{1}{2}(e \times (0{\cdot}13)^2 \times \text{Annual Value of Corn})\end{aligned}$$

Remembering the analysis in the text, it follows that the increase in annual consumer surplus $=$ Annual Value of Corn $\times$ Proportion of acreage under new seed variety $\times\, 0{\cdot}13 \times (1 - \tfrac{1}{2}e\ 0{\cdot}13)$.

[27] 'The Benefit and Cost of Government Support for Research and Development: A Case Study', K. Grossfield and J. B. Heath, *EJ*, September 1966.

engineering firm, but the logic of the Heath and Grossfield analysis of the benefits of the research work is that these royalties were quite arbitrary, small, and unrelated to the market value of the research services—notwithstanding that such a value, in any case, would be difficult to define. Further, they assumed that despite the semi-monopolistic position of the engineering firm, the sale price of harvesters to farmers was competitive in that the firm faced potential competition from other harvester manufacturers. The major benefits of the research were taken to be the cost saving experienced by potato farmers who purchased the new models. Medium-sized growers (twenty to fifty acres) were the ones expected to derive most advantage, and it was estimated that for such farms the average saving per harvester per annum (allowing a capital charge for the harvester) would be of the order of £80 to £90. Granted data on the number of the new harvesters in use from 1960 onwards, the total savings to farmers were calculated for each year. The principle is not very different from Griliches' approach, save that by concentrating attention on the change in market prices he raises the possibility of total supplies being increased. Heath and Grossfield do not estimate the consumer surplus triangle though, if extra supplies are not possible because of quota restrictions, this may not be an omission. Finally, the horizon involved is fairly short—no values after 1967 are considered—because the NRDC's contribution was essentially one of providing money at a crucial stage for NIAE, and providing licensing know-how and enterprise in exploiting the invention. Some harvester producer would probably have taken up the invention after a time-lag. In the absence of NRDC, the costs would have been the same but the benefits would have been delayed.

Irrigation projects

In many countries an important function of projects developing water-resources is the provision of irrigation water. Economic analysis of such projects has been proceeding for a long time in the USA but other countries, for example, India,[28] are now attempting to undertake such analyses. The immediate beneficiaries of these schemes are of course farmers, and in the USA—mostly in the Western states—quite a large range of crops draw on irrigation facilities; not only sugar beet, rice, and soya beans but grain, fruit, vegetables, seed crops, and livestock. The basic problem is that, while revenue is often received from water-users:

> . . . it is not generally practicable to sell the water by the acre, foot or even year by year; rather, the beneficiaries must sign long-term contracts to meet the total obligations for the project before construction is started . . .

[28] See for example *Some Economic Aspects of the Bhakra-Nangal Project*, K. N. Raj, and *Economics of a Multi-Purpose River Dam*, N. V. Sovani and N. Roth. Both issued in 1960 by Asia Publishing Co.

and in addition

> ... one of the main objectives of the [US federal] programme is the creation of new family-farm opportunities and of a new life for relatively poor families ... [so that] ... payments for irrigation water must be sufficiently low to leave them significantly better off.[29]

So there appears to be both some 'public good' characteristics in irrigation facilities and, in addition, the US programme is motivated partly by 'non-efficiency' objectives. Willingness-to-pay is not therefore indicated by revenue; this is not only because of the factors mentioned above, but also because even the 'long-term' revenue receipts are fairly small: often they are spread over forty years free of interest and free also of repayment obligations over the first ten years.

Since the benefit of water is not indicated by its market value, the Bureau of Reclamation—the body in the US authorized by the 1902 Reclamation Act to build irrigation projects—undertakes farm budget studies to estimate the changes in the farmers' net income caused by the new facilities, and this is used as (part of) a measure of the benefit of these schemes. So, again, one is imputing a value to project outputs by estimating benefits as they accrue to project 'consumers'. Benefit is taken as the profitability of the farm outputs occasioned by the project. Sugar-beet and rice producers, for example, use water to increase the supplies of these agricultural products. The market value of these supplies, net of the cost of accompanying factors, is the profit measure in question. And this, in principle, is the demand price which would have emerged if water could itself have been sold. An important characteristic of this situation is that the effect of projects is to promote *extra* supplies of farm products, and we shall be considering some of the implications of this

[29] Eckstein, *op. cit.*, pp. 197 and 227. If the second point *is* an important objective, there seems little point estimating willingness-to-pay, since even if this fell short of project costs the acceptance of such a project is consistent with the objective. Eckstein, in addition, gives some other curious reasons why revenue is not or would not be a good measure of benefit. He says that

> '... if farmers had to pay as much for the water as it was worth in terms of additional output, there would be no incentive for them to bother moving to the project or to engage in the long and back-breaking task of bringing the irrigable acreage into intensive cultivation.' (p. 197)

and further on, that

> '... direct benefits, which measure the increase in income of the settlers, do not provide a measure of revenue potential since it is impossible to charge a price for water which would leave the incomes of irrigators unchanged' (p. 227).

There is some price that could be levied on farmers—if only there were not 'public good' problems—which would be just small enough to induce them to cultivate; this constitutes a measure of the farmers' willingness-to-pay. If this price is practically zero, then the 'benefit' of the irrigated water is zero. Neither is there any presumption that this price is approximated by the value of the farmers' additional output; at the most, it would be this value less the cost of accompanying factors of production.

in the next section. One final point may be noted here; water is one of the products of some of the water-barrages under review at present in the UK—the Dee, Morecambe Bay, etc.—though these are not irrigation schemes. At present, UK data precludes attempts to impute the value of water from the profitability of using firms. The only economic analysis, at present, is the computation of the cost of water emanating from each scheme and the use of this in choices between different barrages.[30]

With these examples as an indication of some of the approaches used in cost-benefit analysis, we may now proceed to consider some general problems of valuation common to many of them.

9.4 Economy-wide effects

Alternative costs

One valuation problem that has cropped up time and again is the use of the so-called 'alternative-cost approach' to measure benefits, and we may briefly tie together some of the points already made about this. It is an approach used in many guises. The benefits of new roads are estimated as being, at most, equal to journey costs on alternative road routes (net of costs on the new routes). Similarly, in the cases of research into corn varieties and potato harvesters, the limit to benefits was indicated by the yields with alternative farming techniques (net of yields with new techniques). In two other examples a comparison is made between proposed public facilities and alternative private supplies. One writer attempted to estimate the UK demand curve for North Sea Gas, by assuming willingness-to-pay was equal to the cost to industrial and domestic consumers of existing alternative fuel supplies. Similarly, the Ministry of Transport's study group on the Channel Tunnel have imputed maximum demand prices for the Tunnel from data on the cost to transporters of using private (and public) ferries and airways.[31] Finally, the nearest alternative to the use of canals and rivers for transport in the USA is usually the railways, and the benefits of navigational improvements to inland waterways is often taken to be at most the cost of transportation by railway.

Three points can be made about this general method. Firstly, when the aim of analysis is to estimate what real resources are saved by the construction of the new project, the data available for alternative facilities needs to be closely examined. Commentators on the techniques used by the US Army Corps of Engineers for navigational improvements, have stressed that to the extent that railway rates are often not equal to marginal costs, the difference

[30] See for example *Dee Crossing Study Phase I*, Ministry of Housing and Local Government, HMSO, 1967, part 4 and appendices E1 to E9.

[31] See 'What Price North Sea Gas', G. Polyanyi, *Hobart Paper 38*, Institute of Economic Affairs, 1967 and 'The Channel Tunnel: Investment Appraisals', A. H. Watson, *Public Administration*, Spring 1967.

between rail prices and canal costs may not indicate the real resource saving involved. However, there is a problem here, since project beneficiaries do actually have to pay rail prices rather than rail costs, and to this extent rail prices do reflect transporter's willingness-to-pay. We shall reconsider this issue in a later section (see p. 308). The second point is simply to emphasize again that, when output rises, the use of alternative cost may over-estimate benefits. The third point follows close on from the second. In some of the examples the alternative to the public project's output is private supplies. If we wished to be sure that 'efficient' quantities of public supplies are produced, then the safest form of analysis is to enlarge the basic maximand to embrace the possibility of alternative private facilities. The point is similar to our previous discussion of the alternative uses of project inputs—the land site for public or private water-resource development (see pp. 287–8). The maximand would then relate to the social benefits and costs of public projects plus the social[32] benefits and costs of private supplies. The solutions to this decision problem will involve optimal quantities of both public and private outputs and optimal sizes for public and private projects. Now, the criterion for choosing between one source of supply as opposed to another, implied in this problem, *will* in some circumstances be equivalent to measuring the benefits of public projects as the cost of private supplies; and *in some circumstances it will not*. To give one example of this,[33] suppose the problem is to decide on the appropriate sizes of a public project and a private project; what size of Channel Tunnel and how many private cross-Channel hovercrafts; what size of public water-barrage and what size of private HEP plant. If the benefits of both, at all size levels, are exactly the same, then the maximand would imply a simple cost-effectiveness approach—one compares the cost of two methods of pursuing a common objective. The public project is undertaken if its cost is less than the private project. Alternatively, if the benefit of the public project is measured as the cost of the alternative method, then using the criterion 'undertake public project if benefit exceeds cost', gives the same result. In other circumstances, when benefits are different, for example, this approach will be wrong and in general it is safer to include both sets of projects in the maximand. Whether it is ultimately worthwhile to adopt this general approach will depend on the ease—or more formally the costs—of obtaining all the relevant information.

The benefits of producer goods

In this chapter, and the previous two for that matter, we have brushed over a problem that merits close attention. Willingness-to-pay as a criterion for

[32] This is worth emphasizing: to the extent that there is some government control over private sector operations, then it is the social evaluation of private projects rather than their private profitability (which in some cases may be equivalent) that is the relevant consideration.

[33] P. O. Steiner has explored this whole area systematically in his paper 'The Role of Alternative Cost in Project Design and Selection', *op. cit.*

allocating resources originates in the idea that consumers derive utility or satisfaction from the goods and services they consume, and their willingness-to-pay for any service indicates their relative preferences for this service over others. To the extent that demand curves indicate consumer willingness-to-pay, then the benefits of goods and services have been taken to be indicated by market prices or, in their absence, estimates of what those prices would have been. However, many of the illustrations used do not refer to goods which enter consumer preference functions. Research and development expenditures, farming equipment, irrigation water, routes for road haulage, electricity for industrial usage, are all producer goods. Stemming from their use ultimately, of course, are the potatoes, music, and cigarettes which are consumer goods. We have so far assumed that the willingness-to-pay of the *immediate* consumers of project outputs is the measure needed for 'efficient' resource allocation. How can we be sure this is the right measure for producer goods which do not enter utility functions?

To illustrate this problem, take the case where the services emanating from a public product have the effect, simply, of increasing the supply of all goods 'downstream'. A new river barrage, for example, enlarges the cultivable area of a region because of irrigation water provided, and this increases the supply of wheat or field rice and eventually increases supplies of bread and rice in final goods markets: or one can think of a new electricity generating plant whose supplies go initially to distribution companies and ultimately takes the form of domestic electric heating. The consumer goods, therefore, require the use of factors of production at each stage, from the public project to the final goods producer. The criterion would then be that the benefit from the extra supplies of final goods ultimately emerging should exceed the summed cost of all inputs at all stages.[34] To simplify the example, suppose that there is only one production process in between the public agency and the consumer. It follows, then, that the surplus of consumer valuation of final goods over the cost of inputs used in the final goods sector, is the relevant amount to compare with the costs of the public project. When the extra supplies in question are fairly small in relation to total market supplies, this is precisely the measure calculated in some of the approaches described before. Thus, in the case of water-resource developments which increase farm output supplies, benefits are estimated by measuring the profitability of these extra supplies of grain, rice, sugar-beet, etc.; this profitability is nothing more than the market value of these supplies net of the cost of factors used at the farming stage. Notice, however, two implicit assumptions in this approach; one is that farmers are profit-maximizers, so that all the calculated profits will be realized; the second is that the farming industry and any other industries downstream, like millers and bakers of bread, should be competitive. This will guarantee that the farmers' willingness-to-pay falls

[34] The implicit assumption behind this being that no rental elements or producer surplus accrue to the intermediate stages *as a result of the change*.

short of the market value of final consumer goods by an amount *no greater* than the opportunity cost of factors (including capital and entrepreneurship) used at each stage. The same points apply when public projects produce saleable services like electricity supply. Consider electricity consumed by the metal-using industries, which themselves produce kitchen utensils. Provided the extra electricity is small in relation to total supplies, then the prices of electricity and kitchen utensils will be virtually unchanged. To the extent that the extra electricity facilitates the production of extra kitchen utensils, then the benefit to final consumers is indicated by the extra receipts of the metal-using industry. The surplus of these receipts, over the opportunity cost of all inputs (other than electricity) in the metal-using industry, is the amount that has to be compared with the production costs of the extra electricity. But this surplus is precisely the demand price of the metal-using industry for electricity supply. That is, provided the firms are profit-maximizers, and the industry is competitive, its demand curve for electricity is equal to its marginal revenue product from electricity. For small changes, marginal revenue product is equal to the market value of the extra kitchen utensils net of the costs of other inputs.

But what if the change is sizeable? The water-barrage scheme, for example, might significantly increase farm outputs. The key effect here is when the price of final products fall. To the new farmers, profitability is indicated by the surplus, above input costs, of their agriculture produce *valued at the new lower prices*. In addition, this might well be the measure of benefit that emerges from the farm-budget studies of analysts in this field. However, if the price fall is sizeable, consumer valuation of the extra supplies exceeds the farmers' receipts. For the intra-marginal units of the *extra* supplies, consumer's willingness-to-pay exceeds the new market price, and so this *consumer surplus on the extra output* would be left out of benefit measures which related to farmers' profitability. Clearly, the significance of this omission depends on the size of the price change. The same point applies to the public agency when its outputs are marketable, as in the case of electricity supply. This we recognized clearly in the previous two chapters by specifying that, for an indivisible increase in capacity, the benefit of extra output is approximated by $\frac{1}{2}(P_1+P_2)$, where P_1 and P_2 were the old and new prices respectively. The same point also applies, as we saw in the previous section, to generated traffic in the case of road investment and to the additional corn quantities in the case of Griliches' new seed varieties.

There are three points to bear in mind in all these cases. Firstly, the effects of public projects cannot always or even usually, be characterized as causing extra supplies of produce downstream.[35] Projects like those involving research and development into new farming techniques, new roads, the

[35] This context dominates S. A. Marglin's discussion of these sorts of problems, since he is primarily concerned with water-resource projects which boost farm outputs. See 'Objectives of Water-Resource Development: A General Statement' *op. cit.*, especially pp. 22–28 and 55–58.

Channel Tunnel, and many others, not only increase total supplies of various goods and service but have, as perhaps their main effect, the result of reducing costs. This is why their benefits take the form of consumer valuation of extra supplies net of input costs + the increase in consumer surplus from the reduced price of existing supplies, this latter representing a reduction in the costs of existing road users, potato growers, wheat farmers, etc. When projects are characterized as simply involving extra supplies, then, when these supplies are large, market prices fall; in which case, since the price of existing supplies will also fall, why is this not included as a benefit? The answer lies in the *possibility* of increasing supplies when no significant *cost changes* have occurred. This must mean that, initially, for some factors of production, earnings included some rental payments. Thus, some farmers may have been earning excess profits because limited water facilities kept down supplies; or, alternatively, land-owners earned sizeable rents.[36] On the advent of extra farm produce, these rental payments would fall. On the basis that the efficiency criterion is concerned with the maximization of benefit minus cost, that is, the sum of consumer and producer surplus, then the price fall induces an increase in consumer surplus just offset by the fall in producer surplus. A second point, worth bearing in mind, is that many changes in private industries which are fairly competitive could still involve sizeable real price changes; if private projects are evaluated on profitability considerations, then their economic worth—using the 'efficiency' criterion—is understated. In other words, how do we reconcile the recommendation that public agencies should make allowances for consumer surplus when ICI, English Electric, etc., do not (understandably) take such things into account? One could get out of this difficulty only by arguing that most large changes take place in the public sector, but one would be hard pushed to support the argument. The third and final point is that when public projects do cause such shifts in market prices, the whole basis of surplus analysis becomes shaky in any case, (cf. section 3.5). If consumers purchase more than one of the goods whose prices are changing, then one can no longer accurately infer willingness-to-pay from market price information. Thus, if the Channel Tunnel is expected to have a significant effect on final good prices, its evaluation by surplus analysis becomes rather dubious. When the whole structure of relative prices is affected, traditional cost-benefit analysis becomes inappropriate—though there may well be nothing else to use!

Secondary benefits

A particularly troublesome problem, in evaluating public projects, is the range of benefits generated. It has been shown that when project outputs are producer goods, the willingness-to-pay of 'consumers' of these goods will,

[36] Cf. Marglin, *ibid.*, p. 57, footnote.

under certain circumstances, reflect final consumer valuation of the goods ultimately emerging. But are there any other benefits arising? Take the case of North Sea Gas when used as a producer good. Firms and industries using the new product may experience increases in incomes, either because of the reduced cost of fuel, or because of a general increase in activity. Similarly, manufacturers of gas appliances will have more business and, therefore, experience a rise in profits. Should not these extra incomes and profits be treated as a benefit generated by the public project in question? These so-called secondary benefits have been a source of contention in the evaluation of water-resource projects in the USA. For example, in the case of irrigation, the farm-budget studies of the Bureau of Reclamation estimate the effect of new projects on the profitability of farmers using the new water. But these are only 'direct' benefits. In addition, project analyses have included some 'indirect' benefits from the further processing of project outputs—so-called stemming benefits—and from the increased incomes of farm suppliers of fertilizers, equipment, and household goods ('induced benefits'). A 'Bureau of Reclamation Manual' in March 1952, for example, said:

> Indirect irrigation benefits are project effects which comprise the *increase* in:
>
> A. Profits of local wholesalers and retailers from handling the increase in sales of farm products consumed locally off the project without processing.
>
> B. Profits of all other enterprises between the farm and the final consumer, from handling, processing, and marketing the increase in sales of farm products locally and elsewhere.
>
> C. Profits of all enterprises from supplying goods and services for the increase in farm purchases for family living and production expenses.
>
> D. Land value of local residential property.[37]

To give a final and oft-quoted example, if a new road stimulates the construction of new garages nearby, should their profits be included as a benefit of the road?

The problem of secondary benefits is one of specifying what items to include in the basic maximand of eq. (9.1). So far we have concentrated on benefits and costs 'near' to the project. Suppose these are re-defined as TC*p* and TB*p*, respectively, the latter being in the irrigation example, the increased profits of farmers 'consuming' project outputs. What is now being mooted is that there are certain other benefits at the secondary stage, say TB*s*, so that the basic maximand becomes:

$$TBp - TCp + TBs \tag{9.5}$$

By formulating the issue in this way, the character of secondary benefits is revealed since two questions immediately arise:

[37] Paragraph 2.2.4, quoted in McKean, *op. cit.*, p. 155.

(a) Are there no secondary costs to set against the secondary benefits? This is the key point made by economists commenting on procedures in the analysis of US water-resource projects.[38] Thus, it may well be that the processers of the farmers' outputs—millers and bakers, for example—increase their activity and, therefore, their profits, but *has not the capital so attracted any opportunity cost*? The point applies to all factors of production. The public project attracts more factors to both 'stemming' activities and to 'induced' activities. But, unless these resources have no alternative use value elsewhere, the incomes so generated cannot be taken as an additional net benefit of the project. If the opportunity cost of the factors in question are denoted by TC*s*, the maximand becomes:

$$\mathrm{TB}p-\mathrm{TC}p+\mathrm{TB}s-\mathrm{TC}s \qquad (9.6)$$

In the case of garage construction stimulated by a new road, the issue is whether the capital so attracted could be put to some profitable use elsewhere.
(b) Are the secondary benefits completely offset by secondary costs? If they are, then secondary effects can be completely ignored. Of course, some small margin must exist to induce the factors to move, but one normally ignores this type of change. In general, most writers have made the point that, if the economy is fully employed, then extra resources in the sector in question can only be obtained by attracting them from other occupations, in which case they will have an alternative use value which, with full employment, will not fall far short of their value in their new locale. Resources for the new garage, therefore, do not necessarily come from old garages located on routes now only lightly used. It is better to think of resources moving out of the latter into a general pool, and from this pool come new resources. Even if there were a direct switch and even if the change in profitability were large, this does not mean that there is a surplus of benefit over cost, for one has to compare profitability in the new garage with profitability *in the next best locale*, which in the new situation would certainly not be the old garage site.[39] As a theoretical point, it is probably safer to say that the significance

[38] Good discussions of the secondary benefits problem can be found in J. Margolis' article 'Secondary Benefits, External Economies and the Justification of Public Investment', *R Econ. Stat.*, August 1957, reproduced in *Readings in Welfare Economics*, *op. cit.*, and in chapter 9 of McKean, *op. cit.*

[39] The characterization of this sort of example—by a number of writers—as a pecuniary externality or spillover does not seem particularly useful. In fact, the concept of a pecuniary externality is itself unhelpful and probably not necessary (cf. chapter 3 p. 55). Prest and Turvey characterize the garage example in this way, and comment that in the case where one garage closes and another opens, any

> '... net difference in profitability and any net rise in rents and land values is simply a reflection of the benefits of more journeys being undertaken, etc., than before, and it would be double counting if these were included too.' (*op. cit.*, p. 688)

The allusion to double-counting is misleading since it really only explains how, in general, one evaluates the benefit of a producer good (cf. our previous sub-section). The real question is whether the next best opportunity to investing in the new garage offers a significantly lower

of secondary effects depends not on the level of employment but more on the relationship between prices and marginal costs. If in all sectors price equals marginal cost, then the value of factors in any one use approximates their next best value elsewhere. It is clearly possible to construct a model of an economic system where unemployment exists, in the sense that some factor rewards are very low; but then no secondary effects need be taken into account as long as these rewards are reflecting low marginal products. In the Keynesian sense, we think of unemployment more as a situation where existing rewards for factors in employment exceed the factor's marginal product—because of market imperfections, minimum wages, etc.—with some resources left idle, and it is in this sense that writers have seen unemployment as leading to secondary effects. Posing the problem in terms of prices and marginal costs does raise another issue. If the economy is only moving towards equilibrium, prices can exceed marginal costs. Put another way, when resources do shift, these are not 'marginal' changes, i.e., not near the margin of profitability; intra-marginal changes may be involved. After all, if the surplus of TB*p* over TC*p* is sizeable, is not the project itself an intra-marginal opportunity? When public projects involve fairly radical departures from past practices, there seems to be a case for bearing this point in mind.[40] One final point must be made on secondary effects. If resources are being relocated from the prosperous Midlands to development areas like Northern Ireland, then the 'efficiency' criterion takes cognisance only of any *difference* in the 'benefit' of these resources in the two regions. But, clearly, if we are interested in either altering the distribution of income or promoting the development of a region—and the latter concept is not easily amenable to the language of static welfare economics—then the gross size of benefits is of additional interest. We return to these issues in the next chapter.

Market imperfections and shadow prices

Throughout this section, numerous hints have been given of the importance

---

return. If such alternative returns are low, then there is a real net secondary benefit generated by the road construction.

'We are concerned ... [they continue later on the same page] ... with the value of the increment of output arising from a given investment and not with the increment *in* value of existing assets.'

Suppose that the new road is aesthetically pleasing (displeasing) to nearby residents; this would be a real externality as defined in chapter 5 (or a 'technological' externality in the terminology of many writers), and the increased (decreased) market value of the residents' houses would represent the present discounted value of the flow of extra real benefits (costs) so created. Presumably this *should* be added to the other 'efficiency' benefits of the road.

[40] It is not, moreover, a clear-cut theoretical point. If there is a surplus of secondary benefit over secondary cost, why is this not expropriable by the farmer in the example of irrigation water which is not priced, or by the Gas Council in the case where the outputs of the public project are priced? Similarly, in the case of unemployment, why cannot the increase in incomes and any other multiplier effects be expropriated by the initiator of these effects?

of a correspondence between prices and marginal costs. It is, time, now, to face up to this matter squarely. Discrepancies between prices and marginal costs can occur for a number of reasons, and here we consider those occurring in private markets, through both imperfections in the degree of competition and government imposed 'distortions' such as taxes and subsidies.[41] To the extent that these are relatively permanent features of the economy, we are thrust into the difficulties of second-best problems. As we suggested in chapter 4, where a general approach to these sort of problems was considered, to get a precisely correct solution in any particular case is practically impossible because of the widespread nature of such market imperfections. The approach of sub-optimizing within broad sectors was suggested as one approach. In the field of cost-benefit analysis, something like this is often attempted by a concentration on the more immediate and tractable issues. This certainly seems to be an area where some empirical estimates of the general 'inadequacies' of conventional methods of correction for taxes, for example, would be most useful.

The main issue in question is that, if the market price of an input or output diverges from its marginal cost because it is subject to a tax or a subsidy, or because it is produced by an industry with monopolistic elements, then one is no longer certain that the market price in question carries the same interpretation that it has in resource allocation models, where these imperfections are absent. Whereas in the model of chapter 3 such prices reflected the underlying real production transformation rates and subjective substitution ratios, there is no guarantee of this when markets are imperfect. And, of course, we cannot concern ourselves simply with project inputs and outputs since there may be imperfections upstream and downstream—and side-stream!—relevant to the public project. Thus, if some of the industrial users of North Sea Gas are in semi-monopolistic positions, then their demand price for natural gas does not carry the same information about final consumer demand as it did, before, in our discussion of producer goods. Demand prices facing the public agency do not reflect the ultimate consumer benefit net only of opportunity costs at each stage. The same point applies when no prices are charged for the outputs of public projects. In general, the suggestion in these sort of situations is to calculate the benefits of such projects as the actual (or imputed in the case of water-resource projects, for example) demand price *plus* any excess profits of firms and industries downstream from the project.[42]

However, even if one has been able to identify where the distortions arise

[41] Externalities, of course, are another source but we explained most of these problems in chapter 5, though some of the general points made here are applicable to this kind of market imperfection. Note also that quota restrictions and similar government controls also mean the value of additional outputs has to be carefully considered in these circumstances. (Cf. discussion of the Heath and Grossfield Study of potato harvesters in section 9.3.)

[42] See for example Marglin, 'Objectives of Water-Resource Development: A General Statement', p. 49, *op. cit.*

and one has some rough estimates of these distortions, it is not always clear how allowances should be made. For example, in UK road investment evaluations, it has now become accepted practice to estimate benefits, as we have already seen, by reference to the journey and accident cost savings occasioned by road improvements, and to exclude from such journey costs the petrol tax that forms part of a vehicle-owners' operating costs. The exclusion of petrol tax from estimates of journey costs is sometimes justified on the grounds that the tax is a pure 'transfer' item.[43] The argument behind this is that the value of resources used in making car journeys—looking at the fuel item only—is equal to the price of petrol net of tax since such a figure represents the costs of producing petrol, that is the prices of the inputs used in producing petrol (or rather, refining, in the UK environment). To the extent that these input prices reflect their opportunity cost, then the concern is with measuring the value of these inputs when not used for petrol production. Similarly, when new roads save on the capital part of operating costs by reducing, for example, the number of lorries needed to carry out a given number of journeys per annum, then the appropriate cost concept here is the lorry purchase price (or replacement price) net of purchase tax, since the aim is to get a measure of the alternative use value of inputs at present employed in the lorry-producing industry. As a final example, consider the agricultural labour-savings resulting from the introduction of new corn varieties and new potato harvesters, in our examples in section 9.3 of research and development work. If employers of this labour were subject to a payroll levy like the Selective Employment Tax, what are the costs that are saved? Following the previous argument, the costs saved would not include SET—even though this *is* saved by the employer—on the grounds that only the wage-rate reflects the alternative use value of labour, granted, that is, that market forces do play some part in the determination of such wages.

On the other hand, one might argue in a different way. In assessing the benefits of, say, new roads, one is interested, to start with, in discovering the valuation that road users attach to making existing journeys. Since petrol tax is unit related to the number of journeys, then the 'marginal' journey or the marginal unit of traffic will be characterized by the equality of marginal benefit (from the journey) and marginal journey cost *where this includes petrol tax*. The point can be easily illustrated if the reader will turn back to Fig. 9.1. The equilibrium points B and F associated with the old and new routes, respectively, are determined by the relationship between what the road-user is prepared to pay—as indicated by the demand curve—and what he has to pay indicated by the C and C^1 lines. What the road user has to pay will include petrol tax and, therefore, his saving as a result of the new road includes petrol tax saving. In other words, if the concern is with the actual

[43] Cf. '. . . the exclusion of savings in fuel tax, is, however, essential since such taxes must be levied in any case and their saving represents no net benefit to the community.'
Coburn and others, p. 43, *op. cit.*

benefit accruing to the road user, then the tax has to be included. Since, moreover, the alleged aim of road investment analyses is often to calculate 'benefits'—that is, estimates of willingness-to-pay—then it would appear to be incorrect to exclude petrol tax or purchase tax from journey cost saving. Another example arises in the way that the US Army Corps of Engineers has calculated the benefits of navigational improvements to inland waterways, by comparing the cost to transporters of using the improved waterways with the alternative of rail prices. Eckstein,[44] amongst others, has criticized this procedure on the grounds that rail fares on particular routes are unrelated to marginal costs; but if it is benefits to transporters that matter, then the engineers' method is not necessarily wrong. Similarly, savings in SET would be included in estimates of the labour-saving benefits to farmers of new seed varieties and new harvesters. In all these cases, the argument has concentrated on the inputs used by the farmer, road haulage firms, etc. The point can be made more general if one looked at the outputs of these producing units. If such outputs are subject to a tax whether a tax on inputs or purchase tax on sales, and if secondly, the concern of the analysis is estimating the value of extra supplies or the loss through reduced supplies—value interpreted as consumer valuation—then the appropriate measure is the price of the product gross of tax (or subsidy for that matter) since this is equal to consumers' marginal valuation of the product.

Whether taxes and subsidies should be excluded from market prices really, therefore, depends on what question is being asked. On the one hand, one might be concerned with ascertaining the value to consumers of goods lost or increased as a result of a public project. Here, the price actually paid by the consumer is the item which approximates to consumers' (marginal) valuation, and so the tax and subsidy would not be excluded. If, however, the concern is with ascertaining the cost of these supplies in terms of the next best use value of the resources involved, then the price should be taken net of tax or subsidy.[45] So it depends on the nature of the investigation. There is another problem with related characteristics. A public agency may purchase inputs from a particular firm and this, in practice, in some circumstances might mean a reduction in sales to other consumers, and in other circumstances there may be no such detraction. Thus, if the firm in question is a monopolist selling at a price above marginal cost, the 'real' value of the inputs used by the public agency would be equal to consumer valuation of the monopolist's product in the case where the public agency's purchases reduce other consumers'. That is, no allowance need be made for the excess

[44] *Op. cit.*, pp. 167–75.

[45] Notice that, taking the petrol tax example, the petrol price net of tax equals the sum of the prices of inputs in the petrol production industry. The alternative outputs—say transistor radios—which these inputs might produce might themselves be subject to purchase tax, but this does not matter since it is consumer valuation of alternative outputs that we are trying to estimate. Professor A. R. Prest has pointed out to me that the distinction between the two approaches is similar to that between valuing national product at factor cost or market prices.

of price above marginal cost. When there is no contraction of sales to other consumers, then the value of the resources used to supply the public agency is equal to their value in another firm or another industry—that is, it is equal to the monopolist's marginal cost rather than price, and so an allowance needs to be attempted in these circumstances.[46]

The point that the appropriate valuation depends on the aim of the analysis, explains some of the procedures that have been recently suggested for the public sector's use of capital funds. When investment funds are transferred from the private sector to the public by taxation or government borrowing, the question of the opportunity cost of these funds arises. The problem is that the profits that would have been earned in the private sector are subject to corporate taxes. Is the opportunity foregone equal to the private sector's net yield? Many economists have suggested that the opportunity foregone is the value of the goods and services that would otherwise have been produced, net of running costs. Since this is equal to capital's income before tax, then the conclusion is that the opportunity cost of such funds is approximated by the gross profit yield in private industry.[47] The point is general to all factors of production; the value of the goods and services that labour, employed in the public sector, would otherwise have produced is approximated by their wage-rate gross of tax and, of course, the public sector does in practice pay such a rate. The use of capital does involve many further problems, and it is to this area that we turn in the next section. One final point can be made in the context of market imperfections. Even if decision-takers were interested only in the 'efficiency' aspects of project evaluation, there are many constraints of an intangible nature which would suggest that outright use of 'rules' derived from the sort of arguments developed above might be very inappropriate. Take the case of costing supplies of project labour inputs when there is unemployment. The standard conclusion from the neo-classical resource allocation model would suggest the imputation of a very low shadow price to such labour, on the basis of its low alternative use value. One difficulty, of a theoretical nature, is that capital used by the project may itself have some such labour embodied in it so that to make an allowance for one thing and not another might distort the choice of factor-combination in the project. But a much more difficult point is that project analysts might require, from the government, information on expected (or planned!) unemployment levels over the relevant time-horizon. There seems some sense in Prest and Turvey's suggestion[48] that unemployment, certainly at the national

[46] A fuller discussion and analysis of this point can be found in R. N. McKean's 'The Use of Shadow Prices', chapter in Chase, *op. cit.*

[47] This is part of the logic of the 8 per cent interest rate which the Nationalized Industries are required to use for discounting capital projects. That is, allowances have been made for the fact that rates of return in the private sector reflect profit taxes and investment grants. See *Nationalised Industries: A Review of Economic and Financial Objectives*, Cmnd 3437, p. 5, HMSO, November 1967.

[48] *Op. cit.*, p. 695.

level, is a matter better left to central government rather than project analysts.

9.5 Public investment: effects on the private sector

Introduction

Much of public expenditure is, in fact, investment expenditure in the sense that the activities in question have effects which are spread out over time. Moreover, public investment has, over the post-war period, become an increasingly important portion of total national investment. The time-stream aspects of public investment appraisal—in particular, the search for appropriate interest rates—has generated an abundance of literature in the economic journals. Now, it is true that the choice of interest rate can, in principle, have a significant effect on choice of production technique and the value of the public sector's claim on investment funds.[49] To this extent, economists' concern with interest rates and investment criteria is well founded. However, in practice, the worthwhileness of many public sector schemes is often unaffected by the choice of a particular investment criterion. This is because the estimates of costs and particularly benefits—in even the first year of a project's operation—are themselves subject to wide margins of error. That is, the acceptability of a project is often affected just as much (if not more) by the confidence attached to the estimates of benefits and costs themselves as by, for example, the particular level of the interest rate used for weighting benefits and costs in different years. It is important to bear this in mind before despairing of the difficulties associated with discovering 'correct' investment criteria. I am suggesting, therefore, that the bulk of effort in the public expenditure field can probably be—and is increasingly, now—most usefully directed to the measurement and estimation problems mentioned in the previous part of this chapter and the preceding two chapters. Nevertheless, in situations where benefit and cost estimates are reasonably firm, and granted that techniques will improve over time, the refinements of particular investment criteria need to be closely examined.

In chapter 6 we explored the time-stream aspects of public investment, with reference primarily to the choice of interest rate. Granted, in other words, that the benefits and costs of a project have been estimated, one needs a weighting system to make items, incurred or received at different points in time, commensurable. Converting items to present value terms by use of an interest rate is, in fact, to use such a weighting system. This 'net discounted present value' (NDPV) of a project could be estimated by using a market rate of interest—such as the government bond-rate or average yields on

[49] A good example of this is the illustration by R. L. Meek of how choice of interest rate can have a significant effect on choice of nuclear or coal generating plants in electricity supply. See 'Investment Choice in the Electricity Supply Industry: Some Recent Developments', *District Bank Review*, March 1965.

equities—but we described in chapter 6 a number of reasons why this approach had little theoretical validity. In taking these factors into account, those responsible for the over-all planning of public investment may decide eventually on an interest rate which is different from the market rate. We are concerned partly, in the rest of this chapter, to see the implications of this so-called planners' or social time-preference rate for decision rules involving capital, that is, for investment criteria. In addition, of course, investment criteria are not simply concerned with interest rates. To the extent, for example, that the public sector draws on funds from the private sector we need to examine the implications of this transfer. Further, the net yields of private investment are affected by profits taxes and the way risk and uncertainty enter these decisions; again, this was considered in chapter 6, and our concern here is with the way one allows for these factors in formulating decision rules. Two further general points can be made at this stage. Firstly, the public sector draws on private sector funds by taxation or borrowing, and we shall be concerned, in parts of analysis, with the effect that this transfer has on the private sector. These funds, of course, represent the face value of the expenditure on inputs needed for those public sector activities not receiving sales revenue. To this extent, the concern is with whether the face value of these expenditures reflect the 'true' cost to the economy. Now, one aspect of this has already been dealt with in the previous part of this chapter, namely, whether the price paid for these inputs reflects the opportunity cost of these inputs—that is, their value in their next best locale. A divergence could occur because of market imperfections of one sort or another, because of externalities or indivisibilities, and so on. We are now to be concerned with those divergences that occur through the *methods of financing* the employment of these inputs—the transfer-of-funds effect rather than the transfer-of-resources effect.[50] The second point is that, since every part of the public sector is involved in investment, then the issues in question are common to the public sector as a whole. Since a large part of government revenues from taxes and borrowing are pooled, then one cannot say whether the investment funds of, say, the electricity industry or government research, 'come' from this tax or that tax. The relevance of this point is that, if it be decided to take some of these issues into account, then the appropriate source of decision-taking is not the board of a nationalized industry or a committee in the Ministry of Housing and Local Government; these are issues that have to be decided centrally by the Treasury or some such body.[51]

[50] How these two matters are jointly allowed for in costing input supplies will be discussed in the last section of this chapter.

[51] The decision about the level of interest rate to use for discounting the benefits and costs of projects in the UK Nationalized Industries was, in fact, made by the Treasury, and the arguments were presented in the Treasury White Paper, Cmnd 3437, *op. cit.*

Plan of analysis

Since the rest of this chapter involves a rather extended chain of argument, it will probably be useful to indicate here how the analysis has been arranged. Six major points can be seen, namely:

(a) The effect of public investment in displacing and generating private investment is considered in the very next sub-section.

(b) Social time preference is then introduced in section 9.6.

(c) A digression is made to explore whether some of the suggested allowances for social time-preference are really necessary.

(d) The use of shadow multipliers is then considered.

(e) Taxes and uncertainty are brought into the argument at this point.

(f) Finally, the relevance of sales revenue is considered.

A conventional investment criterion

The general context of these issues can be indicated if, first of all, the very simplest sort of environment is taken. Suppose that no projects in the public sector yield any direct sales revenue. All the benefits of these projects are in a non-cashable form—research and development, education, many water-resource projects, and roads approximate this situation. Assume, secondly, that risk, uncertainty, and corporate taxes are absent. If public expenditure is partly financed by government borrowing, then the rate of interest on such government bonds will, in this risk-free world, tend to approximate other interest rates in the capital market. Now, to start with, suppose that decision-takers in the public sector have decided that the relative weights on present and future consumption, implied by the market rate of interest, are 'right'; that is, the social time-preference rate coincides with the market rate. How then should individual public projects be evaluated, granted the primary concern with 'efficiency'? For any defined set of projects or production possibilities, we have previously thought of eq. (9.1) as summarizing the nature of the decision problem. The totals of benefits and costs in the maximand more correctly need time labels, and also need standardizing by a time-weighting system. Following the logic of the present assumed simple environment, eq. (9.1) needs to be replaced by:

$$\text{Max.} \sum_{t=0}^{t=n} [(TB)_t - (TC)_t]/(1+r)^t \qquad (9.7)$$

s.t. constraint of production function

Here, a planning horizon of n years (or whatever is deemed to be the appropriate time span) is taken; each benefit and cost is given a time label of t, and the conversion to present values is effected by the discount rate, $1/(1+r)^t$, where r is the market rate of interest. Associated with this maximand is the criterion for evaluating any changes in output supplies or any particular project. If the net social worth (in present value terms) of any one project is denoted by N, then we have[52]

$$N = \sum_{0}^{n} (B_t - C_t)/(1+r)^t \tag{9.8}$$

and the criterion would be to invest if N is positive. Equation (9.8) involves, basically, the same idea as the criterion in eq. (9.4); now each project can involve benefit increases in each year; thus B_t denotes the change in benefit in year t—the j subscripts of eq. (9.4) have now been dropped in order to avoid unnecessarily complicated formulations. Since costs can also be incurred each year, the change in costs in year t is denoted by C_t. Granted that, as assumed, the benefits are in a non-cashable form, and that all costs are financed by taxation and borrowing, what effect would the use of the proposed investment criterion have on resource allocation?

The cost items represent the face value of the expenditure on inputs, and we may assume that such outlays also indicate the alternative use value of these particular inputs. Since the public agencies have no revenue account, an alternative method of finance has to be sought. Now, if there were some slack in the economy by way of unemployed resources and spare commercial bank funds, then the government could finance these projects by borrowing from the central bank. We shall, however, ignore this possibility which means that funds will have to be obtained from the private sector either by lump-sum taxation or the floating of government bonds. In any year, t, the face value of such transfers is C_t. The problem is that such transfers imply a real income loss for the private sector;[53] against this has to be balanced the stream of benefits generated by the public investment. Economists have been concerned, therefore, with examining whether public investment criteria, such as that implied in eq. (9.8), ensure that the benefits of the public project compensate for the stream of benefits that would otherwise have accrued to the private sector in the absence of government taxation and borrowing. On the costs side, the issue is then one of ascertaining whether the face value of transferred funds indicates the 'true' opportunity cost of public investment.[54] Since it is

[52] Note that there is no constraint on the availability of funds in eq. (9.7). The use of benefit-cost ratios as an investment criterion is, therefore, irrelevant; cf. the latter part of section 9.2. Budget limitations are introduced in the next chapter. Each of the items in the production function mentioned in eq. (9.7) would have a time dimension, so that formally one might have to differentiate the maximand with respect to not simply each good typified by j, but also with respect to extra j in year 1, extra j in year 2, and so on. A rigorous derivation of these criteria is given in the appendix of the next chapter.

[53] If hoarded cash balances are used to finance the purchase of government bonds or to meet tax payments, no sacrifice of consumption or investment is involved.

[54] A pioneering article was P. O. Steiner's 'Choosing Among Alternative Public Investments in the Water-Resource Field', *op. cit.* This was stimulated by some earlier work on investment criteria by Eckstein, *op. cit.*, chapters III and IV; McKean, *op. cit.*, chapters 5 and 7; and also chapter IV of *Multi-Purpose River Development*, by J. V. Krutilla and O. Eckstein, John Hopkins, 1958; a review of this earlier work can be found in J. Margolis' 'The Economic Evaluation of Federal Water Resource Development', *AER*, March 1959. The full emphasis on opportunity costs came in a paper by S. A. Marglin elaborating on Steiner's work; see 'The Opportunity Costs of Public Investment', *QJE*, February 1963.

consumption that enters utility functions, we wish to discover the consumption benefits that would have accrued from the funds in question. Part of the tax and borrowed funds would have been devoted directly to consumption, and to this extent the opportunity cost of such funds can be taken as equal to their face value. But not all of the funds need have been devoted to consumption. Part of them may have been saved, generating investment in the private sector. Moreover, one cannot assume that only the funds used to purchase government bonds would otherwise have gone to private investment. In principle, both tax and borrowed funds could have been devoted to both consumption and investment. The real problem is: what is the opportunity cost of those funds (either tax or bonds) that would have stimulated private investment? Suppose that such investment would have generated, over the planning horizon, a stream of income which was consumed; it follows that the opportunity cost of these funds is the present value to the private investor of this consumption stream. This poses a problem, since it suggests that the funds' opportunity cost can only be ascertained by a knowledge of the effects of the foregone private investment. However, under certain circumstances, this is not necessary. If the private investment in question can be treated as being 'marginal' to the whole of the national private investment, the net present value of such investment is roughly zero. Since this means that the present value of the income generated is just equal to the initial investment then, clearly, the latter can be taken as a measure of the former. With the assumption of 'marginality', the face value of funds approximates the present value of the benefit stream that would otherwise have been generated. This certainly simplifies matters, since it means that all of the £C transferred in year t have an opportunity cost equal to their face value, whether they would otherwise have been consumed or invested. This happy result emerges as a consequence partly of the 'marginality' assumption and partly because of the absence of profits taxes, uncertainty, and the equivalence of the market interest rate with the social time-preference rate. While the latter points will be the subject of subsequent analysis, the 'marginality' assumption will be retained throughout. Its significance can be better appreciated if we look, first of all, at the benefits of public investment.

The benefit term in eq. (9.8), B_t in year t, is the concept on which much of the previous analysis of this chapter has concentrated. It is a measure of the willingness-to-pay of receivers of the outputs of public projects. In practice, part of this may be recouped as revenue to the public enterprise but, in the present context, benefits are assumed to be in a non-cashable form. So the term relates to the measures that emerge in cost-benefit analysis, of the benefits of irrigation water, roads, and so on. These are then *imputed* measures of the 'market' value of project outputs. In the same way that we inquired about the consumption streams that would have occurred in the private sector in the absence of the funds transfer, it is now relevant to inquire about the consumption stream generated by the public project. The difference between these two consumption streams is, in fact, precisely what the public project contributes to total net efficiency benefits. Since project beneficiaries do not surrender any claims on resources, then the whole of the measured benefits constitute a real income increase. If all of this *is* consumed, then benefits take on their face value. Part of the real income increase may lead to private investment. In other words, we are suggesting, for example, that a farmer's real income rises in year t because he now receives (free) irrigation water. Part of this he may take in the form of extra consumption in year t, but part also would take the form of saving and investment in year t.[55] Again, however, if the 'marginality' assumption is made, then the present value to the farmer of the consumption stream generated by his private investment will be roughly equal to the cost of the investment. The latter can be taken, therefore, as a measure of the stream of consumption benefits attributable to the private investment generated by the public project. The imputed market values emerging from conventional benefit analysis, therefore, in this case *do* indicate the stream of consumption benefits generated by the public project.[56] The more innovatory is the public project the less does 'marginality' become a realistic assumption. For example, in many underdeveloped countries, public construction of the infra-structure of the economy generates investment, which can hardly be treated as 'marginal' in the above sense of the word. In fact, the problem of 'marginality' can become contentious even in developed economies. If we are holding all public expenditure up for examination then, theoretically, this could raise the possibility of public expenditure falling to very low levels. In this light, the face cost of this large volume of taxed and borrowed funds at present transferred to the public sector could not be treated as 'marginal' to private investment; there would be a vast change in the content of private investment if public investment fell

[55] M. S. Feldstein characterizes the effects of project benefits on consumption and investment as being determined *partly* by whether the project produces final consumer goods or capital goods. It may well be—following the farming example in the text—that the farmer's investments in year t will be greater if a public water-barrage supplies him with irrigation water rather than domestic electricity; but in the latter case, the overall change in his consumption in year t (as opposed to year $t-1$) may not be equal to the value of the domestic electricity; obviously, he will consume all of this electricity, but the overall effect on his real income may be to increase his saving over what it would otherwise have been. The basic issue then is his propensity to consume out of income increases, and this is the approach implied in our analysis. See 'Net Social Benefit Calculation and the Public Investment Decision', *OEP*, p. 124, March 1964; the same viewpoint is implied in another of Feldstein's articles, 'Opportunity Cost Calculations in Cost-Benefit Analysis', *Public Finance*, No. 2, 1964.

[56] The effect of public investment in generating consumption and private investment has not received as much *explicit* attention in the literature as the opportunities foregone through that investment. Steiner, *op. cit.*, hardly discusses the matter at all. Although it is an integral part of the models in his paper 'The Opportunity Costs of Public Investment', *op. cit.*, Marglin does not analyse benefits in any depth. To find this, one must turn to his work on *Economic Factors Affecting System Design*, pp. 198–205, *op. cit.*, where more attention is given to the real income effects of project outputs. The benefit problem has received probably most explicit attention by E. J. Mishan on pp. 144–6 of his short paper 'Criteria for Public Investment: Some Simplifying Suggestions', *JPE*, April 1967; occasional allusions to the issue can also be found in his December 1967 *EJ* article on 'A Proposed Normalisation Procedure for Public Investment Criteria'.

to fairly low levels. We have to get round this one by *asserting* that, even limiting oneself to economic efficiency considerations, large parts of public expenditure *will* be justifiable. The area where the choice between public and private becomes important is not, then, sufficiently large to render the marginality assumption irrelevant. We return, in the next chapter, to a discussion of the division of the economy between private and public sectors.

The conclusion is that, in situations where the capital market is well developed, where risk and uncertainty fortunately do not exist, where only lump-sum taxes are levied, and where the government opts for the market interest rate as its normative rate, the 'conventional' investment decision rule involved in eq. (9.8) is satisfactory. The use of the criterion will guarantee that, when all projects for which N is positive have been undertaken, one extra pound or dollar raised in year t by taxation or borrowing means the foregoing of a stream of consumption whose present value is equal to one pound and the generation, by public investment of these funds, of a stream of consumption whose present value does not exceed one pound. Where public and private projects take the form of perpetual constant streams of consumption per £ invested, then this yield per £ will, in final equilibrium, be the same in both sectors. Moreover, it will be equal to the market interest rate and, therefore, to the government bond rate. For example, a private investment of £1 yielding a constant annual consumption stream of £y, into infinity, has a net present value of $(y/r)-1$ (cf. appendix to chapter 6). For 'marginal' investments, this net value is zero, and so $y/r = 1$. Thus, y, the yield per £, equals the market interest rate r.

9.6 Criteria and financing for public investment

The use of a social time preference rate

For a variety of reasons—discussed in chapter 6—governments may desire to reject the time-weighting system implied by the use of a market interest rate. Here, we assume that the government has decided on the level of its social time preference (STP) rate, and the aim of our analysis is to explore how it can be incorporated into investment criteria. At first sight, it would appear that all one has to do is substitute the STP rate for the market rate in the criterion associated with eq. (9.8). That is, with e as the STP rate, the net worth of a public project would be given by:

$$N^1 = \sum_0^n (B_t - C_t)/(1+e)^t \qquad (9.9)$$

and the criterion would be to undertake a project if N^1 is positive. However, a discrepancy between e and the market rate not only suggests that the government wishes public investment to differ in quantity and character from that emerging from the use of a market rate, but also implies that total national investment should be different. Take, for example, the case where it is felt that the market rate gives insufficient weight to the welfare of future generations so that e is less than r. To the extent that private investment opportunities are evaluated with the use of the market rate, then this investment will be sub-optimal. What can be done about this? Two broad possibilities have been canvassed. One is to alter the quantity and character of private investment by direct policy measures. Private investment might be encouraged by investment incentives or direct subsidies; or the government might directly invest in the private sector; or monetary policy might be used to drive down the market interest rate so that it approximates the STP rate.[57] There is nothing wrong with these suggestions; they are quite consistent with the policy objectives. Many economists analysing these problems have felt, however, that these means may be circumscribed by institutional restrictions. It may not be possible to use these weapons if their primary use is for other policy objectives—as certainly monetary policy is. Moreover, even if possible, they are long-term solutions. Because of this, a second suggestion has been made, namely, to use public investment to achieve the policy objectives. This approach accepts institutional forces as constraints on policy objectives, and seeks to accept and select public investment projects in a way which will effect the policy aim. As one of the chief advocates of this approach has suggested:

> This is a problem of 'second best'. The optimal solution, undertaking all public and private investment that has a positive present value at the social rate of interest, is precluded by the institutional structure and we are consequently faced with the necessity of choosing the best of inferior combinations of public and private investment. . . . Clearly the goal in planning public investment should be avoidance of displacement of 'better' opportunities in the private sector. . . .[58]

The reader can probably now appreciate the relevance of the framework discussed in the previous section. Public investment means the foregoing of the consumption stream that the transferred funds would otherwise have occasioned and the generation, through its products, of another consumption stream. We have to discover, now, the appropriate criterion for evaluating public investment which ensures that the consumption stream generated is

[57] This view is particularly associated with J. Hirschleifer, J. C. De Haven, and J. W. Milliman in chapter 6 of their book, *Water Supply: Economics, Technology, and Policy*, University of Chicago Press, 1960. To a certain extent W. J. Baumol also sees this as a possible policy measure in his paper 'On the Social Rate of Discount', *AER*, September 1968.

[58] *Economic Factors Affecting System Design*, S. A. Marglin, p. 199, *op. cit.* Notice that when the government embarks on an investment programme (or if direct incentives to private investment are given) then, in principle, the discrepancy between e and r could diminish to the extent that total national investment is increased. That is, unless the changes in public investment are treated as a marginal addition to total national investment, the level of e cannot be taken as given. The STP rate in final equilibrium, in principle, emerges as a result of confronting the government's social time preference *function*—if we can put the matter so formally—with productive investment opportunities. See Mishan, *JPE* pp. 140–1, *op. cit.*, and also M. S. Feldstein's 'The Social Time Preference Discount Rate in Cost-Benefit Analysis', *EJ*, June 1964.

'better' than the consumption stream foregone, taking into account that time-streams are evaluated with reference to the STP rate.

Looking at the costs side first, we know that these represent foregone private consumption and investment, whether the costs are financed by taxation or borrowing. The private opportunity cost of funds, that would have been used for investment, is the present value of the stream of consumption that such investment would have generated. By use of the 'marginality' assumption, this opportunity cost could be taken as equivalent to the money cost since, if the investment is marginal, the money cost will be just equal to the present value to the individual of the consumption stream. This still holds good. Where the difference occurs now is that the present *social* value of the consumption stream diverges from its present private value and, therefore, from the money cost of the investment.[59] For example, if £1 of private investment yields a constant annual stream of consumption of £y over a longish period, then its present private value is y/r if r is the market interest rate; its present social value is y/e and is, therefore, higher if, as we are assuming, the fraction e is less than r. If, then, £C of transferred funds would otherwise have been invested, then we may say that the social opportunity or shadow costs of these funds is CT; since the 'marginality' assumption implies that the money cost of the investment, C, is just equal to the private present value, Cy/r, then it follows that, in this simple example, T is equal to r/e. Those funds, which would otherwise have been consumed, may be taken as having an opportunity cost equal to their face value. The simple approach of the previous section has now to be abandoned since the money-cost item, C_t, in eq. (9.9) no longer reflects social opportunity cost. It is now necessary to ascertain what part of these funds would have been consumed and what part invested, and the latter must be imputed a value different from their face value.[60]

[59] This was a key point in the paper by Steiner and in the further elaborations by Marglin and Feldstein. However, we must note that Steiner's exposition differs from ours because he persists in using the rate of return approach; similarly, Eckstein, Baumol, and others talk of a social discount rate which combines the idea of a social interest rate and alternative yields in the private sector. Now, in some instances (cf. appendix to chapter 6), the rate of return approach and the present value approach are equivalent. In addition, we shall, in the text, allude now and again to empirical estimates of alternatives foregone in the private sector and, in these cases, rough empirical data will probably be in the form of rates of return. Subject to this, we keep to the present value approach because of the reasons summarized in chapter 6. In fact, the discussion of private sector alternatives foregone indicates clearly the point of the present value approach, since it explicitly draws attention to the stream of consumption benefits. For a good critique of the social discount *rate* approach see M. S. Feldstein's 'Opportunity Cost Calculations in Cost Benefit Analysis', *op. cit*.

[60] Notice that the social value of a private investment project is taken here as the stream of income accruing to the private investor, discounted at e. It is the discounted stream of profits—that is, the value of goods produced less running costs. Feldstein, in the three articles cited, suggests that the social 'productivity' of private investment is greater than this, to the extent that private investors ignore income payments to other factors. He is suggesting, in other words, that the value of goods should be taken gross of running costs. As we argued in section 6.4 (see the sub-section entitled 'The Social Productivity of Investment'), this is not relevant as a general rule; it holds only if the accompanying factors have no alternative use value.

A digression

However, before rushing into these complications, it is important to consider an argument—advanced most explicitly by Mishan[61]—which suggests they may be unnecessary. Basically, the argument is that there is no need to distinguish between consumption and investment since, for individuals in the private sector, the two are equivalent. Take the case where £2 of transferred funds is split equally between consumption and investment. The present social value of the £1 of private investment, is, to pursue the simple case, equal to y/e and its present private value is y/r. But when individuals are in equilibrium with respect to consumption and investment decisions, £1 has the same value in all cases. The £1 of consumption is equivalent to the individual to *y/r and, therefore, the social value of* £1 *of consumption can be taken as y/e.* On these grounds, it is unnecessary to distinguish between consumption and investment. £C has a social value of Cy/e, irrespective of the split of these funds between consumption and investment. If, further, it were true that tax funds are more likely to decrease consumption than would government borrowing,

> the social opportunity cost of one dollar ... is (y/e) ... irrespective of whether the funds are raised wholly by taxation, wholly through the bond market or by a mixture of both methods.[62]

Now, this argument is particularly attractive when it is taken in conjunction with an additional but different point. In attempting to estimate the value of displaced private investment, in practice some rough measures will probably have to be used. In particular, it may well be that empirical knowledge of the growth path of income generated by investment is so limited that significant differences between public and private investment do not appear in this respect. Certainly estimates of the effects of private investment have, in UK discussions, often taken the form of saying that pre-tax 'returns' are of the order of 15 per cent;[63] that is, each £1 of private investment yields benefits which are roughly equivalent to an annual constant consumption stream of £0·15 per £ invested. If public investment yields consumption benefits which are also constant or, more generally, grow at similar rates to private investment, then it is possible to demonstrate that STP loses its significance completely! For example, suppose a public project yields benefits over a long period of £b per annum, all of which are consumed. The money costs of the project are taken, for simplicity, as involving a base-year outlay of £C. Following the Mishan argument, this can all be treated as foregone private

[61] In his article in *JPE*, April 1967, *op. cit.*; occasional references to this viewpoint can also be found in his *EJ*, 1967 paper, *op. cit.* Baumol, *op. cit.*, takes a similar methodological view in his analysis of corporate taxes—to be discussed later. Finally, it is implied in Steiner's article, *op. cit.*, if only because he treats all alternatives to public investment as private investment.

[62] Mishan, *JPE*, p. 143, April 1967, *op. cit.*

[63] Cf. the 1961 White Paper on *The Financial and Economic Obligations of the Nationalised Industries*, Cmnd 1,337.

investment; if this would have yielded constant annual consumption benefits of y per £, then the social opportunity cost of the transferred funds is, as before, CT, where T is r/e. It follows that the net worth of the project (N_1) and the investment criterion are given by:

$$N_1 = (b/e) - CT \qquad \textit{Investment criterion} \qquad b/r > C \tag{9.10}$$

That is, since e is common to both sides of the investment criterion, it cancels out, and we are left with a conventional decision rule which involves comparing the face value of the funds with the stream of project benefits discounted at a market rate of interest. The conclusion holds if benefits vary over time, as long as the growth rate is roughly the same on both public and private investment.[64] Any interest rate would accept all those projects which are accepted using e. Their acceptability simply depends on the relative sizes of b and Cy.

There are two reasons why this conclusion is dubious. Firstly, the argument, that private consumption can be taken as equivalent to private

[64] Subject, that is, to any allowances for profits taxes, risk, uncertainty, and sales revenue. The proof is as follows. Suppose that the benefits of the public project grow at x per cent p.a. If B_1 denotes benefits in the first year then the present value of this stream, discounted at e, is:

$$\sum_0^n B_1(1+x)^t/(1+e)^t.$$

Similarly, if the base-year outlay, C, would otherwise have yielded in the private sector an initial consumption benefit of A_1, which then grew at x per cent p.a., then the social present value of this stream is:

$$\sum_0^n A_1(1+x)^t/(1+e)^t.$$

The private value is similarly defined, with r substituted for e, so that if the social opportunity cost of the transferred funds is denoted by CT then, granted the 'marginality' assumption that C is equivalent to the present private value, T is equal to:

$$\sum_0^n (1+x)^t/(1+e)^t \div \sum_0^n (1+x)^t/(1+r)^t.$$

The net worth of the project is, therefore:

$$N_{11} = \left[\sum_0^n B_1(1+x)^t/(1+e)^t\right] - CT.$$

Since the criterion is to invest if N_{11} is positive, then, cancelling out, this is equivalent to

$$\sum_0^n B_1(1+x)^t/(1+r)^t > C.$$

This conventional investment criterion emerges because, with similar growth paths, the interest rate loses all its significance. Abandoning the terminology of social opportunity costs, the net worth can simply be written as:

$$N_{11} = \left[B_1 \sum_0^n (1+x)^t/(1+e)^t\right] - \left[A_1 \sum_0^n (1+x)^t/(1+e)^t\right].$$

The criterion of investing if N_{11} is positive is equivalent to observing whether B_1 is greater than A_1. Any interest rate could be used for discounting! The use of e simply tells us the equivalent present social worth of the investment.

investment, seems inconsistent with the basic premise that the feasibility of direct policy measures is circumscribed. Consumption and investment are not adjusted in a socially optimal manner, and to treat the two as equal implies that one is indifferent between £1 drawn from consumption and £1 drawn from investment. But, if the generation of future benefits by public investment is financed more from present consumption rather than private investment, then this is a good thing from the point of view of the basic policy aim. It is like saying that one would be indifferent between 1,000 extra daily travellers on congested roads and 1,000 extra daily travellers on lightly-used railways; if the price mechanism were fully operative (congestion taxes, etc.) the mode of transport would be immaterial—at least on 'efficiency' grounds.[65] If government were able to effect direct policy measures on road-users, and *did do so*, then we might perhaps retain the indifference. Similarly, if the government could and did directly attempt to discourage present consumption by taxes or investment incentives, again one could ignore the distinction between the two. But the basic assumption of this whole approach to public investment criteria is that such policy measures are constrained,[66], and this is why public projects are to be evaluated with respect to a social opportunity rather than a money cost concept. The second point is that it would clearly be unrealistic to assume that all of the benefits of public projects can be treated as consumption. As we explained in the previous section, part of the real income increase, experienced by project beneficiaries, may be reinvested. To the extent that this also is evaluated with respect to r rather than e, then the market imputed estimates of benefits will not reflect their full social value. A shadow value has again to be given to an effect of public investment, and this time the item is that portion of benefits which will be reinvested.

Shadow multipliers

To return to the main stream of the analysis, a discrepancy between the market time-weighting system and that viewed as socially desirable by the government, implies that the investment decision rule associated with eq. (9.9) has to be altered, to allow for the fact that the market values of foregone and generated private investment do not correctly reflect the social value of such investment. The decision rule has to be such that it encourages those public investments which, through their method of financing, involve least sacrifice of private investment, and whose benefits do most to stimulate private investment.

[65] I was finally persuaded to this viewpoint after a discussion with Mr W. Peters who suggested the transport analogy.

[66] In contrast to foregone private consumption, Mishan in the two articles cited characterizes that part of public project benefits which are directly consumed, as 'constrained' consumption. It is '... consumption which is constrained to take place within the period' (*EJ*, December 1967, p. 779) and its social value is taken as equal to its face value.

For example, if the benefits of irrigation water tend to go to low-income farmers with low marginal propensities to invest and meagre investment opportunities, whereas the benefits of electric energy tend to go to industrial entrepreneurs with high marginal propensities to invest and excellent investment opportunities, electric energy will be relatively more attractive than irrigation.[67]

Let us briefly indicate how one formally allows for this, and then we can comment on its significance. Looking at the costs side of eq. (9.9), we may denote the social opportunity cost of £C of expenditure in year t as $C_t \times M_t$ where:

$$M_t = c_t + (1 - c_t)T_t \tag{9.11}$$

Here c_t represents the portion of transferred funds (via taxation or borrowing) that would otherwise have been consumed. The remaining portion, $1 - c_t$, representing investment, has a shadow value, T_t, which represents the present social value of the consumption stream that such an investment would have generated. Thus M_t represents the social opportunity cost of one pound or dollar of transferred funds. The social value of one pound of project benefits could be denoted as M_t^b and defined in a similar way, with C_t^b and T_t^b replacing the items in eq. (9.11), to indicate that in principle the propensity to consume out of benefits and the character of reinvestment opportunities afforded by the project, could differ from the propensity to consume out of taxes or loanable funds and the character of the foregone private investment. We, therefore, finish up with an expression for the net worth of a public project:

$$N^2 = \sum_0^n (B_t M_t^b - C_t M_t)/(1+e)^t \tag{9.12}$$

and the investment criterion that projects are undertaken if N^2 is positive.

There are two general points that can be made about this approach. One is that, despite the formidable statistical estimates which are necessary to calculate the value of N^2, equations (9.11) and (9.12) are, in theoretical terms, grossly simplified. True, we have allowed that the C's and T's could vary each year and that they could be different on the benefits side from the costs side. But to start with, propensities to consume usually differ over varying groups or income classes in the economy; in theory, one might allow for this by distinguishing between different groups of recipients of project benefits and groups of taxpayers. In addition, the T_t^b and T_t expressions themselves would be fairly complicated, if one allows that private investment does not simply generate a constant stream of consumption benefits as we suggested before. If part of the income generated by the initial investment is itself reinvested, then we will need to know how this propensity to reinvest differs from the other investment propensities, or how it differs among different

[67] *Economic Factors Affecting System Design*, S. A. Marglin, *op. cit.*, p. 204, footnote.

income groups; and then we could go on further by considering the reinvestment of the income generated by the reinvestment of the initial stream of income emanating from the initial investment.[68] But is this a relevant and feasible exercise for those people responsible for formulating general criteria for public investment decisions? The relevance of these sorts of models, is that they have certainly clarified some of the methodology of making allowance for social interest rates. In practice, rough estimates will have to be made. Equation (9.12) indicates that if the shadow 'multipliers' were equal and, moreover, constant each year, i.e., $M_t^b = M_t = M$, then while knowledge of the present social worth of any project still requires an estimate of M, it is basically unnecessary for making investment decisions. Since the criterion is to invest if N^2 is positive, then M cancels out to give the criterion:

$$\sum_0^n B_t/(1+e)^t > \sum_0^n C_t/(1+e)^t \qquad (9.13)$$

which, of course, is the same as the criterion associated with eq. (9.9). Granted knowledge of the level of e, eq. (9.13) seems to be a feasible decision rule for operational purposes. If, further, one accepts that the acquisition of the information necessary to use the more sophisticated eq. (9.12) is not a costless exercise, then it is my own view that one needs to focus on a key question: are there good reasons for guessing that the private investment generated by public sector investment is significantly different from the private investment foregone through the transfer of funds? If there are such reasonably based informal hunches, then one might then go ahead to track the detail down more precisely; and this, in the end, may involve nothing more than adding, say, a rough multiplier to the present value of project benefits. This seems to be the chief operational significance of the theoretical literature on the relationship between social interest rates and public investments which yield non-cashable benefits. And public officials may take an awful lot of persuading to accept even this mild suggestion.

Taxes and uncertainty

Whereas in the above analysis any taxes have been assumed to be levied on a lump-sum basis, in practice they are, of course, related to economic magnitudes like wage-income, corporate profits, sales, and so on. Our particular concern in this context of public investment criteria is not simply that the immediate sources of finance for public projects are themselves distortive—

[68] In addition, all taxes in our present model are of an assumed lump-sum nature. Since, as we shall argue in the next section, incomes generated should be taken gross of tax but reinvestment rates will relate to net of tax incomes, then more complications enter the shadow value term. Those who like the algebraic gymnastics involved in these formulations should consult Marglin's 'The Opportunity Costs of Public Investment', *op. cit.*, the 'Comment' by A. Nichols in *QJE*, August 1964, and in particular Feldstein's 'Net Social Benefit Calculations and the Public Investment Decision', *op. cit.*

as most taxes are in the 'efficiency' sense—but that, in particular, the yield to private investors will be subject to corporate profits tax. The money cost of transferred funds will, to the extent that it displaces private investment, be equal, on the 'marginality' assumption, to the present value of generated income, net of tax. But the gross income generated is the item that represents the value of goods produced, and it is this item that matters,[69] so that again we have that the private valuation of private investment falls short of its social valuation. The problem of risk and uncertainty can also be crudely conceptualized in the same way. The uncertainty and risk, attached to the realization of the benefits of public projects, can be dealt with directly in making estimates of these benefits. However, if one accepts the argument, discussed in section 6.3, that allowances for risk and uncertainty by private investors exceeds the social degree of uncertainty involved, then again the money cost of a private investment will understate its social valuation, even though the former equals the present value of the stream of 'privately expected' incomes. We shall assume that private allowances for uncertainty are made on the values of yearly benefits that a private investor expects to receive, rather than by altering the time-weighting system; it is true that, in some cases, allowances are made by adding a risk premium to the interest rate, but we shall ignore this. Note that this last point does not imply that market rates of interest do not reflect risk allowances; they might well do, as we shall see.

The proposition, now being advanced, is that the present social value of private investment differs from its present private value, not because the disposition of private individuals towards present rather than future consumption differs from the social evaluation of these items, but because the yearly benefits themselves represent a private yield different from the social yield. Take the case of profits tax as an example and, moreover, let us provisionally assume there is no divergence between the STP rate and the market rate that would emerge in a risk-free world. As a starting point, one might consider the investment criterion associated with eq. (9.8), where the money costs and market imputed benefits of a public project are converted to present value terms by the use of a market interest rate. The problem is that public projects, whose benefits are non-cashable, require financing from taxation and government borrowing. To the extent that this reduces private investment, the money cost of the funds understates the social cost, since the stream of investment income that would otherwise have emerged is subject to a profits tax. Now, at first sight, it would appear all that needs to be done is to impute a tax figure to the benefits of the public project. In this way, the public investment and the private investment that might be displaced would be evaluated

[69] Another way of looking at this is to say that the profits taxes, that would otherwise have been generated, represent part of the opportunity cost of the transferred funds, to the extent that in their absence the government will have to levy taxes elsewhere. Cf. M. S. Feldstein, *OEP*, p. 119, 1964, *op. cit.*

on a comparable basis. In fact, this only holds under fairly restricted circumstances. Suppose that the benefits of the public project are all directly consumed, and, secondly, that all transferred funds would otherwise have been invested. The funds transferred in the base year, C_0, would otherwise have generated a stream of annual benefits, A_t in year t, whose net value to private investors after tax is given by vA_t. The symbol v, therefore, indicates disposable income as a fraction of gross income. We may keep matters simple by supposing that all income generated by the initial private investment *is* consumed. We have, then, that the present social value of the investment is

$$\sum_{0}^{n} A_t/(1+r)^t,$$

and the present private value is

$$\sum_{0}^{n} vA_t/(1+r)^t,$$

which, with the marginality assumption, is equal to C_0. If the social value is represented as C_0T^*—that is, money cost times a shadow multiplier—then, clearly, in this example T^* is equal to n/v.

The same points apply to funds in other years, and in this simple example T^* may be taken as constant each year.[70] We may then write the investment criterion as:

$$\sum_{0}^{n} B_t/(1+r)^t > T^* \sum_{0}^{n} C_t/(1+r)^t \quad \text{or} \quad \sum_{0}^{n} (vB_t - C_t)/(1+r)^t > 0 \qquad (9.14)$$

One, in other words, imputes the tax rate, $(1-v)$, to project benefits so that each year the actual benefit entry is vB_t. With this modification, the conventional investment decision rule still applies, using a market rate of interest. In fact, we might have to accept that, in the rough and ready world of applied studies, we will probably have to work with data that gives investment returns in only a fairly general way; for example, that project benefits are £b per annum and each pound of private investment yields £y of gross annual income. In this case, an additional point can be seen. If we take the case where only a base-year expenditure of £C is involved, then the investment criterion is:

$$b/r > CT^* \quad \text{or} \quad b/y > C \qquad (9.15)$$

In this second version of the criterion we have implied that r/v is equal to y. Why is this? Projects in the private sector which are on the margin of profitability will be such that the net present private value is roughly zero. For such projects then, the present private value of the stream of after-tax profits per £ of initial investment—vy/r—will just be equal to 1. When the

[70] That is, in any year, t, private investment would have yielded a stream of income over n years.

capital market is in final equilibrium the market interest rate is, therefore, equal to vy, and the appropriate public investment criterion is equivalent to comparing the face value of costs with the present value of the stream of project benefits discounted at a rate, y, equal to the gross annual yield obtainable from each £ of private investment. This is the conclusion that Baumol makes in his 1968 paper.[71] If after-tax 'returns' in the private sector are of the order of 8 per cent ($vy = 0{\cdot}08$), and the corporate tax rate is 0·46 per £ ($= 1—v$), then the social discount 'rate' should be 17 per cent ($y = 0{\cdot}17$). In fact, a similar point applies to risk allowances. If the net annual yield to a private investor is taken to fall short of the social yield, partly because of taxes but also because of the 'over-allowance' for risk and uncertainty, then the use of the gross yield per £ figure, in discounting the benefits of public projects, will again be the correct procedure. On this basis, Baumol would say that, if the gross yields of a private investment are 17 per cent comprising a 2 per cent risk premium, a 7 per cent tax 'yield', and an 8 per cent net yield to private investors, then the appropriate rate to use for discounting public projects is 17 per cent and not the market rate 10 per cent.

While this certainly illustrates some of the broad relationships that are involved, the particular conclusions are subject to the same criticisms that we levied at some of the simplifications proposed in the use of social interest rates. First of all, one cannot realistically assume that public projects do not themselves stimulate private investment. In this case, the character of such generated investment would have to be examined with respect to taxes and risk allowances. At one extreme, for example, if all benefits were reinvested and the same factors operated we would have to attach the shadow multiplier, T^*, to the observed benefits, £b per annum in eq. (9.15), as well as to C. This would then simplify to the criterion: invest if $b/r > C$. No imputation of tax rates to public projects is necessary. One would, for both tax and risk purposes, simply discount at the market rate. The more important point is that transferred funds cannot be all treated as though they were foregone private investment. One must, in theory, use the sort of approach involved in eq. (9.12) for N^2. That is, shadow values would have to be attached to both benefits and costs, reflecting not only the relevance of e, but also that private investment is subject to profits tax and perhaps also to over-allowances for risk. Though £1 of consumption is the same for the individual as £1 of investment, from the point of view of resource allocation the social value of the latter is underestimated because of the presence of profits taxes. So, as with the STP discussion, it is relevant to distinguish the two. One must, therefore, *disagree* with Baumol in the following passage:

> That the government's use of resources does deprive consumers of some goods is true but beside the point because consumers implicitly but very definitely indicate how they feel about this foregone consumption through

[71] *Op. cit.*

the rate of return they are currently providing to business firms. And the costs of taxation versus borrowing are considerations relevant to the choice of strategy of stabilization policy. They should not determine whether or not a specific project is undertaken.[72]

We will not go into the algebraic manipulations necessary to get expressions for shadow costs and benefits which allow for profits tax and risk as well as the STP rate. Sufficient indication has been given of how, at a fairly simple level, the items M_t^b and M_t in eq. (9.12) would have to be modified. Again, the key questions would appear to revolve around the difficulties of getting all the necessary information and whether, therefore, it is not better first of all to make some informed guesses of the extent to which public projects generate private investment of a different quantity and nature from that which it displaces. If it does, and quantitative estimates are not going to be impossibly difficult, then one can perhaps get down to more detail.

Sales revenue

Public sector activities range from defence and education where little direct sales revenue accrues, to roads where large amounts of tax revenue accrues but much of it is in fact more of a tax than a tax-price, and finally to enterprises like the UK Nationalized Industries who have not only been obliged by statute to break-even but, recently, have been advised to relate prices closely to economic costs. We have spent much of the book looking at the relevance of prices in these various situations. What we propose to do, now, is briefly indicate its relationship to the investment decision rules analysed so far in this chapter. Firstly, we may note that sales revenue in one sense serves as an alternative source of finance to government taxation and borrowing. In addition, in many cases, it constitutes an expropriation of the project's benefits into a cash inflow for the public sector. The larger is sales revenue the smaller is non-cashable benefit and the smaller, therefore, is the real income increase of project beneficiaries. At the extreme, if all the market's willingness-to-pay was recaptured as revenue, then no (or only a marginal) increase in real income would be experienced by the project's consumers. For that part of benefit not captured as revenue, clearly, the same factors apply as before, namely, that the market imputed value of standard cost/benefit studies will understate their social value to the extent that the STP rate is lower or higher than the market rate of interest, to the extent that investment income is subject to profits tax and so on. What is the social value of the revenue received by the public sector? We can, perhaps, better approach this problem by inquiring how the government will dispose of the cash balances. On the one hand, it could return the balances to the private sector, there to be spent or saved. That is, for example, it could keep taxation and borrowing

[72] *AER*, pp. 792–3, 1968, *op. cit.*

lower than they would otherwise have been. Ignoring macro-economic effects, this really means that sales revenue is a substitute source of finance to taxes and borrowing and would have its own social opportunity cost, to the extent that providers of sales revenue have different consumption propensities and tax rates from the initial providers of tax finance and the purchasers of government bonds. Granted these measures of the social opportunity cost of the public investment outlays, they would then be compared with the social value of the real income increase to project beneficiaries.[73]

However, this characterization of sales revenue does not seem to be satisfactory when taken in conjunction with the proposition, affecting previous formulations, that total national investment is non-optimal. Take the case where investment is deemed to be sub-optimal on the grounds that the STP rate is less than the market rate. To treat sales revenue in a similar way to taxation and borrowing is, in fact, to condone the private sector's allocation of income between consumption and investment. If, in other words, sales revenue is treated, in investment decisions, as a substitute for, say, taxation, then the government is exerting no influence on the rate of investment. It would be more relevant to suggest that the government should be ploughing back all of this sales revenue into further public investment; the aim, in other words, would be to pre-empt as many private sector claims on resources as possible and finance 'this year's' project costs from taxation and borrowing. The net worth of a public project might then be characterized in the following way. Let sales revenue in year t be denoted by S_t. Let the social value of each £1 of this sales revenue be denoted by M_t^p, an item which would reflect the stream of future consumption generated through reinvestment of this sales revenue. We may retain the notation of M_t^b and M_t for the shadow values of costs and non-cashable benefits, but in contrast to equations (9.11) and (9.12), we now reinterpret these symbols to cover allowances for profits taxes, and risk, as well as the STP rate. The net worth of a public project may then be defined as:

$$N^3 = \sum_0^n (S_t M_t^p + B_t^s M_t^b - C_t M_t)/(1+e)^t \tag{9.16}$$

The multiplier, M_t^b, is therefore applied to benefits not matched by sales revenue $-B_t^s$. In the case where prices are closely related to unit sales, then the concept in question is the consumer surplus enjoyed by project beneficiaries.

9.7 Summary of time-stream issues

(a) Many public sector activities involve the use of real resources which

[73] This seems basically to be Feldstein's position. See *OEP*, 1964, pp. 122–6. Our next paragraph is closer to the approaches of Marglin (in his 'Economic Factors . . .') and Mishan in the two articles cited above.

produce a stream of goods and services over time. Such streams, in addition, may themselves require the use of resources in more than one year. The basic maximand used in this chapter, therefore, involves benefits and costs with time-labels.

(b) In examining the time-stream aspect of these investment decisions it was found useful to assume, on the one hand, that a public agency's outlay on resources reflected opportunity costs in terms of their use value in other parts of the economy and, on the other hand, that all the problems of estimating the imputed market values of yearly benefits had been overcome.

(c) A conventional allowance for the time-spread of benefits and costs would be to convert all items to present values, using a market rate of interest. However, arguments have been developed in chapter 6 to suggest that public decision-takers may wish to use a different time-weighting system from that implied by current market interest rates. If such a system of weights is represented by the use of a social time preference rate, *e*, then at first sight it would appear that all one has to do is convert benefits and costs to present values using such a rate. However, this would overlook the point that the public sector's ability to purchase resources relies on a transfer of purchasing power from the private sector. In the case where public project benefits yield no sales revenue, this transfer is effected by taxation or the issue of government bonds. The face value of these funds however, may understate their true opportunity cost,[74] since any subsequent decrease in private sector investment involves a social loss different from the private loss, to the extent that private rates of discounting diverge from the social rate. By a similar token the imputed market values of public project benefits may diverge from their social value, to the extent that any investment stimulated via the real income increase of project beneficiaries is also evaluated with respect to a market rather than a social interest rate. In addition, the volume and character of private investment may diverge from its optimal level because its returns are subject to a profits tax, and also because private allowances

[74] This is probably the appropriate point to reconcile the transfer of funds problem with the transfer of resources. Suppose the public project purchases services whose money price (£10) exceeds, because of market imperfections, their economic cost (£7). In the previous part of this chapter we have argued that these services would have to be given a shadow cost equal to £7. However, since £10 has actually to be paid, this is the amount of, say, taxation that has to be raised. There is no guarantee that suppliers of tax funds would have otherwise devoted all of the £10 to consumption. To the extent that it would have been invested, another shadow value, reflecting the forces of the social interest rate and so on, would have to be attached. In terms of social accounting, one approach to this would be to treat costs as £10 × shadow multipliers for the investment problem, and then credit the benefits of the project with £3, to allow that the supplier of the inputs in question receives a consumer or producer surplus to the extent that his factor reward exceeds its economic cost. This is not to say that the issue is straightforward. To the extent that the supplier of tax funds would otherwise be ultimately putting claims on resources, then these resources could themselves be subject to other (or even the same) market imperfections. This is the real problem of second-best. When public agencies make allowances for market imperfections, etc., the concentration on the more immediate and tractable items does not, by definition, always solve the problem.

for risk and uncertainty may overstate the risk and uncertainty to the economy as a whole involved in such private investment projects.

(d) One approach to solving these problems would be the use of monetary policy, investment incentives and so on, to directly alter private investment plans. To the extent that there are limits to the effectiveness of this policy method, an alternative approach is to so select public investment projects that the generation and sacrifice of private investment, caused by such public expenditure, takes on a character which best fits in with the basic aim of altering private investment. The basic technique is to attach a shadow value to costs, representing the *social* value of the consumption stream sacrificed by the transfer of purchasing power to the state; similarly a shadow value is attached to benefits. In the case where sales revenue does accrue, these shadow values could allow for the opportunity that such revenue afforded for future public investment. These streams of shadow values are then converted to equivalent present worth terms by use of the social interest rate.[75] We saw that the shadow terms in question could become quite complicated. Under certain conditions, the two effects cancelled out and so it was suggested that, prior to undertaking the vast effort involved in calculating these shadow items, it would probably be worthwhile to consider in broad terms whether public investment was going to have a significant effect on private investment. In the end, some fairly crude allowances may have to be made.

[75] Those who prefer rates of return to present value can be accommodated if the streams of shadow benefits and costs are subjected to Mishan's 'normalization' process (*EJ*, 1967, *op. cit.*). Basically, the idea involves compounding benefits forward to some pre-determined terminal date, and discounting costs back to the base year. One then has an investment option with only two years involved. As we demonstrated in the appendix to chapter 6, in such circumstances the following two criteria are equivalent:
(a) Accept the project if the present value of the terminal stock of benefits exceeds the base-year outlay, and,
(b) Accept the project if the internal rate of return (between the terminal stock of benefits and the base-year outlay) exceeds the chosen interest rate.
In fact, the interest rate loses all its ranking significance in this context. One could use a market rate! Where the social interest rate does exert its significance is in the initial compounding and discounting which generates the base-year and terminal items.

10. Alternative objectives and additional constraints

10.1 General issues

In the search for decision rules for allocating public expenditure between uses, for determining the amount of direct revenue accruing in some sector, for the commitment of resources to public investment ventures, and so on, it is a fairly obvious point but one that bears repeating that two questions have to be answered:

(a) What is being maximized? Or, more formally, what is the objective function?

(b) What constrains the maximizing process?

To the extent that the utility functions of the constituent members of the (present and future) population contain outputs as positive items and input supplies as negative items, the maximand dominating this second part of the book has been related to consumer willingness-to-pay for outputs and to input suppliers' required rewards. On occasions certain policy constraints have been suggested—such as that considerable short-run price fluctuations should be avoided—but the only constraint examined in any depth has been that provided by the technological possibilities of physically transforming inputs and outputs. The decision rules under discussion have been derived, therefore, by constraining the maximand by the production function. If different objectives are taken, or additional constraints postulated, different rules emerge. Arguments about decision rules are, therefore, invariably arguments about (a) objectives, or (b) the relevance and existence of constraints, or (c) the logic of the maximizing process. The rejection of a particular urban renewal programme on the grounds that benefits fall short of costs, both defined in the conventional way, may be disputed if willingness-to-pay for services is thought to be an inappropriate way of defining the 'advantages' of such projects. Arguments against reducing electricity tariffs in off-peak periods because of a fear of a drop in revenue, may well be simply a reflection of a policy constraint that because of the need to avoid managerial laxness, budget deficits should be avoided. Much of the argument about short-run or long-run pricing discussed in chapter 7, concerns the logic of the optimizing process rather than objectives or constraints.

Now economists have had most to say about the 'simple' situation where 'efficiency' benefits and costs are constrained only by a production function. Looking at the constraints side of the issue, this concentration partly reflects the very real difficulties of formalizing some of these constraints. Besides the constraints provided by the production function and funds limitation, we should recognize, as Eckstein[1] has suggested, that there are administrative and legal constraints. Recognition is, however, all that can be done in some cases. Particular types of tax and licensing approaches to the problem of road congestion have been considered recently in the UK. Since the 1965 budget, the tax authorities have been very busy dealing with the new capital gains tax and the changes in corporation tax; then, shortly afterwards, came the Selective Employment Tax. We may recognize that certain types of road 'solutions' may involve a bigger administrative burden on the Inland Revenue than others, but whether this could be formulated as a constraint on the overall road maximand, so that any emerging decisions rule contains an allowance, is of course dubious to say the least. When economists make recommendations they do in practice (sometimes!) make a rough guess at the way the constraint affects the overall maximization problem. While, therefore, it is very useful to remind ourselves that formally the production function is but one of many constraints, we must also recognize that it will be a very long time, if at all, before some of the intangible factors can be fully formalized as a part of the decision process. Now, a familiar characteristic of the public sector is that any particular enterprise or agency is limited in its access to funds. This applies not only to those activities which are completely financed from taxes or government bonds, but also to revenue-generating bodies like the UK Nationalized Industries whose investment programme is directly financed from government loans and, therefore, indirectly from government borrowing or taxes. Since the access to funds can be interpreted as an additional constraint on an agency's operations, then it means for one thing that the investment decision rules discussed in the previous chapter are not necessarily appropriate even if one keeps to the 'efficiency' maximand. Since the constraint can be formalized in a reasonably tractable manner, economists have been able to analyse its implications for decision rules. Section 2 of this chapter therefore examines budget limitations in more depth.

Turning now to objectives, it is true of course that theoretical welfare economics is very much concerned with exploring the meaning of various policy objectives. In more applied work, 'efficiency' concepts of benefits and cost have however dominated the scene. Partly this has been because the 'efficiency' approach is related to the criterion of accepting a project, or a change in output etc., as long as the gainers *could* compensate the losers. As we shall see later on in this chapter, this ability to compensate losers means that *in principle at least*, devices like the tax system could be used to offset

[1] 'A Survey of the Theory of Public Expenditure Criteria', O. Eckstein, chapter in *Public Finances: Needs, Sources, and Utilisation*, Ed. J. M. Buchanan, NBER, Princeton, 1961.

any unfavourable distributive effects of investment projects, pricing policies, and so on. However, there are limits to this ability and, in any case, there are other objectives besides willingness-to-pay which are in practice pursued in the public sector. The important issue, here, is examining the contribution that economics can make when these 'unfamiliar' objectives are pursued. Historically, for example, it would appear that a guiding objective behind the operation of the UK National Health Service has been that people with similar degrees and types of sickness should have equal amounts and equal qualities of medical care, irrespective of their willingness-to-pay for them or their apparent demand for such services. A similar sort of 'minimum or equal consumption' objective can also be canvassed for, say, education for individuals up to age 18 or beyond. At the risk of stating the obvious, there is nothing in economics to suggest that these objectives are 'incorrect'. In this context when people talk of 'the economics' of this or that, they mean the comparison of benefits and costs which, in a micro-setting, are defined in relation to willingness-to-pay. One has to be careful that stated objectives do not hide more tractable issues. For example, if the health objective mentioned above is concerned only with avoiding consumption patterns which reflect income distribution, then it *may be* that alternative devices, like the tax system, could offset the distributive aspects; in which case the 'efficiency' criterion is still basically dominant. In fact, the health objective probably includes in addition a paternalistic concern over consumers' knowledge of health requirements. Public expenditure would, in general, appear to be motivated by many considerations other than 'efficiency'. The contribution of economics need not be negligible, however. With an objective which is no more sophisticated than the minimum or equal consumption approach, there is still the problem of choosing between inputs to meet this objective. What sort of teaching methods in education; how much equipment relative to lectures, where to locate hospitals, what type of surgery service? And without suggesting new objectives one can still ask why we 'need' X scientists per annum, and so on. This seems a fruitful line of inquiry for economists in such parts of the public sector but it is, at present, only in its formative stages. It stems, basically, from economists' traditional concern with a comparison of benefits and costs, where these are now defined in the wider sense of advantages and disadvantages. It means examining alternative courses of action taking into account stated objectives, or examining the logic of different objectives and constraints. What we propose to take up in section 3 of this chapter, however, is the somewhat more ambitious task of incorporating income distribution objectives into expenditure plans and expenditure criteria. On the one hand, it is an issue which has long been recognized by economists as being closely linked with—if not indiscernible from—'efficiency objectives' and, secondly, though the conclusions of our analysis will be pitifully modest, it is an issue which is more tractable than some of the other social objectives that influence public expenditure.

10.2 Budget allocation

Meaning of funds limitations

A characteristic of the expenditure criteria, discussed in the previous chapters, is that if all parts of the public sector used such criteria then the marginal social value of £1 would be the same in each part. On the margin, £1 of (present value) expenditure this year would produce the same (present value of) benefits whether used in hospitals, technical colleges, or crime prevention. Value and benefit have been interpreted as willingness-to-pay, but the same general significance of the expenditure criteria would hold if different objectives were the case and different interpretations given to 'value'. In addition, the value of this marginal £1 would also be the same if left in the private sector, provided that public expenditure criteria attaches to transferred funds, the sort of shadow multipliers discussed in chapter 9. When the availability of funds to particular government departments, agencies, or enterprises is limited, clearly the aim will still be to achieve this equivalence of 'returns' to various sectors, and it is the search for decision rules which will guarantee this, which forms the subject matter of this section.

Notice to start with that even in the analysis of the previous chapters some form of funds restriction applied. To talk of 'the public sector' implies some division of function and funds in the economy. The size of the public sector is a type of constraint which, in one sense, is easy to handle analytically. For it is probably not too wide of the mark to suggest that the division of the economy between private and public sectors has been affected by the historical development of the country, is affected by macro-economic, purely political, and other non-tractable considerations, and is little affected by any *systematic* analysis of advantages and disadvantages.[2] We may, then, realistically treat the split as arbitrary; more precisely, that the operating scope of public agencies and the annual volume of funds raised by taxation and/or borrowing is outside the purview of our analysis. If this constraint on the size of available funds existed in the context of our analysis of public investment, why did this

[2] In the models of Steiner and Marglin, both relating to the US water-resource development sector, the ranking devices for sector projects incorporate an allowance for the economic worth of alternatives in a 'pool' of projects in other parts of the public sector. This would be unnecessary if there were no restrictions on the size of the public sector. In this context the procedure of the two writers is rather curious. They are developing investment criteria for one sector, but assume that such criteria will not be developed or will not be used in other sectors; this is why the 'pool' becomes relevant. However, their analysis presumes knowledge of returns in other sectors and, in any case, if 'efficiency' is not the chief objective in other sectors then the efficiency return in these sectors is not the correct measure of the 'loss' if their investment programme is cut down. See P. O. Steiner's 'sector 3' in his paper 'Choosing Among Alternative Public Investments in the Water-Resource Field', *AER*, December 1959. S. A. Marglin's discussion of this point appears briefly on p. 204 of his 'Economic Factors Affecting System Design', chapter 4 of *Design of Water-Resource Systems*, A. Maass and others, Harvard University Press, 1962 (and MacMillan, 1967), and is, in fact, quite separate from his discussion of budgetary constraints.

not affect the criteria developed there? Basically, two factors were at work. On the one hand, our so-called 'marginality' assumption—that projects in the private sector foregone and generated as a result of the public investment programme had a present private value of benefits no greater than their cost—guaranteed that the private value of displaced private investment, for example, was indicated by the face value of the funds transferred. Granted that allowances were made in the shadow multipliers for problems like social time preference and corporate taxes, then, to undertake public projects as long as benefit exceeded costs would ensure the equality of marginal returns in both sectors. The second factor, which was more implicit than explicit, was that the government budget was big enough to ensure that all public projects with positive net present social values would be undertaken. To raise the possibility that the budget is inadequate brings us right to the problem at hand, since if such projects cannot be undertaken then the investment criterion which *accepts* all projects whose benefits exceeds costs, must be wrong. At first sight it might appear that, even in these new circumstances, the appropriate investment criterion is fairly obvious, namely, to rank projects on the basis of their benefit/cost ratios and move down the list of all possible projects in the public sector until the budget is exhausted. Setting aside the problem of taking such an embracing view of government expenditure, we must query the cost item in the suggested ratio. Is it this year's costs, next year's, or all of them summed? Is it capital or running costs, or both? The appropriate decision rule clearly needs analysing in more detail.

Economists writing about public expenditure decisions have stressed that, not only is there a constraint on the total volume of government funds, but also funds are limited to each sector. Now, clearly, budget plans and allocations have to be made in advance. As such the Post Office or primary school education do have a funds 'limitation'. What is at issue is the significance of this restriction. At one extreme, one might assume that the allocation of funds between different parts of the public sector is completely arbitrary. Within each sector returns to expenditure are calculable, but this has no effect on the way funds are allocated by higher-level decision-takers as between sectors. What then is the nature of the problem facing the economist concerned with the development of expenditure criteria within a particular sector? He might take the line that nothing can be done unless higher-level decision-takers alter their allocation criteria. On the other hand, he might accept the constraint and sub-optimize within each sector. That is, we take the Post Office's allocation of investment funds this year as unalterable, and then consider how best to allocate these funds between various postal services. There is, clearly, a danger in this since there could be widely disparate returns in different sectors. In the end it is probably more sensible to accept these funds constraints as a fact of life, and hope that eventually light will filter through above. But this is an extreme. In practice, the overall allocation of the government budget between sectors is not arbitrary. On the one hand, there is some rough approximation to equalizing returns, but one would be hard put to see this clearly for the important reason that these 'returns' reflect a very complex set of objectives. If the government decides to spend more on roads next year in Scotland because of electioneering considerations or because of regional policy, this is certainly not arbitrary though the objectives in question are obviously difficult to quantify. The safest conclusion is that any actual annual allocation of funds is determined by a mixture of political factors, aggregate, and regional policy aims, some 'non-efficiency' considerations, some 'efficiency' considerations, plus some rules of thumbs like 'add 2 per cent to last year's figures'. Now, the significance of all this is that, if we develop investment criteria for any particular sector based on certain manageable and measurable objectives, we must not be surprised if the allocation of funds by higher-level decision-takers does yield disparate returns in different sectors, where these 'returns' are defined in relation to the manageable and measurable objectives. This is quite consistent with a rough equality of 'returns', from the point of view of the higher-level decision-takers' objectives. On the other hand, of course, it seems realistic to assume that additional precision for certain objectives and decision rules is something that would be welcomed at higher levels, and this provides the justification for our analysis. What we propose to do is to consider one particular sector whose access to funds is restricted. For illustrative purposes the efficiency objective is taken and we then consider appropriate decision rules in this context. Later on, the wider implications for overall allocation of the government budget is re-considered.

The general tenor of our approach has been one of viewing a funds limitation as a constraint on the overall maximization process, and this is the approach which will be analysed in more detail. Historically, however, the derivation of, for example, investment criteria has been confused by losing sight of the basic maximand. One can see intuitively that, if funds are restricted to a particular sector, then the use of a normal (social) interest rate and the face value of funds will be inadequate in determining the worthwhileness of particular projects, for such methods are derived from a setting where funds are not restricted. A common suggestion has been to raise the required 'rate of return' in this sector and this, it is said, could be done by raising the interest rate used for discounting. One of the more sophisticated versions of this approach was advanced in 1958 by R. N. McKean.[3] Given a range of possible projects, one initially calculates the internal rate of return on each, and then makes a provisional list of projects to be included in the budget by ranking projects on the basis of these rates of return. The return on that project which just gets into the programme is the sector marginal rate of return. McKean recognizes that such a ranking may differ from present value methods, and so he then compiles a new list of projects using the rate of return on the initially selected 'marginal project' for discounting the time-stream of

[3] *Efficiency in Government Through Systems Analysis*, Wiley & Sons, chapters 5 and 7.

benefits and costs of each project. Should the 'marginal' project on the new list be different from that on the old, further iterative runs are conducted to get a stable list. In principle, the sector marginal rate of return could then be used for comparing returns in different parts of the overall public investment programme. There are two misconceptions in this. One is to use internal rates of return at all. They are misleading, as we suggested in chapter 6.[4] Secondly, the idea that funds rationing necessitates a change in the interest rate is also wrong, as we shall demonstrate, though it is a common misconception.

Limits to capital expenditure

The form that budget limitations take can vary considerably. Limitations on the size of a public enterprise's capital expenditure is characteristic of the UK Nationalized Industries, dependent as they are on government loans for their investment programmes. Similarly, in many of the water-resource development projects in the US, a distinction is made between federal and local expenditure. Since the latter relates primarily to running costs, limits to federal funds imply limits to project capital items. In other situations, as in education and health in the UK, there are limits to both capital and running expenses. Further, in some circumstances sales revenue accrues; to the extent that this is treated as enterprise revenue (and it is reinvested) rather than central government revenue, the funds constraint is applicable only to the non-reimbursable portion of costs. Finally, of course, the time span of the funds limitation will vary in different cases. We cannot cover all contingencies in our analysis which, therefore, will be purely illustrative, though we shall indicate that most forms of actual budget constraints make the derivation of appropriate decision rules a formidable problem.

The nature of the effect of budget constraints can be best indicated in the context of some fairly simple types of constraint on capital expenditure. To start with, let us re-consider the formulations of the decision problem presented in section 9.5. Broadly, the problem was presented as one of maximizing total benefit less cost, subject to the constraint of a production function. The items in equations like (9.7) were designed to embrace a range of possible projects, products, inputs, and production possibilities. This basic setting will be retained, subject to two modifications. Firstly, no reference will be made to the shadow multipliers introduced as an allowance for the effects on the private sector of social interest rates, corporate taxes, and so on, though we shall continue to convert public sector benefits and costs to present value terms by the use of the social interest rate, *e*. The relevance of these shadow multipliers is largely a separate issue to that of budget constraints, though the relationship between the two will be briefly explored later on. Secondly, a distinction will be made between operating (or running)

[4] See the introductory part of section 3.

costs and capital outlays, since this distinction is relevant for certain types of funds constraint. In the spirit of the discussion in the previous chapter the overall sector decision problem, in the absence of a funds constraint, is given by:

$$\text{Max.} \sum_{t=0}^{t=n} [(TB)_t - /(TO)_t - (TK)_t]/(1+e)^t \qquad (10.1)$$

s.t. constraint of production function

Over the horizon of n years there is an expression for total benefits which will be functionally related to the various products and services relevant to this sector. That is, there will be an equation for $(TB)_t$ such as eq. (9.2) in the previous chapter, except that now each item will have a time label. Similarly operating costs, (TO), and capital costs, (TK), will be functionally related to the quantities of operating and capital inputs respectively. The technological relationship between all these products, services, and inputs will be given by the production function. Projects and activities involving extra inputs and outputs will be warranted if the extra benefit exceeds the extra cost. Equilibrium will, following the logic of the previous chapter, be characterized by the equality of extra benefit and extra cost. Putting it another way, and allowing for the time-stream effects, the net present social value of marginal supplies and marginal projects will be zero. There are two aspects of this on which it is useful to focus. Firstly, in principle, it may be possible to increase supplies in any one year by incurring either operating costs *or* capital costs, in that year or previous years. Near equilibrium the marginal benefit from doing this will just be equal to the marginal costs in question. As in the previous chapter, let the extra benefit from increasing the output of some product or service in year t be denoted by B_t. Similarly let the change in costs in year t, as a result of increasing this output, be denoted as O_t when operating costs are involved, and K_t when capital costs are involved. Marginal supplies are, therefore, characterized by:

$$B_3/(1+e)^3 = O_2/(1+e)^2 \qquad 2, 3 = 0\ldots t\ldots n \qquad (10.2)$$

$$B_3/(1+e)^3 = K_2/(1+e)^2 \qquad 2, 3 = 0\ldots t\ldots n \qquad (10.3)$$

Taken together the two expressions indicate that, when variations of this sort are possible, the cost of achieving some particular objective (extra benefit in year t) should be the same for the different methods available. A second feature of equilibrium arises if we look at the conventional characteristic of investment projects, namely, that a stream of benefits over time is produced by occasioning capital and operating costs in a number of years. To distinguish this sort of project from the possibilities implied in (10.2) and (10.3), let us denote the extra benefit, extra running cost, and extra capital cost in year t as ΔB_t, ΔO_t, and ΔK_t, respectively. Such projects are to be undertaken if their net present social value is positive, that is,

$$\sum_{t=0}^{t=n} (\Delta B_t - \Delta O_t - \Delta K_t)/(1+e)^t > 0 \qquad (10.4)$$

For marginal projects the ratio of the present value of benefits, net of operating costs, to (the present value of) capital costs is unity.

We are now in a position to examine how funds limitations affect these decision rules and, to start with, we may suppose the enterprises's capital expenditure is limited. In particular, consider the somewhat unrealistic situation where all activities and projects within this sector involve capital outlays in only the base year of the planning period. Clearly, this would mean that in the absence of a funds constraint the capital entries in the above expressions would be replaced by $(TK)_0$, K_0, and ΔK_0. If capital expenditure is precluded from exceeding a certain fixed sum, then we have effectively an additional constraint on the maximization process. Formally, this could be written as:[5]

$$(TK)_0 \leq (\overline{TK})_0 \qquad (10.5)$$

where $(\overline{TK})_0$ is the assumed fixed volume of base-year funds available for capital expenditure. The key point of such a constraint is that *the face cost of capital outlays for any particular project understates the real—i.e., opportunity—cost to the enterprise of committing these funds to this purpose.* The face cost, in the absence of constraints, indicates the value of using these funds elsewhere—that is, in other projects in this sector, in other parts of the public sector, or more generally in the private sector. In these other sectors all projects whose benefits exceed the face cost will be undertaken; as long then as *this* project's benefits exceed its face costs no comparison with other projects is necessary. If funds are restricted for the public enterprise in question, then there is no guarantee that all its other projects showing an excess of benefit over cost, will be undertaken. It, therefore, becomes necessary to ensure that if this project is selected, it does not preclude undertaking other projects with a greater value. Capital outlays, therefore, have an opportunity or *shadow cost* greater than their face cost. We may analyse this in two stages. Firstly, let the shadow cost of each £1 of capital outlay for particular supplies or projects within this sector be denoted by $1+\phi$. After briefly considering the logic of this for decision rules, we may then move to the crucial question

[5] Notice that the equation says that actual capital outlays must be no greater than the fixed amount. If all activities involved only small capital outlays, then we could be sure that the budget would be precisely exhausted. In that case we could write eq. (10.5) as an equality; that is, actual outlays must equal the prescribed budget. This latter situation is the one common to marginal economics, and is used in the appendix. Where projects differ in size and some are quite large, then the assumptions of marginal analysis are no longer applicable. There may not be enough small projects to fully exhaust the budget. In addition, when a small project, x, has a net present value per £ of capital outlay greater than large project, y, it may be necessary to include y in the budget and leave out x. That is, y has to be compared with x plus a number of other projects whose total capital outlay is equivalent to that of y. These sorts of problems are the ones dealt with by linear programming techniques.

of how the value of ϕ is to be discovered. Clearly, the benefit from extra supplies of goods and services has to be compared, not with the face cost of capital outlays but with their shadow cost and so, while eq. (10.2) is unaffected, equations (10.3) and (10.4) will be replaced by:

$$B_t/(1+e)^t = K_0(1+\phi) \qquad t = 0 \ldots\ldots n \qquad (10.3a)$$

$$\sum_0^n [(\Delta B_t - \Delta O_t)/(1+e)^t] - \Delta K_0(1+\phi) > 0 \qquad (10.4a)$$

As far as the separate use of operating and capital inputs is concerned, since the opportunity costs of the former are unchanged, then there will be inducements for planners to rely as much as possible on operating costs as a substitute for capital expenditure[6]—fewer new roads, but increased volumes of maintenance costs. For projects involving the joint use of operating and capital costs, the present value of benefits net of operating costs has to exceed the base-year capital outlays by an amount which reflects returns in other parts of the enterprise.

The shadow cost of funds

How is the value of ϕ to be determined? Formally, the matter is straightforward. If the enterprise could be viewed as considering all its potential activities simultaneously, then it would attempt to solve an overall problem like eq. (10.1), namely to maximize total benefits less costs subject to the production function. Except that now there is, in addition to the production function, a constraint on the size of possible capital outlays. Now, in such maximization problems mathematically we use a symbol to constrain the production function, and another symbol would then be necessary to constrain the amount of capital expenditure. If λ and ϕ, respectively, are used for these purposes, then the overall maximand in eq. (10.1) becomes

$$\begin{aligned} &\sum_0^n [(TB)_t - (TO)_t]/(1+e)^t \\ &-(TK)_0 \\ &-\lambda(\text{Production Functions}) \\ &-\phi[(TK)_0 - (\overline{TK})_0] \qquad (10.1a) \end{aligned}$$

The last part of this expression introduces the constraint that base-year capital expenditure should not exceed the given amount $(\overline{TK})_0$. Now, it can be demonstrated that the solution to this problem involves precisely the decision rules associated with eq. (10.3a) and eq. (10.4a). A proof of this is relegated to the appendix to this chapter, partly because it is a rather cumbersome process, but more importantly because the general reader

[6] Cf. Marglin's formulations in *Economic Factors Affecting System Design*, pp. 164–70, *op. cit.*

should not need this to appreciate what is the key point, that capital outlays involve an opportunity cost greater than their face cost. Moreover, it is unrealistic to assume, at least with present knowledge, that a public enterprise could conduct such an exercise. The relevance of the formulation of the maximization problem is to give a guide to rough ways of approximating the solution. Within any part of the public sector there will be a large number of possible projects, and analyses will be proceeding in numerous places. The beauty of the decision rules, developed in the absence of funds constraint, is that they are conducive to a considerable amount of decentralized decision-taking. Project analysts need compare benefits with simply the face value of expenditure.[7] When funds are constrainted, writers like Marglin and Feldstein[8] have suggested the following sort of approach. Projects which just get into the budget are 'marginal' projects and, for these, benefits net of operating costs are just equal to the shadow cost of capital. Equations like (10.4a) will be equalities rather than inequalities. If the net present value of such a project, *including only the face cost of capital outlays*, is denoted by N_m, and if these face capital costs are denoted by ΔK_{0m}, then, for such a project:

$$N_m/\Delta K_{0m} = \phi \qquad (10.6)$$

Thus, ϕ is the net *face* present value per £ of capital cost on marginal projects. It represents the cost of the funds constraint,[9] since projects which are just excluded from the budget will also have a net present value per £ of capital outlay roughly equal to the left-hand side of eq. (10.6), and this is what is foregone as a consequence of the constraint. The tighter is the budget the greater will be the value of ϕ. The central authorities in the industry might then proceed as follows. Having some idea of the worth of projects undertaken in this sector in the past, and knowing the amount of funds available in this base-year, they might make an informed guess at the value of ϕ; that, for example, the return per £ on marginal projects will be of the order of 20 per cent. Project analysts would then be instructed to evaluate projects, giving capital a provisional shadow cost of 1·2 per £. This would be the value for $1+\phi$ in equations like (10.4a). To anticipate some future problems, this might be expressed in a slightly different way. Some particular project, is to be provisionally accepted, if:

$$N > \Delta K_0 \phi \qquad (10.7)$$

[7] Bearing in mind chapter 9's treatment of social interest rates, corporate taxes, and so on, these face values would have to be adjusted for the shadow multipliers discussed there. As we stressed in that discussion, the appropriate allowance is one common to all parts of the public sector, and decisions on this will have to take place at a fairly high level; it is not a matter to be left to project analysts in individual sectors.

[8] S. A. Marglin, *op. cit.*; chapter 4, Maass; and M. S. Feldstein, 'Net Social Benefit Calculation and the Public Investment Decision', *OEP*, March 1964.

[9] Cf. the discussion in chapter 2 of Lagrangean multipliers.

where N is its net *face* present value, ΔK_0 is the base-year capital outlay, and ϕ is 0·2 in this example. Projects are sometimes mutually exclusive and care is needed in formulating the choice involved—different sizes of a water-barrage, different locations for an airport, and so on. Thinking of two projects, A and B, the criterion would be to choose A if:

$$N_A - N_B > (\Delta K_{0A} - \Delta K_{0B})\phi \tag{10.8}$$

that is, if the extra face present value of project A more than compensates for the alternatives foregone as a result of its heavier requirements on capital outlays. Now, with projects provisionally selected in this way, there is no guarantee that the budget will be precisely exhausted.[10] If there are spare funds, then 20 per cent was too high a value for ϕ, so some recalculations will be necessary. Similarly, if the provisional list of projects more than exhausted the budget, then the central authorities will have to ask analysts to re-consider their projects, using a higher value for ϕ. This trial and error method is like a market for capital funds, where demand is matched against the fixed supply. In fact, if initial analyses have been conducted in some detail, this job could be done centrally without further resort to 'field' analysts, and the development of computers and programming techniques will greatly facilitate this central assessment.

The example is greatly simplified, since capital outlays occur in only one year. Some different forms of budget constraints can be dealt with in roughly the same manner while, in other cases, considerable complications arise. Before looking at these, there are two points that need to be made to tie up this subject with previous discussions. Firstly, we described in section 9.2 how the US Bureau of Reclamation and the Army Corps of Engineers have used benefit/cost ratios in evaluating water resource projects. Our formulations are consistent with the use of some such ratios, since eq. (10.4a) and eq. (10.7) both imply that a project is acceptable if:

$$\sum_{0}^{n} (\Delta B_t - \Delta O_t)/(1+e)^t \div \Delta K_0 > 1+\phi \tag{10.9}$$

This does not give any more information. The ratio of benefit, net of operating costs, to capital costs has to exceed unity by an amount which is not *a priori* precisely known. The basic problem of discovering ϕ still remains. It is not enough, moreover, to rank projects by the size of this ratio, for the type of projects provisionally accepted will depend on the size of ϕ. In terms of the choice between the two projects A and B, one has first of all to calculate the incremental benefits and costs for A over B; then A is accepted if the ratio of incremental benefits minus incremental operating costs, to incremental capital costs, exceeds $1+\phi$. When different degrees of capital intensity are

[10] Note that this is a different point from that mentioned in the footnote of p. 339, where it was suggested that indivisibilities in capital outlays would mean that budgets are not fully exhausted.

involved, the size of ϕ is relevant to the choice of production technique. Notice also that the ratio in eq. (10.9) has only capital outlays in the denominator. Some agencies in US water-resource development have used both operating and capital costs as the denominator, so that the ratio becomes one of benefit to all costs.[11] The crucial point is that the denominator should contain the item which is constrained. Operating and capital costs may, as we shall see, be relevant for some types of constraints, but the denominator need not, as a general rule, refer to all costs.

Finally, an implication of the above analysis is that the presence of budget limits does not necessitate tampering with the interest rate used for discounting. Restrictions on the size of the budget imply a scarcity of funds which in this simplified example, occurs simply at one point of time. The suggested investment criterion essentially incorporates a valuation of these scarce funds: it does not affect the way one *wishes to weight* present and future benefits and costs.

Other forms of budget limits

In practice, even if it is only capital expenditure that is limited, we must recognize that the set of opportunities in any sector will include some projects starting at a later date than the base-year and, in practice, funds constraints may apply in each year. However, if all separately defined activities and projects involve capital outlays in only one year, no further problems arise. The process spelled out above would have to be repeated each year with ϕ taking on a different value each year. Complications arise when we allow that projects may involve capital outlays in more than one year. Even these may be reasonably tractable to the previous approach. In some cases, budget limits may be prescribed over a planning period. Thus, the reviews of public expenditure in the UK include planned allocation of funds over the next four or five years.[12] When plans like this allow some transfer of funds from one period to another then we could, to be more sophisticated, think of the constraint as relating to the present value of funds that can be spent over some planning period. If this period is taken to coincide with the horizon set by the productive opportunities open to the public enterprise in question, then such a constraint effectively takes the form of

$$\sum_{t=0}^{t=n} (TK)_t/(1+e)^t \leq (\overline{TK}) \tag{10.10}$$

Outlays on capital expenditure over the period in question should have an

[11] Benefits and costs are also often expresssed in annually equivalent terms, and, while this may also be questionable if some items are growing over time, it is a separate point to the one under consideration. See *Water-Resource Development,* O. Eckstein, Harvard University Press, 1958, chapter III.

[12] See, for example, *Public Expenditure: Planning and Control,* Cmnd 2915, HMSO, February 1966.

equivalent present value no greater than $(\overline{TK})$. Following the logic of eq. (10.7), the investment criterion for any particular project which involves capital outlays in more than one period is:

$$N > \sum_{0}^{n} \phi \Delta K_t/(1+e)^t \tag{10.11}$$

The crucial term, ϕ, now relates to projects which are marginal to all the opportunities over the planning period; more precisely, it is the net face present value per £ of capital outlay on such projects, where the latter is given in present value terms. Similarly, if there are constraints on all types of expenditure whether capital or operating, then, provided they are transferable in the manner of our previous example, one simply adds ΔO_t to the capital item in the summation series of eq. (10.11). Or, putting the matter in terms of benefit/cost ratios, the investment criterion is:

$$\sum_{0}^{n} \Delta B_t/(1+e)^t \div \sum_{0}^{n} (\Delta O_t + \Delta K_t)/(1+e)^t > 1+\phi \tag{10.12}$$

Here we see the most direct analogy with the practices in US water-resource development, since all the cost items appear in the denominator of the ratio. However, its appropriateness depends on the circumstances and, as we suggested before, the formulation in terms of ratios does not mean one has escaped from the problem of discovering ϕ. Moreover, when separate constraints exist on capital and operating costs, it is obvious that the appropriate investment criterion will attach a different shadow cost to operating inputs than capital inputs. For a particular project, the appropriate criterion changes from eq. (10.11) to:

$$N > \phi_o \sum_{0}^{n} \Delta O_t/(1+e)^t + \phi_K \sum_{0}^{n} \Delta K_t/(1+e)^t \tag{10.13}$$

The expression ϕ_o, therefore, indicates the net face present value of marginal activities involving the use of operating costs, expressed per £ of present value operating costs; a different value now applies for ϕ_K. Those readers wishing to pursue the logic of this in more detail should refer to the appendix to this chapter. It goes without saying that simple benefit/cost ratios are no longer useful since capital and operating costs are separately constrained. The left-hand side of eq. (10.12) has no relevance for the evaluation of projects. The reader is also left to work out the expression for the choice between the two projects A and B, the point now being that the excess of the net face present value of A over B has to be compared with the differences (positive or negative) in both running and capital costs in each project, each difference having a separate shadow value.

An important point to which we now must turn is that, although there may be some possibilities of transferring funds as between years, the budget planning period may be less than that which embraces the full effects of sector projects. At one extreme, there may be funds constraints in every year, but even if periods of five years were involved the issue could still arise. To hint at these difficulties suppose operating costs are not restricted but there is limitation on capital expenditure each year. This means that $(TK)_0$ must not exceed $(\overline{TK})_0$, that $(TK)_1$ must not exceed $(\overline{TK})_1$, and so on. Setting aside the very unlikely possibility of the value of marginal projects in each year being the same, the general implication is that ϕ takes on a different value each year. In terms of eq. (10.11), ϕ has to be replaced by ϕ_t. Written out in full, this means that a particular project is warranted if:

$$N > \Delta K_0 \phi_0 + [\Delta K_1 \phi_1/1+e] + [\Delta K_2 \phi_2/(1+e)^2] + \dots + [\Delta K_n \phi_n/(1+e)^n] \qquad (10.14)$$

Whether or not it is worthwhile to undertake a project which would start in, for example, the base-year (ΔK_0 is positive), requires a knowledge of constraints and project values in future years. In fact, it is even more complicated than that since the value of ϕ_2, for example, is itself determined by project values and constraints in the years from two onwards. To determine ϕ_2 it is necessary to know ϕ_3, ϕ_4, etc. There is an escape from this dilemma if, as we allowed before, there are projects involving capital costs in year two only. Making an informed guess at which of these would be marginal, will give a value for ϕ_2, since this is equal to the net face present value per £ of year two capital outlay on such marginal projects. But, generally, the problem becomes so interconnected that any one project can be evaluated only by solving the over-all maximization problem which, in this context, could involve some complicated programming problems. Additional complications would arise, of course, if operating costs are separately constrained. Clearly, some short-cuts might be used, but it does mean a much bigger role for the central authorities of the industry than that anticipated in the absence of funds constraints.

Conclusions

(a) When enterprise funds for expenditure on particular purposes are limited in any time-period to prescribed amounts, expenditure for any one purpose involves an opportunity or shadow cost greater than its face cost. Investment criteria, for example, in the presence of constraints on capital expenditure, should therefore involve a comparison of a project's present value of benefits net of operating costs with the shadow present value cost of capital outlays; they do not require an adjustment of the interest rate for discounting. For any project, the excess of shadow cost over money cost reflects the returns that are foregone in not using these funds for other projects; more precisely they reflect the net face present value per unit of the restricted funds, on projects which are just left out of the budget. While the shadow costs can formally be obtained as solutions to the over-all sector maximization problem, it is more likely that, at present, enterprises will have to make rough guesses at these shadow magnitudes, and to ensure that the budget is fully used by some trial and error adjustments to the initial estimates. In some cases, theoretically correct solutions cannot even be approximated by such methods and this suggests that, on the other side of the coin, there are advantages in not making budget allocations too restrictive or refined.

(b) In principle, the logic of the process, whereby funds are allocated among projects within a public agency or enterprise, has direct relevance to the allocation of the overall government budget to the various government departments, agencies, and public enterprises. At this level it is necessary to ensure not only that, say, a harbour development scheme has larger benefits than any other transport project which it might preclude, but also that transport projects in general do not take place if larger benefits can be obtained by transferring scarce funds to other public enterprises. Ideally, there will be, in other words, a solution opportunity cost for all public funds; its level will be determined by the returns to those potential public projects which, in any year or time-period, do not get into the government budget. While it is useful to see the logic of this overall allocation of public funds, it is of course an abstraction. Not only are objectives diverse and complex, as we suggested in section 10.1, but even if one looked at only one objective, as we have done in this section, the development of expenditure criteria has only just started at the enterprise level let alone any higher levels.

(c) Finally, it is worth noting that the effect of budget constraints is somewhat similar to the effect of our allowances, in the previous chapter, for social interest rates, taxes, and so on. Both cause the use of public funds to have an opportunity cost different from their money cost. One is an external opportunity cost, while budget limits impose an internal opportunity cost.[13] When both exceed the face cost of funds, it is the higher of the two that is relevant. In other words, if the public budget is tightly limited, then the rise in the internal shadow value of the input or 'purpose' in question may make outside considerations entirely irrelevant.

10.3 Income distribution objectives and expenditure criteria

Those responsible for determining the content of public expenditure do, in practice, take account of a number of different policy objectives. The criterion of determining which projects, what resources, what functions, by reference to consumers' willingness-to-pay is but one of these. In addition, whereas some of the early writers in resource allocation tended to ascribe considerable significance to this criterion, the development of welfare economics has

[13] Cf. S. A. Marglin, *Economic Factors Affecting System Design, op. cit.*, p. 205. See also pages 217–19 for a discussion of the effects on project design when there are private alternatives to the public project.

indicated the many qualifications to which it is subject, from the point of view of human or economic welfare. It is relevant to remember two of the qualifications discussed in chapter 4, namely:

(a) The criterion of undertaking some activity if consumers are willing-to-pay for it is, sometimes, advocated on the grounds that such a criterion ensures that the allocation of resources between uses reflects consumer preferences: that is, it will reflect consumers' free choice of one thing instead of another. Whether one ascribes any welfare significance to this criterion depends, partly, on whether one ascribes any significance to the free choices made by an individual. Are all individuals the best judge of their own well-being?

(b) Willingness-to-pay will also reflect, in part, a consumer's income. Whether one ascribes any welfare significance to the criterion, therefore, partly depends on whether differences in income can be ignored. It is this aspect of the criterion which we examine in this section.

The tax/transfer solution

It was suggested, in the introductory part of this chapter, that the 'efficiency' criterion can be reconciled with income distribution objectives by the use of taxes and transfers among different groups in the economy. Let us consider, first of all, a number of examples where a particular policy decision departs from 'efficiency' considerations because of a desire to allow for distributive objectives. The way these objectives can be accomplished by retaining the efficiency criterion but introducing tax-transfer changes can then be explained. This will pave the way for a discussion, in the next sub-section, of the limitations of the tax-transfer solution. Four different situations illustrate the main characteristics of this problem:

(a) In an interesting exercise, briefly alluded to in the previous chapter, G. Polanyi attempted to construct UK supply and demand curves for North-Sea Gas.[14] Figure 10.1 is a rough sketch map of his results. The *D* line purports to be the annual partial demand function likely to be relevant towards the end of the 1970s. It is constructed by making consumers' willingness-to-pay synonymous with the costs of alternative fuel supplies. The LMC line is estimated as the set of prices needed by suppliers to give a minimum compensation to the required factors of production, a 15 per cent return on capital being assumed to be sufficient to attract resources to these schemes. The limits to North Sea Gas are in the neighbourhood of 40,000 million therms per annum, but such quantities will not be realizable for quite a while, and certainly in the 1970s the maximum quantities assumed to be initially available are, according to Polanyi, in the region of 15,000 million therms. Initially then, the short-run marginal cost function takes the

[14] 'What Price North Sea Gas', Hobart Paper 38, *Institute of Economic Affairs,* January, 1967.

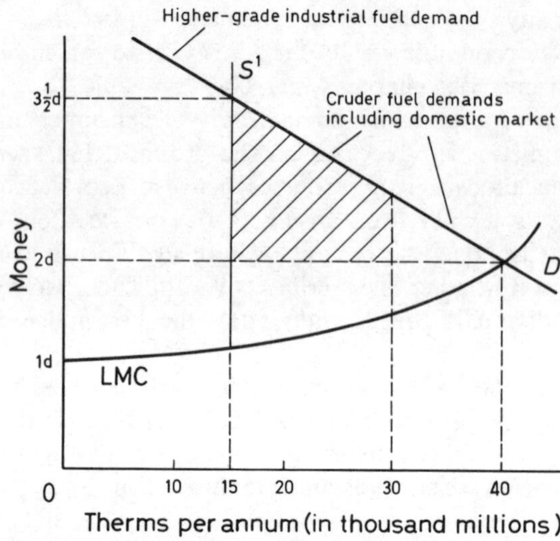

FIG. 10.1

path of S^1, so that the 'efficient' price is $3\frac{1}{2}$ pence per therm. Keeping price at the efficient level would mean, over time, a gradual reduction, in real terms, to the long-run level of 2 pence per therm. This

> . . . system of allocation, by placing each successive investment of gas on offer in a free market, constitutes an automatic mechanism for ensuring that, at any point in this long-term process of making the full potential reserves of gas available, priority of use is always given to those applications of the gas which yield the highest return to the national economy by the substitution of the gas for alternative fuels.[15]

Here 'return', of course, means simply the surplus of consumers' willingness-to-pay over the minimum compensation required by input suppliers. In this case, with the price of $3\frac{1}{2}$ pence, a large part of this surplus accrues as producer surplus.

Now, there is increasing evidence that the government wishes to keep the price fairly low and make sales to the domestic market. This would entail rationing on the part of the Gas Council. This policy measure would be consistent with a policy aim of increasing the relative real incomes of lower money income groups. To the extent that such groups spend a higher portion of their money income on fuel than high income groups (and that the indirect use of gas provides smaller benefits for the former), and to the extent that benefits will be conferred *now* rather than in twenty years' time, this could have an impact, albeit perhaps modest, on relative real incomes now. There

[15] *Ibid.*, p. 27.

is nothing 'economically unsound' about this; formally, we are departing from the case where each £1 of benefit has the same weight to whomsoever it accrues. In conventional benefit/cost terminology some benefit would be lost, since excluded industrial demanders will make outlays on other resources which give a smaller surplus of benefit over cost. But when, as here, market indicators of people's 'needs' are being replaced by different indicators, such terminology is irrelevant. Now, the standard argument against such procedures is to use the tax-transfer mechanism to effect the distributive aims. Take, as an example, the situation where the initially available 15,000 million therms of gas is sold, not to the 0–15 group in Fig. 10.1, but instead is sold at 2 pence per therm to the 15–30 group, which includes part of the domestic market. This latter group, therefore, experiences a real income increase equivalent to the shaded area of consumer surplus in Fig. 10.1. If, instead, a free market price of $3\frac{1}{2}$ pence had been set, then suppliers would have earned excess profits roughly equal to ($3\frac{1}{2}$ pence–1 pence) $\times$ 15,000 millions. A tax on these profits could be used to effect transfer payments to those individuals who would, in the other policy proposal, have received gas at 2 pence per therm. It can be seen, from the diagram, that these profits will always be more than enough to compensate the excluded domestic consumers. The 'efficient' course of action in moving from a price of 2 pence to one of $3\frac{1}{2}$ pence, has embedded in it the guarantee that the gainers could over-compensate the losers. In fact, the suppliers' net of tax price can be taken as high as 2 pence, and the compensation requirement could still be met.[16] However, all this depends on the taxing process having, in general, no effect on supplies—in this case, it is assumed to have no such effect, since the LMC line purports to represent minimum supply prices—and on the feasibility of transferring income to the domestic consumer in question. To these general issues we turn in the next section, but before that let us consider some further examples.

(b) Consider a hypothetical case where the optimum size of a large-scale project is in question. No sales revenue accrues from the project's services, costs being financed by taxation, and rationing can, it is assumed, restrict demands to whatever is deemed to be the appropriate level. Although it does not exactly correspond to these assumptions, the reader might think of extensions to a road system in one particular region of a country, and the benefits of the project's services are revealed by studies of the effect of the extensions on the journey costs of road-users. The MC line of Fig. 10.2 depicts, in a very rough way, the construction costs of increasing the size of this project. The 'efficient' solution is at q_1 where the extra benefit from a marginal increase in the size of the project—as indicated by the ordinates of

[16] This net of tax price received by suppliers could be raised further if discrimination is possible in the selling price of gas, for then parts of the consumer surplus could be expropriated. One is, in other words, changing the content rather than the total of social surplus, by increasing producer surplus at the expense of consumer surplus. Notice that, in some cases, full redistribution of benefits to excluded parties may necessitate such discrimination.

the demand curve—is just equal to the extra cost of construction. Those groups of consumers typified by the range q_1q_2, whose valuation of the project's services falls short of the costs of supplying them, are effectively excluded. To the extent that the locale of the project is a fairly underdeveloped part of the country, the government might argue for an extension of project size on the grounds that willingness-to-pay does not reflect needs. The effect of this would be to give the needy group a real income increase equal to the shaded area of the diagram, since no prices are levied. Again, the tax-transfer solutions can be shown to be superior, in principle. The point, in

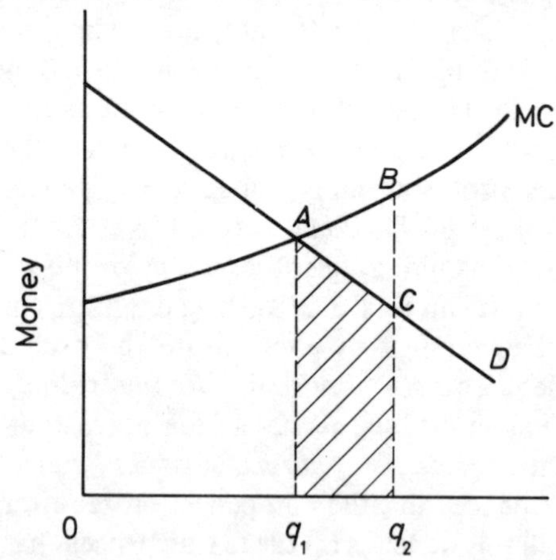

FIG. 10.2

this example, is that the extra benefits conferred involve outlays on construction resources equal to the area under the MC line between q_1 and q_2. In standard 'efficiency' terminology, there is a loss of social surplus equal to the area *ABC*. It would be cheaper, therefore, to give the group in question a direct transfer payment equal to the shaded area rather than incur the costs of increasing the scale of the project's benefits. In the contraction of scale from q_2 to q_1 the gainers—tax-payers, in this instance—could more than compensate the excluded group of potential consumers.

(c) A nice example of the choice between efficiency and distribution has been provided by S. A. Marglin.[17] A multi-purpose water-resource project can be designed towards providing irrigation water for the American Indians or towards providing hydro-electricity for industry. If geared towards irrigation water, the efficiency benefits are only $20 million per annum, while the electricity design yields $30 million per annum; the two options are indicated by points *A* and *B* in Fig. 10.3. Clearly, the federal government might be very

[17] 'Objectives of Water-Resource Development: A General Statement', chapter 2 of Maass, *op. cit.*, pp. 63–64; figure 10.3 is a rough sketch of Marglin's Fig. 2.9.

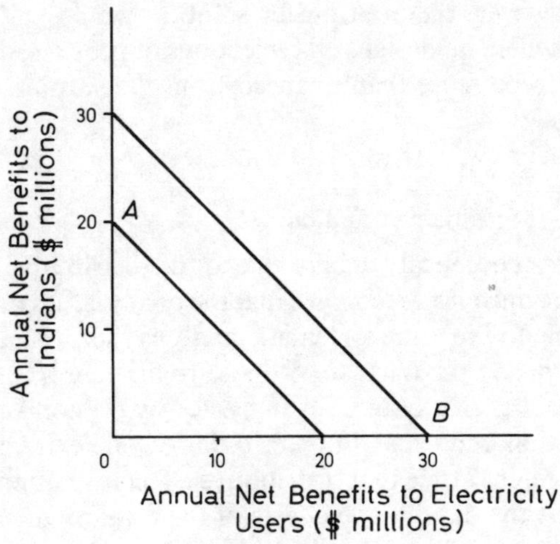

FIG. 10.3

interested in the irrigation possibility, despite its apparent inferiority. In principle again, however, any concern with the relative real income of the Indians can be accommodated by designing the project for electricity, expropriating industry's benefits, and using them for effecting direct income transfers to the Indians. The line connecting point *B* to the vertical axis indicates the various distributions of benefits between the two groups, granted that all re-distributions are feasible. Since the line from *A* to the horizontal axis indicates the scope of such allocations, if the project is designed towards irrigation, then on these grounds it is inferior. The key question is again whether the expropriation and transfer of the benefits accruing initially to electricity users' is feasible.

(d) Finally, it is useful to recall that in standard cost/benefit practice, so-called secondary benefits are not recommended for inclusion in the benefits of a project, on the grounds that the resources in question involve an opportunity cost. That is, real incomes rise in one area, but to the extent that resources are drawn from elsewhere, there are falls experienced elsewhere. But, if there is an electrification scheme in, say, the Scottish Highlands, then the generation of incomes in such an area may be part of the government's policy on income distribution. The fall elsewhere may be deemed to be of no consequence, so that on these grounds secondary benefits should be included. In fact, one writer has gone further by saying that there

> . . . is no such thing as a secondary benefit. A secondary benefit, as the phrase has been used in the benefit-cost literature, is in fact a benefit in support of an objective other than efficiency.[18]

[18] 'Benefit/Cost Analysis: Its Relevance to Public Investment Decisions', A. Maass, *QJE*, p. 211, May 1966.

Here again, however, the tax-transfer solution would suggest that, rather than making 'inefficient' designs and selections of projects, direct transfers to such regions can be more than financed from the surplus from 'efficiently' chosen projects.

Attitudes towards income distribution

Given this basic theoretical background to the distributive effects of public expenditure, one must now recognize that the policy issues in question are not always amenable to the same systematic analysis that we have considered in other parts of this book. What we propose to do here is survey, briefly, the different approaches that have been suggested by economists, in the context of project selection and expenditure criteria. At one extreme, if I might use that word, one might argue that distributive effects are unimportant: this on the grounds that the distributive effects of the total of government projects are neutral and, therefore, may be disregarded. However, this is largely irrelevant since it presupposes the existing distribution is 'proper' in some sense. Or, alternatively, there are those who argue that present income differentials do reflect relevant economic forces and these should not be disturbed. In general, however, most economists accept that projects have distributive implications and, moreover, that the existing distribution of income cannot be viewed as ideal. Three groups of approaches seem to stem from this:

(a) Economists should keep to the efficiency measures, on the grounds that they have no special competence in assessing the relative importance of £1 received by person *X* as against £1 received by person *Y*. Project analysis and suggestions for design and selection would, therefore, reflect efficiency considerations; thereafter, these would be modified and doctored by the political process.[19] The point, it seems to me, is that 'economic efficiency' is a fairly empty concept in terms of people's welfare; on its own it has little social significance. By stressing 'efficiency' alone there is a great danger that economists will merely be supporting the existing distribution of income. Though they have no special competence in weighting the pounds mentioned above, project analysts implicitly would be introducing the judgement that £1 has the same welfare significance to whomsoever it accrues.

(b) The particular method used to design and select projects is but one way of attacking the distributional issue. Another is the tax-transfer device, described in the previous section: to the extent that this approach is fully

[19] The reader might like to turn back to the introductory part of section 3.4 to see the quotation of J. M. Buchanan's view that, in this sort of context, economists should not kid the general public that they have a hot line to God. Something of this approach appears also in R. Dorfman's recommendations—reported in Maass's article, *op. cit.*—to the West Pakistan government, that project design should reflect efficiency criteria. The more extreme view, alluded to in the opening paragraph, can be found in chapter X of M. Friedman's *Capitalism and Freedom,* University of Chicago, 1962.

feasible, the solution is superior to that which effects distributive aims in a project selection. Some economists then support this line of reasoning, which, in addition, does have the advantage of being consistent with a fair amount of decentralized decision-taking. A. V. Kneese, for example, has

> . . . felt particularly uneasy about the recent rash of economic studies which endeavour to insert an explicit income redistribution value in public project evaluations. . . . [The] . . . traditional economist's [sic] prescription . . . [involves] . . . confronting the income distribution problem directly in actual transfers of income, and programs which help the underprivileged to render those services which society values . . . [and] . . . this still makes a lot of sense to me. [The economist] . . . is almost duty bound to make a nuisance of himself among decision-makers by never failing to proclaim that . . . [these] . . . policies may be more in accord with a decentralized decision-making process.[20]

Present practices in the UK public sector seem implicitly to take this line. The 1967 White Paper on the Nationalized Industries[21] hardly mentions distributional factors at all, while advocating the use of marginal-cost pricing and conventional cost/benefit analysis. Most cost/benefit studies of particular issues have had, as yet, hardly anything to say on distribution, though one must remember, as we have stressed throughout this book, that this is still a fairly young subject area, and there are plenty of problems in the present search for appropriate efficiency measures of benefits and costs. However, these tendencies are not without implications. Maass suggests that US water-resource development is moving in the reverse direction.[22] In the original Flood Control Act of 1936, it was stated that a general standard should be that, for a project to be undertaken, 'the benefits to whomsoever they may accrue should exceed the costs'. By 1950 the 'Green Book', mentioned in the previous chapter, gave overwhelming emphasis to the efficiency ranking functions. Maass views this as a trend away from consideration of distributive effects, particularly since the Bureau of the Budget in 1952 nailed this emphasis into national policy.

(c) Finally, there are those, including myself, who would be reasonably content with the above approach if the distribution of income (i) can be easily altered independently of any resource using project, and (ii), it *will* be so altered. There are a number of points to bear in mind in this respect. Firstly, it is possible to argue[23] that certain methods of redistribution inherent

[20] Discussion comments in *Problems in Public Expenditure Analysis,* Ed. S. B. Chase, p. 66, Brooking, 1968.

[21] *Nationalised Industries: A Review of Economic and Financial Objectives,* Cmnd 3437, HMSO, November 1967.

[22] *Op. cit., QJE,* pp. 212–13, May 1966.

[23] Cf. Marglin, *op. cit. (Objectives of water-resource . . .),* pp. 17–18; and Maass, *QJE,* May 1966.

in the tax-transfer system, such as unemployment pay, are unattractive because the recipients become socially condemned. In addition, and this is a key theoretical point for the tax-transfer solution, in principle such devices would themselves have to be of a lump-sum nature, for otherwise the levying of taxes and transfers would simply create further 'inefficiencies'. Income and profit taxes have been well publicized as having disincentive effects. If we want to be rigorous about this we can say, following Freeman,[24] that there are costs involved in using the tax-transfer solutions. A third point is that it may not be possible to use the tax-transfer system in a way that effectively achieves the distributional aims. In the example of the multi-purpose project providing irrigation water or electricity, it would be necessary to tax the industrial users of electricity. Since in some instances the full willingness-to-pay may have to be exploited, this may well necessitate price or tax discrimination—a course of action which is not always feasible. Finally, it is relevant to mention that the full distributive impact of a set of public projects is probably not only unknown—in terms of magnitude—by both decision-takers and analysts unless they have been instructed to pursue the distributive effects, but also the impact is probably also not realized, at least by decision-takers. It seems likely that recognition will take place slowly and thus, in practice, the tax-transfer mechanism will take a long time to adjust.

Methods of allowing for the distributional effects of projects

Emanating from the approach in (c), above, have been a number of suggestions in which project assessment could take account of distributional effects. Putting the matter at its strongest, these suggestions are only in the formative stage, and should be treated as such. Clearly governments do take income distribution into account in any actual selection of projects, and we have already described how public expenditure decisions can reflect distributive aims in particular cases. Our concern here is with a systematic allowance for income distribution in all cases of government activities which do not give rise to revenue. We suggested in chapter 4 that, in those parts of the public sector where a price system is already in existence, it would be extremely difficult to incorporate distributional objectives into the routine management activities of bodies like, for example, the UK Nationalized Industries. In such circumstances, we felt it relevant and feasible to introduce distributional considerations when major pricing policy decisions were under review, such as the introduction of North Sea Gas, or pricing the use of roads, or using the price system over long periods for rationing scarce supplies, or shifting from average to marginal cost pricing. However, this is a matter of judgement only, and those who wish to use the whole of the public

[24] 'Income Distribution and Planning for Public Investment', A. M. Freeman, *AER*, June 1967.

sector as a vehicle for changing the distribution of income may extend the logic of what we have to say for projects giving rise to non-priced benefits. The various suggestions that have been made in this context may be arranged under three headings:

(a) *The Display Method.* Essentially the idea here is simply to *describe* to decision-takers the distribution of the benefits and costs of a project. Although this appears to be a pitifully modest proposal, it is, in my opinion, for reasons that will become apparent in looking at the alternatives, the limit to which practising project analysts are likely to be able to go during the foreseeable future. The idea would be to set out the totals of benefits and costs by categories deemed likely to be relevant. For a large project, like the bridge across the Humber Estuary near Hull, the proposal would involve identifying the sources of traffic likely to use the bridge, their origin and destination by region, and possibly the nature of the goods transported. Now, while the proposal of simply describing the distribution of benefits and costs may appear unadventuresome, the exercise could be quite formidable. The construction of tables showing the size of benefits for different money-income groups and different geographic regions will involve plenty of work but, clearly, decision-takers may well be interested in other dimensions, such as age, sex, family size, religion, and education; and of course, in the United States poverty programmes, race becomes an important category. B. A. Weisbrod[25] has conducted an interesting exercise from data relating to the recreational benefits of two State Parks in the USA, one at Beaver Creek, Ohio, and another at Hammonasset, Connecticut. As he points out, if one specified six subdivisions for income, six for age, eight regions, and two races, then six hundred 'cells' of required data emerge! Moreover, the distribution of project benefits will usually involve greater measurement problems than the totals. (Recreational benefits are often approximated by calculating journey-cost savings effected through the particular location of a facility.) In Weisbrod's State Parks example, the benefits to the categories of white and non-white subdivided by age groups 0 to 18, 19 to 64, and 64 plus, and by income bracket (two divisions above and below $3,000 per annum), were obtained by allocating total benefits on the basis of census data on the distribution of population in the vicinity—a procedure beset with reservations.

However, the magnitude of these exercises is a self-made problem and reflects the ambitiousness of the suggested approach; to start with fairly modest categorizations will have to be made. Notice also that a concern with distributive effects may well necessitate the tabulation of secondary benefits and costs, particularly when important development areas are involved. An additional piece of information, which might interest decision-takers, is how

[25] 'Income Redistribution Effects and Benefit-Cost Analysis' chapter in Chase, *op. cit.* The display method has also been canvassed implicitly by Maass, *op. cit., QJE,* 1966, and by R. N. McKean in *Efficiency in Government Through Systems Analysis, op. cit.*

the selection from a list of projects is affected by the use of different possible weights to benefits and costs. If a public agency has a fixed annual budget, for example, then one could attach, say, weights of more than £1 to each £1 of benefit accruing to low-income project beneficiaries and, say, zero values for fairly high income groups. The sensitivity of project selection to certain changes in these weights could then be examined.

(b) *The Existence of a Specific Policy Goal.* In some instances project analysts may be able to wrest from decision-takers specific, if rough, quantitative estimates of distributional aims. This could be in the form of a requirement that the percentage unemployment rate on Merseyside should this year drop by one point, or that real incomes in Northern Ireland should rise by £150 million per annum over the next ten years. When there are public investment projects likely to have some effect in such regions—such as improved communications or urban renewal programmes—clearly these aims can be incorporated in project selection procedures. As Marglin[26] has suggested, these aims could be accommodated formally by attaching them as constraints on the efficiency maximization process. In the case where some group's real income has to rise by at least a certain amount over some period, then such a constraint is similar to the budget limits discussed before. Without going into this rigorously, one can guess that for any one project the present value of efficiency net benefits per £ of income accruing to the group in question will have to exceed some cut-off level. Or, if the aim is to increase the real income of the group in question as much as possible, subject to efficiency benefits and costs not being negative, then this also is clearly amenable to the sort of analysis we have discussed before. The real question, however, is whether goals are often specified in such a clear form. Hedging by keeping vague seems much more characteristic and so this whole approach may only have limited usefulness.

(c) *The Derivation of General Weighting Systems.* Both the previous approaches skirt round the key theoretical point, which is that to alter expenditure criteria, in order that they incorporate distributional objectives, requires that project analysts are given some fairly general information on government policy with respect to income distribution. In using the efficiency criterion for selecting projects, one is implicitly maximizing a function where each person's welfare is linked to increases in his income, and each £1 of income received or surrendered is given the same weight. If a complete set of 'government' weights were available, then one could clearly use these in project selection. When weights are available for broad groups of people, then one way to allow for this would be to maximize total efficiency net benefits plus a weighted measure of the benefits accruing to the group in question. A more general formulation would be simply to attach social weights to each potential project beneficiary; Freeman, for example, has

[26] Cf. Marglin, *op. cit.*, pp. 67–84.

canvassed this approach.[27] Thinking of the case where projects are financed from taxes or government bonds, he would work out expenditure criteria by maximizing the difference between benefits and costs where each benefit to each person (and the same for costs) has a specific weight. For example, let $(TB)_i$ be the total benefit accruing to person i from projects and supplies in some particular sector, and $(TC)_a$ be that part of taxation or borrowing supplied by person a, all expressed in present value terms. One might then maximize the following expression:

$$\sum_{i=1}^{i=m} (TB)_i \alpha_i - \sum_{a=1}^{a=x} (TC)_a \pi_a$$

where α_i is the social weight attached to person i, and π_a is the weight given to person a. If costs and benefits are, in this case, functionally related to the volume of services provided, then equilibrium will be characterized by the usual equality of marginal benefit and marginal cost, though each item now has a social weight attached to it. While it is useful to have this sort of formulation, the particular form of the expressions and the mechanics of their solution are really secondary; it is the discovery of the weights that is the crucial item. The manipulations involved in the above expressions are, therefore, particularly academic when one recognizes that the weighting system is, of course, a great unknown.

A number of suggestions have been made, in the context of public expenditure decisions, to *infer* a system of weights from past and present government action. Eckstein,[28] for example, advanced the hypothesis that government acts, in its income-tax programme, on the basis of equi-marginal sacrifice. In this case, one might deduce that the effective marginal tax rates at different income levels imply a social or governmental evaluation of the marginal utility of income; that is, the marginal utility of income is less the higher one moves up the income scale. Appropriate weights could be deduced for different income levels, and these weights used in project evaluation. Freeman counter-argued that, if the government did act on this principle, there would be a tendency for equalization of net incomes; incomes above a certain level would be taxed away and no taxes would be levied below that level. More significance can be attached to the present differences in marginal effective tax rates, he argues, if one accepts that the tax-transfer mechanism involves the difficulties described before—incentive and administrative costs, un-

[27] *Op. cit.* (The first approach is suggested as a possibility by Marglin, *op. cit.*, pp. 78–81). Incidentally, Freeman's concern over income distribution is fairly limited.

> 'If... [project]... beneficiaries bear full cost there is no subsidy and no redistribution problem of any consequence.'

(p. 495, footnote).

[28] 'A Survey of the Theory of Public Expenditure Criteria', pp. 447–8, *op. cit.*

favourable aspects of certain methods of transfer, etc.; an increasing marginal tax rate thus reflects both a declining social evaluation of marginal income increases and, in addition, the 'costs' of taxation. However, these attempts to deduce distributive goals from government action are clearly dubious. Whether any consistency can be imputed to government actions, and, whether action reflects only distributive factors, is questionable. This latter point is exemplified in Weisbrod's exercise.[29] He proposed a model where it was assumed that any departures of *actual* government choice of projects from those choices suggested by efficiency measures, was attributable to a concern with the projects' distributional effects. From this scheme it is possible to deduce a system of weights for various benefits and costs, consistent with the government's actual choice. In fact, he considered a number of water-resource projects proposed by the Corps of Engineers in 1950. For purposes of analysis he ignored that the engineers' implied efficiency ranking criterion, a benefit/cost ratio, may not be correct on efficiency grounds. The ranking of projects by benefit/cost ratios was then compared with the ranking implied in Congressional decisions; the latter was taken to be implied in the date at which any one project was recommended to be started. From this information Weisbrod was able to use his model to deduce a system of weights for various groups of beneficiaries likely to be affected by these projects. The trouble is that such Congressional decisions will reflect not only distributional considerations but also intangible efficiency benefits and costs, electoral implications, pressures groups, and so on. While it *is* easy to be critical of these heroic exercises, one must conclude, as we said initially, that these developments are in but a formative stage. Exploratory use of the display method may tell us a lot about income distribution, about decision-takers' concern over these matters, and about the administrative problems involved in incorporating allowances for these matters into project selection procedures. In the applied parts of the subject area this would seem to be a useful advance.

Appendix

INVESTMENT CRITERIA IN THE PRESENCE OF BUDGET CONSTRAINTS

A rigorous derivation of some standard investment criteria

In chapter 9 investment criteria were examined in some detail. Their rigorous derivation was omitted since the relationship between the basic maximand and such criteria was fairly clear. When an enterprise's budget is limited in one way or another, the appropriate investment criteria are not so obvious, and this appendix indicates more rigorously than the text of this chapter how such criteria are related to the basic maximand. To start with, we must spell

[29] *Op. cit.*, pp. 190–213. Maass also in *QJE* article *op. cit.*, used a similar approach in a context of highways, housing, and urban renewal.

out in more detail the logic of the 'simple' case where there is no funds restriction. In this situation the overall sector maximization problem is given by eq. (10.1) in the text of this chapter. More rigorously, the Lagrangean expression to be maximized is L where:

$$L = \sum_{t=0}^{t=n} [(TB)_t - (TO)_t - (TK)_t] D^t - \lambda [F(X, H, V)] \qquad (10.A1)$$

The undetermined Lagrangean multiplier, λ, constrains the production function, which we shall discuss shortly. The first part of eq. (10.A1) contains the totals of benefits and costs, and the symbol D^t is used in this appendix as a simpler form of the discount rate, $1/(1+e)^t$, used in the text of this chapter. Now benefits and costs will themselves be functionally related to outputs and inputs respectively. Let the volume of the jth product or service in year t be denoted by x_{jt}, the volume of the lth operating input (labour, raw materials, fuel, etc.) by h_{lt}, and the volume of the gth capital input by v_{gt}. The functional relationships between benefits and products, and between costs and inputs, may be written as:

$$(TB)_t = \sum_{j=1}^{j=s} f_{jt}(x_{jt}) : (TO)_t = \sum_{l=1}^{l=z} f_{lt}(h_{lt}) : (TK)_t = \sum_{g=1}^{g=w} f_{gt}(v_{gt}) \qquad (10.A2)$$

Each term allows for a different functional relationship for different years and different products or inputs. Each of these inputs and outputs appears in the production function, $F(X, H, V) = 0$, implied in (10.A1). The symbols X, H, and V, are summary terms relating to products, operating inputs, and capital inputs, respectively. For products we have:

$$X = x_{11}, \ldots, x_{j1}, \ldots, x_{s1}; x_{12}, \ldots, x_{j2}, \ldots, x_{s2}; \ldots; x_{1n}, \ldots, x_{jn}, \ldots, x_{sn} \qquad (10.A3)$$

and H and V would be defined in a similar way. In the case where every item is treated as partially variable, we have the following first-order conditions for a maximum:

$$\delta L/\delta x_{jt} = B_{jt} D^t - \lambda F_{jt} = 0 \qquad j = 1 \ldots s, t = 1 \ldots n \qquad (10.A4)$$

In this expression, B_{jt} is used as a shorthand for $\delta(TB)_t/\delta x_{jt}$, and F_{jt} is the shorthand for $\delta F/\delta x_{jt}$. Using similar terminology for operating inputs would give:

$$\delta L/\delta h_{lt} = (-)\, O_{lt}\, D^t + \lambda F_{lt} = 0 \qquad l = 1 \ldots z, t = 1 \ldots n \qquad (10.A5)$$

Here, and henceforth, we recognize that changes in inputs would have a negative sign in the production function. Instead of leaving F_{lt} as implicitly negative, we have treated it as positive and prefaced it with a negative sign so that $-\lambda(-)F_{lt}$ takes its simpler form in (10.A5). Finally, optimal use of capital inputs implies:

$$\delta L/\delta v_{gt} = (-)\, K_{gt} D^t + \lambda F_{gt} = 0 \qquad g = 1 \ldots w, t = 1 \ldots n \qquad (10.A6)$$

Assuming that the second-order conditions are met, the three equations above are sufficient conditions for optimality. They may be rearranged into the more familiar formulations of:

$$B_{j3}D^3 = O_{l2}D^2F_{j3}/F_{l2} \qquad 2,3 = 0\ldots t\ldots n \qquad (10.A7)$$

and

$$B_{j3}D^3 = K_{g2}D^2F_{j3}/F_{g2} \qquad 2,3 = 0\ldots t\ldots n \qquad (10.A8)$$

The ratios, like F_{j3}/F_{g2}, represent production transformation rates between input in one year and output in another year, so that the right-hand side of (10.A8) indicates the present value of the marginal cost of producing extra j in year three by the use of capital in year two. The two equations (10.A7) and (10.A8) represent the required equality between marginal benefit and marginal cost, when operating and capital costs are taken to be separately adjustable. They correspond to eq. (10.2) and eq. (10.3) in the text, where the notation has been simplified by leaving out the j, l, and g labels, and where cost terms like 0_2 are equivalent to $0_{l2}\ F_{j3}/F_{l2}$ in eq. (10.A7) above.

Now, in the main text of the chapter, we considered projects which involved the use of capital and operating inputs in more than one period, and which generated a stream of benefits over time. We can analyse such a simultaneous change in several variables by taking the total differential of the production function with respect to j, l, and g. Denoting this as δF, then, if the set of inputs and outputs is optimally organized, $\delta F = 0$, that is:[30]

$$\delta F = \sum_{t=0}^{t=n} F_{jt}\delta x_{jt} - \sum_{0}^{n} F_{lt}\delta h_{lt} - \sum_{0}^{n} F_{gt}\delta v_{gt} = 0 \qquad (10.A9)$$

Now, when the enterprise is near equilibrium, we know from equations (10.A4) to (10.A6) that $F_{jt} = B_{jt}D^t/\lambda$, that $F_{lt} = O_{lt}D^t/\lambda$, and so on. Substituting into eq. (10.A9) gives:

$$\sum_{0}^{n} [B_{jt}\delta x_{jt} - O_{lt}\delta h_{lt} - K_{gt}\delta v_{gt}]\, D^t = 0 \qquad (10.A10)$$

Since the three items in the brackets are nothing more than the extra benefits, running, and capital costs in year t of a particular project, then eq. (10.A10) says that, in equilibrium, the net discounted present value of the benefits and costs of such a project will be zero. Projects are, therefore, worth undertaking if such present values are positive. Simplifying the notation by writing ΔB_t for $B_{jt}\delta x_{jt}$, ΔO_t for $O_{lt}\delta h_{lt}$, and so on, the rule is to invest when:

$$\sum_{0}^{n} (\Delta B_t - \Delta O_t - \Delta K_t)D^t > 0 \qquad (10.A11)$$

which is precisely the criterion suggested in eq. (10.4) of the main text.

[30] This section draws on parts of Marglin's formulations in 'Economic Factors Affecting System Design', *op. cit.*, pp. 164–70.

Introducing budget constraints

Although considerable space has been devoted to discussing the situation where no funds limitations exist, it provides a background which allows one to introduce such limits fairly easily. The first situation examined in the text was one where capital outlays were incurred in only the base year, and the total of such expenditure was limited. The former point on its own would simply mean that, in the equations for capital inputs and costs, t needs to be replaced by 0. The funds restriction means that:

$$(TK)_0 = (\overline{TK})_0 \qquad (10.A12)$$

where $(\overline{TK})_O$ is the fixed sum of funds available for capital expenditure. This, effectively, means an additional constraint on the maximand so that eq. (10.A1) is now changed to:

$$L' = \sum_0^n [(TB)_t - (TO)_t]D^t - (TK)_0 - \lambda[F(X,H,V)]$$

$$-\phi[(TK)_0 - (\overline{TK})_0] \qquad (10.A1a)$$

where ϕ constrains actual capital outlays to the prescribed amount. Many of the equilibrium conditions are unaffected. What does happen is that eq. (10.A6) changes to:

$$\delta L'/\delta v_{g0} = (-)K_{g0} + \lambda F_{g0} - \phi K_{g0} = 0 \qquad g = 1 \dots w \quad (10.A6a)$$

implying that eq. (10.A8) changes to:

$$B_{jt}D^t = K_{g0}(1+\phi)F_{jt}/F_{g0} \qquad t = 0 \dots n \qquad (10.A8a)$$

and, working through, eq. (12.A10) becomes:

$$\sum_0^n [B_{jt}\,\delta x_{jt} - O_{lt}\,\delta h_{lt}]D^t - K_{g0}\,\delta v_{g0}(1+\phi) = 0 \qquad (10.A10a)$$

By rearranging terms, we get the solution for ϕ, namely, that it is equal to the net *face* present value of 'marginal' projects per £ of capital outlay, as we indicated in eq. (10.6) of the main text. Using the simplified notation of eq. (10.A11) above, we have that the investment criterion associated with eq. (10.A10a) is to accept those projects for which:

$$\sum_0^n (\Delta B_t - \Delta O_t)D^t - \Delta K_0(1+\phi) > 0 \qquad (10.A11a)$$

which is precisely the criterion suggested in eq. (10.4a) of the main text. The present value of the flow of benefits, net of operating costs, has to exceed not the face cost of capital but its shadow cost, which is $1+\phi$ per £.

The derivation of investment criteria with different constraints involves the same basic process. Take the case where there are separate constraints on operating and capital costs, and there are funds limitations applicable to each year in the planning horizon. Such a situation implies the following set of constraints:

$$\begin{aligned}
(TO)_0 &= (\overline{TO})_0 \qquad & (TK)_0 &= (\overline{TK})_0 \\
(TO)_1 &= (\overline{TO})_1 \qquad & (TK)_1 &= (\overline{TK})_1 \\
&\vdots & &\vdots \\
(TO)_n &= (\overline{TO})_n \qquad & (TK)_n &= (\overline{TK})_n
\end{aligned} \tag{10.A13}$$

If the amount of funds to be spent in year t is constrained by ϕ_{ot}, for operating costs, and ϕ_{kt} for capital costs, then the relevant Lagrangean expression to be maximized is:

$$L'' = \sum_0^n [(TB)_t - (TO)_t - (TK)_t]D_t - \lambda[F(X, H, V)]$$

$$- \sum_0^n \phi_{ot}[(TO)_t - (\overline{TO})_t]D^t - \sum_0^n \phi_{kt}[(TK)_t - (\overline{TK})_t]D^t \tag{10.A14}$$

Notice that we have multiplied the funds constraints by D^t. This is permissible since multiplying both sides of each of the equations in (10.A13) by D^0, D^1, etc., does not affect the conditions. Now, the first-order conditions for a maximum are:

$$\delta L''/\delta x_{jt} = B_{jt}D^t - \lambda F_{jt} = 0 \tag{10.A15}$$

$$\delta L''/\delta h_{lt} = (-)O_{lt}D^t + \lambda F_{lt} - \phi_{ot}D^t = 0 \tag{10.A16}$$

$$\delta L''/\delta v_{gt} = (-)K_{gt}D^t + \lambda F_{gt} - \phi_{kt}K_{gt}D^t = 0 \tag{10.A17}$$

On rearrangement these give:

$$O_{l2}D^2(1+\phi_{o2})F_{j3}/F_{l2} = B_{j3}D^3 = K_{g2}D^2(1+\phi_{k2})F_{j3}/F_{g2} \qquad 2, 3 = 0 \ldots n \tag{10.A18}$$

Here we have joined into one equation the required equality of marginal benefit and marginal (shadow) cost, relevant to the situation where inputs can be separately varied in each year. Working through, as before, we would have, instead of eq. (10.A10), the following conditions for equilibrium with respect to projects involving simultaneous changes:

$$\sum_0^n [B_{jt}\delta x_{jt} - O_{lt}\delta h_{lt}(1+\phi_{ot}) - K_{gt}\delta v_{gt}(1+\phi_{kt})] = 0 \tag{10.A19}$$

In the simpler terminology of eq. (10.A11), the criterion is to invest if:

$$\sum_0^n \Delta B_t D^t - \Delta O_t(1+\phi_{ot})D^t - \Delta K_t(1+\phi_{kt})D^t > 0 \tag{10.A20}$$

Finally, if we adopt the convention in the main text of denoting the net *face* present value of the project by N, then the investment criterion becomes:

$$N > \sum_{0}^{n} (\Delta O_t \phi_{ot} + \Delta K_t \phi_{kt}) D^t \tag{10.A21}$$

This, then, is a general expression which covers all the cases discussed in the main text. For example, if there are no constraints on running costs, ϕ_{ot} is zero, and, if the constraint on capital expenditure applies to all the planning horizon with no specifications for each year, then ϕ_{kt} is replaced by ϕ and eq. (10.A21) simplifies to the case of eq. (10.11) in the text. If there is a constraint on operating costs, but this also allows transfers between years, then ϕ_{kt} and ϕ_{ot} are replaced by ϕ_k and ϕ_o, respectively, so that eq. (10.A21) simplifies to eq. (10.13) in the text. Finally, if there is no constraint on operating costs but capital expenditure is limited separately each year, then ϕ_{ot} is zero, ϕ_{kt} is replaced by ϕ_t, and eq. (10.A21) simplifies to the investment criterion in eq. (10.14) of the text.

11. Conclusion

The content of this book provides a point of departure in the sense, I hope, of encouraging readers to examine the subject area in more depth but also in the sense that other areas of inquiry stem from it. For example, the theory of welfare economics has been concerned with the analysis of some fairly simple objectives. Granted certain assumptions concerning welfare or happiness, one can deduce certain propositions about the allocation of resources. These should be treated as no more than starting points. The assumptions have proved unhelpful in some cases, and the systematic analysis of more complex policy objectives in areas such as health, education, and defence seems an important line of advance in the future; the objectives associated with Pareto-type efficiency may well become less important. A second focal point has been the pure theory of public goods, which now looks as though it might provide a launching-pad for the development of positive theories of public expenditure. There are two aspects of this worth noting. One is to examine the particular technical characteristics of public goods and see how this fits into conventional welfare economics—what size of fire-station, and how to finance it. This approach has been the one adopted in this book. The other approach, and one more directly related to the positive aspects of public good theory, recognizes that our conventional price theory is not only concerned with the determination of the market prices of private goods but also has embedded in it a theory of how such markets develop; how, for example, self-interest can encourage the growth of markets. Some of the apostles of public good theory want also to look at not only the technical characteristics of public goods but why and how they came to be provided, not by a market, but by the political process. This is certainly an intriguing line of thought, but where it will lead to remains to be seen.

Associated more closely with the general principles discussed in this book, is the empirical work now being undertaken in the context of particular goods and services in the public sector. As well as the more well-known work in transport, electricity, and education, other areas in the UK such as the Gas Industry, the Post Office, and the health services look as though they will be involved in detailed economic work. This is an extremely healthy development in this whole subject area and one that is long over-due. At the same time, it is probably useful to mention here that some of these developments are not above criticism. One of the key dangers is that attention will be devoted to detailed statistical exercises and complicated maximization processes, partly at the expense of considering some of the more fundamental problems concerning the basic objectives of policy. In some respects it is quite frightening how techniques like cost-benefit analysis can be uncritically embraced, and even when criticisms are made they are often of a technical kind—the inability to deal with intangibles for example, or the limitation to partial equilibrium changes. It is important not to let such techniques mask decisions which require attention to quite proper social objectives.

With this qualification, the advent of empirical work in the public sector is to be welcomed. This book has been concerned with issues common to many of the particular public sector products. At this *general* level two items —among many—that could be emphasized as requiring some detailed empirical content may be mentioned here. The first relates to the analysis of public investment criteria. On the one hand, if we could assume that the context of the discussion in the latter part of chapter 9—broadly that inter-temporal 'efficiency' is a useful guide—was roughly correct, then it would seem important to consider the general allocative effect that public investment has on total national investment. This means, to start with, considering to what extent the private investment that is foregone and the private investment that is generated, can be treated at all as being marginal to the whole private investment programme. In addition, one needs to discover the effect of the switch on the character of such investment. Are more long-term investments encouraged? What kind of regional displacement is involved? If any use is to be made of the theoretical analysis of these transfers of funds, it will have to be supplemented by some such empirical content. A second important area is that of second-best. Again some of the formidable aspects of the theory may not prove all that relevant once one gets down to detail. The broad relationship between prices and marginal costs in sectors involving public enterprises is the first thing that comes to mind. But just as important is to examine the 'distortion' effect that particular taxes, subsidies, or government controls have on the prices of inputs and outputs that appear in cost/benefit studies. How, in transport for example, purchase taxes on vehicles distort computations of resource saving. How imported items might be valued given our balance of payments position. Some generally agreed treatment of such issues is necessary if project analysts are not to be continuously burdened with studying these problems every time a project is assessed.

Reading Guide

Those readers who are already familiar with some of the work in this field can simply use the footnote references in the text to explore the literature in more depth. This guide is directed more towards those who have to come to the subject for the first time, with the aim of providing a starting point in their reading. For simplicity, the subject has been arranged under five headings. Only a few references are given for each topic, but the first section looks at some of the literature in more depth, since the first few chapters of the text contain few literature references.

Basic welfare economics (*chapters* 1 *to* 4)

The coverage of these chapters forms the basis of the theory of welfare economics. Three texts covering most of this, and more besides, are I. M. D. Little's, *A Critique of Welfare Economics*, Second Edition, Oxford University Press, 1957; J. de V. Graaf's, *Theoretical Welfare Economics*, Cambridge University Press, 1957; and S. K. Nath's, *A Re-appraisal of Welfare Economics*, Routledge and Kegan Paul, 1969. However, these are fairly advanced treatments, and for the 'unexposed' student it is often useful to look at those texts on price theory which have a section on welfare economics. The chapter in W. J. Baumol's, *Economic Theory and Operations Analysis*, Prentice-Hall, 1965, provides a good bird's-eye view of much of the area. An extremely good survey, relying mainly on diagrams, has also been written by F. M. Bator in 'The Simple Analytics of Welfare Maximisation', *American Economic Review*, March 1957, reproduced in *Readings in Micro-Economics*, Ed. W. Briet and H. M. Hochman, Holt, Rinehart & Winston, 1968. With this as a background the reader could then turn to the three texts mentioned above, as well as E. J. Mishan's 'A Survey of Welfare Economics', *Economic Journal*, June 1960, reproduced in *Welfare Economics: Five Introductory Essays*, Random House, 1967, and in *Surveys of Economic Theory*, I, American Economic Association and Royal Economic Society, Macmillan, 1965. Those who wish to explore the foundations of welfare economics can take advantage of the collection of articles in Part I of the American Economic Association's *Readings in Welfare Economics*, Ed. K. J. Arrow and T. Scitovsky, Allen & Unwin, 1969; this book ranks, in coverage, with some of the other texts on welfare economics.

Turning to more specialized topics within the first four chapters of our book, it is not easy to find a full exposition of consumer and producer surplus analysis without going to the source material of J. R. Hick's work, referred to in sections 3.4 and 3.5. However, the chapter in I. M. D. Little's *Critique*, *op. cit.*, on indivisibilities and consumer surplus is a very good starting point, although his evaluation of the usefulness of surplus concepts is different from the approach taken in this book and, moreover, from the many applied economists who have made use of them. C. D. Foster's discussion of 'Surplus Criteria for Investment, *Bulletin of the Oxford University Institute of Statistics*, November 1960, is a good example of an attempt to put surplus concepts on an operational footing. The analysis of compensation tests has been on a much wider canvas than the partial equilibrium setting of chapter 3. Those readers wishing to explore this area could probably not do better than look at Mishan's survey (*EJ*, 1960, *op. cit.*) and then follow the issues of the *Economic Journal* during the 1960s to observe a debate which was primarily stimulated by the chapters in Little, *op. cit.*, on welfare criteria. The subject of interest in the first part of chapter 4 is, of course, concerned with the whole relevance and methodology of welfare economics. Most of the texts referred to above have a lot to say on this subject, and S. K. Nath's evaluation of what he calls 'the *a priori* welfare economics' is particularly useful. The reader might also like to look at one of the few articles on the methodology of welfare economics by G. C. Archibald entitled 'Welfare Economics, Ethics and Essentialism', *Economica*, Nov. 1959. The reader who wishes to delve into second-best problems must be prepared for a fair amount of mathematics. However, it is also useful to get a feel for the subject by looking at the contributions of J. E. Meade in chapter VII of his *The Theory of International Economic Policy, Vol. II: Trade and Welfare*, Oxford University Press, 1955; or M. J. Farrell, 'In Defence of Public Utility Price Theory', *Oxford Economic Papers*, February 1958, reproduced in an amended form in *Public Enterprise*, Ed. R. Turvey, Penguin Modern Economics, 1968; or E. J. Mishan in his article 'Second Thoughts on Second Best', *Oxford Economic Papers*, October 1962. Then the reader can look at the more technical discussion of R. G. Lipsey, R. K. Lancaster, O. A. Davis, and A. Whinston referred to in chapter 4, and at the symposium on second-best in the July 1967 issue of the *Review of Economic Studies.*

Public goods, externalities, and returns to scale (*chapter* 5)

There have been quite a number of surveys of externalities, but an excellent starting point for this whole area is F. M. Bator's, *Anatomy of Market Failure*, Q.J.E. 1958 reproduced in *Readings in Micro Economics, op. cit.* Chapters 1 and 4 of R. A. Musgrave's *The Theory of Public Finance*, McGraw-Hill, 1959, provides a general view of the whole area and, in addition, an excellent history of the analysis of public goods. This latter topic is also evaluated in J. G. Head's admirable paper on 'Public Goods and Public Policy', *Public Finance*, No. 4, 1962, and has the advantage of being linked to the problem of indivisibilities and joint supply. The reader should then be in a good position to explore the subject in more depth in the footnote references of chapter 5, particularly the work of P. A. Samuelson and J. M. Buchanan. In fact, the latter's book on *Demand and Supply of Public Goods*, Rand McNally & Co., 1968, itself provides a systematic exposition of public good theory, as well as a detailed guide to the literature. Much of the International Economic Association's 1966 conference was concerned with theoretical aspects of public goods, and their proceedings have been published as *Public Economics*, Ed. J. Margolis and H. Guitton, Macmillan, 1969.

Public investment criteria (*chapter* 6 *and parts of chapter* 9)

A useful survey can be found in P. D. Henderson's 'Notes on Public Investment Criteria for the UK.' *Bulletin of the Oxford University Institute of Statistics*, February 1965, reproduced in an amended form in *Public Enterprise*, Ed. R. Turvey, *op. cit.*, O. Eckstein and J. V. Krutilla have also written a good introduction to this area in chapters III and IV of *Multi-Purpose River Development*, Johns Hopkins, 1958, though the particular conclusions they come to have been subject to a battery of criticisms. A non-rigorous exposition of these criticisms can be found in M. S. Feldstein's 'Opportunity Cost Calculations in Cost-Benefit Analysis', *Public Finance*, No. 2, 1964. The reader should then be able to get a lot of advantage from the various works referred to in the footnote references of chapter 6 and sections 9.5 and 9.6. For those wishing to explore the wider problems of efficient capital accumulation, Part VII of *Readings in Welfare Economics*, *op. cit.*, contains a selection of pioneer articles.

Pricing (*chapters* 7 *and* 8)

Although there was an abundance of work on marginal-cost pricing in the immediate post-1945 period, particularly in the UK, the reader would probably be better advised to look at more recent writings to start with. Though it is primarily directed at the problem of peak loads, O. E. Williamson's article 'Peak-Load Pricing and Optimal Capacity under Indivisibility Constraints', *American Economic Review*, September 1966 (reproduced in *Public Enterprise*, Ed. R. Turvey, *op. cit.*), provides the kernel of marginal-cost pricing theory. Similarly, R. Turvey's all too brief article on 'Marginal Cost Pricing in Practice', *Economica*, November 1964, contains the essence of the short-run/long-run discussion. The first part of R. L. Meek's exposition of 'An Application of Marginal Cost Pricing: The Green Tariff in Theory and Practice', *Journal of Industrial Economics*, July and November 1963, contains a useful diagrammatic treatment of the short-run/long-run issue. R. Turvey's *Economica* article is, in fact, a review of the collection of translated French articles, *Marginal Cost Pricing in Practice*, Ed. J. R. Nelson, Prentice-Hall, 1964; and M. Boiteux's 'Marginal Cost Pricing', and G. Dessus's 'The General Principles of Rate Fixing in Public Utilities', both constitute fairly simple introductions to the subject. The reader should then be able to explore the footnote references of chapters 7 and 8.

Project appraisal (*chapters* 9 *and* 10)

It would be silly to try to indicate reading in this vast subject area, since much of it relates to individual parts of the public sector. The reader is invited to consult the footnote references on p. 290 of chapter 9, where some of the main surveys of cost-benefit analysis are described. References to many of the individual areas of the public sector are given in the other references in this chapter and in chapter 10.

List of abbreviations

In some cases the title of a journal, publishing body, or a similar publication has been abbreviated in the text. Below is a full list of the abbreviations and details of the full title of all journals referred to in the text.

American Economic Association	AEA
American Economic Review	AER
Applied Statistics	
Bulletin of the Oxford University Institute of Statistics	BOUIS
Canadian Journal of Economics and Political Science	
District Bank Review	
Econometrica	
Economica	
Economic Journal	EJ
Her Majesty's Stationery Office	HMSO
International Economic Association	IEA
International Economic Papers	
International Economic Review	
Journal of Business	J Business
Journal of Industrial Economics	JIE
Journal of Law and Economics	J Law Econ.
Journal of Political Economy	JPE
Journal of the Royal Statistical Society	JRSS
Lloyds Bank Review	
Ministry of Housing and Local Government	M of Housing and Local Government
Ministry of Transport	M of Transport
The Manchester School	
National Bureau of Economic and Social Research	NBER
Oxford Economic Papers	OEP
Oxford University Press	OUP
Proceedings of the Institution of Civil Engineers	
Public Administration	
Public Finance	
Quarterly Journal of Economics	QJE
Scottish Journal of Political Economy	SJPE
Review of Economic Studies	R Econ. Studies
Review of Economics and Statistics	R Econ. Stats.
Revue Francaise de l'Energie	
Royal Economic Society	RES

Index

Aaron, H., 138n
Accounting costs (see Costs, accounting)
Aggregate demand curves:
  for peak loads, 270–2
  for public goods, 134–6
Agriculture:
  evaluation of research expenditure on, 294–6
  in United States, and farm budget studies, 303–4
  United States Department of, 294–5
Airports, 151–2, 154, 280
Alchian, A. A., 177
Annual capital charge, 215–16
Army Corps of Engineers, United States, 278, 279, 282, 298–9, 308, 342–3, 358
Arrow, K. J., 21n, 60n, 280n, 281n
Ayer, A. J., 197–8

Bailey, M. J., 184n
Bates, R. W., 224n
Bator, F. M., 47n, 112n, 120n, 130n, 141n, 262
Baumol, W. J., 26n, 186n, 188, 190n, 198n, 317n, 318n, 319n, 326–7
Beesley, M. E., 75n, 213n, 280n
Behavioural rules, 39, 43, 92–5
Benefit:
  alternative cost method of measuring, the, 61–2, 282, 292, 298–9
  marginal, meaning of, 24–6, 40
  measurement in cost-benefit analysis, examples of, 290–8
  secondary, and cost-benefit analysis, 302–4, 351–2
  theory of taxation, the, 137
Benefit-cost analysis (see Cost-benefit analysis)
Bergson, A., 48n
Boiteux, M., 116n, 120n, 209, 210n, 217n, 219–20, 241, 244, 246, 249, 267n, 271n
Bonds, government, as finance for public investment, 310–30
Boulding, K. E., 69n
Box diagram, explanation of:
  in exchange, 19
  in general optimum, 20–2
  in production, 14–15
Briet, W., 47n, 112n, 262n
British Rail, 239, 240
Broadcasting, 140, 141
Buchanan, J. M., 59n, 127n, 137n, 138n, 139n, 141n, 143–5, 147n, 149, 156–7, 272n, 352n
Budget, of public enterprise:
  constraints on, 334–46, 358–63
  exhaustion of, and returns to scale, 12–13, 50–3, 112–31, 218–20, 244–51, 255–65
Bureau of Reclamation, United States, 296–8, 303, 342
Bus services, indivisibilities in supply of, 257–60

Canals, 298–9, 308
Cannon, C. M., 224n
Capacity, productive:
  excess, 236–42, 245
  expansion of, and long-run marginal cost, 226–36
  optimal volume of, 209, 218–26
  rigid limits to, 123–8, 209–11
Capital:
  charge, annual, 215–16
  markets, 173, 185–6
Cassell, F., 238n
Central Electricity Generating Board, 266–7, 272n

Channel Tunnel, the, 123–5, 298
Charlesworth, G., 294n
Chase, S. B., 290n, 309n, 355n
Clapham, J. H., 128n
Clemens, E. W., 284n
Coal, pricing of in the United Kingdom, 228
Coase, R. H., 145n, 150, 153n, 154, 156, 160, 247n, 249n
Coburn, T. M., 280n, 307n
Cohen, K. J., 217n
Collard, D., 197
Collective goods (see Public goods)
Compensating income variations (see Income variations, compensating)
Compensation:
  and project evaluation, 280
  by law, and externalities, 145–62
  tests and income variations, 59–60, 73–84, 158–60
Constraints:
  budget, 334–46, 358–63
  general significance of, 3–4, 284–5, 331–3
Consumer:
  choice,
    and needs, 90–2, 97–8
    theory of, 9–11
  rationality, 90–1, 97, 196–9
  surplus,
    and externalities, 145–62
    pure theory of, 62–9
Contract curve, 15, 17, 19
Cost-benefit analysis:
  and the alternative cost method of measuring benefits, 61–2, 282, 292, 298–9
  basis of, 87, 278–83
  and cost-benefit ratios, 288–90, 342–5
  and the distribution of income, 246–358
  and marginal-cost pricing, 282–3
  and producer goods, 299–302
  and project selection criteria, 288–90, 358–63
  and secondary benefits, 302–5, 351–2
  and shadow prices for market imperfections, 305–10
  and the specification of a project, 283–90
  time-stream aspects of, 310–30
Costs:
  accounting and economic, 244–51
  alternative, as a method of estimating project benefits, 61–2, 282, 292, 298–9
  decreasing,
    and falling input prices, 118, 130–1
    and increasing returns to scale 53, 118–31, 218–20, 245
  exclusion, and externalities, 138–41, 152–3
  historic, 205–6, 236–42, 244–6
  increasing industry, 53–6
  joint (see Joint supply)
  marginal (see Marginal cost)
  minimization of, and choice of technique, 211–18
  opportunity, of public investment, 313–14, 318–28
  secondary, in cost-benefit analysis, 302–5
Crew, M. A., 224n
Cyert, R. M., 217n

Davis, O. A., 43n, 93, 101, 104n, 107, 108, 156n
Decision rules, meaning of, 3–4, 85–100
Defence expenditure, 279
Demand curves:
  for peak loads, 270–2
  for public goods, 134–6
Dessus, G., 241n, 257n, 258n
Dictator, benevolent, 12, 35, 163–5
Discounted cash flow (see Present value)
Discounting:
  and conversion to annual equivalent terms, 213–16, 255–6
  continuous, 266n
  meaning of, 172
Discriminatory pricing, 120–1, 248, 272n, 272–3, 349n
Distribution:
  of income,
    and compensation tests, 73–84
    and externalities, 161–2
    and marginal-cost pricing, 247
    and market interest rates, 196
    and public expenditure criteria, 346–58
    and public goods, 137–8
  of wealth, and market interest rates, 196

Distribution—*cont.*
of welfare, 32, 23–5
Divisibility (see Indivisibilities)
Dolbear, F. T., 156n
Dorfman, R., 187n, 290n, 352n
Dupuit, J., 125, 248n
Durability, of assets, 236–9
Durbin, E. F. M., 244n

Eckstein, O., 168, 185, 187n, 195n, 252n, 254, 279n, 296–7, 308, 313n, 318n, 332n, 343n, 357
Economies:
external (see Externalities)
of scale (see Returns to scale)
Economist:
French (see French economists)
omniscient, 12, 35, 163–5
Education, economic evaluation of, 11, 196–8, 280–1
Efficiency:
economic (see Pareto efficiency)
managerial, 247, 248
Pareto (see Pareto efficiency)
technical, 17
Electricity supply:
cost structure of, 204, 207, 272
global and marginal problems of, 213n
and security margins, 224n
tariffs, 265–78
and transmission lines, 219–20
Electricité de France, 116n, 211n, 221, 246, 249, 267, 272n
Ellis, H. S., 55n, 128n
Equilibrating income variations (see Income variations, equilibrating)
Exchange, Pareto optimum in, 18–19
Exclusion:
costs, 138–41, 512–3
principle, the, 139
External:
economies and diseconomies of scale (see Externalities)
effects (see Externalities)
Externalities:
and compensation, 58–9, 145–62
definitions of, 110, 143–5, 156–7
and the distribution of income, 161–2
and efficient solutions, 145–61
in the form of external diseconomies, 112–18, 142
in the form of external economies,
characterization of, 131–3
and Marshallian competition, 128–31
and public goods, 131–46, 154
joint supply, and public goods, 138–41
and keeping up with the Jones', 110–11
and the legal system, 145–62
and private and social valuation, 86–7, 109, 306n
pecuniary, 53–5, 304n, 305n
and the tax/subsidy solution, 113–18, 142, 154–7

Factors of production:
elasticity of supply, 53–6
fixity of supply, 17–18, 24n, 39, 41–2
optimal distribution,
between firms, 13–18
between individuals, 18–19
unpaid, and externalities, 112–18
Farrell, M. J., 95n, 245n
Federal Inter-Agency River Basin Committee, 289
Feldstein, M. S., 184n, 189, 196n, 198, 290n, 315n, 317n, 318n, 323n, 324n, 328n, 341
Fellner, W., 55n, 128n
Flemming, J. S., 184n
Flood relief programmes, 279–80, 296–8
Foster, C. D., 70n, 75, 249, 258, 280n
Freeman, A. M., 354, 356–8
French economists, 2, 209, 242, 245n
Friedman, M., 352n
Future generations, provision for, 163–6, 189–99

Gas:
Council, 88
North Sea, 298, 347–9
General optimum, the:
and community indifference maps, 19–23
significance of, 23–6
Generations, future welfare of, and provision for, 163–5, 189–94
Goods:
intermediate (see Producer goods)
optimal distribution of,
between firms, 12–18, 25–6
between individuals, 18–19

Government bonds, as finance for public investment, 310–30
Graaf, J. de V., 12n, 28n, 88, 96, 164n, 198
Green Book, the, 289–90
Green Tariff, the, 211n, 249, 267, 272n
Griliches, Z., 294–5
Grossfield, K., 295–6, 306n
Guitton, H., 100n, 110n

Haven, J. C. de, 317n
Hayek, F., 109n
Head, J. G., 138n, 141n
Health, 10, 11
Heath, J. B., 295–6, 306n
Henderson, A. M., 67n, 77n, 247n
Henderson, J. M., 26n, 36n
Henderson, P. D., 184n, 187n, 189
Hicks, J. R.:
  and the compensating income variation, 62–7, 69, 70, 72–3
  Kaldor- test, 60
Hirschleifer, J., 177n, 178n, 180n, 184n, 185, 211n, 271n, 273, 317n
Hochman, H. M., 47n, 112n, 262n
Hotelling, H., 247n, 248n
Housing and Local Government, Ministry of, 281n, 298n
Houthakker, H. S., 267
Howard, A., 97n
Howe, M., 239n, 240n

Income:
  distribution (see Distribution of income)
  marginal utility of (see Utility, marginal, of income)
  national, and welfare, 24–5
  variations,
    compensating, 59–60, 73–84, 79–82
    equilibrating, 75–82
    and externalities, 157–60
Indifference maps:
  for illustrating time-preference, 169–71
  meaning of,
    for individuals, 10–11
    for the community, 20–3
  use of, in box diagrams, 19
Indivisibilities:
  and joint supply and increasing returns to scale, 120–8
  and pricing, 253, 255–65
  and project evaluation, 280
  and social surplus analysis, 58, 60–73
  and transport examples, 257–60
Inputs (see Factors of production)
Intangibles, 285
Intermediate goods (see Producer goods)
International trade, theory of, 16
Investment:
  criteria (see Private investment, Public investment)
  decisions and marginal-cost pricing, 173–7, 218–26
  private (see Private investment)
  public good aspects of, 198–94
Irrigation projects, 296–8, 303
Isoproduct map, meaning of, 14–16

Johnson, H. G., 89n
Joint supply:
  and competition, 125–8
  definition of, 123–4
  and increasing returns to scale, 123–5
  and multi-purpose projects, 254–5
  and peak loads, 270–2
  and pricing in public enterprises, 252–7
  and public goods and externality, 138–41

Kahn, R. F., 48n
Kaldor, N., 60n
  –Hicks test, 60
Kneese, A. V., 353
Knight, F. H., 115, 116
Kritilla, J. V., 313n

Labour, supply of, 12, 17–18
Lagrangean multipliers:
  explanation of, 26–7
  significance of, 28
Lancaster, R. K., 100
Lange, O., 52
Lees, D. S., 132n
Lerner, A. P., 40n, 52, 244n, 247
Lewis, W. A., 239, 242, 248n, 261n, 267
Lind, R. C., 193n
Linear programming, 285n, 339n
Lipsey, R. G., 100
Little, I. M. D., 9n, 161, 74n, 79n, 88, 258–9

Lloyd, F. J., 280n
Lump-sum taxes, 46–7, 92, 247

Maass, A., 68n, 187n, 284n, 334n, 341n, 350n, 351n, 352n, 353, 355n, 358n
Marginal cost (see also Costs):
and economic rent, 53–7, 69–73, 115
and marginal benefit, 23–6
and marginal productivity, 17
pricing (see Marginal cost pricing)
short-run and long-run, 205–9, 216–18
Marginal cost pricing:
and accounting deficits, 244–51, 255–65
and choice of production technique, 211–18
and excess capacity, 236–42
general outline of, 48–57
and income distribution 91–2, 97–9
and increasing costs, 112–18
and increasing returns to scale, 118–31, 220, 244–51, 255–65
and investment decisions, 173–7, 218–36
and joint supply, 123–8
and peak loads, 265–77
and physical capacity limits, 209–11, 222–4
and second-best problems, 92–5, 99–108
short-run and long-run, 205–9, 216–44
and social surplus maximization, 69–73, 207–8
and technical change, 236, 245
and theoretical welfare economics, 88–90
and the theory of the Pareto optimum, 38–42
Marginality assumption in public investment criteria, the, 314–16
Marglin, S. A.:
on budget constraints, 334n, 340n, 341, 346n, 360
on cost-benefit analysis, 284n, 287n, 301n, 302n, 306n
on income distribution and public investment criteria, 350–1, 353n, 356n, 357n
on partial equilibrium analysis in water-resources development, 68n
on time-stream aspects of public investment criteria, 164n, 182n, 189–94, 197, 313n, 315n, 317, 318n, 322, 323n, 328n
Margolis, J., 100n, 110n, 304n, 313n
Market imperfections:
and shadow prices in cost-benefit analysis, 305–10
and the theory of public investment criteria, 185–6
and the theory of second-best solutions, 94–5, 98–100
Marshall, A.:
and consumer surplus, 62–9, 77n
and external economies, 128–31
and joint supply, 139n
Masse, P., 267n
Mathematics, use of, 5
McGuire, M. A., 138n
McKean, R. N., 289n, 303n, 304n, 309n, 336–7, 355n
McManus, M., 107n
Meade, J. E., 74n, 117, 130n, 247n
Meek, R. L., 211n, 213n, 215n, 217n, 267, 272n, 310n
Merrett, A. J., 215n
Methodology, 3–4, 96
Milliman, J. W., 317n
Mills, E. J., 239n, 240n
Millward, R., 138n, 294n, 253n
Minasian, J. R., 141n
Mises, Von F., 52n, 121
Mishan, E. J.:
on compensation tests and welfare criteria, 67n, 74n, 80
on externalities, 55n, 117n, 144n, 145n, 147n, 157n, 159n
on general welfare economics, 40n
on public investment criteria, 184n, 198n, 315n, 317n, 319–21, 328n, 330n
on rent, 70n, 71n, 83
on second-best, 45n
Monopoly, 47–8, 118–23
Munby, D., 75n, 114n, 180n, 210n, 280n
Musgrave, R. A., 123n, 137–9

Nath, S. K., 88, 150–7
Nationalized Industries, United Kingdom, 87–8, 180–2, 248–9, 309n, 353

National Prices and Incomes Board, 87–8
National Research and Development Corporation, 295–6
Nelson, J. R., 116n, 120n, 209n, 220n, 241n, 245n, 246n, 267n, 272n, 291n
Nelson, R. R., 281n
Neutse, G. M., 216n, 263n
Nichols, A., 323n

Objectives:
  income distribution, 346–58
  a review of, 85–100
  welfare, 3–4, 24, 331–4
Optimum conditions (see Pareto optimum)
Outputs, optimal distribution:
  between firms, 13–18
  between individuals, 18–19, 23–4

Paisley, J. L., 294n
Pareto:
  criterion, the, 11, 18–19, 56–60
  efficiency,
    and accounting deficits, 246–7
    and price patterns, 35–42
    and private enterprise, 42–8
    relevance of, for policy, 95–100
    time-dimension of, 166–82
  optimum, the, 13–26
    formal analysis of, 26–30
    as a necessary condition for welfare maximization, 33–4
Peacock, A. T., 2, 213n
Peak loads:
  general nature of, 253–4, 265–7
  shifting, 270–3
  theory of pricing with, 268–77
Perfect competition, and Pareto efficiency, 45
Peston, M. H., 131–2, 279n
Peters, G. H., 290n
Peters, W., 321n
Phelps-Brown, E. H., 238n, 244, 247n, 249n
Pigou, A. C.:
  on externalities, 109–10, 131, 142–3, 154–7
  on increasing costs, 55, 113–15
  on increasing returns to scale, 119, 128–31
  on provision for future generations, 196–7
  on public expenditure, 137n
  on public utilities, 1
  on road congestion, 115–18
Plott, C. R., 155n
Polanyi, G., 298n, 347–9
Poole, Lord, 97n
Posner, M. V., 182n
Post Office, the, 87–8
Preference:
  distributional, 73–5
  function (see Utility, function)
  individual, 10–11, 32–3
  political and market, 197–8
  and welfare in context of investment decisions, 196–9
Present value:
  meaning of, 172
  net discounted, of a project,
    and marginal cost pricing, 220–6
    meaning of, 174–5
    and public investment, 175–8
  versus internal rate of return controversy, 177, 182–4, 195n, 199–200, 330n
Prest, A. R., 137n, 138n, 290n, 291n, 304n, 305n, 308n, 309–10
Prices:
  accounting, 24
  discriminatory (see Discriminatory pricing)
  fluctuating, 240–2
  and Incomes Board, the (see National Prices and Incomes Board)
  and marginal costs (see Marginal-cost pricing)
  patterns of, and Pareto efficiency, 35–42
  in public enterprises (see Public enterprises, pricing)
  shadow, and market imperfections, 305–10
Private enterprise:
  and income distribution, 45–9
  and Pareto efficiency, 42–5
Private investment:
  criteria, 173–5, 177n
    multi-period aspects of, 182–4
  displacement of, and generation by, public investment, 298–330
  financing of, 178–82

Private investment—*cont.*
public good aspects of, 189–94
social productivity of, 189, 318n
Producer goods, 41–2, 299–302
Product, marginal, meaning of, 15–16, 18
(see also Productivity, social)
Production:
frontier, 17
function,
of community, 17 (see also Transformation, function, social)
of firm, 13, 14, 26, 36n
optimal organization of, 13–18, 36–7
possibility curve, 17 (see also Transformation, function, social)
Productivity:
marginal, 15–16, 18
social, of investment, 189, 318n
Programming, 285n, 339n
Projects:
evaluation of,
and marginal-cost pricing, 220–6
and indivisibilities, 280
multi-purpose, 252–5
public sector,
and selection criteria, 288–90
specification of, 283–90
time-stream aspects of, 310–30
and valuation of costs and benefits, 282–3, 298–310
Property rights, 12, 145–62
Public enterprises:
and increasing returns to scale, 118–31, 220, 244–51, 255–65
and market socialism, 48–9
and mixed economies, 49–53
pricing policy of, 87–8, 94–5, 240–4
(see also Marginal-cost pricing)
Public expenditure, positive theories on, 3, 136–7, 364
Public goods,
and external economies, 131–3, 154
general implications of the pure theory of, 136–8
and income distribution, 137–8
and joint supply and externality, 138–41
positive theories on, 3, 136–7, 364
and provision for future generations, 189–94
and relationship to peak load problems, 271n
and Samuelson's polar model, 133–6, 154
Public Investment:
Criteria,
and adjustments for market imperfections, 185–6
formal derivation of, 358–60
and marginal-cost pricing, 173–7, 218–36
marginality assumption in, the, 314–16
multi-period aspects of, 182–4
and Pareto efficiency, 175–8
and sales revenue, 327–8
and shadow multipliers, 321–3
and taxes and uncertainty, 323–7
and the use of social time preference, 195–9, 316–23
and effects on the private sector, 310–16
financing of, 178–82, 316–30
public good aspects of, 189–94
Public sector, size of, 2–3, 86–7, 136–7, 315–16, 334–6

Quandt, R. E., 26n, 36n

Railways:
British, 239–40
costs of, 239–40
rates of, 298–9, 308
Raj, K. N., 296n
Rate of return, 171
internal, 117, 182–4, 195n, 199–200, 330n
Rees, R., 99n
Rent, 53–7, 69–73, 82–4, 115
Research and development activity:
evaluation of projects involving, 294–6
by governments, 281
Returns:
to scale, 12–13, 233n
constant, 50–1
decreasing, 112–18
increasing, 53, 118–31, 220, 244–51, 255–65
rate of (see Rate of return)
Reynolds, D. J., 280n, 292n
Ridley Committee Report, 228
Risk, 187–9 (see also Uncertainty)
Roads:
congestion of, 114–16, 261–5

Roads—*cont*.
indivisibilities in provision of, 261–5
and investment criteria, 280, 290–4
Robertson, D. H., 128n
Robertson, D. J., 213n
Robinson, J., 122n
Roth, N., 296n
Ruggles, N., 242n

Sales revenue, and public investment criteria, 327–8
Salter, W. G., 236n
Samuelson, P. A., 31, 188n:
on decreasing costs, 122–3, 127–8, 140–1
on public goods, 110n, 133–6, 137n, 139n, 140–1, 154
Scale, returns to (see Returns, to scale)
Scitovsky, T. B., 21n, 60n, 79n, 111n, 280n
Scrap value, 206
Secondary benefits (see Benefit, secondary)
Second best, the problem of, 32, 50, 92–5, 99–100, 365
and cost-benefit analysis, 305–10
formal analysis of, 100–8
and public investment criteria, 317
Second-order conditions, 27n
Shadow multipliers, 321–3
Sharp, C., 114n
Social costs (see Externalities)
Socialism, market, 48–9
Solomon, E., 177n, 178n
Sovani, N. V., 296n
Sraffa, P., 128n
Stasi, P., 120n
Steiner, P. O., 62n, 265, 271n, 273n, 287n, 299n, 313n, 315n, 318n, 319n, 334n
Stiglitz, J. E., 123n
Stubblebine, W. C., 143–5, 147n, 149, 156–7
Subsidies:
and income distribution, 46–7, 91–2, 97–8, 347–54
as solution to external economies, 129, 142, 154–7
treatment of, in cost-benefit analysis, 305–10
Substitution, marginal subjective rate of, 19, 25
Supply, separate and single, 124, 140
Surplus:
analysis and factor rewards, 82–4
consumer (see Consumer, surplus)
producer, 72, 82–4
social,
and indivisibilities, 58, 60–73
and marginal-cost pricing, 69–73, 207–8
maximization of, 69–73
Sykes, A., 215n
Systems analysis:
and peak loads, 273–6
and pricing, 234–6

Tariffs:
electricity, 265–75
two-part, 248–9
Tarif Vert, the, of Electricité de France, 211n, 249, 267, 272n
Taxes:
and accounting deficits, 247
benefit theory of, 137
congestion, 114–16, 261–5
and externalities, 113–18, 142, 154–7
income, 46–7
and income distribution, 46–7, 91–2, 98, 347–54
inheritance, 190
lump sum, 46–7, 92, 247
on private investment, and public investment criteria, 323–7
selective employment, 307
as source of finance for public investment, 310–30
Technical change and pricing, 236, 245
Technique, choice of production, 211–18
Time preference:
individual, 166–8, 196–7
planners' (see social)
rate of, 167
social, 195–9, 316–23
Transfer:
earnings, 69–73
payments by the state,
and distribution of income objectives, 46–7, 91–2, 97–8, 347–54
and external economies, 129, 142, 154–7
Transformation:
curve (see Production, possibility curve)
function, social, 28
marginal rate of, 15–18, 25 (see also Productivity, marginal)

Transport:
and indivisibilities, 257–60
Ministry of, 53n, 114n, 125, 240n, 253n, 291, 298
Users' Consultative Committee, 240
Tullock, G., 193
Turvey R., 72n, 95n, 222n, 296n
on cost-benefit analysis, 290n, 304n, 305n, 309–10
on electricity economics, 204, 213n, 275n, 277n
on externalities and public goods, 112n, 138n, 147n, 153n
on income distribution, 98n
on marginal-cost pricing, 211n, 220, 221n, 232n, 236, 241, 244
on methodology, 97n, 244n
on public investment criteria, 184n, 195n
on second-best, 100

Uncertainty:
in demand for electricity supply, 224
and externalities, 111
and investment decisions, 187–9
and public investment criteria, 323–7
Unemployment:
and secondary benefits, 304–5
and shadow prices for labour, 309–10
Utility:
cardinal, 10–11, 19n
function, 10–11, 12, 22–3
marginal, 10–11, 18–19
of income, 62–8, 157–62

Value:
present (see Present value)
private and social (see Externalities)
scrap, of assets, 206
Value judgements, 10–11, 90–1, 164–5, 198–9
Viner, J., 55

Walker, G., 248n
Walters, A. A., 75n, 114n, 210n
Warford, J. J., 265n, 286n
Water:
supply,
industry in the United Kingdom, investment in, 286
in rural areas of the United Kingdom, 281–2
resources, development of,
and flood relief, 279–80, 296–8
and irrigation, 296–8, 303
and project-selection criteria in United States, 289–90, 342–4, 353
in the United Kingdom, 298
Watson, A. H., 123n, 298n
Webb, M. G., 213n
Weisbrod, B. A., 355, 358
Welfare:
and choice, in context of investment decisions, 196–9
of different generations, 163–6, 189–94
economics, conclusions of, 88–90
function, social, 32–4, 75
meaning of,
community (see national)
individual, 9–11
national, 3–4, 9–11, 20
social (see National)
West, R., 97n
Whinston, A., 43n, 93, 101, 104n, 107, 108, 156n
Williams, A., 137n
Williamson, O. E., 72n, 222n, 256n, 272n
Wilson, T., 249n
Winch, D. M., 64n, 69, 68
Wiseman, J., 2, 243–4

Printed Offset Litho in Great Britain by
Cox & Wyman Ltd., London, Fakenham
and Reading

